The Bronze Age in Europe

The Bronze Age in Europe

An introduction to the prehistory
of Europe c.2000–700 BC

& J. M. COLES
A. F. HARDING

METHUEN & CO LTD

First published in 1979
by Methuen & Co Ltd
11 New Fetter Lane London EC4P 4EE
Typeset by CCC and
Printed in Great Britain by William Clowes & Sons Limited,
Beccles and London

ISBN (hardbound) 0 416 70640 1
ISBN (paperback) 0 416 70650 9

Contents

Preface

This book was written because of the continuing lack of general surveys of the European Bronze Age, and the persistent difficulties both students and teachers had in obtaining and reading the enormous literature concerned with Bronze Age matters. Gimbutas wrote in 1965: 'This year is not yet the date for a fluently readable book on the Bronze Age of Europe', and though this may still be true we have decided to take the plunge. The task of covering so vast a topic posed, as can be imagined, many problems, and some of these we have managed to overcome with the help of those friends and colleagues whose names appear below; others may turn out to have been insuperable. We have relied on the published work of many people, and we hope that we have accurately represented both the factual evidence and their views. Wherever possible, we have visited sites and museums to inspect the material at first hand; we have visited and worked in almost every country considered here, J.M.C. in the west, north and south, A.F.H. in the south, east and central areas. The main exception as far as detailed study is concerned is the Soviet Union.

Because the literature on the European Bronze Age is so vast, we have naturally had to be selective, and important sites and controversies have had to be omitted because of lack of space. On the other hand, there are certainly other useful reports which we have simply failed to find. The literature is not always readily available, either in Britain or abroad, and the proliferation of journals and monographs continues at a rate which often exceeds the ability of libraries to purchase and readers to read. We have attempted to provide a bibliography of some important works of reference, and we refer to these using the Harvard system within footnotes at the end of each chapter; the many other references simply cite journal number and page, or monograph title.

The difficulties of relating chronological divisions as proposed for many areas have been overcome, we hope, by ignoring the minutiae of periods, horizons, phases and groups (except insofar as they are appropriate to individual chapters) and by adopting an arbitrary Early Bronze Age and Late Bronze Age (sometimes more accurately if tediously called earlier and later) for each area; for this we have used a combination of radiocarbon dates, periodization schemes and stratigraphies where available; the appearance of central European Urnfields has been taken as a prime indicator of the start of the Late Bronze Age.

Radiocarbon dates for the Bronze Age are increasingly important as they begin to appear in sufficient quantities to allow greater precision and reliability. There are still gaps, of course, but the overall picture of the total life of certain groups is becoming clear. Although the publication of radiocarbon dates is still sporadic, with many dates not appearing in *Radiocarbon*, or quoted elsewhere without laboratory number or s.d., we have assembled as many as were available and reliable and these appear at the end of the relevant chapters.

The regions described have been devised where possible using geographical, not modern political, boundaries, as well as Bronze Age distributions of material that may reflect territorial constraints. In each of the two main sections of the book there are five chapters: central Europe (from the Rhine to the Carpathians), eastern Europe (including European Russia and the eastern Balkans), southern Europe (the Adriatic shores and the central Mediterranean), western Europe (the Atlantic countries and islands) and northern Europe (the north European plain and highlands). We have found it convenient to treat the central European area first, and in considerable detail, because we believe that this vast region created many of the developments of the European Bronze Age, it is central to the whole, and it is far more fragmented in terms of the current available literature.

Both authors have read and discussed every part of the book, but the original composition of the chapters was divided as follows:

Central Europe (chapters 2 and 7): A.F.H. with contributions from
J.M.C.

Eastern Europe (chapters 3 and 8): A.F.H.

Southern Europe (chapters 4 and 9): J.M.C. and A.F.H.

Western Europe (chapters 5 and 10): J.M.C.

Northern Europe (chapters 6 and 11): J.M.C.

Introduction and Conclusion were written jointly.

For each region we have attempted to include the most important sites on a location map; other sites can be found, with luck, in any good atlas by reference to the district names which follow them. These are of varying size and significance, depending on the unit of local administration within each country; in general they are either of district size (e.g. German

Kreis) or of county size (e.g. French *département*); sometimes both are provided, as with the Soviet Union. In some cases, sometimes deliberately for the purposes of the book, or inevitably because the precise location could not be found, sites are less accurately located by reference to larger geographical or political areas, such as the German *Länder* or French regions. These wider geographical areas are useful when discussing cultural or economic zones or boundaries.

Many of the illustrations have been taken from published works and their quality is regrettably varied; a number have been redrawn. It is sad that so many illustrations of important sites and material are still published without scales and details. A few of our own illustrations have had to suffer in this way.

The balance of evidence for the Bronze Age is not uniform through our areas, and each chapter has deliberately been designed to suit its own area evidence rather than forced into an arbitrary overall design. Nonetheless, each chapter contains some discussion on settlement and economy, distributions, burial customs, material culture, art, religion and ritual behaviour. These headings are not the most suitable, given a free choice of data, but they have to reflect the work done and published. Our own interest in and concern for future developments in Bronze Age studies are expressed in the conclusion.

Many people have helped us during the writing and preparation of this book, and though we cannot mention them all, we are sincerely grateful to them. We particularly thank Dr Jan Bouzek of the Charles University, Prague, for his unfailing guidance and help, especially over the central European Bronze Age. Most of his suggestions have been included here. Among those who read and commented on various parts in draft, we thank Drs L. Barfield, J. Bill, J. Butler, J. C. Chapman, G. Eogan, B. Gräslund, D. W. Harding, R. J. Harrison and S. Shennan. For help in museums, supplying off-prints or other data, for discussion on particular points and correspondence, we thank A. Beneš, V. Furmánek, J. Hrala, O. Kytlicová, E. Neustupný, J. Ondráček, J. Paulík, I. Pleinerová, E. Plesl, J. Poláček and J. Vladár (Czechoslovakia); G. Behm-Blancke, R. Breddin, D.-W. Buck, W. Coblenz, H. Kaufman, K. Kroitzch, K. Simon and K. Peschel (DDR); A. Jockenhövel, H. Koschik and H. Müller-Karpe (BRD); T. Kemenczei, T. Kovacs, A. Mozsolics and I. Stanczik (Hungary); I. Aldea, I. Ordentlich, D. Popescu and T. Soroceanu (Romania); P. Doluchanov (Soviet Union); P. Pavlov (Bulgaria); K. Wardle (north Greece); A. Ammerman, A. M. Bietti Sestieri, G. Barker, C. Gamble, T. Potter, L. Vagnetti and R. Whitehouse (Italy); M. Korkuti and F. Prendi (Albania); B. Gediga, M. Gedl, W. Hrebenda, K. Jażdżewski, Z. Kaszewski, J. Kraussowa, L. Krzyżaniak, J. Machnik,

J. Ostoja-Zagórski, T. Sulimirski, T. Wegrzynowicz and W. Wojcie-chowski (Poland); G. Burenhult, D. Damell, B. Gräslund, A. Hyenstrand, C.-A. Moberg, J. Nordbladh and S. Welinder (Sweden); E. Lomborg, K. Randsborg and H. Thrane (Denmark); A. Siiriäinen and J. P. Taavitsainen (Finland); J. Briard (France); P. Ashbee, O. Dickinson, F. Lynch, J. J. Taylor, J. Turner, G. J. Wainwright, D. Gurney and many others (Britain); J. A. Bakker, J. J. Butler, S. J. de Laet, P. Modderman, J. D. van der Waals and H. Waterbolk (Low Countries); A. ApSimon, H. Case, L. Flanagan, and P. Harbison (Ireland); M. Almagro, R. Chapman, O.-H. Frey, R. Harrison, E. Sangmeister and H. Savory (Iberia). For drawings and maps we thank Y. Brown and B. Gill; for photographic copies of line-drawings we thank G. Owen and T. Middlemass. We are grateful to several museums and other persons who supplied plates, which are acknowledged separately.

A great deal of literature could only be consulted in the library of the Institute of Archaeology, London, and to its Director and Staff we are most grateful. A.F.H. further has to thank the Research Fund Committee of the University of Durham and J.M.C. the University of Cambridge for grants which made possible the travel necessary for the writing of this book.

Our most particular thanks go to our wives for much help during the writing, typing, editing and preparation of the book for the press.

July 1977   J.M.C
                                                             A.F.H

List of tables

(Radiocarbon dates are expressed in years bc; calendar dates are expressed
in years BC.

List of maps

List of plates

Transliteration of Cyrillic

а	– a	п	– p	
б	– b	р	– r	
в	– v	с	– s	
г	– g (even in Ukr.)	т	– t	
д	– d	у	– u	
е	– e	ф	– f	
ж	– ž	х	– ch	
з	– z	ц	– c	
и	– i (even in Ukr.)	ч	– č	
й	– j	ш	– š	
і	– i (Ukr.)	щ	– šč	
ї	– ji (Ukr.)	ъ	– ”	
к	– k	ы	– y	
л	– l	ь	– '	
м	– m	э	– ė	
н	– n	ю	– ju	
о	– o	я	– ja	

Ukrainian and other scripts have slightly different values for some letters (e.g. и, г - strictly y, h) but to avoid complication we have used the Russian system throughout. Place-names are transliterated directly unless a familiar English usage exists (e.g. Moscow, Belgrade for Moskva, Beograd). Ukrainian place-names are mostly given in Ukrainian.

Abbreviations

BRGK   *Bericht der römisch-germanischen Kommission.* Frankfurt a/M

BROB   *Berichten van de Rijksdienst voor het Oudheidkundig Bodemonderzoek.* Amsterdam

BSA   *Annual of the British School of Archaeology at Athens.* London

BUSS   *Buletin per Shkencat Shoqërore.* Tirana

B Vgbl.   *Bayerische Vorgeschichtsblätter.* Munich

CAH   *Cambridge Ancient History.* Cambridge

EAF   *Ethnographisch-archäologische Forschungen.* Berlin

ESA   *Eurasia Septentrionalis Antiqua.* Helsinki

FA   *Folia Archaeologica.* Budapest

FAP   *Fontes archaeologici Posnanienses.* Poznań

FvfD (Führer...)   *Führer zu vor- und frühgeschichtlichen Denkmälern.* Mainz

Fundb. aus Baden-Würt   *Fundberichte aus Baden-Württemberg.* Stuttgart

Glasnik Kos i Met.   *Glasnik muzeja Kosova i Metohije.* Priština

GNAMP   *Godišnik na narodnija archeologičeski Muzej Plovdiv.* Plovdiv

GZMS   *Glasnik zemaljskog muzeja u Sarajevu.* Sarajevo

IAI   *Izvestija na archeologičeskija Institut.* Sofia

INMV   *Izvestija na narodnija muzej-Varna.* Varna

Inv. Arch.   *Inventaria archaeologica.* By countries

IVAD   *Izvestija na varnenskoto archeologičesko družestvo.* Varna

JAS   *Journal of Archaeological Science.* London

JFA   *Journal of Field Archaeology.* Boston

JIES   *Journal of Indo-European Studies.* Butte

JIVUF   *Jahresschrift der Institut für Vorgeschichte der Universität Frankfurt am Main.* Frankfurt a/M

JMV   *Jahresschrift für mitteldeutsche Vorgeschichte.* Halle/Saale

JVSTL   *Jahresschrift für die Vorgeschichte der sächsisch-thüringischen Länder.* Leipzig

KSIIMK   *Kratkie soobščenija instituta istorii material'noj kul'tury.* Moscow

KSIAM   *Kratkie soobščenija instituta archeologii.* Moscow

KSIAK   *Kratkie soobščenija instituta archeologii.* Kiev

KSAMO   *Kratkie soobščenija o polevych archeologičeskich issledovanijach.* Odessa

Mat. Arch.   *Materiały Archeologiczne.* Kraków

Mat. Staroż.	*Materiały starożytne.* Warsaw
MCA	*Materiale şi cercetări arheologice.* Bucharest
MIA	*Materialy i issledovanija po archeologii SSSR.* Moscow
Mitt. der präh. Komm.	*Mitteilungen der prähistorischen Kommission der Akademie der Wissenschaften.* Wien
Mon. Ant.	*Monumenti Antichi.* Rome
Not. Scavi	*Atti della Accademia nazionale dei Lincei-Notizie degli scavi di Antichità.* Rome
PA	*Památky Archeologické.* Prague
PBSR	*Papers of the British School at Rome.* London
PPS	*Proceedings of the Prehistoric Society.* Cambridge
Preist. Alp.	*Preistoria Alpina.* Trento
Przeg. Arch.	*Przegląd Archeologiczny.* Poznań
PZ	*Prähistorische Zeitschrift.* Berlin
RSP	*Rivista di scienze preistoriche.* Firenze
RVM	*Rad vojvodjanskich muzeja.* Novi Sad
SA	*Sovetskaja Archeologija.* Moscow
SAA	*Soviet Anthropology and Archeology.* New York
SbČSSA	*Sborník československé společnosti archeologické.* Brno
SCIV	*Ştudii şi cercetări de istoria veche.* Bucharest
Sl. A.	*Slovenská archeológia.* Bratislava
SNMP	*Sborník narodního muzea v Praze.* Prague
Stud. Alb.	*Studia Albanica.* Tirana
ŠZ	*Študijné Zvesti AÚ-SAV.* Nitra
TGIM	*Trudy gosudarstvennogo istoričeskogo museja.* Moscow
TP	*Trabajos de Prehistoria.* Madrid
UISPP	*Union international des sciences pré- et protohistoriques.*
WA	*Wiadomości Archeologiczne.* Warsaw
WMBH	*Wissenschaftliche Mitteilungen aus Bosnien und Hercegovina.* Sarajevo
ZfA	*Zeitschrift für Archäologie.* Berlin
ZSAK	*Zeitschrift für Schweizerische Archäologie und Kunstgeschichte.* Zürich

1 Introduction

This book has as its theme the development of the Bronze Age in Europe outside the Aegean area. In geographical terms, the territories surveyed range from the Atlantic islands and maritime coastlands to the Carpathians and the Black Sea, and from the great river valleys and plains of the north to the coasts of the Mediterranean. Within this great variety of environments we have attempted to describe some of the important developments in European prehistory from c.2000 to c.700 BC.

We do not see the European Bronze Age as a period that can be easily separated from preceding or succeeding prehistoric developments, and in many ways the divisions Neolithic – Copper Age – Bronze Age – Iron Age become more and more artificial as cultural and environmental evidence for continuity accumulates through landscape as well as typological studies. However, for the purposes of this book, we have had to adopt a chronological framework based upon an arbitrary definition for the Bronze Age. What we have taken as defining features are the regular occurrence of metal-working in many communities, and a general date of c. 2000 BC for certain areas where metallurgy was never, or only later, established as a major industry.

Copper had been used since the earliest Neolithic in those parts of Europe where its appearance on the surface was most obvious, and the later Neolithic groups in east-central Europe are more properly termed Copper Age, so great was the quantity of implements produced. But metal forms in the Copper Age are simple and restricted: awls, ornamental discs of sheet bronze, hammered flat and perforated for attachment to clothing, tanged daggers, spectacle-spiral pendants, spiral beads, and – in greatest profusion – shaft-hole axes and axe-adzes of massive appearance. Hand in hand with this production of copper went that of gold, which was used in quantity for ornaments, especially ring pendants, spiral beads and a few other forms. Copper Age communities in central Europe built fortified villages by lakes or on hilltops, and many settlements were placed near copper ore deposits; there is much evidence for local metallurgy, as well as general similarity throughout the region in total industrial assemblages. The differences between this Copper Age evidence and that of the traditional Bronze Age are often minimal in certain areas, and this is why Müller-Karpe would have us now take a large part of the traditional 'Early Bronze Age' as 'Copper Age',[1] but we feel it is still possible to draw a line between an 'Incipient Metal Age' and a 'Full Metal Age', regardless of the actual alloys used. It will be objected that such a line will be as arbitrary as any other, including Müller-Karpe's, and to this we can only reply that in the first place changing the established system will be misleading, and, in the second, a simple and reasonably objective test may help to eliminate these difficulties. In Central Europe the criterion of a Metal Age should be that *most* of its tools and weapons and at least *some* of its ornaments, should be of metal; and that there should be evidence of extensive and local extraction and working of metal.[2]

In Central Europe, hoards of tools (for it is on hoards and not single finds that one should depend) continue, right up to the threshold of the Bronze Age, to be made of stone and bone. In Austria, for example, the Lengyel and related Late Neolithic groups like Wolfsbach and Kanzianberg contain large stone-axe and flint collections, as does the succeeding Baden group.[3] Only with the advent of the late Copper Age groups like Ossarn does metal start to appear in any quantity, and not until the time of the *Ringbarren* hoards can we speak of an absolute predominance in tool and weapon types of metal over stone.[4]

The vast increase in the quantities of metal found as tools and implements is a natural reflection of increased working of copper veins at the main mining centres of central Europe. It is now forty-five years since Pittioni concluded that the famous mines of the Bischofshofen-Mühlbach area in upper Austria started to be exploited intensively during the period of the *Ringbarren* hoards, that is, in the Early Bronze Age.[5] The finds from the settlement on the Klinglberg near St Johann in Pingau included pottery with slag inclusions and the association of these sherds with a flanged axe clinched the matter. It now seems quite clear that the extensive mining of copper, such as we have discussed elsewhere (p. 63), is, in central Europe, the concomitant, if not actually the cause, of the development of the Early Bronze Age in the area. The date of this transition to the Bronze Age is likely to be in the late third millennium BC, although naturally it will always remain impossible to pinpoint the exact time and place of our artificial transition to the Bronze Age. A further help, however, can come from the recognition of the alloying of copper with tin or arsenic, to produce the metal bronze, and here the analyses of metal objects (noted below) can be of value; using these, we may point to the first objects made of tin-bronze, or the first two-piece moulds, and suggest these as general *termini ante quos* for the Bronze Age. Such beginnings, however defined, were not of course uniform over the European continent, either in time or amplitude, and previous and recent studies of material of Copper Age and Bronze Age character, utilizing terminologies based upon local finds and sites, have led to the identification of a bewildering variety of differing cultural groups in the early stages of the Bronze Age of central Europe and elsewhere. We have tended to avoid the proliferation of names of archaeological groups in this book wherever possible.

Fig. 1 Opening of the Trindhoj barrow in 1861, under instructions of King Frederik VII of Denmark. The oak coffin exposed had already been emptied before the archaeologists Worsaae and Herbst, anatomist Ibsen and artist Kornerup (whose drawing this is) had arrived on the scene. Further in the mound lay another oak coffin with a clothed body (see fig. 92 for reconstruction).
(From *Skalk*, 1963, no. 3)

The history of Bronze Age studies is concerned with two main aspects. The first, in the earlier nineteenth century, resulted in the excavation of thousands of burial monuments (fig. 1), and the destruction of evidence of all kinds; there were few areas possessing museum facilities and adequate provision for storage of records, and many of the outstanding monuments were rifled for precious metals. The early conservation of organic materials from a few burials in the north are a welcome exception.[6] These matters are referred to in the relevant chapters below.

The second major aspect of Bronze Age studies, initiated in the nineteenth century and continuing up to the present time, is the attention paid to typology, particularly of metal products but also pottery and stone.[7] The fine quality of workmanship, the opportunity to express local stylistic preferences in shape and decoration, the deposition of products in hoards or graves with other objects, all have created the chance to describe and discuss the evolution of types, the changing fashions and preferences of Bronze Age communities, the regular association of objects and the possible trading patterns developed for the dissemination of products. These studies, and there are thousands of them, can create opportunities for the further understanding of Bronze Age societies, but not if they are taken in isolation and treated as end products in themselves. In this book we have attempted to reduce the typological content to an acceptable minimum, while emphasizing that such studies are still vital to an overall picture of the Bronze Age. A short survey of the major forms appears elsewhere in this Introduction.

The surviving evidence for the Bronze Age is massive. Apart from the many thousands upon thousands of metal artifacts and pottery vessels, quantities of flint and stone work exist, and the decorated rock surfaces as well as clay and metal objects also form a body of data suitable for study. Cemeteries of inhumed or cremated remains abound, from a few burials to many hundreds. Settlements in a variety of situations are becoming increasingly well-known through discoveries of new sites and further examination of the old. Although stratified settlements are not widely distributed, the tell-type occupations in east-central Europe, and cave sites in the west, allow some measure of stratigraphical detail which is lacking from the open flat settlements so characteristic of many areas in Bronze Age Europe. Lake-side settlements, preserved by peats or muds, create their own unique opportunities. Increasingly, environmental data and organic remains are becoming available for study, through re-examination of old sites and selection of new areas for research. The development of patterns of land-use, the take-up of new land, and the methods of exploitation for food-production, all of these are under examination in many areas of Europe, and this is one of the most encouraging aspects of Bronze Age studies.

Closely related to these landscape studies are questions of alterations in natural conditions through land-take (*landnam*) and land-exhaustion, through forest clearances, alterations in water levels, and through climatic changes. Some of these matters are referred to elsewhere in this book. In terms of climate, the Bronze Age falls within Pollen Zone VIII (in the Blytt-Sernander system), that is, the Sub-boreal period which lasted about 2,500 years, *c.* 3000–500 BC. A variety of approaches have shown that the climate of the Sub-boreal was warm and rather dry, with considerable variation in humidity, in contrast to the warm but wet conditions of the preceding Atlantic period and the cooler, wetter conditions of the succeeding Sub-atlantic.[8] During the Sub-boreal, brown soils predominate, and the process of podsolization was temporarily halted; the growth of peat bogs similarly slowed down, and periodic desiccation occurred in them. Lake levels fell considerably but still fluctuated wildly; sea levels were generally higher than before but close to present-day values.

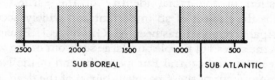

Fig. 2 Climatic oscillations during the later Sub-boreal and early Sub-atlantic phases in Europe. Stipple represents relatively cool and/or moist episodes; unstippled areas represent relatively warm and/or dry episodes.
(After Frenzel 1966, fig. 4)

Within the limits of the Sub-boreal, numerous smaller oscillations occurred (fig. 2).[9] Three main cool and/or moist spells have been recognized: the first a century either side of 2000 BC, the second around 1600–1500 BC and the third early in the first millennium and carrying on into the markedly wetter conditions of the Sub-atlantic. The date of this last deterioration is not certain: in central Europe it appears to have been around 800 BC, in some other parts, including Britain, rather earlier. The impact of such an alteration in climate had serious consequences in many parts of Europe.

There are other approaches to the study of Bronze Age Europe that might reward modern studies. Among these are the problems of the racial affinities and physical characteristics of Bronze Age populations.

The great majority of anthropological studies of the skeletal remains of Bronze Age populations have proceeded by means of metrical analysis, in particular of skulls.[10] The 'cranial index' is still frequently quoted although it is now widely agreed that it is of little value in distinguishing large-scale patterns. More recent analyses quote large numbers of measurements and ratios, but so far little homogeneity has been found in the skeletal types of populations attributable to the same culture. At Grossbrembach (Sömmerda), for instance, four main skull types were distinguished, but these accounted for under 50 per cent of the population; the remainder were 'mixed forms'.[11] It is also clear that Bohemian, Moravian and Thuringian Únětice groups varied considerably from each other; there is no question of distinguishing a single skeletal type attributable solely, or even mainly, to groups making Únětician artifacts. In our opinion the time is still far off when sensible conclusions can be reached concerning the racial affinities of Bronze Age populations, but current work may well begin to differentiate physical groups through large scale sampling of completely excavated cemeteries.

The question of the racial identity of the earliest Bronze Age populations is the subject of an important and widely-accepted theory whose principal proponent has been M. Gimbutas.[12] Broadly speaking, this involves the spread of people on a large scale out of the south Russian steppe into eastern and central Europe at the end of the Neolithic. The archetypal monument of these people is burial of the dead in a grave-pit under a mound of earth (Russian *kurgan*). Such barrows are widely found in south Russia and the Ukraine in the late Neolithic where they are referred to as *Pit Graves*, part of the *Pit Grave culture*. Other features said to be typical of the 'Kurgan culture' include the dismemberment of the corpse before burial, the orientation of the grave so that the face looked east or south and the practice of sprinkling red ochre over the corpse. Tumuli containing some or all of these features are found in Eastern Europe in the Eneolithic and even more so in the Early Bronze Age; it is therefore assumed that the people who erected barrows like this to bury their dead were related to – in fact descended from – the late Neolithic groups on the Russian steppe. Round barrows do not normally appear in the Neolithic; how natural then to assume that a new people was responsible for their introduction in the Bronze Age.

Once this step is accepted, everything else follows. The Corded Ware groups of Europe can be seen as descendants of the 'Kurgan culture'; barrow-graves of the Early Bronze Age similarly. Gimbutas can thus postulate a 'Kurgan' origin for the Coţofeni and Monteoru groups in Romania, the Otomani group in east-central Europe and the generalized Únětice groups in west-central Europe. Since the middle and late phases of the Bronze Age can be shown, in the west at any rate, to have followed on the early phase without a significant cultural break, the people living then must have been of Kurgan origin too; and since one cannot descry any major invasion of people into central Europe between the Urnfield period and the (presumably Celtic) Early Iron Age, it follows that all these groups must be ancestral to the Celts, in other words of Indo-European stock. For this reason Gimbutas can view the 'great Kurgan expansion which proceeded out of the European steppes into Europe and the Near East' as 'Proto-Indo-European'. In the same way tumulus burials in Albania and Greece have been regarded as the distinctive hallmarks of the Indo-European 'Kurganers', arriving there during the third millennium BC and thus responsible for the arrival of the Greeks in Greece.[13]

How can this hypothesis be tested? It seems to us that there is only one sure way, and that is by absolute dating. If the south Russian tumuli can be shown to be consistently earlier than the central and eastern European, then the theory can stand. If not, then it must fall. At the time of writing some forty radiocarbon dates are available for Pit Graves and another six for the late variant called Catacomb Graves (table, p. 154). The great majority fall between 2400 bc and 1700 bc, though a very few are earlier (only a couple significantly so). The only dates for 'Ochre Graves' in east-central Europe are very similar – 2315 ± 80 bc from Kétegyháza, 2140 ± 160 and 2110 ± 160 bc from Baia-Hamangia. Dates for Corded Ware fall in much the same bracket (the range is 2600 – 2100 bc) although it is remarkable that many of these come from the opposite end of Europe and are not from barrows. Broadly speaking, the supposedly derivative groups in Europe are in fact *contemporaneous* with the Pit Graves in south Russia, and not appreciably *later* than them.

Further dates will help to clarify this picture which is still far from complete; other considerations encourage the scepticism that this pattern suggests. Should the spread of a particular burial type be taken as an indication of racial affinities? Could not the barrow be taken rather as a fashion, just as supine inhumation in a coffin with grave-stones at head and foot has been the prevailing fashion in Europe for centuries, more an indicator of the Christian religion than of anything else? Barrow burial occurs in many areas, especially in western Europe, where a primary spread of 'Kurgan people' cannot possibly have occurred. Even if one interprets the Wessex group of southern England as of Kurgan derivation, how is one to explain the occurrence of round barrows and cairns in the Neolithic of Britain, Ireland and Brittany? The fact is that barrow-burial is widespread in time and space and cannot possibly be taken as indicative of a unitary racial situation. That it has been is proof of the force of habit – the habit of introducing invaders from the east, and in particular from the vast unknown of Asiatic Russia, to account for change in the cultures of Europe.

Instead, we see little in the Bronze Age of Europe that needs external influence either to initiate or sustain its unique character. The distribution of Bronze Age occupation in Europe is essentially that of the preceding Neolithic, except that a greater density of population seems attested, by size and number of settlements and cemeteries and by the taking of new lands hitherto uncultivated. The economic practices and industrial processses of the Bronze Age are also logical progressions from the European Neolithic, although there are one or two aspects of significance.

The first is that metallurgy, although known before, created opportunities for the accumulation of material wealth, however that is interpreted. Copper and gold products, unlike stone and clay, were still valuable even when broken or worn, as they could be put back into circulation through the melting-pot or hammer. In time, therefore, more and more metal came into circulation, as more natural supplies were exploited without accompanying wastage. A second feature of the Bronze Age, not seen before, was that for the first time regions in Europe had to create some mechanism to ensure regular and ample supplies of a raw material, metal, which was only available well outside their territories;[14] the precise arrangements by which northern Europe, for example, acquired copper, tin and gold throughout the second millennium are a continuing subject of research.

The metal resources of Europe were otherwise quite widespread (fig. 3). Copper in accessible deposits is reported from the Atlantic coasts, the Alpine area and Bohemian Ore mountains, the Carpathians, the southern Balkans and the Caucasus, and there are other smaller sources as well.[15] Only the northern parts of Europe were well outside the spread of copper-bearing deposits. Tin, however, was much more restricted, and its sources seem to have been limited to the Atlantic coasts, to the Bohemian Ore mountains and to north-western Italy. These supplies, or some of them, must have been quite rapidly discovered and exploited,[16] and mechanisms developed to allow for wider distributions of this essential element in bronze-casting. Gold, highly-valued for its ornamental qualities, was available in north-western Europe, in the Carpathian region, in east Germany and central Jugoslavia, with perhaps other smaller sources as well.[17]

The importance of European metallurgy, in terms of invention and character, when compared with the evidence from the near and middle East, should not be forgotten; copper, tin and gold all occur in the near East, and in Egypt as well, but their exploitation was by no means earlier than, or superior to, that of the European continent. The denigration of coppersmiths in Egypt, with fingers like a crocodile and a smell like fish excrement, may not relate to the standing of metal-workers in Europe, but the importance of such craftsmen should perhaps not be exaggerated. Specialized work with wood, stone, flint, clay, glass and amber is also

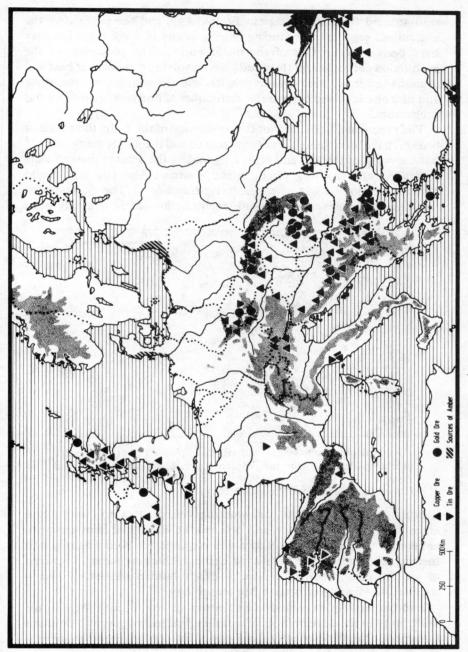

Fig. 3   Sources of copper, tin, gold and amber in Europe. (After Gimbutas 1965)

Copper Ore ◣
Tin Ore ▶
Gold Ore ●
Sources of Amber ▨

9

well-attested from the European Bronze Age, and the position of the
individuals capable of producing objects in any of these materials may
have been equal to that of the metal-worker. The processes for the
production of bronzes, pottery and glass, involving control over heat and
draught and time, were broadly similar, and the winning of ores, stone
and flint also involved comparable techniques of prospect, quarrying and
preparation.

The precise methods used for the production of the many thousands of
bronzes have been the subject of experiment and theory for many years,[18]
but the work of Pittioni and others, in tracing the actual mines and the
separating and smelting places in the Austrian Alps (fig. 4), should
perhaps be singled out as a major contribution.[19] The processes of
smelting oxide ores, roasting and smelting the deeper sulphide ores,

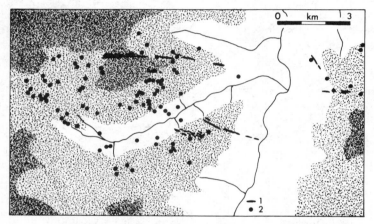

Fig. 4   Mining hollows (1) and smelting places (2) at Mühlbach,
Salzburg, Austria, near the Salzach River. Contours at 1,000 and
1,500 m.
(Based on Zschocke and Preuschen 1932)

melting and casting, and cold-working the product to harden and
embellish it, are well known and need not be elaborated here except to
emphasize that some form of kiln was required for both smelting and
melting. The importance of tin as an element which, at about 10 per cent
of the finished product, created a much harder artifact, is also a
standardized feature of Bronze Age technology.[20]

Another and quite remarkable feature of the Bronze Age is the
uniformity in the development of metallurgical techniques and products
throughout the various natural regions of Europe. In almost every area
the development of metallurgy proceeded in much the same way. The

first copper tools were simply hammered into shape; the first moulds were shallow depressions on blocks of stone, and only at a later stage did finely-made two-piece moulds with valves come into use. The natural result was that similar types of implements were produced in different areas at the same time; or, at any rate, that assemblages contained a comparable variety of implements. This is most obvious in cemetery material in the earlier period – compare the metal finds from, say, Kisapostag (p. 83) and Adlerberg (p. 53) – but by the middle of the second millennium, hoards, too, had similar contents (sickles, palstaves or flanged axes, bracelets, etc.). The invention of a new form, like the sword, spread rapidly throughout the continent so that its first appearance in Austria more or less coincided with that in Romania. The most obvious correspondences in hoard content come in the later Bronze Age; by the thirteenth century a hoard in Transylvania contained similar classes of object to a hoard in Saxony, though not, of course, identical types. We may notice a progression from an earliest phase, during which simple flat objects of pure copper were made – tanged daggers, flat axes, occasional beads – through a period when arsenic or tin was starting to be used, and triangular daggers, flat racket-headed pins, spiral beads, and simple finger-rings of doubled and folded wire were commonly found in graves; to a full 'Bronze Age' development with the regular deposition of large amounts of metal in hoards – flanged axes and *Ringbarren* to start with, then palstaves and spiral-ended bracelets or leg-rings, and finally swords, flange-hilted daggers and sickles, fibulae, solid bracelets of round, hemispherical and lozengic section, leaf-shaped spearheads, bronze vessels, winged and socketed axes, and so on. The list is seemingly endless.

Grave-finds also show close correspondences. Grave assemblages with simple flat sheet or folded wire ornaments (earrings or bracelets), bone beads, faience beads, spiral bronze beads, and triangular daggers may appear anywhere in central Europe in the earlier part of the 'Early Bronze Age'; while trapezoidal-hilted dirks and daggers, long pins with ribbed shank, spiral-terminal leg-rings and heart-shaped pendants characterize the period traditionally called 'Tumulus'. A wide variety of related forms may occur; yet in spite of regional differences, there *is* an overall pattern to be found, and the experienced worker has little difficulty in putting an unfamiliar hoard or grave-find into its correct time-bracket, simply because most bronze forms, in one shape or another, are ubiquitous. Not so with pottery, of course; a closer acquaintance is needed to slot pots into their appropriate pigeon-hole; yet even here a modicum of order may be found. The Early Bronze Age in central Europe produced a very characteristic cup shape, with low belly and funnel-like neck, that appears everywhere; the Tumulus culture is most often characterized by bowls with incised geometric decoration, pedestal bases, and, often, peaked rims; while in the Late Bronze Age cinerary urns, often biconical or with globular body, cylindrical neck and flaring rim, were the universal form. Such forms serve as chronological indicators to the trained eye, while the more exact attribution of types to phases, and their relation to one another, is a matter for the local specialist.

By such specialized typological study, various distributions of related materials can be seen, and production centres and exchange mechanisms suggested. The problems with such an approach are several. We must rely upon known distributions with all their uncertainties about uniformity of discovery, equal degrees of research and recognition, and similar preservation of evidence, in different areas. We must also recognize that burial of such material as bronzes, or pottery, may have been made for very different reasons, and simple uncorrected comparisons of find-spots may well be totally unjustified; a glance at a few possibilities for the disposal of objects will show some, but doubtless not all, of the differences in the ultimate place where objects came to reside.

Deposition of objects

	local areas	*foreign areas*
contemporary use	in grave	gift
	in votive deposit	plunder
	loss during use	tribute
	thrown away	exchange or sale
	abandoned in settlement	
future use	in scrap metal hoard	in scrap metal hoard
	unused in hoard	unused in hoard
	inheritance	

Burial with the dead or loss during use, for example, should reflect the chronological and cultural spheres of the producing society, but acquisition through plunder, or inheritance, or exchange mechanisms, may take material out of its original position in space or time, and it may then again be subject to various methods of and reasons for deposition. Distribution maps which take no account of such variation must be of uncertain value.

One way by which archaeologists have attempted to arrange their material, and to find the sources of the products, is by analysis of the metal composition. Spectographic analysis can determine if the metal is a deliberate alloy (of copper and tin) and can identify and measure the impurities in the metal.[21] When comparisons are made with the possible or probable ore bodies themselves, as has been done in Austria, it theoretically allows a direct correlation between mine and product, and the importance of this need not be stressed. Many different analytical studies have been made of Bronze Age metals, and among these studies we might single out the ambitious Stuttgart programme which now encompasses many thousands of Early Bronze Age objects.[22] Using five main elements, nickel, bismuth, arsenic, antimony and silver, in varying proportions, the analyses are grouped and distributions plotted. Various regional metal-groups are identified, and although there are some groups so heterogeneous that they cannot possibly be attributed to a single source or industry, others are restricted to geographical areas and can, for the moment, be claimed to represent the major and probably local metal source for that area.[23]

There are many other programmes of analyses, none so ambitious as the Stuttgart studies, but more rewarding in terms of locally-defined groups.[24] The work of Pittioni and Neuninger in Austria has already been noted; here the absolute quantities of the elements are not measured, only their presence, or a trace, or absence; comparisons with the ore bodies have readily been made.[25]

The problems with these programmes of analysis are many. They include the demonstrable fact that the composition of the ore varies with its position in the parent rock and can be affected by weathering, smelting, melting and casting; the analytical techniques can vary and produce different results. Much current work attempts to assess these uncertainties, and to devise more consistent procedures. Most heavily criticized has been the Stuttgart school, but this is mainly directed towards the interpretation of results rather than the analytical data.[26]

For gold, the analytical work has proved useful if also controversial. Analysis of many hundreds of gold objects has allowed the identification of a number of groups which may relate to local gold sources. The products of the Bronze Age workshops centred near the gold-bearing deposits of Brád and Verespatak in Transylvania are readily identified by composition and character (fig. 5) and the correlation of Irish Bronze Age products with Irish Wicklow gold is a useful if undramatic revelation.[27]

These programmes of analyses must be seen as only one small part of the study of Bronze Age communities in Europe. They may provide a guide to the mechanics of industry in certain areas, but the whole question of the interpretation of metalwork in the European Bronze Age is unresolved. Basically, the evidence of Bronze Age societies suggests a large number of small communities almost entirely self-sufficient and under little pressure. Within and between these societies there is a range of materials, mainly metal, which sometimes demonstrates long-distance distribution of raw metal or finished products. The mechanisms by which

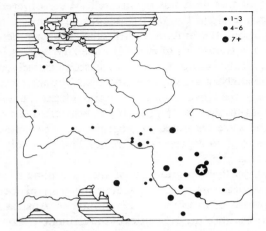

Fig. 5   Distribution of gold finds of Groups A3 according to Hartmann 1970. The gold source at Brád is shown as a star, and the majority of large finds lie close to source in the middle Danube region.

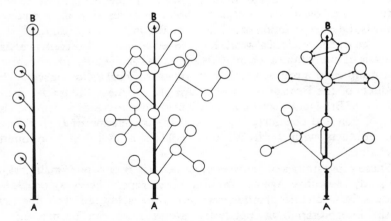

Fig. 6   A model of distributive mechanisms which may reflect the ways by which Bronze Age objects were spread out from source A to destination B through direct or indirect means. The circles represent intermediate or diversionary destinations.
(After Stjernquist 1967 and Thrane 1975, fig. 117)

such materials were obtained, worked and distributed are not well-known, and although ethnographic evidence may provide some suggestions,[28] the situation of Europe in the Bronze Age was unique and we cannot attempt to create an artificial model without much more evidence at our disposal to guide us towards the most appropriate theoretical position. We may talk of random exchange, local redistributions, highly organized regional and longer-distance trade (fig. 6), and many maps of Bronze Age materials purport to demonstrate these systems (fig. 7). But we suggest that much more work on sources, analyses, settlement locations and geographical territories is required before we can begin to assess the importance or otherwise of the movement of objects and materials over appreciable distances.[29]

Important as metals and their procurement were to the peoples of Bronze Age Europe, we would not wish these remarks to imply that we believe such things to have been their main preoccupation. While a fair

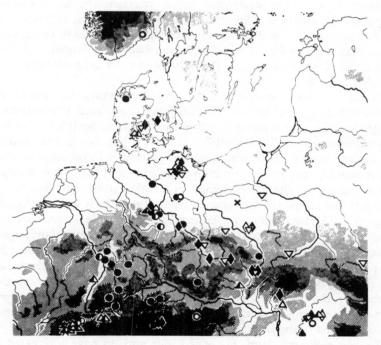

Fig. 7 Distribution of beaten metal cups of various Late Bronze Age types, perhaps produced in several centres, or disseminated from a single source.
(From Thrane 1975, fig. 81)

number of people must have been engaged in the various processes that led from the extraction of ore to the distribution of finished products, many more must have been involved with metals only peripherally. Though objects of metal conferred a degree of 'wealth' on their owner by reason of their intrinsic value both as raw material and as artifact, such wealth was presumably restricted in its distribution through society. One can hardly doubt, indeed, that for the majority of people inhabiting small agricultural villages of the types we describe in this book, the procurement and possession of metal was of little concern: the demands of the farming year would afford little time, and the returns of agriculture little opportunity, for active seeking after wealth. Metal tools, where functionally superior, would naturally be in demand, and Bronze Age farmers must have tried to ensure their availability by providing other commodities for barter, including their own labouring services. For such people, the aspects of life that would remain of unchanging importance would be the provision of food, clothing and shelter, and the more abstract factors that determine social relationships and emotional responses. In archaeological terms, it is the evidence for settlement, for economic practices and for social division that probably encapsulate, more than any number of metal finds, the essence of Bronze Age life. It is in the study of these aspects, then, that we expect the most informative insights to occur.

Much has been written in the past purporting to demonstrate population chnge on the basis of artifact typology. Such attitudes are no longer tenable, at least not in the simplistic guises under which they have generally appeared.[30] Instead, the evidence for population continuity on the basis of settlement forms, economic patterns and religious practices has mounted, and once freed from the shackles of the simple equation artifact change = population change, typological study can often be used to refute the supposition of change where formerly it was employed to support it. Archaeologists are becoming increasingly aware that what they view in the artifactual record is essentially a static landscape, a frozen moment in time, whereas what should more properly be sought is the dynamic aspect, based on the processes of development in the various interlocking subsystems of the whole. It is with the study of these processes—the processes by which cultural systems alter and adapt to take on the various tangible shapes we see before us—that archaeology, including that of the Bronze Age, will be principally concerned.[31]

We can make no claim, nor was it our aim, to have interpeted the material remains of Bronze Age Europe from any strict 'processualist' standpoint. This book presents the results of other people's researches and excavations; it is mainly a review of the current state of Bronze Age studies, and processualist interpretations have so far had little impact in this area of prehistory. At the same time, we have attempted to avoid simplistic interpretations of artificial remains and to present a broad spectrum of evidence which will be amenable to a variety of approaches. At the very least, we would like to think that we have cleared the decks for further study.

Notes

1 Müller-Karpe 1974. It is interesting, though perhaps fruitless, to speculate on the absolute percentage figure which would be required for an objective standard by which to judge a culture 'Full Metal Age' rather than 'Incipient Metal Age'. Different figures would no doubt be obtained for different areas, and it would in any case depend on what materials one was using (whether hoards alone, or graves etc.). Theoretically it would be convenient to imagine a 50 per cent metal level for graves (more than 50 per cent of the non-ceramic content) but the numerous 'ametallic' Bronze Age finds would render this impossible. Some such estimate in combination with a 'hoard coefficient' might be more satisfactory.

For a recent detailed discussion of terminology (from a Marxist standpoint) see L. S. Klejn, *Neolithische Studien* I (1972), 7–29. And see R. Pittioni, *Norddeutsche Affinerie* (April 1966), 33–9, for a view of the significance of metal.

2 The situation in Northern Europe is clearly different (p. 283).

3 Pittioni 1954, 164, 170ff., 200 etc.

4 Pittioni 1954, 206, 284ff., 288, 290.

5 R. Pittioni in Zschocke and Preuschen 1932, 155–68.

6 Glob 1974.

7 Among many, the works of Montelius and Reinecke; descriptions and references occur in relevant chapters.

8 Several papers in *Proceedings of the International Symposium on World Climate 8000–0 BC*, Royal Geographical Society, London, n.d. (1966), especially L. Starkel, B. Frenzel, S. Jelgersma; for a reconstruction of atmospheric circulation *c.* 1200 BC, H. H. Lamb *et al.*

9 Frenzel 1966, 106ff.

10 The standard view is C. Coon, *The Races of Europe*, 1939, 154ff, 162ff.

11 Ullrich 1972, 112ff.

12 Gimbutas 1956; 1965, 21ff., 185ff., 250, 259 etc., *JIES* 1–2 (1973), 163–214.

13 Hammond 1967.

14 Other materials (flint, obsidian, stone and shells, for example) were quite widely distributed in parts of Europe in the fourth or third millennia, but were perhaps not quite so dominant materials as bronze eventually became. The possible agencies of distribution, and a useful set of maps, are discussed by A. Sherratt, in *Problems in Economic and Social Archaeology* (ed. G Sieveking, I. H. Longworth and K. E. Wilson), 557–81, London 1976.

15 The utilization of surface ores probably took place at an early date. Deeper mining in the areas with the richest deposits, however, was in progress in the early centuries of the second millennium BC. The ore mountains of the Carpathians (especially the north side of the Transylvanian Alps, the Munţii Metalici near Hunedoara and elsewhere),

Jugoslavia (in various parts of the mountainous zone, notably the mines in the Carpathian extension near Rudna Glava) and the central Alps (the Salzburg district) were intensively exploited.

16 By panning rather than by mining, according to analytical evidence.

17 Gold-panning was probably the most common method of retrieval of the metal, but mining was also practised in the Transylvanian region of eastern Europe: Hartmann 1970. See also H. Neuninger, E. Preuschen and R. Pittioni, *Archaeol. Austriaca* 49 (1971), 23–35.

18 R. Tylecote, *Metallurgy in Archaeology*, 1962;
R. Forbes, *Metallurgy in Antiquity*, 1950;
A. Oldeberg, *Metalteknik und förhistorist Tid*, 1942—3;
H. Drescher, *Der Uberfangguss*, 1958;
W. Lorenzen in *Helgoland und das früheste Kupfer des Nordens*, 1965, 13–19;
H. Coghlan *Pitt Rivers Occas. Papers Technology* 4 (1951) are but a few of the substantial contributions.

19 R. Pittioni, *Der urzeitliche Kupferzbergbau im Gebiet um Kitzbühel. Stadtbuch Kitzbühel* 2 (1968); Zschocke and Preuschen 1932.

20 Antimony, lead and arsenic (the last within the ore itself and not as a separate toxic and volatile metal) were used on occasion as substitutes, but none as successfully as tin. Arsenical copper was an important source of metal in the early Bronze Age; see H. McKerrell and R. F. Tylecote *PPS* 38 (1972), 209–18; E. R. Eaton and H. McKerrell, *World Archeol.* 8 (1976), 169–91 with refs. The temperatures required for most processes must have involved some form of kiln: smelting copper ores, *c.* 1100°C; melting copper *c.* 1100°C; melting gold, *c.*

1050°C. The processes of smelting oxide ores such as cuprite and malachite:
$$2\,CuO + C \rightarrow 2Cu + CO_2;$$
for sulphide ores such as chalcopyrite (copper pyrites), roasting before smelting:
$$2\,Cu_2S + 3O_2 \rightarrow 2Cu_2O + 2\,SO_2$$
$$2\,Cu_2O + Cu_2S \rightarrow 6Cu + SO_2$$
H. Hodges *Artifacts* (1964) chapter 4.

21 In general, the trace elements found in an object of bronze are assumed to have come in the copper ore and not in the tin.

22 Junghans, Sangmeister and Schröeder 1960, 1968 (hereafter JSS).

23 Summarized in A. Hartmann and F. Sangmeister, *Angewandte Chemie* 11 (1972), 620–9; S. Junghans and H. Schickler, *Germania* 46 (1968), 1–19; *Ausgrabungen in Deutschland* 1 (1975), pt. 3.

We may most conveniently summarize the results from central Europe. Throughout the Copper Age (JSS use this term in the traditional sense) the most important metal group was E oo, but E oi and E oiA were also in use, especially for flat axes. In the Early Bronze Age proper, the situation becomes much more complicated, though certain features stand out. Ingot torcs, for instance, overwhelmingly cluster in group C2, with high figures for FC as well. There is no clear preponderance for the Early Bronze Age in south-east central Europe in the early phases, though C2 is high and A, B2, E11A and E11B are fairly high. The south-west part shows a clear dependence on groups A and A1, the north part on A and C2, but with many others as well. In the later stages of the Early Bronze Age the definition of objects by given metalgroups is impossible, for nearly all of them are represented; but there are indications that new groups, like FA and FB1, were coming into use, a trend which Tumulus bronzes continued.

What do these groups mean in geographical terms? Metal-group E oo is widely distributed throughout Europe and cannot be attributed to a given source. Eo1 and Eo1A both show a marked preference for Iberia, but occur widely elsewhere. The important group C2 is impressively homogeneous and is almost certainly to be attributed to the Austrian ore-sources. It is interesting, therefore, to observe that objects of metal-group C2 occur all over central Europe, and further east as well if the analyses are to be believed. Group A in the Early Bronze Age is more northerly-oriented, showing a concentration on the lower Elbe, but with a fair scatter around central Europe as well. E11A looks as if it may have a strong Scottish-Irish bias; E11B, A1 and B2 are not restricted to any one area, and the same is true of the later FA and FB1 groups. It appears, then, that only C2, and possibly E11A, are attributable to particular ore-sources, and therefore trade; it is unfortunately impossible to distinguish from the remainder any clear pattern.

24 E.g. H. Coghlan and H. Case, *PPS* 23 (1957), 91–123; H. Case, *Palaeohistoria* 12 (1966), 141–77 for Ireland; D. Britton, *Archaeometry* 4 (1961), 39–52 for south Britain; H. T. Waterbolk, *Helinium* 5 (1965), 227–51 for the Netherlands and a widely accepted method of presentation of analyses in graph form; J. M. Coles, *PPS* 35 (1969), 330–44 for Scotland; M. A. Smith and A. Blin-Stoyle, *PPS* 25 (1959), 188–208 for Late Bronze Age Britain; P. R. Giot, J. Bourhis and

J. Briard, *Travaux du Laboratoire d'Anthropologie Préhistorique* 1964–65, 1969, for Brittany; A. Boomert, *Helinium* 15 (1975), 134–61 for Gemeinlebarn, Austria; F. and E. Schubert, in A. Mozsolics 1967, 185–203 for Hungary; E. Sangmeister, in A. Mozsolics 1973, 215–49 for Hungary; F. R. Hodson, *World Archaeology* 1 (1969) 90–105 for a multivariate technique for clustering analyses.

25 R. Pittioni, *Arch. Aust.* 26 (1959), 67–95 as well as continuing series of analyses reported in the same journal.

26 A. Boomert, *Helinium* 15 (1975), 134–6 gives a useful summary, and full bibliography of reviews; one of the first reviews of the Stuttgart school was J. J. Butler and J. D. van der Waals, *Helinium* 4 (1967), 3–39.

27 Hartmann, 1970; A. Hartmann, *Germania* 46 (1968) 19–27; A. Hartmann and E. Sangmeister, *Angewandte Chemie* 11 (1972), 620–9. H. Neuninger, E. Preuschen and R. Pittioni, *Arch. Aust.* 49 (1971), 23–35.
Critical review of Irish evidence: P. Harbison, *J. Roy. Soc. Antiq. Irel.* 101 (1971), 159–63.

28 E.g. M. J. Rowlands, *World Archaeology* 3 (1971), 210–24; Rowlands 1976; Stjernquist 1967.

29 We do not further pursue the varying schools of thought about the existence and role of 'specialist smiths', 'itinerant merchantmen', 'travelling salesmen', 'craft schools' and the like, although all of these have had their support from a wide variety of prehistorians: V. G. Childe, *The Bronze Age*, 1930; C. F. C. Hawkes, *The Prehistoric Foundations of Europe*, 1940; Clark, 1952; D. L. Clarke, *Analytical Archaeology*, 1968; Gimbutas 1965.

30 Originally set out by J. G. D. Clark, *Antiquity* 40 (1966), 172–89; the

debate continued by W. Y. Adams,
Antiquity 42 (1968), 194–215.
31 For tentative applications to Bronze
age Europe, C. Renfrew, *The*
Emergence of Civilisation, 1972, and
in C. B. Moore (ed.), *Reconstructing*
Complex Societies, 1974.

PART 1
Earlier Bronze Age

2 Central Europe

By central Europe, we mean the area called in German *Mitteleuropa*:
extending from central Germany to the edge of the Carpathians and the
Vistula, from Berlin and Warsaw in the north to the Austrian and
Hungarian borders in the south; comprising the whole of Austria,
Czechoslovakia and Hungary, and most of East Germany and Poland.
We also wish to consider here some of the earlier Bronze Age groups on
the western fringes of central Europe – mainly in the Rhine valley, which
touches on western and south-western Germany, eastern France and
northern Switzerland.

Geographically, central Europe falls into a number of distinct zones.[1]
In the north (northern Germany and Poland) is the vast tract of low-
lying land that comprises the north European plain, interspersed with
lakes and extensive forests. Glacial action has rendered many of the soils
sandy or boggy. South of this area lie the hills that border on Germany
and shut in Bohemia and Moravia, rolling upland country with
intermittent forest, brown forest soils, and in many parts a thin layer of
loess. To the south again one comes to the Danube valley, and in Austria
and Switzerland to the foothills of the Alpine massif, where the brown
forest soils give way to poorer mountain soils, and where the relief is
naturally more marked as the mountains become higher. To the west, the
long valley of the Rhine stretches southward from the North Sea, some
600 km (as the crow flies) to the Alps; in its central area the rolling hills
and plains provide fertile soils. The upper Rhine valley, like that of the
Danube, is dissected by many streams flowing from the mountains and
high plateaux of south Germany.

Terminology[2]

The attribution of archaeological finds in central Europe to a 'Bronze
Age' started in the second quarter of the nineteenth century, following

C. J. Thomsen's invention of the Stone–Bronze–Iron sequence. By the latter decades of that century it had become apparent that there were many sub-phases within the Bronze period; in particular it was evident that the earlier part was characterized above all by inhumation burial, often in a barrow, and the later part (usually referred to as the Hallstatt period in the early German literature) characterized by cremation. We now know that the second phase should be sub-divided again, so that the earlier part of it (Hallstatt A and B) belongs to the Late Bronze Age, the later part (C and D) to the Early Iron Age. Although it was realized from an early stage that internal development was discernible in each main period, precise definition – or at any rate labelling – of the phases was not attempted until Paul Reinecke, living in Munich and working in south Bavaria, applied a series of phase-letters to the material. Each period, Bronze and Hallstatt, was divided into four – A to D – on the basis of typological development of hoards and grave material; but although the system came into general use during the first quarter of this century, Reinecke never gave more than an outline of the suggested characteristics of each stage.[3]

The ordering of the 'Bronze Age' into A, B, C and D was in general correct, as is shown by the fact that the scheme continues in use today; but even in its home area it is restricting, and when applied to more distant lands it becomes no more than a general framework onto which material can be pinned. As long as one knows what one means by the individual phases, this system can greatly aid the understanding of sequences of material in areas other than Bavaria. In general, Br A refers to what is traditionally called the Early Bronze Age, and B and C to the Middle, or Tumulus, Bronze Age; D (the 'Late Bronze Age' in the old sense) witnessed the start of widespread cremation burial and is nowadays taken as the early part of the ensuing 'Urnfield' period.[4]

Reinecke himself subdivided his phases A and C, and a good deal of shuffling of material between periods has gone on since then. Br A was divided into A1, which included material from flat inhumation cemeteries like Straubing and Adlerberg as well as hoards with metal-hilted daggers like Gaubickelheim (Oppenheim) and Neunheilingen (Langensalza), and A2, which was composed of hoard material like that from Trassem (Saarburg), Langquaid (Rothenburg) and Tinsdahl (Hamburg-Rissen), characterized by daggers and rapiers with ogival blades, flanged axes, socketed spearheads, and pins with perforated spherical heads. In 1960 a third phase, A3, was suggested by Milojčić;[5] Točik and Vladár,[6] among others, later amplified this to account for a collection of material identified by them in south-west Slovakia, patently later than the usual A2 but earlier than B1. The usage Br A3 has not, however, found its way far into

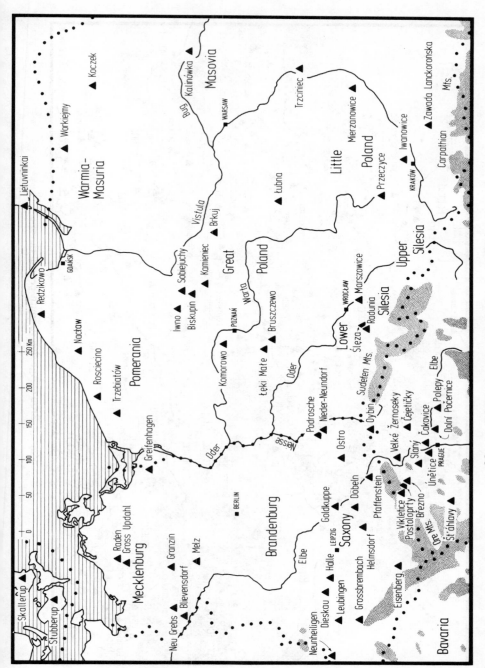

Map 1   **Bronze Age sites in north-central Europe.**

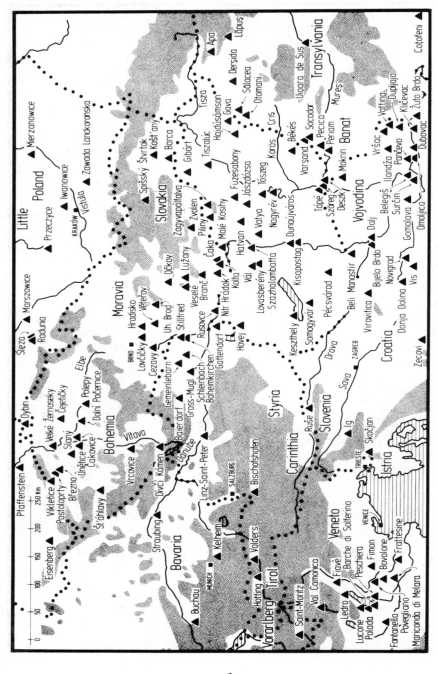

Map 2   Bronze Age sites in south-central Europe.

26

the literature, even though the material (Ilvesheim, Ackenbach, Bühl etc.) is clearly anomalous.

The B and C periods were also sub-divided by Reinecke and again by Holste; their systems included illogicalities, however, and only considerably after the event has Torbrügge established a more or less accepted scheme for Bavaria[7] (fig. 8).

These outline schemes provide a broad framework for the study of the period in central Europe, but they are based almost entirely on typology, and mostly that of bronze objects. Since these are the most numerous and distinctive artifacts found, they naturally act as a focus of attention; they do not, however, account satisfactorily for other cultural manifestations, like pottery, ornaments or grave forms. To try to fill this gap, several other schemes have been adopted. Christlein[8] has worked out a fourfold, and Stein[9] a threefold, development of the Early Bronze Age at Gemeinlebarn on the basis of the horizontal stratigraphy at the cemetery there; only in the final phase do graves contain material comparable to that of Br A2 (fig. 9). Adler,[10] by the use of incidence tables of the artifacts in graves, was able to divide the material at Linz-St Peter into three chronological groups, the main innovation being a late phase of Br A1 which seemed to be transitional to A2. Moucha's work proceeds mainly by means of pottery typology;[11] he distinguishes six phases in the Únětice group in north Bohemia (fig. 10). Other authors have also provided pottery sequences for individual areas.[12]

Proceeding from a metallurgical viewpoint, Schubert[13] has distinguished four phases of metal-working in the Early Bronze Age on the middle Danube, going from the simple wire and beaten sheet ornaments of early Nitra and related groups, through a phase characterized by more elaborate, but still fairly small, forms, to the main period of metallurgical production: characteristic forms are large knot-headed pins, finger rings (*Noppenringe*) and ingot torcs. Finally comes a late phase transitional to Middle Bronze Age.

The name that dominates the study of the early part of the Bronze Age in central Europe is that of *Únětice* (in German, *Aunjetitz*). Únětice is a village a few kilometres north-west of Prague,[14] not far from the Vltava. In the second half of the nineteenth century a cemetery of sixty flat graves was excavated by the local doctor, and the material from them was seen to be typical of many such cemeteries in Bohemia – triangular daggers, ring-headed and eyelet pins, leg- or arm-spirals, spirally-folded finger-

Fig. 8 (*overleaf*) Bronzes, pottery and tomb types typical of the earlier Bronze Age in the upper Palatinate. A-D phases after Reinecke etc.; triangles contain types found in hoards.
(After Torbrügge 1959a)

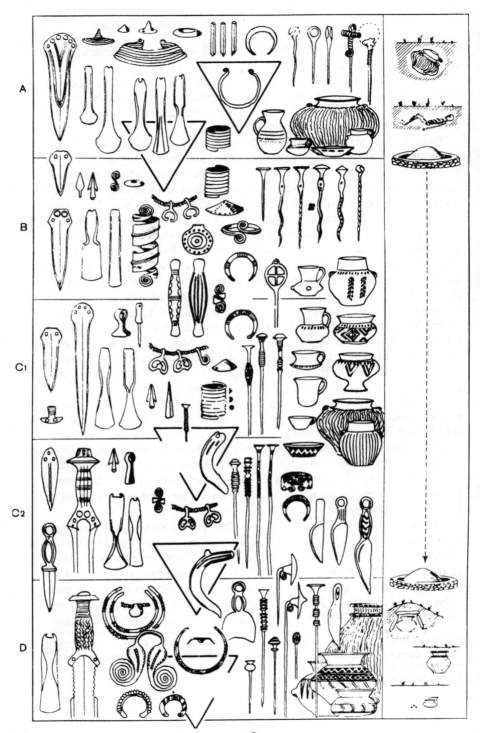

28

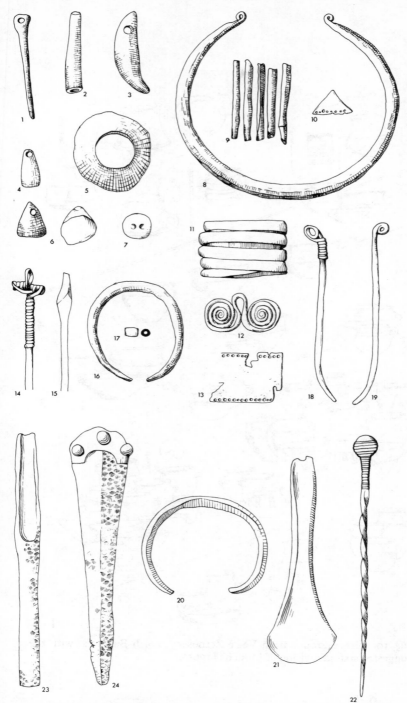

Fig. 9   Types found in graves at Gemeinlebarn (St Pölten) with the
suggested fourfold division of Christlein (1964). 1–7, phase 1; 8–13, 18–19,
phase 2; 14–17, phase 3; 20–24, phase 4. Varying scales.

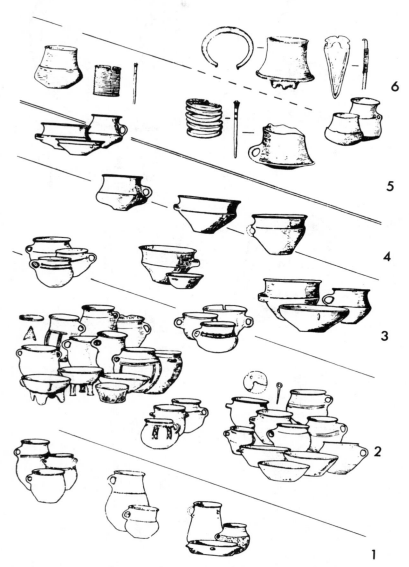

Fig. 10   Grave-groups from Velké Žernoseky, north Bohemia, with the suggested sixfold division of Moucha (1961).

30

rings known as *Noppenringe*, 'droplet' earrings, spiral beads, amber beads of various shapes, and a variety of cups and jars, notably 'hour-glass cups' and miniature vessels. This collection, when amplified by other finds from Bohemia, was seen to be analogous, or in some cases identical, to material in Moravia, as well as western Slovakia, Austria, Bavaria, Thuringia, Saxony and Silesia, so that the cultural name was applied to the whole area covered by these provinces. More recently, some authors have applied the term further afield – to eastern Slovakia and even Hungary and Romania – though in a loose sense only. Strictly speaking, material like that from the classic cemeteries of the Únětice area is found only in Bohemia and the immediately adjacent areas; even the famous 'princely graves' are not a Bohemian phenomenon, and certainly not paralleled at Únětice itself. But it is convenient, and not seriously misleading, to refer to the wider area – up to the boundaries of the Hungarian province – as that of Únětician culture or, more accurately, group of cultures. In Reinecke's terminology this corresponds to Br A; the early, mostly metal-less graves being A1, and the rich graves of the classic phase being A2. The latest finds form a separate group, sometimes called A2/B1 and sometimes A3, though the universal validity of such a phase is by no means certain (cf. above, p. 24).

In the succeeding period, the traditional name 'Tumulus Bronze Age' (*Hügelgräberbronzezeit*) indicates that the period was one in which graves were situated under barrows, and in many areas this is the prevailing form. The concept of a culture characterized solely by graves is not, today, an appealing one; nor are the reasons why these graves are separated from Únětice graves intelligible without an understanding of the historical development of Bronze Age studies. The period and its phases were defined by Reinecke on the basis of certain closed grave groups (Lochham, Göggenhofen, Asenkofen and Riegsee) at a time when settlement material was virtually unknown and scholarly interest centred around attribution of types to given phases of development. Reinecke pretended to do no more than this; and his attributions were, in their relative order, more or less correct. The 'Tumulus Bronze Age', however, was a period of at least 200 years, during which people lived as well as died; the importance traditionally attached to it can be seen from the fact that it is often simply called 'Middle Bronze Age'. By the end of the Tumulus period, that is by Br C2/D, the first signs of a different tradition, involving cremation as the dominant funeral rite rather than inhumation, are beginning to appear; it is at that point that we will stop in this chapter.

It is our intention in this survey to make regular use of none of the chronological systems we have described, which we believe are inappropriate for general study of the European Bronze Age. It will be found necessary, however, to have some familiarity with them since they are normally used in the literature. Our framework is to be much looser, and we will in general refer only to events or sites as being part of the 'earlier' or the 'later' Bronze Age, the dividing line being drawn at around 1300 BC. Sometimes more precise definition is called for, and here we have occasionally introduced elements of the traditional framework (especially that of Reinecke in central and Montelius in northern Europe). In these cases, reference can be made to table 1.

Table 1   Comparative chronological schemes for central Europe: earlier Bronze Age

Reinecke (*modified*)	Montelius (*North Europe*)	Bóna (*Hungary*)	Hachmann (*North Europe*)
		(EBA)	
Br A1		MBA 1	
			Horizon I
A2		MBA 2	
	I		Horizon II
(A3)			
B1		MBA 3	Horizon III
B2/C1	II	LBA 1	Horizon IV
C2		LBA 2	
D	III	Transitional	

Environment

Environmental evidence from pollen analysis has provided a fairly full and consistent picture for central Europe over many years. We can do no more than touch on these matters here, for the literature is truly vast.[15] The Sub-boreal, in central Europe pollen zone VIII, is identified by palynologists as the period of the spread of the beech in the mixed oak forest.[16] Such is the picture obtained from very many lowland areas,[17] though of course the sequence is rather different in the mountains; there hornbeam flourished in this period. Numerous diagrams show that forest clearance was under way, and continued to take place sporadically between phases of regeneration. Cereal pollen is usually present throughout, as well as cultivation weeds like *Plantago*; occasionally charcoal layers appear. Climatically, it is thought that the decrease of the mixed oak forest and the increase in shade-loving species indicates a cool period, with some increase in precipitation perhaps around 2000 bc.[18]

During the course of the earlier Bronze Age there were apparently two oscillations that brought about cooler, wetter conditions (cf. above, p. 5), though it is not possible at present to correlate these with known archaeological events.

Western Part

The later Copper Age in west-central Europe was dominated by the companion and complementary cultural groups, Corded Ware and Bell Beakers. Copper objects, especially tanged daggers and simple ornaments, appear in graves of these groups with some regularity; but it is not that fact that leads one to consider them of paramount importance in the formation of the local Early Bronze Age groups, but rather the remarkable similarity in pottery forms. Both groups are, in central Europe, known mainly from inhumation cemeteries; and though in some areas they must have overlapped in time, the evidence is unequivocal that Corded Ware started earlier than did Bell Beakers.[19] Elements of both groups were apparently available when the crystallization of the succeeding Bronze Age groups took place. In central Germany, Poland and Slovakia the inheritance was from Corded Ware; in Bohemia, Moravia and southern Germany it was from Bell Beakers. Pottery forms from both go through virtually unchanged, and in widely separated areas: for instance the Chłopice-Veselé group in south Poland and north Slovakia,[20] and those elements of early Únětice which used to be called 'Marschwitz' (Marszowice) by German scholars,[21] are clearly of Corded Ware derivation – indeed in some cases the pot forms have not changed at all – while cemeteries like Straubing and München-Sendling in Bavaria,[22] or Polepy in northeast Bohemia,[23] show a clear continuation into the Únětice culture-group of the simple one-handled cup or polypod bowl. Some cemeteries are in fact 'transitional' from Bell Beaker to Early Bronze Age,[24] and it has been shown that Beaker and (to a lesser extent) Corded Ware grave furnishing continued on into the Bronze Age.[25] There can be no doubt – at least insofar as artifacts can lead to historical conclusions – that direct local development from Corded Ware and Bell Beakers led to the formation of the cultural groups of the Early Bronze Age of west-central Europe.

Settlement

Early Bronze Age houses in central Europe have left few traces. Often they seem to have been no more than rough shacks erected over simple pits, in which grain storage, and in some cases cooking, took place. For the earliest phases – 'proto-Únětice'[26] – knowledge of settlements is negligible, and settlement patterns have to be deduced from cemetery distributions. Only with the development of the period are more sites found[27] but it is still quite rarely that regular house-plans occur, and Bohemia is among the most prolific areas for them. Postoloprty (Žatec), with sixteen houses known and a possible total of forty in the village (not all contemporary), is the most notable, but the same area of north-west Bohemia has produced many other finds.[28] The two houses of the earlier period at Postoloprty were rectangular (about 6 × 4 m; fig. 11); one had four central posts that were taken as a support for a ridge roof, the other also had four posts, but the middle two were deeper, suggesting a higher central construction.[29] The excavator suggested that twenty to thirty houses were in use at one time, with a population of 100 to 200. More recently, excavations at Březno (Louny) have revealed a series of Únětician houses; the total is not yet known but runs into some tens – composed of posts inserted very close together forming rectangular structures up to 20 m long, and mostly oriented east–west: both internal and external storage and rubbish pits are numerous.[30] Březno was occupied continuously from the early Neolithic to the Iron Age, so that its situation, on light sandy loess, and only a few hundred metres from the River Ohře, is of importance; this is typical for Early Bronze Age settlements in north Bohemia. Raised sites beside rivers were also typical for Silesia,[31] where the settlement type was indistinguishable from that current in the Neolithic.

North Bohemia is an area where open settlements of this (and many other) periods abound, in contrast to the situation in most of the lands occupied by the Únětice culture-group. Isolated pockets of denser settlement do occur: in north Austria, for instance, the Salzburg area has produced a disproportionately large number of habitation sites,[32] important through their connection with the exploitation of the nearby copper sources. In Austria, again, is the well-known site of Grossmugl (Korneuburg) where six house-plans were recovered,[33] but the irregular placing of these and their 'semi-subterranean' nature does not inspire confidence that a true picture was obtained from excavation, though the site was undoubtedly used as an Early Bronze Age settlement as well as a later Bronze Age urnfield.

North of the Únětician area, an interesting enclosure comes from Biskupin (Żnin: not to be confused with the late Lausitz stockade nearby, p. 356).[34] A roughly pear-shaped area 90 m long was enclosed by a ditch, broken at two points, and no doubt a bank; abundant settlement debris included pottery named after the type-site of Iwno. The site has been interpreted as a stock enclosure, and is estimated to have been able to hold 500 cattle (p. 287).

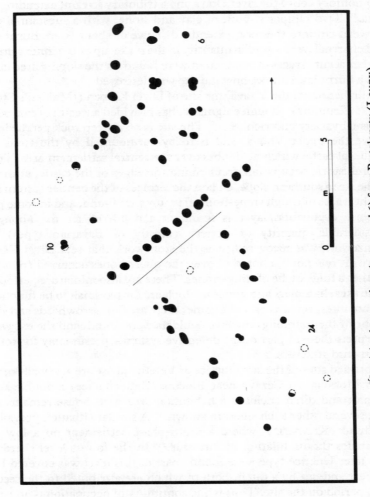

Fig. 11 Únětician house-plans (24, 10 and 6) from Postoloprty (Louny). (After B. Soudský, *AR* 5 (1953))

At the end of the Únětice Bronze Age, especially in that late part of it named after Věteřov, settlements changed from being low-lying open sites on terraces beside rivers to being fortified sites, often on steep and highly defensible hill-tops. At Vinoř north of Prague the settlement, which contained part of a house 6 × 2.8 m, was fortified by a ditch and possibly a palisade.[35] At Vrcovice (Písek) the site occupies a rocky promontory above the river Otava and a tributary stream, extending over 1 ha.[36] Two ramparts, built of clay and stone, with a substantial ditch between cut into the rock, extend a distance of about 60 m. Burnt daub and charcoal were found in quantity in the make-up of the inner rampart. Rather scanty traces of occupation were found on the sloping area inside, and a burnt layer shows how the site was destroyed.

Further down the Vltava, the site of Dívčí Kámen ('Maiden's Stone', Český Krumlov), though enigmatic, has provided a wealth of material of unusual variety and richness.[37] The site is on a steep rock perched high above the upper Vltava, and is today surmounted by the ruins of a medieval castle which no doubt cover the central settlement area. Traces of prehistoric occupation occur round the edges of the castle, at the top of the steep southern slope, and on the terraces of the gentler eastern side. Slight traces of rough stone-built structures are found, and in some parts a dense occupation layer is found at a depth of 1.1 m. Though a considerable quantity of pottery (mostly of Bavarian types) and bronzework was recovered, it is the stonework that sets Dívčí Kámen apart. At one point a hoard of over 120 quernstones occurred (pl. 5), at another a huge cache of sling-stones. There are also miniature perforated stone axes, hammers and gouges, which are far too small to be functional and are interpreted as part of a game; there are flint arrowheads and saws. In one of the soundings massive boulders were found, and the excavator interprets these as part of the defensive system – presumably for rolling down onto attackers.

Fortified sites of the late Únětice or Věteřov phase are also well-known from Moravia. At Cezavy near Blučina (Židlochovice) a double stone rampart and ditch enclosed a habitation area with house remains and pits; several other such sites are known.[38] A similar situation prevails at Hradisko (Kroměříž), where a multi-phase settlement on a low hill dominates the undulating countryside.[39] In the lowest level sherds of local later Únětice type were found: part of this level was covered by a rampart and cut by a ditch, both of which are attributed to the second main period on the site. Thus while continuity of occupation is attested, there is some evidence (for the rampart was insubstantial) for a break, with defensive measures being taken at a time that coincides with the end of Únětice.[40] In the second layer, the excavator identifies elements in the

pottery (notably bossed ornament) that link it with the succeeding
Lausitz culture, and comparable sherds have been found at other sites in
the district.[41] The succession is clearly an important one, but it is hard to
deduce historical conclusions from the evidence that Hradisko provides.
The fact of fortification, and the transitional nature of the middle layer
ceramics, are not enough, in our view, to suggest an 'invasion' of Lausitz
people; it is the continuity of settlement and pottery types that should be
stressed. The same situation, leading either to Lausitz or to 'Danubian
Tumulus' settlement, may be seen in Austria, Bohemia and Slovakia.[42]

Settlement sites of the Tumulus period are less well-known though
such evidence as there is suggests that they continued much as before.
Indeed a number of sites have been found which actually span the
transition from Únětice to Tumulus, like Meclov-Březí (Domažlice)
where a series of post-holes formed a roughly trapezoidal house; the total
settlement area was 2,722 sq m, and it included four hut-plans and ovens,
with over 200 pits and post-holes.[43] Many other comparable sites are
known.

Fortified sites continued to be occupied in this period; among these we
may mention Přítluky in Moravia, with ditch and double rampart, and
traces of occupation inside; a fire had brought an end to settlement.[44]

North of the area of the Tumulus groups, in Poland, some extensive
and important sites are known from this period (Montelius I–II). One
such is at Bruszczewo (Kościan, Leszno) in Great Poland.[45] The site is
a low peninsular mound in flat open country, and was once surrounded
by water. From its numerous pits came large quantities of pottery as well
as the usual settlement debris – wattle-and-daub remains, stone tools
including weights, axes, grinders etc., bone handles and hafts, as well as
large numbers of animal bones. Five open hearths delimited by stone
circles 1 m in diameter were recovered; a bank surrounded the whole site
and is supposed to represent a means of enclosing stock. Perhaps the most
important finds from Bruszczewo, however, are the tools of trade of a
bronze-smith – tuyères, a clay crucible, clay mould supports, a stone
mould, slag fragments and so on.

Such a site seems clear evidence of permanent settlement based on
agriculture. The relative scarcity of settlements in the Tumulus area,
however, has led some authorities to envisage a pastoralist basis for the
Tumulus population, without permanent habitation sites. We do not
believe this to have been the case. Tumulus settlements are now much
better known than they used to be, and tend to occupy the same situations
as in the Early Bronze Age. Material culture, which we discuss below,
similarly suggests an agricultural economy, with finds of sickles, grain
storage pits etc. It is in any case intrinsically unlikely that a well-

established agricultural community should suddenly take to pastoralism as its economic foundation. Any possible change visible is much more likely to have been connected with the apparent change in the climate during the fifteenth and fourteenth centuries BC (p. 5).

Burial

So far we have been looking at areas where settlements predominate, but there are many more where cemeteries are the only sites found. It is in general true to say that the standard rite in western central Europe at this time was inhumation, but there are numerous exceptions, particularly in the later part of the Únětice period. The burials are most commonly flat (i.e. not under barrows) and the bodies contracted, laid on one or the other side: frequently this was according to sex, men on their left sides, women on their right.[46] Later Únětician burials could be in large barrows, but such burials are uncommon and the exception rather than the rule; nor do they appear in the central Únětician area.[47] In general, Únětician cemeteries contained several tens of graves (seventy-seven at Dolní Počernice, sixty at Únětice itself), but they could go into hundreds.

Burial types vary not only according to geographical location but also through time. Typical early graves – that are clearly Únětician, but have little or no metal in them – come from cemeteries like Dolní Počernice[48] (Prague – rural, north), where simple pits were used, and the dead, more or less tightly contracted, placed on their right sides, usually one to each pit. Variations on this may be seen at Velké Žernoseky[49] (Litoměřice) in north Bohemia, where stone settings are found lining the grave pits (fig. 12) or at Hlízov (Kolín) where multiple burials occurred in a hut-like construction.[50] In Moravia, similarly, pit-burial was the standard grave-form in the earliest ('proto-Únětician') cemeteries as well as the early classical ones.[51] As the period progressed, grave forms began to diversify and though the commonest single form was still the contracted inhumation in lined or unlined pits, double graves,[52] burials in storage pithoi,[53] wooden coffins,[54] storeyed graves,[55] grouped graves or graves in rows,[56] and other forms are found.

The information that can be obtained from scientific excavation of one of these cemeteries is potentially very great: the cemetery of Grossbrembach (Sömmerda) in Thuringia is especially important.[57] It started in the early phases of Únětice and went on to the late, though not the latest. The head typically pointed to the south and looked to the east (that is, the body lay on the right side); and in some cases burials took place directly above each other (storeyed graves), but strangely enough the bodies in such cases were usually male. A horizontal stratigraphy has been established by the excavator, but the most important conclusions concern the existence of family groups, which more or less correspond to the location of the graves in the cemetery. Among eighty-one graves and 108 skeletons five of these groupings were observed, based on physiological characteristics (like metopic sutures or wisdom teeth) as well as the position of the graves; and inside these larger units even smaller groupings were observable, which are taken on the basis of close anatomical similarities to represent first-degree kinship. Forty-seven such families were present, and the total population at any one time, assuming an average age at death of between twenty and thirty, is estimated at something over 100. These figures compare well with those obtained for other Únětician cemeteries where both smaller and larger familial groupings may be distinguished.[58] It seems that, in the larger cemeteries at least, the positioning of burials depended not on temporal sequence but on kinship. To demonstrate, as some have attempted, that the positioning depended also on social structure, is much more difficult, and in our view

Fig. 12 Burial-types from the Únětician cemetery at Velké Žernoseky (Litoměřice).
(After Moucha 1961)

possible only in rare instances. Cases where the individual was bound
with rope – as at Roggendorf and Schleinbach (Nö) – may be indicative
of slaves or criminals: at Schleinbach the skull of the skeleton, which was
female, had been deliberately smashed.[59]

Detailed analysis of Early Bronze Age grave forms in Saxo-Thuringia[60]
has demonstrated the unity of this area with Únětician Bohemia, at least
so far as burial form is concerned. The great majority of cemeteries are
'flat', and granted a twofold division of the period it is possible to attribute
a massive preponderance of simple pit or cist graves to the early phase,
with walled stone graves and barrows becoming more common as time
went on. The orientation of the body, as in Bohemia, is strictly north–
south (head at the south). On occasions traces of wooden constructions,
grave stelae (tombstones) and other elaborations can be descried, features
which recall the 'mortuary chambers' of Leubingen or Helmsdorf.
Cremation is almost unknown; double and multiple burials occur
commonly, for instance in the cemetery at Nohra (Nordhausen):[61] there
they date to the early part of the period. A few pithos burials are also
known, as in Bohemia.

The aspect of burial traditions in Early Bronze Age central Europe that
is usually associated with the 'classic' phase of Únětice is a group of
unusually large and rich barrows in the northern part of the area, though
in fact neither the burial rite nor the grave-goods are typical of the
Únětice culture properly so-called. These unusually large barrows in
Saxo-Thuringia are often called 'princely burials', and they are
remarkable not merely for their internal construction but also for their
extraordinarily good state of preservation. The massive cappings of stone
inside the barrows at Leubingen (Sömmerda) and Helmsdorf (Hettstedt)
enabled wood to survive, rotting but plainly discernible, until excavation
in 1877 and 1906 respectively. It is not impossible that if similar conditions
had prevailed elsewhere wooden 'mortuary chambers' would be a better-
attested phenomenon.

The barrow at Leubingen[62] was 34 m in diameter and 8.5 m high (pl.
3; fig. 13, 2). The central cairn was delimited by a ring-ditch 20 m in
diameter and estimated to contain 209.5 cu m of stones – a considerable
quantity in view of the fact that the immediate vicinity is completely
stoneless. The stones of the cairns were large overlapping slabs that
successfully kept dampness out of the wooden chamber underneath.
Eighteen wooden posts were set in a rectangular arrangement 3.9 × 2.1 m,
seven each side leaning in to a ridge-roof, and four supporting one end
(the southern); the other, northern, end was left open. In the middle of
the south end a massive upright beam supported the ridge-roof. In both
this and the ridge-pole, mortice-holes had been cut to receive the supports

leaning in from the sides. Similarly the side-supports had the planks for the floor recessed into them. Above each of these side-supports was a wide wooden board which almost joined with its neighbours; gypsum mortar was smoothed into the cracks. Above this roofing was a layer of thatch and above that the stone cairn.

On the oaken floor (all the timber was oak) lay the extended skeleton of a man who was judged by the state of his teeth and the gouty condition of his joints to be 'old'. Across his hips, at a right-angle, lay another body, in a very poor state of preservation: from the slenderness of the bones this was considered to be an adolescent or even a child. The original report stated this skeleton might be female on account of the gold jewellery found in the grave, but this is not certain. At the left side of the man's feet was a globular pot, rusticated in its lower half, surrounded by a setting of stones; nearby were a whetstone and serpentine pick. At various other points were a halberd with one rivet surviving in the fragments of the wooden haft, three small triangular daggers, two flanged axes, three chisels (both of the latter groups no doubt useful for constructing wooden chambers) and a group of gold objects: two massive eyelet pins, one spiral bead, one massive bracelet and two *Noppenringe* (pl. 3).

The barrow at Helmsdorf[63] was about 34 m in diameter, and had been constructed over earlier Corded Ware burials (fig. 13, 1). An encircling stone wall retained the central cairn. Under this lay a massively solid wooden grave-chamber. The floor area, 3.9 m long, was paved with sandstone slabs at the north end, and merely covered with reeds at the south. The ridge-roof was constructed of oak planks which leaned in to fit against each other at the centre without a ridge-pole; stone revetment held them in place at the bottom, and the exterior was sealed with a brownish material that had turned into sandy loam, and with a layer of thatch. To prevent the whole construction being crushed by the weight of the cairn an extra-strong outer roof of massive oak beams was erected over this whole area, ten to each side and joining in a central ridge.

The corpse was laid on a wooden bier on the paved part of the floor. The skeleton, which was barely preserved, was contracted and lay on its right side, head to the south, looking east; it was judged to be that of an adult man. The grave goods consisted of a large and very smashed pot in a stone setting on the floor, a diorite hammer, a flat bronze axe, two bronze objects that were probably a dagger and a chisel, a massive gold bracelet, two gold earrings, a gold spiral bead, and two gold pins. All the small grave-goods were found on the bier.

Everywhere were found traces of ash and burning. The fill of the chamber was ashy, and there were specks of burnt material here and there. The skull showed signs of scorching, while it was suggested that

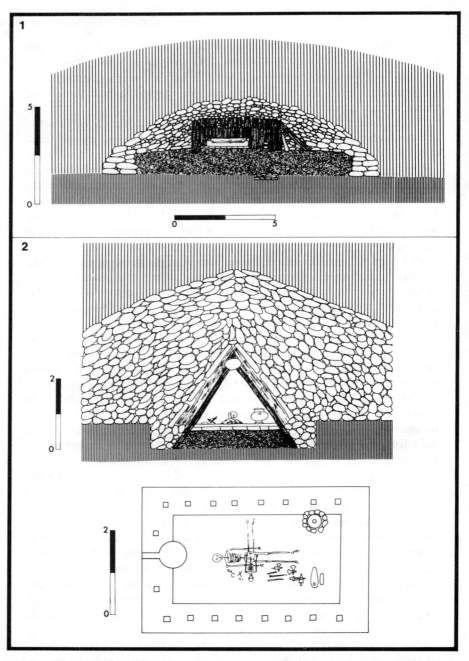

Fig. 13   Rich Early Bronze Age barrows from Saxo-Thuringia. 1. Helmsdorf (Hettstedt).
2. Leubingen (Sömmerda).
(After H. Grössler, *JVSTL* 6 (1907); P. Höfer, *JVSTL* 5 (1906))

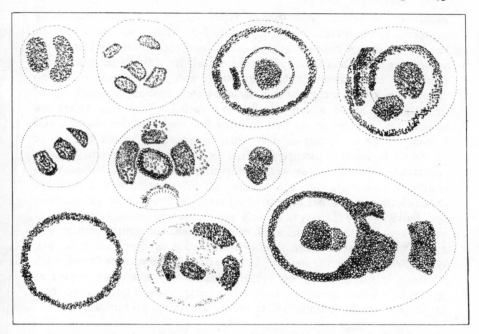

Fig. 14   Types of barrow construction, Tumulus period, West Bohemia.
(After Čujanová-Jílková 1970)

stains on the vertebrae were evidence of fumigation. But the clearest signs
of burning came from the southern roof-gable and the eastern plank of
the south wall; ashes were also found above the roof. Whether this
represents an attempt at firing the whole structure we do not know.

Other very large barrows with rich grave-goods are known from
Poland, where the excavations at Łęki Małe (Leszno) have amplified
some of the details of barrow construction and the funeral rite.[64] It seems
necessary to see in these rich barrows the proof of social stratification; but
it is notable that they are restricted to the latter part of the Early Bronze
Age and are by no means typical of the whole.

The emergence of burial under a barrow as a common Únětician form
is strong evidence for direct and unbroken continuity from this into the
post-Únětician period. The Tumulus Bronze Age (*Hügelgräberbronzezeit*;
Middle Bronze Age in conventional terminology), as its name implies,
adopted burial under a barrow as its standard grave type. Various
authorities have distinguished regional groups extending over the entire
central European area and well to the west in Germany;[65] these are based

primarily on pottery and bronze types. The burial type was fairly uniform, and showed little change from later Únětician times, though the great numbers concentrated in some areas (e.g. western Bohemia) are something new. Details vary, but the general idea is the same; burials are either by inhumation or by cremation, and there seems to be no correlation between barrow size, internal construction, and richness of grave goods, all of which can be very varied[66] (fig. 14). There are indications in some areas that inhumation was used for women and cremation for men, but as it is usually impossible to tell the sex of cremated bones this picture may not be correct. Coffins and wooden constructions occur in the well-preserved barrows around Schwarza in southern Thuringia (fig. 15), where rich information is also available about clothing and other funeral offerings.[67] At Dolný Peter (Komárno) and Šalka (Nové Zámky), as well as at other tumulus cemeteries in south-west Slovakia, recent work has uncovered substantial numbers of graves with either pit-cremation or inhumation predominating, as well as inurned cremation at Šalka.[68] In some cases grave pits are found, with offerings but apparently no burials, which the excavators regard as 'symbolic'; sometimes, too, as in other parts of the Tumulus world, a single grave could contain both cremated and inhumed burials.[69]

Fig. 15 Women's dress as reconstructed from finds of the Tumulus period around Schwarza, Thuringia.
(After Feustel 1958)

A third general class of site, ritual or religious, is scantily represented in the earlier Bronze Age of central Europe. From the Únětice period there is little that can be reliably interpreted as a cult place, though miniature vessels and figurines occur in late contexts.[70] In the succeeding period a couple of sites are known. At Černčín (Bučovice) in Moravia was found a stone construction in the form of a rough Maltese cross, the arms 2.5 m long and 0.5 m wide and oriented exactly on the cardinal points: in the middle of each terminal stood a vase, with a fifth in the very centre. No other finds indicated whether this was part of a cemetery or a settlement. At Viničné Šumice (Slavkov near Brno) was a shallow bowl-like depression, and on one edge a small container full of carbonized wheat: a cup, jug, bowl and clay disc were found nearby, and the excavator interprets the whole as an agricultural offering. In a settlement at Uherský Brod a bovine skeleton, extended north–south, was surrounded by stones and had a pottery vessel under its head. Other cow jaw-bones and skulls, with pottery and stone settings, were nearby. To the west was a circular depression 0.5 m deep, the sides baked red by fire, and to the north another, similar, but at a higher level and with concentric ridges of terracotta surrounding. A rectangular depression with white clay sides – unfortunately in a very bad state of preservation – completed the picture, and the accompanying finds, including miniature vessels, zoomorphic vases, etc., indicate that this was a cult place. Similarly at Černý Vůl (Black Ox) near Prague a clay 'altar' was recovered, bearing parallel raised ribs on its face, in the form of a flat facade with points or horns and, it seems, representations of birds.[71]

Certain aspects of the earliest Lausitz culture material have also been seen as ritual in nature. At Hradisko (Kroměříž) the early Lausitz levels contained a variety of unusual bone placements, including a child's skull placed alone in a shallow pit with pottery ranged around and a flat stone slab on top.[72] The head had apparently been detached in the region of the 4th–5th vertebrae and buried separately for 'ritual' purposes. 'Partial' burials of this sort are attested at a number of Moravian Lausitz sites, including Bezměrov, Hulín (Kroměříž) and elsewhere. At Hradisko and Rataj pits with the scattered bones of numerous individuals were also found, as well as evidence of dismemberment and cannibalism (cf. later practices, below, p. 362).

Material remains

The earliest stages of the Bronze Age include the phase customarily termed 'proto-Únětician'.[73] Many features of pot technique and shape that derive from Bell Beakers are present – notably squat S-sided cups and polypod bowls. At Velké Žernoseky (Litoměřice) on the Elbe the earliest graves contain medium to tall one-handled cups and jugs, usually with globular belly, incurving neck and outcurving rim; low conical bowls also occur (fig. 10).[74] Metal-work is rare in graves of this phase in Bohemia, though it was commoner on the middle Danube. In general, pottery forms became more angular and less globular as the early Únětice period developed; the bellied globular cups and bowls give way to conical and carinated-conical bowls, and 'Únětice cups', so typical of the main phase, developed by way of the one-handled cup with long conical neck (pl. 4). The Únětice or 'hour-glass' cup is very characteristic: the sides are markedly concave in profile, the base low, the single handle placed low down. Few later Únětice pot-forms are so diagnostic.

On settlement sites, the most typical single vase is an ovoid storage jar, the outside rusticated over all or part of the surface, and with knobs below the rim for the attachment of a leather lid (fig. 16).[75]

Metal types accompanying earlier Únětice graves are few and simple. Pins are the most common; other objects include ingot torcs, spectacle-spiral pendants, arm- and leg-spirals, and, occasionally, simple triangular daggers. In the earliest stages of the Únětice development graves were regularly accompanied by boar's-tusk pendants, bone beads, simple copper tube or pendant ornaments, tanged flint arrowheads and so on. Graves of this period may be seen in the closely related local group at Straubing,[76] though similar material can be discerned throughout the central area (fig. 17). These metal and other types constitute what Torbrügge has called the 'Weapon Combination A1' – that is, triangular daggers with arrowheads and wrist-guards, which implies a method of warfare (i.e. bows) similar to that employed in Beaker times, and quite separate from that current later in the Únětice and Tumulus periods.[77]

Later Únětice graves may contain a wider variety of metalwork, and this manifests itself particularly in weapon and ornament types. Daggers are ogival, or, if triangular, longer than hitherto, and acquire solid metal hilts and rich incised decoration on the blade; axes are flanged; special forms like the Polish metal-hafted halberds are found. But the greatest variety occurs in the pins, and particularly characteristic of Reinecke's Br A2 was the pin with perforated spherical head. Spiral arm-rings and tutuli (pointed boss-like objects) occur, but the advent of the solid bronze bracelet is perhaps the most notable addition to the repertory – usually round in section, penannular, and having incised decoration on the surface.

Beads of bone, shell or boar's tusk were a frequent accompaniment of the dead; metal spiral beads (saltaleoni) and spectacle spiral pendants often occur. Amber is widespread, reflecting the proximity of the Baltic

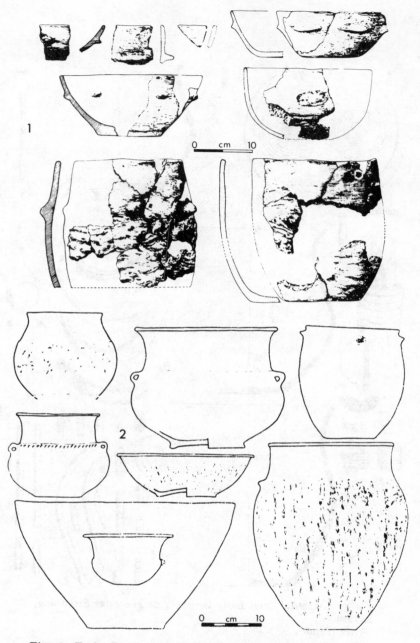

Fig. 16 Early Bronze Age pottery from settlement sites. 1.
Grossbrembach (Sömmerda). 2. Bruszczewo (Kościan).
(After G. Behm-Blancke, *AuF* 19 (1974) and Z. Pieczynski, *FAP*
20 (1969))

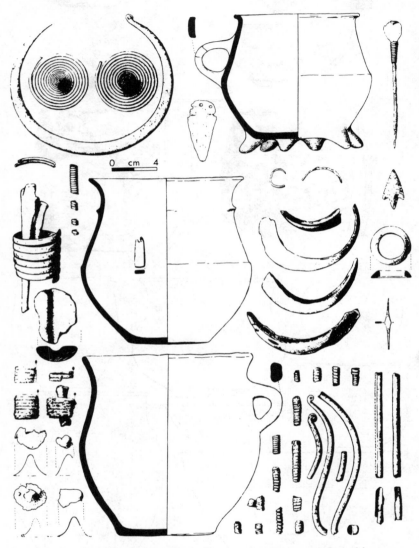

Fig. 17 Material from Early Bronze Age graves at Straubing, Bavaria.
(After Hundt 1958)

48

sources, and the trading network that secured its distribution. More controversial is the origin of the small annular or segmented beads of a glassy material described as faience.[78] These beads are made of crushed sand or quartz and are coloured blue or green by the addition of copper oxide and cobalt. On firing, the surface of the bead tended to become glassy (fusion started to take place), while the interior stayed opaque. The manufacturing process, however, is not so different from that of pottery, and we consider that the necessary technology for local production of these beads was present; the idea of importation from Egypt or the Near East is an uneconomical hypothesis.[79]

In metalwork, hoards of ingot torcs appear from an early phase.[80] The hoards that are typical of Reinecke's A1 are those with solid-hilted daggers. We may take as typical of these the hoard from Bresinchen (Guben)[81] which contains 103 flanged axes, one double-axe, two solid-hafted halberds, eight daggers, ten ingot torcs, nine heavy rings, two 'Thuringian rings', and eleven 'leech-shaped rings' – a total weight of 30 kg – contained in two coarse ovoid storage vessels (pl. 5). The size of these hoards is enormous: the second hoard from Dieskau (Saalkreis) contained 293 flanged axes.[82]

Characteristic of Reinecke's later (A2) phase were the hoards like Langquaid (fig. 18), containing narrow flanged axes, Bohemian palstaves, spearheads (with straight-sided triangular blades and incised decoration at the base), pins with perforated spherical head, a variety of penannular tapering bracelets, and the first rings with antithetic-spiral terminals.[83]

In the pottery of the Tumulus period most characteristic is the globular bellied pot with cylindrical or conical neck and rich incised or rusticated

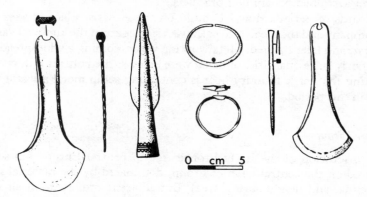

Fig. 18 Objects from the Langquaid (Rothenburg) hoard.
(After Hachmann 1957)

decoration (fig. 19, 21);[84] this vase-form takes on many varieties, and can have a more or less carinated belly, and flaring or everted mouth. The great number of related forms includes a simpler urn-like pot, less globular, but also having cylindrical neck and handles on the shoulder; and an elaborated form with 'drooping' embossed sides. Very common too are the pedestalled bowl, also with rich incised and embossed ornament, the tall one-handled cup, usually with bosses on the lower part of the belly, and sometimes with feet, and the low conical bowl, very often with 'peaked' rim. In Austria the pottery from the later part of the period (Br C) is very fine: at Herzogenburg (St Pölten) exceptionally well-polished black ware, in a variety of one-handled high-necked jugs, was found in a kiln.[85] Further west, the southern German material makes extensive use of incised and excised decoration on a range of shapes that shows many local forms.[86]

Among bronzes[87] the long pin is present from phase B (fig. 20), though the longest forms appear later; in Bavaria it is square-sectioned but wavy in profile and with a flat disc head, in Bohemia the shank may be striated and head more seal-like (*Petschaftnadel*), in Thuringia it may be wheel-headed. Thin-sectioned wide ribbed bracelets and sheet metal pendants and bosses also occur, as well as small two-riveted triangular daggers or dirks. By the end of the period the sword had been invented and occurs in both solid- and flange-hilted forms, the former with elaborate spiral decoration on the hilt. Other distinctive forms of Reinecke's phase C are finger- and arm-rings with antithetic spiral terminals (fig. 20, 7, 9), heart-shaped pendants, palstaves and flanged axes, tweezers, tutuli, and dirks with rounded or trapezoidal heel, as well as a great variety of incised round-sectioned penannular bracelets.

Hoards of periods B and C build on the A basis. Flanged axes first accompany and then lead into palstaves; sickles are of the knobbed variety at first, and later flanged. Metalworking was becoming a widespread art, and fairly large quantities of metal were being turned out; it is, however, striking that large foundry hoards containing scrap metal are still very rare in this period.

Related groups

The discussion of the Early Bronze Age in central Europe has so far centred on the central Únětice group, dominated by the material from Bohemia, and neighbouring areas. But adjacent provinces on all sides fostered related archaeological groupings. In Bavaria the early Straubing group[88] was turning out ingot torcs, sheet bronze bosses, spectacle spiral pendants, spiral bracelets and finger-rings, metal tubes and plaques, and

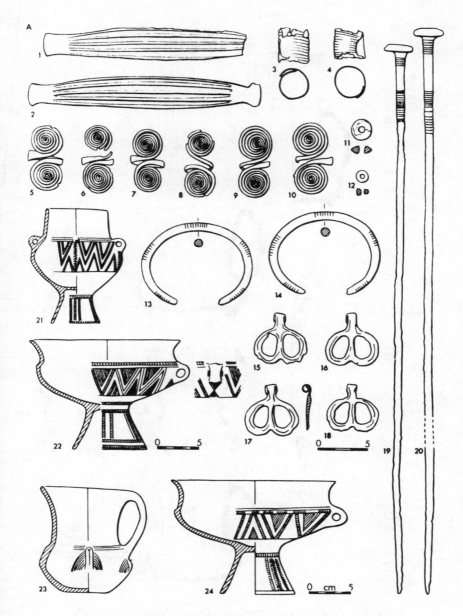

Fig. 19 Finds from Tumulus period barrows at Št'áhlavy
(Plzeň south).
(After Čujanová-Jílková 1970)

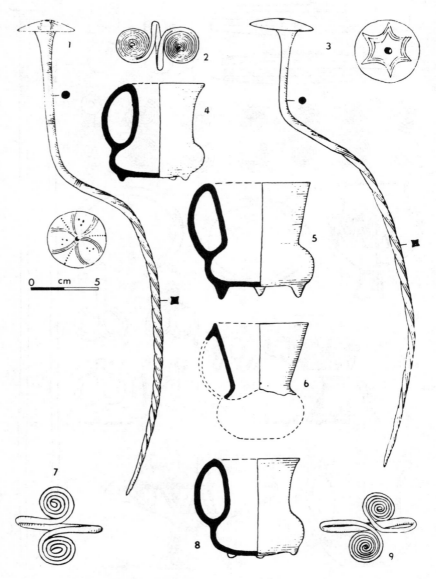

Fig. 20 Finds from barrows at Dolný Peter (Komárno),
Tumulus period.
(After Dušek 1969)

racket pins with folded tops, as well as pottery forms related closely to those in Bohemia (tall cups with tapering neck, S-profiled cups and jars etc.) to adorn the flat graves of its population (fig. 17). In neighbouring Austria, in addition to a true Únětice element, local groups are named after cemeteries at Wieselburg, Unterwölbling and elsewhere, though most of these have such close parallels in Bohemia or Hungary that it is an unnecessary complication to add new names. Particularly detailed work has been carried out on the cemetery at Gemeinlebarn (St Pölten),[89] attributable to the Unterwölbling group.

Related to Únětice, and indeed a generic part of it, is the late facies of the Early Bronze Age that appears in Moravia, west Slovakia, Austria and north-west Hungary – the so-called Věteřov group. The term was originally defined by Tihelka to distinguish a group of Moravian cemeteries which contained material that was strongly homogeneous but related to that from the best-known Únětice cemeteries in Bohemia.[90] The type-site is near Kyjov (fig. 21). Closely comparable to, and for practical purposes indistinguishable from, this Věteřov material is that from Lower Austria described as Böheimkirchen by Pittioni,[91] and, as in Moravia, the material there is found on hill-top settlements (like the type-site) as well as in cemeteries.[92]

Comparable Early Bronze Age groups have been recognized in the middle and upper Rhine valley, and present-day western Germany, eastern France and northern Switzerland. The widespread elements of the contemporary Rhône-Alpine group are discussed elsewhere (p. 185). The Rhine, and its major tributary the Main, may have formed an important route in the earlier Bronze Age, and although the Adlerberg group of the middle Rhine is often singled out as the major western contemporary of Straubing and Únětice, other small groups have been recorded along the Rhine and Main, from Westphalia southwards through Württemberg and Alsace into the Jura. The Adlerberg group itself is represented principally by cemeteries of inhumations, sparsely furnished with copper and bronze daggers, pins of metal or bone, flint arrowheads and handled pottery cups. The cemeteries tend to be rather small, the type-site with about twenty graves[93] (fig. 22).

At the Rhine-Main confluence, other Adlerberg graves and finds are known,[94] and this area in particular is quite thickly sown with finds of the earlier Bronze Age – graves, hoards and single finds;[95] more detailed regional studies have begun to isolate particular areas, which show, among other things, the preference for river valley occupation even in the upper reaches.[96]

West of the middle Rhine, small and rather isolated earlier Bronze Age groups have been recognized in the Saarland, and in the lowlands of

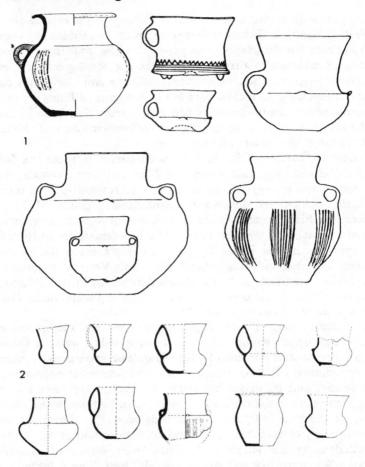

Fig. 21   Pottery of Věteřov (1) and Mad'arovce (2) types from
Věteřov and Malé Kosihy (Štúrovo). Varying scales.
(After J. -W. Neugebauer, *Arch. Aust.* 59/60 (1976); A. Točík,
Nitra Kommission, 1958)

Lorraine and Champagne;[97] bronze itself tends to be sparsely represented
except in occasional hoards,[98] and these are in general not of the earliest
Bronze Age (fig. 23). The contents of graves, and probably settlement
debris, tend to consist of stonework including flints, and in this aspect
Neolithic traditions continued. These areas are best considered as
expressing the westernmost extension of the central European earlier
Bronze Age.

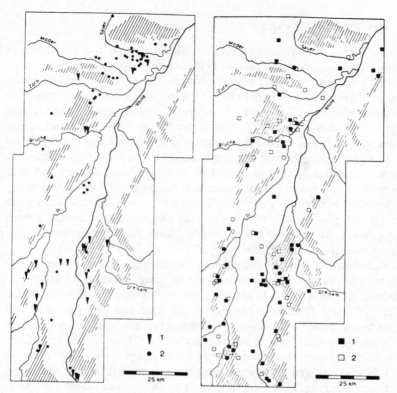

Fig. 22   Distribution of Bronze Age burials in the upper Rhine valley.
Left, 1. Beaker and Early Bronze Age, 2. Middle Bronze Age. Right, 1. Late
Bronze Age, 2. Early Iron Age.
(After Balkwill 1976)

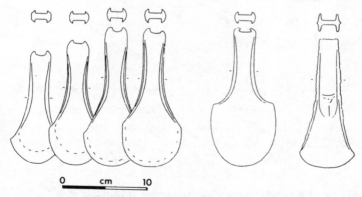

Fig. 23   Hoard of axes from Habsheim (Haut-Rhin).
(After Zumstein 1976)

55

The upper Rhine valley, through Alsace and into the highlands of northern Switzerland, has yielded evidence for Bronze Age occupation of both plains and uplands, the latter not extensively exploited before the second millennium. The earlier Bronze Age is represented essentially by cemeteries of inhumations with or without earthen or stone mounds, and by hoards of metal objects.[99] The cemetery at Singen on the upper reaches of the Rhine near lake Constance contained about fifty Early Bronze Age graves; the rite was contracted inhumation, sometimes in a wooden coffin and usually protected by a stone setting around and over the grave. The bodies of both males and females faced east, and many were supplied with metal grave-goods, females with necklet, spiral armlet or anklet, and pin, males with dagger, ring and awl. Pots were not placed in the graves; their deposition is not commonly found in earlier Bronze Age communities in the Rhine valley.[100]

The evidence, then, for the earliest Bronze Age communities in the Rhine valley is very restricted, essentially to cemeteries and a few hoards. Settlement traces (fig. 24), mainly pottery scatters, have been noted regularly,[101] and their position suggests a first and perhaps intensive exploitation of major upland areas. Clearances on the plains of Alsace and other areas of eastern France have been noted,[102] but there is little firm data about economic activities except from a few Swiss sites such as Arbon Bleiche on Lake Constance. This settlement, containing a number of houses measuring from 3 × 4 m to 8 × 4 m and supported on a massive understructure of upright and horizontal timbers, contained a population engaged in activities involving major forest clearances and the establishment of pasture.[103] The animals herded were cattle, pig and sheep, but

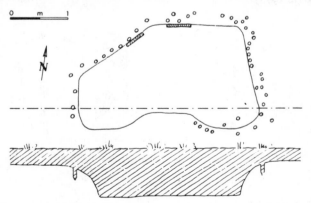

Fig. 24   Plan and section of sunken house at Bundolsheim (Haut-Rhin).
(After Zumstein 1966)

wild animals were also taken when available.[104] The materials recovered from the settlement include many bronze weapons and ornaments, stone implements, some bone tools and rather coarse pottery with either finger-impressed cordons and handles, or incised geometric decoration. The quantity of metal and its character suggests that this occupation belongs to a developed stage of the Early Bronze Age, at a time when further exploitation of metal resources and industries in the Alpine region had begun, and these are reflected all along the Rhine valley from Switzerland to the north European plain.

The Tumulus Bronze Age in central Europe runs parallel to a variety of developments in the north. In the west and centre of Poland it is usual now to distinguish a 'pre-Lausitz' culture (*Vorlausitz, przedłużycka*) which is the immediate forerunner of the full Late Bronze Age Lausitz.

Although the earliest true Lausitz material dates to Br D there is a whole group of finds in the Lausitz area that is plainly ancestral to Lausitz proper, dating to Br B and C.[105] Three phases of development are distinguished. Special pin types (notably cylindrical, spindle- and semi-conical-headed) characterize the period as a whole; other elements are less definitive (fig. 25). At no time is pottery prolific, and it is extremely rare at the start; when it appears, it comes in two main forms, an ovoid jar with rusticated surface, and a globular 'terrine' with cylindrical neck. The inhumation rite is standard, and the usual variety of stone settings and pits occurs in the tumuli (fig. 26).

The Tumulus Bronze Age represents for much of the Rhine valley the first period when metal became widely available, and the Rhine itself presumably had a role in the movement of such materials; the distribution of metalwork of this phase is very closely related to the course of the Rhine and its major tributaries.[106]

Other regions, well away from the major rivers, had had little or no trace of a Bronze Age until now; areas along the middle Main and further north along the Lippe, now yield very abundant signs of a population with a full complement of traditional Bronze Age material culture, in both metals and pottery; burial traditions are, as elsewhere in this period, of the developed Bronze Age (p. 44). An area along the rivers Lippe and Alme with hardly any recognizable early second millennium occupation yields over 500 known barrow burials of this later period, arranged in distinctive cemeteries and furnished with ample metal and ceramic equipment,[107] which reflects both north European and Rhine valley features. The explanation for this sudden appearance of Bronze Age communities in the Rhine valley is not perhaps merely to be sought in the fact that flat graves of the earliest Bronze Age are unrecognized while the upstanding barrows of the later period are clear and obvious.

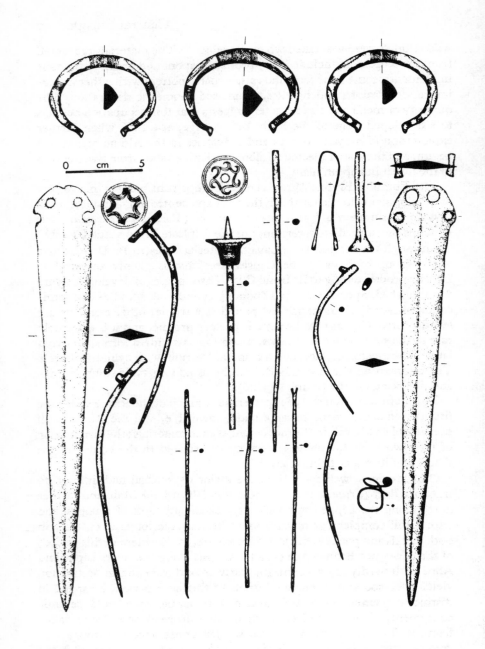

Fig. 25 Finds from 'pre-Lausitz' barrows in Poland.
(After Gedl 1975)

58

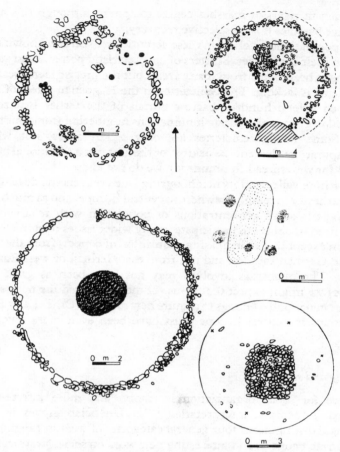

Fig. 26   Plans of 'pre-Lausitz' barrows in Poland. The burials are in pits (shaded) or stone settings; post holes (centre right) indicate a mortuary structure, solid circles pottery.
(After Gedl 1975)

Many of the barrows cover extended inhumations, furnished with a bewildering array of personal ornaments and weapons. Local preferences in styles of pins, bracelets, necklets and anklets, as in pottery shapes and decoration, are marked, and have been the subject of many detailed studies which may help to distinguish small centres of activity but mask the essential uniformity of ideas along the entire Rhine valley and its adjoining regions.[108]

Bronze hoards of axes, sickles and other equipment are now more commonly found throughout the region,[109] and preference for their deposition in rivers or marshes begins to appear, although this may be deceptive based as it is on selective recovery.

The populations involved in these activities are scarcely known except through their cemeteries. Scatters of characteristic pottery, and stone or flints, have been noted from many areas, but the precise identification of settlements is lacking. The cemeteries in the Haguenau forest of Alsace contained several hundred barrow burials of the earlier Bronze Age, arranged in groups of separate inhumations numbering from four to over forty. Some major cemeteries are only 2 km apart, but whether contemporary settlements lie nearby, or the area was a traditional burying ground for widespread communities, we do not know.[110]

The Rhine valley and its neighbouring lands reflects the development of the earlier Bronze Age elsewhere in central Europe, and as much as any area suggests small concentrations of population with relatively little desire, need or ability to participate in any wider issues of subsistence or tradition except that of increasing acquisition of copper, from the Alpine or north German sources, and tin, from east German or west European sources. The quantities involved may not have been as great as we imagine; we might expect that re-use of metal reduced the necessity for constant major undertakings to acquire new material. Other Early Bronze Age groups in central Europe must have been even more favourably placed.

Economy and society

Evidence for social organization is scanty, and more inferred than observed. A Marxist interpretation[111] of Ůnĕtician graves in Saxo-Thuringia distinguishes four general categories of wealth, ranging from chieftains to paupers, and interesting new work on social stratification in the Nitra group at Brank confirms that even in relatively poorly equipped cemeteries certain graves stand out as 'rich' – graves which cannot be satisfactorily segregated on the basis of sex, position in cemetery, age etc., and so suggest a distribution of wealth dependent solely on social factors.[112] That society was stratified may reasonably be inferred from the size of the great barrows of Saxo-Thuringia, whose construction represents many man-days of productive labour.

The lack of detailed modern work on economic aspects prevents a thorough appraisal. There is good evidence for agriculture and stock-rearing, as well as spinning and weaving, potting, and metal-working. Plough-marks have been found under barrows in a number of different areas;[113] querns, pounders, sickles and other agricultural implements are widespread.[114] An interesting find from Döbeln-Masten in Saxony[115] comprised a pit about 1.5 m in diameter and 1.2 m deep, with five storage vessels of typical Únětice type (placed upside down) and two quernstones (fig. 27). Filling most of the pit was a mass of carbonized grain, mostly emmer; such a practice must have been common to many Únětician settlements.[116] The produce of normal agriculture was supplemented, where possible, by food from hunting and fishing: at Janówek (Dzierżoniów) numerous shell-fish remains came to light, as well as large numbers of animal bones, quernstones, etc.[117] Bovine bones are said to have accounted for over half the total at that site, and in general it is true to say that where work has taken place, cattle predominate in the faunal sample. The regular finding of pottery strainers for cheese-making probably indicates the importance of dairy produce in the Únětice culture-group. Similarly, the great quantity of spindle-whorls and loom-weights must reflect an active textile industry, and the extensive exploitation of sheep for their wool.[118]

The abundant evidence for stock-rearing in the form of animal bones and for crop agriculture in the form of grain impressions, carbonized cereals (mainly emmer, but also einkorn and spelt) and agricultural implements, indicates a mixed economy. It has been said[119] that the Úněticians were predominantly stock-breeders, but we feel that agriculture must have played a large part in the Early Bronze Age economy. The same is probably true of the Tumulus period, in spite of assertions to the contrary.[120] Finds of agricultural implements, especially sickles, continue; sites attributable to the Middle Bronze Age include many settlements and not just a proliferation of barrows as interpreted by Childe. The character of the Early Bronze Age economy probably continued unaltered with minor changes of emphasis throughout the period. Only full analysis by modern methods, however, can finally solve this problem.

A factor that has come to be regarded as important, even crucial, in the Early Bronze Age is the production and distribution of salt.[121] The best-known salt-mines in continental Europe are those at Hallstatt and Dürrnberg bei Hallein in the Salzkammergut in Upper Austria, and though the most intensive working did not take place until after the Bronze Age, isolated finds of Bronze Age objects indicate that the importance of the area was already appreciated during it. More certain evidence comes from central Germany, however, in the area around Halle/Saale (both names connected etymologically with the word 'salt').[122] Specialized pottery vessels of various forms are found, frequently containing a high proportion of organic material in the clay, constituting 'briquetage' – cylindrical and oval 'pedestals' (spindle-shaped objects), troughs, beakers (often with pointed bottom) and

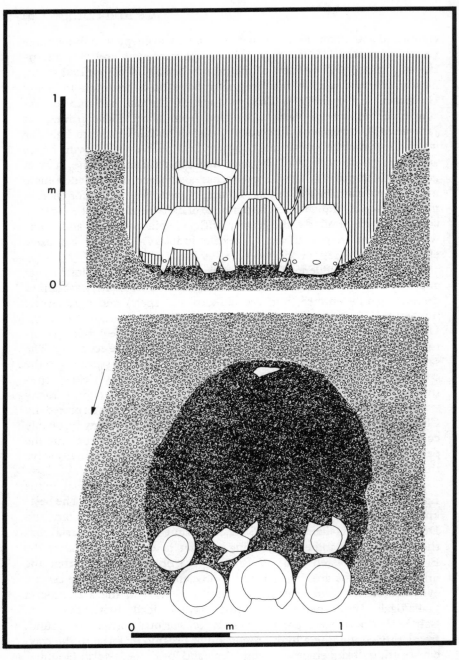

Fig. 27 Plan and section of a pit containing pottery and carbonized grain from Döbeln-Masten, Saxony.
(After Coblenz, *AuF* 18 (1973))

moulds. The method was that of evaporating salt-solutions, and briquetage-sites were usually on level ground beside brine springs or salt lakes.[123] A flat clay floor would be constructed, the pedestals placed on it at regular intervals, and the troughs or other evaporation pans balanced on them, filled with salt water. A fire would then be lit between the supports to evaporate the water (more of which would be constantly added until crystallized salt filled the whole pan). Wet salt crystals would be pressed into the beakers or other moulds, and dried off to form a salt cake. Thousands of fragments of these vessels came from Halle-Giebichenstein, and many hundreds of cylinder-supports. Of some interest for our immediate purposes is the fact that certain forms – the 'oval supports' (used in pairs) and the flat troughs – have been shown conclusively to be of Early Bronze Age date.[124]

The daily intake of salt for an adult human is estimated at 12 to 15 g (considerably more for large animals), though diet normally accounts for an essential minimum of only 3 to 7 g. In addition salt is used as a preservative, in leather-working, as a fertilizer, in the making of cheese and so on.[125] Its importance as a commodity thus cannot be overestimated. There are numerous cases in the historical and ethnographic record of peoples adopting desperate courses to obtain salt; the same must have been true in prehistory. Areas like Hallstatt or Halle must have acquired a considerable importance in the pattern of Bronze Age trade and exchange.

Perhaps the most important single industry was metallurgy. We are fortunate in having good evidence for several aspects of Bronze Age metal production, especially mining. It has been shown that the first use of the Austrian copper mines dates back to at least the Early Bronze Age and possibly earlier, for sherds of Early Bronze type containing small slag inclusions have been found, and finds of each succeeding period show that the mines continued in use throughout the Bronze and into the Iron Age. Investigation of the mines of the central Alps (the Salzburg area) has provided valuable evidence of the technology employed.[126] The ores, which concentrate in the Bischofshofen-Mühlbach area (notably Mitterberg) and the upper Salzach and Saalach valleys, are found as 2 m thick lodes in faults in the rock; they often go down into the earth at a steep angle, reflecting the way in which cracks in the earth's crust were filled with the molten substances that became copper ore. The miners followed these bands down (where the angle was not impossibly steep), and devised an ingenious series of tools and methods for bringing the ore to the surface. The rock would be heated by wood fires at the spot where working was being carried out, and then cracked by pouring cold water onto the working face. Wooden wedges and bronze picks were then used to prise out large chunks of the rock (fig. 28). As the tunnel became longer and deeper, wooden platforms were erected to bear the waste rock, protecting the miners from the smoke of the fire and enabling a draught to pass freely down the tunnel. Wooden aqueduct sections, mallets, shovels, wedges, buckets, spatulae, sieves and a variety of carrying implements (the purpose of some still imperfectly understood) have been found preserved in the shafts,[127] as well as huge metal hammers for breaking up the rock, long socketed picks,[128] and crude stone pounders and pounding querns for extracting the copper-bearing veins from the rock prior to separation in water. The ore would then be taken down the mountain for roasting with charcoal in a roasting-bed and then loaded into stone-built shaft furnaces (fig. 29). Cake-like copper ingots and slag are both found. It was calculated that one working area comprising three open-cast galleries would produce 12.6 tonnes of mined material a day,

Fig. 28　Reconstruction of Bronze Age mining operations at the face. The heated lode has been cooled and the fire cleared away; note the timbering of the gallery, the tree-trunk ladder, the long-handled bronze picks and gads, the shovels and troughs, and the lamps of wooden chips.
(After R. Pittioni, *Inst. of Arch. 7th Ann. Rep.* (1951))

Fig. 29   Reconstruction of roasting and smelting of copper ore.
(After R. Pittioni)

of which about 315 kg would be turned out as raw copper. This volume would, of course, be reduced further with separation, smelting and refinement, but still represents a significant quantity, especially if more than one area was being worked at once. To keep the work going, 180 men (or women) would be needed, allowing for miners, separators, transporters, overseers, and timber-men (to supply 20 cu m of wood per day). Since more than one area was probably open at any one time, this figure can certainly be doubled.

Following the mining and smelting of the ore came its distribution from the source to the place of manufacture into implements (and, eventually, to the place of archaeological deposition). The particular problems concerning Bronze Age exchange and distributive agencies have been briefly touched upon in the Introduction (p. 12), where reference to the analytical work conducted upon the metal itself is also made. We are unable to comprehend fully the organization, or lack of it, that caused many thousands of objects of metal to be transported over short or long distances, but there can be no doubt that materials were indeed moved through central Europe.

While local exchange and contact was a regular and integral part of Early Bronze Age life,[129] long-distance trade is attested only in certain commodities and with certain areas. The most famous case concerns objects of supposed Egyptian or Mycenaean provenance – faience beads, amber spacer-plates, and bone cylinders with spiraliform motifs. The value of this evidence is far from certain. Faience beads are likely to have been manufactured locally,[130] and the amber spacer-plates are mostly different in detail from the well-known Greek and British pieces and form a local group connected with the rest only in general terms. The trade in amber to central Europe from the Baltic is, however, indisputable; in return, bronzes of central European manufacture found their way to the north (below, p. 311–12). Stone for chipping or grinding was also traded, though not over large distances (in central Europe); shells (especially *Dentalium*) were brought from the Adriatic and Black Sea coasts.

Chronology

The absolute chronology of the earlier Bronze Age in central Europe is very far from secure; there are few stratigraphical successions which would allow the relative position to be ascertained. In the absence of a long sequence from a deeply stratified site, we are forced to rely on isolated instances of temporal ordering, based either on typological study of the pottery or on the relative placing of graves. In cases where, for instance, Únětice sherds underlie Lausitz or Tumulus material[131] the information is crude and gives little opportunity for closer refinement.

The absolute chronology rests on the supposed connections with southeast Europe, and on a handful of radiocarbon dates (table 3). For the former, we have already mentioned our belief that the faience beads are of local manufacture, and do not indicate any precise synchronism with Egyptian chronology. The same may be said of the pottery cup from Nienhagen (Oschersleben) in Middle Germany and a 'stirrup' lid from Věteřov (Kyjov),[132] though both are striking pieces in their own contexts. The spiraliform designs on bone and antler objects in Moravia and southwest Slovakia should be seen in connection with similar pieces in Hungary and Romania (below, p. 153) which we believe represent a local school of ornamentation, the products of which occur in metal and clay as well as antler and bone. Only amber spacer-plates found in south Germany and Bohemia in Tumulus contexts indicate any kind of precise synchronism.[133] If their date is of the order of 1500 BC then the Tumulus context of most of the continental pieces can be reconciled with the uncalibrated radiocarbon dates.

From the few dates available for the Early Bronze Age of west-central Europe the general pattern is that the Únĕtice period started by 1900 bc and ended by at the latest 1400 bc, perhaps earlier. Late aspects of the group fall between 1700 and 1500 bc, the Tumulus period between 1500 and 1300 bc; the Late Bronze Age (Br D) then starts about 1300 bc.

Comparison of the radiocarbon and historical chronologies for the central European Bronze Age is difficult while radiocarbon dates are so few. In general the uncalibrated dates fit better with traditional notions of chronology, which are, however, largely dependent on the cross-links discussed above and therefore of uncertain value. If one admits, though, that at the very least the evidence of the amber spacer-plates must indicate a synchronism, the dilemma can be described quite simply. If the early Tumulus period in south Germany is to be placed within the fifteenth century, then the picture derived from calibrated dates as tabulated in table 2 is considerably in error; the uncalibrated dates provide a much closer fit. Further comment must be withheld until the extensive programme of dating by Groningen and other laboratories is complete, though possible ways out of the dilemma have been suggested. One of these is to derive both the supposed 'imports' and the prototypes from a hypothetical place of origin in the northern Balkans.[134]

Eastern part

The Bronze Age in Hungary, Slovakia and south-east Poland followed a separate, though related, course to that further west. The cultures of the Hungarian plain in particular form a unit which developed in its own

Table 2 Absolute dating, earlier Bronze Age, central Europe

Traditional		Uncalibrated C14	Calibrated C14[135]
c. 2000 BC	Transitional from Copper Age	c. 2300 bc	c. 2500 BC
c. 1800–1500 BC	Early Bronze Age, earlier part	c. 1900–1700 bc	c. 2300–2100 BC
	Early Bronze Age, later part	c. 1700–1500 bc	c. 2100–1700 BC
c. 1500–1300 BC	Tumulus Bronze Age and related	c. 1500–1300 bc	c. 1800–1500 BC
c. 1300 BC	Start of Late Bronze Age	c. 1300 bc	c. 1500 BC

Table 3   Radiocarbon dates, west-central Europe, earlier Bronze Age

Site	Lab no.	bc
Early Únětice		
Prasklice (Kroměříž)	Bln–475	1895 ± 80
Developed Únětice		
Helmsdorf (Hettstedt)	Bln–248	1663 ± 160
Łęki Małe (Leszno), barrow 1	GrN–5037	1655 ± 35
,,	M–1325	1950 ± 150
Větefov		
Slanská Hora (Slaný)	LJ–2047	1650 ± 200
,, ,,	LJ–2503	1530 ± 40
Budkovice	LJ–2048	1700 ± 200
Middle Bronze Age		
Bruszczewo (Kościan)	GrN–5047	1370 ± 40
Rosdorf (Göttingen)	GrN–5603	1170 ± 35
East French		
Les Mournouards (Le Mesnil, Marne), cave-site	Gsy–114	1800 ± 150

individual way. We describe this first, and then move to contemporaneous developments in the mountains to the north.

Culturally, as geographically, the Great Hungarian Plain forms an independent and homogeneous unit. It is possible to list a series of small cultural groups lying in and on the fringes of the plain, but it seems more profitable to take the plain as the focal point and see the peripheral groups in terms of what occurred in the centre; in this way parts of Slovakia, Jugoslavia and Romania can be considered under the same general heading as Hungary. The Great Hungarian Plain (which with Transylvania comprises the Carpathian Basin) is an area of around 150,000 sq km, traversed by fast and wide rivers like the Danube, Tisza, Sava and their tributaries, and hemmed in at the edges by extensive mountain ranges.[137] Most of it lies less than 200 m above sea-level, and consists of loess-derived black-earth or brown forest soils suitable for intensive agriculture – conditions that were fully exploited from the early Neolithic on · and naturally led to prolific and long-lasting settlement. The consequent formation of tell sites from the massive accumulation of debris from mud and wattle houses is an outstanding feature of settlements throughout the earlier Bronze Age of Hungary. Where excavation techniques permit, it is possible to discern many building levels within a single period; the great tell sites, like Tószeg, were complete villages where houses were numerous and frequently rebuilt. It

Table 4   Radiocarbon dates, east-central Europe, earlier Bronze Age

Site	Lab no.	bc
Transitional to Early Bronze Age		
Csepel Island (Budapest)	Q-1122	2220 ± 90
Dates quoted by N. Kalicz and R. Kalicz-		
Schreiber:[136] early Nagyrév with Bell		2285 ± 100
Beaker		1820 ± 60
Nagyrév		
Baracs (Dunaújváros)	Bln-340	1785 ± 80
Vatya		
Dunaújváros–Koszider, grain from EBA vessel	Bln-341	1555 ± 80
Kosziderpadlás (Dunaújváros)	GrN-1994	1320 ± 50
Otomani		
Gánovce (Spišská Nová Ves)	GrN-7319	1465 ± 35
Mad'arovce		
Nitriansky Hrádok (Nové Zámky)	LJ-2044	1400 ± 200
Chłopice-Veselé		
Iwanowice (Miechów)	M-2688	1770 ± 180
,,	M-2325	1750 ± 170
,,	M-2328	1850 ± 170
Trzciniec		
Iwanowice (Miechów)	M-2169	1450 ± 160
Miernów (Kielce), barrow II	K-1838	1500 ± 100
Mierzanowice		
Iwanowice (Miechów)	10 dates between 1750 and 1600 bc	

is only at a few sites, however, that detailed plans have been recovered: recent work at Tószeg and Jászdózsa, for instance, has pioneered the way by showing us the wealth of information retrievable.

Terminology

The terminology of the earlier Bronze Age in east-central Europe makes use of several conflicting schemes. In Slovakia and southern Poland the Reinecke system for Bavaria is widely used; in Hungary things are quite different (though Reinecke himself proposed a scheme for Hungary which was never widely adopted[138]). The basis for chronology until ten years ago was the sequence established by Childe and Tompa at Tószeg[139] – Nagyrév (A or I), Hatvan (B or II), Füzesabony (C and D or III and IV). Subsequently Mozsolics reduced this sequence to three phases (A–C) and by comparison with other tell stratigraphies devised her own threefold chronology (I–III), later extended to include the Tumulus period (IV) and Ha A and B (B. V and VI).[140] Bóna's dissatisfaction with the complexities of this scheme has led him to create another, which (alas!) is equally confusing to the neophyte.[141] He distinguishes an Early, Middle and Late Bronze Age, but in such a way that the divisions are far from corresponding to the German phases. Thus Nagyrév, Hatvan and their relatives are Early Bronze Age; Füzesabony and Vatya Middle Bronze Age; and everything thereafter Late Bronze Age, until the time of the Urnfield period (table 1). This is logical in some ways, and indeed the Hungarian Early Bronze Age *does* seem to have started earlier than the Czech and German; but it leads to a situation where a culture can be called Early Bronze Age in one country and Middle Bronze Age in another – as is the case with Gáta-Wieselburg, for instance. The most recent scheme, that of Hänsel, avoids this to some extent by relating the phases much more closely to the central European divisions (Early, Middle and Late Danubian Bronze Age, each divided into three). His work has been severely criticized, however, both inside and outside Hungary on methodological grounds and on grounds of accuracy, and seems destined to sink without trace.[142]

There are also in use large numbers of 'culture' and 'group' names with a purely local significance. These we consider in turn as we come to them. We shall continue to refer to an 'earlier Bronze Age', meaning the whole period up to the start of the Urnfields (i.e. up to the end of Br C, B. IVa, and Bóna's 'transitional phase').

The earlier Bronze Age in Hungary is exceptionally well-documented by comparison with other regions,[143] and though the cover at the edges of the area is less full, one may gain a clear picture of the sequence of cultures from Hungary itself. In general the *Vučedol-Zók* group is the immediate precursor of those groups traditionally described as Bronze Age.[144] In north-east Hungary there is a dense distribution of Zók sites clustering in the *Nyírség* (Borsod-Abaúj-Zemplén and Szabolcs-Szatmár counties); scattered more loosely through central Hungary, and in south-west Slovakia, are sites with material typified by that found at *Makó* – Vöröskereszt (Csongrad, on the river Maros);[145] this group is known in Slovakia as the *Kosihy-Čaka* group.[146] In Hungary settlements tend to be at the base of tell sites, in Slovakia they are on raised terrace-like banks near rivers, on fertile black or brown loamy soils with a loess or sand underlay.[147] Houses are not well-known, but appear to have been simple post-constructions, accompanied by storage pits; the best examples come from Tiszalúc-Dankadomb near Miskolc (Borsod-Abaúj-Zemplén), but they occur too on other sites better known in the succeeding, Hatvan, period – Nitriansky Hrádok (Nové Zámky) and Malé Kosihy (Štúrovo). Burials were usually by cremation.[148]

The general picture of the Bronze Age sequence of the Hungarian plain is one of parallel local development. Because of the nature of archaeological research, however, many different culture names have been used, and it is our intention to examine the whole before its parts. If we start from the middle and work outwards, after the Zók group we have to deal with the *Nagyrév, Hatvan* and *Füzesabony* groups which succeed or run parallel with one another on tell sites on and around the Tisza; on the Danube are the *Kisapostag* and *Vatya* groups; in the south of Hungary and the Banat (both Jugoslav and Romanian) the *Periam-Mokrin-Szöreg* groups of sites; west of the Danube are the related groups of *north Pannonian* and *Encrusted Pottery*; in southern Slovakia appear the *Nitra* and *Košt'any*, related to the south Polish *Mierzanowice*, and giving way to the *Mad'arovce* group (related to early and late Únĕtice respectively). This group has elements in common with the local Tumulus culture which succeeds it; elsewhere on the plain the earlier groups we have mentioned either continue (like Füzesabony) into the 'Middle Bronze Age' or give way to various urn-using cultures, the most important of which is *Piliny*. In the Vojvodina one can find both Tumulus sites and urn-using groups, the most important being first *Vattina* and later *Belegiš*. Finally, in south-east Poland, and extending into the Ukraine, is the group that succeeds Mierzanowice –*Trzciniec*, seen by some authors as part of a larger grouping (Trzciniec-Komarov-Sosnicja).

Levels of the Zók culture, resting directly on the natural ground surface, underlie those of the true Bronze Age at many of the tell sites on the Hungarian plain, and it is likely that the latter succeeded the former by means of a gradual transition. There are many stratified tells in Hungary, and it has long been customary to cite the example of the mound at Tószeg-Laposhalom (Szolnok) as an exemplar of the sequence.

The mound (pl. 9) rises some 6.5 m from the plain, and forms what must originally have been a roughly elliptical hillock just beside the river Tisza in its mid-course (where its width is still very considerable). It is thought once to have been about 360 m long and half that wide, covering some 7 ha, and since over half of it has now vanished through erosion and artificial means, it appears today as a large sheer bank in the section of which numerous habitation layers can be discerned – some, like those where a level of burning is present, more visible than others. The course of the Tisza has changed since prehistoric times, and would originally have been a little further away; but the terrain would, in the absence of efficient drainage systems, have been marshy and – if the situation today is anything to go by – mosquito-ridden. Outside the marshy areas, however, the land is very fertile and would no doubt have supported a rich grain crop.

There were numerous layers of occupation, but the Bronze Age pottery falls into three main groups, which were distinguished in broad outline by the original excavators in the early years of this century, though only attributed finally to their correct cultural groups in 1952.[149] Above Neolithic and Chalcolithic (Tiszapolgár) levels came those with pottery identified at the nearby tell at Nagyrév; above that, and as sherds barely distinguishable from it, pottery of the type found at the Strázsahegy site at Hatvan; and above that, various levels attributable to the group known from numerous cemeteries and settlements in eastern Hungary – Füzesabony. In fact many of the less elaborate pottery forms continue unchanged from start to finish, and it is only characteristic decorated sherds that enable a precise chronology to be established. It is indicative of the difficulty that occurs in tying down pottery to particular cultures that Márton did not recognize the important Hatvan level, and that different authorities have variously seen three or four Bronze Age levels at Tószeg.

The same stratigraphy occurs frequently both in Hungary and in Czechoslovakia.[150] In Hungary we shall look in more detail at the typical tell-site of Jászdózsa-Kápolnahalom (Szolnok) (pl. 2), and of the many other examples it is worth mentioning the eponymous site of Hatvan-Strázsahegy (Heves) and the rich tell-sites at Tiszafüred-Ásotthalom (Szolnok) and Tiszaluc-Dankadomb (Borsod-Abaúj-Zemplén).[151] In Czechoslovakia similar stratigraphies are known from Malé Kosihy (Štúrovo),[152] Nitriansky Hrádok (Nové Zámky)[153] and Barca (Košice).[154]

Unfortunately the matter is very much more complicated than this straightforward stratigraphy would suggest. No sooner had the true affinities of each pottery level been established than it was shown that this sequence is valid only for certain areas: elsewhere the positions of Nagyrév and Hatvan relative to other groups and to each other were quite different. In north-east Hungary, for instance, there is no Nagyrév and the Hatvan levels follow directly on from Zók levels and can be shown to be contemporaneous with Nagyrév elsewhere, even to have started earlier. From the stratigraphy at Tiszaluc Kalicz has distinguished three separate phases of Hatvan development, and the start of Füzesabony should fall within the late phase.[155] On the other hand in Transdanubia it is Hatvan that is missing: broadly speaking, Nagyrév groups are succeeded by Vatya ones around the Danube and by Encrusted Wares in western and southern Hungary.[156]

Most of these tell sites are 'fortified' – that is, they are provided with an encircling bank and ditch or simply a ditch, and very often situated on defensible tongues of land in the bends of rivers. No traces of encircling palisades have yet been recovered. Whether or not these earthworks were truly defensive in nature has not been established: they may have been no more than a means of keeping wild animals out of the village compound.

Fortified tell-sites are also a distinctive feature of the Vatya group,[157] though at Százhalombatta (Pest) the same site was occupied from Nagyrév times through to the time of the Tumulus culture. The investigation of one such site at Lovasberény-Mihályvár[158] revealed a double row of earthworks on the west side, and a single one on the east – though it was suggested that the site was not lived in but used as a cult area; it also contained a bronzesmith's workshop. The ditches were up to 6 m deep, and the area enclosed an irregular triangle on a low hill: the impression is very much one of a genuine hill-fort, for defensive purposes. Twenty-six such sites, mostly on or near the north–south stretch of the Danube, have been identified.

House plans of the several phases do not differ greatly. In a tell-site houses are built more or less in the same way and to more or less the same plan, century after century. Recent work at Tószeg, however, has revealed certain differences in the architecture of different levels. Houses in the Nagyrév levels were built of clay only, both walls and floors, and had an unusual internal arrangement with partition-walls projecting only slightly from the main side-walls; there was no evidence of burning in these houses, which must presumably have just crumbled away – fireproof but not rain-proof. In the Hatvan and Füzesabony levels houses are rectangular and of wattle-and-daub, as usual, and succeed one another with great frequency.[159] At Jászdózsa the Hatvan houses have a post frame and are up to 12 m long and 6 wide, with two or three internal hearths; the Füzesabony houses vary in size: one measured 11 × 5 m, another, higher up, 7 × 5 m.[160] A good series of houses came from Hatvan itself:[161] they were long rectangular post-structures oriented E–W or NE–SW, and of various sizes: one measured 17 × 6 m. A central row of posts supported a ridge-roof. Other houses are known from Barca and Tiszaluc; the latter has provided evidence for the internal arrangement of the houses, with clay hearths being the most important feature, either flat or with a rim, and usually oval in shape. Kalicz has distinguished a development of hearth types in Hatvan houses, with more elaborate types usually appearing later, and in smaller houses.[162] As for the positioning of houses, the site of Barca contained in the excavated quarter twenty-three houses, nineteen oriented north–south and four at right-angles to these. The group of nineteen is divided into two opposing rows of six with seven buildings half the size between them, and it has been suggested that Barca was a special site, perhaps a chieftain's residence; it may, on the other hand, indicate no more than an unusual attention to detail.

The typical settlement form of the other important groups on the Hungarian plain was also the tell, though these are less well documented.[163] The Periam-Szöreg group has the important type-sites of Periam and Pecica (Arad), and corresponding tells are known near the main cemeteries at Szöreg and Oszentiván-Nagyhalom (Csongrad); the lack of recent excavations with modern techniques prevents a fuller knowledge of houses, which have been said to be 'pit-dwellings' and 'megara'.[164] Much settlement debris, though no proper houses, was also recovered from the allied type-site of Gerjen-Váradpuszta (Tolna). Of much greater importance are the findings from the Vărşand sub-group of Füzesabony, at the type-site and at Békés (Városerdö and Várdomb).[165] The latter is one of the best-excavated and best-published settlement sites in the central European Bronze Age, so that its findings are especially valuable. The dense superposition of layers, and the skilful removal of one after another revealed a series of rectangular houses, of varying plans. The most numerous were post-hole constructions composed of stakes (mostly under 0.1 m in diameter) supported by some larger posts and interwoven with wattle and daub. The size of these houses varies from some 10 × 8 m to 22 × 16, though it is impossible to reconstruct their functions. In addition, there are the scanty remains of curvilinear post-constructions. Less tenuous in outline are the houses composed of wooden planks and beams, the construction of which recalls Swiss lake-dwelling houses. Usually the floors were constructed of parallel beams laid side by side and tied in at each end, or each side, by dowelled cross-beams. The largest of these, house H I;222, is oriented NNE–SSW and measures more than 5 m long and 2.5 wide, the width of the planks being between 0.21 and 0.28 m. In the northern part of the floor (as in most of these houses) was a raised round hearth on a clay platform with modelled clay rim. The positioning of the open hearths in the houses is alleged to have made a ridge-roof unlikely; the absence of post-holes is said to indicate that the whole house was of log construction, but we do not feel this case is proven: a central row of post-holes is not essential for a ridge-roof.

By far the majority of these sites have been tells, but there remain other sites which are of the greatest importance in their local context – fortified hill-sites. In Hungary a number of such sites are known in the hillier districts, though they are scarcely impressive in scale. Kalicz has distinguished five situations in which they may occur in the Hatvan culture,[166] of which the commonest is that found on the Földvár ('citadel') at Gibárt (Borsod-Abaúj-Zemplén): a high terrace was cut off by a deep ditch from all the easier approach-routes, leaving a substantial part of the site undefended (a situation also found on tell-sites). Here, as always in such cases, fortified hill-sites make use of natural defences, especially high slopes by rivers, promontories and so on.

Hill settlements are also found in the group called by the Romanians after the site of Otomani, which is equivalent to the Hungarian Füzesabony. Its distribution extends deep into Slovakia and the north Carpathian foothills; Barca is there the best-known name, Spišský Štvrtok the most impressive site. It is convenient to treat all these as one group, but really only the distinctive pottery links the various sub-units; and in Romania even that merges imperceptibly at the edges with Wietenberg to the east, while the type of settlement there renders it more Transylvanian than otherwise.[167] The distribution of Otomani sites in Romania – numbering some eighty-six in 1971 – is concentrated in the north-west of the country, principally along the edge of the west Carpathian foothills, but extending into Transylvania along the valleys of the Mureş and Someş, with a scatter of sites in the intermediate upland.[168]

The general situation of Otomani sites varies. In all cases it is said to have been usual for them to avoid hilly terrain and concentrate on low ground with abundant water; but this statement is to some extent biased because it is clear that the Otomani group was in fact primarily a lowland phenomenon (Füzesabony), and did not extend far into the area of upland conditions. In hilly terrain, like Slovakia, sites appear not on hill-tops but on eminences of middle height, conveniently placed for exploitation of arable land and for ease of obtaining water. When one considers the total number of sites attributable to the Otomani-Füzesabony grouping, an overwhelming majority occur on the Hungarian plain and its adjacent river-valleys: the fortified Otomani sites represent no more than a local phenomenon.

Detailed study of settlement location and fortification systems[169] in the Romanian Otomani sites has enabled five main situations to be identified: settlements on promontories, in angles formed by streams and rivers, mound-like settlements, open sites, and 'island sites' in marshy areas. Some of these, as we shall see, have chronological significance.

At Otomani itself (Marghiţa, Crişana) there are three localities which have yielded material of the culture. The earliest in date, as well as the best-known, is that called Cetăţuia (Citadel), in a typically dominating position on the bluff of hills overlooking the extreme eastern edge of the great Hungarian plain. Investigations were begun here in 1925 by Roska, and continued more recently by Horedt and others.[170] A fairly small area is enclosed by the earthworks, which consist of one encircling ditch and rampart and one supplementary work cutting off the northern projection of the spur of land. The ditches are either round- or V-bottomed, and of some depth; the inner works were probably supplemented by a palisade. The presence of the outer works at the north side, where the slope is steepest, and the absence of something similar at the unprotected south end, is problematical; nor is the chronological position clear, for sherds of both main phases were recovered.

A similar site, a few kilometres away, is Sălacea, important for its ritual building (below, p. 86f.). This site also lies on a promontory of land overlooking the plain; here too an encircling earthwork enclosed the whole site, with irregularly cut round-bottomed ditches and rather broad ramparts giving a total width of 21 m. There was also some evidence of an outer fortification at certain points.[171]

It has been shown that 90 per cent of Otomani settlements were either artificially or naturally fortified.[172] This fact alone indicates the very different nature of Otomani settlement from that of Füzesabony. The lowland site at Otomani on an island in the river Er, on the other hand, fits in with the Hungarian distribution rather than the Romanian. This site ('fortress of earth') lies only a metre above the water-level and is therefore presumed not to have been fortified by banks and ditches. The occupation was lengthy, however, as no less than eight separate habitation layers were observed. Remains of elaborate pile-structures were recovered, including a double ring of posts 15 m apart.[173] Of the other types of Otomani settlement, we may mention here Potău (Satu Mare, Maramureş), in the bend of a river – the only example to have been systematically investigated – and protected by a rampart; Socodor and Vărşand, both tell-sites; and, in the later stages, Pir (Carei, Crişana), in marshy land with fortifications added to an existing settlement and cemetery.[174]

The number of houses known is not large, but several different types are recorded.[175] At Otomani-Cetăţuia both round and rectangular buildings are said to have been found, with clay floors and a single door flanked by double-posts; the round house was only 2 m in diameter.[176] In the more recent excavations a rectangular house 3 × 4 m was recovered, with scattered remains of clay daub preserving reed impressions, and the copious ashes of reeds that are assumed to have formed part of a roof. Two hearths were found inside, directly on top of the beaten earth floor, oval in shape and one metre long. A comparable building, delineated by a mass of baked clay, was found at Sălacea. In other places burnt beams and post-holes indicate a wooden-framed construction. As for the internal arrangement of Otomani houses, dividing walls are said not to occur; a couple of hearths and a number of storage pits (of inverted bell shape) are invariable. There is some evidence from the tell-sites that houses were disposed in a ring around an open area, and it is even alleged that community leaders were separated off in specially designated raised areas.

All that has been said so far refers to the first two phases of the culture, and in phase III we have the additional evidence of several large house-plans from Otomani-Cetatea de Pamînt, of which only one, the largest, is yet published in detail.[177] On a platform of baked clay 24.5 × 12.5 m, a post-framed wattle-and-daub structure had been erected, and traces of the mouldings of the windows were preserved. Three rows of three posts, stouter in the middle than at the sides, supported the roof. No less than eight hearths were found (? all from the one house), circular, with a diameter between 0.6 and 0.8 m, and having a groove round the rim.

In Hungary hill-forts are not a common feature of Füzesabony settlement, but in Slovakia they occur more frequently.[178] The site of Barca is not exactly a hill-fort, but it lies on a tongue of land 12 m above the valley of the river Hornád; where the southern and western slopes run down to the plain a ditch and rampart are present. More dramatic than this, however – indeed one of the most important sites in the central European Bronze Age – is the hill-fort of Spišský Štvrtok (Spišská Nová Ves) at Myšia Hôrka.[179] This hill rises some 50 m from an undulating valley in the Spiš or Slovenský Raj ('Slovak Paradise'), very steeply on the western side, but more gradually at the east, where a neck of land joins it to higher ground (pl. 6). It is here that the defences are concentrated, and not only was a substantial encircling and stone-lined palisade ditch dug but a rampart with inner and outer stone facings was provided. These stone walls now survive to a height of 1 m and are built of rather thin stone slabs (pl. 6) which petrographic analysis has shown to have been brought from a distance of 2–3 km. The main entrance through the rampart is at the east, and there round tower-like bastions were erected, nearly 6 m in diameter. The assumed length of this fortification wall is 160 m, its width 4.8 m at base and 4 m at the top, its height 3.5 to 4 m – higher if we postulate that a wooden palisade surmounted it. Inside these fortifications were laid a series of house-foundations, twenty-six to date, lying in a row oriented north–south. At the west side they adjoined the palisade, arranged so as to leave a 'town square' in the shape of a U with a form of stone paving. The houses themselves were mostly rectangular two-roomed affairs, and produced rich finds of gold and bronze objects hidden in chests under the floor. Some buildings contained finds – like moulds – which enabled them to be identified as work-shops. A cult area was also noted (see below, p. 88).

Fortified sites occur, too, with some regularity in south-west Slovakia, where the material from them is usually named after the finds from Mad'arovce (Krupina). Veselé-Hradisko (Piešt'any), Vráble (Nitra), the castle hill at Nitra (appropriately enough now the home of the Archaeological Institute), Nitriansky Hrádok (Nové Zámky) and Malé Kosihy (Štúrovo) all have substantial encircling ditches and banks; stone fortifications are uncommon, however, and restricted to Veselé and Ivanovce-Skala (Trenčín), though Moravia has a few examples of such construction. The site at Nitriansky Hrádok-Zámeček lies beside the river Nitra in a low-lying situation; it was rendered defensible by a double-ditch and rampart. The outer ditch was V-shaped, 10 m wide and 4.5 deep, the inner ditch shallower and more curved in profile. The rampart was a timber-framed construction 4.5 m high (estimated) and 5 m wide, the outer sides sloping slightly and having a wattle retaining structure (fig. 30).[180] Little information is as yet available on the finds in the interior of this site: more is known from Veselé, where, on the other hand, little is known of the defences.[181] Numerous storage pits were

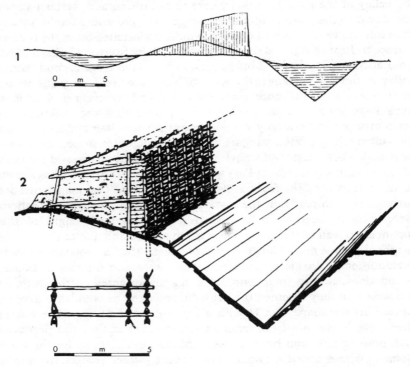

Fig. 30   Reconstruction of the defences at Nitriansky Hrádok, west Slovakia. (After Vladár 1973b)

found, and remains of houses in the form of beaten earth floors, hearths and burnt daub. The accumulation of material in tell-like layers assigns these Mad'arovce sites to the Hungarian plain group; many of them are on low loess terraces above rivers in situations differing little from those of the true Hungarian tells.

Considerable numbers of settlements occur in south-east Poland in the latter part of the Early Bronze Age in the Trzciniec culture, which is closely related both to pre-Lausitz and to the Tumulus groups (above, p. 57). The type-site is a settlement near Bełżyce (Lublin),[182] an area especially prolific in sites, with house-foundations sunk well into the ground; large numbers of extensive settlements have been recovered, mainly in dune areas.[183]

We may note in conclusion that some areas of east-central Europe have produced virtually nothing in the way of settlement sites. This is particularly true of the Nitra group which preceded Mad'arovce in south-west Slovakia, and its relatives in east Slovakia. We should perhaps expect Nitra settlements to turn up in a form hitherto unsuspected.

Important though settlements are, it is the burial sites that have been most used for classification of cultural groups, if only because the objects recovered from them are more complete and more distinctive. Broadly speaking, cremation was commoner in earlier Bronze Age Hungary than in most other areas, and inhumation is restricted to certain groups, especially west of the Danube. The sequence is essentially one in which urn-burial alternates with inhumation burial in simple pits: one can divide cultures up into those which used cremation urns and those which inhumed. This alternation is especially obvious if we follow the Tószeg culture-sequence that we have discussed above.

Urn-burial was the standard form in Nagyrév cemeteries, which are numerous and prolific. Bóna, who has published the standard work on this aspect, distinguishes four main types of Nagyrév cemetery, which he names after Tószeg-Ökörhalom (lying one kilometre from the tell), Sövényháza-Kötörés (Csongrad), Szigetszentmiklós (Csepel Island, Budapest) and Kulcs (Dunaújváros, Fejér):[184] the differences are mainly reflected in the pottery forms but to some extent in the burial rite too. The second group, for instance, includes four graves at Szöreg (Csongrad) which contained contracted skeletons that had, apparently, been burned at some subsequent stage; the first and the third have cremations that may or may not be inurned. In the last, Kulcs, group, on the other hand, inurned cremation was universal: the graves were put in groups (?familial), with about twenty metres between them. Inside a group, the urns were laid in rows, up to seven in one row. Grave-goods were few. Each urn was covered by a bowl, and in one group at Kulcs it was customary for the bowl to be laid bottom downwards, suggesting a practice restricted to a single family. Accessory vases were put inside the urn: usually a handled jug and a pedestalled cup. A few graves stand out as pre-eminent: either by especially rich offerings or by multiple burials.[185] The rich Makó and early Nagyrév finds in the Budapest area have enabled a threefold chronological division for the culture to be made.[186]

Much less is known about burials in the Hatvan culture, but cremation was universal there too.[187] Urns were used in perhaps half the cases recorded. Rectangular or oval pits were dug, and the ashes or urn laid in the middle with accessory vessels round about. More than one cemetery can apparently belong to a single settlement, and Kalicz notes that the two are usually well separated: cemetery in the valley if the settlement is on a hill, or across a river if on the plain. In Slovakia notable cemeteries are at Salka (Štúrovo).[188]

By contrast, inhumation was the commoner rite in Füzesabony times, though cremations do sometimes occur (as at Streda nad Bodrogom) in the same cemeteries.[189] Mounds or raised sites were used; graves may be arranged in rows and groups, as at Megyaszó (Borsod-Abaúj-Zemplén). The body was buried in contracted position, knees usually bent at about 60°, arms bent and hands in front of the face. There was considerable differentiation between the sexes: men's graves were rather deeper than women's, and at Megyaszó Tompa observed that men were laid on their right sides, oriented approximately south–north, women on their left sides, oriented north–south; the faces of both thus look to the east, and there are few exceptions to this rule. Similar rites were followed at other sites, and it is suggested that such practices have an Eneolithic origin. In general, grave-goods are rich, though some graves have none; weapons, axes and richly decorated pottery appear in quantity in men's graves; gold and bronze ornaments, tutuli and amber beads in women's. The position of pins in graves reveals no essential difference between men's and women's dress, nor do they indicate with any clarity what clothing was like. Finally we may mention grave 122 at Hernádkak (Borsod), where a man's skeleton had a spearhead embedded in the pelvis.[190] These cemeteries are numerous, but they are not often found beside their companion settlement; an exception to this is at Tiszafüred (Szolnok), where Kovács has excavated more than 1,000 graves, belonging to both Füzesabony and Tumulus cultures, and utilizing both inhumation and cremation.[191]

The cemeteries of the Periam-Szöreg-Mokrin group have been intensively studied, and it is the rich and well-known material from sites like Pitvaros, Őszentiván, Deszk (2) and Szöreg (Csongrad), Battonya

(Békés), Mokrin (Kikinda) and Beba-Veche (Timiş) that has caused the group to be so frequently cited in the literature.[192] Burial was usually by contracted inhumation in oval or rectangular grave-pits, on left or, more commonly, right sides in various orientations but a preference for north–south. Grave-goods vary with time, and with sex, but are in general rich. A few graves, on the other hand, are in urns or pithoi, as at Szöreg and Deszk A. The fullest picture comes from Mokrin: a roughly elliptical area on sloping ground contained some hundreds of graves, of which 312 were examined.[193] About half were sub-rectangular in shape, and most were oriented north–south or south–north, the skeletons contracted on left or right sides (fig. 31); five cremations were found. Only two graves were found oriented east–west, both unfurnished. Males had the head to the north and lay on the left side. The most interesting feature about the disposition of the cemetery is the fact that the graves are arranged more or less in eleven lines, spreading north and north-west from the central part of the cemetery, and the excavator suggests that these may represent familial groupings. The infrequency with which grave-pits cut one another also leads him to suppose that grave markers must have been placed above the interments. Recent work on Mokrin has given an elegant demonstration that the northern part of the cemetery must be the earliest, for it is there that the greatest numbers of unfurnished graves, as well as of stone axes, simple bronze buttons, spectacle pendants and so on occur.[194] This conclusion has been of considerable importance in unravelling the pottery sequence which is by no means as obvious, and also the local chronological situation: Mokrin is said to cover the entire time-span of the cemeteries that cluster round the river Mureş (mentioned above), starting earlier than any other and continuing as late as the latest (Deszk A).

In the eastward, Romanian, extension of the Füzesabony and related groups, burials have not been found in quantity: only recently has this aspect become at all familiar. A cremation cemetery at Ciumeşti (Carei, Maramureş)[195] has been attributed to the Otomani group, though the urns found there are, of course, quite different from settlement pottery. No definitive mode of disposal was observed there, nor at Pir (Carei).[196] Single inhumation burials have been observed at various settlement sites; at Sălacea there was a multiple grave, containing a man aged about 50, a woman of about 54, a girl of about 15, and an infant. According to the excavator, the man's right hand lay on the girl's pubis, and a finger of her left hand was extended in the region of his phallus: not unnaturally, this is interpreted as a 'sexual grouping', whatever that may mean.[197] There was another burial – this time of a child – outside the 'temple' at Sălacea (below), and a third, by cremation, in the centre of the site. At Otomani

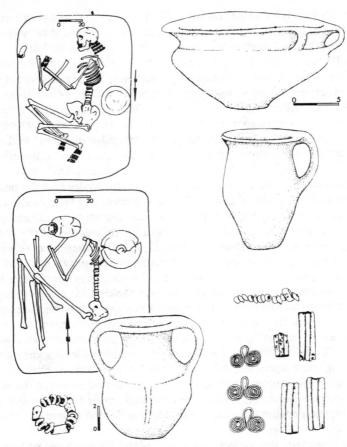

Fig. 31   Graves and grave goods from the Early Bronze Age
cemetery at Mokrin (Kikinda), Banat. *Scales in cm.*
(After M. Girić, *Mokrin, I,* 1971)

itself there was a contracted inhumation on the left side with a single jug
as grave-goods.

The Tumulus culture left an impression on the cultures of the
Hungarian plain, but it cannot be said to have formed any sizeable group
there; it is mainly at the northern and western edges that the Middle
Danubian and Carpathian groups appear (above, p. 44). Some sites in
northern Hungary are a real part of the Tumulus culture; elsewhere
Tumulus influence is present as at Hajdúbagos (Hajdú-Bihar), where a
cemetery of more than twenty graves contained pottery that clearly
demonstrated the Tumulus affinities.[198]

In the remaining earlier Bronze Age groups in the Hungarian plain, we may separate those that utilized urn burial (Kisapostag, Vatya, and Encrusted Pottery on and around the Danube; Piliny in the north) from those that inhumed (Somogyvár and Gáta in the west, some of the Vărşand cemeteries in the east), though biritual cemeteries also occur, as at Tápé (Szeged). As far as the cremations are concerned, it is less worth detailing the individual points of difference than examining the development of the rite. We have already seen how the Nagyrév group practised inurned cremation, and the Kisapostag cemeteries represent a late facet of this:[199] Kisapostag leads straight into Vatya, in which the cremation rite is taken over virtually unchanged.[200] The cemeteries may be very large, as at Dunakészi (Pest) or Dunaújváros (Fejer). Parallel to this runs the Encrusted Pottery culture to the west of the Danube, and though inurned cremation was standard, there are a number of instances recorded where children are inhumed in pithoi.[201] Piliny is somewhat anomalous: its bronzework shows it must be contemporary with the later Tumulus period, but earlier than the true 'Urnfields'. Though many hundreds of Piliny graves have been found, including nearly 1,000 at Nagybátony alone, there is little information available on the precise form of Piliny cemeteries. They concentrate in northern Hungary and southern Slovakia (the type-site is not far from Salgótarján) and are especially numerous towards the area of the Carpathian foothills – no doubt reflecting the settlers' need for the metal ores which occur in those regions. The grave-pits are either simple or stone-lined; in some cases a stone marker was put over the top. The standard contents were an urn with an inverted bowl placed on top, and sometimes little cups and storage jars.[202] At Šafárikovo (Rimavská Sobota) animal bones were found, unburnt, in the body of the pit, possibly remains of the funeral feast.[203] The cremated bones, on the other hand, were carefully collected and put in the urn. At Barca (Košice) seventy-two graves were excavated in an urnfield separated from the Otomani hill-site (where Piliny sherds also occurred): some of these had stone grave stelae.[204]

At Tápé (Szeged) nearly 700 graves were excavated, a majority of them contracted inhumations in simple pits and without barrows, but including also extended and pithos burials and inurned cremations. The pottery shows clear analogies both with Tumulus groups to the north and with the richly decorated wares of the Vojvodina (Vattina-Vršac). The bronzes are exclusively of the Koszider phase and later (Br B–C); cf. below, p. 93.[205]

In the Vojvodina the rich cremation cemeteries of Vattina and related types succeeded the Mokrin-group sites; further to the west tumuli with inhumations are found, containing Vattina material but perhaps rather to be connected with the more general spread of Tumulus burial. Contemporary with these were the cremating groups of the Vojvodina, among which the sites of Belegiš, Omoljica and Surčin may be mentioned (below, p. 202).[206]

Continuing round the fringes of the plain, we find in the west of Hungary cemeteries of the Gáta (Gattendorf) group.[207] At Gattendorf itself (Burgenland) the cemetery lay in and under a large tumulus, 35–40 m in diameter; at other sites, like Rusovce (Bratislava; formerly Oroszvár) and Hainburg-Teichtal (Lower Austria) grave groupings were observed, though the precise nature of these groupings varied from site to site. At Hainburg-Teichtal rows of graves were found, as has been noticed in Únětician cemeteries at Kolín and elsewhere. Burial was here invariably by inhumation, and no one orientation was dominant: at Gattendorf (Gáta) the graves were thoroughly mixed; at Rusovce (Oroszvár) there was a tendency for a west–east direction of the burials. The bodies were more or less tightly contracted, and no firm observations have yet been made as to whether there was a sexual differentiation in burial form. Animal bones sometimes accompanied the corpse.

To the north, in Slovakia and southern Poland, almost all the information we possess about the Nitra group (or more widely the Nitra-Košt'any-Mierzanowice group) comes from cemeteries. Since Točík published the basic study of the south-west Slovakian material,[208] excavation in both Slovakia and Poland has added considerably to our information about the group. At Branč (Nitra) Vladár has excavated 237 graves of the Nitra group;[209] these were usually simple rectangular pits, sometimes with a wood lining and in one case with a wooden 'chamber'; the bodies are disposed according to sex, men west–east with head to the west and looking south, women east–west with head to the east but on their opposite sides – that is, they also looked south (fig. 32). The cemetery at Košice of the Kost'any group was similar;[210] here the graves were laid in rows, oriented north–south, with some 1.5 m between graves. The skeletons were usually laid on their sides, but some were on their backs; the knees were either tightly contracted or only slightly bent. Considerable numbers of graves of this group have recently been excavated in Poland;[211] one of the largest cemeteries is Iwanowice (Miechów), where Machnik has found over 160 graves and established a radiocarbon chronology (below, p. 101).[212]

Grave types of the Trzciniec culture of south-east Poland were very diverse, being either by inhumation or by cremation, and either flat or under barrows. The large number of sites of all sorts has enabled five local sub-groups to be distinguished.[213]

We may sum up this analysis of grave form in the cultures of east-

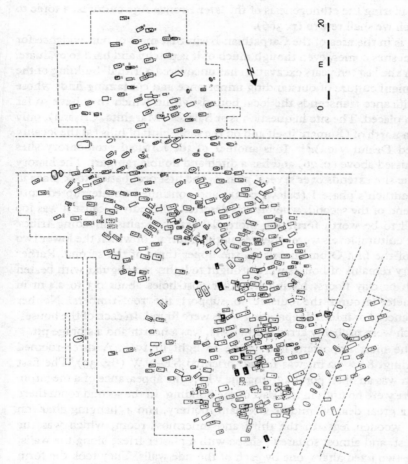

Fig. 32 Plan of the Nitra-group cemetery at Holešov (Moravia).
(After J. Ondráček)

central Europe by remarking that there was a continual interplay of differing traditions, in particular of inhumation versus cremation. The cemeteries using each rite can be seen to show broad similarities, and the major difference lies between those groups that cremated and those that inhumed. The fact that the cremation rite can be traced back to the very beginning of the Bronze Age in Hungary is of great importance in considering the ethnogenesis of the later Bronze Age cultures, a topic to which we shall return (p. 366).

It is in the area of the Carpathian Basin that most of our evidence for ritual sites comes, even though much of it is patchy and hard to evaluate. Over the last ten years excavation has uncovered a 'ritual' building of the Otomani culture of outstanding importance and containing finds whose significance transcends the local bounds within which they have so far been placed. The site in question is at Sălacea (Marghiţa, Crişana), only 8 km north of Otomani itself and on the same bluff of hills (at the locality called Dealul Vida).[214] It is another of the fortified promontory sites discussed above (p. 76) and has a ditch and double rampart. The history of the site extends over several phases; the first occupation took place in Ordentlich's phase I (below, p. 91) and continued uninterrupted until the end of the second, when it was deserted, allegedly because it was too small to be worth fortifying more elaborately against invading tribes. Five cultural levels were observed in the interior, of which the lower two are of the first Otomani period, the upper three of the second. Rather scanty remains of houses were brought to light, rectangular with beaten earth or clay floors, having irregular post-holes about 0.3 to 0.4 m in diameter around the outside to support the roof-timbers. Neither entrances nor internal separating walls were found. In each of the houses, which were probably arranged in rows, was a hearth and a storage pit.

The most important finds came to light in 1968. A three-roomed building, 8.8 × 5.2 m, was found, oriented SE–NW (fig. 33). The first room was an open porch, giving the whole the appearance of a megaron. There were no finds in this part of the building. In the second room there was a great deal of 'middle Otomani' pottery, and a 'hanging altar' on four wooden legs. In the third and innermost room, which was the largest, and almost square in shape with a plaster frieze along the walls, were two fixed altars, one by each of the side walls. They took the form of clay platforms, and one was pyramidal, tapering from 1.6 m at the base to 1.2 m above. Six holes in the floor are interpreted as settings for timber roof-supports, above which was a reed roof. On each of the side altars were found nine pyramidal clay objects, not unlike loom-weights, but unperforated and therefore interpreted as 'fire-dogs'; three curved stone knives; and a spool-like cylindrical clay vase-support with cut-out sides.

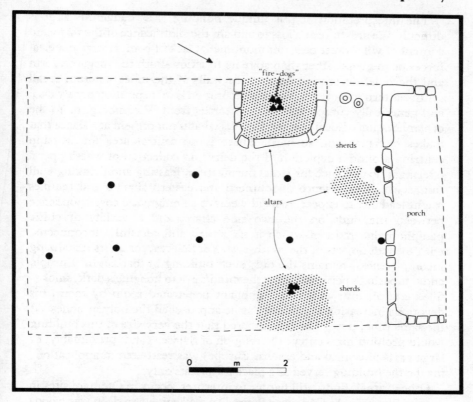

Fig. 33   Plan of the Otomani 'temple' at Sălacea.
(After Ordentlich 1972)

A great variety of other cult objects was found in different parts of the
site, including figurines, a model altar in clay, model wheels, eleven
miniature carts in clay, a stone macehead (said to be of alabaster), a clay
boat model, a miniature *rhyton* decorated in the Otomani style with
knobs, two similarly decorated *askoi*, a variety of cult vessels bearing feet,
five bone horse-harness cheek-pieces, weights, rattles, and a good deal of
richly decorated pottery in the Otomani II style.

Outside the temple was an inhumation burial of a child in a simple pit,
1.1 m in diameter and with vertical sides 1.3 m deep. In the pit was
another of the spool-like cylinders found on the altars, and this, together
with the child's disarticulated bones, suggested to the excavator some
function as an 'offering pit'.

The interpretation of this unique building is as dangerous as it is difficult. We are quite at a loss to explain the significance of the form and content of what must be a cult monument; lack of comparative material forces us to guess rather than state its function. Both the megaron form and the relief decoration on the side walls of the inner sanctum recall south-eastern prototypes. Yet this decoration is in inspiration purely local and generically comparable to the hearths from Wietenberg, or to the ornamentation of local pottery. But it is what is not present at Sălacea that makes interpretation so hard. There is no central area for worship centring around a depiction of the deity; no collection of worshippers' offerings; no evidence for ritual purification, feasting and drinking – all things which experience of southern and eastern shrines and temples might lead one to expect. Instead we have an enigmatic correspondence between the finds on the two side altars, and a variety of cultic paraphernalia, most of which is *sui generis* and certainly unconnected with the cult objects of the south-east. Yet Sălacea, for all its tantalizing incompleteness, remains the only such building in 'barbarian' Europe, and it is perhaps permissible for the mind's eye to imagine a dark, smoke-filled edifice, into which the suppliant penetrated room by room, his devotions increasing in intensity as he approached the holy of holies. At the same time, it must be remembered that the very size of this building would prohibit mass entry: the religion of Sălacea (and, presumably, of large parts of central and eastern Europe) was restricted in application; maybe the building served as a place for priests only.

Other 'ritual' finds, still harder to interpret, occur in Otomani sites in central Slovakia. At Gánovce (Poprad) a well some 2 m deep was wood-lined, containing animal and human bones, split and often burnt, and domestic vessels with applied plastic breasts, birch-bark vessels, and (most strange of all) an iron dagger.[215] It is claimed that 'ritual cannibalism' took place both here and at other sites at this time.[216] At Spišský Štvrtok a large rhomboidal stone was found on the acropolis not far from two cremations in pottery vessels, which led the excavator to suggest a ritual function for the area. A number of other sites have produced clay fragments, shaped into rectangular edges and the like, reminiscent of the structures from Uherský Brod[217] (above, p. 45).

In most of the other cultural groups of the Carpathian Basin, the evidence for ritual is extremely scanty. Askoid and footed vessels with elaborate plastic and other decoration, from Nagyrév and Kunszentmarton may have been used as *rhyta*: such forms are present too in the transitional phase preceding Nagyrév on Zók sites like Pécs-Makárhegy.[218]

Material culture

Although it is on the basis of material culture that so many and various separate groups are distinguished, and although certain distinctive forms can be seen to be characteristic of certain areas, there is a remarkable homogeneity in the finds from the different groups of the Hungarian plain. It is possible to group them by phases. In the first, to which we may assign the Nagyrév, Hatvan, early Periam-Szöreg-Mokrin, Kisapostag and Encrusted Pottery groups, the *Leittyp* or universal form is the one- or two-handled cup with tall funnel-like neck, in a polished black fabric; or with conical neck springing from a rather squat globular belly and rich incision and white encrustation (fig. 34, top centre). Another very common form is the low conical bowl with broad furrow round the rim and one or two small strap-handles. In metal, the simplest of triangular riveted daggers, spiral beads, tubes, flat sheet ornaments with curled edges, spectacle pendants, ivy-leaf pendants, *Hülsen-* and *Schleifennadeln*, buttons and coiled finger-rings appear; and in other material one finds faience beads, bone and shell beads, and bone pins. Of course each group has its specialities: Nagyrév urns are rather coarse ovoid vessels with rusticated decoration; vases with pedestal bases and cut-outs are common; incised ornament reminiscent of Beaker patterns is found.[219] Periam has many two-handled *Kantharos*-type vases, decorated with ribbing and elaborate arcaded incised ornament;[220] Kisapostag has large urns with globular body, small everted neck and four small strap-handles on the belly.[221] Hatvan has more elaborately decorated cups, urns with tall trumpet-mouth and applied ornament, low flaring drinking-cups, and a huge and varied quantity of settlement pottery – ovoid storage jars, straight-sided cups, biconical vessels, jugs of all shapes and sizes etc.;[222] the commonest decorative technique was that of rustication – brushing, by impressed textile or matting, pinching-up, or finger-smoothing – and most of the sherds lying on the surface of a Hatvan site will be found to

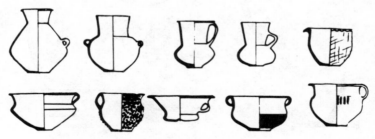

Fig. 34   Forms of Hatvan pottery.
(After Kalicz 1968)

be of this sort. Hatvan material also includes copious bonework (pins, hafts, sleeves etc.), stone hammers and axes, clay spindle-whorls and loom-weights, spatulae and ladles, animal figurines and zoomorphic vases, lids, trays etc.; several wheels for model carts have been found.

In the second main phase we include Füzesabony and Vărşand east of the Danube, with Otomani in the Romanian foothills, Vatya along the Danube and west of it, Mad'arovce in south-west Slovakia and eastern Austria, and the early urn cultures of the Vojvodina (Vattina and related). To it we may also assign a distinctive group of bronzes, sometimes named after the site of Kosziderpadlás near Dunaújváros (Fejér).

The most famous aspect of Otomani-Füzesabony is its fine polished black pottery, typically decorated with channelling and bosses (fig. 35). The commonest shapes are elegant one-handled cups with rather prominent bellies, open bowls, often footed or pedestalled, and jugs with wide belly and narrowing trumpet neck, recalling the shape of Únětician

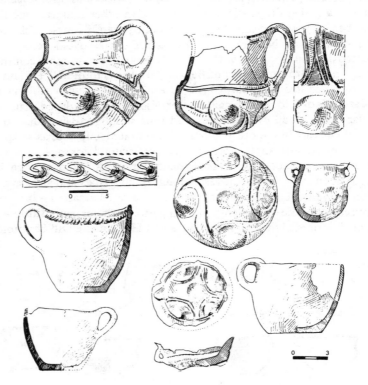

Fig. 35 Vărşand. Pottery of Otomani (Gyulavarsand) type. (After D. Popescu, *MCA* 2 (1956))

cups. As for decoration, spiral designs commonly occur, usually in association with bosses, but also triangles, motifs made up of groups of parallel lines, zig-zags etc.[223] Recent work by Ordentlich in Romania[224] and Bóna in Hungary[225] has enabled a chronological development of Otomani pottery to be established, on the basis of stratigraphical observations at the type-sites. Three phases are distinguished: the first characterized by poorly fired medium-sized vessels with brushed or cloth-impressed rusticated ornament, notched rims and flat bosses, a preponderance of low-bellied cups and jugs, sometimes with incised garland decoration; the second by cups that are taller than they are broad, 'fish-bowls', vases with strongly curved profiles, handles that do not rise above the rim, arcade ornaments, hatched triangles and a few incised spiral motifs, together with (in Hungary) the start of channelled and bossed decoration; and the third by well-fired cups and jugs with high handles and channelled spiraliform decoration on the belly, large bellied vessels with cylinder neck and small handles, and bowls and plates with the same characteristic decoration. Specialized forms of the Füzesabony aspect include tube-footed vases, cylindrical beakers, footed bowls and so on, while fish-bowls, strainers, spoons, spindle-whorls, vase-stands and waggon-models occur; other specialities are portable hearths of clay, four-footed grills and pyramidal fire-dogs. The ceramic inventory of the adjoining 'Gyulavarsand' (Vărşand) group of Bóna is not essentially different, with the overridingly common form being the low rounded cup with rather raised handle, and channelled decoration being universal. The more unusual pot forms (including waggon models) also bear out the idea that 'Gyulavarsand' is but a local variant of Otomani-Füzesabony – which, indeed, is how most authors have regarded it.[226]

The cemeteries – and settlements – of this broad grouping are unusually rich in metalwork, a fact which has often been seen as a direct reflection of the proximity of the ore-bearing mountains of northern Hungary and Transylvania. Lumps of casting waste come from Füzesabony and Tószeg; moulds for flat axes, shaft-hole axes, pins and spearheads are known. As far as finished products are concerned, other axe types include the flanged, shaft-tube (Křtěnov type) and disc-butted varieties; there are triangular or ogival daggers, awls, pins with roll-top, Hülsenkopf, spherical or biconical head, and sewing needles; also Noppenringe, arm-rings, tubes and pendants. Hoards, on the other hand, are hardly known. The range of types from the Vărşand area is similar, but it is here that a rich series of hoards come into the picture, including in the early stages the well-known Apa-Hajdúsámson series (below, p. 93).

The cultural material of these groups has been used to divide the period into sub-phases, and each of these may be seen to have wider analogies.

The early stages of Otomani (in Ordentlich's classification) are similar to the Nagyrév and Hatvan stages in Hungary, or to Tószeg A and early B; phase II corresponds to Tószeg B and C, phase III to later Tószeg C. In terms of the German sequence, this must range from Br AI to Br C or even D: hoards attributable to Br D occur on sites of phase III.[227] A hoard of bronze phalerae, tutuli and *saltaleoni* from Otomani itself (Cetatea de Pamînt) is attributed to Br D – Ha AI.[228] On the basis of these pottery divisions different types of site can be placed in different phases of the culture: fortified promontory sites occur only in phases I and II, and island sites only in phase III. The alleged connection between the disappearance of hill-sites and the start of island sites on the one hand, and the spread of Tumulus elements and 'Koszider' bronzes on the other is not, in our view, a plausible reconstruction of what must have been a complex situation. The late island sites perhaps represent a quite separate development, related to events on the plain, and do not necessarily imply that the previous occupants of the hill-sites had been ousted from their traditional homes.

Pottery of Piliny type is highly characteristic and rather unvaried. The urns are dark-faced and highly polished, usually with swelling belly and conical or cylindrical neck. Decoration consists of channelled vertical or horizontal lines and small bosses with concentric channels. Small loop handles are commonly placed on shoulder or belly. The other common form is the low bowl with raised ring-base and wide channel below the rim: peaked bowls recall Tumulus types, while small one-handled cups are especially characteristic of the Barca cemetery.[229] An unusual find from Radzovce (Lučenec) was a rich grave in a large cemetery containing seventeen pottery vessels, a group of small bronzes, and a portable one-piece pot-and-stand, assumed to be for cult purposes but no doubt equally serviceable for cooking. The Piliny bronze industry was also prolific.

Analysis of the contents of the large cemeteries of Barca, Nagybátony and Zagyvapálfalva has enabled a division of the Piliny cultural material to be made, though geographical variation makes general rules difficult. An eastern and a western group are generally distinguished, Barca typifying the former, and the large Hungarian cemeteries the latter; within each an early and a late phase is claimed. In the pottery the decline of rich linear decoration is characteristic of the later phase: the bronze-work enables us to synchronize Piliny with Br B2–C for the earlier, and Br C–D for the later phase.[230]

Throughout the Hungarian earlier Bronze Age the production of metal and metal objects was of signal importance, a situation that continues into the later period when vast quantities are known. The reason we may presume to have been the proximity of the metal ores of Transylvania:

the smiths of Hungary were apparently able to secure unrivalled access to the ore supplies to their east, and to an extensive market in central Europe (products of their work-shops have been found far north of the Carpathian ring). The evidence from moulds and smithing hoards makes it likely that metalworking was carried out locally in numerous workshops and not distributed from a few specialized centres.

Mozsolics has divided the bronze hoards into a series of 'horizons', much as Hachmann has done for hoards in the north. None of these is demonstrably contemporary with Nagyrév; Bányabükk, the earliest, predates it. The hoard horizon Kömlöd-Ercsi has shaft-hole axes with drooping blade, flat axes and a rich funerary inventory: it is set by Mozsolics parallel with Hatvan (B.II). The Hajdúsámson horizon is notable for its richly decorated and exotic forms: solid-hilted swords with wide swelling blades, disc-butted axes, shaft-tube and 'eastern' axes of bronze with elaborate incised spiraliform decoration, hand-guard spirals, and a few daggers with incised decoration. In terms of the German sequence this collection runs parallel with Br A2, or the Langquaid horizon. Locally, it is contemporary with the earlier part of Otomani-Füzesabony (B.IIIa); the find of Hajdúsámson metalwork with Füzesabony pottery at Nagykálló is unequivocal in its association.[231]

The succeeding Kosziderpadlás series of hoards contain some old and some new types.[232] Certain forms of disc-butted axe continue to be produced; shaft-tube axes now have short conical tubes, while other bronzes have a distinctly 'Tumulus' appearance – leg- and arm-spirals, ivy-leaf and heart pendants, long pins with disc head and twisted shank, bracelets with tapering or expanded ends, flanged axes and (more important) palstaves, and solid-hilted daggers in increasing numbers. The distribution of such hoards covers not only all of Hungary, especially along the Danube, but also extends far into Czechoslovakia.[233] Hoards containing Koszider types even appear in Poland and, to a lesser extent, in eastern Germany.[234] In Hungary they are to be set parallel with the later part of Otomani-Füzesabony, in Germany with Br B. Most interesting and important, however, is the fact that this time is precisely that when the major tell sites of the Hungarian plain, occupied since the Eneolithic, come to an end, or at least suffer a destruction: Malé Kosihy, Nitriansky Hrádok, Veselé, Barca I, Pákozdvár, Kosziderpadlás, Százhalombatta, Baracs, Füzesabony, Tószeg, Pecica, Békés, Vărşand, and Otomani III, as well as Romanian sites like Verbicioara and Monteoru IIb, all exhibit this phenomenon. The succeeding layers show strong Tumulus influence, or else are Tumulus relatives like Piliny. It is not surprising, therefore, that several authors have suggested that the Koszider hoard horizon is to be connected with the arrival in the

Hungarian Plain of new peoples, perhaps from the east, and perhaps the bearers of 'Tumulus culture'.[235]

Following this phase of apparent upheaval come two further hoard horizons corresponding to Br C and D in the west, here named after Forró and Ópályi.[236] In Hungary the cultures contemporary with them are Tumulus groups in the north, Piliny, and other early urn-using groups like Gava (B.IV). The material found is much more varied than hitherto, and also more prolific: some types of disc-butted axe continue, while solid-hilted octagonal swords, palstaves with rayed faceting, large pins with multiple swellings on the shank, and numerous types of arm- and leg-spirals form the main bulk of the material, which correlates with Br C in south German terms. In Slovakia the Forró hoard horizon is named after the finds of Dreveník (Spišská Nová Ves) and Vel'ký Blh (Rimavská Sobota);[237] the Ópályi after the find at Ožd'any (Rimavská Sobota). We may find related metal forms in groups like Piliny: a recently discovered hoard from Zvolen, for instance, included a chisel, five palstaves, two long pins, two arm-spirals, an elaborate pendant, and three leg-spirals (sometimes called 'Salgótarján rings'), characteristic of Br C or even D. Funerary material is similar.[238]

The time of the Hajdúsámson hoard also saw a great flourishing of gold-working, and the production of superb and elaborate gold ornaments, many of them found in Transylvania near the ore sources.[239] A number of distinct forms may be recognized: discs and roundels, such as those from Ţufalău, Şmig, Graniceri and Ostrovul Mare (fig. 52); cups and other vessels, like the pieces from Biia and the former Bihar county (now in Romania); arm-bands, bracelets and smaller rings, as from Bilje (Osijek), Biia (Mureş Autonomous Region), Pipea (Braşov) and elsewhere in Transylvania; and a few weapons, like the 'eastern' axes from Ţufalău (fig. 52). Mozsolics also attributes the extraordinary sword from Perşinari and the daggers from Măcin to this horizon, in the absence of any closer indications. Some of these objects, and especially the gold cups, are masterpieces, showing elaborate attention to detail in the shaping of the piece (e.g. fluted sides of the Bihar cups) and in the decoration (there are incised and repoussée spiraliform designs on these cups and on many of the discs). The bracelet from Bilje which we illustrate (pl. 7) was found in 1840 in unknown circumstances; its decoration is of knobs and multiple incised lines, forming wavy bands, 'pot-hook spirals' and so on; the shape is remarkable for its ribbed band and wide curling ends; it weighs nearly 205 grams. Some of the larger pieces weigh well over half a kilogram, and the total weight of the finds from Şmig, for instance, is similar. Mozsolics is able to suggest that one or two groups of these objects emanated from the same workshop or even the same hand. These gold objects, while not numerous, represent the work of a school of smithing that was on a totally new plane, both technically and artistically.

Gold finds are not very common in the Kosziderpadlás hoard phase, though perhaps no less than in the preceding one: spectacular pieces were not, however, produced.[240] Nor can many pieces be attributed with certainty to the Forró (B.IVa) horizon: an exception is the find from Derecske (Hajdú-Bihar), where two bracelets with antithetic-spiral terminals indicate broad contemporaneity with Br C; three rings with flattened leaf-shaped bands (*Lockenringe*) complete the find. By contrast the Ópályi phase saw a great expansion in the quantities of goldwork.

Copper sources are especially numerous in the Carpathian zone of east-central Europe, though little success has yet been achieved in attributing precise composition patterns to given sources. At the start of the Bronze Age considerable numbers of imported axes are found – disc-butted and 'eastern'; but a recent find at Špania Dolina (Banská Bystrica) has produced clear evidence of local working of copper, for stone pounders and other implements were found in ancient slag-heaps.[241] During later Hungarian phases (B.IIIb) ingot and smithing hoards became quite common; 'tongue-shaped ingots' are known from half-a-dozen sites (including a hoard from Dunaföldvár in the British Museum), and lumps of copper and gold from several more.[242] Ingot torcs are the more common form in Slovakia, however, where hoards like those from Gajary and Stupava (Bratislava) exhibit this type.[243] Moulds are also quite common in B.III from an early phase, mostly of sandstone though a few are of clay or schist. Central Hungary east of the Danube has no stone, so that one must postulate trade and transport of both raw material and the means of fashioning it. Most of these moulds are for axes (shaft-hole axes from Tószeg, Szihalom, Vattina, Pecica level XIII, etc.; also shaft-tube axes), but daggers, spearheads and other forms are also represented. Most of the moulds occur on settlements. In B.IV numerous sandstone moulds are found, as in the large collections from Piliny and Soltvad-kert.[244] In each of the periods concerned, Mozsolics has been able to distinguish at least some workshops, which turned out their own distinctive products: some finds come from the same mould, like two of the daggers from Kelebia (Bács-Kiskun); in many other cases one can observe identical or almost identical decoration on pieces from different moulds. This is especially true of the Hajdúsámson material, where the elaborate curvilinear decoration – seen in an interesting experimental form on the sword from Hajdúsámson itself – must be the product of a single school, if not a single workshop. Moszolics suggests that the leading and most spectacular display hoards were the work of a single master, or at any rate of a specialist smithy where each process was done by a single person. On grounds of distribution, one would have to place such a workshop in Transylvania.[245]

Spectrographic analysis of Carpathian basin bronzes has shown an overwhelming concentration of $F_{A/B}$ metal, which is presumably to be identified with one or more of the Transylvanian copper sources.[246] This group accounts for the great majority of B.III hoard finds, in Transylvania as in Hungary and Slovakia. In each case the sequence starts with group A for the earliest finds (pure copper), goes through a phase with mixed metals of varying provenance, and finally settles down on $F_{A/B}$. A similar situation prevails in B.IV, though by this time thorough mixing of the copper stock must have taken place.[247]

Most characteristic of the Nitra group is the 'willow-leaf ornament' in copper, usually for use as a bracelet, but sometimes as finger-, ear- or hair-rings[248] (fig. 36). Various types have been distinguished: most typical in the classic area is that with cast solid midrib. The same leaf-like shape is also found on knives, and other frequently-occurring bronzes are *Noppenringe* (in simple forms with twisted ends), thick wire spiral rings of various sizes, thin sheet metal 'headbands', knot- and racket-headed pins, basic triangular daggers, and (occasionally) awls, axes and adzes. The non-metallic grave-goods, besides bone and faience beads, include antler buttons, bone pins, boars' tusks (for bracelets) and flint objects (hollow-based arrowheads, scrapers, blades). Pottery is not common, and comprises mainly one-handled S-profiled cups, biconical jars, and simple two-handled jars; sometimes corded decoration betrays the immediate ancestry of the group in Corded Ware (Chłopice-Veselé group). Three phases of development have been distinguished.[249] Identical material comes from the cemeteries of the Mierzanowice group in little Poland and in eastern Slovakia the Košt'any group has very similar material: particularly notable in the latter are spool-headed pins and very numerous beads.[250] Willow-leaf ornaments are found even further east, as far as the cemeteries around Kiev (below, p. 120). The ancestry in Corded Ware and Globular Amphorae is particularly apparent in Poland, where forms closely reminiscent of the Amphorae occur. Machnik has stressed the importance of the group as a whole in the general development of culture both sides of the Carpathian basin, and shown convincingly that close contact took place between the two sides of the north Carpathian ring.[251]

Nitra-group material is succeeded in south-west Slovakia by Únětice-type finds, and somewhat later by Mad'arovce finds.[252] These have been temporally subdivided and can be seen to span a period from pre-classical Únětice down to early Tumulus times; the pottery types are similar to

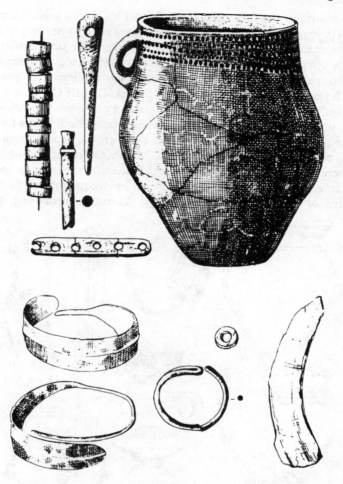

Fig. 36 Finds from Nitra-group graves at Brančk (Nitra). Not to scale.
(After Vladár 1973a)

those of Věteřov in Moravia on the one hand and to those of Encrusted
Pottery on the other: they form a sort of transitional zone or continuum
between the two. The typical pottery form is a version of the high-necked
one-handled cup, often with pronounced flare of the neck (fig. 21, 2). On
a number of south-western Slovakian sites a 'late-Mad'arovce' or 'post-
Mad'arovce' level has been recognized (as at Majcichov) which lies on
the threshold of the full 'Tumulus Bronze Age'.

The northern part of east-central Europe includes, too, sites where the 'pre-Lausitz' group has been identified. This is discussed more fully above (p. 57): suffice it to mention here the very early cemetery at Martin where some material has been placed as early as Br B2. Similarly it is possible – with hindsight – to detect the first flowerings of later Bronze Age groups like Čaka in the earlier material, leading to a 'pre-Čaka' horizon starting locally (in south-west Slovakia) in Br C.[253]

In the Trzciniec group, S-profiled jars and bowls are the commonest forms, with one-handled angular cups and flaring-neck bowls following not far behind; decoration is by large deep grooves and flutings, ribs, bosses, cording and coarse rustication. Metalwork is typical for Br B–C and includes antithetic spiral-terminal bracelets, tapering penannular bracelets and leg-spirals in great numbers; less frequently one finds dirks and pins of types that resemble central Tumulus forms (fig. 37). In

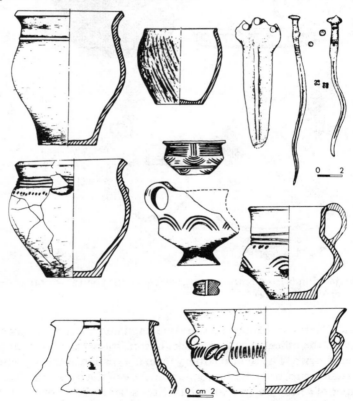

Fig. 37   Material of the Opatów group of the Trzciniec culture, south-east Poland.
(After Dąbrowski 1972)

general, however, metal is scarce in the Trzciniec culture, and hoards of ornaments like that from Dratów (Opole Lubelskie) are the exception rather than the rule;[254] their typological connection with the prolific hoards of the Koszider series in Hungary stresses the fact that Trzciniec was distinctly southward-looking.

Economy

Economic conditions in east-central Europe do not differ greatly, so far as we know, from those further west. The information available is scanty; excavations at Békés and Spišský Štvrtok (two of the most important recently dug sites) have revealed only the presence of emmer and einkorn or both, summer wheat and rye at the former, barley (undifferentiated) at the latter.[255] Evidence from bones is still worse: we only know that the main domesticates were present, but have no idea of the relative proportions in even one cultural layer with any certainty. Kovács has suggested [256] that the absence of plaster-built houses and tell-settlements from the Tumulus and Piliny periods in Hungary is to be attributed to the predominance of animal-breeding (pastoralism?) rather than crop agriculture: that is, to a mobile or semi-mobile rather than a purely sedentary economy.

One animal that is implied, even if its bones are not numerous in excavation, is the horse. Bridle cheek-pieces in bone and antler, perforated in various ways, appear quite commonly on sites of all periods at least from Hatvan times onwards (fig. 38), while horse bones occur from the Chalcolithic and are especially numerous on Bell Beaker sites.[257] It was, apparently, during later Br A1 and Br A2 that the main spread of horse-riding took place: the evidence from south-east Europe suggests that the practice was becoming common by 1600 BC, and Near Eastern contexts are rarely earlier and mostly later. The development in Hungary was thus as early as any in Europe: and a derivation of the practice from the steppe zone of eastern Europe is not implausible in view of the fact that objects interpreted as cheek-pieces have been found in Catacomb Grave contexts.[258]

Horses were not, however, used as draught animals, and representational evidence indicates that this was the exclusive domain of oxen. Model waggons are known in Hungary from the Chalcolithic on: models and wheels occur with some regularity on earlier Bronze Age sites.[259] Less information is available from later periods of the Bronze Age, so that the representation of a two-wheeled waggon on a late Piliny pot from Vel'ké Raskovce (Trebišov) is of great interest.[260]

For ordinary domestic activities our evidence is surprisingly full. Many

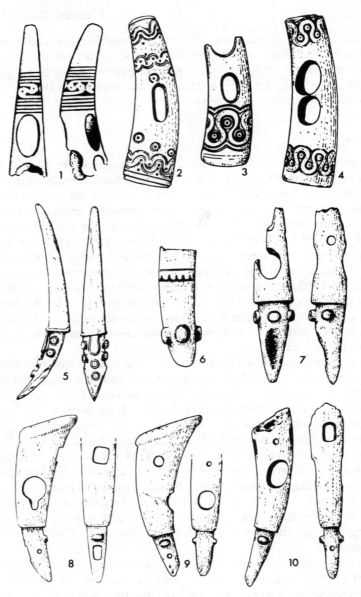

Fig. 38 Antler cheek-pieces for horse harness, earlier Bronze Age. 1. Monticelia, 2. Vattina, 3. Veselé, 4. Malé Kosihy, 5. Mende-Leányvár, 6. Barca, 7. Nitriansky Hrádok, 8–10. Castione dei Marchesi (north Italy).
(After H-J. Hundt, *Preist. Alp.* 10 (1974))

sites of all cultural groups have produced spindle-whorls and loom-weights in considerable numbers; the activities of potters and bronze-smiths we have already discussed. A skill not often attested in this part of the world is that of wood-working. The houses at Békés provided ample evidence of elaborate dowelling, beam construction and so on, to a high level of competence. Such wooden houses go back at least to the time of the Hatvan group.[261]

Chronology

Radiocarbon dating provides little help for most of east-central Europe in the earlier Bronze Age. The transition to Nagyrév can be seen to have occurred by 2000 bc, and the later part of the period, around the start of the Tumulus-type cultures, apparently falls around 1400 bc. There are no relevant dates available to indicate when the later Bronze Age – the beginning of true urnfields – starts.

We have already discussed the application of cross-dating to the central European Bronze Age (p. 66). Br A2 and the Hajdúsámson horizon in Hungary (B.IIIa) are roughly synchronous. Hajdúsámson should therefore fall somewhere between 1700 and 1500 bc (2100–1700 BC). The uncalibrated dates therefore support the idea of a connection with the Shaft Graves of Mycenae; calibrated they rule it out. The Nagyrév-Hatvan phase was a long one and could easily go back beyond 2000 BC. On the other side, the Ópályi horizon must fall in the thirteenth century, since it is equivalent to Br D; other groups will be equivalently earlier, and the Kosziderpadlás horizon should fall around 1500 BC.

The chronology of the Nitra-Mierzanowice group has become much clearer since the publication of dates from Iwanowice. Three graves of Corded Ware type (Chłopice-Veselé) gave dates between 1850 and 1790 bc, while ten dates from Nitra-Mierzanowice graves are between 1750 and 1600 bc (see table 4). These dates, when calibrated, could be in agreement with traditional notions of chronology: they support the idea of the developed earlier Bronze Age straddling the sixteenth century, though it should be noted that the faience bead horizon to which they refer is placed considerably earlier than would allow for an 'Egyptian connection'. This conclusion must also have relevance for other areas where faience beads are found, especially southern Britain.

The Trzciniec group had apparently started by 1500 bc, rather earlier than anticipated, though too few dates are available for detailed comparisons. In any case the precise chronological relation to central European material is not clear: some types may well have appeared earlier in the east than in the west.

Conclusions

The Bronze Age in east-central Europe got under way earlier than in the west-central part, and the succeeding periods started there at least as early as, if not earlier than, their counterparts to the west. Metal-working, too, reached impressive proportions at an early stage, and the impression one has of the first half of this period is one of continuous and peaceful settlement, as shown by the long accumulation of debris in the tell sites.

A marked change occurred in this pattern around 1500 BC. Many tell sites were burnt or deserted (some permanently); numerous hoards of bronzes were deposited in the ground; in the succeeding levels, where they are present, new elements are visible in the material culture that link it with the Tumulus culture. At the same time (so far as it is possible to judge) a new 'horizon' of metalwork (*Kosziderpadlás*) appears containing many Tumulus forms and representing a uniform metal industry. This was also the time, further north, of the rise of the Trzciniec culture which has many forms in common with Tumulus.

The inference normally drawn from this is obvious. Most authors have seen a causal connection between the various phenomena, interpreting the situation as meaning that a new people, closely related to the bearers of the Tumulus culture further north, swept into the Hungarian plain by force, causing widespread desertion and the loss of much metal to the ground. Such a quasi-historical interpretation is attractive, but an alternative hypothesis presents itself. Although some tells are deserted, others are not; the shift in population could as easily be explained in economic or demographic terms as in political. The metalwork horizons are, in our view, to be seen as the products of their age – in other words, certain types are bound to be universal at certain times; the widespread distribution of Koszider bronzes need reflect no more than improved communications between areas and the successful marketing of high-quality products. Only physical determination of race in skeletal material will identify the arrival of new peoples.

Notes

1 Mellor 1975, 4ff., 30ff.
2 Useful summaries of this matter have appeared recently: V. Moucha, *PA* 65 (1974), 244–52; Gerloff 1975, 1–5.
3 The Bavarian material was published piecemeal in succeeding parts of *Altertümer unserer heidnischen Vorzeit*

5 (1903–9), ed. Lindenschmidt. The first statement of the chronological division appears in *Korrespondenzblatt der deutschen Gesellschaft für Anthropologie, Ethnologie und Urgeschichte* 33 (1902), 17ff., 27ff. Reinecke modified his scheme on more than one occasion; the clearest statement

of it appears in *Germania* 8 (1924), 43–4. A collection of Reinecke's contributions to *AuhV* 5 is republished as Reinecke 1911/1965.

4 The German terminology is very confusing at this point. *Spätbronzezeit* is applied to Br D when *Bronzezeit* and *Urnenfelderzeit* are regarded as separate entities; nowadays, especially outside Germany, it is sometimes applied more generally to the entire period from Br D to Ha B. The Germans also use the terms *Jüngbronzezeit* (approximately equivalent in meaning to English Late Bronze Age), *Jüngstbronzezeit*, and *Endbronzezeit* (referring to the latest material before the Iron Age, Montelius V or V/VI in the north). In a similar way, the early stages of the Bronze Age are often called *älteste* and *ältere Bronzezeit*.

5 V. Milojčić, *Germania* 38 (1960), 227–31 (review of Hachmann 1957).

6 Točik and Vladár 1971, 389ff.

7 Torbrügge 1959b. Most of the trouble arises from the fact that Holste (1953b, 21ff.), in dividing B into B1 and B2, included under B2 material that properly belongs to Reinecke's C phase. Holste's B2 in fact equals Reinecke's and Torbrügge's C1.

8 Christlein 1964.

9 Stein 1968.

10 Adler 1967.

11 Moucha 1963.

12 Neumann 1929.

13 Schubert 1973, 72f. Each individual type is also discussed. More specifically, on this basis he divides cultural groups as follows: Nitra, early and late (cf. p. 84); Unterwölbling, I, II and III; Únětice (in the Weinviertel), I and II (first appearing there in a developed form).

14 Not south of Prague, as Childe stated (1929, 226 n. 1), and as other authors have repeated (Pittioni 1954, 283; Gimbutas 1965, 269 fig.

176). Material from the Únětice cemetery itself is well illustrated in Stocký 1928, pls X–XI. The selection in Gimbutas 1965, fig. 176 seems a strange choice, especially for the pottery. Finds in the National Museum, Prague, and the regional museum of Roztoky u Prahy, a few km north-west of Prague, where photographs of the site are also on display.

15 For a comparative chart of the various attempts at periodization, see E. Lange, *Botanische Beiträge zur mitteleuropäischen Siedlungsgeschichte*, 1971, 22.

16 The basic work is F. Firbas, *Spät- und Nacheiszeitliche Waldgeschichte Mitteleuropas nördlich der Alpen*, 1949, 1952, 2 vols, Jena.

17 E.g. H. Müller, *Nova Acta Leopoldina*, n.s. 110, 16 (1953), 1–67; or at the Wasserburg, where a dominant mixed oak forest with abundant hazel (Atlantic) gives place to a massive increase of beech (Subboreal), which, however, declines dramatically in the topmost layers: Reinerth 1928, 26ff. Cf. also numerous pollen diagrams in Firbas, *op. cit.* vol. II.

18 K. Rybníček and E. Rybníčková, *Folia geobot. phytotax.* 3 (1968), 117–142; M. Ralska-Jasiewoczowa, *Ber. Deutsch. Bot. Ges.* 85, H. 1–4 (1972), 101–12. We thank Dr Judith Turner for these references and for other help on botanical matters.

19 Cemeteries where both groups occur are listed by O. Kytlicová, *PA* 51 (1960), 468ff.

20 V. Budinský-Krička, *Sl.A.* 13 (1965), 51–106; J. Machnik, *Arch. Polski* 11 (1966), 376–400.

21 Childe 1929, 223ff.; cf. Wojciechowski, *Arch. Polski* 12 (1967), 108–18.

22 Hundt 1958; Müller-Karpe 1974, nos 506, 529, pl. 517. Cf. too Adler 1967, 88f.

23 Moucha 1963, 11ff. (cf. *AR* 6 (1954), 502ff.); Müller-Karpe 1974, no. 426, pl. 525A.

24 Like the cemetery of Brandýsek (Slaný): O. Kytlicová, *PA* 51 (1960), 442–74. The combination of one-handled jugs (esp. fig. 8.2), polypod bowls, copper objects and beakers shows that these graves stand on the threshold of the Bronze Age. For the relationship of bell beakers to the Early Bronze Age, cf. Christlein 1964, 52: a possible synchronism of the two at Nähermemmingen.

25 Ruckdeschel 1968.

26 Moucha 1963, 12, 24ff.; J. Ondráček, *SlA*. 15 (1967), 389–446.

27 E.g. Trinum (Köthen): E. Schmidt-Thielbeer, *AuF* 19 (1974), 3–5; Blšany (Louny) and Lipany (Praha): I. Pleinerová, *PA* 51 (1960), 520ff.; cf. Billig 1958, 160ff., Holste 1953a, 5,15 (Straubing settlement). For the scarcity of Early Bronze Age settlement sites in general, cf. Sarnowska 1969, 13ff.

28 I. Hnízdová, *AR* 5 (1953), 380–92, 431–2, who states that 163 Únětice settlements have been traced.

29 B. Soudský, *AR* 5 (1953), 308–18, 426–7.

30 I. Pleinerová, *AR* 24 (1972), 369–372, 469–70. Dr Pleinerová was kind enough to provide further information about her latest finds on site at Březno in 1975.

31 Sarnowska 1969, 16.

32 Pittioni 1954, 347ff. J. Reitinger, *Arch. Aust.* 23 (1958), 1–50 (sites at Linz-Reisetbauer and St Florian am Inn, with a prolific series of pits and possibly a rectangular house).

33 E. Beninger, *Mitt. der prähist. Kommission der Akad. der Wiss.* 4 (1941), 49–89. Pittioni 1954, 302f., figs. 208–9.

34 L. Rauhut, *WA* 20 (1954), 252–9; Z. Rajewski, *Archeology* 11/1 (1958), 42–3.

35 Sklenář 1973, 126f., with refs.

36 Sklenář 1973, 127 with refs.

37 J. Poláček, *Dívčí Kámen, Hradiště z doby bronzové*, 1966, and *Další výsledky výzkumu na Dívčím Kámeni* (*Dívčí Kámen, a Bronze Age fortress*, and *Further results of research at Dívčí Kámen*), Jihočeské Muzeum, České Budějovice. Sincere thanks are due to Dr Poláček for providing information and conducting us round the site in 1974.

38 K. Tihelka in *Nitra Kommission* 1958 (1961), 78, 92; Middle Bronze Age settlements: Vochov (Plzeň), V. Čtrnáct, *PA* 45 (1954), 335–55; Tuchlovice (Kladno): V. Moucha and V. Trnka, *AR* 11 (1959), 617–637.

39 Hradisko is rather a hill settlement than a hill-fort (Gimbutas 1965, 270). The rampart and ditch are far from obvious to the visitor.

40 V. Spurný, *PA* 45 (1954), 357–77; *Nitra Kommission* 1958 (1961), 125f.

41 Hulín and Bezmerov (Kroměříž): Spurný, loc. cit.

42 E.g. Pittioni 1954, 367ff., 373f.

43 E. Čujanová-Jílková, *AR* 23 (1971), 683–99. An increasing number of sites are producing pottery of both Br A2 and Br B1, e.g. Esslingen am Neckar: E. Gersbach, *Fundb. aus Baden-Wurt.* 1 (1974), 226f.

44 Z. Trnáčková, *AR* 6 (1954), 746–751, figs. 318–20; *Investigations* 1966, 135.

45 Z. Pieczyński, *FAP* 20 (1969), 268–271; *Actes du VIIIᵉ Congres ISPP* (1973), III, 49–51; *AAC* 15 (1975), 205–10. Material in Poznań Museum.

46 Ruckdeschel 1968.

47 See e.g. K. Tihelka, *PA* 44 (1953), 235ff. on Moravia.

48 I. Hásek, *The Early Únětician Cemetery at Dolní Počernice near Prague*, Fontes Arch. Pragenses 2, 1959.

49 Moucha 1961.

50 J. Filip, *Pravěké Československo*, 1948, 180.

51 J. Ondráček, *Sl.A.* 15 (1967), 389–446. Cf. *AR* 24 (1972), 514–19 (Vyškov), where a gold ring and flint knife-dagger accompanied the burial; the gold ring is the first example in a Moravian phase 1 grave.

52 E.g. Rebešovice (Židlochovice): Ondráček 1962, 61.

53 J. Neustupný, *PA* 3 (1933), 14–20.

54 Rebešovice: Ondráček 1962, 57ff. with refs to other examples; detailed study by I. Pleinerová, *AR* 12 (1960), 13–27.

55 Grossbrembach (Sömmerda): Ullrich 1972, and unpublished information by the kindness of Prof. G. Behm-Blancke (Weimar).

56 V. Moucha, *AR* 6 (1954), 523–36.

57 Ullrich 1972, 39ff. for analysis of familial relationships.

58 I. Pleinerová, *AR* 11 (1959), 379–408.

59 F. Scheibenreiter, *Arch. Aust.* 23 (1958), 51–86.

60 Fischer 1956, 170ff.

61 E. Schmidt-Thielbeer, *JMV* 39 (1955), 93–114.

62 P. Höfer, *JVSTL* 5 (1906), 1–99.

63 H. Grössler, *JVSTL* 6 (1907), 1–87. This account of the opening of the barrow, which took place under 'rescue' conditions, makes fascinating reading; especially such details as the finding of some fragments of the *Saalezeitung* for 4 January under the topmost stones of the cairn – year unknown, but presumably not Bronze Age! The barrow was completely quarried away for the construction of railway sidings, though wood from the coffin survives and has been used for radiocarbon dating (table 3). The extraordinary degree of preservation in the barrows at Helmsdorf and Leubingen, in complete contrast to anything else known from Early Bronze Age

barrows, must be accounted for by the fact that the stone roofing kept conditions in the chambers very dry, and that the wood used must have been heart-wood. Fungi and bacteria would not be formed in such conditions, and the floors cannot have permitted the dissemination of water through the area, even though they themselves had begun to suffer from damp-rot. The heart-wood of oak is especially resistant to attack by fungi, so one must imagine that the timbers used were selected with this in mind. We thank Miss J. Cronyn, who has advised us on this problem.

64 M. Kowiańska-Piaszykowa and S. Kurnatowski, *FAP* 4 (1953), 43–77; M. Kowiańska-Piaszykowa, *FAP* 7 (1956), 116–38; *FAP* 19 (1968), 6–31.

65 Childe 1929, 296; Holste 1953a, 24ff.; Ziegert 1963; Gimbutas 1965, 284. The various groups in central Europe are: Middle Danubian (Lower Austria, Moravia, southwest Slovakia, west Hungary); Bohemian; Upper Palatinate (Regensburg area); south Bavarian; Swabian (Württemberg); east Hessian-Thuringian.

66 Čujanová-Jílková 1970, 14.

67 Feustel 1958, 2f., 28ff., 50ff. Gimbutas 1965, 284f.

68 Dušek 1969, 50ff.; A. Točík, *Die Gräberfelder der karpatenländischen Hügelgräberkultur*, 1964.

69 As at Dolný Peter, grave 17: Dušek 1969, 59.

70 V. Hrubý, *PA* 49 (1958), 40–57; I. Hnízdová, *PA* 45 (1954), 195ff. (Vinoř).

71 J. Neustupný, *SNMP* ser. A, 14 (1960), 3f., 167; the fragments, which have not been satisfactorily reconstructed, are in the National Museum in Prague.

72 V. Spurný, *Beiträge* 1969, 283–93. The cult of the severed head is of

course a common Celtic occurrence; the evidence from Hradisko
could be important in this respect.

73 Ondráček (personal communication) follows the six-part division
of Moucha, and has been able to
refine and correct details of the
chronology and synchronisms of
Točík (1963).

74 Moucha 1963, 24–7, 40–2, 48. For
Eneolithic-influenced shapes, see
esp. fig. 8.

75 E.g. Grossbrembach, G. Behm-
Blancke, *AuF* 19 (1974), 247ff.

76 Hundt 1958.

77 Torbrügge 1959b, 18–22, fig. 5.

78 So called after true faience, the
glazed majolica emanating from the
workshops of Faenza.

79 The classic works on faience in
prehistoric Europe are H. C. Beck
and J. F. S. Stone, *Archaeologia* 85
(1935), 202–52 and J. F. S. Stone
and L. C. Thomas, *PPS* 22 (1956),
37–85.

80 On Early Bronze Age hoards generally: von Brunn 1959; Billig 1958,
79ff.; Tihelka 1965. Ingot torcs:
Stocký 1928, pl. VI; Pittioni 1954,
288ff.; B. Bath-Bilková, *PA* 64
(1973), 24–41; F. Moosleitner *et al.*,
Arch. Aust. 53 (1973), 30–46.

81 R. Breddin, *Veröffentlichungen des
Museums für Ur- und Frühgeschichte
Potsdam* 5 (1969), 15–56.

82 Von Brunn 1959, pls. 12–23.

83 Hachmann 1957, 112ff.

84 Torbrügge 1959a, 35, fig. 10, 15
(Mantlach); Čujanová-Jílková
1970, pl. 108,16 (Šťáhlavy), pl.
115,19, pl. 100,22 (Vrhaveč).

85 Willvonseder 1937; Pittioni 1954,
382ff.; J.-W. Neugebauer, *Mitt. der
Österreichischen Arbeitsgemeinschaft
für Ur- und Frühgeschichte* 25 (1974–
1975), 65–89; *Arch. Aust.* 59–60
(1976), 49–86.

86 Holste 1953a, 31ff., 56ff.

87 Detailed discussions and corpora
of Tumulus bronzes: Willvon-

seder 1937; V. Furmánek, *Sl.A.* 21
(1973), 25–145 (central
Danubian).

88 Hundt 1958.

89 Christlein 1964; Stein 1968; J.-W.
Neugebauer, *Arch. Aust.* 59–60
(1976), 49–86.

90 K. Tihelka, *Obzor Prehistorický* 13
(1946), 51–7; Tihelka 1958, 77ff.;
K. Tihelka, *PA* 51 (1960), 27–135.

91 Pittioni 1954, 367ff.; Grosswei-
kersdorf: J.-W. Neugebauer,
Arch. Aust. 58 (1975), 5–74.

92 Cf. Cezavy near Blučina
(Židlochovice).

93 G. Illert, *Führer...* 13 (1969); E.
Gropengresser, *Führer...*3 (1965).

94 U. Schaaf, *Führer...* 21 (1965).

95 G. Behrens, *Bronzezeit Süddeutschlands*, Mainz, 1916; G. Pescheck, *Führer...* 8 (1967); B.
Stümpel, *Führer...* 11 (1969).

96 G. Pescheck, *Führer...* 27 (1975),
28 (1975) in the middle Main
valley; P. Schauer, *Führer...* 22
(1973), and O. Höchmann,
Führer... 23–24 (1973), in upland
areas.

97 F. Stein, *Führer...* 5 (1966);
Thévenin 1976; Chertier 1976.

98 E.g. Trassem: G. Behrens,
Bronzezeit Süddeutschlands,
Mainz, 1916, no. 63.

99 Cist burials at Eguisheim, Alsace:
Zumstein 1966, 96–8, fig. 29; Sandars 1957, 14–15; and at Donau-
berg: Sandars 1957, 13.

100 W. Kimmig, *Neue Ausgrabungen
in Deutschland*, Berlin, 1958, 107–
126.

101 E.g. Zumstein 1966.

102 B. Guillet *et al.* in Guilaine 1976,
82–7.

103 W. Ludi, in Guyan 1954, 92–109.

104 The pigs were slaughtered between 17 and 23 months old, and
the cattle were consistently killed
at 3 years old: Higham 1968, 65–8.

105 M. Gedl, *Kultura przedłużycka*,
1975. The term 'pre-Lausitz' was

introduced by J. Kostrzewski, *Przeg. Arch.* 2 (1924), 46.

106 E.g. U. Schaaf, *Führer...* 15 (1969), 21 (1972); B. Stümpel, *Führer...* 11–12 (1969); C. Pescheck, *Führer...* 27–8 (1975).

107 W. R. Lange, *Führer...* 20 (1971); the cemeteries of Kirchborchen and Etteln at Paderborn are particularly notable.

108 E.g. Ziegert 1963 with many maps and illustrations, which may represent time-groups if local prefences are believed to have been strictly evolutionary and consistent; Holste 1953a provides useful summaries of Tumulus Bronze Age typologies over a wide area of central Europe, with adequate maps. Excellent illustrations of some selected items in W. Kimmig and H. Hell, *Vorzeit am Rhein und Donau*, Lindau and Konstanz 1958.

109 E.g. Thévenin 1976, 640; W. Kubach, *JIVUF* 1974, 29–50, on local metal preferences in graves of the Early and Late Bronze Age in Hesse.

110 C. F. A. Schaeffer, *Les Tertres Funeraires Préhistoriques dans la Forêt de Haguenau*, 1, 1926; Zumstein 1976; Sandars 1957, 66ff.; geographical discussion of continuity and population in the upper Rhine valley, C. J. Balkwill, *PPS* 42 (1976), 187–213.

111 K.-H. Otto, *Die sozialökonomischen Verhältnissen bei der Stämmen der Leubinger Kultur in Mitteldeutschland*, 1955.

112 S. Shennan, *Antiquity* 49 (1975), 279–88.

113 E.g. Okalew (Wielun), Dąbrowski 1972, 98; Nebel on Amrum Island, *Offa* 13 (1954), 17ff.; Wendelstorf (Bad Doberau), *AuF* 2 (1957), 69–70, pl. 11a.

114 Cf. A. Harding in *Problems in Economic and Social Archaeology*

115 W. Coblenz, *AuF* 18 (1973), 70–80.

116 Cf. the remarks of G. Behm-Blancke on Grossbrembach: *AuF* 19 (1974), 247–55. Settlement pottery was found in the field adjoining the cemetery, as well as pits; the proven use of such a pit for storage at Döbeln indicates the most likely function for these.

117 W. Wojciechowski, *Silesia Antiqua* 8 (1966), 42.

118 E.g. Hradčany (Prostejov – in Moravia, not Bohemia) cited by Gimbutas 1965, 250; Linz-Reisetbauer: J. Reitinger, *Arch. Aust.* 23 (1958), 29 fig. 20.

119 Gimbutas 1965, 250

120 Childe 1929, 296ff.; cf. Gimbutas 1965, 297 for our viewpoint.

121 On prehistoric salt in general, Nenquin 1961; Clark 1952, 127.

122 K. Riehm, *JMV* 38 (1954), 112–156; 44 (1960), 180–217; *Antiquity* 35 (1961), 181–91; *Germania* 40 (1962), 360–400; Matthias 1976.

123 Nenquin 1961, 120ff.

124 Matthias 1976, 373–94.

125 Nenquin 1961, 139ff.

126 R. Pittioni in Zschocke and Preuschen 1932, 155–68. For the Mitterberg mines in general, Zschocke and Preuschen 1932, passim; R. Pittioni, *7th Annual Report of the Institute of Archaeology* (1951), 16–43.

127 The most remarkable series comes from Kelchalm bei Kitzbühel in the Austrian Tirol: E. Preuschen and R. Pittioni, *Arch. Aust.* 15 (1954), 3–97, figs. 11, 12, 13, 36–8.

128 E.g. from the Mitterberg at Mühlbach am Hochkönig (St Johann): Wien, Naturhistorisches Museum, nos. 36477 and 4902.

129 E.g. I. Pleinerová in *Nitra Kommission* 1958 (1961), 111–24; H.-J. Hundt in *Nitra Kommission* 1958

(1961), 145–76; W. Sarnowska, *Preist. Alp.* 10 (1974), 137–41.

130 Harding and Warren 1973.

131 E.g. Hradisko (Kroměříž), see above pp. 36–7.

132 H. Mötefindt, *Archäologischer Anzeiger* 1 (1912), 99–103; Tihelka 1958, 85 pl. II,5.

133 N. Sandars, *Antiquity* 33 (1959), 292–5; Gerloff 1975, 198ff., 260ff.

134 C. Strahm, *AAC* 15 (1975), 233–234.

135 Calibration based on R. M. Clark, *Antiquity* 49 (1975), 251–66, esp. 264, table 8.

136 *Preist. Alp.* 10 (1974), 188.

137 Mellor 1975, 20ff.

138 P. Reinecke, *AE* n.s. 19 (1899), 225–51, 316–40; V. Furmánek, *AR* 29 (1977), 554–63.

139 Childe 1929, 261f.; Tompa 1934–1935 (1937).

140 Mozsolics 1952, 35ff.; 1957, 119ff.; 1967; 1973.

141 First published in Bóna 1958, some details added 1975.

142 Hänsel 1968; reviews in *Alba Regia* 12 (1972), 237ff. (T. Kovács); *Fundb. aus Baden-Würt.* 1 (1973), 705ff. (H. Schickler); *AAH* 23 (1971), 386ff. (N. Kalicz); etc.

143 This has a long tradition: see Tompa 1934–5, Patay 1938, Kalicz 1968, Bóna 1975. For metalwork, the publications of A. Mozsolics are pre-eminent: 1966, 1967, 1973.

144 Kalicz 1968, Ch. II. Both Patay and Kalicz include in their Bronze Age what we would describe as Copper Age cultures – Baden, Bodrogkeresztúr, Bell Beaker, 'Kurgan grave', and Vučedol-Zók. All of these singly and in combinations occur in pre-Bronze Age situations.

145 J. Banner, *Dolgozatok* 15 (1939), 73–92; Kalicz 1968, 77ff.

146 The importance of the Čaka material was first recognized by Točik and fully discussed by J. Vladár,

Sl.A. 10 (1962), 319–40; *Sl.A.* 12 (1964), 357–90; *Sl.A.* 14 (1966), 245–336. Further refs in Kalicz 1968, 77 n.34

147 Fortified hill-sites are found in parts of Hungary, too: cf. Nagygörbö-Várhegy (Veszprém), where a rampart enclosed an area 115 × 85 m; Gy. Nováki, *AE* 92 (1965), 168–75.

148 N. Kalicz, *AE* 94 (1967), 3–19, where a house-plan from Nyírpazony is also published; Kalicz 1968, 81f.

149 The results of both older and modern excavations are summarized in J. Csalog, *AAH* 2 (1952), 19–33; Mozsolics 1952; J. Banner, I. Bóna and L. Marton, *AAH* 10 (1957), 1–140. Gimbutas (1965, 194f.) has a convenient summary.

150 Important sites other than those discussed in the text: Vesztö (Békés), where the transition from Chalcolithic (Tiszapolgár) to Early Bronze Age and Middle Bronze Age is found: Artö (Borsod), where the earlier Bronze Age of Hatvan and Füzesabony types leads into a Tumulus horizon; Százhalombatta (Pest): T. Kovács, *AE* 96 (1969), 161–9.

151 Kalicz 1968, 120, 127, figs. 6–14.

152 A. Točik, *Nitra Kommission* 1958 (1961), 17–42.

153 A. Knor, *AR* 2 (1950), 56–60; Gimbutas 1965, 276; Točik 1964; cf. generally T. Nešporová, *Sl.A.* 17 (1969), 369–402, with distribution map. A final report on Nitriansky Hrádok has not yet appeared.

154 L. Hajek, *Nitra Kommission* 1958 (1961), 60ff.

155 Kalicz 1968, 178ff.

156 G. Bándi, *Alba Regia* 6–7 (1966), 11–25; Bóna 1975, 28ff. For these authors Kisapostag is a cross between Nagyrév and Vatya: Bándi, for instance, sees it not as an

independent culture but as a late sub-group of Nagyrév, comparable with the group named after Szigetszentmiklós. Cf. too *AMFME* 1969/2, 47–60; *AJPME* 14–15 (1969–70), 97–111 (synchronisms and connections of Encrusted pottery, notably its Szeremle group).

157 Bóna 1975, 57ff.

158 Gy. Nováki, *AE* 79 (1952), 3–19 fig. 7; E. F. Petres and G. Bándi, *AE* 96 (1969), 170–7.

159 We thank Dr Ilona Stanczik of Szolnok Museum for this information.

160 Houses were also found in the earlier excavation by S. Gallus, quoted Bóna 1975, 147. Cf. too Tompa 1934–5 (1937), 91–2 fig. 8.

161 F. Tompa, *AE* 48 (1935), 17–34.

162 Kalicz 1968, 139ff.

163 Important, though unspectacular, settlement material of the Kisapostag group has recently been reported from Balatongyörök-Becemajor: I. Torma, *AVMMK* 11 (1972), 15–39. Continuity of such open sites into the Tumulus period is well represented at sites like Bag: T. Kovács, *FA* 17 (1965), 65–86.

164 M. Roska, *Dolgozatok* 3 (1912), fig. 83 and other articles: quoted by Bóna (1975, 84f.).

165 Banner and Bóna 1974, 31ff. T. Kovács, *AE* 96 (1969), 161–9.

166 Kalicz 1968, 133f.

167 Gimbutas 1965, 200, treats Otomani and Wietenberg as part of the same cultural group.

168 I. Ordentlich, *Marmatia* 2 (1971), 19–35. We are indebted to Dr Ordentlich for his kind help at Oradea Museum.

169 Ordentlich 1969.

170 M. Roska, *Dacia* o.s. 2 (1925), 400ff. K. Horedt *et al.*, *MCA* 8 (1962), 317–24. Ordentlich 1969,

459ff. Cf. too *Dacia* n.s. 7 (1963), 115ff.

171 Ordentlich 1972.

172 Ordentlich 1969, 469.

173 I. Ordentlich, *Dacia* n.s. 7 (1963), 129 fig. 11; n.s. 12 (1968), 150.

174 Ordentlich 1969, 466–7. Socodor (Criş, Crişana): D. Popescu, *MCA* 2 (1956), 43ff.; *Dacia* n.s. 17 (1973), 391. Vărşand: D. Popescu, *MCA* 2 (1956), 82ff. Investigation of Otomani sites continues, e.g. at Girişul de Criş (Oradea): *Dacia* n.s. 17 (1973), 377; Sacuieni (Marghiţa, Crişana): *Dacia* n.s. 17 (1973), 384.

175 I. Ordentlich, *Dacia* n.s. 12 (1968), 141–53.

176 M. Roska, *Dacia* o.s. 2 (1925), 401 fig. 1.

177 I. Ordentlich, *Dacia* 12 (1968), 151f., fig. 3.

178 M. Novotná, *Musaica* 2 (1962), 27–32.

179 Vladár 1973a, 273ff., Map 1. Fortified Otomani sites also occur at Kežmarok, Spišský Štvrtok, Dreveník-Žehra, Barca, Nižná Myšl'a and Streda nad Bodrogom.

180 A. Točík, *Nitra Kommission* 1958 (1961), 8ff.; Vladár 1973a, 276ff.

181 Točík 1964.

182 A. Gardawski, *WA* 20 (1954), 369ff.

183 A. Gardawski, *Mat. Staroz.* 5 (1959), 7–189, esp. 89ff. Dąbrowski 1972, 100f. The regional sub-groups are: Lublin, Opatów, Masovia-Podlasie, and the 'zone transitional to Tumulus culture'.

184 I. Bóna, *Alba Regia* 2/3 (1963), 11–23.

185 I. Bóna, *Alba Regia* 1 (1960), 7–15.

186 R. Schreiber, *AE* 98 (1971), 151–166, esp. the comparative chart on p. 164.

187 Kalicz 1968, 143ff.

188 T. Nešporová, *Sl.A.* 17 (1969), 369–402.

189 Bóna 1975, 148ff. B. Polla, *Birituelle Füzesabonyer Begräbnisstätte in Streda nad Bodrogom*, in B. Chropovský, M. Dušek and B. Polla, *Gräberfelder aus der älteren Bronzezeit in der Slowakei* I (1960).

190 Bóna 1975, 150 pl. 155,4.

191 Information kindly supplied by Dr T. Kovács, National Museum, Budapest.

192 Popescu 1944, 68ff.; I. Bóna, *Alba Regia* 4/5 (1963–4), 17–63; A. Gazdapusztai, *AAA Szeged* 12 (1968), 5–37; M. Girić, *Mokrin I* (1971); Bóna, 1975, 85ff.

193 M. Girić, *Mokrin I* (1971).

194 T. Soroceanu, *PZ* 50 (1975), 161–179.

195 I. Ordentlich and C. Kacsó, *SCIV* 21 (1970), 49–63.

196 Z. Székely, *SCIV* 17 (1966), 125ff.

197 Information through the kindness of I. Ordentlich, Oradea Museum.

198 T. Kovács, *FA* 21 (1970), 27–47; *FA* 17 (1965), 65–86.

199 A. Mozsolics, *Der frühbronzezeitliche Urnenfriedhof von Kisapostag* (1942).

200 Bóna 1975, 31ff.

201 Bóna 1975, 198ff.; north and south groups are sometimes referred to as Veszprém and Szekszárd groups. In Slovakia the group is called Hurbanovo: Dušek 1960, 187 (and ff. for description of graves at Patince). G. Bándi, *AVMMK* 11 (1972), 41–58 distinguishes four separate areas of Encrusted Ware settlement (on the basis of cemetery distribution) in northern Transdanubia, and three in the south of the area.

202 P. Patay, *AE* 81 (1954), 33–49, with refs. to other cemeteries.

203 V. Furmánek, *AR* 20 (1968), 9.

204 E. Jílková, *Sl.A.* 9 (1961), 69–106.

205 O. Trogmayer, *Das bronzezeitliche Gräberfeld bei Tápé*, 1975.

206 Garašanin 1958, 75ff.

207 Bóna 1975, 231ff. In Austria this group, absurdly enough, is known as Wieselburg: absurd, because Gáta is in fact Gattendorf in Austria, while Wieselburg is Mosonmagyaróvár in Hungary!

208 Točík 1963.

209 Vladár 1973b. Cf. too similar recent work at Holešov (Moravia) where the final phase is also of Únětice date: J. Ondráček, *AR* 24 (1972), 168–72. Ondráček has shown that the Nitra group is equivalent to early Únětice in central Moravia and western Slovakia and can therefore only be followed by developed Únětice. We thank Dr Ondráček for information on and permisssion to study unpublished material from Holešov.

210 J. Pástor, *Košické pohrebisko* (1969). Similar cemeteries appear elsewhere in the Košice area, e.g. Všechsvätých: J. Pástor, *FA* 17 (1965), 37–50.

211 Among others, Pieczeniegi (Miechów): A. Krauss, *Mat. Arch.* 9 (1968), 159–65; Świniary Stare (Sandomierz): J. and A. Krauss, *Mat. Arch.* 12 (1971), 109–31.

212 We are grateful to Dr J. Machnik (Archaeological Institute of the Polish Academy of Sciences, Kraków) for information on Iwanowice. A settlement lies beside the cemetery: *Preist. Alp.* 10 (1974), 57–66.

213 Dąbrowski 1972, 89ff.

214 I. Ordentlich, *Satu Mare – Studii și Comunicări* 1972, 63–84, pl. xi–xviii.

215 Vladár 1973a, 293f. E. Vlček and J. Hájek in *A Pedro Bosch-Gimpera en el septuagésimo aniversario de su nacimiento* (1963), 427–39. This celebrated find is the subject of continuing controversy. It has usually been considered an import from the Near East; a radiocarbon

date of 1465±35 bc has now been obtained from wood in the well, J. J. Butler, *IXe Congres UISPP*, 1976, Résumés, 431.

216 J. Jelínek, *AR* 6 (1954), 633f.; C. Ambros, *Sl.A.* 7 (1959), 61.

217 J. Paulík, *ŠZ* 10 (1962), 27–57.

218 Janus Pannonius Museum, Pècs.

219 Patay 1938, 32ff., pl. III.

220 Patay 1938, 53ff.; Bóna 1975, 92ff., 113.

221 Patay 1938, 42ff.; Bóna 1975, 44.

222 Kalicz 1968, 149ff.

223 Popescu 1944, 89ff.

224 I. Ordentlich, *Actes du VIIe Congrès UISPP, Prague 1966* (1970), I, 619–22; *Dacia* 14 (1970), 83–97.

225 Bóna 1975, 151ff.

226 But cf. N. Kalicz, *AE* 97 (1970), 23–31, for a different view.

227 M. Rusu, *Dacia* 7 (1963), 185, 205, 207.

228 I. Ordentlich, *AMN* 5 (1968), 397–404.

229 V. Furmánek, *AR* 20 (1968), 3–11, 157–63.

230 The difficulties involved in classifying Piliny material can be seen in (e.g.) T. Kemenczei, *AE* 92 (1965), 3–26: in the eastern group of Piliny a *Muhi* phase is sometimes distinguished, though there are in fact two sites at Muhi, each characteristic of a different phase. Kemenczei advocates the use of Barca as the type-site and 'first' and 'second' to divide its material chronologically.

231 Mozsolics 1967, esp. 109, 152–3, pl. 8,12.

232 Bóna 1958; Mozsolics 1967, *passim*.

233 M. Novotná, *Musaica* 6 (1966), 9–26. Particularly important hoards come from Včelínce and Hodějov.

234 Dąbrowski 1972, 28ff.

235 The main discussions of this 'horizon' stem from Mozsolics 1957 and Bóna 1958, and figure prominently in the subsequent publications of both these authors.

236 Mozsolics 1973, *passim*; pp. 105f. for the criteria for defining the horizons.

237 Novotná 1970, 20ff.

238 V. Furmánek, *Sborník Práci Fil. Fak. Brněnské University* E16 (1971), 106–7.

239 Mozsolics 1966.

240 Mozsolics 1973, 90.

241 Točík and Vladár 1971, 382, 418.

242 Mozsolics 1967, 96ff.

243 M. Novotná, *Musaica* 1 (1961), 35–43.

244 Mozsolics 1973, 80, pls 108–9.

245 Mozsolics 1967, 102, 142f., pl. 4, 1–2 for the Kelebia axes; two others are very similar. On workshops in general, 1967, 102ff.; 1973, 84f.

246 F. and E. Schubert, in Mozsolics 1967, 185ff.

247 E. Sangmeister, in Mozsolics 1973, 215ff.

248 Točík 1963, 746, figs. 242,258.

249 Točík and Vladár 1971, 383, 418. The three phases are included within Br A1 and correspond to 1. Bell Beaker, Kosihy-Čaka and late Corded Ware (Veselé) influence; 2. Classic phase, Únětice influence; 3. Transitional, influence; 3. Transitional, influence of pre-classic Únětice.

250 J. Pástor, *Košické pohrebisko* (1969), 86ff. Three phases have been seen here too, culminating in the emergence of Otomani elements (Br A2).

251 J. Machnik, *Sl.A.* 20 (1972), 177–188.

252 Patay 1938, pl. viii, 1, 11–12; ix, 2 (Magyarád).

253 Točík and Vladár 1971, 406, 421; Z. Benkovský-Pivovarová, *Sl.A.* 20 (1972), 253–312.

254 Dąbrowski 1972, 81ff., pls. I–XI (Trzciniec), XII–XIII (Sosnica).

255 Banner and Bóna 1974, 81; Vladár 1973a, 291.
256 T. Kovács, *FA* 17 (1965), 65–86.
257 A. Mozsolics, *AAH* 5 (1953), 69–111; *AAH* 12 (1960), 125–35; *Preist. Alp.* 10 (1974), 107–11.
258 A. M. Leskov, *SA* 37 (1964), 299–303.
259 I. Bóna, *AAH* 12 (1960), 83–111.
260 J. Vizdal, *Sl.A.* 20 (1972), 223–31.
261 Banner and Bóna 1974, 34ff.

3 Eastern Europe

The term 'eastern Europe' covers a huge and varied area, much the largest that we shall consider in this book. We include here the south-western part of the Soviet Union, Romania, Bulgaria and northern Greece. Strictly speaking, our account should go further east than it does: we have taken the river Don as our eastern boundary, whereas Europe extends to the Urals, and to the borders of Kazachstan, Turkey and Iran. The omission of the important Caucasian area is intentional; it would greatly extend the length of this section; it is perhaps more relevant to students of Near Eastern than European archaeology; and it has in any case been covered thoroughly in relation to neighbouring Turkey and Iran in an excellent recent account.[1]

Within our chosen area, it is possible to distinguish two main sub-areas. The first is the huge expanse of the steppe in south Russia and the Ukraine, and the forest-steppe and forest zones to the north in central Russia. As far as one can tell, life in the Bronze Age in these areas was not on a very high level of material culture. Settlements are rarely more than undistinguished open sites with domestic debris; burials are not notable for their richness; arts and crafts were not highly developed. By contrast, in the second sub-area, the mountains and plains of Romania and Bulgaria, permanent settlements were soon established, copper extraction proceeded apace, and in many areas social stratification is evident from the contents of graves. It is not, of course, possible to draw a firm line between the two traditions, but in general one may say that the geographical change marked by the start of the steppe saw also a cultural change. It is in any case likely that the inhabitants of the steppe zone would have been unable, at least in the early part of the period, to undertake arable agriculture on any scale because of the rather arid conditions then prevalent. The onset of cooler, moister climate after 1000 BC may well have changed this situation.

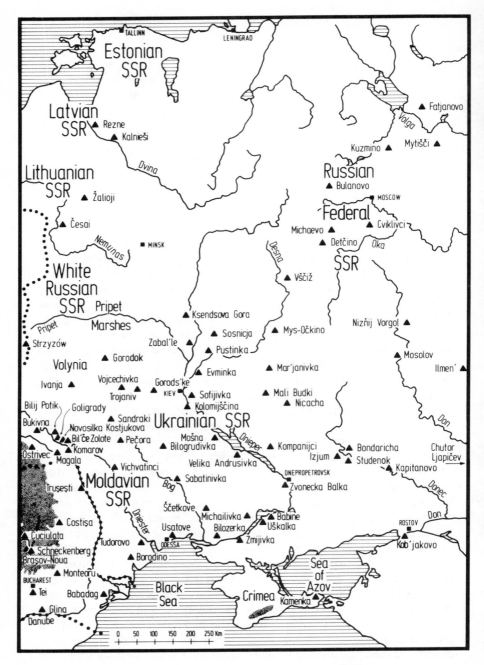

Map 3   Bronze Age sites in the western USSR

114

Geography and environment

Broadly speaking, the western part of the Soviet Union can be divided into a steppe zone in the Ukraine and a forest zone in Belorussia, with a broad transitional band of wooded steppe in between. The steppe zone is characterized by its Black Earth soils, rich in organic matter and highly fertile, and its markedly continental climate. The forest zone has mostly brown forest soils, varying from true podsols in the north to degraded black earths in the south; the climate is less severe than on the steppe, and large tracts of deciduous forest are still to be found. The relief of the land is rather unvaried: vast areas of undulating country are punctuated by occasional morainic ridges (the Smolensk-Moscow ridge) and low plateaux (the Central Russian Heights, the Volynian-Podolian Heights, the Donec Heights, seldom over 300 m above sea level) as well as broad rivers (Dniester, Bug, Dnieper, Donec, Don) and marshlands (Pripjat Marshes).[2]

South-west of the Soviet Union is a very varied landscape. Bulgaria includes two barren mountain ranges, the Rhodope and the Balkan Mountains (extending west into Macedonia and Serbia), while the north of the country can be seen to be part of the Lower Danubian province that also includes lowland Romania. This is a fertile area of intensive agriculture, though the Bulgarian side is rather dry and even steppe-like in the east, just as the Dobrogea in Romania is arid though fertile. In central and northern Romania is the beautiful and mountain-locked province of Transylvania, formerly Hungarian. The Carpathians encircle this land in a tight ring, and only at the west are the approaches less than Alpine. Access from the Danubian plain to Transylvania is controlled by a few river valleys through the towering mountains, and it is hardly surprising to find that in prehistoric times, as at the present day, culture and environment are quite separate in the two zones. Nowadays the German and Austro-Hungarian heritage is responsible for many of the more obvious differences in architecture, field lay-out, and racial affinities; but the very nature of the landscape of Transylvania, with its pleasantly rolling green hills and pastures, its wooded valleys and terraced hill-sides, ensures that the culture of its occupiers will be uniform within itself, and separate from that of neighbouring areas. The middle and higher slopes of the Carpathians, if not actually wooded, must have supported flocks of sheep and goats, while the rolling fertile meadows in the extensive upland plateaux gave scope for arable farming. A further special significance of Transylvania in the prehistory and early history of eastern Europe lies in the fact that it conceals a treasury of metal ores.[3] To this day the iron and gold sources are among the most productive in

Europe, and copper and silver are known to have been present in commercial quantities. It is even said that tin is found, and if that were so, it would naturally have become a focus of attention for metal-using cultures all over eastern Europe. Exploitation of the copper and gold sources is assured from the late Neolithic on; hoards of copper axes and axe-adzes, and finds of copper and gold ornaments are frequent in Salcuţa, Gumelniţa and late Cucuteni contexts. It is highly probable, though not yet proven by metal analysis, that it was the Transylvanian sources which supplied the rich metal age cultures of the Hungarian plain (p. 93). It has even been suggested that the gold, if not the copper, in the Shaft Graves of Mycenae was of Transylvanian origin.

Environmental evidence from eastern Europe is not extensive, but recent pollen work has provided some information. For the Macedonian area the diagram from Philippi covers the entire period from the Neolithic to Iron Age.[4] The Early Bronze Age vegetation is reconstructed by Greig and Turner as lowland mixed oak forest, with thinner woodland than previously and some maquis; on the hills was a typical mountain forest with beech and fir. This is the vegetation that accompanies phase Vb at Sitagroi, and it is striking that it changes at much the same time as the abandonment of that site (p. 132). Subsequently the forest was reduced in density; lime virtually disappeared and elm was much reduced. The appearance of the olive at this time suggests human activity, and though the amount of olive fluctuates and is even absent for a time during the later Bronze Age, the overall pattern remains much the same for the rest of the period. This evidence for the start of olive cultivation is supported by diagrams from the Peloponnese though in central Greece it appears to come rather earlier.[5]

From the Soviet Union comes evidence of a relatively dry and warm phase in the second millennium bc, followed by a considerably cooler, wetter period from around 1250 bc. Spruce in particular reached a maximum in the late Sub-boreal, falling off somewhat in the Sub-atlantic. Each zone tells a different story; pine was still dominant in the Ukraine, though the mixed oak forest and the birch were also of importance.[6]

Detailed pollen sequences for Romania and Bulgaria have not yet succeeded in subdividing the Sub-boreal period. In the Romanian mountains, the hornbeam reached its maximum everywhere, with spruce a less important element; throughout this period, the beech was rising until it became dominant in the next. There was still a substantial mixed oak forest, and numerous diagrams show the presence of weeds of cultivation. A very useful diagram has been obtained from the muds of lake Varna, synchronous with the Early Bronze Age settlement there.

This indicates a mixed flora, with tree pollen fairly constant at 50 per cent of the total. The forest is of mixed oak type; walnut is present throughout, but is probably native to the area. Grasses, cereals and weeds of cultivation, as well as aquatic species, complete the picture. This remains fairly constant except for a subsequent marked fall in tree pollen and increase in non-tree pollen; this clearance was, however, short-lived.[7]

The Soviet Union[8]

A variety of Chalcolithic groups is distinguished. In Moldavia and the south-west Ukraine the *Tripillja* (Tripolje) culture had metal as a regular concomitant from an early stage;[9] just to the north, in Volynia and Ruthenia – and the sub-Carpathian part of the Ukraine more generally – the *Barrow-Grave* culture connected with the makers of *Globular Amphorae* and *Corded Ware* is found; while on the lower Dnieper and in the steppeland across the Don *Pit Graves* were still in use. During the currency of these groups the *Gorods'ke, Usatove* (Usatovo) and *Middle Dnieper* groups started. In White Russia to the west the so-called *comb-pricked pottery* culture gave way to the *Dnieper-Desna* group, while in central Russia the Corded Ware group named after the cemetery of *Fatjanovo* continued through the earlier Bronze Age.

The principal full Bronze Age groups we may distinguish are the *Bilij Potik,* followed by *Komarov,* in Podolia and Volynia; *Sosnicja* around the Desna; and the *Catacomb Grave* culture in the north Pontic area, the successor (or contemporary?) of Pit Graves.

The development of the Tripillja (Tripolje) culture led to a variety of innovations. The latest stages of Tripillja itself (phase C2) correlate with new sub-groups named after settlements and cemeteries at Gorods'ke (Korostišiv, Žitomir), Vichvatinci (Ribnicja, Kišinev), Usatove (Odessa), Evminka (Oster, Černigiv) and Sofijivka (Borispil, Kiev). There is no accepted generic name for these groups but all occurred at roughly the same time and bordered on each other. They are, in effect, 'transitional' from Copper to Bronze Age. Their common inheritance was elaborately decorated pottery drawing on Tripillja roots, with large piriform and biconical amphorae, wide open bowls with incurving rim, decorated in massive swirling designs in the Tripillja fashion, or undecorated except for cordoned finger-impressions, cording, etc. In some of these groups, particularly in the 'Black Earth' area, extensive plateau settlements, with many house plans in an encircling pattern, continued from earlier times (as at Kolomijščina village near Chalep'ja, Obuchiv, Kiev).[10] The basis of the economy is said to have been stock-breeding, but crops no doubt played an important role too. In some areas

(e.g. Usatove, Sofijivka) only cemeteries occur in any number: these were either flat inhumations with stone settings (Vichvatinci), barrow-graves (Usatove) with crouched inhumations in shafts or cists and an encircling ring of stones,[11] or cremations (Sofijivka) in urns or simply in pits. Recent excavations on barrows of Usatove type have confirmed many details of barrow construction. At Tudorovo (Kaušan, Kišinev), a large barrow 20 m across contained a series of burials, the richest in a pit at the perimeter of the mound covered by stones. In the centre was a wood-lined grave pit disturbed by a later burial; two 'ritual pits' were also found, containing pottery.[12] In the fill of the mound were found stone and copper objects – a chisel, an awl and a fragmentary knife, while with burial 1 were five vases and a lid, a necklace of animal teeth, a copper knife and an awl; the body, which was tentatively identified as that of a woman, was crouched on its left side, the head to the east. Similar constructions – and finds – may be seen at Usatove itself, where numerous grave-pits were cut in the ground both beneath and around the primary mound[13] (fig. 39). Grave-pits without mounds also occur.[14] In material culture other than pottery, barrows of the Usatove group are especially prolific in metal: triangular riveted daggers, of forms closely related to those of the Aegean Early Bronze Age,[15] flat axes, awls, knives and so on occur, while ornaments of boar's tusks and beads of faience are found too.[16] Arsenical bronzes were the dominant type.[17]

There are indications, however, that Usatove itself is a special phenomenon: graves elsewhere are much less rich, and the barrows here form a cemetery which lies beside a settlement surrounded by a stone wall and containing stone-built houses.[18] One of the tombs, moreover, contained a small corbel-vaulted chamber, the inspiration for which is alleged to have been Aegean. The further connection of Usatove with areas to the south and south-east is shown by the presence of ox skulls and sculptured bulls' heads on grave stelae; while amber probably came from the Baltic and silver and antimony from Anatolia. The dating proposed by Sulimirski,[19] which suggests that Usatove ran parallel to the Sixth City of Troy, seems to us far too low; the analogies show, rather, a synchronism with the Early Bronze Age in the Aegean (Troy II, Early Minoan II in Crete etc.) and with the start of the true Bronze Age in central Europe (Br AI, as shown by the faience beads etc.). The long sequence of development in the Usatove tumuli is shown by the original Usatove barrow which comprised a double ring of stones, and had no less than thirty-two grave-pits and cists at various levels, with a clear sequence of pottery from Pit Grave through Catacomb to Timber Grave types.[20]

On the middle Dnieper, barrow graves were also common,[21] and the burial rite was very similar to that of the pit graves of the late Neolithic

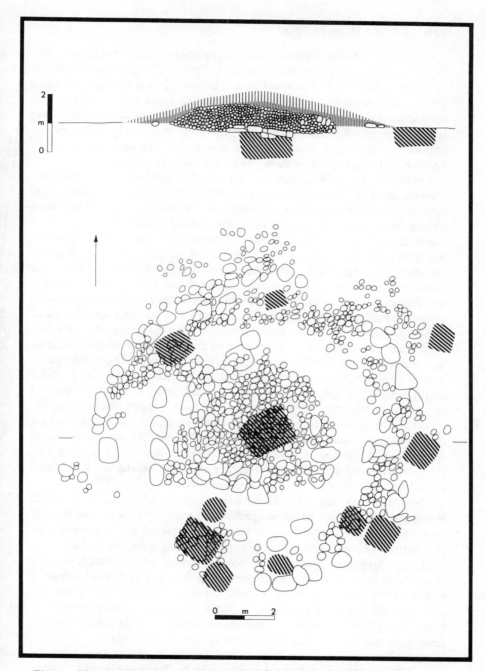

Fig. 39   Usatove (Odessa), barrow 12, plan and section. Grave pits hatched.
(After E. F. Patokova, *KSAMO* (1962))

– contracted inhumations in shafts. A number of settlements have also been investigated, as at Ksendzova Gora (Bychov, Mogilev) and Zabal'le (Rogačev, Gomel').[22] The finds cannot be described as spectacular, since they usually comprise rubbish pits containing flints and potsherds, but they at least show that domestic sites of the culture are recoverable. That trade in precious commodities was not forgotten can be seen by the appearance of amber in sites of this group, but we have no means of knowing whether it was of Baltic or local provenance.[23]

From the Gorods'ke group in Volynia (the type-site lies on the river Teteriv west of Kiev)[24] there is evidence of substantial numbers of settlements, either platform constructions or pit-dwellings. It has been shown that sites are usually on high ground above river valleys;[25] excavated examples include Trojaniv (Žitomir)[26] and Cviklivci (Kamenec Podolskij, Chmel'nickij).[27] From these settlements come copious stonework (polished axes, triangular arrowheads, scrapers etc., as well as stone axe-hammers), bonework (awls, sleeves etc.) and pottery, which is divided into two main groups – unpainted cord-impressed storage vessels, pithoi, stands and cooking pots, and slipped or painted dark-on-light vessels in the Tripillja tradition. Stylized clay figurines and spindle-whorls are also common. Of the material from the sites on the Desna or in the cremation cemeteries near Kiev particularly notable are the riveted copper daggers, flat spearheads, flat axes, tubes, rings and other ornaments. The material indicates a variety of dates: some sites appear to lie firmly in the true Bronze Age, others have copper objects that are typologically among the earliest. The late Tripillja site of Sabatinivka I (Gruška) produced a knot-headed pin (*Schleifennadel*), equivalent to Br AI in central Europe; a cave at Bil'če Zolote (Borščiv, Ternopol') in Podolia produced a three-riveted dagger of copper on the one hand, and a bead said to be of dark blue glass on the other.[28]

The area north-east of the Carpathians – the provinces of Volynia and Podolia – is a complex net of small cultural groups in the earlier Bronze Age. At least two Eneolithic elements may be recognized – barrow-graves and pottery of the Corded Ware group, and cist-graves and amphorae of Globular Amphora type.[29] The barrow-graves of the north-eastern Carpathian foothills form a homogeneous group: a large mound is usually raised over a shaft containing a crouched inhumation. Grave goods are poor, but the pottery is true Corded Ware – beakers and amphorae, with battle-axes; flint daggers and other objects, simple copper ornaments and some gold also occur. That the culture should be contemporary with the Nitra-Mierzanowice group to the west (above, p. 96) is shown by the sporadic occurrence of faience beads, which also occur in the related Strzyżów group in south-east Poland. All these groups show several stages

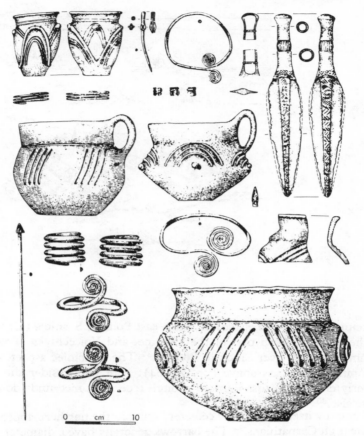

Fig. 40   Ivanja (Dubno, Rovno). Grave-goods from barrow of the Komarov culture.
(After I. K. Svešnikov, *SA* 1968/2)

of development, and the latest part of the series must correlate with Br A1 or even A2 in the west.[30]

The first true Bronze Age culture in the sub-Carpathian zone was a cultural group that is found more widely in Romania under the guise of the Monteoru-Costişa group: that named after the site of Bilij Potik (Čortkiv, Ternopol') – in Russian Belopotok – which is discussed below (p. 142). This in turn gave way to, or even formed part of, a wider cultural grouping of the 'Middle Bronze Age' named after the barrow-cemetery of Komarov[31] (Galič, Ivano-Frankovsk) in the Middle Dniester basin, and seen to be closely related to material named after the sites of

Trzciniec (Opole Lubelskie) in south-east Poland, Sosnicja (Černigiv) in the north-western part of the Ukraine, and Vojcechivka (Polonne, Žitomir) on the river Sluch in Podolia.[32] The Trzciniec aspect of this grouping we discuss above (pp. 79, 84): here we consider the more easterly end of the distribution, though true Trzciniec finds do occur there also.[33]

Komarov itself is a barrow cemetery lying in the northern approaches to the high Carpathians.[34] The barrows generally have a diameter of up to 20 m and contain many secondary burials – typically up to six, in addition to the primary one; men are frequently laid on their right side, women on their left, with their heads pointing in opposite directions. Multiple burials of various sorts are found, and at Vojcechivka a triple grave contained two men and a woman, the woman laid in the opposite direction with her legs under the left leg of one of the men. Recent excavations at Ivanja (Dubno, Rovno) in Volynia produced a single cremation along with four inhumation burials in two lined pits in a large tumulus, with a rich accompaniment of pottery and bronzes; two of the burials had been made on the spot where the cremation had taken place (fig. 40).[35]

The domestic side of this cultural grouping can be seen in the Sosnicja facies around the river Desna, where some twenty sites are known on raised sandy land beside rivers.[36] A recent example is at Pustinka

Fig. 41 Pustinka (Černigiv). Reconstruction of settlement of the Sosnicja group.
(After S. S. Berezans'ka, *AK* 23 (1970))

(Černigiv), where Berezans'ka found a roughly rectangular house, 12.8 m × 7.2 m, divided into two rooms; one contained a large hearth and two pits, the other had post-holes around the perimeter (fig. 41). A second hearth lay outside.[37] The construction of all the houses was of wood, with a central row of post-holes and walls of horizontal timbers held in place by inner and outer uprights. A number of internal fittings have been tentatively assigned to particular places in the houses. The agricultural buildings are generally areas of multiple post-holes interpreted as structures raised on stilts, probably for drying grain; of the two 'cult buildings' one was circular, 12 m in diameter, and contained four post-holes assumed to have supported benches, and a gully leading from the centre to the side of the building. A smashed pot lay nearby. The cult interpretation rests solely on the fact that this building is quite different from the ordinary houses. The high standard of observation and the detailed publication make Pustinka a site of exceptional importance, and the excavator's reconstructions of great interest. Other, similar, finds have been made by the same scholar around both Desna and Seima;[38] and rich settlement material – including much bone- and stone-work, spindle-whorls, tuyères etc. – has come from the site of Mošna (Čerkasy).[39]

In both groups, the typical pottery form is an upright beaker-like or pithoid jar without handles; the decoration is usually deeply incised and the ornament invariably geometric. The commonest motifs are pendent hatched triangles, herringbone designs and groups of parallel lines set in a V-formation but not actually joining in the middle. In the Komarov area, Costişa-type two-handled cups with knob-terminals also occur, as well as a variety of smaller shallow cups and jars, but this probably merely reflects the difference between the funerary and domestic aspects of the culture. A further speciality of this cemetery is one-handled cups with pedestal base and boss ornament, and these reflect contact both with Poland (Trzciniec) and with the Slovak-Hungarian province (above, p. 98); so, too, do later vessels in this series, like the tulip-shaped bowls and pots from Bukivna (Tovmač, Ivano-Frankovsk) on the Dniester.[40]

The metalwork of Komarov and related groups is particularly significant, as Hungarian bronze-types characteristic of the Koszider horizon do appear on these sites with some regularity. At Komarov, for instance, antithetic spiral-terminal rings and bracelets, massive bracelets, tutuli and long pins are all considered to have been imported from south of the Carpathian ring.[41] Metalwork of rather later date also occurs: at Zazime (Borispil', Kiev), for instance, several moulds for socketed axes were found, eloquent witness to the existence of local metal-working.[42]

The extraordinary hoard from Borodino (Odessa), containing elaborate ornaments and weapons, should also be mentioned here, though its date is a matter of continuing debate.[43] It includes four shaft-hole axes of nephrite and serpentine, a silver dagger with gold plate decoration, three polished maceheads, possibly of alabaster, two silver spearheads with gold decoration, and a silver pin with rhomboidal head. On the pin is found the 'pulley' decoration commonly known from gold objects in the Shaft Graves at Mycenae; on the dagger are triskele and related designs; running spirals go around the base of one spearhead, and elaborate zigzags around the other. Though some of these pieces and motifs are clearly locally derived, it seems hard to escape the conclusion that the dagger, at least, and possibly the pin, were manufactured in imitation of early Mycenaean prototypes.

The vast steppe zone of the southern Ukraine – the north Pontic region – is characterized during this earlier part of the Bronze Age by variations on one main theme – the barrow burial. Already in the Neolithic burials under tumuli (*kurgans*) with characteristic pottery and bone objects became widespread; in both Late Neolithic and Bronze Age the method of tomb construction lends its name to the period. The late Neolithic-Eneolithic tumuli are called 'pit graves' (*Jamnaja kultura*) and those of the earlier Bronze Age are called 'catacomb graves' (*Katakombnaja kultura*). Pit graves are characteristically deep shafts in the ground, usually square or rectangular, lined with timber and covered with planks.

Burial was by inhumation in a contracted position, and red ochre was used in quantity to cover the body; grave goods were poor. The presence of red ochre has led German scholars to call the whole series of barrow burials from the third and second millennia bc the *Ochre Grave culture*,[44] a concept little different from the 'Kurgan culture' of Gimbutas. The barrows are then typical of the so-called 'Kurgan people',[45] being widespread in their dispersal through Europe and west-central Asia. Radiocarbon dates indicate that pit graves belong to the later part of the third millennium bc (table 5), but this is also the time-span of most dates that refer to catacomb graves as well; this fact alone should make us suspicious of separating the two traditions too far.

The 'Catacomb Grave culture' covered much of the north Pontic region between the Dnieper and the Volga whereas pit graves had extended even east of the Urals. In the central area, burial is in a pit with a side chamber – like an underground, vertically-dug chamber tomb (fig. 42). Burials were usually contracted inhumations, but orientations differ. A special practice of the eastern groups, more rarely found to the west,

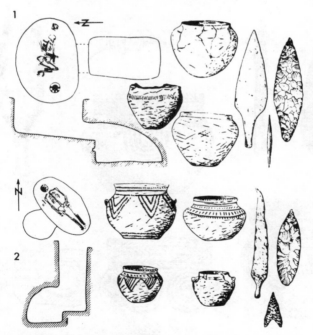

Fig. 42   Catacomb graves and typical grave-finds from the Crimea.
(After A. A. Ščepinskii *SA* 1966/2)

is that of deformation of the skull of the deceased; it was also common to provide joints of mutton or beef for the dead, or even whole skulls.[46]

Objects regularly found in catacomb graves include copper beads and pendants, daggers of flint and, occasionally, bronze, flint arrowheads, stone battle-axes, bone hammer-headed pins, stone and faience beads, arrow-straighteners, and pottery (fig. 43). The latter is not very informative and certainly not aesthetic, but it may be said in general to be rather coarse and heavy, coming in globular shapes related to those of the pit graves but generally having flat bases. Decoration is heavy, either by deep incision or by impression (especially of cord); comb- and shell-stamping also occur. Motifs include concentric circles and semi-circles, various linear geometrical ornaments, alternating cord or zig-zag bands,

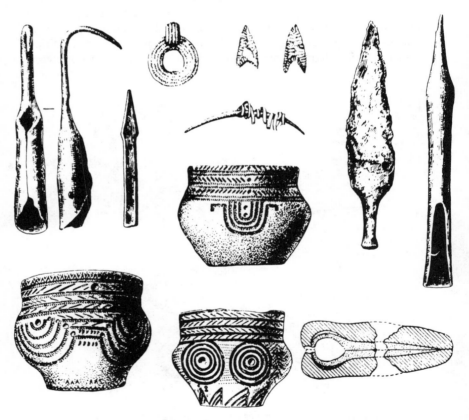

Fig. 43   Grave-goods from catacomb graves of the Donec group. Not to scale. (After *Archeologija Ukrajins'koj RSR*, 1971)

arcading and so on. A particular form seen as characteristic of the culture as a whole, but also indicating links with the west, is the bipartite 'incense-burner' or 'censer', a pedestalled bowl unevenly divided into two parts. Of considerable interest too is the regular occurrence of cart-wheels and other cart equipment, as well as cart models in clay. Also important is the considerable quantity of metalwork, mostly of arsenical bronze, imported from the Caucasus.[47]

An important series of settlements, mostly from the west of the area (around the Dnieper), provides the domestic aspect of the catacomb graves. The site at Kamenka (Kerč, Simferopol'), recently dug, is especially important. Here roughly round or oval stone-built houses were found, 6.5 to 7 m in diameter or 8 m long, and attributable to two phases of the same cultural aspect (fig. 44).[48] At Babine (Verchnij Rogačik, Cherson) site III, on a terrace beside the river Komka, settlement debris and the foundations of a roughly rectangular hut were found, measuring 8 × 3.3 m. An oval pit is said to be a dwelling too, but is more likely to be for rubbish only. The scanty remains of a post-framed daub construction with clay floor seem to be indicated. The finds included flint daggers and arrowheads, stone axes, spindle-whorls, bone awls, and copper and faience beads. All the main domesticated animals were represented, cattle and sheep/goat each accounting for about 30 per cent of the total, pig for 12 per cent and horse for 10 per cent.[49]

Various groups have been distinguished in the large numbers of barrows recorded.[50] Chief among these are the western or Donec group and the southern or Azov Sea group; related examples occur to the east (Don-Manyč) and north (Dnieper bend). The most characteristic types are to be found in the Donbass, beween Donec and Don.

There is disagreement about the origins of the catacomb graves. Broadly speaking, scholars are divided into those who favour a local origin and development from pit graves,[51] and those who see the culture as intrusive.[52] This is not the place for a detailed discussion, but one or two points may be made. First, the standard of the early excavations was not high, and it has been suggested that V. A. Gorodcov, the father of Russian barrow-excavation, missed many of the side-chambers charac-teristic of the 'catacombs'. Second, the basic idea of the catacomb grave is similar to that of the pit grave: an underground chamber. Indeed, some cases are recorded where it is difficult to decide whether a grave belongs to the pit or catacomb variety (the so-called 'transitional' types). Third, the area involved is very large, so that one should not expect identity of culture everywhere. Fourth, radiocarbon determinations indicate very similar dates for both series of graves, though a long sequence of development is suggested by the finds. For these reasons, we prefer to

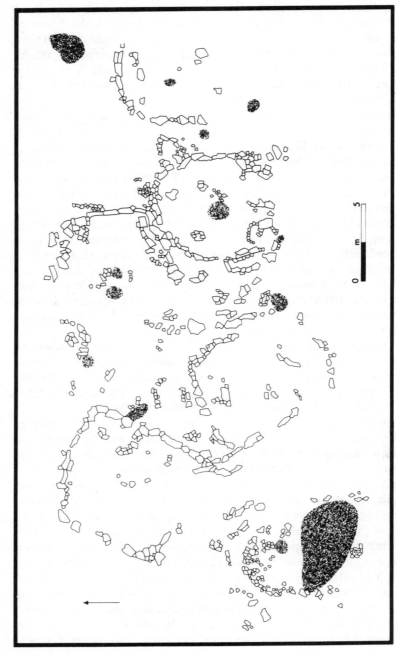

Fig. 44 Houses from the settlement at Kamenka (Kerč), late Catacomb period. Hearths and pits shaded. (After V. D. Rybalova, *Arch. Sbor.* 16 (1974))

think of catacomb graves as a specific local variant in the general sequence of barrow development, not as an independent cultural manifestation.

In the west and centre of Russia the transition to a full Bronze Age economy was apparently a slow business. Both the Dnieper-Desna culture of White Russia and the Fatjanovo group of western central Russia are clearly of Corded Ware derivation; and since copper appears in Corded Ware contexts from the start, and true bronzes are few and far between even in the developed stages of these cultures, it is extremely difficult to know to what date any given site should be assigned. Further, the lack of radiocarbon dates rules out a strictly objective chronology.

Most sites with material attributable to the Dnieper-Desna group are settlements and lie north of the forest-steppe zone: they are unprolific and short-lived.[53] Surface ground-plans of huts accompany rubbish pits with flints and sherds. Both barrow and flat graves occur, though it is claimed that to start with barrows are found only at the eastern end of the distribution. A typical barrow-cemetery is Moška (Chodoviči, Gomel') on the Dnieper:[54] typically multiple-use kurgans contained burials with a rich variety of stone and metal objects – chipped flint arrowheads, knives and scrapers, polished flint axes and ground stone hammer-axes, copper battle-axes, spearheads, spectacle-spiral pendants, and the characteristic beaker-like pottery with round base and belly and cylindrical neck, decorated by cord or other impressions, in bands of geometrical motifs. Foreign connections are shown by the forms of the metal objects, which suggest Caucasian and central European analogies, as well as by analysis of the metal (both Caucasian and Transylvanian ores have been identified) and the occurrence of faience and amber beads. The cultural assemblage as a whole is clearly hybrid, containing elements related to the Middle Dnieper, Corded Ware, Trzciniec-Sosnicja and Fatjanovo groups: theories concerning its origin and development are purely speculative, though it seems to us reasonable to assign it to part of the late Corded Ware grouping. The considerable number of stone battle-axes found makes this view the more possible.[55]

The same can be said of the adjacent Fatjanovo culture, part of the same general group as the Dnieper-Desna.[56] Again, one can assume that the culture lasted many centuries, for some cemeteries are quite clearly in the Corded Ware-Battle Axe and Globular Amphora grouping, while others contain bronzes of advanced types. The two main groups in this culture are named after the areas in which they occur: Moscow and Jaroslav-Kalinin. The type-site is near Jaroslav. Most sites are flat cemeteries, with crouched inhumations in shallow pits; it is said that men were buried with their head to the south-west, women with their head to the north-east. The commonest grave-good is the battle-axe, with a variety of ornaments in copper, bone, boar's tusk, etc.; a most interesting find is that from Vladyčino (Rjazan') of wide Únětician wrist-bands, willow-leaf and spiral ornaments, and flat copper plate ornaments, as well as typical Fatjanovo pottery (fig. 45).[57] This find must correspond in date to Br A in central Europe; and there are indications that the culture started much earlier and went on much later: from one site came a copper disc covered with iron. Such a find may, of course, reflect contact with early iron-using communities of the Near East rather than the spread of iron across Europe. Further evidence for the longevity of the culture comes from apparently stratified sequences like that at Mytišči (Tejkovo, Ivanovo): one grave containing a 'Thuringian' amphora (Globular Amphora culture) was prior to another with a wide Únětician wrist-band of the type already mentioned.[58]

The origins of the culture are disputed: most scholars agree that the Fatjanovo group represents a local variant of the Corded Ware-Globular Amphora continuum, and indeed the 'Thuringian' amphorae are plausibly seen as of western derivation. In spite of this, more than one author has attributed the source of development of the group as a whole to an eastern origin, either within the area of the Pit Grave culture or, more specifically, the Caucasus.[59]

Absolute chronology

Most of the cultures discussed above fall in the second millennium bc. Those of direct Corded Ware derivation belong to its early part, those with Tumulus-type bronzes to its later part. The position of the Borodino hoard is uncertain, but a date in the fourteenth century BC seems reasonable.[60]

A good collection of radiocarbon dates is now available (table 5), which indicates the approximate positions of the various groups. Of them, Usatove is much the earliest, flourishing in the second half of the third millennium bc or even earlier. Pit graves go from about 2500 bc to around 1700 bc; catacomb graves fall within that bracket, in the centuries around 2000 bc. The single date from a Komarov context is much later, as expected.

Bulgaria and North Greece

The Early Bronze Age in Greece started soon after 3000 BC and reached its zenith in Early Bronze II, a period of considerable trade, metallurgical expansion and large-scale settlement; this was the period of the second city of Troy, of the major settlements of Poliochni on Lemnos and

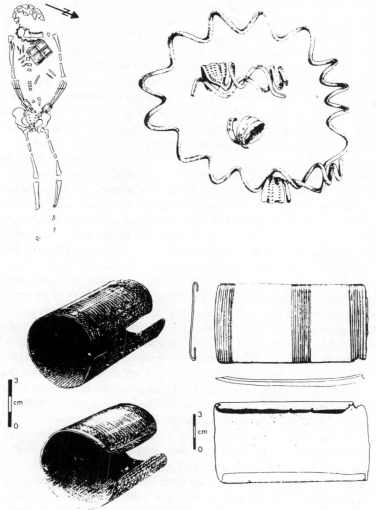

Fig. 45   Vladyčino (Rjazan'). Grave of the Fatjanovo group, with spiral wire necklace, wrist-bands and plate ornaments.
(After O. N. Bader, *SA* 1971/1)

Thermi on Lesbos, of the House of the Tiles at Lerna, the Round Building at Tiryns, and a host of other important sites. The history of Early Bronze I I I and Middle Bronze I is tied up with the problem of the arrival of the Indo-European speakers later known to us as the Greeks;

by Middle Bronze I the relatively rich cultures of the Early Bronze Age had given way on the mainland to a materially poorer culture in which a most characteristic element was the pottery. In many places a finely levigated and well-fired grey ware, often called Grey Minyan, appears or a decorated ware with painted designs in matt dark paint on a light ground – Matt-Painted Ware. More common, however, is a coarse dark ware decorated with applied knobs or incised patterns. Burials were usually in cist graves, and metal uncommon. Only at the end of the period, towards 1600 BC, did new developments take place, so that by 1580 BC the Mycenaean period had started.[61] The relative poverty of the mainland in the Middle Bronze Age was not reflected on the islands, where sites like Phylakopi on Melos or Agia Irini on Kea flourished.

In Macedonia, a key site is Kritsana on the west coast of Chalcidice, where six successive settlements are all attributed to the Early Bronze Age.[62] The pottery is linked on the one hand to the Early Bronze Age wares of central and southern Greece via forms like the bowl with incurving rim, the askos, the pyxis and other specialized forms, and the use of *urfirnis* (semi-lustrous paint), and on the other to the late Bulgarian tell pottery via the great number of one- and two-handled cups and mugs.

The recent British excavations at Sitagroi in the plain of Drama have produced material that provides a clear and useful link between Greece and Bulgaria in both Neolithic and Early Bronze Ages.[63] From the brief reports published so far, it is clear that levels IV and V are those which should be attributed to the Bronze Age proper. In phase IV the pottery, which is mostly undecorated, is said to show affinities to Baden on the one hand (high-handled cups), and to Thessalian Early Bronze I on the other; while in phase Va simple conical bowls and tall-necked narrow jugs are said to be 'not unlike those of Troy I'. In phase Vb, finally, a range of one- and two-handled cups, conical bowls with incurving rim and cordoned barrel-like storage vessels, mostly in dark burnished ware, as well as stone shaft-hole axes and clay anchors and hooks, indicate affinities with Troy I and II and with the Ezero series in Bulgaria (below, p. 134). Level V also contained well-preserved remains of buildings,[64] including a structure 17 m in length in Vb, and the 'Burnt House' in Va. This was an apsidal building 8 m long, the main room 6 m square, with a small apse at the north containing two clay bins, two ovens, pithoi and other pottery (fig. 46). These included rare encrusted forms. In the main room, which was separated from the apse by a pisé partition wall, were a hearth and several complete pots. The main part of the house was timber-framed, with wattle-and-daub walls and a central retaining post, but the apse was of flimsier construction; the roof was of brushwood bonded with clay. In general shape and layout this house relates quite

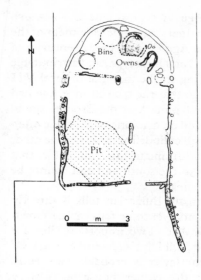

Fig. 46   Sitagroi (Drama), level Va, the 'Burnt House'.
(After C. Renfrew, *Antiquity* 44 (1970))

closely to the Ezero series, as well as to earlier Baden culture houses at Vučedol. A generic connection with Early Helladic III and later houses in central and southern Greece also seems likely.

Thrace is an area which could potentially exceed Macedonia in importance for an understanding of the relationships between the various cultures of the east-central Balkans. It lies on the threshold of three major culture-provinces – the Anatolian, the Bulgarian, and the Macedonian – and is favourably placed to receive influences by land or sea from south, east or north. Yet in spite of a substantial level of Neolithic settlement, Thrace remains in the Bronze Age an almost total blank, with only a few sites (and those not rich in material), even recognized.[65]

For subsequent developments in northern Greece, our information is very scanty. The second millennium BC is known mainly from pottery sequences and not from extensive excavation. In the Chalcidice, Middle Bronze Age levels are represented at Agios Mamas and Molyvopyrgo;[66] in central Macedonia at Kilindir, Vardaroftsa and elsewhere. The appearance of grey ware and ring-stemmed goblets of 'Minyan' type is of interest; more characteristic, however, are incised white-filled wares, with spiraliform decoration, in wide bowls with wish-bone handles. This ware continues into the 'Late Bronze Age', when it is found on globular pots with two high handles and elaborate, almost metopic, decoration on the belly. These forms correlate closely with pottery in Bulgaria and Romania (p. 135). Mycenaean sherds appear only rather later.[67]

In Bulgaria, very few tell sites can be shown to have been occupied after the earliest part of the Bronze Age. A typical case is Karanovo (Sliven), where level VII represents the final stage of development of the tell but a very early stage of the Bronze Age.[68] It succeeds centuries of occupation by people making pottery of Gumelniţa type, and attributable to the Copper Age; nor is there anything in the material of level VII which would in itself lead one to suppose that the true Bronze Age had started by this time. In the pottery, the hallmark of the Bronze Age in Bulgaria is the high knobbed handle, found on drinking cups; these often have a rounded base and sometimes a high cylindrical neck. On the other hand, *askoi* and low conical bowls with incurving rim show that connections with contemporary groups to the south and east cannot be ignored; 'Trojan' forms occur on a few sites.[69]

It is possible that the desertion of many Bulgarian tells is directly attributable to the arrival of new occupants; yet some tells can be shown to have continued through the Bronze Age. Two important sites are Razkopanica near Manole (Plovdiv) and Tell Dipsis (Ezero, Sliven). Of the two main levels at Razkopanica, the lower is probably very early Bronze Age, the upper rather later; the earlier house-plans were rectangular, but two of the later ones had apsidal ends.[70] At Ezero a Bronze Age layer comprised nine building levels, distinct but part of the same cultural group; originally an encircling wall was built, though it subsequently went out of use. In horizon 4, the houses are laid out carefully on the same orientation. They are said to have been wattle-and-daub constructions, with horseshoe-shaped ovens and open round hearths inside.[71] The finds from this and other sites include a variety of stone tools (axes and adzes, sickle blades etc.) and very many bone and horn tools (hoes, hammers, sleeves, needles etc.) as well as pottery, which we summarize below. Trapezoidal houses up to 6.5 m long, attributable to a rather later stage of the earlier Bronze Age, have been identified by Katinčarov at a tell near Nova Zagora, and, to a later stage still, an apsidal-ended house nearly 13 m long.[72] This find clearly corresponds to those from Sitagroi and Razkopanica, and – perhaps – Middle Helladic Greece.[73]

Caves were also occupied during the Bronze Age in Bulgaria, as is shown by several sites on the north side of the Rhodope mountains: Devetaki, Emen, Magura. In the last-named were found several flimsy brushwood huts with ovens and hearths on beaten clay floors; the material was very similar to that from Ezero.[74] Rather more information is available from lake-side sites near Varna. One site at Ezerovo was found because the wooden piles of the houses were partly visible: the largest of them are 3 m long and 0.9 m in circumference.[75] At other sites like Strašimirovo substantial remains of pile-constructions were found, though complete house-plans are not known. It is not clear how far into the Bronze Age these sites continue: they were certainly most prolific in the Copper Age, and may not have long outlived the events which caused the desertion of the great tells.

The finds from these lake-dwellings are similar to those from land-sites, though much more organic material is preserved.[76] Early Bronze Age pottery in Bulgaria is invariably handmade with a fine sand temper; it is rather unevenly fired, varying from brilliant red to smoky grey.[77] In general the repertoire of shapes and decoration is similar to that in the Eneolithic: characteristic new types are the vase with pointed base and the cross-hatched panel. Otherwise the earlier Bronze Age assemblage includes *askoi*, small rounded cups, conical bowls with incurving rim, biconical jars (several of these forms similar to those in the Early Helladic II repertoire), and, invariably, elaborate pointed and *ansa lunata* handles, recalling those in Macedonia. At Razkopanica the shape that appears in overwhelming numbers in the upper layer is the globular bowl with two high handles, though biconical jars and one-handled cups are also very common. The globular bowl is also known from an important well find near Plovdiv.[78] A chance find revealed a pit 4.5 m deep composed of six consecutive layers of earth-filled pottery and covered with four layers of stones. Forty-four whole and many fragmentary vases were recovered; it is clear that the best analogies are with the Zimnicea-Tei-Verbicioara group of Romania (below, p. 143), and with the Macedonian Middle Bronze Age forms (p. 133). Other shapes are crude one-handled straight-walled cups, biconical or ovoid storage jars, and globular cups. Decorative techniques are shown by the material from Magura cave, where grooving, channelling, pitting and incision are used to construct borders, herring-bone patterns, all-over rustication, panelling and so on.[79]

Other noteworthy finds include anthropomorphic bowls from Ezerovo, stylized anthropomorphic figurines in antler from Ezero,[80] and a strictly limited range of metal goods. Copper shaft-hole axes had been known in Bulgaria from the late Neolithic, but the advent of the Bronze Age did little to stimulate metal production. Until the time when hoards of sickles and socketed axes start to occur, bronzes are rare and usually made from unalloyed copper – flat axes, awls, pins and the like. The great wealth of Troy II and Early Helladic II found no reflection in contemporary Bulgaria.

Few graves are known, although of considerable importance are the recent finds from tumuli at Tărnava and Kneža (Vraca), where both inhumation and cremation burials occur. Most of the tombs are rectangular pits, lined with stone or wood; the skeletons were covered with red ochre in the steppe manner (fig. 47). The pottery is of Coţofeni

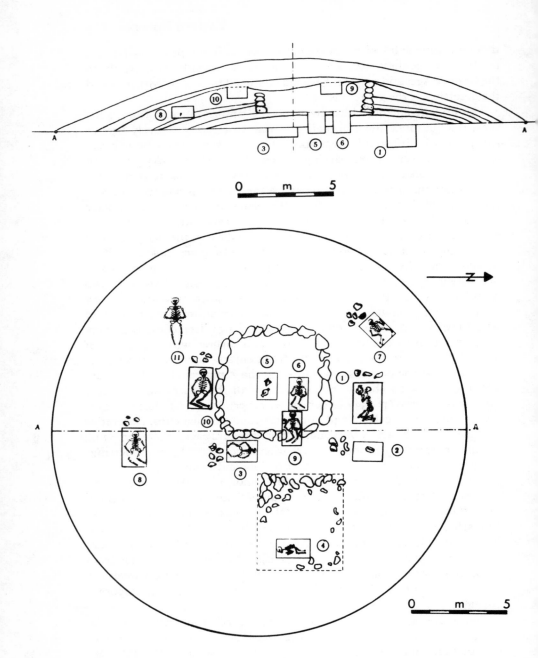

Fig. 47   Tărnava (Vraca). Plan and section of Early Bronze Age tumulus.
(After B. Nikolov, *Arch.* 18/3 (1976))

type (below, p. 158). The appearance of cremation, and the unified nature of the burial rite in the Vraca area, marks an innovation in the Chalcolithic practices.[81] From Loveč comes a male inhumation in a pit covered with a dome-like structure of stones; beside the body lay a dog. The finds comprise a deep two-handled jar, a conical bowl, a small biconical cup, a simple bronze dagger, a gold rivet and a gold spiral ornament.[82] The largest cemetery is at Bereket (Stara Zagora), where crouched inhumations on the left side, head to the south, were accompanied by ochre as well as pottery and copper tools; other tombs have been found in the lowest levels of later Thracian tumuli, a fact which lends support to the idea of Bronze – Iron Age continuity.[83]

The varied and scattered nature of the sites in Bronze Age Bulgaria, and the almost total lack of dating evidence and stratigraphic sequence through the period, lead us to conclude that the rôle and significance of the area in the Bronze Age cannot yet be properly assessed, though the situation has improved immensely in the last ten years.[84] The greatly extended range of archaeological cover in the country, however, makes us sceptical that the position will change very much in the future; the scarcity of known sites can no longer be attributed to a lack of research. That Bulgaria was an important area in the Bronze Age can be judged both from its geographical position and from its early role as a copper-producer. This is shown both by workings at the ancient mines of Aibunar (Stara Zagora)[85] and by the rich finds of grave material in the Chalcolithic.[86]

Romania[87]

The present-day country of Romania divides naturally into three main parts – the lowland area on the lower Danube, the mountain-locked upland zone of Transylvania, and that part of the Hungarian plain in the Romanian Banat. These divisions are in general reflected in the archaeological record too. We include the last in our consideration of the Hungarian plain as a whole (p. 69); the two former we treat here. Cultural groups occasionally cross the natural barrier of the Carpathian Ring; more usually they are confined to one side or other. This fact, combined with the proliferation of cultures that have been identified in the area, makes the situation there especially confusing, and a more generalized coverage such as we have attempted for central Europe impossible. There is, furthermore, considerable disagreement among Romanian scholars about the nature of the first Bronze Age cultures in Romania, for one man's Neolithic is another's Bronze Age; in general, however, it is convenient to regard the Bronze Age as starting when cultures belonging to or related to such typically Eneolithic groups as Salcuţa come to an end.[88]

Among such transitional groups we may mention *Coţofeni*[89] in Muntenia, Oltenia and parts of Transylvania; *Cernavoda*[90] in the Dobrogea and lower Danube; *Folteşti* (phase II)[91] in Moldavia; and a group of inhumation burials containing red ochre which are apparently synchronous with the latest phases of the groups already mentioned.[92] Following these, we have *Glina* (phase III) in Muntenia and Oltenia, and its relative *Schneckenberg* in Transylvania; in the lowland zone a variety of cultural groups characterized by the presence of cups and bowls with two high handles ('Kantharos cultures') and named after sites at *Tei, Verbicioara, Zimnicea, Coslogeni* and *Monteoru*; in the upland zone an independent and widespread group named after the *Wietenberg* at Sighişoara; and elements of 'Hungarian Plain cultures' like *Otomani, Periam*, and so on. In the latest part of the earlier Bronze Age, we may find in the Banat and areas adjoining it cultures that are part of the Dubovac/Žuto Brdo group of Jugoslavia and in Romania are named after the sites of *Gîrla Mare* and *Cîrna*.

In considering the start of the Bronze Age in lowland Romania, we are assisted by a number of good stratigraphical sequences. One such is that from the deep deposits at the settlement of Verbicioara (Calafat, Craiova) in Oltenia. Six main strata were distinguished:[93] at the bottom were levels of the early and middle Neolithic, then those of the Eneolithic (Salcuţa culture); the fourth contained pottery of Coţofeni type, the fifth of the type known from the site of Glina, level III; and the sixth a type that was first identified at Verbicioara itself. The top two levels are the most important for our purposes. The fifth (Glina III – Schneckenberg) is named after a large mound site near Bucharest and a hill site in Braşov; in the lowland aspect of the group such sites have several periods of occupation, with the Glina III levels typically overlying those of Salcuţa, Gumelniţa or Cernavoda without the interposition of Coţofeni.[94] Graves include flat inhumations and cists but are poorly known; recent excavations at Zimnicea (Teleorman)[95] have revealed a flat inhumation cemetery with material hitherto unknown but related both to Bulgarian and to Glina III finds. The burials were crouched, with head to the south: the face usually looked to the east, that is, the body was on its right side; in a few cases stone settings were present. The pottery differs from the run of Glina III forms – to which we return shortly – in having a series of askoid jugs with high beaked cylindrical neck and one handle going from rim to shoulder; conical bowls, bellied jars and globular vessels with high funnel-like neck and small strap or lug-handles are also found (fig. 48). In metalwork we may mention the variety of copper and

Fig. 48   Zimnicea (Teleorman). Burial and grave-goods from early Bronze Age cemetery.
(After A. D. Alexandrescu, *Dacia* n.s. 18 (1974))

139

silver pendants, spiral rings, crescentic earrings and beads, all of which seem to indicate a date contemporary with the earliest Bronze Age in the region.

The Transylvanian aspect of this culture is named after the site of Schneckenberg (Dealul Melcilor – Hill of the Snails) in Braşov, and in the same city are two other hill sites with material that is complementary – the Gesprengberg (Dealul Şprengului) and the Steinbruchhügel (Dealul Pietrăriei). Though these sites produced considerable quantities of material, more detailed information is available from the recent excavations at Cuciulata (Braşov).[96] Two main levels were distinguished, with traces of houses in each: in the first an oval fireplace 0.83 m in diameter rested on an earth floor, though few walls survived; in the second there were remains of a rectangular house 4.05 × 3.65 m with a floor of limestone slabs daubed with yellow clay, resting directly on the natural rock. In the centre was a round hearth on a base of small stones; also in the hut were charcoal and burnt clay fragments, bone and stone tools, and three small oval plates. At the north and north-east sides of this room was a raised bank or bench of stone slabs. Outside the hut to the east were two opposed hearths, but without clear traces of the house that contained them.

Cuciulata is but one of many such hill-top sites in south-eastern Transylvania, between the river Olt and the Carpathians. They cannot be described as hill-forts, rather as hill-top settlements; what little analysis has been done of their location indicates a preference for sites above river-valleys in high, commanding, positions without artificial fortifications. That the situation is more complex than this, however, is indicated by the very fact that the same culture is found on the Romanian lowlands in sites like Glina and Verbicioara: the depth of deposits at most Glina sites makes it likely that there, at any rate, permanent occupation took place. Schneckenberg material also occurs in cave sites, notably Gura Cheii (Braşov) and Almaş (Odorhei), but this represents only a continuation of occupation during the Chalcolithic. More important are a number of cemeteries, like Rotbav (Feldioara, Braşov), where Wietenberg crema-tions followed Schneckenberg inhumations,[97] and Codlea (Braşov);[98] contracted inhumations in small stone cists were standard.

Among typical pottery forms on the lowland are jugs with a tall cylindrical neck and two high handles, and globular bellied flasks; decoration is often excised and encrusted in large geometrical patterns, especially herring-bone (maybe indicating a Coţofeni ancestry) or burnished brown with applied lugs and nipples.[99] A related pottery style is named by the Romanians the style 'with successive impressions', as found at Craciuneşti (Hunedoara).

In Transylvania the material from the Schneckenberg has been divided into three phases, but these divisions were typological and not founded on stratigraphical observations;[100] the sequence at Cuciulata is thus very important. There is no evidence at this site for the separate existence of a third phase.[101]

The most important single find at Cuciulata, however, was a clay model waggon, which came from level I. This piece, which is rectangular, made in coarse clay, and undecorated, is one of a large group of such pieces.[102] Other examples come from Wietenberg and Otomani sites,[103] and that from Cuciulata is demonstrably the earliest of the group; a connection with the Hungarian examples of the Baden culture is therefore unlikely. It is reasonable to assume that these waggons and carts represent the actual types in use at the time they were made, and discussion invariably arises over the purpose of such models. They could be votive; they could be designer's models; most likely they were toys. A standard type seems to be represented, rectangular, with sloping sides, fixed axles, and wheels fixed to them so that the whole axle turned, revolving in a projecting ring or 'ear' at each lower corner of the cart (fig. 51).

Miniature wheels were also found at Cuciulata and at many other earlier Bronze Age sites in Romania, especially of the Glina-Schneckenberg and Wietenberg groups, but also later on in sites of Tei, Monteoru and Otomani affinities. All these examples are solid, and one can imagine the weight of the originals they were copying. Bovines were probably used to draw the solid-wheeled carts, as well as for milk and food, while horses came into use during the later part of the earlier Bronze Age (cf. above, p. 99). At Cuciulata all the cow bones are from mature animals, though the breed was apparently a small one.[104]

A related group recently identified in Transylvania is named after old finds at Jigodin, but better known from the excavations at Leliceni (Sîncrăeni, Harghiţa).[105]

Returning to the site of Verbicioara south of the Carpathians, we have still the topmost stratum to consider. It is convenient to include various other local groups under the one heading, and refer to the 'two-handled bowl' complex, for material closely similar to that from Verbicioara has turned up at many sites throughout lowland Romania and north Bulgaria.[106]

Settlements of this phase in lowland Romania are well-known. Verbicioara material occurs on tell sites occupied since the early Neolithic; sites with Tei material are found near water on raised terraces or hilltops, and are characterized by an abundance of tools in the artifact assemblage.[107] Tei itself, though, was a lake-site (near Bucharest) with rather scanty evidence of pile-dwellings. Sites with material of Coslogeni type are found to the east of this, especially around Călăraşi, and are again near rivers.[108] The type-site (Grădiştea Coslogeni, 'La Cliçci', Dichişeni, Ialomiţa) lies in south-east Muntenia on a low hill, about 600 m × 300 m, between the Danube and its parallel tributary, the Borcea. The Bronze Age layers were stratified above Hamangia material in a metre-thick stratum, prolific in sherds and animal bones. Finally, in eastern Muntenia and Moldavia are the sites named after Monteoru: Sărata-Monteoru itself is a hill-fort (Buzău) at the extreme end of the Carpathian foothills overlooking a stream (the Sărata), and its local name, Cetăţuia (Citadel) reflects its commanding position.[109] It is a multi-phase monument, and the relationship of the different parts to each other is not yet fully known: it seems to have made use of box-like ramparts made either of wooden beams or of gravel-filled stone walls. In the interior of the fort were a number of house-platforms. In the north of Moldavia are the related finds of Costişa type;[110] at Costişa itself (Buhuşi, Bacău) there was a stratigraphical sequence in which pottery of middle Monteoru type overlay that typical of and restricted to Costişa, showing that the latter is but an early local variant of the former. Like Sărata-Monteoru it is a fortified site, in this case on a terrace on the left bank of the river Bistriţa, and made defensible by cross-ditches; similar sites occur north of the border in Podolia and Soviet Moldavia where they are named after the site of Bilij Potik (Čortkiv, Ternopol'), though cemeteries are at present the commoner in this group.

Of the funerary finds those of Zimnicea and Sărata-Monteoru are outstanding. At Zimnicea (Teleorman) recent excavations have revealed a cemetery of sixty-four inhumations, later used by an Iron Age community;[111] the burials were contracted, most commonly on the left side, oriented east-west with the head to the west. In each grave-pit was a single skeleton, accompanied by one pot; occasional exceptions to this rule included the burial of a mother and baby and a couple of instances where two pots were found. In such a situation it is perhaps not surprising that only two pot-types occurred: the two-handled bowl, and globular one-handled jugs, both in a coarse slipped grey-brown fabric. Other cemeteries with material of this kind are as yet hardly known, but the distribution of the characteristic pottery suggests that they will turn up eventually.

At Sărata-Monteoru, we have the rare case of a cemetery lying beside the settlement, for four large grave groupings were found adjoining the citadel, and it has been possible to correlate the various phases of both. The burials were usually contracted inhumations on the left side, often oriented east-west; grave goods were typically a Monteoru bowl or cup, a bronze ornament (leaf earring, knob-headed pin with perforation, spiral finger-ring, or *Noppenring*) and beads, of stone or faience. More specialized forms include bone arrowheads with three barbs and bone plaques decorated with circles; more rarely stone hammers and mace-heads. In the northern part of the distribution cemeteries of tumuli contained contracted inhumations in cist or built stone structures, and the finds suggest a direct ancestry from the Globular Amphorae. At Popovci ('Ternopol'), for instance, stone battle-axes and cord-impressed pottery in Costişa-Bilij Potik shapes occurred in large slab-built cists.[112]

Material from these various groupings has led to multiple divisions of the sequence. Five phases have been distinguished within both Verbicioara and Tei.[113] An especially rich and important find of Verbicioara pottery came from Govora-sat,[114] where many whole vases were represented. In addition to the two-handled bowl (often with knob-terminations on the handles) one finds cups with globular body, flaring conical neck, applied 'warts', and a single handle, and hour-glass vases with rounded body, omphalos base, oval mouth, and groups of vertical incised lines. The surface is dark and burnished, with profuse incised or 'stabbed' decoration, often encrusted with white paint (fig. 49). The shapes of Tei pottery are similar; ornamentation includes simple zig-zags, bands of parallel lines, 'stabbed' decoration, but no spirals.[115] In the Coslogeni group pottery is much less common and mainly known from sherds of domestic vessels on habitation sites: it is also usually unornamented. High-handled cups with knob terminations indicate a general affinity to the rest of the group. That the potters of Coslogeni were concerned with functional objects for immediate practical use is shown by a huge storage vessel from the site at Călăraşi, decorated with a large incised zig-zag on the neck and an incised horseshoe pattern with attendant dots above each of the four handles and the four knobs. Such a vessel, presumably for grain storage, must attest grain production on a very considerable scale. Two main fabrics were noted by the excavators: one coarse and porous, usually grey, the other finer with a polished surface, brick-red or maroon in colour.

The phases of Monteoru are many and complicated, for the type-site has a long stratigraphy. It is, nonetheless, clear that two main divisions may be made.[116] There are many features in Monteoru pottery that link it with Verbicioara-Tei, and equally some that indicate affinity with Coslogeni. In addition to the commoner domestic forms, such specialized shapes as storeyed *askoi* and pointed-base vases appear, no doubt connected with similar vessels in the Bulgarian series. Handles may be high and thick or channelled, knobbed, pointed, ledge and so on, a sure indication of relation to the Bulgarian-Macedonian province. Surface decoration is incised, and a characteristic repertoire of motifs sets

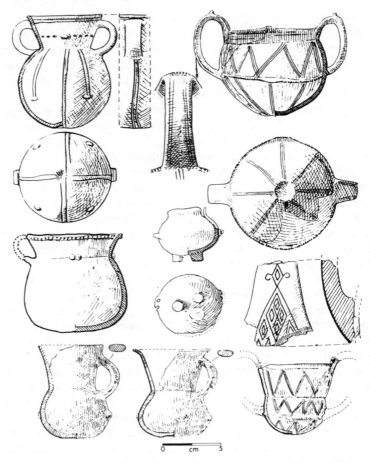

Fig. 49   Verbicioara (Dolj). Pottery from the upper (Verbicioara) stratum. (After Berciu 1961)

Monteoru aside as a regional group: pendent festoons (very popular), oblique parallel lines, vertical and horizontal bands, wavy lines and so on. In the northern area, the two-handled bowl is squatter, but otherwise still has the pendent triangles and elaborate knob-handles. The fabric, unlike that from most other Early Bronze Age pottery groups in Romania, is light and unburnished. Metal finds are not plentiful; in addition to those mentioned above (p. 143) we may add willow-leaf ornaments and spectacle pendants.

In Jugoslavia, the 'two-handled bowl complex' or 'Kantharos culture' is represented by the group of sites named after Vatin (Vattina) in the

Banat, which we discuss more fully in chapter 4. Some of the traditions of Vatin continue in the succeeding groups, which are remarkable for the fineness of their ceramic art. They are found along both banks of the Danube between Oltenia and south Hungary – that is, in north-west Bulgaria, western Oltenia, and the Banat on both sides of the Jugoslav-Romanian border. Its best-known manifestations – in Romania at any rate – occur rather late in the period we are considering, straddling the border between earlier and later Bronze Age; if we include some of these developed sites here it should not be forgotten that in the earliest phases things were rather different. In Romania this group is named after the urn cemetery of Gîrla Mare (Dolj) on an island in the Danube, Cîrna and Ostrovul Mare (Dolj);[117] in Jugoslavia the group is called Dubovac-Žuto Brdo, after the type-sites close to the Romanian border, and the most important finds have come from Korbovo (Negotin).[118]

In Jugoslavia, not a lot is known about the details of this group, though rich ceramic material, including figurines, has been recovered.[119] In Romania sites are on flat terraces above rivers, like Gîrla Mare on the Danube; fortified sites do not occur. A great deal is known about the funeral rite. The site of Cîrna[120] lies by a stream south of lake Cîrna in an area periodically flooded by the Danube. There were originally more than 200 tombs, containing over 500 vases; the rite was by cremation, in urns, which were put in pits something over a metre deep. The standard contents were an urn containing the ashes, with two or three accessory vessels, including a bowl used as a lid, two-handled bowls, cups and so on (fig. 50). In one case two lids had been put on an urn, with other vases in between. Most of the burials are single but there are a few cases of double and even triple burial; there is also some evidence of horizontal stratigraphy, for the latest burials lie closest to the water's edge. Differential wealth is also clearly observable, for at Cîrna forty-two of the graves contained only one vase and were classed as 'poor', fifty-four were of 'medium wealth', fifteen were 'rich', and five 'very rich' – numerous vases, metalwork and figurines being found in them (fig. 50).

The material culture of the group is rich and varied. The most characteristic forms of the early phase are the two-handled bowl – often having peaked rim and fluted belly, simple one-handled cups, conical lids for 'hanging vases' which are pedestalled with globular fluted body, and ovoid pots with two small handles at the neck. Later on one finds globular urns with cylindrical or funnel neck, two-handled amphoroid urns, often with peaked rim, conical bowls, commonly with pedestal foot and peaked rim, and globular cups and jugs with cylindrical neck, pedestal base and furrowed handle. Features like the pedestal bowl with peaked rim indicate clearly a synchronism with the central European Tumulus groups, but

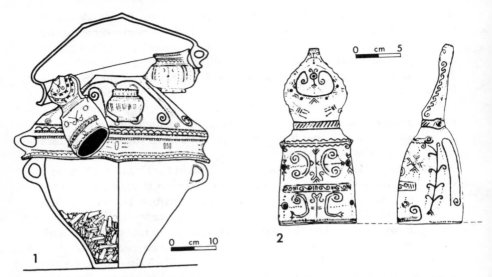

Fig. 50   Cîrna (Dolj), material from cremation cemetery. 1. Urn with accessory vessels, 2. Figurine.
(After Dumitrescu 1961)

the decoration is purely local. It is mostly incised, cord-impressed or stamped, and it is invariably encrusted with white paint. The motifs include arcading, garlands, pendent spirals, zig-zags, floral bands, dots, dot-and-circle designs, sun motifs etc. – a repertoire almost rivalling (and in many respects appearing very similar to) what is found on Mycenaean pottery. Zoomorphic vases do occur, but in general the figurines for which the culture is so famous appear later on (below, p. 408). In bronzework one may find moon and heart pendants, rings and bracelets, *Hülsennadeln,* seal-headed pins and other ornaments (though these are not well-preserved in the cremation cemeteries we are considering); in contemporary hoards one finds flanged axes, shaft-tube axes, tutuli and so on. These features all become more pronounced and elaborate with the passing of the centuries.

Transylvania was occupied by a completely different cultural group during this time. As one travels north-west from Braşov, crossing the Olt near Cuciulata, one moves out of the area in which Schneckenberg sites occur. From the top of the clock-tower of the beautiful German town of Sighişoara one can see to the west a spur of land projecting from the line of hills along the valley of the Tîrnava Mare. Closer up one can see that this hill has a flat plateau-like summit and banks and terraces on the west side (pl. 2). This hill is the Dealul Turcului ('Hill of the Turks') or

Wietenberg, and on it excavations before the First World War revealed traces of extensive settlement that gives its name to, and remains typical of, a cultural group that covers almost all of Transylvania through the earlier part of the Bronze Age.[121]

Regrettably little is known about the actual settlement of Wietenberg.[122] The early excavations exposed a large area but found nothing in the way of house-plans; there were, however, many pits which, as was the fashion, were interpreted as dwelling-pits but which we can safely assume were first for storage and later for rubbish. The famous plaster hearth, decorated with running spirals (discussed below), lay in the centre of the plateau but apparently unassociated with any structures. The plateau is about 190 m × 90 m at its widest point, and cut off from the rest of the spur system by a ditch and bank (pl. 2, lower). Cuttings through the dividing bank on the neck of the spur and straight down the slope of the hill showed that the Bronze Age occupation was confined to the very summit and did not extend beyond to the adjacent plateau-top, unlike the later La Tène occupation. It would be reasonable, then, to see the Wietenberg as a *Höhensiedlung* or hill settlement, not as a hill-fort; but its occupiers can hardly have been unaware of its defensive possibilities, and its commanding position must have served it in good stead in time of upheaval. The situation of the Wietenberg is typical of Wietenberg sites in general which tend to be on medium-sized hills beside rivers and are not fortified.[123] Another typical site, recently excavated, is Derşida near Bobota (Sălaj) in north-west Romania and thus well separate from the focal area of Wietenberg settlement.[124] The site is at the 'Dealul lui Balotă', a gentle hill some 200–250 m high on the right bank of the river Crasna, and is especially important in showing a deep stratigraphic succession. Five phases were distinguished, and this is important for an understanding of the development of the pottery, and of the house-types. The lowest level (phase I) contained three 'dwelling pits' of irregular oval shape up to 9 m long; one or more rubbish or storage pits lay at the end of the long axis, and hearths were found inside lying directly on the natural earth. This was succeeded by a level (phase II) characterized by fairly large pit houses with open hearth and central storage pit; here there was evidence of posts, though not in any particular plan. Level 3 (also phase II) produced evidence of stout post constructions, and in this and the succeeding levels 2 and 1 there were many and various storage pits with a rubbish fill. The excavator claims to be able to see this as a full and legitimate house development, but one must again express reservations about the concept of the 'pit-dwelling'. Similar observations, however, have recently been made at other sites, like Palatca (Cluj).[125]

Wietenberg funerary sites are relatively few. A cemetery of thirty-eight cremations is known from Bistriṭa (Cluj): these were inurned and accompanied by rich ceramic, though no metal, finds.[126] At Obreja (Mihalṭ, Alba) on the other hand, the body was inhumed in a contracted position in a pit.[127] At Vinṭu de Jos and Sibişeni (Alba) cemeteries involving both rites are definitely known,[128] though cremation was apparently the dominant type. Finally, a cemetery at Ocna Sibiului contained fourteen cremation urns, and among the ashes were small bone plates and accessory vases, covered by lids or sandstone slabs.[129]

The main area of distribution of Wietenberg sites is central Transylvania, especially along the Mureş.[130] It is arguable whether true Wietenberg sites are found outside Transylvania: Monteoru sites with Wietenberg material on them are regarded as a separate group that should not be included with the main corpus.[131] Well over 200 sites are known, the vast majority in central and north-central Transylvania; the visitor to the storerooms of Alba Iulia museum cannot fail to be impressed with the quantity of material from Wietenberg sites. This is a cultural group remarkable for its abundance, its uniformity over a wide area, and for the contrast between its rich pottery and its poor – almost non-existent – houses and graves.

Very characteristic of Wietenberg pottery is the decoration, especially in bands which may be infilled with vertical or diagonal lines and dots and form meanders (both square and spiral), and in channelling and incision, which are so arranged as to produce elaborate spiraliform and other geometric motifs.[132] Eleven main categories of vase-shape have been distinguished, of which the most characteristic are the 'peaked bowls', the flat plates, the fluted one-handled cups, and the various theriomorphic forms, including vases with multiple mouths, with bird and animal heads, etc. The stratigraphic results from Derşida have enabled a general development to be discerned.[133]

Finds of stone and bone are numerous on Wietenberg sites; the type-site has produced a long and well-documented series of stone implements, while metal, though undoubtedly in common use during the life-time of Wietenberg, is not normally found in association with settlement material. The stonework usually consists of small celts, perforated hammers and hammer-axes, mace-heads and knobbed club-heads (*Buckelkeule*), and curved knives (*Krummesser*), in addition to small pounders, querns, whetstones and so on. There is also a great quantity of bonework on Wietenberg sites, used for awls, needles, knobs, handles, arrowheads and so on; a recent find of interest and importance is that of a 'sceptre' of bone from Lancrăm (Alba).[134] It has a large transverse perforation and a knob on the side, but the decoration is the most important – compass-drawn dot-and-circles, 'pulley motifs', dentated bands, and so on; these are also found on horse-harness cheek-pieces (one from Wietenberg itself).[135] Further evidence for transportation comes in the form of model carts (fig. 51).

No description of Wietenberg material would be complete without mention of the famous hearth from the type-site. It was found 0.6 m below the surface in the very middle of the settlement, and is made of a grey-white cement-like fabric. It is estimated to have been 1.5 m across originally, though now it is much broken. Round the outside runs a circle of large running spirals in the Wietenberg style (that is, made up of groups of parallel channellings); this is separated by a double border of three lines from another similar circle of smaller spirals. Inside this is a zig-zag pattern made by excision, leaving the pattern standing out in relief; while in the middle is a clear open circle 0.5 m across.

There are two interesting aspects to this hearth. The first concerns its significance in its local context. It was surely no ordinary fire-place – traces of burning are nowhere mentioned. It has been suggested that it had an astronomical use: the inner ring of spirals has thirteen parts, while the innermost ring of zig-zags may have had fifty-two notches, very convenient (if correct) for measuring a 52-week, 13-month, 364-day year. Quite why the outer circle consists of ten spirals is not clear, though; nor is it easy to support the idea that the hearth was 'oriented according to the four directions of the heavens', seeing that it is round. An interpretation as an offering table is preferable.[136] A fragment of a second

Fig. 51   Model carts from Wietenberg and Otomani sites. 1. Vărşand, 2. Novaj, 3. Wietenberg.
(After Bóna 1961)

hearth, similarly decorated, was found 7.5 m to the south of the first. The second point of importance concerns the fact of decoration with running spirals, for this is always seen as a link with the Mycenaean, or at any rate Aegean, world; the great hearth from the megaron at Pylos has running spirals painted on its plaster.[137] The form of decoration on the Wietenberg hearths is, however, purely in the local style and identical to that found on ceramic productions. The question thus becomes a more general one: were the artistic styles of Transylvania influenced by those of the Aegean world? Vases had been decorated with spirals for centuries before the Bronze Age started; so that it seems wisest to regard any connection with the Aegean on the basis of spiraliform decoration as being of a very general nature, and not the result of direct influence.

Transylvania, rich in metal ores, is naturally also a centre of metallurgical production, and the variety and quantity of objects produced was very considerable from the start of the Bronze Age. The main problem is that of tying the metal forms into their cultural position, for metal finds are usually rare on settlement sites. In goldwork, we may mention the famous hoards from Ţufalău and Şmig (fig. 52) with axes, gold discs, necklace of lock-rings, spirally-wound wire, cylindrical beads, and lumps of gold.[138] Drop-shaped earrings were also common, and occur too at Sărata-Monteoru. In bronzes, especially important were the disc-butted axes (*Nackenscheibenäxte*) which are extremely numerous both in Romania and in Hungary. Several types have been distinguished.[139] One famous hoard containing these is that from Ighiel (Alba): they were richly decorated on the disc-butt, and the find also included spiral leg-rings.[140] Solid-hilted swords, like those from the hoard of Apa (Satu Mare, Maramureş) are well-known, though not many in numbers (fig. 53).[141] Other forms include rather simple triangular daggers, flat axes, knot-, seal- and sphere-headed pins and a group of hilt-less rapiers which have long been considered to be of Mycenaean inspiration. Detailed comparison, however, coupled with the fact that one of these has been found in a Br D – Ha A hoard in Bulgaria (1200–1000 bc) makes this extremely unlikely. Finally we may mention the finds of moulds that occasionally turn up: they are not at all common in most of Romania, and only in the Banat does any substantial number occur.[142] Elsewhere, the odd find of disc-butted axe moulds in stone makes the lack of them the more obvious.

Chronology

Radiocarbon dates, though few and far between for this area, indicate a start to the Bronze Age on the lower Danube in the later centuries of the

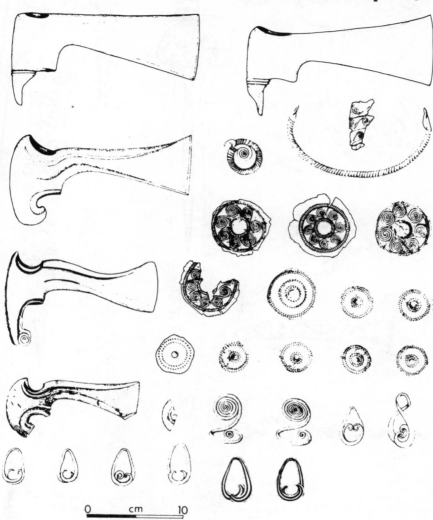

Fig. 52 Ţufalău (Trei-Scaune), hoard of gold axes, discs and earrings.
(After Hachmann 1957)

third millennium bc, and a transition from it by 1400 bc (table 5). The
evidence from cross-dating is not extensive in this area, and depends
either on direct cultural links (as between Bulgaria and Macedonia) or on
assumed contact between high 'barbarian' cultures such as those in
Transylvania and centres of civilization in the Aegean, as shown
particularly by spiral designs on goldwork (especially discs). The pieces

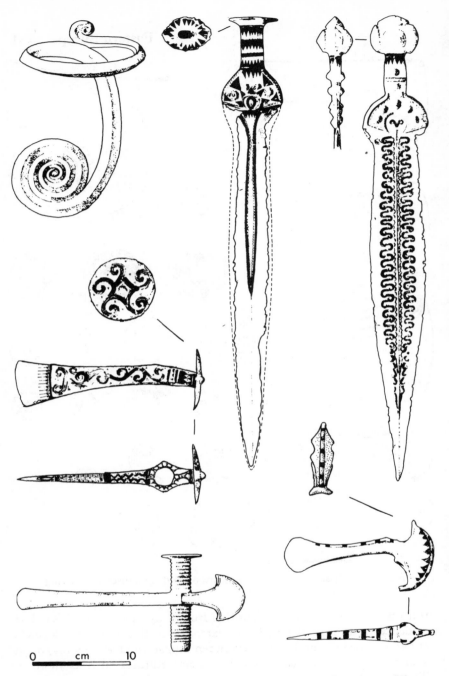

Fig. 53 Apa (Satu Mare). Hoard of bronze swords, axes and arm-ring.
(After Hachmann 1957)

from Ostrovul Mare, Țufalău and Șmig are cases in point.[143] These designs, however, though admittedly very similar to those on Mycenaean objects (especially from the Shaft Graves of Mycenae), can in fact be seen to be part of a local school of artistic production: the spirals on the discs from Ostrovul Mare, for instance, are identical to those on Wietenberg pottery, similar – but not identical – to those on Mycenaean material. The same is true for the spiral designs on the Apa and Hajdúsámson swords. No great chronological significance can, then, be imparted to these pieces showing 'artistic' connections with the south; but a date in the mid-second millennium BC is perfectly plausible.[144]

Table 5 Radiocarbon dates, eastern Europe, earlier Bronze Age

Site	Lab no.	bc
Late Tripillja/Usatove		
Majaki (Beljaevka, Odessa)	Bln–629	2450±100
,,	LE–645	2390±65
Danku (Kotovsk, Moldavia), burial pit	LE–1054	2650±60
Pit Grave[145]		
Michajlivka (Cherson), site 1, early PG	Bln–630	2380±100
,,	LE–355	2100±150
Caca (Volgograd), kurgan 6, grave 3	UCLA–1270	2260±80
Us'man (Rostov), kurgan 1, grave 13	UCLA–1271	2200±80
Girejeva (Rostov)	RUL–136	1920±130
Borisovka (Tatarbunary, Odessa)	LE–856	1970±50
Demitrovsk (Dnepropetrovsk),		
,, kurgan 10, grave 12	LE–824	1970±50
,, kurgan 1, grave 5	LE–822	1900±90
,, kurgan 1, grave 16	LE–823	1730±60
Catacomb Grave		
Rostov, kurgan 6, grave 12	Bln–694	2265±100
,, kurgan 6, grave 11	Bln–697	2115±120
,, kurgan 1, grave 5	Bln–696	2055±100
,, kurgan 5, grave 6	Bln–693	1975±160
,, kurgan 7, grave 3	LE–624	1930±90
Kudinov (Rostov), kurgan 2, grave 6	UCLA–1273	1910±80
Komarov		
Ivanja (Rovno)[146]	GrN–	1285±35
Sosnicja		
Pustinka (Černigiv)[147]	KI–	1190±100

Table 5—cont.

Site	Lab no.	bc
Middle Dnieper and related		
Krasnoe Selo (Volkovysk, Grodno), flint mines		
,, Shaft 125	LE–799	1640±150
,, Shaft 13	GIN–148	2360±45
,, Shafts 2, 3 and 12	LE–636	1240±60
,, Shaft 12	LE–680	1420±50
,, Shaft 106	LE–915	1560±110
Karpovci (Volkovysk, Grodno), flint mines		
,, Shafts 1, 2 and 4	LE–913	1400±80
,, Shaft 5	LE–914	1540±70
,, Shaft 13	LE–1032	1050±30
Krivina (Bešenkoviči Vitebsk) bottom of cultural layer		
	LE–757	1930±60
	LE–1062	1850±60
,, ,, ,, Osovec site II (Bešenkoviči, Vitebsk)	LE–936	1930±80
,, ,,	LE–756	1400±60
,, ,, Kut (Zozov, Rovno)	LE–753	1550±50
	GIN–152	2140±80
Bulgaria		
Tell Dipsis, Ezero (Nova Zagora) series[148]		
Occupation horizon I–4, average of 3 tests:		2300
,, ,, I–6, average of 2 tests:		2370
,, ,, I–7, average of 6 tests:		2485
,, ,, I–8, average of 3 tests:		2455
,, ,, I–9, average of 3 tests:		2375
,, ,, I–10, average of 3 tests:		2290
Varna, lake sites	KI–89	2260±60
Macedonia		
Sitagroi (Drama), phase Vb, average of 4 tests:[149]		1980
,, phase Va	Bln–877	2220±100
,, phase Va	BM–652	1853±59
,, phase IV–Va	Bln–782	2360±100
,, phase IV	BM–650a	2413±56
,, phase IV	BM–651	2382±79

Notes

1 C. Burney and D. M. Lang, *The Peoples of the Hills*, 1971.
2 J. Dewdney, *A Geography of the Soviet Union*, 1972, 4f., 33ff.
3 Copper occurs especially in the north around Baia Mare, at Balan, in the Dobrogea, and in other parts of Transylvania. Some idea of the extent of the deposits of eastern and east-central Europe may be gauged from M. Maczek, E. Preuschen and R. Pittioni, *Arch. Aust.* 12 (1953), 67ff. Tin is mentioned by Berciu (1967,16) but not by J. Dayton, *World Archaeology* 3 (1971), 49–70.
4 J. R. Greig and J. Turner, *JAS* 1 (1974), 177–94.
5 H. E. Wright in *The Minnesota Messenia Expedition: Reconstructing a Bronze Age Regional Environment* (ed. W. A. Macdonald and G. R. Rapp), 1972, 188–9.
6 N. A. Chotinskij, *ZfA* 10 (1976), 161–72; id and D. A. Krajnov, *SA* (1977/3), 42ff., figs. 1–3. Full documentation for each area is to be found in M.I. Nejštadt, *Istorija lesov i paleogeografija SSSR v golocene*, 1957. Nejštadt's scheme on p. 18 (Hl₃ = Sub-boreal); deciduous forest zone, 150ff.; Eurasian steppe zone, 191ff.; European-Siberian forest-steppe zone, 172ff.; 'Mediterranean forest' zone, 207. Summary of events in the Middle Holocene, 357-66. Cf. too *Paleopalinologija*, vol II, ed. I. M. Pokrovskaja, 1966 (translation published by NLLST Boston Spa, 1970), 399ff.; fig. 6 (p. 406) shows twenty-five of Nejštadt's different types of regional diagram.
   Of less use, though with details of many pollen sequences from Belorussia, is N. A. Machnač, *Etapy razvitija rastitel'nosti Belorussii v antropogene*, 1971 (Stages of the Development of the Vegetation of the Byelorussia during Anthropogen [sic]).
7 The main work in Romania has been that of E. Pop, who first synchronized the Romanian sequence with the central European. See E. Pop, V. Lupşa and N. Boşcaiu in *Progrese în palinologia românească*, *Simpozionul de palinologie*, Cluj 1970 (1971), 219–25 for a table and bibliography; also other articles in this volume. Lake Varna: E. Božilova and M. Filipova, *INMV* 11 (1975), 19–25.
8 On this area in general, Ja. Pasternak, *Archeologija Ukrajini* (Toronto 1961); Gimbutas 1965, 389ff.; T. Sulimirski, *BIA* 7 (1968), 43–83; Sulimirski 1970, 147ff. (ch. 3), and review by L. S. Klejn, *PPS* 40 (1974), 211ff.; *Archeologija Ukrajins'koj RSR*, vol. 1, 1971, 288ff.; *Eneolit i bronzovyj vek Ukrainy*, 1976; cf. general studies on specific areas, e.g. A. A. Ščepinskij, *SA* (1966/2), 10–23 (the Crimea).
9 E.g. R. Tringham, *Hunters, Farmers and Fishers of Eastern Europe, 6000–3000 B.C.*, 1971, 195ff.
10 Sulimirski 1970, 171, after T. Passek, *MIA* 10 (1949), 132, fig. 70.
11 V. I. Selinov and E. F. Lagodovskaja, *SA* 5 (1940), 239–63.
12 A. I. Meljukova, *KSIAM* 88 (1962), 74–83.
13 E. F. Patokova, *KSAMO* 1961, (1963), 12–16; 1962 (1964), 102–123.
14 V. G. Zbenovič, *KSAMO* 1962 (1964), 37–45; V. Selinov and E. Lagodovskaja, *SA* 5 (1940), 257ff.
15 V. G. Zbenovič, *AK* 20 (1966), 38–46.
16 T. S. Passek, *MIA* 10 (1949), ch. 6, fig. 97.
17 E. N. Černych, *UISPP* – IXᵉ Congrès, Colloque XXIII, 1976, 190.
18 T. S. Passek, *MIA* 10 (1949), 194ff. with refs., esp. notes 75, 76, 80 etc.
19 Sulimirski 1970, 183f.

20 V. G. Zbenovič and A. M. Leskov, *KSIAM* 115 (1969), 29–38.

21 Sulimirski 1970, 176ff.

22 I. I. Artemenko, *KSIAM* 88 (1962), 64–73; cf. too S. S. Berezans'ka, *AK* 17 (1964), 170ff.; *AK* 20 (1966), 47–57, with analysis of the pottery. The discussion by I. I. Artemenko in *MIA* 148 (1967) is a comprehensive study which clearly shows the Chalcolithic basis of most of this material.

23 I. I. Artemenko, *MIA* 148 (1967), 53ff. fig. 41.

24 V. Petrov and E. Kričevskii, in *Tripils'ka kultura*, 1940, 339–451.

25 M. M. Šmaglij, *Zapiski Odesskogo Arch. Obščestva I*, 34 (1960), 302–8 (quoted Sulimirski 1968a, 53); *AK* 20 (1966), 15–37.

26 M. M. Šmaglij, *AK* 13 (1961), 20–37, (esp. 22 n. 11).

27 T. G. Movša, *SA* (1964/1), 131–45.

28 Sulimirski 1970, 173f., 176 fig. 41.

29 Sulimirski 1968b.

30 Sulimirski 1970, 158.

31 Komarów, the type-site, was excavated by Sulimirski in the 1930s while the area was under Polish administration.

32 Recent detailed studies of the Trzciniec-Komarov group in the Ukraine: I. K. Svešnikov (Swiesznikow), *Arch. Polski* 12 (1967), 39–107; S. S. Berezans'ka, *SA* (1967/2), 120–36; Vojcechivka: O. Lagodovs'ka, *AK* 2 (1948), 62–78; O. Lagodovs'ka and Ju. M. Zacharuk, *AP* 6 (1956), 69–74.

33 A. Gardawski, in *Beiträge* (1969), 81, fig. 13 (Nezvika).

34 T. Sulimirski, *BIA* 4 (1964), 171–188; Sulimirski 1968b, 105ff.

35 I. K. Svešnikov, *SA* (1968/2), 159–168.

36 Detailed studies: S. S. Berezans'ka, *KSIAK* 10 (1960), 36–47, esp. 41ff.

37 S. S. Berezans'ka, *AK* 23 (1970), 152–61; id., *Pustynka, poselenie epochi bronzy na Dnepre*, 1974.

38 S. S. Berezans'ka, *AK* 11 (1957),

87–94; M. B. Barbon and S. S. Berezans'ka, *AK* 23 (1970), 162–5.

39 V. A. Il'inskaja, *KSIAK* 10 (1960), 48–58.

40 R. Rogozińska, *Mat. Arch.* 1 (1959), 97–114.

41 E.g. Gimbutas 1965, 71ff., figs, 35–37; Sulimirski 1970, 159, map XV (cf. too *BIA* 4 (1964), 186ff.).

42 M. B. Barbon and S. S. Berezans'ka, *AK* 23 (1970), 162–5, figs 2–3.

43 O. A. Krivcova-Grakova, *Bessarabskij Klad*, 1949; Hachmann 1957, 170ff., 221, pl. 67; Gimbutas 1965, 65f., pl. 12; V. A. Safronov, *Problemy Archeologii* 1 (1968), 75–128; V. S. Bočkarov, *Problemy Archeologii* 1 (1968), 129–54.

44 E.g. Häusler 1974.

45 Gimbutas 1956, 70ff.; 1965, 21ff.

46 Sulimirski 1970, 223ff.

47 Ju. O. Šilov, *AK* n.s. 17 (1975), 53–61; Sulimirski 1970, 227f.; E. Černych, *UISPP*, IXe Congrès, Nice 1976, Colloque XXIII, 192.

48 V. D. Rybalova, *Arch. Sbor.* 16 (1974), 19–49. The site spans the transition from Catacomb to timber grave periods, and is not typical of earlier Catacomb settlements.

49 A. V. Dobrovolskij *KSIAK* 7 (1957), 40–5. Sites with pottery like that at Babine III are usually described as belonging to the area of 'multiple-cordoned' pottery.

50 Detailed description and analysis of Pit and Catacomb Graves: Häusler 1974. Divided into (a) Donec area, (b) Volga-Ural area, (c) Volga-Don area, (d) North Azov area and bend of the Dnieper, (e) Moločnaja valley, (f) northern area. Detailed examination of grave form, orientation etc. Clear differences between true Catacomb Graves and ordinary Pit Graves are established, but the difficulty of working with the poor information obtained by Gorodcov is stressed. Häusler believes, as we do and as the radiocarbon dates bear out, that Catacomb

Graves were a grave form for a particular element of the population, and were contemporary with Pit Graves. For other groupings: O. G. Šapošnikova, *Archeologija Ukrajinskoj RSR*, 1971, 320ff. (Donec, Charkiv-Voronež, Azov-Crimea; Dnieper-steppe.); *Origini* 3 (1969), 85–118.

51 Notably O. A. Krivcova-Grakova, *Genetičeskaja svjaz jamnoj i katakombnoj kul'tury*, *Trudy GIM* 8 (1938), 33–8; T. B. Popova, *Plemena katakombnoj kul'tury*, 1955; Häusler 1974, 49ff.

52 Notably S. S. Berezanskaja and O. G. Šapošnikova, *SA* (1957/2), 273; L. S. Klejn, *SAA* 1/4 (1963), 27–37; *SA* (1970/1), 49–57.

53 I. I. Artemenko, *MIA* 148 (1967).

54 I. I. Artemenko, *Pamjatniki kamennego i bronzovego vekov v Evrazii*, 1963, 46f., figs 10–11; quoted Sulimirski 1970, 192ff., figs 46–7.

55 E.g. Ja. G. Rier, *SA* (1975/3), 141–148 on axes from the Mogilev district of White Russia.

56 I. I. Artemenko, *KSIAM* 93 (1963), 57 (cemetery of Oločino, Kesovo-Gorsk, Kalinin). On Fat'janovo generally, D. A. Krajnov, *Archeologija SSR*, V, 1–19 and V, 1–20, *Pamjatniki fat'janovskoj kultury* (1963 and 1964).

57 O. N. Bader, *SA* (1971/1), 55–72. The plate wrist-bands are very similar to those recently published from Nový Bydžov in Bohemia: V. Moucha, *PA* 65 (1974), 244–53.

58 O. N. Bader, *KSIIMK* 75 (1959), 143–53; quoted Sulimirski 1970, 199.

59 P. M. Kozin, *SA* (1963/3), 25–37; *MIA* 130 (1965), 124–7; J. Ozols, *Ursprung und Herkunft der zentralrussischen Fatjanowo Kultur*, 1962, 74ff.

60 The date of the Borodino hoard is much discussed. Reinecke attributed it to the Iron Age (*Germania* 9 (1925), 52), but most authors have put it about the time of the Shaft Graves – 16th–15th centuries BC, e.g. Hachmann 1957, 172; Gimbutas 1965, 65. Sulimirski (1970, 341) attributes it to the time of the 'Timber Grave expansion', c. 13th century. The detailed analysis by V. A. Safronov and V. S. Bočkarov in *Problemy Archeologii* 1 (1968) has similarly produced a divergence of opinion between 15th–14th and 13th centuries.

61 J. L. Caskey, *CAH* 3rd edn, vol. I, part 2, 1971, chapter 26a; vol. II, part 1, 1973, chapter 4a.

62 Heurtley 1939, 17ff., 79ff., 166ff.

63 C. Renfrew, *PPS* 36 (1970), 295ff., esp. 302 and fig. 8.

64 C. Renfrew, *Antiquity* 44 (1970), 131–4.

65 Prehistoric material is known in small quantities from Mesimvria in west Thrace (*Ergon* 1970, 66, figs 64–5), from the cave of Maroneia (*Ergon* 1971, 94–104, figs 119–120), from Paradimi, and from Python and Asar Tepe on the Turkish border. Elsewhere a few sherds occur: D. Theocharis, *Prehistory of Eastern Macedonia and Thrace*, Ancient Greek Cities vol. 9 (n.d.).

66 Heurtley 1939, 89ff., 204ff.

67 Heurtley 1939, 93ff., 214ff., esp. nos. 403, 405, 427, 435, 449.

68 G. Georgiev, in *L'Europe à la fin de l'âge du pierre*, 1961, 87–9 and Beil. A and B.

69 E.g. vessels of Trojan type (*depas amphikupellon*) from Michalič (Svilengrad): V. Mikov, *Razkopki i proučvani ja* 1 (1948), 20ff., fig. 12.

70 P. Detev, *IAI* 17 (1950), 171–90.

71 G. I. Georgiev and N. Ja. Merpert, *IAI* 28 (1965), 129–59; *Arch.* 8/3 (1966), 10–15; *Antiquity* 40 (1966), 33–7; *Arch. Aust.* 42 (1967), 90; R. Katinčarov, *Arch.* 16/1 (1974), 3 fig. 1; Katinčarov 1975, 91ff. Another tell site that continues through to the Bronze Age but no further is Azmak (Stara Zagora):

G. I. Georgiev, *Arch.* 4/1, (1962), 59–65.

72 R. Katinčarov, *Thracia* 1 (1972), 53; *Arch.* 16/1 (1974), 4–5, figs 2–3; *Arch.* 17/2 (1975), 5; Katinčarov 1975, 96f.

73 Since the Burnt House at Sitagroi is said to have contained pottery akin to Troy I, it may be too early to be considered in this connection. On the other hand the presence of apsidal-ended houses in EH III at Lefkandi and Lerna would seem to fit with the Bulgarian examples very closely, and may lend support to the supposed northern or north-eastern connections of Middle Helladic, where apsidal-ended houses are standard.

74 N. Džambazov and R. Katinčarov, *Arch.* 3/3 (1961), 56–64; *IAI* 34 (1974), 107–38.

75 G. Tončeva and A. Margos, *Arch.* 1/1 (1959), 96–99.

76 G. Tončeva and A. Margos, *IVAD* 12 (1961), 128–131; *IVAD* 13 (1962), 1–16; *INMV* 3 (1967), 3–19 (anthropomorphic stelae); *INMV* 9 (1973), 267–84; I. S. Ivanov, *INMV* 9 (1973), 285–8.

77 P. Detev, *GNAMP* 2 (1953–4), 101–10; the study is based on the material from Razkopanica, Kapitan Dimitrievo, Bikovo, Plovdiv. Cf. now Katinčarov 1975, 100ff.

78 P. Detev, *Arch.* 6/4 (1964), 66–70.

79 N. Džambazov and R. Katinčarov, *IAI* 34 (1974), 107–38.

80 R. Katinčarov, *IAI* 33 (1972), 71–77.

81 B. Nikolov, *Arch.* 18/3 (1976), 38–51.

82 G. Kitov and P. Pavlov, *Muzei i pamatniči na kulturata* 13/2 (1973), 4–9. Material in Loveč Museum.

83 R. Katinčarov, *Arch.* 17/2 (1975), 11f.; the finds from Bereket (Stara Zagora) remain unpublished. For continuity to later tombs: L. Getov, *IAI* 28 (1965), 203–29.

84 Cf. now the review articles by R. Katinčarov, *Arch.* 17/2 (1975), 1–17; Katinčarov 1975.

85 E. N. Černych, *UISPP* – IXᵉ Congrès, Nice 1976, Colloque XXIII, 183. Cf. too now the evidence for early mining activity in the Donec region of the Soviet Union: S. I. Tatarinov, *SA* (1977/4), 192–207.

86 E.g. Devnja: H. Todorova-Simeonova, *INMV* 7 (1971), 3–40; I. S. Ivanov, *INMV* 8 (1972), 246–59; graves with goldwork in *Thracian Treasures from Bulgaria* (London: British Museum, 1976), 27–8, and Iv. Ivanov, *Muzei i pamatniči na kulturata* 14 (1974), 44–7.

87 General summaries by Nestor (1932, 69–73, 94–104) and Berciu (1967, 67ff.). Gimbutas (1965, 218ff.) is concerned mainly with the Monteoru culture, which she sees as having 'definite roots in the Kurgan culture'.

88 The question of terminology and the transition to the Bronze Age is much discussed, e.g. by D. Popescu, *SCIV* 16 (1965), 129–48 and 323–340 and elsewhere; S. Morintz and P. Roman, *Dacia* n.s. 12 (1968), 45–128; P. Roman, *AAC* 15 (1975), 145–58; A. Vulpe, *SCIV* 24 (1973), 217–37.

89 Coţofeni is near Craiova (Dolj) in Oltenia. The characteristic pottery tends to be stratified above late Salcuţa or Cucuteni material. The sites are often on raised ground near rivers. The pottery is richly ornamented with deeply incised and stroked decoration in short multiple designs; shapes include the one-handled cup with rounded base and globular bowl with everted rim. Three phases have been distinguished.

90 Cernavoda is in the Dobruoge; the group has been identified by Berciu (*Sl.A.* 12 (1964), 269–80) as belonging to a wider grouping, including Ezero and Donja Slatina.

Both tell-sites and hill settlements are known. Radiocarbon dating indicates a lifetime in the third millennium bc.

91 M. Florescu, *Arh. Mold.* 2–3 (1964), 105ff., believes this to be among the earliest Bronze Age cultures in Moldavia; the stratigraphy at Bogdaneşti (Tîrgu Ocna, Bacău) and Mîndrişca (Adjud, Bacău) showed that it comes immediately before the Monteoru IC3 level.

92 Nestor 1932, 65ff. Ochre Grave tumuli contain contracted inhumations, sometimes multiple, and often with stone settings around the skeletons. Copper and silver objects occur, as at Decea-Mureşului (Alba) or Vládháza (Cacova).

93 D. Berciu, *SCIV* 12 (1961), 227–240; *Dacia* n.s. 5 (1961), 123–61.

94 P. Roman, *PZ* 51 (1976), 26–42; I. Nestor, *Dacia* o.s. 3–4 (1927–32), 226–52.

95 A. D. Alexandrescu, *Dacia* n.s. 18 (1974), 79–93.

96 G. Bichir, *Dacia* n.s. 6 (1962), 87–114. The term Schneckenberg culture was originally coined by Schroller and adopted by Nestor (1932, 69ff) and others. It is no accident that the culture is still known by its German name; this part of Transylvania is one of the most German-dominated and the scholars involved, Schroller and Prox, were both Germans. A 'proto-Schneckenberg phase' has now been identified: Z. Székely, *SCIV* 21 (1970), 201–8.

97 D. Popescu, *Dacia* n.s. 6 (1962), 519.

98 Popescu 1944, 47.

99 P. Roman, *PZ* 51 (1976), 30ff.

100 Prox 1941. Only the last phase was considered to be equivalent to full Bronze Age of Periam type.

101 G. Bichir, *Dacia* n.s. 6 (1962), 96ff.

Bichir has demonstrated that many of the forms of the first level at Cuciulata continue into the second; no evidence came to light for the existence of a third phase.

102 G. Bichir, *Dacia* n.s. 8 (1964), 67–86.

103 Wietenberg: the Wietenberg itself Pietriş-Gherla, Podei Lechinţa de Mureş; Otomani: Otomani-Cetăţuie, Vărşand-Movila dintre Vii.

104 G. Bichir, *Dacia* n.s. 8 (1964), 67ff. esp. 82.

105 P. Roman, P. Iános and C. Horváth, *SCIV* 24 (1973), 559–74.

106 Cf. Bóna 1975, 179ff.

107 Leahu 1966. Nestor (1932, 101–104) has the first description. Other important sites: Bucureşti-Noi, upper levels of Căscioarele (Ilfov) on the Danube, Fundeni, Baneasu and Catelu Nou. Tei material also occurs in south-east Transylvania, in a Wietenberg-like form: Popescu 1944, 80–88.

108 V. Leahu, *SCIV* 20 (1969), 17–32; S. Morintz and N. Anghelescu, *SCIV* 21 (1970), 373–415.

109 Nestor 1932, 95; more recent work on the site: I. Nestor, *SCIV* 1 (1950), 53–6; *SCIV* 2/1 (1951), 159–69; *SCIV* 4/1–2 (1953), 69–89; *SCIV* 6 (1955), 497–513; *Istoria României* I (1960), 100–5; cf. too Gimbutas 1965, 219, pl. 35, 1; Berciu 1967, 90ff., pl. 41.

110 A. Vulpe and M. Zamoşteanu, *MCA* 8 (1962), 309–16.

111 A. D. Alexandrescu, *Dacia* n.s. 17 (1973), 77–97. This cemetery should not be confused with the early Bronze Age graves from the same locality.

112 Ju. N. Zacharuk, *KSIAK* 8 (1959), 129–32.

113 Berciu 1961, Leahu 1966. Verbicioara extends from the east Banat and the Iron Gates to Muntenia, and from the Carpathians to north

Bulgaria (Devetaki): D. Berciu, *SCIV* 12 (1961), 227ff.

114 D. Berciu *et al.*, *MCA* 7 (1960), 134–7.

115 Leahu 1966; *SCIV* 14 (1963), 309–21.

116 M. Florescu, *Arh. Mold.* 4 (1966), 39–118. The subdivisions of Monteoru are many and complex. No clear statement of their meaning and origin is easily available, but Gimbutas (1965, 223) provides a useful comparative table. The earliest cemetery is no. 2, which corresponds to the end of Monteoru I (Ia); nos. 4, 3 and 1 follow in that order, corresponding to different parts of Monteoru II (IIa, IIb). In addition, finds from the so-called 'sacrificial area' and 'sanctuaries' cover a wide span, appearing early in each main phase. Berciu (1967, 91) identifies four main phases in the development of Monteoru and adopts a different system; it seems likely to cause confusion, however, and is not generally used.

117 Berciu 1967, 87–9.

118 Garašanin 1958, 82ff.; Brukner et al. 1974, 229ff. and note 163.

119 Garašanin 1958 85ff., pl. 18; V. Trbuhović and Z. Letica, *Starinar* n.s. 19 (1968), 47–57; S. Karmanski, *Nalezi bronzanodobske idoloplastike iz okoline Odžaka*, 1969.

120 Dumitrescu 1961.

121 Gimbutas 1965, 200; Horedt and Seraphin 1971, 12f. Gimbutas includes Wietenberg as part of the Otomani culture.

122 The recent book by Horedt and Seraphin (1971) is edited by Horedt from the large quantity of notes Seraphin left. One must hope that Horedt's own excavations will produce something more substantial. The banks visible on the west side are partly modern terraces.

123 Berciu 1967, 94.

124 N. Chidioşan, *Dacia* n.s. 12 (1968), 155–75.

125 T. Soroceanu, *Centenar Muzeul Oradean* (1972), 165–72.

126 I. Crişan and Şt. Dănilă, *MCA* 7 (1961), 145–50.

127 T. Soroceanu, *AMN* 10 (1973), 493–515; Berciu 1967, 96; Horedt and Seraphin 1971, 7f.

128 Horedt 1960, 114; *SCIV* 14 (1963), 455; Sibiu Museum.

129 Horedt 1960, 128.

130 Horedt 1960, fig. 4.

131 Horedt and Seraphin 1971, 12f.

132 Horedt 1960, 115ff.

133 N. Chidioşan, *Dacia* n.s. 12 (1968), 155–75.

134 I. A. Aldea, *Apulum* 11 (1973), 25–35.

135 Horedt 1960, fig. 13,10.

136 Horedt and Seraphin 1971, 74f.

137 C. Blegen *et al.*, *The Palace of Nestor at Pylos in western Messenia* vol I (Princeton, 1966), 85ff., figs 65–6, 73.

138 Popescu 1944, 131.

139 I. Nestor, in *Marburger Studien* (1938), 178–93.

140 Popescu 1944, 115ff., figs 50–1.

141 Popescu 1944, 122ff.

142 Popescu 1944, 73ff., figs 26–8.

143 Popescu 1944, 131.

144 Opposing views on the significance of the spiral ornament may be found in Vladár 1973 and A. F. Harding, *The Extent and Effects of Contact between Mycenaean Greece and the rest of Europe*, unpublished dissertation, Cambridge 1972.

145 See now 40 dates for Pit Graves listed by D. Ja. Telegin, *SA* (1977/2), 5–19.

146 I. K. Svešnikov, *SA* (1968/2), 167.

147 S. S. Berezanskaja, *Pustynka, poselenie epochi bronzy na Dnepre* (1974), 143.

148 H. Quitta and G. Kohl, *ZfA* 3 (1969), 229ff.

149 C. Renfrew, *Antiquity* 45 (1971), 276.

4   Southern Europe

Europe south of the Alps presents a very different face from those parts we have been considering so far, and the nature of the Bronze Age is correspondingly different. We include in this chapter Italy and most of the countries or areas that adjoin it – Jugoslavia and Albania to the east; Switzerland to the north; the Rhône-Saône valley to the west; and the islands of the central Mediterranean – Corsica, Sardinia, Sicily and the Aeolian islands, and Malta; Greece, which might properly appear here, we specifically omit except when it is of direct importance to an understanding of the situation further north or west; Spain we consider in chapter 5.

Geography and environment

The extreme north of Italy is Alpine, and closely connected culturally, then as now, with Switzerland and Austria. To the south lies the vast plain of north Italy – the provinces of Piedmont, Lombardy, Emilia-Romagna and the Veneto – dominated by the Po and its tributaries, but containing other important rivers like the Adige and Piave which flow directly into the Adriatic. This is naturally an area of high agricultural productivity with mainly alluvial soils and a heavy preponderance of arable farming: it also contains the main modern industrial complexes. South again is the 1,000 km chain of the Apennines, mountains of a different sort to the Alps; the characteristic formation is of a high central chain pierced by numerous river valleys, on the east side running straight to the sea, on the west side tending to run more north-south. To the west, too, are extensive plains and the upland area of the 'Anti-Apennines', marshy plains surrounded by gentle hills. In the south-east of the country there is a certain amount of flat land, especially in Apulia; its suitability for intensive agriculture is seriously impaired, however, by a tendency to aridity.

Map 4   Bronze Age sites in central-southern Europe

162

The whole peninsula is a mixture of vegetational and climatic zones: true Mediterranean vegetation occurs in the south, and in the coastal areas of the centre; temperate forest covers the Apennines. There are typically poor mountain soils in the upland areas, with alluvium in the river valleys; the big plains of the north, on the other hand, have rich black-earth soils, very fertile and susceptible of intensive exploitation.

The valley of the Rhône and Saône rivers in south-eastern France forms part of an important route from the Mediterranean northwards into the valley of the Rhine and central Europe through the Belfort Gap. Bordering the Rhône and Saône rivers are the uplands of the Massif Central and the French and Swiss Alps. It seems likely that the delta of the Rhône during the Bronze Age was an area hardly suitable for permanent settlement, and the evidence for activity in the middle and upper valley tends to be on the eastern side, particularly in the lower parts of the Jura, and beyond into the Swiss plateau. Here the lakes and glacial soils created conditions suitable for early agriculture, particularly around Lake Geneva. The local and regional conditions, and the problems of the Alpine passes, are noted below (p. 190).

Jugoslavia also falls into a number of different geographical regions, for the area it covers is very large. Most of the coastline is dominated by mountains – from the Julian Alps in Slovenia through the Velebit and Dinaric mountains in Croatia to the massive ranges of Hercegovina and Montenegro. Certain parts – notably Istria and the more northerly Dalmatian coast – boast a coastal plain, but it is usually arid and poor in soils. In most other parts subsistence farming and extensive pastoralism were until recently the rule, especially in the south. By contrast, most of the north of the country is a huge flat fertile plain – part of the Pannonian plain – and the prehistoric cultures may more properly be considered with the Hungarian region (above, p. 70ff.). In the east, the rolling hills of Serbia soon turn into inhospitable mountains around the Iron Gates, the Balkan Mountains of Bulgaria, and the upland area centred on Kosovo-Metohija. Finally Macedonia, with which we may include Albania, is an area of high hills and deep-scouring river valleys. Macedonia focuses on the Vardar valley, taking us to the Aegean near Thessaloniki, while Albania looks to the Adriatic via rivers like the Drin, Shkumbi and Vijosë. In between the two lies range after range of towering mountains, made the more impenetrable by their scrub or dense forest cover, their lack of well-formed river-systems, and the land-locked nature of the few upland plains that occur.

Environmental evidence from southern Europe is not extensive, though the quantity and quality of work done varies from region to region. A number of pollen sequences are available from Italy, especially the north, and of particular importance are those from the Polada lake-sites. At Lake Ledro, for instance, the prevailing vegetation was mixed oak forest with high values for beech.[1] Cereals were present from the Atlantic, but reached a high point during the Sub-boreal, when the elm suffered further regressions. It is interesting to observe that although a great many of the wooden piles at Molina di Ledro were of needle-bearing softwoods, these species show little change in the pollen diagram during this time. Diagrams elsewhere in north Italy bear out the likelihood that the Sub-boreal was relatively warm and dry by comparison with the Atlantic, though the reappearance of *Artemisia* and increase of alder in the Sub-atlantic suggest a cooler phase at that time.[2]

In Switzerland and the Rhône-Saône valley pollen analysis suggests that quite extensive clearances for upland pasture took place, as well as lowland cultivation. Tree lines were at their highest in the Alpine regions during the earlier Bronze Age;[3] evidence from tree-ring analysis suggests a more continental climate in this period in north-east Switzerland than prevails today, though subsequently (in the later Bronze Age) a dry spell set in.[4] In general the picture obtained in Switzerland is similar to that known from continental Europe as a whole.

There are, apparently, no pollen diagrams available for Albania, but work in north-west Greece may help to fill the gap.[5] A series of radio-carbon-dated diagrams from Epirus show that the area was well-wooded throughout the later Holocene, though from the latter part of the Early Bronze Age on anthropogenic effects become increasingly important, with weeds of cultivation and in some cases cereal pollen starting to appear. At Edessa the olive appears by 1330 ± 55 bc together with the walnut and chestnut, and there are indications, too, of vine cultivation. There is, however, nothing yet available in the pollen record from north Greece to lend any firm support to the 'drought theory' for the end of Mycenaean civilization.

In Jugoslavia, anthropogenic indicators are virtually absent until the Graeco-Roman period, when the walnut, chestnut and other species were introduced (the '*Juglans* line').[6] The natural vegetation shows relatively little variation of any sort through what we may assume is the Bronze Age, apart from that determined by latitude. Thus diagrams from Palu (Istria), Mljet (south Dalmatia) and Vid (lower Neretva valley) show the presence of Mediterranean evergreen species like *Quercus ilex, Phillyrea, Pistacia* (pistaccio), *Olea* (olive) and *Erica* on the one hand (typical maquis plants), and deciduous species (oaks, ash, hornbeam, and *Ostrya*) on the other.

From analysis of sediments and marine deposits in the northern Adriatic region come indications of a change to a warm humid climate near 1000 bc. The sea level was higher than that of today;[7] the level of the water-table at inland lakes rose, causing the abandonment of at least one site.[8] Such a climatic change seems to be in accord with information available from other areas (cf. above, p. 5).

Italy

The terminology of the Italian Bronze Age has grown up piecemeal. The normal practice is to use local culture-names defined by type-sites. Thus in the north the earlier Bronze Age lake sites are named after *Polada,* giving way to those named after *Peschiera.* In Emilia the celebrated *terremare* were in use from the Middle Bronze Age (of traditional terminology), though chronological division of them is lacking. Only in central and southern Italy is a system present: The *Apennine culture* covers the whole period from the Copper Age up to the time when elements of the Iron Age Villanovan culture appear. The most basic divisions are those of Peroni,[9] who divided the Apennine proper from a 'Sub-apennine' (where the typical Apennine incised pottery was absent, even though some other forms continued), and this again from the 'Protovillanovan'. The Apennine culture continued throughout the Bronze Age, but of course much local development is discernible: Trump defined six phases in a twofold pottery tradition.[10] It has been customary to refer to an early, middle and late phase: a 'proto-Apennine' phase has also been isolated, though this has little to do with the true Bronze Age Apennine culture and it is more likely that the early Apennine developed directly on a Chalcolithic basis.[11]

The Bronze Age in Italy succeeded a well-developed Eneolithic phase that consists of the cultural groups of Remedello (centred on the Po plain), Rinaldone (Tuscany, Umbria and Latium), Conelle (Marche), Ortucchio (Abbruzzo), Gaudo (Campania), Cellino or Laterza (Apulia) and Piano Conte (Lipari and the adjacent mainland).[12] In Sicily this is the time of the rich cultures and pottery styles first of San Cono and Piano Notaro, then of Serraferlicchio, Sant' Ippolito, Malpasso, Conca d'Oro as well as the Bell Beakers. There are, naturally, regional specialities and differences in this material, but in general one may point to open village sites and caves for settlements; single contracted inhumations in the north, collective tombs in the south; dark burnished pottery; tanged and leaf-shaped flint arrowheads; a variety of ground stone tools including perforated axes and hammers in some areas; and, rather infrequently, triangular riveted daggers, halberds, flat axes, awls, and buttons or beads of copper. Copper slag has been found on the acropolis at Lipari in Diana (late Neolithic) levels (which have a radiocarbon date of 3050 ± 200 bc), and other Neolithic copper objects are known; it has recently been argued that the technology may have been learnt from Balkan metal-using peoples.[13] Certainly it seems to have developed in Italy at least as early as it did in the Aegean, and neither the radiocarbon chronology nor study of the metal types involved favours the idea of Aegean influence on the development of Italian metallurgy.

The richest and best-documented cultural group in Early Bronze Age Italy lies in the north, principally along the great valleys and lakes of the southern Alpine foothills, but extending also to the Po plain. The greatest concentration lies around (but not on) Lake Garda, where the lake-site of Polada gives its name to the group. Barfield has given an excellent concise account of the group as a whole; Peroni's more detailed study is indispensable.[14]

The most productive, though not the only, type of Polada site is the lake-dwelling. This offers the same advantages and disadvantages that we have noted on lake-sites elsewhere: on the one hand organic material is very well preserved, especially wooden objects; on the other the generally haphazard nature of the investigation of such sites and the difficulty of recovering evidence of stratification, leads to a situation where the chronological and economic development is barely known or understood. Peroni divides the constructional types of the Polada group into *palafitte*, which consist of vertical beams sunk into the lake-bed, and *bonifiche*, successive horizontal layers of timber, supporting hut-floors.[15] As for huts, fragments have been recovered at many sites but complete house-plans more rarely. There was no standard house-shape, though most consisted of closely-spaced upright posts enclosing clay or stone-paved floor-areas with rectangular hearths. Huge quantities of material have been recovered from some of the excavated sites: among these Molina di Ledro (Trento),[16] Barche di Solferino (Mantova) and Lucone (Brescia) may be singled out for the richness of their finds. Among the best recently excavated sites is Fiavè (Trento).[17] The site lies high among the hills north of Lake Garda, on the shores of what was once the lake of Carera, now a marsh. The site has been known and sporadically excavated since the middle of the nineteenth century; systematic work by Renato Perini has been under way since 1969. Two main zones have been investigated, the sequence different in each: in one, late Neolithic and Eneolithic levels are succeeded by late 'Middle Bronze Age' and Late Bronze Age; in the other Early and Middle Bronze Age material accounts for the entire development. By the time of the Early Bronze Age the site was concentrated on the south-east corner of the lake, composed of *palafitte* and surrounded by a palisade. Massive posts were driven into the lake bed, their length reaching 9 m or more, 5 m below the surface, and 4 above. By the time of the late Middle Bronze Age this had been many times repaired, so that the whole area of settlement was shifted and the houses started afresh. It is from this phase that most is known of the methods of construction. A horizontal network of beams either singly or in pairs was laid on the bottom of the lake. In between the pairs of beams were inserted vertical posts perforated near the bottom for the insertion of a horizontal cross-piece which actually rested on the sleeper-beams; this was a method of distributing the weight over the sleepers and preventing the piles sinking further and further into the lake-bed. A layer of mud containing freshwater molluscs and cultural debris enveloped these foundations; this was succeeded by a layer full of charcoal, the result of the conflagration which brought this phase to an end. In sector seven the cultural layers contained large quantities of organic material – bones and carbonized grain – mixed in with abundant pottery. As it was impossible to distinguish individual buildings, it has been suggested that this section was intended for consolidation of the main *palafitta*, providing at the same time a convenient rubbish tip.[18]

Lake-side settlement continued as the dominant form in the northern valleys right on into the later Bronze Age. Some Polada sites, like Ledro and Lucone, remained in use; others were abandoned and replaced by new ones, like Bor di Pacengo on Lake Garda.[19] Little is known of this phase in detail; it saw a natural development in artifact types (in particular including bronzes attributable to Br B north of the Alps), without any very significant change in the economy.

To the south, on the Po plain, the earliest part of the Bronze Age is not well-known, but subsequently the area supported the famous (though hardly understood) *terremare*. The sites concerned are often mounds of fertile black earth rich in organic matter and domestic debris, probably raised above the flood level of the surrounding plain by deliberate dumping of rubbish. Italian prehistorians, following in the steps of Säflund,[20] have defined the area of the *terremare* as delimited by the Po in the north, the Apennines in the south and the river Panaro (a southern tributary of the Po) to the east; Barfield suggests that certain sites outside this area, notably on the Lombard plain to the north-west and in the Adige area and beyond to the north-east, may be included under the same general heading. East of the Panaro the cultural material becomes mixed, including elements of the Apennine group, which eventually established its own sites down on the plain. The almost total absence of reliable stratigraphical observation on *terremare* has meant that the chronological development and position of the group is virtually unknown. That it spans the Bavarian phases Br B, C and D is apparent from the bronzes found on the sites; that they have a high degree of internal development is known from Gorzano and other sites where clearly distinguishable layers were present, with recognizably different pottery in each.[21] But a precise and detailed stratigraphy is wholly lacking, a fact which, sad to relate, makes this important group one of the less well-known in Bronze Age Europe.

The *terremare* were enclosed by a bank and ditch, the former sometimes timber-laced with a box-like construction.[22] Excavation has usually revealed a forest of post-holes, though house-plans are hardly known. At Monte Leoni (Parma), however, recent work has brought to light a roughly rectangular hut-floor measuring 9 × 5 m, with rounded corners on one side.[23] The house was cut into the side of a hill and the walls were of wattle-and-daub with a frame of oak beams. The roof was also of timber, which had fallen into the interior when the house was destroyed, along with much other debris. The situation of Monte Leoni on a low hill about 100 m above sea level in the Apennine foothills raises the question of the unity or otherwise of the *terramara* 'culture', for it has always been supposed that *terremare* were restricted to the plain. Settlement sites of all periods on the Po plain consist mainly of black earth, however; this feature is not peculiar to the *terremare*. Once liberated from that idea, we are free to admit the possibility of *terramara* sites in the hills, and we can see that it is in fact the cultural material which distinguishes the group – pottery styles above all, but also the abundant presence of metal and other domestic utensils. At Monte Leoni, for instance, a number of bronzes characteristic of Br D were found *in situ* inside the house. Such finds would be unthinkable in the hills further south.

Central Italy was occupied in the earlier Bronze Age by people whose material culture was remarkably uniform, even though their technological plane seems to have been considerably lower than that of most peoples around them. Metal hardly appears, but pottery is ubiquitous and extremely elaborate. The tendency for these sites to concentrate in and around the mountains has led to the coining of the term 'Apennine Culture'.[24] The great majority of Apennine sites are simple affairs, apparently without surviving structures and containing only scatters of domestic refuse. Various settlement situations have been distinguished, in particular the contrasting upland and lowland settings; typical of the former are caves and other sheltered sites, while the latter are very mixed. The standard thesis, proposed by Puglisi, is that the impermanent nature of the sites, and the complementary distributions of upland and lowland sites, indicate an economy based on transhuming pastoralism, exploiting two main environments in turn according to the season.[25] The discoveries at Luni sul Mignone, however, and recent palaeoeconomic work, have shed grave doubt on this hypothesis.

Luni sul Mignone (Viterbo) lies to the west of the Apennine chain in southern Etruria, about 20 km from the sea.[26] There are two main areas of occupation: Luni proper, occupying a tuff plateau 550 × 140 m above the river Mignone (later an Etruscan stronghold in the territory of Tarquinia); and below it to the east a small plain named Tre Erici, where a considerable depth (6 m) of occupation debris was found, spanning the Neolithic to Iron Ages. From this stratified sequence a series of radiocarbon dates was obtained, and the scanty remains of Bronze Age and Chalcolithic huts. Much more of Bronze Age date was found on the acropolis. On the western part of the plateau three house-foundations were found, roughly in line, cut down into the bedrock to a depth of up to 2.2 m. The middle house is the smallest at 7 m long, the south house the largest at 42 m; that to the north is about 30 m long. All three houses are 4 m wide (fig. 54). On top of the rock the walls are built up of flattish stones: the excavator suggests a simple reed roof. Several hearths were found, and there were multiple entrances, suggesting that interior divisions once existed for separating different social groups, perhaps families. The substantial nature of the houses at Luni, and the fact that the economy was clearly based on farming and stockbreeding, enabled Östenberg to suggest that the Apenniners of *that* area, at any rate, were more than the backward pastoralists depicted by Puglisi.[27] The exciting discovery of imported Mycenaean sherds in the Bronze Age layers opens up the possibility that these people were involved in some way in the export of copper ore from the Tuscan mountains to the Aegean world – even though they did not, apparently, use the ore themselves.

SECTION
0 1 m 2 3

Fig. 54 Apennine houses at Luni sul Mignone, reconstruction.
(After Östenberg 1967)

In complete contrast to Luni, one may take a typical upland site – like the rock shelter at La Romità di Asciano (Pisa) or the cave of Grotta a Male near Assergi (Abbruzzo), both of which have produced stratigraphical successions of some importance.[28] The latter is a large cave nearly 1,000 m above sea level (unlike La Romità, which is only in the foothills of the Apennines) in an upland basin, with a major part of the surrounding land being suitable only for rough grazing. A thin Eneolithic layer was succeeded by over 2 m of Bronze Age deposit, half of it attributed to the 'latter part of the Bronze Age'. A stone mould for a flanged axe was recovered from this layer. The faunal remains indicated a change during the Bronze Age from mixed hunting and pastoralism to a broader stock-rearing economy in which cattle and caprines and, to a lesser extent, pigs, formed the principal sources of food, and it has been suggested that during the later part of the earlier Bronze Age a permanent settlement was established in the cave.

Different from both of these sites, though closer to Luni in that the site nestles up against an acropolis, is Narce (Calcata) in southern Etruria, where a long stratified sequence covers the entire Bronze and Early Iron Ages. The excavator has distinguished three Bronze Age building phases, with rectangular stone and timber structures in the earliest, and semicircular or oval in the second and third; an encircling wall was probably added in the second. The history of the site, which increased considerably in size during the course of the Bronze Age, is intimately involved with the local history of the river Treia, for periods of occupation alternate with levels of thick silt deposited by the river as it changed its course.[29]

Our knowledge of the details of life in the Italian Bronze Age becomes scantier as we progress down the peninsula. The number of informative and stratified sites in the south is very few. Among these may be mentioned Tufariello (Buccino), where, on a terrace of middle height above the confluence of two rivers, a surrounding wall enclosed a substantial number of rather flimsy stone-built square or rectangular houses;[30] and La Starza near Ariano Irpino (Avellino).[31] This is a gypsum hill that rises 80 m above two streams that delimit and defend it on the entire western and northern sides. The original area of the hill-top is estimated by Trump at 175 × 50 m, though much of this is rocky. The site is not far from the central point of the Apennine chain at the spot where it is crossed by the important road known in Roman times and today as the Via Appia Traiana. In the little that was left of the Bronze Age habitation layers there are small hearths at various levels; not, apparently, inside houses. The occupation at La Starza was, however, a long one even if it was seasonal; evidence for the latter view is provided by the fact that one of the main *tratturi* of central Italy passes directly beneath the site.

On the southern coasts a few sites provide evidence of long-lived and large-scale occupation. Coppa Nevigata at the mouth of the Cervaro started life at this time, maybe surrounded by a massive wall;[32] at Porto Perone (Leporano) on the southern coast of Apulia, near Taranto, a different situation prevailed.[33] Its maritime situation and consequent potential importance as a trading station are clear, though it is far from certain that imported Aegean pottery is really present from Middle Helladic on. The main excavated area is a terrace below a ridge of land projecting out to a headland in the Ionian Sea, and a considerable depth of deposit was found, with a stout stone encircling wall. In trench 1 an important sequence of Apennine material was found. Scanty remains of post-built houses were found near the bottom in levels attributed to 'proto-Apennine'; four complete plans were recovered from level e, called 'Middle Apennine'. These are roughly circular affairs, defined by small stone settings and having beaten clay floors, between 2 and 2.5 m in diameter with an outer ring of post-holes, perhaps for posts to support an

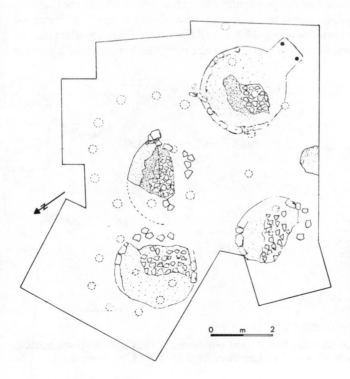

Fig. 55 Porto Perone, Leporano (Taranto). House-plans from 'middle Apennine' layers. (After Lo Porto 1963)

overhanging eave. One of the structures had a porch-like entrance at the south side (fig. 55).

In Sicily and the Aeolian Islands a considerable number of habitation sites are known from the earlier Bronze Age. The islands had, in fact, reached a level of material culture and density of occupation that one may assume stemmed from their favourable position on the trade route to Greece. Influence and importation from the Aegean increased over the course of the Bronze Age, and it is even possible to argue that Mycenaean settlement occurred during the Late Bronze Age. House plans, arranged in villages, are known from hilltops and from plains in the Aeolian Islands: these are the sites of the *Capo Graziano* culture. Capo Graziano itself is a rocky peninsula on Filicudi with a series of stone-built oval huts (fig. 56), but much larger is the oval house at the Lipari acropolis, measuring some 12 × 8 m.[34] Other houses on the site are smaller, like those from Capo Graziano. A conical building, truncated at the top, is interpreted as a granary. By contrast, settlement sites on Sicily are much less common than tombs, though parts of the south coast have produced villages. Of these the best known is Monte Sallia, the importance of which is attributed to the proximity of the flint mines of Monte Tabuto.

In the ensuing centuries (the 'Middle Bronze Age') a series of important settlements are found – Milazzese on Panarea, Portella on Salina, and Capo Graziano and Lipari again.[35] The first of these is among

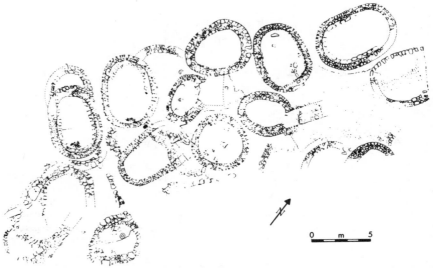

Fig. 56   Filicudi (Aeolian Is.). Plan of settlement of the Capo Graziano culture. (After L. Bernabò Brea and M. Cavalier, *BPI* n.s. XVII, 75 (1966))

the more extensive, with thirty-three excavated huts, mostly oval; there were areas of paving inside, and a series of stone slabs thought to have been used as furniture. The position of this site, perched on a spur of rock projecting into the sea, is about as impregnable as it is possible to be: but whether its occupants lived in it all the time, or simply retired to it in time of trouble, is hard to say. Since Panarea is a small island transhumance is hardly possible!

Outstandingly important is the 'palatial' complex at Thapsos (Augusta), on the projecting headland of Magnisi a few kilometres north of Syracuse.[36] These buildings came to light in excavations since 1968 and are not yet fully known. The settlement extends over a huge area 1 km × 200 m, though only a small part has been investigated. At least three phases of building are discernible: round and sub-rectangular houses date to the period of the Thapsos cemetery (Middle Bronze Age) and are comparable with those from Milazzese and Salina. Somewhat later, but probably still during the Thapsos cemetery period (imported Maltese pottery of Borg in-Nadur types was found), large rectangular buildings were laid out with paved courts, corridors, antechambers etc., and a double fortification wall was erected. The excavator has distinguished two main complexes, A and B, in the central area (fig. 57) and although the relative functions of these are not known, the whole undeniably bears an Aegean stamp and recalls the layout of Mycenaean palatial sites. Mycenaean pottery is not reported from the habitation area, but it does come from the Thapsos chamber tombs; much Thapsos material from the houses indicates contemporaneity with the main period of Mycenaean importation. Might there not even have been Mycenaeans living at Thapsos? It is certainly tempting to think so. The only surprising thing is that buildings of this size and importance have not been found elsewhere in south Italy.

Burial sites in the Italian earlier Bronze Age are very rare. From the Polada group comes only a handful of inhumation burials in caves and rock-shelters. On the Po plain, contemporary with the early *terremare*, come cemeteries, like that at Povegliano Veronese, containing both extended inhumation and cremation burials – 'biritual' sites that appear to represent a specific cultural feature. For the *terremare* themselves, on the other hand, cremation is likely to have been the dominant rite, though most datable *terramara* cemeteries so far discovered fall into a rather later time-bracket. Much the same is true of the north-west. The rest of the country is more or less a blank: Apennine burials are virtually unknown, though in some cases – the Gaudo area in Campania, for instance, or in Apulia – Eneolithic funerary traditions seem to have continued, with the use and re-use of rock-cut chamber tombs or dolmens. Examples include

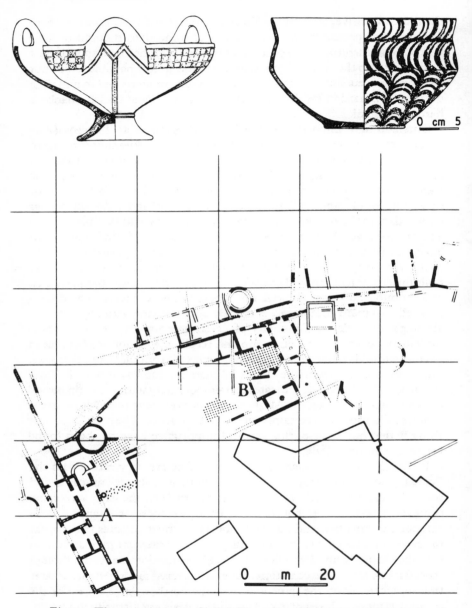

Fig. 57   Thapsos (Augusta, Sicily). Plan of the Thapsos-period settlement showing well-planned 'palatial' blocks and sub-rectangular houses
of an earlier period, and pottery from the site.
(After Voza 1973)

174

Laterza (Taranto) and Cellino San Marco (Brindisi), where sizeable cemeteries of these tombs occur.[37]

On Sicily burials are extremely common in the earlier Bronze Age, mainly because they took place in rock-cut chamber tombs which have survived where earth graves have not. In the earlier period they are named after the site of Castelluccio (Noto), later after Thapsos (Augusta).[38] Many hundreds of tombs are known, frequently in cemetery groups. At Castelluccio the tombs are small oval chambers, less than 2 m in any one direction, with small *stomia* (doorways) and in some cases antechambers. The most famous examples have their doorways blocked with stone slabs that bear carvings, mainly spiral designs, clearly reminiscent of, though chronologically later than, megalithic art in general and Maltese temple art at Tarxien in particular. By contrast the tombs in the area around Etna, where the lava is so hard as to make rock-cutting impracticable, are usually in caves, but the finds in them indicate broad similarity to the rest of the Castelluccio culture.

Chamber-tombs continued a popular form on Sicily for many centuries, and in the period following the time of Castelluccio they became large in scale, either cut down vertically into level rock or else horizontally into the side of a hill. The provision of a *dromos* (entrance-passage) in these, the occurrence of *tholos*-like beehive chambers, as well as the finds of Mycenaean pottery and bronzes, must indicate contact with the Aegean.

For ritual and religion northern Italy provides a rich mine of information – often difficult to interpret – in the form of rock art. The most famous collection is in the Val Camonica, lying north of Brescia, between Lake Iseo and the Swiss border. A series of places along this valley, which is penetrated by the river Oglio, have rock carvings, though conventional prehistoric sites are very few.[39] By the study of palimpsest carvings, superposition, patina and wear, Anati has identified four main phases in the Camonica ('Camunian') rock art, ranging from the Neolithic to the Roman period. It is principally his phase III that affects us here, for phase I is claimed to be Neolithic, and II Chalcolithic; but to some extent we have to consider the whole chronological range in order to appreciate the varieties of symbolism and style that are present (fig. 58).

One of the principal elements in Camunian religion seems to have been the solar disc or sun-motif.[40] Cup-and-ring marks (of solar significance?), cup-marks alone, wheels, discs with rays attached to them, and linked discs appear in great profusion. These are frequently linked with animal figures (especially stags), less commonly with humans; houses are also found linked with the sun – thus, temples. Altars are represented, frequently in scenes interpreted as involving sacrifices of animals. There

Fig. 58   Rock-art from the Val Camonica. Height of panel *c.* 2 m.
(After Anati 1961)

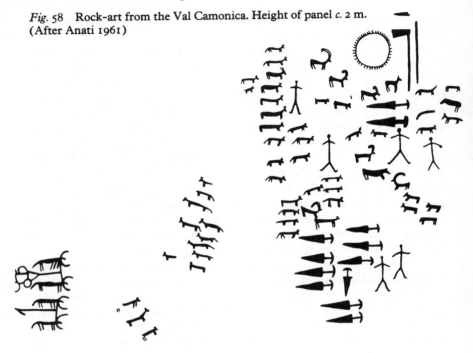

are numerous scenes depicting various kinds of worship – of animals, humans, or inanimate objects, and Anati has stressed the similarity of many of these elements to known features of Celtic religion. Figures clad in strange plumage or other ritualistic garb appear, often wielding weapons (themselves allegedly the object of veneration). In a number of cases funeral scenes are clearly represented, with a line of mourners, their arms upraised, beside a prostrate corpse. There are also numerous 'enigmatic objects' which may have had cultic significance: the so-called 'paddles' are one such feature.

Contemporary rock carvings in Switzerland at Carschenna near Thusis, at an altitude of 1,100 m, are not so extensive in subject matter, but depict horsemen as well as cups, circles and wavy line designs.[41]

Other religious sites worthy of mention here are the Pertosa cave (Salerno) in southern Campania and Belverde di Cetona (Siena) in southern Tuscany. Both sites were used throughout the Bronze Age and well into the Graeco–Roman period. At Belverde there is an ordinary Apennine settlement and above it, pushed into crevices in the rocks, numerous pots and broken sherds (some containing charred grain) and some skeletal material. Further, many of the rock-summits are artificially shaped, like the 'Anfiteatro' with its tiered seats on three sides. Comparable sites are known from elsewhere in Tuscany.[42] At the Grotta Pertosa the situation was rather different: the site is a large cave high above the river Tanagro (and not far from Tufariello). Through it flowed a stream beside which stream was a settlement on wooden platforms and piles. The exceptional interest lies in the fact that, in addition to prolific domestic debris, large numbers of miniature votive vessels were found, eloquent testimony to the veneration of a river or water deity.[43]

Material culture

It is above all the pottery of Bronze Age Italy that marks it as a period of considerable artistic achievement. Through most of the peninsula potters seem to have been much more numerous and influential than smiths; it was to their pottery that they devoted the time and artistic effort that they were not spending on production of metal work. This fact is the more surprising in that most of it was made for domestic, not funerary, purposes. It is possible to distinguish two main fabrics: a coarse ware, for large containers often decorated with impressed cordons; and a fine burnished ware, dark-faced and in the centre and south richly decorated with incisions and other ornamentation. In the north the forms include (most characteristically) straight-sided cylindrical and conical bowls, cups and mugs (the 'Vapheio cup' from Ledro is, surely, one of these),[44] rounded and carinated cups, some large storage vessels, and a great variety of individual forms.[45] Of the handles, most typical is the strap type sharply bent upwards in an 'elbow'. Similar shapes, even including this last feature, are found in wood, telling evidence for the one-time commonness of such objects. Many of the Polada forms continue into the Bor phase, notably the range of one-handled cups, but new types appear also – wide-mouthed bowls with carination, decoration by grooving (in concentric bands around the vessel), incision (in geometric motifs) or bossed ornament – features which have been seen as Hungarian in origin. Handles, always an Italian speciality, become more elaborate – horned in the northern lakes area, knob- or keel-shaped in the north-east. *Terramara* pottery includes many of these elements, as well as forms of its own, like the crested handle and the knobbed biconical jar.[46]

The Apennine range of pottery is still richer (fig. 59). The ubiquitous form is the *capeduncola* – a shallow cup with one handle, in a great variety of forms, usually carinated. Other common forms are biconical jars, platters, jugs and a number of special forms, like milk-boilers for cheese-making. Trump has shown[47] how Apennine pottery varies regionally – a variation particularly apparent in the handle forms, for in the south one

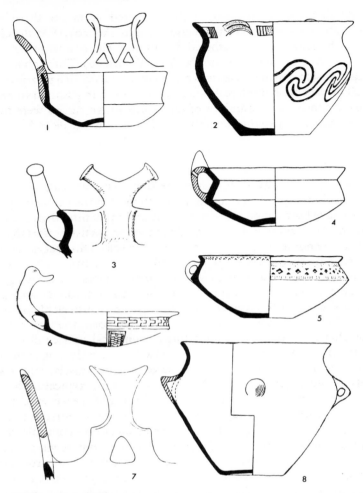

Fig. 59   Apennine pottery. 1–4. southern forms, 5–8. northern
forms. Varying scales.
(After Trump 1958)

finds a predominance of 'elongated tongue handles', often flaring or
outcurving at the ends, in the north knobs and column handles, with
horned or crescent-shaped termination. There are two types of milk-
boiler which also have exclusive distributions.

Other aspects of material culture may be dealt with more briefly. It is
the Polada sites above all that have produced domestic material: spindle-
whorls and loom-weights, wooden bows and tanged or hollow-based flint

arrowheads, together with other organic material – textiles, dug-out canoes and so on; there are beads of bone, amber, limestone and paste.[48] A special feature of *terramara* finds is the large quantity of bone used for handles and hafts, discs and other ornaments, bridle cheek-pieces and so on; it is frequently decorated with compass-drawn ring-and-dot motifs.

We have already mentioned that metal-working is not much in evidence in the remains of earlier Bronze Age Italy, and this is in spite of the existence of ore sources (notably in Etruria and the Trentino) and the depiction of smiths at work on Val Camonica carvings. From Ledro come moulds, crucibles and tuyères, and copper slag occurs elsewhere.[49] The range of objects produced on Polada sites is very similar to that known from Austria and southern Germany, and includes hammered sheet bronze objects of *Blechkreis* type. Subsequently Tumulus bronzes appear, notably swords, spearheads and dirks; the swords, of Cowen's Sauerbrunn and Boiu types, are especially important in indicating that northern Italy was party to the development of the standard central European types, for these swords appear otherwise in Austria, Hungary and Romania.[50] On *terremare* one finds less martial objects such as winged axes, pins, razors and so on – more of them datable to the later than the earlier part of the Bronze Age. Most notable among hoard finds are the Ripatransone (Ascoli Piceno) collection of daggers, showing the spread of solid-hilted triangular daggers of northern type; and the Cascina Ranza (Milan) hoard, containing south German swords, socketed spearheads, and spatulate flanged axes of Swiss type (fig. 60).[51]

Economy

The economic situation of northern Italy is comparatively well-known as a result of the large quantities of organic material that survive. An agricultural basis was considerably supplemented by hunting and gathering. Wheat, barley and flax are found, together with the agricultural implements used to cultivate them (including a crook-ard); in addition to the common domesticates, bones of red and roe deer, wild pig, and bear occur. Fishing implements are common, and pike is the most frequent fish represented, though this may merely reflect the greater chances of finding pike bones than those of other species. Numerous pips and stones from fruits and berries have been found, including wild cherries, apples, plums, strawberries, raspberries, elderberries, and grapes; various nuts and acorns also occur. Also found was 'a burnt hemispherical mass which may have been a loaf of bread' from Ledro, and 'carbonised balls ... which strangely resemble the present-day pasta speciality of the Veneto known as *gnocchi*'.[52] There is no reason to suppose

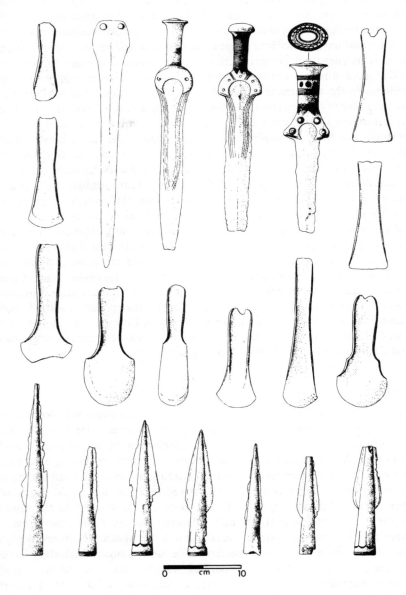

Fig. 60 Bronze hoard from Cascina Ranza (Milan).
(After Hachmann 1957)

180

that Italian cuisine was not as polished and elaborate in the Bronze Age as it is today, even if it used a more restricted range of materials; though one could not have ordered a *capuccino* let us not suppose that the contents of the Graubolle man's stomach (admittedly of Iron Age date) indicate the general fare of prehistoric temperate Europe. We do not know when the roux sauce may have been invented, or who made the first *spaghetti*; but the range of foodstuffs available must have offered tempting opportunities to the imaginative Poladan.

On the more strictly economic side most information is available to us from Fiavè, where bone was exceptionally well-preserved (more complete bones being found in one area than broken fragments), and extensive sieving has resulted in the recovery of good samples. By far the greatest proportion of the whole were the caprines, perhaps approaching 60 per cent of the total.[53] Cattle accounted for well over 20 per cent and pigs for 6.5 per cent of the precisely identified bones. Other animals were not numerically significant, though a variety of wild species do occur – red deer, roe deer, chamois, bear etc. Fish bones, though preserved, hardly figure at all – surprising on a lake-site. The pigs were unusually small individuals, and many of those found had been killed young, as is common in economies that keep pigs under intensive control. The young age at death of some of the cattle further suggests that pressure on food resources – particularly in a small upland basin like Fiavè – led to economic strategies designed to conserve limited winter fodder. The apparent absence of evidence for transhumance in a situation where it would surely have been desirable has been taken as a possible indicator of rising population in the area during the earlier part of the Bronze Age, a suggestion that is further supported by the increase in the number of sites during that period over the total in the Eneolithic.

The economy of prehistoric central Italy has been the subject of special study by Graeme Barker.[54] His basic thesis is that 'although short-term changes in the economy were not uniform and contemporary from area to area, the overall view is one of increasingly intensive exploitation systems'. By contrast to some Neolithic economies which utilized year-round settlements in the hills and winter camps in the lowlands, in the Bronze Age permanent lowland settlements were established as well. For example the Luni community, which was based on stock-raising and cereal agriculture, was a permanent settlement, but it depended, too, on distant hill shielings like the Grotta a Male, with a network of transit camps on the *tratturi* in between.[55] At Luni itself cattle accounted for about half the faunal sample, with caprines and pigs sharing the other half: these two species were mostly killed young. A wide range of cultivated plants was recovered, even though the natural environment is more suited to grazing than to arable agriculture. At Narce much more winter pasture and arable land is immediately accessible; caprines are much the largest component of the faunal sample, though stock policy seems to have been similar to that at Luni. It is only at the upland sites, especially caves, that wild species (notably deer) are represented in substantial numbers (nearly 25 per cent at the Grotta a Male).

Arable agriculture was an important element of at least some Apennine economies. Preserved seeds from the Luni acropolis (Apennine II levels) include emmer, einkorn, spelt and bread wheat, barley, horse-beans, bitter vetch and grass pea: agricultural implements were also found. Similar plant remains have been recovered from many different sites.[56] Further evidence for the tilling of the land comes from the rock art of the Val Camonica, where there are scenes depicting paired animals pulling a crook-ard, followed by human figures carrying what may be picks to break up the clods of earth.[57] Field walls, perhaps of prehistoric date, occur in the area. If the carvings are to be believed, however, hunting was a much more popular practice – or was it simply more risky, demanding more in the way of preparatory ritual? Or, simpler still, more exciting to depict? These scenes show straightforward pursuit with spears; trapping and snaring of various kinds; netting; and what appears to be the use of the boomerang. The commonest animal depicted in these hunt scenes is the stag.

Among the other evidence for economic activity, allegedly of Bronze Age date, to be gleaned from these carvings we may mention fishing (with nets) and various types of handicraft – smithing, wood-working, building, weaving and wheel-making. The latter also bears on the question of transportation; numerous carts, drawn by two beasts, are depicted. The draught animals were mainly oxen, but horses appear during Anati's period III, further important evidence for the spread of this animal across Europe.[58] The roads on which the wheeled vehicles travelled are not known in Italy, though they do, of course, occur elsewhere (cf. p. 252).

Trade and exchange in the earlier Bronze Age of Italy undoubtedly took place, though on what scale we cannot be sure. The importation of Middle Helladic pottery has been claimed at Porto Perone, and the continuance of this southern trade into the Mycenaean period is usually taken as having been caused by the Mycenaeans' quest for mineral sources – the copper and possibly tin of Etruria. In the north, on the other hand, metal in ingot form may have been imported, since ingot torcs of typical central European form occur in Polada contexts.[59] A connection with lands to the north at this time is made the more plausible by the occurrence of amber at Ledro, and of a series of clay plaques impressed with stamped geometric symbols (fig. 61) closely similar to those discovered in Hungary and Slovakia in Mad'arovce contexts and Jugoslavia in Vattina contexts.[60] It has been suggested that these may have been trading tallies; they have sometimes been called 'loaf-of-bread idols' or 'pintaderas'. Though the similarity rarely verges on identity, the occurrence of objects with (we may assume) identical functions in three rather widely separated areas is certainly suggestive. Other features which may be elements in long-distance trade include spoked wheels (again

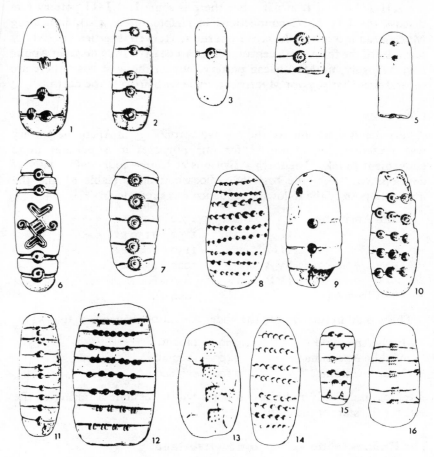

Fig. 61   'Loaf-of-bread idols' from Early Bronze Age Europe: 1–4. Nitriansky Hrádok, 5. Stefanovo, 6. Dubovac-Vattina, 7. Veselé, 8–10. Polada, 11. Villa Capella-Cerasare, 12. Lucone, 13–15. Cavriana, 16. Cattaragna. (After H.-J. Hundt, *Preist. Alp.* 10 (1974))

commonly found in east-central Europe, as in Mycenaean Greece) and the so-called 'Vapheio-cup' from Ledro, a straight-walled conical cup with flaring rim and strap handle joining it.[61] It is certainly possible that a Creto-Mycenaean prototype could have inspired this extraordinary vase, but the range of Polada pottery includes many straight-walled forms, from which this cup diverges comparatively little.

In the south an increasing quantity of Mycenaean pottery is known; imported objects have been found on some forty sites.[62] Many of them are LH IIIA and B in date, but there is some LH I-II pottery (we discuss the LH IIIC connections in chapter 9, p. 420), indicating Mycenaean interest in the area from the start, even if settlement did not occur until the fourteenth century. The east coast of Italy north of Apulia has, strangely, no Mycenaean pottery, but on the west coast there are several sites that suggest Mycenaean trade with areas to the north.

Chronology

A very detailed scheme for the relative chronology of Apennine pottery was presented by Trump;[63] for our purposes it is perhaps more convenient to take Östenberg's divisions at Luni – four main phases of development.[64] On the basis of radiocarbon dates (table 6) and the imported pottery the following sequence was suggested:

Luni Apennine	I	*c.*1350/1300 – 1250 BC
	II	1250 – 1150 BC
	III	1150 – 1000 BC
	IVA	1000 – 850 BC
	IVB	850 – 800 BC
Luni Iron Age		800 BC

This would in turn fit into the wider Apennine sequence as follows:

Early Apennine	?*c.* 1600 – 1400 BC
Middle Apennine	1400 – 1100 BC
Late Apennine	1100 – 850/800 BC

Increasingly early radiocarbon dates will necessitate a raising of the date for the start of the culture.

The Rhône-Saône Valley and Switzerland

The Early Bronze Age is remarkably well-represented in this region which consists of a broad and fertile valley with equally rich plateaux, the largest inland lakes and the highest terrain in southern and central Europe. The land is one of contrasts and complementary zones and these are some of the factors which have made this area one of the most informative about Bronze Age activities.

The distribution of Early Bronze Age settlement in this region is irregular. From the middle Rhône northwards to the upper Saône, and eastwards into the Jura and Swiss plateau, there is ample evidence for occupation which is intensive when compared with that from the lower Rhône and the uplands of the Massif Central to the west. The Mediterranean coastlands themselves were consistently employed throughout the Bronze Age, both for permanent settlement and for transitory occupation during the movement of materials or people from mainland to islands.

The Rhône-Alpine group of the Early Bronze Age is often considered to be a western equivalent of the Únětice-Straubing-Adlerberg complex, but we have suggested that these terms disguise the presence of numerous separate communities, some more distinctive archaeologically than others. The distribution of the Rhône-Alpine group is wide, 300 km from the Rhône-Saône confluence into the southern Swiss Alps, and well-represented along the major parts of the valley systems. The group is identified by distinctive pottery, bronzes, burials and settlements.

Occupation of caves, lake-sides, plateaux and promontories are known. The Gonvillars cave (Haute-Saône) was defended by walling, and defences were erected on upland spurs such as La Roche-Maldru and Grandchamp (Jura).[65] Open settlements near Salins (Jura), and along the banks of the Saône, are also known, and Rhône-Alpine pottery has been recovered from as far west as the western Massif Central, some 200 km distant from the Rhône valley.[66] Lake-side settlements in the Jura include Clairvaux and Chalain, but stratigraphical details are not available.[67]

The evidence from Alpine Switzerland is equally impressive. Settlement of Rhône-Alpine character is known from the Valais eastwards across the Alpine plateau towards the upper Rhine. The lower slopes of the mountains, and rocky ridges above the valley floors, were occupied in order to exploit both fertile lowland and mountain pastures. The settlements, as at Crestaulta (Grisons) and Muota-Fellers (Grisons), were small, mostly undefended, and houses of 4 × 5 m have been recognized.[68] The occupation debris at Crestaulta included some bronze tools, many stone and bone implements, and much cordoned pottery.

The pottery in particular has for long been considered one of the principal features of the group. Large jars with flat bases, and decorated with applied cordons, finger-impressed, with bosses or left unadorned, form a characteristic element, but handled cups of general widespread Early Bronze Age type also occur.

Metalwork of the Rhône-Alpine group is also distinctive, but only rarely are associations found between settlements and fine metal products. Flanged axes of Neyruz and Roseaux types, trefoil pins and metal-hilted daggers are among the impressive products made in this region,[69] and the appearance of the dagger type throughout central Europe is a feature of many Early Bronze Age groups (fig. 62).[70]

Burials within the Rhône-Alpine group are more abundant than has often been suggested. Inhumations beneath barrows, or in unmarked trench graves or cists, occasionally in re-used or re-built megalithic tombs, are widespread, and demonstrate the quite heterogeneous nature of the burial customs, if not of the human communities practising them.[71]

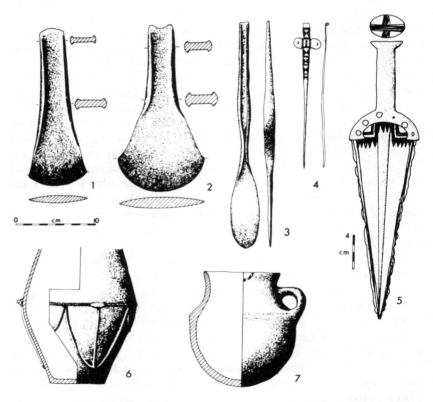

Fig. 62   Early Bronze Age material from the Jura and Languedoc: 1. Neyruz axe, La Chapelle-sur-Furieuse, 2. Roseaux axe, Clairvaux-les-Lacs, 3. Spatulate axe, Chaussin, 4. Trefoil pin, Bois de Parançot, 5. Metal-hilted dagger, Avignon, 6. Cordon-decorated pot, Doucier-Chalain, 7. Handled cup, Broye-les Pesmes. (After Millotte 1976, Roudil and Guilaine 1976)

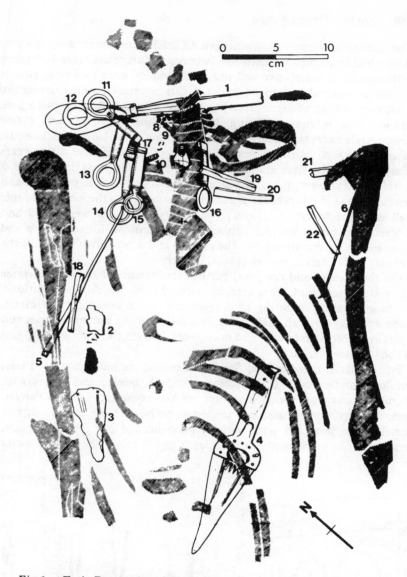

Fig. 63 Early Bronze Age grave at Petit-Chasseur (Valais): 1. spatulate axe, 2. sheet bronze cover for wooden handle of dagger, 3. dagger blade, 4. metal-hilted dagger, 5–6. pins, 7. tooth of bear, 8. bone beads, 9–10, 17–22. bronze tubular beads and pendants, 11–16. bronze pendants.
Dark areas: remains of wood. Hatched areas: human bones.
(After A. Gallay, *Archaeologia* 99 (1976))

The barrow cemetery at Weiningen (Zürich) contained stone-packed graves laid in groups beneath five barrows; adult males were furnished with dagger, bracelet, axe and pin, and females wore two pins, two or more bracelets and perhaps an anklet.[72] The cemetery near the Crestaulta settlement contained cremations placed around a stone block, with a pyre and possible funerary feasting area.[73] Among other burials, a few demonstrate exceptional care and attention; tomb 3 at Le Petit-Chasseur, Sion (Valais), contained the extended body of a young male, 20–22 years of age, encased by slabs and accompanied by an elongated flanged axe, a metal-hilted dagger, pins, necklaces of metal and amber pendants and beads (fig. 63).[74] A structure of a more unusual kind is the wooden double well at Saint-Moritz (Grisons) (fig. 64). The shafts were lined and protected by heavy wooden timbers, and two metal-hilted swords and other bronzes were driven into the ground at the bottom of one well; the site may have been in use for several centuries.[75]

On the plateau and the Jura, further settlements of the early Bronze Age yield material culture not strictly within the Rhône-Alpine traditions, yet in general representing local reactions to the availability of metal, stone and clay with an underlying realization of the current shapes and styles available both to west and north-east, both in the Rhône group and in the Únětice complex.

Pottery from these central Swiss settlements includes cordoned jars, but low-handled cups ('Les Roseaux cups'), bowls, and dishes with geometric and wavy-line decoration are also common.[76] Metal flanged axes, daggers, spearheads, and tanged arrowheads were produced, and burials were provided with various knob-headed pins, bracelets and pendants. The settlements themselves fringe some of the central Swiss

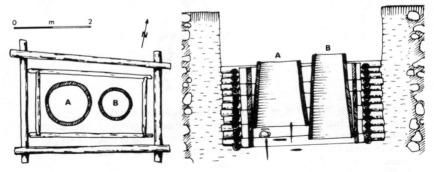

Fig. 64   Plan and section of the wooden wells at Saint Mauritius (Grisons).
Rapiers and other bronze objects were placed at the bottom of Well A.
(After Sauter 1977)

lakes, and often overlie Neolithic occupations. The Baldegg (Luzern) settlement (fig. 65) consisted of at least ten wooden houses, 6 × 4 m, set behind a fence which protected the settlement on the landward side;

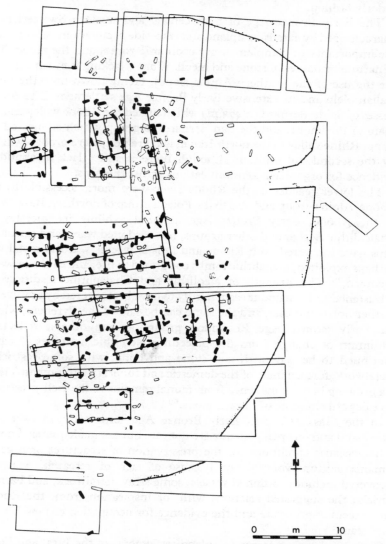

Fig. 65 Plan of the Baldegg settlement near Hochdorf, showing the major wooden uprights and the reconstruction of house plans set inside a palisade.
(After J. Bill, *Archaeologia* 101 (1976))

there was a single inturned entrance, which opened onto an area where very heavy posts were driven in, perhaps to support a raised platform. The enclosed area measured 50 × 35 m, and the houses were set in an orderly fashion.[77]

The Early Bronze Age of both central and western Switzerland is characterized by extensive upland and lake-side occupations, which attest the importance of complementary economic zones, and the recognition of natural resources of stone and metal. What is lacking is much evidence for the use of the southern Alpine slopes, facing down onto the north Italian plain and its extensive Early Bronze Age settlement. The Alpine passes of Saint-Bernard (2,473 m) which linked the Rhône valley and the Plain of Piedmont, and the San Bernardino group which connected the upper Rhine valley to the north Italian lakes region, were probably in use by the second millennium, although there is still a lack of abundant evidence for organized communications across the Alps.

The lower reaches of the Rhône river were more accessible to the Rhône-Alpine group and also to the Polada group of northern Italy. West of the Rhône, Early Bronze Age material exhibits its ancestry in Chalcolithic Beaker and other groups, but cordoned wares and carinated cups have suggested both Rhône and Polada interests. Local metal was perhaps exploited, megalithic tombs continued in use, and cave sites were occupied.[78] The strength of Neolithic and Chalcolithic traditions of subsistence and behaviour seem hardly to have been altered by any events further north and east, and the same can be said of the Pyrenees, where the Early Bronze Age Roussillon group, among others, reflects a minimum of change from the preceding Neolithic activities;[79] caves continued to be occupied, and stone and bone, with some restricted metalwork, formed most of the domestic and funerary equipment. There is a growing body of evidence from faunal remains in the well-preserved cave deposits in some of these regions.[80]

In the Massif Central, Early Bronze Age settlements in caves, in marshland and on open plateaux are not rare but are inadequately known either because conditions for the preservation of structures or organic remains are unfavourable or because of lack of research. Material recovered includes cordoned vessels, some stray metalwork, and barrow burials; the suggested relations with, or inspiration from, the Rhône valley seem appropriate and the evidence for occupation of new land is important.[81]

We have already referred to upland settlements of the Jura, and Early Bronze Age occupation of the French Alps reflects similar interests. The recovery of a bronze axe in a mine-gallery at Moûtiers indicates one of the reasons for these upland settlements, although finished metalwork is not common in the region as a whole. The pottery from the French Alps reflects Rhône-Alpine cordoned ware traditions only in the extreme west; higher up, ceramic continuity with the preceding Neolithic is uninterrupted until the middle of the second millennium.[82]

The coastal plain east of the Rhône delta is a more complex area, as here both Rhône and north Italian together with local Beaker settlement produced a heterogeneity of sites and materials. Metals are rare, and imported, and although some occupation sites are known, burials supply most of the evidence. Caves continued in use, and wheat, barley, beans, peas and olives have been recovered from such a site at Montpezat (Basses-Alpes). Other settlements lay at the delta; the plateau settlement at Camp de Laure (Bouches-du-Rhône) was defended by a heavy rampart, providing a secure area of 1.5 ha.[83] Flint industries continued to be practised until metal supplies in the later second millennium became more abundant. Inhumations in caves, in megalithic tombs, and under

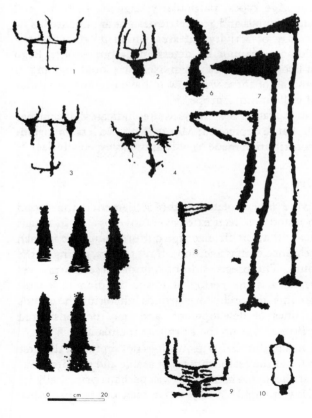

Fig. 66
Rock carvings
from Mt Bego,
Provence:
1, 3–4. plough teams,
2, 9, 10. paired oxen,
5. daggers,
6. sickle,
7, 8. halberds or
standards.
(After de Lumley
et al. 1976)

barrows, were provided with pottery, stone and occasional metal. Polada-type pottery reflects coastal traffic, and perhaps also deliberate movement into the southernmost Alpine area, less than 50 km from the Mediterranean, at Monte Bego with its abundant rock carvings (fig. 66).

The art here has been found on glacially-polished rocks in the chaotic tumble of barren valleys around the mountain, at heights between 2,000 and 2,800 m. It is estimated that nearly 40,000 slates and schists are decorated, comprising 100,000 individual representations. The slabs occur on the rocky valley sides, or at lake edges, and no certain preferences for orientation or composition have been recognized other than those reflected by the focal point of Monte Bego itself. Pecking and grooving were the techniques used in the five main valleys. The subjects consist of human representations, animals, weapons and tools, cupmarks and various geometric designs. The most common animal is the ox, and this is sometimes combined with a plough and a human figure. Oxen are often shown as head and horns only, viewed from above. The weapons appear to be of Early Bronze Age types, particularly daggers, halberds and sickles, but the humans, animals and geometric designs are undated. The significance of this centre of activity, an area which must have been visited over many decades, cannot be determined, but Monte Bego reveals the interest of Bronze Age societies in oxen, in ploughing, and in weapons of bronze, and all of these we know to have been of particular importance in second millennium Europe.[84]

Faunal remains from the rather few analysed sites indicate that caprines were kept as well as the cattle depicted at Monte Bego. No less important at some sites was the contribution made by wild animals, especially deer.[85]

Sardinia and Corsica

Sardinia and Corsica were rather isolated areas of settlement in the second millennium BC. Each island has been extensively investigated in recent years, and it is significant that the Bronze Age cultural sequence in each culminates in the appearance of massive stone-built towers, dating to the later second millennium. The precise chronology of these has not yet been worked out; we discuss the period of tower-building in a later chapter (p. 439). Before this, the prehistoric groups inhabiting the islands pursued independent lines of development, and may be considered marginal to the Early Bronze Age on the European mainland.

In Sardinia,[86] the Chalcolithic *Ozieri* group does not represent the first settlement of the island, but the establishment of arable and pasture land, and the introduction of sheep, oxen and pigs was perhaps principally its work. Collective burials were made in impressive rock-cut tombs. Other cultural groups, *Monte Claro* and *Bonnanaro,* are known as well as Beaker-related material, but the interaction of these, and their contribution to the first full Bronze Age communities of Sardinia, are outside our scope here. Before the end of the second millennium, perhaps as early as 1500 BC, the first towers of the Nuraghic phase were being constructed, eventually to be contained within the stone-built houses of villages. The earliest of these settlements were probably no more than farmsteads, and it was not until later that larger communities began to form again. The wide areas of lowland on the western side of the island were suitable for major cultivation and for pastoral activities, and elsewhere the local silver, lead and copper was available for exploitation, as well as obsidian.

Sardinia lies 200 km from the nearest point of the Italian mainland, yet only 10 km from Corsica. Intensive study on Corsica has shown that the appearance of the tower-building phase there is probably contemporaneous with the Nuraghic phase of Sardinia.[87] Before this time, a population of Neolithic pastoralists and builders of megalithic tombs, stone statues, and stone villages, had effectively controlled the island.

Malta

Evidence for Bronze Age settlement on Malta is not extensive.[88] It is clear that the temple period falls before the advent of regular copper metallurgy; equally, that the succeeding 'Tarxien Cemetery culture' belongs to the Metal Age, for its cremation urns are accompanied by flat axes and bronze daggers. All the evidence points to a destruction of the temples and displacement of the temple-builders by an intrusive metal-using people.[89] The temples were destroyed and not, for the most part, rebuilt – there was later occupation at Borġ in-Nadur and some additions at Skorba, though *after* the desecration of the previous building. To the later part of the earlier Bronze Age on Malta belongs a series of defended sites, often associated with bell-shaped pits, that link it with the Milazzo culture. At least one Mycenaean sherd is known from this phase, and confirms this synchronism as well as indicating the possibility of direct contact with the Aegean. The most famous site, and the place where this sherd was found, is Borġ in-Nadur, overlooking a bay at the south-east of Malta.[90] A roughly triangular promontory is cut off by a massive defensive wall including in its fabric truly Cyclopean stones (fig. 67): its construction must have taken place close in time to that of the great Mycenaean citadels. Inside the site was a temple that had originally been built in the late Neolithic but was now reoccupied. At several places behind the great wall remains of oval huts have been found: the best-documented are those found by Trump in 1959. They had crushed stone

floors; stone wall-foundations; superstructures of 'wattle, thatch etc.';
hearths set against the wall (one of them enclosed in a stone setting); a
bench; querns and stone rollers of unknown use. A long and detailed
stratigraphic sequence was obtained from these deposits. In the soil
immediately above bedrock were sherds of Tarxien Cemetery type,
followed by 'Borġ in-Nadur' pottery. In a similar way, the west temple
at Skorba was adapted for domestic use by the addition of internal
partition walls.[91]

In contrast to the monumental inhumation tombs of Sicily the tombs
of the earlier Bronze Age at Tarxien are, for the most part, simple inurned
cremations.[92] The burning of the body had been done extremely
sketchily, however, and very often the remains had to be broken to fit into
the urn. Accessory vases and other grave-goods were invariably present.
In other parts of the islands it has been shown that small dolmens,
presumably for cremations, can be attributed to the Tarxien Cemetery
culture.[93] These small chambers comprise a large capstone slab resting on
rather less massive wall-blocks, and most now contain no archaeological
deposits at all (fig. 67). Evans has suggested that their origins are to be
sought in the dolmens of south-east Italy around Otranto.[94] The
appearance of funerary urns, however, is another matter, and of quite
uncertain ancestry. At a rather later date rock-cut chamber tombs enjoyed
a brief vogue, and their characteristic bell shape suggests influence from
Sicily.

Tarxien Cemetery pottery is pebble-burnished and rather angular in
shape. The forms include bowls with sharply everted rim, amphoroid
jugs, two-handled goblets, piriform urns and *askoi.* Decoration, where
present, is by incision. By contrast pottery of the Borġ in-Nadur phase
makes extensive use of pedestal bases, though the commonest individual
form is a low conical bowl; decoration is by furrowing, encrusted with
white paint. Of the other finds we may mention the stylized clay figurines
of the Tarxien Cemetery phase, its copper daggers, flat axes, and awls.
The quantity of metal no doubt increased in the Borġ in-Nadur phase,
and included tin-bronze alloys, but our finds are few and of a domestic,
not a funerary, nature. A considerable variety of stone and bone objects
are also represented, and faience beads appear in large numbers.[95]

The chronology of the Maltese Bronze Age is dependent on the
stratigraphical work of Evans and Trump, and on a series of radiocarbon
dates (table 6).[96] These suggest that the transition to the Bronze Age,
that is, from Tarxien to Tarxien Cemetery phases, took place around
2000 bc. The date of the Borġ in-Nadur phase is not known, though the
Mycenaean sherd and extrapolation from the radiocarbon dates would
indicate that it had started by about 1300 bc, or a little earlier.

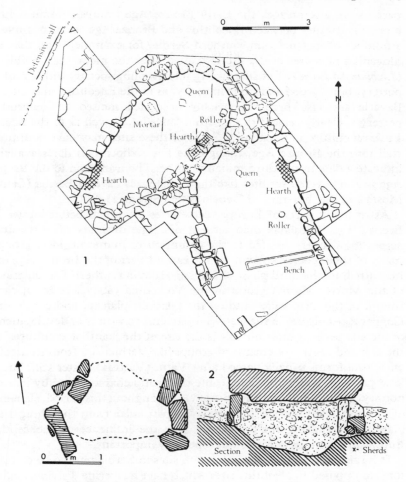

Fig. 67   1. Borġ in-Nadur, Malta: plan of the post-Temple settlement,
2. Ta Hammut, Malta: plan and section of dolmen.
(After Trump, *PPS* 27 (1961), Evans *PPS* 22 (1956))

Jugoslavia and Albania

In Jugoslavia[97] the start of metal-working did not lag far behind similar
events to the north and east. Copper mines at Rudna Glava near Negotin
in eastern Serbia and Bor are among the earliest in all Europe, and rich
metal finds in graves and hoards occur from the Middle Chalcolithic
on.[98] Groups like Baden-Kostolac, Bubanj-Hum phases I–II,
Vučedol, Lasinja and Ljubljansko Barje contained copper as a regular

part of the assemblage; the Early Bronze Age groups contained little more. Continuity between Eneolithic and Bronze Age seems possible in a number of instances; in southern Serbia, for example, or in the rich Slovenian pile-sites of the group named after the moor near Ljubljana (*Ljubljansko Barje*);[99] at sites like Ig pile dwellings occur, with a prolific pottery, bone, wood and stone industry, as in the Eneolithic lake-sites of Bavaria and elsewhere. The richly decorated incised and encrusted pottery is clearly related to that from Vučedol, as well as to the related *Vinkovci* culture in Croatia.[100] Some of these sites may have continued well into the Bronze Age, though the few radiocarbon dates available indicate a date in the third millennium bc. The transition to the Bronze Age is also covered by sites like the Hrustovača cave in Bosnia (Sanski Most) and the 'hill-fort' of Debelo Brdo (Sarajevo).[101]

As in many parts of Europe, cemeteries are much better known in Bronze Age Jugoslavia than settlements. The diversity of grave-finds across the country has led to the definition of numerous local groups, many of them poorly known. To the earliest part of the Bronze Age one may attribute the third phase of Bubanj-Hum in southern Serbia, graves of the Moriš (Maros) group in the Vojvodina (above, p. 8of.), early tumuli in the Drin valley and on the Glasinac plateau, and continuing Copper Age cultures in the west. Subsequently a variety of developments occurred: perhaps most notable is the rise of the 'kantharos cultures' in the east and centre – elements of groups like Verbicioara from Romania, with local forms usually named after Vatin (Vattina). Later still, but at least partly coeval with Vatin, came the group characterized by its rich pottery, Dubovac-Žuto Brdo (p. 144f.). Throughout this period, elements of cultures from outside Jugoslavia, in particular from the Hungarian plain, were making their presence felt; the influence of the central European Tumulus cultures was especially important.

It is said that Bronze Age habitation sites in Serbia tend to be on hill-tops, as opposed to Neolithic sites which have a riverine distribution.[102] The mining areas of the south of the country are protected by a system of 'hill-forts', though these were often placed in positions suitable for the exploitation of arable land.

In southern Serbia a number of stratified habitation sites occur, spanning the Chalcolithic-Early Bronze Age transition. Chief among these are the sites of Bubanj and Humska Čuka (Niš), where phase III has material related to Glina III in Romania (above, p. 138), that is, the start of the true Bronze Age.[103] Other finds are rare, but cave occupation apparently continued from the Copper Age, as at the Gladnica cave (Gračanica) in Kosovo or the Odmut cave (Piva) in Montenegro.[104]

Succeeding the Bubanj-Hum III material, at Humska Čuka and some other sites, comes that typical of the hill-top settlement of Donja Slatina (Leskovac): sites with similar material are distributed in the area of the Morava valley.[105]

Other sites with material that can definitely be ascribed to an early date in the Bronze Age are few and far between. In Bosnia, a fortified site (*gradina*) at Pod (Bugojno) was found on excavation to have four main periods of which the first was attributed to this age: from the lowest levels only pottery was recovered, and this was coarse in fabric with relief bands on the surface, including one- and two-handled vases of types that indicate a synchronism with Belotić on the one hand and Glina III-Schneckenberg on the other.[106]

In northern Serbia, tells are known as well as hill-top sites. Among the most notable is Gomolava (Hrtkovci), which has a long sequence, only partly stratified, from early Neolithic on: the site lies beside the Sava, which has eroded a good deal of it.[107] The Bronze Age layer (IVa) contains evidence of intensive building activity, though whole house-plans have only recently been recovered. Pottery characteristic of the early Vatin group has been found, as well as sherds of later Vatin and the succeeding Belegiš. The succession, then, is a long one, though the investigations so far have not succeeded in separating the various phases stratigraphically. Vatin sites typically occupy raised terraces beside water, and from older excavations numerous house-remains are known. At Vatin itself some twenty-five or thirty houses are suggested, on the basis of the large number of hearths recovered.[108]

In the succeeding Dubovac-Žuto Brdo group, settlements are on high river terraces and usually unfortified, with their attendant cemeteries nearby; houses, where known, consist of rectangular post-settings, or simply scant traces in the sand: this was certainly the case with Grad (Usije, Žuto Brdo) on the Danube,[109] where in two horizons of habitation houses containing ovens and settlement rubbish were found; at Tavan-Ostrovo (Veliko Gradište, Požarevac); and at Kožice (Dobra, Požarevac) on the river of the same name, where a deep series of deposits included levels of this cultural group.[110]

Very much more is known of graves. In Serbia, early material comes from the tumuli in and around the upper Drin basin, as at Belotić and Bela Crkva (Valjevo), and a good many other sites.[111] Cemeteries are known to have been groups of medium-sized tumuli, often with stone settings in the body of the mound. Both cremation and inhumation (crouched) occur. Two of the Belotić examples had traces of fire, and two an irregular stone setting. These burials were accompanied by copper objects as well as pottery in simple one-handled cup and bowl forms; chronologically these finds are attributable to an early stage in the Bronze

Age (Br A), since they compare very closely with metalwork from the Periam-Mokrin group.

The rich series of graves on the Glasinac plateau in the Rogatica area of central Bosnia starts at this time, and the finds from them are partly paralleled in the important settlement at Debelo Brdo (Sarajevo). Graves in tumulus IV at Vrlazije and tumuli VI and VII at Kovačev Do contain daggers with semicircular heel and rivet arrangement, equivalent again to the Periam type on the Pannonian plain (fig. 68). What little is known of the grave rite indicates a predominance of inhumation in stone cairns or settings, a practice which continued far into the Bronze Age.[112]

In Istria there is some evidence for the start of cremation burials in tumuli: at Maklavan (Pula) both inhumed and cremated remains were found together with the bones of horse, oxen and birds in a stone setting in a tumulus that had walls preserved and even an 'entrance' corridor.[113] The few grave-goods recovered suggest an Early Bronze Age date (pins etc.), but in general it is extremely hard to date the barrows in this area.

In Croatia a small local group is named after the site of Višnjica in the north-central part of the country: ovoid pots with vertical channelled decoration come from graves that also contain Noppenringen and knot-headed pins.[114] Other graves from this part of Jugoslavia may contain spectacle pendants and Spondylus shell ornaments – neither of which gives much precision of dating. Subsequently there are some other varieties of site. The cave of Bezdanjača near Vrhovina is one such.[115] Numerous crouched inhumations, shown by their pottery and metalwork to cover the entire Tumulus period and even part of the Urnfield period, were found, often bordered by little hearths with pottery and bones, suggesting ritual feasts. Ochre was frequently added to the grave, and a vessel was found with a powdery ochre deposit in the bottom, no doubt for pouring an ochre mixture over the corpse. The cave perhaps served as the cemetery for the nearby hill-fort at Vatinsovac, and there is some evidence (from the faunal remains) of the importance of hunting in addition to stock-raising and agriculture, for the bones of deer, fox, wolf, brown bear and wild boar accompanied those of the common domesticates. The radiocarbon dates indicate a span of occupation that starts in the fifteenth century bc and goes on till the tenth.

Tumuli like those at Belotić or on the Glasinac plateau continue in use into the succeeding centuries, as finds of Tumulus, Paraćin and Vatin type show.[116] Genuine burials of the Vatin group are not, however, well-known; at the classic sites of the group ordinary inhumation seems to have been the rule. Perhaps the most remarkable thing about the period is the start of barrow-burial of typical central European Tumulus type. In the Vojvodina, for instance, the Velebit site near Kanjiža had such barrows;[117] one may find comparable things in north Croatia or Slovenia.[118]

But by the time of Br C barrows were not the only form of burial in north Jugoslavia. A new tradition was starting, characterized by cremation

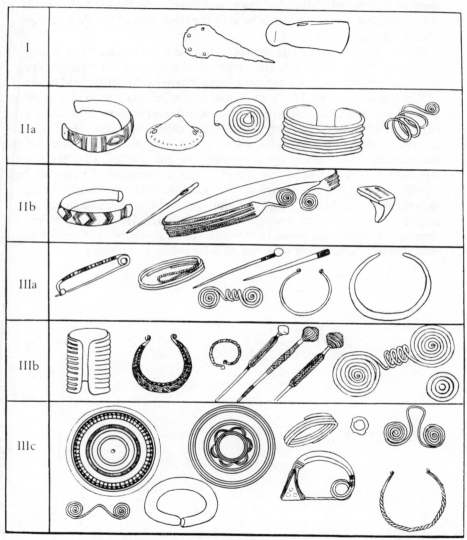

Fig. 68   Sequence of grave-finds in barrows on the Glasinac plateau: I–IIb = earlier Bronze Age, IIIa–c = later Bronze Age.
(After Benac and Čović 1956)

and deposition in urns. The site where this transition has been most fully documented is Belegiš, lying on the Danube in the Srem.[119] The first urns in the cemetery at Štojica Gumno (a settlement was found nearby) were in the character of Vatin pottery, but the later ones broke new ground, having tall cylindrical necks and handles on the belly (fig. 161). This tradition was to continue on into the later part of the Bronze Age (below, p. 444).

In Albania an important sequence has been recovered from Maliq (Korçë).[120] This was a pile-site or group of sites, and the stratigraphy that has been obtained is a composite one. Phase I is Neolithic and phase II Chalcolithic; phase III is attributed to the Bronze Age, and is itself divided into four. No house plans have been found in these levels, but a rich haul of pottery and other settlement debris was recovered. The pottery of phase IIIa includes many conical bowl forms and one-and two-handled cups; decoration is by barbotine and applied relief bands – especially knobs and horseshoe handles. The appearance of wish-bone handles in phase IIIb makes the connection with the Macedonian sequence clear, as do bowls with two high handles; there are also globular-bellied jugs and cups and low open vessels (fig. 69). Many of these forms continue through into phase IIIc which shows a number of forms that indicate contemporaneity with late Middle Helladic in Greece.

Fig. 69   Pottery profiles from Maliq (Korçë), level IIIb. (After Prendi 1966)

The Maliq sequence is one of pottery only, but it is unique in the Adriatic zone in its indication of continuity. Very little other material of this phase occurs in either Albania or Jugoslav Macedonia. A rectangular house-plan was excavated at Demir Kapija:[121] the only example from the area. Elsewhere settlement is attested only from sites with domestic debris like Crnobuki[122] in south-west Macedonia (Bitola) and Mramorić near Čaška (Titov Veles).[123]

The few radiocarbon determinations (table 6) available for Jugoslavia indicate a date around 2300 bc for the end of the Chalcolithic. Dating proceeds mainly by cross-linking; at Humska Čuka parallels for both metalwork (a small curved riveted knife) and pottery (pedestalled conical bowl, goblets and polished grey sherds) have been suggested in Early and Middle Helladic Greece and in Troy I I and I I I–V. Some sherds, indeed, are claimed as true 'Minyan' pottery, finely polished and well-levigated – different from everything else at Humska Čuka, which tends to have a sand temper.[124] The chronological synchronisms suggested are miscellaneous in date and in general radiocarbon dating suggests that Bubanj-Hum I I I should fall well before 2000 bc, which is earlier than the start of Minyan ware on most sites in Greece. The possibility of an ancestry for Minyan ware in the north has often been suggested, though as often denied, and in view of the evidence from Lerna and Lefkandi seems extremely unlikely.[125] More problematical still is the finding of a dagger, apparently of Middle Minoan type, in a grave at Vodhinë in the Drin valley of Albania, for none of the other objects in this barrow can be dated before the very end of the Bronze Age.[126]

The rather patchy nature of our knowledge of the Jugoslav Bronze Age is due not only to the present authors' inadequacies, but also to the relative sparseness of material in relation to the size of the country. Until long stratified sequences are available, as at Gomolava, covering the whole period, and from different areas, our knowledge will remain patchy. It is to be hoped that some of these gaps in this important area will soon be filled.

Table 6   Radiocarbon dates, southern Europe, earlier Bronze Age

Site	Lab no.	bc
Italy – Eneolithic		
La Romità di Asciano (Pisa), layer 10	Pi–100	2298 ± 115
Luni sul Mignone, Tre Erici, level 7 lower	St–2043	2075 ± 100
level 8	St–2042	2005 ± 200
level 8	St–1343	1850 ± 80

Table 6—cont.

Site	Lab no.	bc
Grotta dei Piccioni (Abbruzzo) level III or IV (Rinaldone/Remedello)	Pi–50	2356±105
Buccino (Salerno), rock-cut tombs		
Average of 6 dates, (excluding 1 doubtful)	St–3620 etc.	2202
Grotta del Mitreo, level 4	R–902	1870±50
,, ,, level 5, Ig II pottery	R–903a	1770±50

Italy – earlier Bronze Age

Luni sul Mignone, acropolis, Apennine I, bone	St–2044	1055±75
	St–2047	995±80
Apennine II	St–1345	1245±75
Apennine I and II	St–2045	1170±75
,, Tre Erici level 6, Ap. III – I	St–1147	1125±70
Narce, phase II, Apennine	St–2397	1055±100
S. Maria di Leuca (Lecce), Apennine	F–92	2100±140
Molina di Ledro	Pi–88	1187±105
,, ,, More recent dates:	1950±210, 1709±66, 1692±36	
Cavriana (Mantova)	R–25	1545±60
	R–786a	1570±50
Barche di Solferino (Mantova)	Pi–87	1391±115
Polada	R–294	1380±65
	R–295	1270±55
	R–296	1295±55
Isolone del Mincio (Mantova)	R–96	1280±60
	R–97	1525±60
	R–98	1125±60
Monte Covolo (Brescia)	Birm–469	1890±210
Lucone, Polpenazze (Brescia)	R–375	1410±50
	R–375a	1210±50
Arcevia, level 5. Proto-Ap – Polada	R–275	1315±55
Ortucchio	Pi–80	1416±130
Monte Leoni (Parma), Terramara deposits	GrN–7594	1215±25
	GrN–7595	1295±55
Riparo di Romagnano III – Loc, EBA burials	R–769	1770±50
	R–770a	1680±50

Sardinia

Sa Turricula, Bonnanaro hut	R–963a	1510±50

Malta

Skorba, Tarxien phase	BM–143	2430±150
Tarxien, Tarxien Cemetery phase	BM–710	1336±72
	BM–711	1404±76
	BM–141	1930±150
? Tarxien Cemetery	BM–101	2535±150

Table 6—cont.

Site	Lab. no.	bc
Jugoslavia – Chalcolithic		
Ljubljansko Barje, pile-dwellings	Z–278	2683 ± 117
Veliki Mah No. 1	Z–305	2395 ± 113
Hissar (Prizren), level E4	Bln–351	2220 ± 100
level E3	Bln–350	2340 ± 100
Odmut (Piva), phase VII	Z–409	2330 ± 120
Jugoslavia – earlier Bronze Age		
Bezdanjača cave, Brakusova Draga (Vrhovine)	Z–174	1401 ± 77
	Z–186/II	1349 ± 61
Mediana, Brzi Brod (Niš), MBA pits	BC–5 etc.	1580 ± 60
Omoljica, Banat. Pot in NM Beograd, MBA	BC–2	1580 ± 60
Podgorač, Breški (Našice), pit	Z–300	1460 ± 100
Crnobuki, Tumba (Bitola), horizon 1	Z–364	1650 ± 175
,, ,, horizon 2	Z–365	1710 ± 150
Switzerland		
Mottata (Ramosch), cave	B–149	1620 ± 160
	B–148	1600 ± 100
Southern France		
Salernes, Baume Fontbrégoua (Var), cave	Gif–2100	1720 ± 110
Lorgues, (Var), megalith	Mc–720	1760 ± 90
La Baume Loire, Solignac (H. Loire), rock shelter	Ly–164	1720 ± 130
Le Rond du Lévrier, Salette (H. Loire), rock shelter	Ly–194	1420 ± 210
	Ly–195	1620 ± 130
Clairvaux, La Motte aux Moynins (Jura), lake-side settlement	Gif–1844	1850 ± 110
	Gif–2297	1710 ± 110
	Gif–2299	1930 ± 110
G. de la Baume, Gonvillars (Jura), cave	Gif–467	1480 ± 200
Lac de Chalain, Doucier, (Jura), lake-side settlement	Gif–209	1530 ± 200
Lac de Norlay (Jura), settlement	B–549	1600 ± 200
Varilhes, Carbon (Ariège), occupation	Gif–1354	2050 ± 120
Esclauzels, G. du Noyer (Lot), cave	Gif–1634	1890 ± 120
Les Côtes de Roquefort (Aveyron), cave	Gsy–37	1980 ± 150
Aven du Gendarme (Aveyron), cave	Gsy–38	1940 ± 150
St. Romé de Cernon, G. de Sargel, (Aveyron), cave	Gif–328	1760 ± 186
	Gif–3005	1850 ± 130
	Gif–3006	1670 ± 130
Creissels, G. des Cascades, (Aveyron), cave	Gif–442	1320 ± 150
Moux, G. d'Alaric, (Aude), cave	Mc–593	1775 ± 70
Monclus, G. de Prével, (Gard), cave	Gif–191	1930 ± 180

Table 6—cont.

Site	Lab. no.	bc
Pardailhan, G. Tournié (Hérault), cave	Mc–907	1450 ± 100
	Mc–903	1550 ± 100
Casenovei Vingrau, G. des Châtaigniers (Pyr. Or.), cave	Gif–1275	1480 ± 120
	Gif–760	1170 ± 120
Les Courondes, Ouveillan (Aude), occupation	Gif–1161	1800 ± 130
Carluc, (Basses-Alpes), cave	Mc–364	1790 ± 100
Avignon, (Vaucluse), occupation	Gif–706	1550 ± 120

Notes

1 H.-J. Beug, *Flora* 154 (1964), 401–444.

2 A. Horowitz, *BCSP* 12 (1975), 39–48.

3 J. L. Beaulieu in Guilaine 1976, 59–66; J.-L. Borel in Guilaine 1976, 67–73; G. Jalut in Guilaine 1976, 74–81, 180–5; J.-L. Vernet in Guilaine 1976, 95–103.

4 Frenzel 1966, 118, quoting O. Fürst, *Flora* 153 (1963), 469.

5 S. Bottema, *Late Quaternary vegetation history of northwestern Greece,* 1974; summarized, as are other relevant diagrams, by J. Turner in *Proceedings of the Second International Colloquium on Thera and the Ancient World,* originally intended for 1977 but postponed until 1978. We thank Dr Turner for allowing us to read her contribution in typescript.

6 Summarized in H.-J. Beug, *Problems of Balkan Flora and Vegetation,* Sofia, 1975, 72–7.

7 G. C. Bortolami, J. Ch. Fontes, V. Markgraf and J. F. Saliège, *Palaeogeogr., Palaeoclimatol., Palaeoecol.* 21 (1977), 139–56.

8 H.-J. Beug, *Flora* 154 (1964), 436.

9 Peroni 1959.

10 Trump 1958, 194ff.

11 S. M. Puglisi, *Atti VI Congresso internazionale di Scienze pre- e protostoriche* (Rome 1962), 403–7 Cf. Lo Porto 1963, 363ff.; *BPI* n.s. 15 vol. 73 (1964), 109–42. 'Protoapennine' is the same group as 'Conelle-Ortucchio'.

12 Conveniently summarized by C. Renfrew and R. Whitehouse, *BSA* 69 (1974), 343–90.

13 Ibid. 376ff. This seems preferable to the idea of the local invention of metallurgy.

14 Barfield 1971, 68ff. Peroni 1971, 17ff.

15 Peroni 1971, 36–40.

16 Battaglia 1943; Rageth 1974.

17 R. Perini, *Preist. Alp.* 7 (1971), 283–322; 8 (1972), 199–253; 11 (1975), 25–64.

18 By Mr Clive Gamble, whom we thank for information in advance of publication.

19 A. Aspes and L. Fasani, *Atti e Memorie della Accademia di Agricoltura, Scienze e Lettere di Verona,* 6th series, 19 (1967–8), 69–112.

20 Säflund 1939; de Marinis 1975,

37ff. The name is a corruption of 'terra marinosa', a local designation for particularly rich black soil.

21 de Marinis 1975, 42.

22 E.g. Castione: Säflund 1939, pl. 95.

23 A. Ammerman, personal communication, for which thanks are due; see now *Preist. Alp.* 12 (1975), 1–28.

24 U. Rellini, *Mon. Ant.* 34 (1931), 129–280, esp. 267–72. Major studies of the Apennine group: Trump 1958; Peroni 1959; Puglisi 1959.

25 Puglisi 1959; G. Barker, *PPS* 38 (1972), 170–208; Barker 1975.

26 Östenberg 1967.

27 Östenberg 1967, 242ff.

28 R. Peroni, *BPI* n.s. 14 vol. 72 (1962–3), 251–442; S. Pannuti, *BPI* n.s 20 vol. 78 (1969), 147–247; R. Peroni, *BPI* n.s. 20 vol. 78 (1969), 249–58; Barker 1975, 154.

29 Potter 1976, 41ff. 312f.

30 R. Ross Holloway *et al.*, *JFA* 2 (1975), 11–81.

31 D. H. Trump, *PBSR* 25 n.s. 12 (1957), 1–15; *PBSR* 31 n.s. 18 (1963), 1–32.

32 A. Mosso, *Mon. Ant.* 19 (1908), 305ff.

33 Lo Porto 1963.

34 Bernabò Brea 1966, 97ff.; L. Bernabò Brea and M. Cavalier, *BPI* n.s. 10 vol. 65 (1956), 7ff., fig. 3, 47ff.; cf. too *BPI* n.s. 17, vol. 75 (1966), 143ff.

35 L. Bernabò Brea, *Boll. d'Arte* 1951, 31ff.; L. Bernabò Brea and M. Cavalier, *Meligunìs-Lipára*, vol. III, 1968, 50ff., 144ff., 185ff.

36 Voza 1972, 1973.

37 Polada: Peroni 1971, 22; Povegliano: Peroni 1963, 49ff.; *terremare*: Säflund 1939, 197ff.; central and south: Peroni 1971, 271ff., 283ff., 299ff., 325ff.; M. Gervasio, *I dolmen e la civiltà del bronzo nelle Puglie*, 1913.

38 P. Orsi, *BPI* 18 (1892), 1, 67; 19 (1893), 30; *Mon. Ant.* 6 (1895), 89–150; Bernabò Brea 1966, 110ff.,

123ff. Voza (1972) has suggested that the earliest *tombe a enchytrismos* may be earlier than hitherto thought, and contemporary at Thapsos with *tombe a grotticella*.

39 Anati 1961, and a long series of volumes on all aspects of rock art from the same author, published in Capo di Ponte.

40 Anati 1961, 151ff., esp. 158ff. for sun worship.

41 C. Zindel, *Ur-Schweiz* 32 (1968).

42 U. Calzoni, *Quaderni d' Studi Etruschi* 1 (1954); 2 (1962).

43 U. Rellini, *Mon. Ant.* 24 (1916), 461–616.

44 L. Barfield, *Antiquity* 45 (1966), 48–9.

45 Peroni 1971, 50ff.; Rageth 1974, 127ff., pls 30–86; for the same forms (and numerous other objects) in wood 197ff., pls 104–7. Subdivisions in the Polada material are now possible; L. Fasani, *Memorie Museo Civico Verona*, 1970, 108f.

46 Säflund 1939, 117ff.

47 Trump 1958, 165ff.

48 Rageth 1974, 169ff. (clay), 178 (bone), 186 (stone and amber), 200 (textiles). Glass-paste: L. Barfield, personal communication; dating is Middle Bronze Age.

49 Rageth 1974, 175ff., pls 89–91; 127 pl. 29; A. Aspes and L. Fasani, *Preist. Alp.* 10 (1974), 81.

50 J. D. Cowen, *PPS* 32 (1966), 262–312.

51 Ripatransone: Peroni 1971, 248; O. Uenze, *Die frühbronzezeitliche triangulären Vollgriffdolche*, 1938, 77; Cascina Ranza: Hachmann 1957, 127f., 217, pl. 59; V. Bianco Peroni, *Le spade nell' Italia continentale*, 1970, 98ff., pl. 41.

52 Battaglia 1943, 26ff., pls XV–XVIII; Barfield 1971, 72.

53 H. N. Jarman and C. Gamble, *Preist. Alp.* 11 (1975), 75–6 and unpublished information from Mr. Gamble; M. Jarman, *Preist. Alp.* 11

(1975), 65–73; id. in *Problems in Economic and Social Archaeology* (ed. G. Sieveking *et al.*), 1976, 543ff.

54 G. Barker, *PPS* 38 (1972), 170–208; Barker 1975.

55 Full details in Barker 1975, 153ff.

56 H. Helbaek in Östenberg 1967, 277ff.; cf. material from Fiavè, n. 53 above; cf. now *terramara* evidence from Monte Leoni: *Preist. Alp.* 12 (1975), 19ff.

57 Anati 1961, 115ff.

58 Anati 1961, 142ff.

59 Barfield 1971, 77.

60 First depicted by Točík (1964, 44 fig. 27 and pl. LXI, 15); more fully discussed by L. Fasani, *Memorie del Museo Civico di Storia Naturale di Verona* 18 (1970), 91ff.; Barfield 1971, 77; Vladár 1973a, 321ff., figs 77–8; H.-J. Hundt, *Preist. Alp.* 10 (1974), 171f., fig. 26. For Poland, see now J. Fogel, *Arch. Polski* 22/1 (1977), 97–109.

61 L. Barfield, *Antiquity* 45 (1966), 48–9.

62 W. D. Taylour, *Mycenaean Pottery in Italy and Adjacent Areas*, 1958; F. Biancofiore, *La Civiltà Micenea nell'Italia meridionale*, 1963; F. G. Lo Porto, *Boll. d'Arte* 48 (1963), 123–30; Tinè and Vagnetti 1967; L. Vagnetti, *La Parola del Passato* 134 (1970), 359–80; Bietti Sestieri 1973, 413 n. 1. M. Marazzi and S. Tusa, *Sicilia Archeologica* 9 no. 31 (1976), 49–90; catalogue pp. 83ff.

63 Trump 1958, 194ff.

64 Östenberg 1967, 71, 104, 147ff. The southern house at Luni contained three clear Bronze Age habitation levels, which are thus called Apennine I, II and III: hence one may derive a reasonable basis for the relative chronology of the central Italian Bronze Age. The pot shapes vary rather little from level to level, having a predominance of one-handled carinated cups, miniature vessels and a variety of coarse domestic wares with impressed cordons. The handles progress from mainly raised ribbon types and saddle-shaped horizontal ledge-grips to the great variety one may expect on Apennine sites – very frequently the straight-cylinder knob (*cilindro retta*), but also the horned variety (*cornuta*), or that with animal protomes, the vertical type with median crest and lateral horns, or with 'protruding lobe', and the type with two finger-holes. The reverse process is true in the decorative motifs: in Luni I the commonest forms are bands of dots (*punteggio*) with or without incised bordering lines; there are also rectilinear designs like zig-zags, meanders and lozenges; white encrustation; zoned decoration and excised (*Kerbschnitt*) designs; also a few curvilinear designs. By Luni III, however, many of these were not used at all, while the remainder were infrequent.

65 Millotte 1963, 94; Millotte 1976; Guilaine 1972, 85 for G. des Châtaigniers (Pyr. Or.) occupation; Roudil and Guilaine 1976, fig. 1, 5 for cordoned ware from Les Fournils in the Hérault.

66 Sandars 1957, 24, 26; Briard 1974, 134; Millotte 1963.

67 Sandars 1957, 21–23; Millotte 1976, 495ff.

68 W. Burkart, *Crestaulta; eine bronzezeitliche Hügelsiedlung bei Surin im Lugnez*. Monog. zur Ur- und Frühgeschichte der Schweiz 5, 1946; M. Lichardus-Itten, in Drack 1971, 41–54. Recent excavations of stratified settlements near Savognin, Cunter and Motta Vallac point to more intensive occupation throughout the Bronze Age in the Grisons: J. Rageth, *JSGUF* 60 (1977), 43–101; *Helvetica Arch.* 29–30 (1977), 12–55.

69 Millotte 1976, fig. 1; C. Strahm in Drack 1971, 5–26. Roudil and Gui-

laine 1976, fig. 1, 11 for Nîmes dagger, fig. 1, 14 for trefoil pin from Minerve (Hérault); Guilaine 1976a, fig. 5 for Arnave (Ariège) hoard; Taburles dagger.

70 Rhône-Alpine products: Millotte 1963, pl. 3; Briard 1974, 136, fig. 4, 1–2; daggers: O. Uenze, *Die frühbronzezeitliche triangulären vollgriffdolche*, Vorgesch. Forsch. 11, 1938, Taf. 1–5. The gold cup from Eschenz is an outstanding example of earlier Bronze Age sheet metalwork, and can be compared in general punch and groove technique to the Fritzdorf and Rillaton cups, although there is no need to postulate cultural connections: B. Hardmayer and J. Bürgi, *ZSAK* 32 (1975), 109–20, with excellent photos of the three cups. For recent definition of local groups based on finds of pottery and bronzes, see J. Bill, *ZSAK* 33 (1976), 77–93. Bill 1973 for survey.

71 Sandars 1957, 17; Briard 1974, 134; Millotte 1963; Sauter 1976, 86.

72 J. Bill, *Archaeologia (Dijon)* 101 (1976), 33; C. Osterwalder in Drack 1971, 27–40.

73 Sauter 1976, 95.

74 A. Gallay, *Archaeologia (Dijon)* 99 (1976), 47–53; Sauter 1976, fig. 27.

75 Sauter 1976, 96, fig. 33. Y. Mottier in Drack 1971, 145–56.

76 Sauter 1976, fig. 28; J. Bill, *Archaeologia (Dijon)* 101 (1976), 35–6; C. Strahm in Drack 1971, 5–26.

77 J. Bill, *Archaeologia (Dijon)* 101 (1976), 34; R. Wyss in Drack 1971, 103–22.

78 J. Audibert, *La Civilisation Chalcolithique du Languedoc Oriental.* Inst. Internat. d'Etudes Ligures, Coll. de Monog. Préhist. et Archéol. 4, 1962; Guilaine 1972; Roudil 1972; Roudil and Guilaine 1976.

79 Guilaine 1976a.

80 E.g. Guilaine 1972, 94, who refers to sheep as predominating over cattle and pig, with some evidence for the hunting of wild game on a large scale.

81 Daugas 1976; see also L. Fanaud, *L'Age du bronze en Bourbonnais,* 1965, for northern slopes into the Loire basin where traces of settlement are substantial. F. Henry, *Les Tumulus du Département de la Côte-d'Or,* Paris, 1933, refers to cemeteries of the Early Bronze Age west of the upper Saône.

82 Bocquet 1976.

83 Courtin 1976.

84 H. de Lumley *et al.* in Guilaine 1976, 222–36; J. Nordblah and J. Rosuall, *Val Camonica and Monte Bego. Travel Report,* 1974. Both these recent surveys give useful bibliographies.

85 T. Poulain in Guilaine 1976, 104–115, with comprehensive bibliography.

86 On Sardinia generally: Guido 1963. On the Chalcolithic-Early Bronze Age: W. Bray, *PPS* 30 (1964), 75–98; *RSP* 18 (1963), 155–90; Daniel and Evans 1967.

87 R. Grosjean in Guilaine 1976; Daniel and Evans 1967.

88 On Malta generally: Evans 1959; Evans 1971.

89 D. H. Trump, in *Problems in Economic and Social Archaeology* (ed. G. de G. Sieveking *et al.*) 1976, 605–10. Possible causes for the collapse of the Temple culture have often been suggested and are here reviewed: most popular has been the idea of war or at any rate armed intrusion; other possibilities include 'social instability, leading perhaps to insurrection and civil war', disease, economic collapse (notably through deforestation), drought, or abandonment for religious reasons.

90 D. H. Trump, *PPS* 27 (1961), 254ff.; Evans 1971, 6ff.

91 D. H. Trump, *Skorba,* Society of

Antiquaries, Research Report 22, 1966, 7.

92 Evans 1971, 149ff.

93 J. D. Evans, *PPS* 22 (1956), 85–101.

94 J. D. Evans, *PPS* 22 (1956), 90ff.; 1971, 193, 204.

95 J. F. S. Stone and L. C. Thomas, *PPS* 22 (1956), 57, 81, 84; Evans 1971, 163.

96 C. Renfrew, *Antiquity* 46 (1972), 141–4.

97 On Jugoslavia generally: Garašanin 1959; J. Alexander, *Jugoslavia before the Roman Conquest*, 1972; D. Garašanin and Z. Vinski-Gasparini in *Epoque Préhistorique*, 1971, 305–23; Brukner, Jovanović and Tasić 1974, 185ff.

98 For metal finds in the Eneolithic see rich burials like that from a barrow at Mala Gruda (Tivat Plain, Kotor): M. Parović-Pešikan and V. Trbuhović, *Starinar* n.s. 22 (1971), 129–41.

99 S. Dimitrijević, *Arch. Iug.* 8 (1967), 1–25; P. and J. Korošec, *Fundgut der Pfahlbausiedlungen bei Ig am Laibacher Moor* (Arh. Katalogi Slovenije III, 1969); *Poročilo o raziskovanju neolita in eneolita v Sloveniji III, Kultura Ljubljanskega Barja*, 1974.

100 S. Dimitrijević, *Arheološka iskopovanja na području vinkovačkog muzeja*, Acta Musei Cibaliensis 1 (1966).

101 A. Benac, *GZMS* n.s. 3 (1948), 3–42.

102 V. Trbuhović, *Starinar* n.s. 19 (1968), 39–46.

103 M. V. Garašanin, *Starinar* n.s. 7–8 (1956–7), 269–74; *Starinar* n.s. 9–10 (1958–9), 243–55.

104 J. Glisić, *Glasnik Kos. i Met.* 6 (1961), 133–44; C. Marković, *Arch. Iug.* 15 (1974), 7–12.

105 E.g. Gumnište-Dački Rid (Leskovac): D. Garašanin, *Starinar* n.s. 9-10 (1958–9), 257–61.

106 *Bulletin d'archéologie sud-est Européen* 1 (1969), 120f.

107 N. Tasić, *RVM* 14 (1965), 177–228.

108 Bóna 1975, 181.

109 M. Kosorić and J. Todorović, *Starinar* n.s. 13–14 (1962–3), 267–274.

110 J. Todorović and N. Tasić, in *Stare Kulture u Djerdapu*, 1969, 37, 39.

111 M. Kosorić, *Kulturni, etnički i hronološki problemi ilirskih nekropola podrinja*, Dissertationes et Monographiae, Tuzla 1976; list of sites of each period, 42f. M. and D. Garašanin, *Arch. Iug.* 2 (1956), 11.

112 Benac and Čović 1956.

113 B. Bačić, *Jadranski Zbornik* 4 (1959–60), 197–210.

114 National Museum Zagreb.

115 R. Drechsler-Bizić in *Epoque préhistorique* 1971, 90ff.

116 Bóna 1975, 181, D. Garašanin, *RVM* 3 (1954), 67–73; *Inv. Arch.*, Jugoslavia, 2, Y13–16 (1958).

117 Brukner *et al.* 1974, 461.

118 S. Pahič, *Arh. Vestnik* 13–14 (1962–1963), 349–73.

119 Brukner *et al.* 1974, 462ff.; N. Tasić, *Epoque préhistorique*, 1971, 164ff.

120 Prendi 1966; *Iliria* 3 (1975), 401–6.

121 Garašanin 1958, 122.

122 Garašanin 1958, 123; recent excavations: *Macedoniae Acta Archaeologica*.

123 B. Aleksova, *Glasnik Skopje* 1 (1954), 51–68.

124 D. Garašanin, *Arch. Iug.* 1 (1954), 19–24. Minyan ware is also said to have been found at Kod Cesme (Vrtište, Niš).

125 J. Mellaart, in *CAH*, 3rd edn., vol. I pt. 2, 1971, 700ff.; this view was subsequently retracted: *Journ. Hellenic Studies* 89 (1969), 172–3. cf. too R. J. Howell in Crossland and Birchall 1973, 74ff. For the

view of an autochthonous development of Grey Minyan: D. H. French, ibid. 51ff. Lerna: J. L. Caskey, *CAH*, 3rd edn, I, ch. 26a. Lefkandi: M. Popham and H. Sackett, *Excavations at Lefkandi, Euboea, 1964–66* (1968).

126 F. Prendi, *BUSS* (1956/1), 180ff.; N. Hammond, *Epirus* (1967), 201–204, 350f.

5 Western Europe

The area described here consists of the peninsula of Spain and Portugal, the land mass of western France, and the islands of Britain and Ireland. All parts of this area are associated with the Atlantic Ocean or its European waters, except eastern Spain and south-eastern France which are bordered by the Mediterranean Sea. Throughout, no part is further from a major body of water than 300 km, except the Mesetas of central Spain. In such a position, it is to be expected that maritime resources and navigation would play important roles in the life of Bronze Age societies, just as they have done in historic times. The comparative lack of Bronze Age evidence for such maritime interests is a reflection both of archaeological work and of the character of surviving Bronze Age evidence, and these matters will be discussed below.

Atlantic Europe, however, is much more than a maritime-dominated landscape. The distances involved are great, when we consider them in terms of Bronze Age communities reliant upon wind-powered sails for sea travel, and horse or cart for land transport. The distance between south-western Portugal to the Pyrenees is 900 km, between the Pyrenées and northern France is 900 km, and between northern France and northern Britain is a further 900 km. The evidence of Bronze Age movements and contacts over these distances is not substantial and it should not be expected that a uniform cultural composition existed over such a wide range of territories. Instead, many small cultural groups existed, not evenly distributed over the area, but in pockets; some of these will be described below.

The proximity of the sea, however, is likely to have led to greater territorial knowledge and to more contacts between groups living near the coasts than between land-locked groups where travel and transport would have been more difficult. The relative ease of coasting traffic along shores where landing-places were abundant suggests the manner by which objects of stone, metal or clay were gradually distributed lengthy

Map 5   Bronze Age sites in northern France and the British Isles

distances from their place of origin. Beaching of small wooden[1] or skin boats would have been possible along many of the Atlantic coasts, – on the long stretches of sand-dunes bordering the Bay of Biscay, in many parts of Britain, Ireland and Iberia, or in sheltered coves along the steep cliffs of parts of Brittany, Britain and northern Spain. The longest of these voyages, other than accidental storm-driven journeys, would have been the 150 km between Brittany and south-west England, and between Wales and Ireland; from Spain to the Balearic Islands is 200 km. Contact across the Straits of Dover, and across the North Channel between Ireland and southern Scotland, involved short journeys of 30–50 km only. Such short journeys, made in reasonably calm conditions, might have taken Bronze Age fishermen and sailors about 4–5 hours. The difficulties of narrow channel passages, where the sea will create substantial problems, should not be forgotten, but our knowledge about Bronze Age boats is extremely sparse. What is certain is that many short journeys did take place, and that longer voyages of at least 150 km were also a feature not particularly rare in the life of Bronze Age coastal communities.

The lands of Atlantic Europe are varied. In parts, high plateaux such as the Meseta of Spain, the Massif Central of France, and the Highlands of northern Britain, dominate vast tracts of land and severely affect climate, plants and human occupation. The lowlands of Portugal, of Biscayan France and the Paris Basin, and of eastern England, created uneven opportunities for agriculture. Much of Atlantic Europe, however, contains that variety of landforms which allows arable farming and pastoral activities to operate easily and these were exploited intensively by Bronze Age communities. The temperate climate of northern Spain, much of western France and all of the British Isles, contributed in great measure to these successful activities.

The natural resources of Atlantic Europe were not restricted to varying landforms, equable climate and a maritime environment. As much as any other major area, and more than most, Atlantic Europe contained a variety of other resources that proved to be important to Bronze Age groups. These included substantial supplies of gold, copper, tin and lead, as well as fine-grained rocks and flint. Flint mines, rock quarries and copper mines are known to have been worked in the Bronze Age, and panning of gold and tin, perhaps tin mining, were other industries. The products and technologies are noted below, but an important point here is the unequal spread of these resources. Tin was known only in Spain, Brittany and south-western England, yet these formed a very substantial part of all known European tin sources. Gold could be panned from Ireland, Wales and Scotland, and from Iberia, but was less abundant or absent in other parts of Atlantic Europe; silver was available in Brittany and Spain. Copper, however, was more widespread, available in southern Spain, in Wales, Scotland and Ireland.[2] The fine flint from the chalk mines of southern England, and from Grand Pressigny in France, continued to be utilized in the Bronze Age, and the Neolithic axe-factories of Britain and Ireland yielded stone for finely-made battle-axes and other implements.[3] In all of these, and in other resources, Atlantic Europe was well-endowed, and its position in the Bronze Age of Europe must gradually have assumed more importance as more of its resources came into use and into general knowledge. We prefer not to talk of long-distance movements of trade goods, in the absence of conclusive evidence, but it is sometimes hard to sustain the argument that self-sufficiency, insularity and isolation were the over-riding concerns in the Bronze Age of the west. Such comments are referred to below.

The history of Bronze Age studies in Atlantic Europe is uneven and sporadic. In the nineteenth century, many of the best preserved field monuments, particularly burial mounds, were excavated by collectors of antiquities, and many objects of clay, bronze and gold were gathered into private collections and public museums. Pioneers in attempts to bring some order into the mass of material were active in most regions; the works of J. Evans, J. Déchelette, H. Breuil, and L. and H. Siret, provided corpora of objects and distribution patterns, and Siret in particular recorded the excavation of many monuments.[4] Others were not so careful, and the inadequacy of their recording techniques is still being realized.[5] The excavation of many settlement sites of the Bronze Age is a more recent development, and records are consequently more useful. Yet the chronological schemes for the west European Bronze Age were and are based upon pot and metal typologies and associations, as these were the major objects to be collected and were thought to be suitable for such ordering. There are many schemes for the Bronze Age sequences of western Europe, the most elaborate being that of Burgess for Britain and Ireland;[6] Briard and Guilaine have attempted to bring some order into the French material[7] and Schubart has recently presented a chronological table for Iberia.[8]

The most ambitious of these divide parts of the west European Bronze age into nine phases, either industrial episodes or rather poorly-defined chronological blocks of 100–200 years. We do not believe that such divisions are necessary in a book such as this.[9]

The Bronze Age of Atlantic Europe is closely and logically connected with the Late Neolithic groups which preceded the Bronze Age in most parts of the western province. The point at which the Bronze Age begins is an arbitrary one, and is taken here to be a point in time dated by radiocarbon to c. 1700 bc, and by material cultural evidence to mark the onset of an established bronze-working industry, the appearance of local Bronze Age pottery from Beaker and Neolithic traditions, and the emergence of patterns of land use and settlement not consistently seen before.

Atlantic Europe in the late third and early second millennia was extensively occupied. This is not the place for a detailed outline of the culture-groups and their relationships, but it is important to realize that only minor re-alignments, and degrees of emphasis, mark the arbitrary and purely archaeological inception of the Bronze Age.[10] Agriculture and pastoral activities were established and successful in third millennium Europe, with extensive clearances of forest and ard cultivation as well as hoe plots. Settlements in many areas of Atlantic Europe are sparsely known, but, in others, elaborate stone-built semi-fortified enclosures were constructed. Industries involving an understanding of the properties and potential of fine-grained rock, copper ores, panned gold, wood and clay, were well established, and products were distributed over wide areas through mechanisms still imperfectly understood. Ritual monuments, for the collective burial of the dead, and for single inhumation burial, were constructed, with great regional variability. In some regions, community projects involving earthworks or megaliths were undertaken, and much has been made about the degree of social cohesion that such monuments may imply.[11]

Iberia

The Early Bronze Age in the Iberian peninsula is an episode often neglected in overall studies of the European Bronze Age. The reasons for this appear to be due as much to geographical isolation as to the relative lack of modern work following from the pioneering investigations of the nineteenth century; recent excavations in south-eastern Spain in particular have begun to create new opportunities for re-appraisal.[12] There has been other important work in Valencia and in the south-west as well, but the geographical character of the peninsula as a whole has severely restricted archaeological investigations, just as it would have affected the ability of Bronze Age communities to exploit the great variety of environments. In particular, the central plateau region (the Meseta) remains inadequately explored and the extent of Bronze Age occupation is not well known (fig. 70).

The plateau region, with land varying from 500 to 2,000 m above sea level, contains mixed soils, some poor, but there are many areas in the north in particular where irrigation can create opportunities for successful agricultural activities. The present pattern of transhumance has been

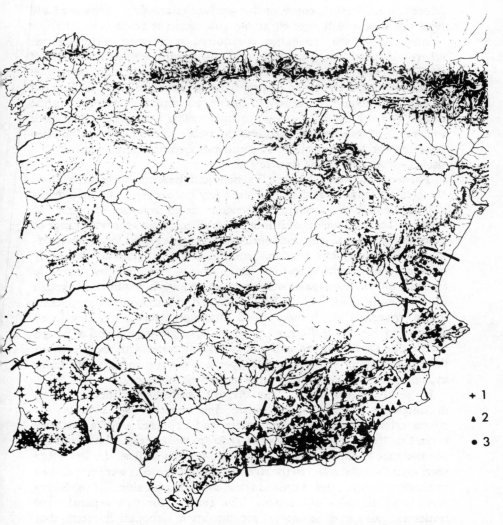

Fig. 70   Map of the Iberian peninsula: 1. south-western Early Bronze Age graves; 2. Argaric sites; 3. settlements of the Valencian group. (After Schubart 1976)

operating on a large scale only since c. AD 1300.[13] To the south-east, the Mediterranean coastland has relatively little arable level land; the dry climate necessitates irrigation of the *huertas* or *vegas*, and with this two crops per year can be harvested in areas such as the Valencian plain and Murcia. The Atlantic coasts of the west are relatively well-watered and here the potential for much arable cultivation is realized on the low rolling coastal plain. Irrigation is required in the very warm Algarve, where conditions are comparable to those of north-west Africa. North of the Tagus, hill-lands link sandy coasts and forested mountains, and small mixed farming activities are appropriate. In northern Spain, looking out to the Atlantic and to the Bay of Biscay, mountains come down to the coasts, and fishing from many drowned valleys is important; the poor soils are used for cattle pasture, and the richer river valleys are exploited for cereals and other crops.[14] The minerals from the north were another useful commodity in the Bronze Age.

Three coastal zones, Almería, Valencia and the south-west have yielded the greatest range of evidence for the Early Bronze Age, but other zones also exist where the surviving evidence is biased in favour of pottery or bronzes. The settlements of Almería and Valencia, and the wide range of burials in both south-east and south-west, provide a basis for understanding the prehistory of second-millennium Iberia. In general, continuity between the Eneolithic and the Early Bronze Age suggests that little external influence or major movement of peoples is required to explain the Bronze Age. Many of the Early Bronze Age communities were semi-urban, possessed much metal, used little stone, had a well-developed agricultural system and buried the dead in single graves, and although the single-grave tradition, and metalwork, contrasts with the preceding third millennium Neolithic and Copper Age groups, there is continuity in some pottery forms, and in some settlement locations.

In south-eastern Spain, the Argaric culture provides the best documentation of an Early Bronze Age society.[15] By 1800 bc the characteristic features of this society had appeared over a territory extending from Granada to Murcia (300 km west to east), and from the Mediterranean shores inland almost 200 km. As well as the low-lying areas near the coasts, and in the river valleys, settlements were established in previously-unoccupied upland areas, including the slopes of the Sierra Nevada to altitudes of 1200 m. The reasons for this expansion of settlement into new territories are uncertain although it seems that climatic factors are excluded.[16] Certainly the question of land use, for cultivation, is important here. Unfortunately, there is very little evidence from pollen, and none from field systems, to show the nature of Early Bronze Age occupation, but a few general comments may be made. The

area is semi-arid, and irrigation is an essential feature today on many
farms. Crops are produced through a fallow system, unless diverted water
allows an annual yield. Stock is managed by forms of transhumance,
summer upland grazing and winter lowland shelter.[17] There is very
slight evidence from the Early Bronze Age site of Cerro de La Virgen
(Granada) for water diversion, but any transhumance pattern, if indeed
present, is unknown.

Argaric settlements are generally described as fortified villages (this
seems an inadequate way of visualizing both the position and the nature
of the settlement). The major sites known are clustered in the south-
eastern corner of Spain, but Argaric metalwork is more widespread over
the large territory noted above. Many settlements occur adjacent to a
river, and are therefore lowland in that they are in valley systems; yet
many sites lie on terraces or, more often, on low steep-sided hills where
they overlook the rivers and where natural defences of slope and rock-
faces make them isolated and inaccessible. Stone walls, of 1–2 m thickness,
sometimes enclose parts of the hill or terrace, but only traces of these
survive in a few areas.

Within the general settlement area, which is rarely over 1 ha in extent,
there was sometimes a fortified enclosure, or acropolis, with thick walls
protecting rectangular huts or a series of large rooms. The connecting
passages and entries to these are inadequately known although in some
cases the huts were laid out in rows on narrow streets. The rectangular
nature of the huts, and the fact that burials of the inhabitants were often
placed within the huts or settlement area, provide contrasts with the
preceding Eneolithic.

The largest known settlement is El Argar, which lies on the left (north)
bank of the Antas river just downstream from a sharp bend in the river.[18]
The settlement covered part of a terrace, 25–30 m above the river, and
although few traces of enclosing walls or huts remained, the 1,000 burials
of the settlement covered an area 300 × 100 m. The river is dry in summer
at the present time and in the past too, but draws water from a wide area
upstream.

The settlement at El Oficio was positioned on a hilltop (fig. 71), and
totally covered the 1 ha available;[19] from settlement to the surrounding
lowland the vertical drop was about 100 m. Thick walling protected the
easiest access on the eastern side, and outer walls were built down-slope
to protect a large rock cistern. The huts on the summit were rectangular,
5–7 m in length and 3–4 m in width, with narrow streets separating
groups of houses with shared walls. The functions of individual houses
and the organization of the settlement are unknown. Burials beneath the
floors represented about 200 people.

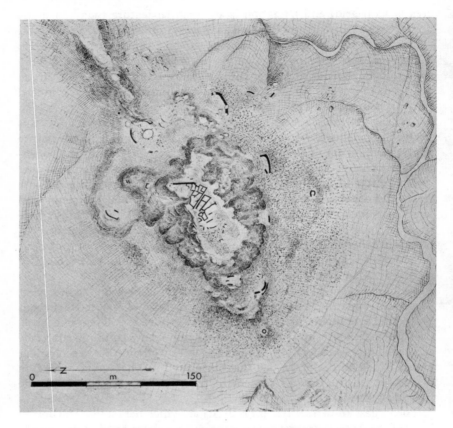

Fig. 71   Plan of the Argaric settlement at El Oficio, Almeria.
(After Siret 1887, pl. 60)

At Ifre the walled settlement was positioned on a rocky hill rising 100
m above a water course, with ample supplies of building stone from the
river banks.[20] An outer set of walls has been interpreted as stock
enclosures, and the inner walling, 2 m thick, protected stone-built huts
each measuring about 6 × 4 m. One of the huts contained a stone and
earth structure interpreted as an oven, perhaps for pottery (fig. 72). A
natural water supply lay within the enclosed settlement area. There were
traces of stairways to upper parts of the huts, and fire-baked impressions
of rope which have suggested roofing materials of wattle and daub.

Other Argaric settlements are positioned in similar defensible and
withdrawn areas. Zapata contained a heavily walled central enclosure on
the summit of a hill, and the Bastida of Totana had rectangular houses set

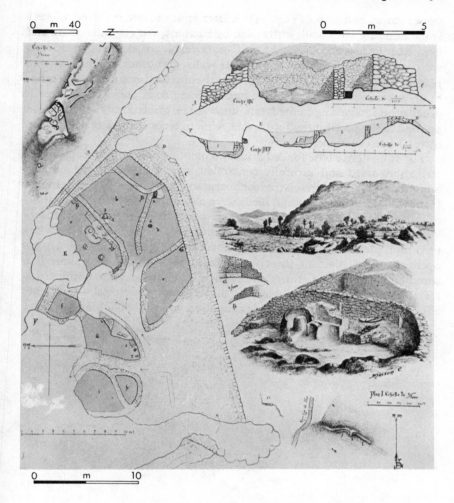

Fig. 72   Plans and views of the Argaric settlement at Ifre, Murcia.
(From Siret 1887, pl. 17)

in a form of terracing on a hill slope.[21] Recent excavations at Cerro de La
Virgen and Cerro de La Encina have added to information about the
internal structures of Argaric settlements;[22] at La Virgen, oval or round
mud-walled huts have been recognized, with burials beneath the floors
as usual. At La Encina, the walls were built of stone with clay binding and
supplemented by posts on both sides of the walls, probably to support an

upper storey and/or roof (fig. 73). A later episode here involved a heavy stone building with walls buttressed by bastions, red clay plastering and evidence of fire and collapse. At the Cuesta del Negro, Argaric round huts were cut into the rock and had timber walls, and crouched burials were placed within the settlement (fig. 74); there was also a mud and stone-built central stronghold and external fortified site.[23] These recent excavations have augmented our knowledge of structural details and pointed to the possibilities for further work in recovering data overlooked by earlier excavations.

The subsistence base for Argaric settlements was agriculture, probably irrigation-based and carefully controlled in a semi-arid environment, and stock-breeding, involving some seasonal movements; supplements from wild animals, fruits and seeds were also important. The occupation of upland areas in the Early Bronze Age would have involved encounters with more hostile seasonal weather conditions. The Cuesta del Negro lies on a high plateau, at an altitude of 1,000 m, the site placed in a canyon opening to the plain of the river Fardes; cold winters and short hot summers, problems of aridity and erosion, must have created difficulties for the inhabitants, yet arable land and pasture were established, and adjacent springs were used. The occupation was probably long-lived, as

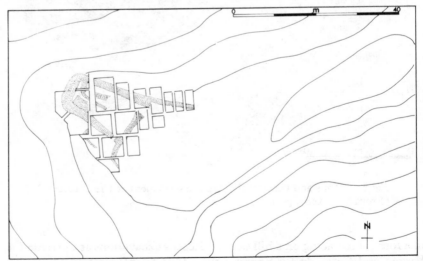

Fig. 73   Hilltop settlement at Cerro de la Encina, Granada, with stone-built walling revealed by partial excavation. The contours are at 1 m intervals, the highest part of the hill to the east, and ground sloping steeply away to north, west and south.
(After Arribas Palau *et al.* 1974, fig. 2)

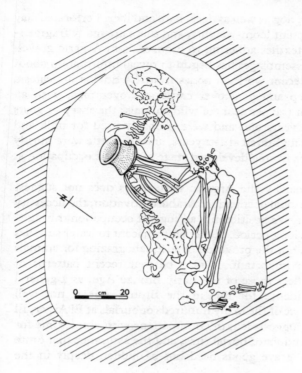

Fig. 74   Crouched inhumation with pottery vessel from the settlement at Cuesta del Negro, Granada. (After Molina Gonzalez and Pareja Lopez 1975, fig. 14)

3–4 m depth of deposits was built up, and the area of the settlement was 6 ha.

There is no certain evidence for dramatic climatic change in the region over the past 8–9,000 years, yet environmental alterations must have occurred through increasingly intensive land use combined with erosion and aridity. Remains of oak at El Argar, La Virgen and Fuente Alamo indicate woodland of some sort, as do deer at La Virgen. To have cultivated successfully, over a long period of time, must have involved the husbanding of water resources, and here the large cisterns at El Oficio and other sites, probable irrigation ditch at La Virgen, and the general site locations of the settlements, suggest that great attention was paid to the problems of water supplies.[24] Exactly how such problems were overcome remains unanswered at the present time.

The crops grown included various forms of wheat, barley, flax, grapes, olives and legumes. Flint sickles were used in the harvest, and saddle querns for grinding.[25] The bread oven at El Oficio represents another stage in this process. Animal bones from Argaric sites include horse, cattle, sheep, goat, pig, dog as well as deer, hare and ibex. Perforated clay plaques probably represent loom-weights, and there are many fragmentary remains of linen textiles adhering to bronzes from Argaric graves. The study of animal assemblages has begun to reveal information about herding practices.[26] Recent work on bones from La Encina indicates a predominance of sheep and goat over cattle and over pigs, with an appreciable component (30 per cent) of wild animals; the sheep or goats were generally over 2 years old, and were probably used for milk and wool. The pigs were slaughtered at 1–2 years, and the cattle were mostly adult. These results are from a developed stage of Argaric occupation at La Encina.[27]

The impression given by the Argaric settlements does not suggest impermanence and seasonal occupation. Arable cultivation, the necessity for irrigation, the defensive positioning, all suggest occupation throughout the year and over a long period. Settlement adjacent to water supplies would have been vital, but the provision of adequate grazing for animals would also have been important. It may be that recent patterns of transhumance may reflect those of the Early Bronze Age, as a general necessity, but the evidence for this in the Bronze Age is not well established. The evidence of the many hundreds of burials at El Argar, El Oficio and other sites suggests lengthy occupations with ample time for the preparation and conduct of burial rites, and the assurance that quite elaborate and wealthy grave goods need not be hidden deeply in the ground.

The grave goods, and the graves themselves, have been the subject of many detailed studies. At very few Argaric settlements have any stratigraphical phases been recognized, although current work will go some way to rectifying this situation. In this absence, the Argaric Bronze Age has been divided into two main phases based upon the material equipment in graves, and upon the grave rite.[28] The burials of Argar A consisted of cist-graves, the inhumed body furnished with metal halberd, triangular dagger, stone bracers, V-perforated buttons, and tall bowls with low carination. The burials of Argar B were in pottery jars, associated with axes, 4-riveted daggers, rare diadems of silver, and pottery chalices.[29] Many of the cist and the jar burials were within the houses, placed beneath the floors, and most were single inhumations. The chronology of these two phases is based upon central European and Mediterranean Bronze Age objects, including halberds and daggers of Argar A and chalice cups and one find of faience beads of Argar B; relations, unspecified, with remote areas are presumed to allow firm chronological separation. We consider precise phasing to be inadequate, as it is based upon forms and shapes of objects from long distances away.

Radiocarbon dates are too sparse and irregular to help, and stratigraphical separations of A and B hardly exist. Nevertheless it seems reasonable to suggest that the material of Argar A is, on the whole, earlier than that of Argar B, without assigning precise dates to the transition, and allowing that some irregularities are likely to occur. Explanations of the differences in other than chronological terms seem overdue.

At El Argar, about 80 per cent of the 1,000 burials were in pithoi or jars.[30] These jars were set into the earth, upright or on their sides, and served as coffins for the disarticulated dead. Male burials were associated with a copper or bronze flat axe, 4-riveted dagger, bracelet and wire pendants, sometimes with ivory, bone and serpentine beads, occasionally with small silver objects, but the variation in number and variety of objects is great (fig. 75). Female burials in jars were often associated with

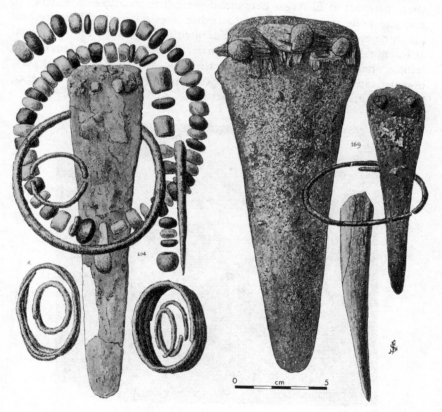

Fig. 75   Argaric grave-goods from El Argar, Almeria.
(Graves 104 and 169 according to Siret 1887, pls 37 and 33)

a small metal knife, an awl and pendants of bronze and silver. Male burials in stone slab cists were accompanied by a copper or bronze halberd, a dagger, bracelet and pendants including silver.

Grave-goods range from almost none to an impressive array of bronze, silver and rare gold objects, and several pottery vessels. A large urn in grave 9 at El Argar contained a female with two pots, a knife, an awl, two sets of triple pendants, a bracelet, a silver ring on a finger, and a necklace of seventy-seven bone, seventy-seven stone, six copper and one tooth beads. Other rich jar graves contain skulls with silver and bronze ornaments (fig. 76); a few pieces in gold also occur. Such division in wealth between graves within the settlement suggests obvious social stratification, but without firmer chronological and demographic evidence there is little more that can be said. Certainly the whole establishment of the settlement at El Argar demanded some firm measure of leadership, and the same may be inferred for other sites where architecture and planning are combined with burials of unequal content.[31] The cist burial at Fuente Alamo, of a male and a female, yielded a silver diadem on the female's head, a bronze sword beside the male, as well as bronze daggers, bracelet, awl, silver pendants, a necklace of ivory, copper and faience beads, a pottery chalice with a copper collar, and six other pots.[32]

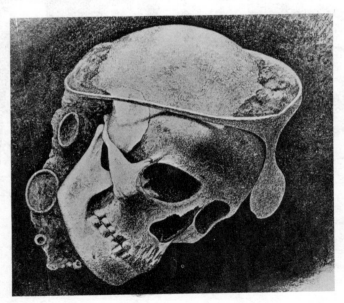

Fig. 76   Diadem of silver and other ornaments on Argaric skull.
(From Siret 1887, pl. 45)

The content of the graves augments the materials recovered from the settlement debris, and all combine to illustrate the wide command of resources and the technological skills available to the inhabitants. The burnished pottery vessels lack much decoration and are well-fired with thin walls and simple shapes. Wide-mouthed shallow dishes, narrow-mouthed jars, jugs with low carinated bases, mugs, and the slender-columned chalices (for wine?) are the most characteristic forms. The jars for burials are extremely large, 1 m in height, and have everted rims probably for tying a cloth cover.

Textiles are preserved mainly as fragments on bone or metal, and some wooden and bone handles or sheaths have also occasionally survived. Bone was used extensively for points and awls, and stonework in the occupation deposits is abundant; pounders, grinders, saws and other industrial equipment were made of fine-grained stone and flint.

Metalworking was extensive as well. Copper sources are known from south-eastern Spain,[33] in the centre of the Argaric region, and traces of copper-working have been found on many sites where arsenical copper, tin-bronze, and an arsenic-tin-copper alloy were cast in stone moulds. A copper mine at Mola Alta de Serelles has yielded moulds for flat axes, and this must be only one of several such Early Bronze Age sources. Closed mould casting was also practised for midrib halberds and daggers, and these would have been more successful with a tin-bronze rather than a copper. Tin sources in Spain are mainly in the north-west, but the south-east also possessed tin sources around Cartagena which are likely to have been used.

Silver was also available in the Argaric region, as well as gold, and both of these metals were used for ornaments. Silver was quite abundant, far more so than in any other Early Bronze Age European society. Over 300 pieces of silver were recovered from El Argar, weighing over 1500 gm, and the majority are from silver cupellated from galena ore, although native silver was also in use.

The entire complex of equipment and activities in the Argaric sites does not suggest much in the way of external stimulus or contact. Self-sufficiency in an environment full of many useful resources, supplemented by control and conservation of those restricted in quantity, whether metal or water, is likely to have been the dominant element in the life of the Early Bronze Age communities. What is lacking from the evidence at the present time is the reason for the defensive nature of many settlements, the degree of social stratification that existed, and the amount of time spent in or on Mediterranean waters; for the last we have no evidence at all. Yet the contrast between the preceding third millennium societies in south-east Spain and the Argaric is great. Increasing specialization in metalwork, the emergence of high-quality weaponry, the development of new fortifications, and above all the change from communal burial to individual burial with accompanying and variable personal equipment, all suggest internal social and economic evolution.[34]

From the northern Argaric settlements to the basin of the river Turía, in an area 200 km along the coast, another series of Early Bronze Age settlements have been recognized, and form the Valencian group.[35] Unlike south-eastern Spain, here any evidence for a previous episode of Eneolithic occupation is rare, and the Bronze Age sites appear as intrusive elements in a lowland environment. The settlements are positioned on hilltops or other initially withdrawn locations, and are walled around like the Argaric sites. Small rectangular huts were built inside the walled area, sometimes (as at Mas de Menente) in a terraced arrangement;[36] each of the eight huts at this site had a hearth, saddle querns and loom-weights. Other promontory or hilltop fortified settlements have heavy walls and occasionally bastions or buttresses. Burials within the huts are rare but metalwork is comparable to Argaric forms. Pottery forms are reminiscent of the Argaric but are essentially local in inspiration as well as manufacture. The evidence for the Valencian Early Bronze Age is rather sparse, and there is so little metal, and no evidence of the social differentiation seen in Argaric graves, that the province is generally considered to represent an entirely separate cultural group.[37] The lack of native metal in the region may explain the Argaric forms brought into the communities.

Further north, along the coastal Mediterranean shores and into the Pyrenées, evidence for Early Bronze Age occupation is sparse, and is essentially restricted to cave sites and some burials. Built settlements are hardly known, but the open occupation near Riner was probably associated with a copper mine; flat axe moulds in the settlement debris indicate some local casting.[38] The valley of the Ebro is one of the largest in all Spain, and it seems likely that the copper sources of the mountains to south, west and north of the basin would have been attractive assets to any exploitation of the lowlands of the plain.

The northern parts of Spain are in fact very inadequately explored for Early Bronze Age occupation. Along the Biscayan shore, and onto the Atlantic coasts of the north-west, no stratified settlements are published, and there is little evidence for the exploitation of the tin sources. Copper was probably mined at Mina de Milagro, as Early Bronze Age daggers and axes have been recovered from the site. This area is, however, part of the postulated Galician-Irish network, bringing essential items to both ends of the system; the evidence for this consists of a few objects of stone, flint, gold and bronze, and rock art of cup-and-ring character.[39] The mechanisms for this sharing of ideas and objects are unknown, and suggestions include the occasional straying of fishermen, or wandering craftsmen (who contributed willingly or unwillingly to the material culture of groups living all along the coastal Atlantic region), or regular exchanges by traders.[40]

Slight traces of Argaric forms and materials are found over much of the peninsula. To the west of the Argaric province itself, in central southern Spain, there are some metal objects and pottery of Argaric character, although settlements have not been excavated. To the north, in the Meseta and in central Portugal, such traces are very sparse, but the whole range of evidence for second-millennium occupation is difficult to interpret. Although the Finca de Paloma, Toledo, hoard contains halberds, Palmela points, a dagger, saw and gold strip, suggesting some common ground with other parts of Iberia,[41] the conditions for settled life on the high plateau are not likely to have attracted an abundance of permanent settlers, yet there are many surface finds of Early Bronze Age material suggesting that settlement may well have been much more dense and persistent than is generally assumed.

The largest expanse of lowland in the peninsula is the south-west, south of the Tagus river, an area also crucial in that it formed the linking agent between the Atlantic world and that of the Mediterranean. For the Early Bronze Age, its role seems to have been almost entirely local, with a well developed agricultural base, settled communities, metallurgy and other self-supporting industries.[42] The archaeological evidence is unfortunately incomplete, with settlement and site location very sparse, yet extensive cemeteries indicate an established series of communities with their own traditions. The area consists of a block in the extreme south-west, 200 km square, clustering along the southern coast and through the basin of the Guadiana river. The lowland environment is suitable for arable cultivation, but the great summer heat suggests that some form of irrigation and water control was necessary in the second millennium BC. There are indications that the settlements were on hills or terraces with defensive walls, but the evidence is very sparse.[43]

The burial tradition of the Early Bronze Age was single inhumation in a stone cist, replacing the well-established communal burials in a megalithic tomb. The cists may have been individual although usually in a scatter forming a cemetery, but more characteristic are cists which are connected physically to others (fig. 77). These cists, or sometimes pits, have slab covers and are buried beneath small and low mounds of earth and stone revetted by dry stone walls. Such structures are clustered around a central and larger primary mound, the whole giving the effect of a single grave tradition in a communal setting. Some of these composite

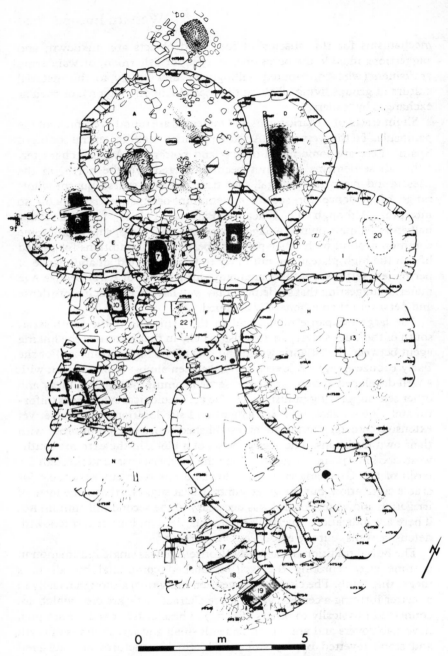

Fig. 77   Grave complex no. 3 at Atalaia, Beja.
(After Schubart 1975, Beilage 5)

and no doubt successive structures are well-built, with carefully selected slabs, and the evolution of a cemetery can be traced.[44]

The range of grave-goods in the cemeteries such as Atalaia, the largest by far, is not as extensive as the Argaric, the objects consisting of a variety of pots and some bronzes. The pots include wide-mouthed bowls, low-carinated bowls and dishes, and narrow-necked jugs, mostly plain although there are a few with punch and groove decoration. Bronze leaf-like points, simple daggers, flat and low flanged axes, and small wire pendants form the bulk of the metalwork. The material has been divided into two phases, Bronze I and II, not the equivalent of Argar A and B as Schubart considers that Argar A precedes his Bronze I of the south-west. The dating of Bronze II is likely to be in the late second millennium or early first millennium bc.[45]

The rare carvings of weapons on cist-covers in the area, as at Assento, Trigaches and Pedreirinha, cannot be firmly dated but seem to be of first millennium date rather than second, notwithstanding their halberds and curved axes.[46] They do, however, add some evidence for the widespread interest in representations of curved axe-blades which occur in northern, southern and western Europe.

In summary, the Early Bronze Age of the Iberian peninsula shows the high technical skills of second millennium communities in developing existing strategies and in evolving new technologies able to cope with expanded settlement patterns, land use and raw materials. There are wide gaps in our knowledge about certain of these groups, but they appear to represent purely self-sufficient societies, each with its own traditional procedures for life and death. There is little doubt that they persisted more or less unchanged well into the first millennium, when new elements gradually began to make some small impact; these matters are dealt with later.

Western France

Any general description of the earlier Bronze Age in western and northern France is hampered by the variations in landscape: lowland coastal areas of the Bay of Biscay, the upland hills and plateaux of the Pyrenées and the Massif Central, estuaries and river basins of the north and west, and the rocky plateau of Armorica. Conditions for settlement in the second millennium bc were different for each of these areas. What can be said as general introductory remarks relies upon a restricted number of observations concerning the evidence for climate, forest clearances and subsistence practices.[47]

The lands of the Paris Basin, parts of Armorica, and the north, are the most suitable for arable cultivation and the pasturing of animals. The large farmholdings of the campagne and of the open plains of Beauce and Picardy indicate the relatively easy way by which these lands can be exploited. In contrast, the south lends itself more to smaller complexes, and to less specialization in food production, with mixed farming even in the rich molasse (marly sandstones and limestones) lands of Aquitaine. In recent times there were as many as 2 million farmsteads of less than 10 ha each, where self-sufficiency in many staples was still attempted, and this should provide some guide to the likelihood of similar smallholdings in the past. The natural mixed forest vegetation of France survives in the region between the Garonne River and the western Pyrénées, and forests still cover parts of the Massif Central as well as other high ground.

Pollen analytical work suggests a second millennium climate somewhat drier than previously, except in highland areas noted below. Beech woodlands were widespread, and oak mixed forest dominated, but clearances for food production were increasingly an encroachment on virgin forests. Cereal cultivation in northern France, pastoral activities in the south, are attested from many sites but such a simplification disguises the variety of subsistence practices employed. Animal bones from settlements indicate a gradual decline in the availability, or exploitation, of wild animals, and some lowland sites contain almost 100 per cent domestic animals; upland sites continue to show heavy reliance on hunting.

Settlements themselves were varied, caves, promontories and hilltops, coastal stations and river valleys all employed on occasion. Widespread exploitation of natural resources for industry is attested, flint and stone, copper and tin, clays and sand, all providing the materials for many specialized as well as local products. Burial practices of the second millennium mark an alteration from the Neolithic, single grave inhumations replacing collective traditions; the variety of receptacles for the dead was great. There is relatively little evidence for ceremonial practices except in a few areas. Travel and transport can be gauged from the wide dissemination of products of stone and metal, and both land and water transport seem necessary, although there is little evidence of wheeled vehicles and only dugout canoes from coastal and inland waters.

The Bronze Age of western and northern France has been the subject of many studies, mostly concerned with the ordering of either burials or metal into successive phases. It is traditional to divide the material into three parts, Early, Middle and Late; here we have combined much but not all of the Middle Bronze Age with the Early Bronze Age, in order to speak of second millennium developments, from c. 1700 bc to c. 1200 bc. It is in any case difficult to point to clear divisions between locally-evolving occupations and industries in western and northern France, areas where Urnfield influence, whatever that may be elsewhere, cannot even be suggested.

The Pyrénées and the western parts of the Massif Central are the only highland areas of Atlantic France, and they provide a geographical link with north-eastern Spain where cave occupation in the earlier Bronze Age is attested. Pollen evidence from the western Pyrénées[48] suggests an episode of increased humidity, perhaps even slightly lowered temperatures, which created conditions in the foothills for widespread beech woodlands, the appearance of fir (*Abies*), and a decline in elm and hazel. Clearances for cultivation in the later second millennium are reported from this zone, but there is very little evidence for much occupation in the higher reaches of the hills. The tendency must be to regard these uplands, and those of the Massif Central, as areas exploited in the Bronze Age mainly for minerals and rocks, and for hunting. Sites in the upper reaches of the Dordogne river, such as l'Igue blanche, have yielded evidence that the hunt for deer and other animals contributed over half of the meat supplies with ovicaprids about one quarter,[49] but there are other sites such as Sargel and the Grotte de la Bergerie where domestic animals made up a large proportion of the fauna recovered.[50]

Settlements in these upland areas, so far as they have been recovered, are in caves and in swallow-holes and other cavities in the rock. There is little evidence about the scale of occupation in terms of density and duration.[51] Structural elements are rarely recorded but a built oven in the Grotte du Noyer contained 11 litres of carbonized grain, almost all of it wheat of *Triticum aestivo-compactum* type.[52] Cereals have also been recovered from other sites in the western part of the Massif Central, and it would seem reasonable to suggest that variable forms of mixed farming, supplemented by hunting and gathering, were practised throughout the earlier Bronze Age in these areas where low-lying plateaux, and river valleys, provided suitable land for arable cultivation. The gross distribution of burials, pottery, stone and metal objects indicates increasingly wide areas of occupation through the second millennium, and this, allied with the rather sparse evidence for forest clearances, suggests an increasing appreciation of the variety of resources in such upland regions of western France.

The industries that were practised in the region show a continuing interest in flint and stone tools, in pottery, and in bone implements, many of which show close affinities with the preceding Neolithic and Chalcolithic communities which formed the sole basis of second millennium populations. Chasséen and Beaker groups, among others, practising these technologies as well as the newly devised gold and copper processes, occupied many of the upland areas where earlier Bronze Age groups have been recognized.[53] Bronze Age industries produced bone points, polishers, daggers, pins and needles, flint knives, scrapers and saws, and stone grinders and pounders. Metal, whether of copper or bronze, tends to be rare on the sites excavated, where only a few knives and pins, occasionally an axe, are found. The pottery industries, however, were prolific, and the variety of domestic ware is great (fig. 78). Most pots are plain although lugs, knobs, cordons and ribbon-handles occur. Globular or biconical jugs, carinated or smooth vases, bowls and large jars are major shapes, but a characteristic form is the polypod pot, with 6–18 feet; these polypods are often linked with similar pots from Aquitaine, and such vessels occur throughout much of the Pyrenées particularly in later second millennium contexts (fig. 81).[54]

Burials in these upland regions also show a continuity in part with the preceding Neolithic and Chalcolithic groups. Caves and collective tombs were used and some chambered tombs were newly built, but single

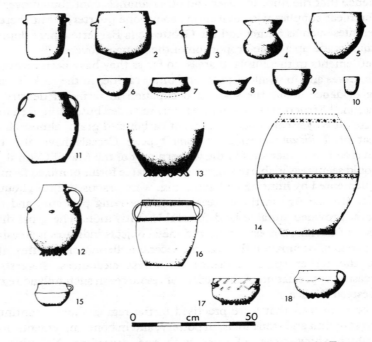

Fig. 78   Early Bronze Age pottery from cave occupations in France. 1–10. Grotte de Marsa, Lot; 11–14. Grotte du Noyer, Lot; 15–18. Grotte de Roucadour, Lot.
(From Clottes and Constantini 1976)

inhumations were also placed in round barrows either in pits or cists.[55] Grave goods tend to be rather sparse, and metal was rarely wasted. An adult female placed in a pit in the Marsa cave was accompanied by two infants' heads.

There is little in the range of material evidence from western parts of the Pyrénées or the Massif Central to suggest an episode of much long-range contact with other communities. The origins of the earlier Bronze Age seem firmly local by internal site stratigraphies,[56] by industrial technologies and by settlement locations. The identification of Polada-type pottery and wares from the Rhône valley, and the Artenacian material from the west (fig. 79), may well represent successful contacts in the ordinary pursuit of desirable objects through seasonal or random relationships,[57] but there is little evidence for organized transmission of materials and ideas from or into what were relatively inaccessible regions.

The same cannot be said of the areas to the west, in the coastal and lowland zone which stretches from the Adour river northwards through Aquitaine, the river basins of the Garonne and the Charente to the Loire with its immense central inland territory. An essentially maritime and riverine landscape, with fertile lowlands, this region provides a contrast to the adjacent uplands of the Pyrénées and the Massif Central.

Earlier Bronze Age settlements in this lowland area are very inadequately explored. In parts, neither settlements nor burials have been found, and the evidence for occupation comes from hoards and finds of metal and pottery. Some cave sites are known where third millennium occupation was succeeded by second millennium interest, but much of the region lacks suitable caves, and open settlements on promontories or terraces or beside estuaries or the shore were chosen.[58]

The economy of such settlements is also inadequately known, but there

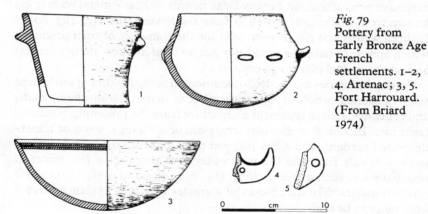

Fig. 79
Pottery from
Early Bronze Age
French
settlements. 1–2,
4. Artenac; 3, 5.
Fort Harrouard.
(From Briard
1974)

are some reports of predominantly ovicaprid-based faunal assemblages from the valleys of the Loire and Charente.[59] The Artenac cave in the basin of the Charente indicates that wild animals were either reduced in numbers or in desirability by the second millennium.[60] The distribution of industrial material, particularly bronzes, suggests coastal occupation, and the presence of dugout vessels on the shores of the Bay of Biscay infers at least some regular fishing or other maritime activities;[61] all of these indicate that coastal settlements should be expected, such as those known from further north and west, in Armorica and Britain.

The origin of the earlier Bronze Age in the region lies in the preceding Neolithic and Chalcolithic groups; in these, copper working is attested, collective burials were placed in chambered graves, and flint and stone work was a major industry. The cave of Artenac contained 100 inhumations associated with flint arrowheads and knives, and these were contemporary with other cave burials, with some burials in barrows or re-used megalithic tombs, and possibly with promontory forts; metal is very rare in such situations but this group is believed to be one of the major contributing elements to the earlier Bronze Age in the west.[62]

The overwhelming evidence for second millennium communities comes from metalwork, as stray finds, as hoards or in burials. In Aquitaine, bronze and copper axes and daggers appear in cist graves in the Dordogne valley,[63] and are believed to represent objects brought in from existing metallurgical centres in eastern France and Atlantic Europe. Further north, in the Loire Valley, arsenical copper was employed to manufacture flat axes and perhaps halberds.[64] There followed, however, a major series of industries all along the coast, producing flanged axes and palstaves, spearheads and bracelets, in a variety of local styles; the Gironde in particular was the centre for quite extensive production, and many large hoards of heavy metal objects are known from this region as well as from the lower Loire area (fig. 80).[65] Inshore waters and rivers were used for the transport of such products, which appear to have been made for purely local markets along the coast and on the coastal plains and estuaries.

Pottery industries are less well-documented in the absence of settlement sites. Cordoned vessels in Aquitaine relate to material from the uplands, and are considered to represent a departure from the preceding Neolithic traditions. Biconical or globular jars, plain or with lugs, warts or finger-decorated cordons, and a few polypod pots, make up the bulk of known pottery vessels from the Gironde valley, but there are a few traces of unusual ware, such as Kerbschnitt (fig. 81), which may represent a few exotic transfers.[66] In the absence of a greater variety of evidence there is little more to be said.

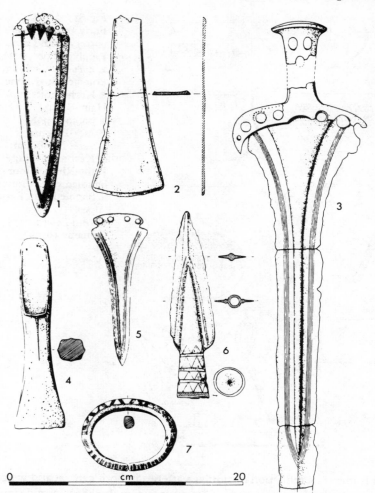

Fig. 80   Early Bronze Age metal products from Atlantic France: 1. dagger, 2. flat axe, 3. Atlantic sword, 4. palstave, 5. dagger, 6. spearhead, 7. armlet. Various sites in western France.
(After Coffyn 1976, Briard 1976a, Cordier 1976)

Our knowledge of burial traditions is equally inadequate. Cist burials and some barrow burials are known from river valleys, but grave-goods are sparse. The human types recovered from these graves include both Nordic long skulls from the Loire-Gironde area, and Mediterranean gracile remains from the Charente, but the intermixing of such types

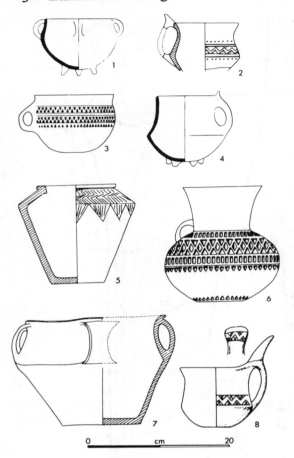

Fig. 81
Early Bronze Age
pottery from France:
1. polypod pot, Ariège,
2. flare-handled jug,
Bouches-du-Rhône,
3. Kerbschnitt cup,
Haut-Rhin,
4. polypod pot,
Basses-Pyrenées,
5. vase, Morbihan,
6. Kerbschnitt jug,
Haut-Rhin, 7. four-
handled vase, Finistère,
8. handled cup, Basses-
Alpes.
(From Briard 1974,
Guilaine 1976a)

here is merely a reflection of similar varieties in both central and western
Europe in the Bronze Age.[67] This situation may reflect a widespread
mixing of original stocks throughout Europe, but here it is likely to be
exaggerated by the possibilities for longer-distance travel by coastal
vessels, which after all might well have linked northern lands with
southern coasts, through gradual and interrupted travel by fishermen,
settlers and others. Certainly connections all along the present French
coast, from the Pyrenées to Normandy, are attested in the Bronze Age,
and from the mainland across to the British Isles as well. A rise in sea-
levels of *c.* 4 m between 1600 and 1000 bc has perhaps masked more
evidence for both coastal traffic and coastal settlement.[68]
Environmental conditions in the peninsula of Armorica are perhaps

better known than for any other area of western France. Pollen analysis of peats and other deposits suggests that climatic conditions were somewhat drier during most of the second millennium. Beech woodland increased, lime and alder declined, and forest clearances were undertaken in new areas. Although earlier Bronze Age settlements are not well known, the evidence of clearance and cultivation is equally important. Cereal pollen has been recovered from a number of sites where traces of habitation exist, and increases in plantain also indicate clearances.[69] At the coastal site of Porsguen, Plouescat, cereal cultivation and grassland increases were associated with remains of sheep or goat and cattle in a peat deposit dated by Bronze Age domestic material to the earlier second millennium bc, but such sites are rare.[70] The acidity of much of the Armorican soils does not allow the preservation of bone, either human or non-human, and this will remain a gap in future assessments of the economic strategies of the Bronze Age. Hunting equipment, described below, may well represent the procurement of wild animals as an important element in food supplies, but its relative value is not known. Bronze sickles clearly indicate cereal or wild grass harvesting.[71] At Le Lividic, on the northern coast, a probably seasonal occupation for the collection of shellfish also involved the gathering of grasses,[72] and there are comparable coastal stations on the southern coasts around the mouth of the Loire river. All of these are low-lying, but promontory settlements in defensive situations are also suggested for the second millennium.[73] The problem of Bronze Age settlements in Armorica is well-known, and although there are hints of very substantial occupation, such as the forty or fifty huts at two sites near Reuniou, Brennilis, the question can only be considered in relation to the pollen evidence and the burial monuments.[74]

Within the earth of such monuments domestic debris has often been recovered, stone mauls, flints, polishers, potsherds, which reflect both Neolithic industrial materials and continuity with the Bronze Age, as much of the pottery is clearly of the second millennium.[75] They also suggest either deliberate incorporation of debris in a burial monument, or the accidental scooping up of material from an adjacent occupation. The final point to make about settlements in Armorica is that the other evidence suggests that occupation is likely to have been continuous, ordered and substantial. In this, the evidence from third millennium sites is important, because there is little to suggest any major incursions of population which formed the basis for the Bronze Age. Beaker settlement along the southern coasts was concerned with copper metallurgy, and gold too, and the distribution of copper axes covers most areas of Armorica.[76] Other Neolithic and Chalcolithic groups were concerned with copper and stone technologies, and their magnificent megalithic tombs, and the *menhirs* and alignments, should not be neglected in any consideration of the Bronze Age. Their positions, and their meanings, to third millennium populations would not have been lost on second millennium groups who were the direct descendants, at least in part if not *in toto*, of the earlier communities. Some large standing stones of Armorica are likely to have been erected during the earlier Bronze Age, including the Grand Menhir Brisé at Locmariaquer.[77]

What sets the Neolithic and Bronze Ages apart, visually, is the alteration in burial tradition, from collective graves to individual graves; less important differences appear in stonework, and in the abundance and elaboration of metal goods. The theories concerning the origins of the earlier Bronze Age of Armorica generally speak of central European influences, direct connections with the 'Wessex Culture' of southern Britain, and the use of the North Sea as a major connecting area.[78] In the absence of new evidence, either of chronology or of human physical characteristics, we can but state that local Armorican evolution from Beaker traditions is a likely base. Relations with southern Britain are also attested in a technological, not cultural, manner, and these are noted below.[79]

The evidence for the earlier Bronze Age of Armorica is essentially that of burial monuments and material culture. Round barrows are restricted to the western part of the peninsula, and line the coastal portions as well as clustering inland along the Blavet river and the southern edge of the Monts d'Arré (400 m). Almost 400 barrows are known, but a majority[80] have few or no records of their contents. The graves, where recognized, contained from absolutely nothing to vast arrays of wealth. Careful study and assessment of the surviving evidence has resulted in the division of the barrows into three sections;[81] one of these consists of perhaps 200 graves where contents and reliability of information are uncertain. There remain almost forty graves with weaponry and wealth, and 140 graves with pottery; the weapon graves form first-series barrows, chronologically earlier (1900–1600 bc) than the second-series barrows with pottery (1600–1400 bc).

First-series barrows are generally large, 20–30 m in diameter, sometimes 50 m, and 5–6 m in height. The earthen body of the barrow covers a small cairn which protects a central cist holding the body. The cist itself may be of wood, of upright stone slabs, or of drystone construction with cover slab. The wooden chambers rest on the soil or in a pit, and were made of planks or tree-trunks or branches. A roof of branches with thatch of reed or ferns formed a mortuary house on occasion.[82] The stone-built cists included large chambers 4 m long but were still used only for single inhumations, albeit with rich grave-goods. Recent descriptions of many of these graves of the first series include commentary on the constructional details which have come to light through modern techniques.[83]

One barrow in particular will serve to indicate the great wealth of first-series barrows. The barrow at Kernonen en Plouvorn was 50 m in diameter and fully 6 m high. The central grave (fig. 82), protected by a cairn, measured 4.7 m by 1.4 m and was built of dry-stone walling with a 7 tonne capstone and two smaller lintels enclosing the chamber, which was paved with stones and wooden flooring.[84] Three oak boxes held grave-goods consisting of 1) three flanged axes, 2) two bronze pins and three daggers (fig. 83) with wooden hilts decorated by minute gold pins and studs, 3) a dagger with bone pommel, c. forty scattered flint arrowheads and an amber bracer; beside the second box was a line of ten flint arrowheads (fig. 84), and a scattered amber necklace (fig. 85). The inhumation, or several, had vanished in the acid conditions. The gold pins decorating the three dagger pommels totalled c. 15,000, each 0.5 mm long and somehow pressed into place forming geometric patterns; tweezers must have been used, and perhaps magnifying apparatus?

Other graves of the first series have also yielded objects of gold and of silver including parts of at least two silver cups, one of which was associated at Saint-Adrien 1974 with gold-decorated daggers and c. forty-five flint arrowheads.[85]

These relatively few graves, furnished with extraordinary objects, have been singled out as marking the burials of an aristocracy, so called 'warrior-priests'.[86] In the absence of further evidence from settlements, or information about the buried persons themselves, it is not possible to comment except to suggest that the connotation 'warrior-priest' infers rather more than can be demonstrated. Yet the exceptional character of these burials indicates distinct stratification in the society, at least in the burial ritual.

The nature of the grave-goods, and the technologies involved, have suggested that cross-Channel relationships between Armorica and Wessex existed in the second millennium. Certainly the phenomenon of very richly-furnished individual graves situated within areas, or cemeteries, with poorer graves, exists in both regions. Typologically the gold pin work on dagger pommels, fine stone axes, amber and flint arrowheads is broadly similar although there are technical differences in most of the materials. Cross-Channel communication seems likely for a variety of economic reasons, but the evidence for a shared political or social strategy is not yet available.[87]

The barrows of the second series are outwardly similar to those of the

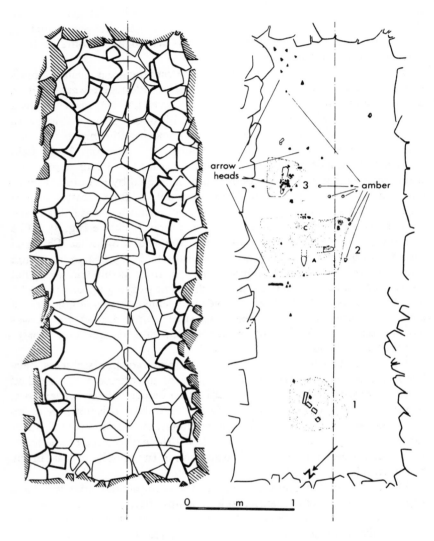

Fig. 82 Plan of the Kernonen, Finistère, central burial chamber. Left: stone paving and the central grave. Right: three wooden boxes in the grave: 1. three flanged axes, 2. three daggers with a line of arrowheads beside the box, 3. one dagger and scatter of arrowheads.
(After *L'Anthropologie* 74 (1970))

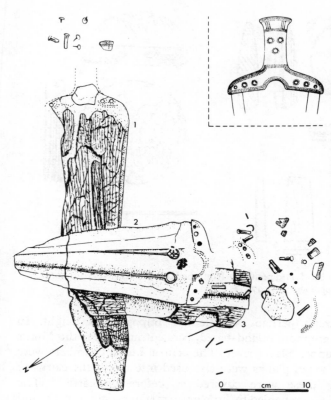

Fig. 83
Grave goods from
the Kernonen
burial, Finistère:
three daggers,
parts of wooden
sheaths, two
bronze pins, with
many gold pins
and rivets for the
dagger handles.
Reconstructed
dagger handle at
top right.
(After
L'Anthropologie 74
(1970))

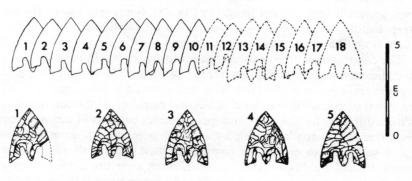

Fig. 84   Flint arrowheads from the Kernonen grave, Finistère. Ten were
in a line, others scattered.
(After *L'Anthropologie* 74 (1970))

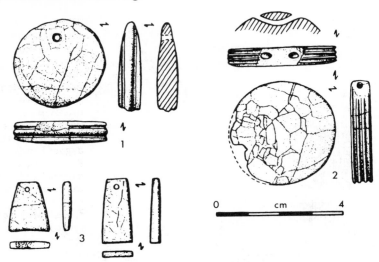

Fig. 85   Amber beads and pendants from the Kernonen grave, Finistère.
(After *L'Anthropologie* 74 (1970))

first series, although perhaps a little less imposing in height. In
distribution they are more inland-based, concentrating near the Monts
d'Arrée and the upper Blavet river. The central burial chambers were
stone built but wooden planks were also used internally; the cairns of
stones protecting these were covered as before by earth.[88] The
inhumations were accompanied by little or no metal, no stone-work, and
by many pottery vessels; in these respects the contrast with the first series
is remarkable. About 100 burials have the characteristic four-handled
vase, generally only one pot per grave (fig. 81). Some pots have only one
strap-handle, others have two. Decoration on these vases is rare, but
other vessels have incised geometric designs.

The conditions of preservation of the dead are so poor in the acidic soils
that the many observations concerning possible shrouds, clothing and
organic grave goods suggest that what has survived is only a small part of
the ritual surrounding the burial of selected members of the community.
With a duration for the first- and second-series barrows of perhaps 700
years it is clear that a large proportion of the population did not achieve
status sufficient to ensure its commemoration in a built tomb. The
recognition of small mounds over cists, often near the large barrows,
suggests that other sectors of the society are represented in recognizable
monuments; without any stone construction, a simple inhumation in a
pit would not survive in a recognizable form.[89]

The problems connected with the first- and second-series burials are considerable. Their division into chronological phases rather than by sex, by age, by social status, has been carefully devised and remains undisputed.[90] Further varieties of evidence are clearly required.

One type of evidence consists of the first of the major sets of metal hoards and products of Atlantic France (fig. 80). The Tréboul group, consisting of flanged axes, unlooped palstaves, long daggers or short swords, and decorated spearheads, appears to be contemporary with the second-series burials.[91] Metal distribution is essentially Armorican, and their high tin content is doubtless the result of exploitation of the tin resources of the lower Loire and Armorica. The peninsula was rich in tin and gold, and copper was also available; however, it appears unlikely that copper was actually extracted locally in the Bronze Age.[92] Contemporary production of axes and palstaves, spearheads and bracelets was underway in other parts of coastal France, and west European rapiers, perhaps of British origin, were also in circulation.[93] The last half of the second millennium was a time when Atlantic Europe metal industries were in full production.

The earlier Bronze Age evidence from areas to the north and east of Armorica are poor reflections of the wealthy societies inferred for Wessex and for Armorica. A few first-series burials are recorded from Normandy, but second-series burials are not known. Beyond this region, the Armorican social structure is totally unknown.[94] Instead, in the basins of the Seine and the Somme, the distribution of earlier Bronze Age material is very sparse.[95] Metalwork reflects the products of the general west European-Atlantic industries, and local Seine productions are known.[96]

Settlements of the earlier Bronze Age in northern France include hill-top and other withdrawn positions. Fort Harrouard is perhaps the best-known, although its precise character may never be understood.[97] Metalwork was rare in the settlement, but Grand Pressigny flint and stone were employed. The occupation at La Roche, Videlles, was contemporary with Fort Harrouard, and much flint work was produced as well as a variety of domestic pottery vessels (fig. 79); metal was extremely rare.[98] Of animal remains, only 40 per cent were domestic, and wild animals hunted were *Bos primigenius*, deer, bear, wolf, fox, wildcat, and beaver. These animals perhaps give a better guide to the environmental conditions than does the mere listing of domestic debris; the herded animals were pig, sheep and cattle. Another large settlement at Cannes-Écluse was unfortunately destroyed with little chance to examine the houses and their disposition (p. 469).[99]

These sites in fact sum up the information about the earlier Bronze Age of northern France, an area which was probably exploited to the full by settlers utilizing the fertile lowlands and the great river valleys, and which provided the possibilities for contact between the lands of the western seaboard and those of the Rhineland and west-central Europe. The evidence for such exploitation is either lost or unrecognized, and this area remains one of the most important territories for future work.

Britain and Ireland

In contrast, the islands of Britain and Ireland, equally well furnished with natural resources, have provided abundant evidence for a variety of Bronze Age activities, and although there are some avenues of research still open, an impressive range of evidence is already assembled.

The islands are geologically very complex, yielding a wide range of topography and soils which defy a brief general description; only a few broadly relevant points will be made here. The traditional division of Britain into a lowland zone and a highland zone (the line running from Lyme Bay in the south-west, to the valley of the Tees in the north-east of England) is valid here. To the north and west of this line are the upland massifs of south-west England, Wales, the Pennine chain and the Uplands of Scotland. To the east of the line are low-lying clays and chalks of eastern England. Ireland is similarly divided, with the massifs of northern and the extreme southern parts separated by the central lowland valley.

The climate of the British Isles is generally temperate and maritime, but the eastern part of Britain is drier and has more temperature variation through the year than the wetter western regions, including Ireland. The mild conditions in Ireland allow arable cultivation as well as pasturing of animals over many parts of the island; dairy cattle and stock-breeding have always been important, as well as large land-holdings for arable cultivation in the eastern and some southern parts. The west coast traditionally has small holdings, with a few beasts, a small plot of cultivated land and crofts with as little as 3 ha of land. About half of Ireland consisted recently of farm holdings of less than 12 ha each. Much the same can be said of Scotland, with arable farming in the eastern lowlands, stock-breeding and long-fallow fields in riverine and some upland areas, hill sheep and crofting in the north-western Highlands, and predominantly dairy farming in the south-west. Pastoral activities, with little evidence for much plough agriculture, are also a feature of highland Wales, where rough hill grazing is important.

A common form of landuse in such conditions was the infield-outfield system, whereby a community of perhaps 2–15 families operated an infield continuously ploughed and manured, and an outfield generally under pasture but periodically cultivated in small sections in shifting fashion to prevent deterioration into rough grazing or moorland. This is almost certainly the pattern of landuse in Bronze Age times.

The evidence for deforestation in the Bronze Age of Britain is considerable, and represents the culmination of clearances begun in Mesolithic times; the matter is referred to below, but such clearances are likely to have been particularly intensive in lowland England, where drier conditions, rolling or flat fertile lands, contributed to a successful arable pattern of landuse. The evidence from Bronze Age sites for such an established economy is not quite unequivocal, but the breadbasket of England today was quite likely to have been just that in the past.

The evidence for second millennium settlement and industry in the British Isles is extensive and varied, as befits a territory of great potential for exploitation. The range of habitats has been indicated, and conditions in the second millennium were particularly amenable for agricultural practices in areas unsuitable today. The populations of Late Neolithic Britain and Ireland were varied and successful in establishing occupation over wide areas, and although certain aspects are imperfectly understood, there is no doubt about their effectiveness in dealing with heavy industries in stone and wood, and in copper and gold metallurgy. Forest clearances and the reworking of scrubland and old grassland are attested, and in some sites a well-controlled animal husbandry existed. Gallery graves, stone circles and other megaliths were erected, henge monuments were embellished, and some alignments point to astronomical observations. Settlements are less well-known but substantial houses, and villages on coastal stations and inland waterways, have been indicated. The density of population represented by these Late Neolithic and Beaker groups is difficult to assess, but the single-grave tradition of burial which became a dominant form at this time cannot have been used for all sectors of the population. Evidence of clearances and cultivation, and large monumental constructions, suggests a sizeable series of communities existing in many parts of the British Isles.[100]

The same can be said of the second millennium populations. Whether the evidence comes from the multiple settlements and field systems, or from burials and metal finds, the density of human occupation in the islands suggests some areas intensively exploited and supporting concentrations of people, and other areas in use but by smaller or less permanent groups.[101] The reason for such widespread settlement is partly climatic, partly population energies. Pollen and other studies have indicated that the second millennium may have been slightly warmer and less wet than now, although most of the evidence is from Britain rather than Ireland where conditions may have been somewhat wetter.[102] Drier conditions in particular would have opened new upland areas for potential agricultural or pastoral activities, and this, with the well-established open field systems of lowland areas would have created opportunities for augmented food production. The information about third millennium agricultural strategies and areas is still inadequate but the important point is that second millennium conditions were appropriate for very widespread activities in both lowland and upland areas.

Two main types of forest exploitation and land use have been suggested for the Bronze Age. The first, in generally lowland situations, involved wide clearances and permanent open country. The second, in more upland regions, was effected by small-scale temporary clearances.[103] Examination of such strategies in association with contemporary settlements provides perhaps the most detailed picture of Bronze Age economies in Europe, other than in fen-edge or lake-side situations.

Evidence from southern lowland England, in areas of light soils, suggests that woodland clearance was widespread in the earlier second millennium.[104] This was not limited to chalk and limestone soils, but included sands and some river gravels. Such cleared areas were regularly put into systematic agricultural use, with regular fields demarcated by banks or ditches.[105] Natural features in the land were used as axes for the laying-out of the field systems, and it seems that large areas were brought into use as a block, with long straight field boundaries agreed and established, from which there extended the individual fields. The axes of the fields often run up and down the slopes of the hills, so that the fields occur on hilltops, on hillsides and in valley bottoms (fig. 86). The fields are rectangular in shape, and each contains from 0.1 to 0.4 ha of arable land. The field system at Chaldon Herring in Dorset encompassed over 300 ha, with major axis lines, field banks, and probable small settlement areas within the fields.[106] Many other examples exist in lowland England, and they can be dated throughout the second millennium. In a few cases, Early Bronze Age barrows post-date field banks, and in most other cases the associated material is of the later Bronze Age.[107] Recent mapping of the surviving field banks, excavations, and experimental work, have indicated that the lynchets forming some of the boundaries may be up to 4 m in height, representing the build-up of soil brought down by cultivation and erosion against an original slightly lower field boundary of uncut turf. The wooden ard, probably tipped with a stone share, was employed in the cultivation of these fields, and criss-cross scratches were made in the soil; original turf, and developed fallow ground, would probably have been removed or cut by hand. The cereals cultivated included barley, wheat, spelt and flax.[108]

A settlement at Winterbourne Steepleton probably represents most of the elements involved in this farming system. The fields covered hilltops,

Fig. 86 Field boundaries and alignments in Central Dorset; the banks are arranged on a north-west to south-east axis and cross both ridge and valley.

(From C. Bowen in Fowler 1975)

247

slopes and valley bottoms, and were over 200 ha in extent. One settlement of four huts within the system had 3 ha of open ground around it, not under ard cultivation. Sunken droveways led to enclosures attached to field banks, and a second settlement consisted of four to five huts. The enclosures may have been for temporary penning of livestock, and open areas perhaps for hoe cultivation plots near the huts.[109]

Upland areas of Britain and Ireland were also widely exploited for food production, through arable cultivation and through herding of animals. Because some of this land became unsuitable for intensive use in later periods, the Bronze Age systems have survived. Large tracts of upland were never brought under control before the second millennium, and these include both areas of poor sandy soil and areas of hard rock such as granite. The evidence for Bronze Age occupation of these upland regions consists of stone banks, hut circles, field banks, burial monuments, pollen and soil analyses.[110] It seems clear that most of these upland areas were forested, and that clearances often took place in a less regular and large-scale manner than in lowland areas, but this was not always the case. The evidence for arable cultivation is weak from some of these areas, and pastoralism is assumed to have been the reason for clearances and for their continuation. But even in a single region such as the North Yorkshire Moors certain sites have yielded ample evidence for cereal cultivation, and others none at all, so the precise land-use pattern was clearly mixed and variable. What is striking is that present-day conditions would not allow such varied strategies in many of these upland regions, the reasons being a combination of erosion and impoverishment of the soils, as well as probable climatic changes for the worse. Podsolized soils with heath vegetation developed in many places as a result of Bronze Age clearances, and the changes were irreversible. This dramatic condition seems likely to have developed in both Britain and in Ireland; even in north-west Scotland continuous open ground is recorded, and field systems were in operation in both Scotland and Ireland in the second millennium.[111]

Stone-built settlements in these upland areas are notoriously difficult to date but the formation of peat over field systems and hut emplacements has allowed many to be assigned to the second millennium; conditions for preservation of organic remains, and poorly-fired pottery, are generally so acidic that only stonework has survived. Many upland areas of Britain contain traces of hut-circles, arranged in nucleated and dispersed settlements, sometimes clearly associated with field banks or territorial boundaries of stones, and with clearance cairns or burial cairns.[112]

One of the major areas where such evidence survives is Dartmoor in south-west England. Many hundreds of hut-circles have been recorded, including groups of twenty to thirty, and these have been divided into pastoral and arable situations.[113] The arable settlements lie between 250 m and 500 m on the rolling country of the eastern part of Dartmoor, in an area of lower rainfall than the west receives. The settlements consist of huts with fields, marked by granite boulder rows, averaging between 0.4 and 1.0 ha. The huts are generally over 6 m in diameter, with rather thin stone-faced walls with a fill of soil and pebbles. Site catchment analysis of the settlements suggests that each was a self-sufficient economic unit; one such site, Blissmoor, consists of three huts associated with six or seven rectangular fields totalling *c.* 1 ha.[114] The lynchets forming part of the field boundaries are explained as the result of soil movement during cultivation, and manuring was probably necessary to maintain fertility in poor soil conditions, for barley and other cereals. An infield-outfield system of land management has been postulated for settlements of this type, where some small parts are permanently cultivated, and where larger areas are worked periodically after periods of regeneration.[115] Lands beyond the outfield could be used for pasture, for both cattle and sheep; pollen evidence suggests woodland clearances around the settlements, with probably less extensive clearances in areas further from the intensive agricultural zones. Wood was employed for buildings and fencing, by inference, and woodlands were perhaps managed for coppiced supplies.

The pastoral settlement at Stannon Down, on Bodmin Moor, is also instructive.[116] Over twenty hut circles, 6–8 m in diameter, covered an area *c.* 150 × 100 m, with strip fields close by for arable cultivation, and large enclosures some distance away for stock control (fig. 87). The fields, sloping downhill from the settlement, were probably ard-cultivated, and totalled less than 1 ha. Smaller fields next to the huts were perhaps for hoe crops. The houses had paved or stamped earth floors, with internal drains or sumps, wooden partitions and furniture, and thatched roofs supported by many posts. Domestic equipment was poorly preserved, some mid-second millennium local pottery, flint tools, and saddle querns. No metal survived, or was perhaps necessary to possess, although a whetstone suggests the possibility of metal blades. Reconstructions of the population are difficult here as elsewhere, but if all the houses were contemporary a group of 100 is possible, requiring either far more arable land (not marked by field boundaries) or reliance upon stock-breeding. The latter seems likely, but it will be apparent that the division of these upland settlements into an arable or pastoral system masks the essential observation that neither system would have been exclusive and that most, perhaps all, such settlements would have had a mixed economic basis only varying in proportions.

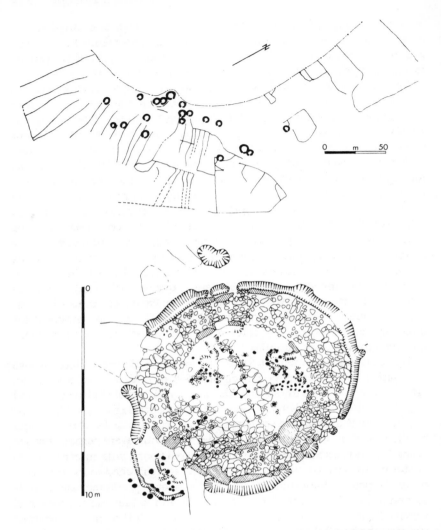

Fig. 87   Stannon Down, Cornwall. *Upper*: plan of the settlement with hut-circles, fields and, at top, edge of disturbed area which masks additional hut-circles. *Lower*: plan of hut-circle, with thick rubble walls, and external drainage gulley, slab-covered channels or sump running out of the entrance, and post-holes marking internal divisions.
(From R. Mercer, *Cornish Archaeol.* 9 (1970), figs 6 and 9)

There is little evidence from such sites of any overall landscape strategy, or of any major controls and perhaps constraints upon the division of the land such as can be seen in the lowland areas where fields were laid out in blocks or along natural or artificial linear divisions.[117] However, upland regions of Dartmoor and probably other highlands were also subjected to overall management; the recognition and significance of this has only recently been understood.[118] Much of Dartmoor and its periphery was divided up by the building of reaves, long stone-built walls which ran across the undulating area up to *c.* 400 m altitude, above which there are no visible reaves. Parallel reaves divide up the drier territories and are terminated by other reaves; above this arable land there are other reaves which may mark grazing allotments, and above this are the hilltops where only burial cairns are the major structures. The individual reaves may be as much as 2 km long, and community territories have been identified, each based upon the upper course of a river. Attached to some reaves, and contemporary, are small enclosures and hut emplacements. Although their study is only now under way, the evidence from pollen and from the reave systems shows an upland area carefully divided to provide that variety of zones essential for successful food production in a landscape undergoing woodland clearance on a large scale and capable of sustaining a large population until deteriorating soils and climate forced abandonment.[119]

Other Bronze Age communities in Britain were also heavily engaged in establishing or maintaining subsistence strategies on the islands to the north and west. The substantial stone-built houses clustered on both the west and east of Mainland (Zetland, map 5), Shetland, and associated with traces of field systems, provide evidence of established farming communities heavily reliant upon stone tools, with no metal, with local traditions of pottery, and with probable participation in the field clearance cairns and cooking sites called 'burnt mounds'.[120] The fields were marked out by stone banks, and seem to have included hoe plots, ard-worked fields and stock enclosures. Cattle, sheep, horse, and pig bones have been recovered, and a cache of 10 kg of carbonized barley lay beside a quern inside one of the houses; the barley provided a radiocarbon date of mid-second millennium bc. The oval houses of these settlements are probably the heaviest known from any area in prehistoric Britain (fig. 88); overall dimensions are 15–20 × 10–12 m, but the walls at the base are consistently 3–4 m thick, so the interiors are not large. Posts held up the roof, and internal house divisions may have been sparse; stone slabs provided some furnishing. The populations represented by these groups of houses may have been of the order of 100.

Within both upland and lowland areas of the British Isles, second

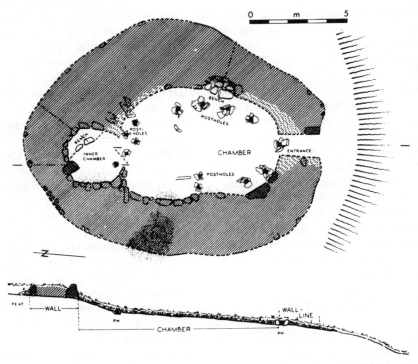

Fig. 88   Early Bronze Age house at Gruting, Shetland with composite section drawn through entrance.
(From C. T. Calder, *Proc. Soc. Ant. Scot.* 89 (1956), 345)

millennium settlements and activities are widespread. Coastal occupation is known from Ireland and from Scotland[121] as well as islands on inland lakes[122] and the advantages of marshland sites were not neglected. At Fengate, in eastern England, a second millennium settlement on the edge of a fenland involved the digging of ditches to contain domestic animals, probably cattle, with access along droveways to both dry land and the rich seasonal pasture of the fen margins.[123] In the marshlands of Somerset, similar activities are likely, but here the evidence suggests a greater interest in the wild products of the marsh waters themselves, fish, eels, fowl and wild plants.[124] Similar marshy areas were used in Ireland where wooden trackways, as in Somerset (pl. 9a) and in eastern England, were built out from dry land.[125] The recognition of Bronze Age hunting stations where game was butchered and cooked by roasting or boiling has relied entirely upon radiocarbon dates, as this activity has extended from prehistoric up to recent times.[126] The Ballyvourney cooking-place, analogous to other dated Irish sites, contained a post-built shelter, an enclosed area for hearths and a boiling pit, and a roasting pit. Several hearths were used to heat the stones for both types of cooking, and experiments showed the effectiveness of this method.[127] The animals hunted in the Bronze Age included deer, *Bos primigenius*, pig and smaller beasts, but many sites suggest that hunting played a relatively small part in the meat requirements of Bronze Age communities,[128] and this may have been due to the progressive reduction of forest, and the success of domestic animal breeding in wide tracts of controlled countryside. The overall picture from Ireland in particular suggests a greater emphasis on animals than on plants, in climatic circumstances more maritime than elsewhere in the British Isles, and wider and wider clearances hastening the podsolization of soils and its eventual disappearance under the growth of peat.

The association between settlements and burials of the second millennium is difficult to assess in the virtual absence of closely-related monuments. Domestic debris from living sites did not often find its way into tombs for the dead, and only general contemporaneities can be assumed on the basis of the character of pottery and a few implements such as knives or pins.

The origins of the earlier Bronze Age single grave traditions lie in Late Neolithic and Beaker ritual, attested from many parts of Britain and Ireland. Burials were either inhumations or cremations, placed either in pits or in wooden or stone coffins, and either left as a flat grave or covered by a cairn or earthen mound. The varieties of burial ritual are great, and cannot be described here.[129] Burials were often placed alone in an area, and often in cemeteries of flat graves or mounds (fig. 89 and pl. 14). The barrows or cairns may be small (3 m across) or excessively large (30 m across). Many burials were associated with varieties of pottery which have been the subject of regional studies,[130] and some rather broad groupings have been established which sometimes had particular burial rites attached to them. Inhumation graves tend to concentrate in eastern Britain where Beaker inhuming groups were most densely represented, and cremation was more dominant in the west. Burials in cists, in flat graves, tend to occur more widely in northern Britain and Ireland, and burials in pits under barrows are a common form in southern Britain.[131]

The pottery associated with these burials are of two main earlier Bronze Age traditions (fig. 90). Food vessels, with inhumations or cremations, are widespread in northern Britain and Ireland, and a number of regional variants have been devised. Urns, accompanying and holding cremations, are found throughout the British Isles, again in regional styles. The association of Bronze Age burials with pre-existing monuments,

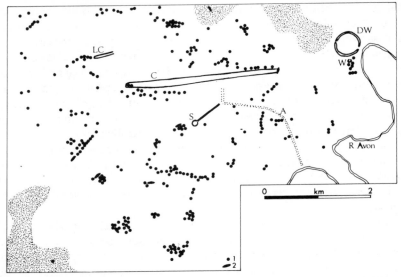

Fig. 89 Distribution of barrow cemeteries around Stonehenge and other
Neolithic monuments: 1. round barrows, 2. long barrows, C. the Cursus,
LC. Lesser Cursus, S. Stonehenge, A. Avenue, DW. Durrington Walls, W.
Woodhenge. Land over 125 m stippled.
(Based on Ashbee 1960, fig. 6)

megalithic tombs in Ireland, stone circles and henge monuments
throughout the area, allied with late Neolithic and Beaker antecedents in
material culture, suggests purely local origins for all these groups. The
complexity of their burial ritual is, however, a continuing study, and
there is increasing evidence that many monuments were not built to hold
only a single body, but were foci for community activity of a ceremonial
nature which may have taken place over many decades. The development
of cemeteries of related burials, with founders' monuments, fits in with
the evidence from settlements and field systems for land organization and
control over long periods of time.[132]

A site such as Cairnpapple, Lothian, where a Neolithic and Beaker
cemetery and henge monument were utilized and transformed into a
Bronze Age cairn cemetery, demonstrates this continuity,[133] and the
monuments at the Brenig, Clwyd, indicate the evolution of a cemetery
and ritual wholly of the Bronze Age.[134] Here the common Bronze Age
features of mortuary houses, stake circle enclosures, the final sealing of
the burials, and the prominent positioning of the primary marker cairn,
can be clearly demonstrated; the cemetery was in use for perhaps only

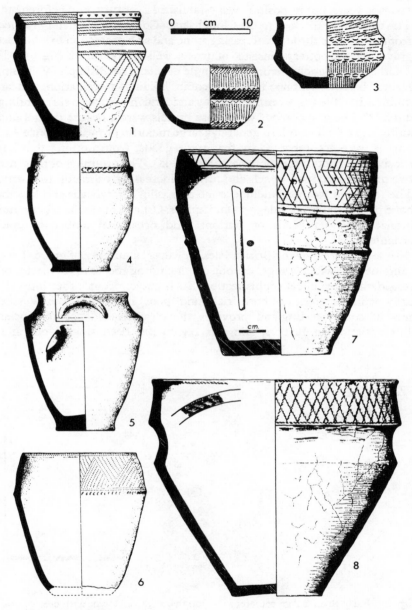

Fig. 90   Early Bronze Age pottery: 1–3. food vessels, 4–6. biconical urns, 7. cordoned urn, 8. collared urn. (1–3 from Simpson 1968; 4–6 from *Victoria County History Wiltshire;* 7–8 from ApSimon 1969)

100–200 years, but its position was established a century or so beforehand. The variation expressed in the Cloughskelt (Co. Down) cemetery ranged from a pit grave through increasing stone and slab protection to a full cist grave, and the pottery consisted of urns as well as food vessels (fig. 91).[135]

Other burial monuments were single events. The Bishop's Waltham, Hants, barrow contained an oak coffin holding a cremation and an inhumation, the grave central to a clay and sand mound with surrounding ditch.[136] The grave-goods with these burials were a bronze dagger and knife, and a food vessel. In general, a large majority of earlier Bronze Age burials were accompanied by few grave-goods, from nothing that has survived to a pot or tool or ornament (fig. 92). The grouping of pots into two main series, food vessels and urns, is increasingly difficult to justify. The tools and weapons include stone axes, flint arrowheads and knives, bone points and bronze daggers and knives. Ornaments include bone and bronze pins, jet beads or buttons, and occasional amber or gold ornaments.[137]

In several areas of the British Isles, however, a number of graves have contained a wider range of objects including decorative pieces of considerable technical sophistication. Such graves occur either individually or in cemeteries of both 'rich' and 'poor' burials.[138] The Wessex area of southern England provides the clearest evidence for social differentiation in Britain, and this region has been singled out and

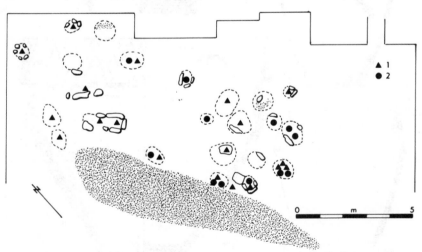

Fig. 91   Early Bronze Age cemetery at Cloughskelt, Co. Down, with cremations placed in shallow scoops or pits, some lined with stones; 1. food-vessel, 2. urn. Stipple: granite outcrop.
(After *Irish Archaeol. Res. Forum* 3 (1976))

Fig. 92 Reconstruction of ceremonies at a single-grave inhumation burial, placed within stake circle, with grave goods, 'ritual pit' offering and funeral feast. Not based upon any single individual archaeological site, but appropriate in general to north-western Europe in the Early Bronze Age. (Drawing by R. Walker)

257

identified as the cross-channel equivalent of the Armorican group. We do not think that any intrusive warrior elements need have arrived in either area to trigger off this episode of local aggrandisement, although this immigrant view has its supporters.[139]

The burial mounds of the Wessex area consist of several thousand graves, mostly built of earth with a surrounding quarry ditch. Several hundred, however, are slightly different and contain either a very large mound or a very small mound separated from the ditch by a berm or flat area. These mounds, called bell or disc barrows, occur within small cemeteries of normal round barrows, and such cemeteries were often situated near impressive Late Neolithic and Beaker monuments.[140] Within these barrows, whether of bell, disc or ordinary bowl types, early antiquarians and a few others have discovered inhumations and cremations furnished with an array of weapons and ornaments not encountered in other areas in such quantities. The original study of these grave-goods led to the identification of a 'Wessex culture', and subsequent work has clarified many details without advancing to a full understanding, or even definition, of the problem.[141]

The most famous burial of this group is the Bush Barrow, excavated in 1808. A probable extended inhumation beneath a large bowl barrow, in a cemetery near Stonehenge, was accompanied by a copper dagger, a bronze axe, dagger and knife, a stone macehead, bone mounts for a shaft, a sheet gold belt-hook, a large gold lozenge plate and a smaller one, and a possible wood and leather shield or helmet (fig. 93,A).[142] The wooden handle of one of the daggers was ornamented with thousands of gold pins in geometric patterns, similar to the Armorican dagger from Kernonen; similarities in daggers, in pin decoration, in social differentiation and in a few other aspects has suggested very close links across the Channel, but these remain to be defined.

Other rich graves include Upton Lovell, where an amber necklace with spacer plates was recovered (fig. 93,B), a form duplicated in jet in northern Britain, and perhaps in sheet gold in the north (pl. 7b) and in Ireland.[143] Many graves in southern England, and elsewhere, were excavated in the nineteenth century and burial details are consequently poor. Both inhumation and cremation were practised, and stone or wooden coffins were used where the remains were not placed directly into the ground or in an urn. Cremations were more numerous than inhumations, and no correlation between these, bell or disc or bowl barrows, rich or poor grave-goods, has been ascertained.

The material found in the barrows of Wessex has been divided into two chronological series. The first, with most of the inhumations and some cremations, contains a majority of the richest graves, including the Bush

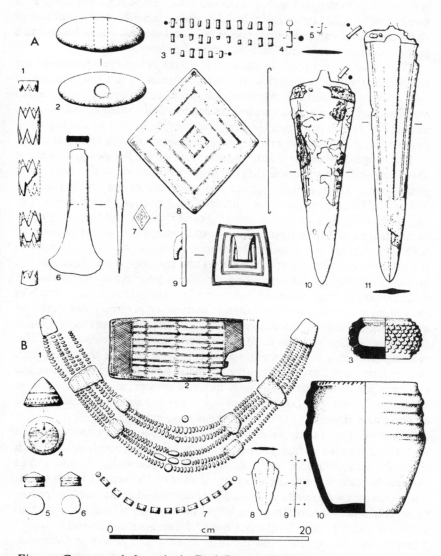

Fig. 93   Grave-goods from A. the Bush Barrow, B. Upton Lovell.
A:1. bone shaft mounts, 2. stone mace head, 3–4. bronze rivets, 5. bronze wire,
6. bronze axe, 7–8. gold plates, 9. gold belt-hook, 10. copper dagger, 11. bronze
dagger.
B:1. amber necklace, 2. gold plate, 3. pottery grape cup, 4. gold-plated shale
cover, 5–6. gold studs, 7. gold beads, 8. bronze knife, 9. bronze awl, 10. pot.
(From S. Piggott, *Victoria County History, Wiltshire,* 1973)

259

Barrow with its daggers, gold pin decoration, gold objects. Female graves were equally richly furnished; the Manton inhumation had a necklace of shale beads and two pendants, one of gold and amber, one of bronze and amber, as well as two small incense cups of pottery.[144]

The material occurring in the second series, when cremation was the universal preference, includes urns as repositories for the burnt bones, as well as small incense cups. A grave from the Wilsford cemetery contained a whetstone, a bronze pin, two bronze daggers and a swan's bone whistle; daggers of the second series are of ogival type.[145] Amber beads and a few faience beads, as well as various pins, are associated with female graves.

The range of material culture represented by the Wessex graves is not abundant, but the technical skills in their production, in the working of stone, bone, wood, amber, bronze and gold, and in the fitting-together of some of these substances, is considerable. The many other contemporary burials in Wessex, and in other areas,[146] contain at best only a few rather simple single-material objects, and form the essential population base upon which the favoured few were supported. Just as in Armorica, the relationship between the rich graves and the poor graves is uncertain, and even definitions for separating rich from poor are unestablished. It might be more appropriate to consider the earlier Bronze Age burials as exhibiting a continuum rather than providing an arbitrary line based on value judgements about scarcity and accessibility of resources. Nonetheless, the evidence for some form of social stratification seems strong. The reasons for such a development are obscure, but must be bound up with the monumental community projects of the later third millennium, the evidence for firmly-established agricultural systems and land control in the earlier Bronze Age, and the possibility that certain areas could provide essential raw materials for Bronze Age technologies.[147]

Major industries undertaken in the second millennium were concerned with the extraction of fine-grained stone for axes and maceheads,[148] with pottery products of great variety, and with metalworking in gold and in bronze. Metallurgy was the growth industry of the second millennium, and its success was based in no small part upon readily-available supplies. Gold could be panned from the Wicklow mountains and elsewhere in southern Ireland, from Scotland, from Wales and perhaps from Devon.[149] Tin was less widespread, and the only known source was in Cornwall. Copper was abundant in most of western Britain and in Ireland, and although it is generally difficult to determine the prehistoric exploitation of particular sources, in view of the very large numbers of metal objects from Britain, and particularly Ireland, it is likely that many metal resources were being used during the earlier Bronze Age, and search for new supplies was perhaps a regular activity.[150] The Beaker introduction of copper and gold-working is generally admitted,[151] and prehistoric mines have been recognized on the eastern side of Mt Gabriel, Co. Cork;[152] these are much smaller than the contemporary mines of the Austrian Alpine region consisting of little more than a narrow entry leading into a pocket quarried out of the rock, with fire-setting and hammers used to loosen the rock. The ores, sulphide and chalcopyrite included, were separated from their parent rock outside the mine. Many casting moulds for a variety of products are known from both Ireland and Britain.[153]

Products of the British-Irish industries included flat and flanged axes, spearheads, halberds, daggers and knives, short rapiers, bracelets and other ornaments; these all occur in a variety of local and regional styles, and occasionally in hoards (fig. 94).[154] The products from the workshops seem to have been designed, in general, for home consumption, and restricted distributions can sometimes be demonstrated. The re-melting of metal, however, must have removed a large majority of such products from the scene, and our distribution maps must therefore be grossly incomplete. Casting in open moulds, in bipartite moulds and in cored moulds was common, and hammer decoration as well as cast decoration could be attempted.

Gold was more abundant in Britain and Ireland than in most European areas, and earlier Bronze Age products were relatively large and heavy. The specialized nature of Wessex goldwork, objects made of thin gold sheet and decorated by punch or line, suggests production for the grave.[155] The larger lunulae or neckplates, found in Ireland and in northern Britain, contain a far greater weight of gold than other earlier Bronze Age objects, and represent various craftsmen or stylistic schools.[156] The lunulae, and other ornaments of the north and west, would impose much greater emphasis on these areas if pure weight of metal was used as an indicator of social leadership, as elsewhere (p. 303).

These objects, and some in bronze, were occasionally distributed outside their areas of origin, and the question of exchange mechanisms, trade across the Channel and across the North Sea, has been considered on many occasions.[157] The maritime nature of travel and transport in Atlantic Europe has been commented upon, and it is perhaps more likely that a few objects should have been unintentionally moved long distances than that major groups of products were deliberately packed and transported to distant markets. The truth may lie in between. For distinct technological specialities, such as the gold pin decoration of dagger handles, or lunulae of particular stylistic decor, it is likely that individual craftsmen were recognized for their skill or artistry, and their products may have been commissioned or otherwise acquired.

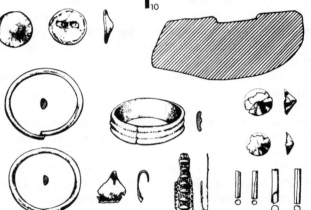

Fig. 94   Early Bronze Age metalwork: 1. part of hoard from
Migdale, Sutherland (consisting of flat axe, armlets, earrings,
beads and buttons), 2. Mould from Kilcronat, Co. Cork, for
flat axe.
(1. from *Inventaria Archaeologica G B* 26; 2. from *Sibrium* 6
(1961))

The organization of a society that allowed or insisted that such
specialized work be done cannot be known to us in the absence of written
evidence. There are other elements in the society that also cannot be
explained in any detail, and these form a heterogeneous group of
monuments that are generally considered in terms of ritual or ceremony.
Such monuments should not be excluded from discussions of burial
structures nor settlements and economies; although broad traditions of

behaviour can be discussed within the earlier Bronze Age, many archaeologically indistinct, yet perhaps socially vital, variations in traditions probably involved other elements in the landscape, natural springs and wells, viewpoints, and human structures such as stone circles, stone alignments[158] and the decoration of rock surfaces.

The deep shaft at Wilsford and other sites dug with axes and picks through 30 m of chalk, and filled with erosion deposits and human debris of the earlier Bronze Age, are incapable of precise interpretation yet foreshadow interest in later prehistoric sanctuaries (fig. 95).[159]

Rock carvings on cists and other stones associated with burial monuments are another element often considered to represent human attempts to influence or commemorate events. The distribution of this art in Britain is essentially northern, between the Tyne and Tay rivers, although there are outliers to the north and large concentrations in the west.[160] Irish rock art is scattered throughout the island, but there are

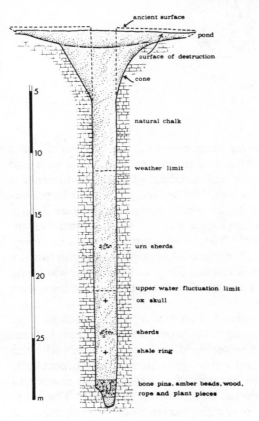

Fig. 95   The ritual shaft dug at Wilsford, Wiltshire, with artifacts found within the filling.

(From S. Piggott, *Victoria County History, Wiltshire*, 1973)

important groups in the east and in the south-west. The objects pecked or grooved into the rock, whether movable or living, are most commonly cups, cup-and-ring variants, with some spirals, discs and human feet (fig. 96). Various stylistic provinces have been identified, and relationships with Breton and Galician art have been postulated. Much of the art clearly has antecedents in third millennium Britain and Ireland, in similar fashion to the Bronze Age stone circles and alignments.

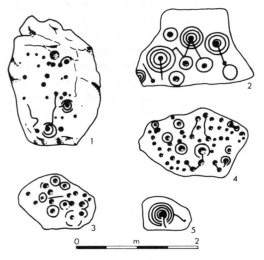

Fig. 96　Rock carvings from Britain:
1. Redhills, Cumberland,
2. Walltown, Angus,
3. Brotton, Yorkshire
4. Bakerhill, Ross,
5. Ingoe, Northumberland
(From Simpson and Thawley 1972)

　Megalithic structures involving the preparation and erection of stones were a common feature in third millennium societies of Britain and Ireland, and the continued use and building of such monuments is attested from the second millennium.[161] The Druids' circle at Penmaenmawr, Wales, and adjacent circles have been dated to the earlier Bronze Age,[162] and alignments and circles such as that at Cholwichtown, Devon, are likely to be contemporary.[163] The re-building operations at Stonehenge were also the work of earlier Bronze Age populations, and this site alone suggests that some overall responsibility and direction was being taken and given, in order to ensure that the necessary actions were correctly completed (pl. 12b).

　The existing monument consisted of an earthen bank and ditch with an entrance and an internal setting of bluestone orthostats brought from southern Wales. In the second millennium, and contemporary with the establishment of field systems and arable agriculture on the adjacent hills, and with the burials in round barrows of richly-equipped males and females, Stonehenge was subjected to rebuilding phases.[164] The bluestones were dragged away, and over eighty sarsen blocks were transported from the adjacent downland; thirty of them, each weighing 25 tonnes, were set up in a circle and capped by thirty lintels of 7 tonnes each. Before this was completed, ten uprights weighing up to 45 tonnes each were set up as pairs inside the circle, and capped by lintels. The axis of the monument pointed towards the midsummer sunrise. Twenty of the bluestones were placed to form an oval setting, with lintels, but this stage was abandoned and the bluestones were re-erected in a horseshoe and a circle. The monument involved Bronze Age society in undertakings of a quite massive character, otherwise unsuspected, and must remain as a cautionary and correcting element in any assessment of Bronze Age society as purely local, self-sufficient and unenterprising. The question of leadership, chieftainship or equivalent, is not necessarily a corollary to such a work as Stonehenge; what it shows quite clearly is the cooperation of large work forces, and these could as well have been from essentially egalitarian societies combining on occasions of high significance, as from communities under the control of individual leaders who possessed great wealth and status.

Table 7   Radiocarbon dates, western Europe, earlier Bronze Age

Site	Lab no.	bc
France		
Etaples, Pas de Calais, settlement	Gif–2677	1470 ± 100
La Chausée Tirancourt, Somme, burial	Gif–1289	1400 ± 120
collective burial	Gif–1372	1750 ± 120
	Gif–1378	1700 ± 120
Guiry en Vexin, Val d'Oise, burial	Gif–3329	1690 ± 100
Soumont St. Quentin, Calvados, occupation	Gif–2316	1400 ± 130
	Gif–2317	1420 ± 150
Saint Jude, Côtes-du-Nord, barrow	Gif–166	1480 ± 160
	Gif–2686	1830 ± 100
	Gif–2687	1920 ± 100
	Gif–2688	1810 ± 100
Abri de la Gourgue, Haute-Pyrenées	Ly–1053	1850 ± 200
Kerno en Ploudaniel, Finistère, barrow	Gif–2421	1500 ± 100
Kervigny, Finistère, barrow	Gif–2481	1560 ± 100
Kerbernard, Pluguffan, Finistère, cairn	Gif–3202	1690 ± 100
Lezommy, Finistère, burial	Gif–188	1650 ± 200
	Gif–189	1200 ± 200
Saint Evarzec, Kerhuel, Finistère, barrow	Gif–482	1630 ± 200
Cleder, le Helen, Finistère, barrow	Gif–748	1300 ± 115
Plouhinec, Lescongar, Finistère, barrow	Gif–749	1620 ± 115
Plouzévédé, Ar Réunic, Finistère, barrow	Gif–1113	1250 ± 120
	Gif–1114	1210 ± 120

Table 7—cont.

Site	Lab no.	bc
Plouvorn, Kernonen, Finistère, barrow	Gif–805	1960 ± 120
	Gif–806	1250 ± 120
	Gif–807	1200 ± 120
	Gif–1149	1480 ± 120
Poulguen, Finistère, burial	Gsy–55B	1610 ± 120
Ile de Geignog, Finistère, megalith	Gif–1477	1650 ± 110
Goarem Goasven, Finistère, barrow	Gif–1313	1850 ± 130
	Gif–1314	1050 ± 130
Lennon, Pendrec, Finistère, burial	Gif–2177	1600 ± 120
Ligollenec, Berrien, Finistère, barrow	Gif–1866	1550 ± 130
Priziac, Finistère	Gif–3201	1980 ± 110
Langolean, Finistère, burial	Gif–2176	1450 ± 120
Elven, Le Boccolo, Finistère, hearth	Gif–1681	1700 ± 130
Melrand, St. Fiacre, Finistère, barrow	Gif–863	1950 ± 135
Cleger, Kervelerin, Finistère, barrow	Gsy–86	1345 ± 150
	Gif–1968	1400 ± 120
Guidel, Tuchenn Cruguel, Finistère, barrow	Gif–235	1320 ± 200
Goerem, Finistère, burial	Gif–769	1520 ± 120
Fay de Bretagne, Loire-Atlantique, pottery	Gif–1465	1350 ± 110
Jard sur Mer, Maine-et-Loire, barrow	Gif–1119	1350 ± 120
St. Aquilin, Dordogne, cave	Gif–1087	1730 ± 130
Villegouge, Roanne, Dordogne, occupation	Gif–783	1750 ± 135
Lescar, Pyr.-Atl, barrow	Gif–2515	1890 ± 80
Sauvagnon, Pau, Pyr.-Atl, barrow	Gif–2516	1670 ± 80
Salies de Béarn, Pyr.-Atl, occupation	Gif–394	1260 ± 200
Cys-la-Commune, Aisne, burial	Gsy–91	1370 ± 110
Les Barbilloux, Dordogne, cave	Gif–1087	1730 ± 130
Iberia		
Cerro de la Virgen, burial, Argar A	GrN–5594	1785 ± 55
occupation, Argar B	GrN–5595	1915 ± 50
Cerro de la Encina, Granada, Argar B	GrN–6634	1675 ± 40
Serra Grossa, Alicante, Valencian BA	Bln–947	1865 ± 100
Terlinques, Villena, occupation	I–4525	1850 ± 115
Montefrio, Granada, Argar B[165]	GrN–?	c. 1865
Cuesta del Negro, Granada, Argar B[165]	GrN–?	c. 1645
Cabezo Redondo, Alicante, settlement	H–2277	1600 ± 55
	GrN–5109	1350 ± 55
Pic de los Cuervos, Sagunto[166]	Q–?	1581 ± 100
Torrello, Castellon	I–6937	1315 ± 90
	I–7250	1350 ± 190
Cueva del Mas d'Abad, Castellón, Valencian BA	I–8936	1460 ± 90
	I–8935	1010 ± 85

Table 7—cont.

Site	Lab no.	bc
British Isles		
Killeens, Co. Cork, Ireland, cooking place	C–878	1763±270
	C–877	1556±230
Mt. Gabriel, Co. Cork, Ireland, mine	VRI–66	1500±120
Ballynagilly, Co. Tyrone, occupation	UB–198	1640±60
Ness of Gruting, Shetland, settlement	BM–441	1564±120
Coney Island, Co. Tyrone, occupation	UB–43	1400±80
Downpatrick, Co. Down, occupation	UB–471	1625±70
	UB–474	1375±75
	UB–473	1315±80
Culbin Sands, Moray, midden	Q–990	1259±75
Amesbury, Wiltshire, barrow	HAR–1237	1670±90
Earls Farm Down, Wiltshire, barrow	NPL–75	1640±90
Bromfield, Shropshire		
barrow	Birm–64	1560±180
cremation	Birm–63	850±71
cremation	Birm–62	762±75
Bleasdale, Lancashire, circle	NPL–69	1810±90
Brightwell Heath, Suffolk, barrow	NPL–133	1770±130
Weird Law, Pebbleshire, cremation	NPL–57	1490±90
Whitestanes Moor, Dumfries, burial	Gak–461	1360±90
Corlona, Co. Leitrim, track	Gro–272	1445±170
Eclipse, Somerset, hurdle track	HAR–680	1510±60
Cambridge, yew bow	Q–684	1730±120
Chapel Flat Dyke, Yorkshire, dugout	BM–213	1500±150
North Ferriby, Yorkshire, boat		
range of 6 dates 1556±110 to 750±150		
Edington Burtle, Somerset, yew bow	Q–669	1320±110
Kirkhill, Northumberland, cremation	SRR–133	1292±90
Mount Pleasant, Dorset, burials	BM–669	1320±51
Harland Edge, Derby, burials	BM–210	1750±150
	BM–178	1490±150
Worgret, Dorset, barrow	NPL–199	1740±90
Snail Down, Wiltshire, pyre	NPL–141	1540±90
Branthwaite, Cumbria, dugout	Q–288	1570±100
Eriswell, Suffolk, barrow	BM–315	1520±115
Swarkeston, Derby, burial	NPL–17	1395±160
Grandtully, Perth, cremation	Gak–603	1270±100
Poole, Dorset, circle	GrN–1684	1260±50
Bedd Branwen, Anglesey, barrow	BM–456	1403±60
	BM–455	1307±80
	BM–453	1274±81
Court Hill, Somerset, cairn	I–5735	1375±100
	I–5734	715±130

Table 7—cont.

Site	Lab no.	bc
Earls Barton, Northants, barrow	BM–681	1264 ± 64
	BM–680	1219 ± 51
Brown Edge, Derby, cremations	BM–212	1530 ± 150
	BM–211	1250 ± 150
	BM–177	1050 ± 150
City Farm, Oxford, cremations	GrN–1685	1510 ± 65
	GrN–1686	1490 ± 60
Barbrook, Derby, cremation	BM–179	1500 ± 150
Stonehenge, Wiltshire, Phase II	I–2384	1620 ± 110
IIIa	BM–46	1720 ± 150
IIIb/IIIc	I–2445	1240 ± 105
Hove, Sussex.barrow	BM–682	1239 ± 46
Amesbury, Wiltshire.barrow	BM–287	1788 ± 55
Chalton, Hampshire.hut	BM–583	1243 ± 69
Edmonsham, Dorset.barrow	BM–708	1119 ± 45
	BM–709	1527 ± 52
Weasenham, Norfolk.barrow	BM–877	1389 ± 56
Tregiffian, St. Buryan, Cornwall	BM–935	1539 ± 59
Wilsford, Wiltshire.shaft	NPL–74	1380 ± 90
Brenig, Denbigh, cairns with cremations		
range of 19 dates (HAR–) 1120 ± 90 to 1680 ± 100		
Fengate, Cambs, ring ditch	HAR–406	1340 ± 80
burial	HAR–400	1460 ± 120
well	HAR–398	1050 ± 70
Heatherwood, Berks, field	HAR–478	1480 ± 70
Moel-y-Gaer, Clwyd, occupation	HAR–605	1640 ± 80
Shapwick, Somerset, wooden fork	HAR–1159	1380 ± 70
Butterbump, Lincoln, burials	HAR–490	1750 ± 80
	HAR–491	1520 ± 80
	HAR–488	1510 ± 130
Shelford, Cambs, burial	HAR–395	1530 ± 70
Cotton Valley, Bucks, hearth	HAR–471	1340 ± 160
Ystrad Hynod, Powys, cist	NPL–243	1500 ± 140
Dunfermline, Fife, burial	SRR–292	1631 ± 40
Crig-a-Mennis, Cornwall, urns	NPL–193	1565 ± 90
Shelford, Notts, cremation	HAR–395	1530 ± 70
Tallington, Lincoln, cremation	UB–450	1460 ± 165

Notes

1 Many dugouts of certain or probable Bronze Age date have been recovered, G. Camps, in Guilaine 1976, 192–201, but the Ferriby boats from eastern England show the elaborate nature, and technical skill, of second millennium boatbuilding techniques: E. V. Wright, The North Ferriby Boats, *Maritime Monographs and Reports* 34 1976.

2 References to sources of metal are numerous and not always consistent. See Schubart 1975, map 35; B. Clayton, *BIA* 11 (1974), 75–129; P. Harbison, *North Munster Antiq. Journ.* 10 (1966), 3–11; J. M. Coles, *Proc. Soc. Antiq. Scot.* 101 (1968–9), fig. 26; J. Briard 1965, ch. 2; A. Hartmann 1970; S. Briggs, J. Brennan and G. Freeburn, *Bull. Hist. Metallurgy Gp* 7 (1973), 18–26.

3 W. A. Cummins, *Antiquity* 48 (1974), 201–5 for summary of stone axe factories in Britain; F. E. S. Roe, *PPS* 32 (1966), 199–245 for battle-axes; F. E. S. Roe, in Coles and Simpson 1968, 145–72 for mace-heads; Clark 1952 for general flint and stone productions, and G. Clark, *Econ. Hist. Rev.* 18 (1965) for comments on trade and traffic in stone.

4 J. Evans, *The Ancient Bronze Implements, Weapons and Ornaments of Great Britain and Ireland.* 1881; J. Déchelette, *Manuel d'Archéologie. Préhistorique, Celtique et Gallo-Romaine.* II.1,1910; H. Breuil, *L'Anthropologie* 10–14, 16, 18 (1900–7); Siret 1913.

5 See Ashbee 1960 for a description of the havoc created by Cunnington, Colt Hoare, Greenwell, Mortimer and others; in regions outside the particular province of these and other collectors, recording was often non-existent.

6 Burgess 1974, esp. 170–1.

7 Briard 1965, 1974; Guilaine 1976, 18.

8 Schubart 1975, 164.

9 Furthermore we do not think that such precision is possible at the present time, although Burgess' work on the metals is useful for certain parts of Britain.

10 For Late Neolithic Atlantic Europe, the literature is enormous. A brief selection: IBERIA: E. Sangmeister, *Palaeohistoria* 12 (1967), 395–408; Savory 1968, ch. 6–7; B. Blance, *Die Anfänge der Metallurgie auf der Iberischen Halbinsel*, Studien zu den Anfängen der Metallurgie 4, 1971; FRANCE: Guilaine 1976, pt C.1; P. Phillips, *Early Farmers of West Mediterranean Europe*, London 1975, ch. 5; G. Bailloud in S. Piggott, G. Daniel and C. McBurney (eds), *France before the Romans*, London, 1974, ch. 4; BRITAIN: I. F. Smith, The Neolithic, in C. Renfrew (ed.), *British Prehistory. A new outline*, London, 1974; D. L. Clarke, *Beaker Pottery of Great Britain and Ireland*, Cambridge, 1970; IRELAND: Herity and Eogan 1977, chs 4–5; H. J. Case, *Palaeohistoria* 12 (1967), 141–78; GENERAL: S. J. de Laet (ed.), *Acculturation and continuity in Atlantic Europe mainly during the Neolithic period and the Bronze Age.* Diss. Arch. Gandenses 16 (1976 a).

11 E.g. Renfrew 1973.

12 See Gilman 1976 for a useful survey of previous work and trends in south-eastern Spain.

13 J. Klein, *The Meseta. A Study in Spanish Economic History 1272–1836*, 1920.

14 Lautensach 1964.

15 Gilman 1976 for recent survey and summary, with references.

16 H. Freitag, *Botanische Jahrbücher* 91 (1971), 147–308, has shown that

the only changes in south-eastern Spanish vegetation since 3000 BC have been due to human interference with the landscape.

17 R. Way, *A Geography of Spain and Portugal*, 1962.
18 Siret 1887, 111–64.
19 Siret 1887, 179–98.
20 Siret 1887, 85–96.
21 Siret 1887, 101–6.
22 Arribas 1976, 156–8; W. Schüle, *Ninth Cong. Arq. Nac. Valladolid*, Zaragoza, 1967, 113–21; F. Kalb, *Tenth Cong. Arq. Nac. Mahóu*, Zaragoza, 1969; Arribas *et al.* 1974.
23 Arribas 1976, 160–1; Molina González and Pareja López 1975.
24 Savory 1968, 194.
25 Renfrew 1973, 121.
26 Dreisch 1973.
27 Arribas 1976.
28 Blance 1964; Schubart 1975a; M. Ruiz-Galvez, *TP* 34 (1977), 85–110.
29 See Almagro Gorbea 1972; less than five silver diadems are known.
30 Siret 1887, 111–64.
31 E.g. El Oficio, Siret 1887, pls 64–66.
32 The short swords of Argar B are widely distributed and include at least one with scabbard mount; representations of the swords exist on rock carvings of the south-west: M. Almagro Gorbea, *TP* 29 (1972), 55–82.
33 Schubart 1975, map 35.
34 This matter has been carefully assessed by Gilman 1976.
35 Aparício Perez 1976.
36 Savory 1968, 203; other settlements: Muntanyeta de la Cabrera and Puntal de Cambra Villar (Valencia). The hilltop settlement at Castellet (Valencia) yielded little metal, and an occupation at Pic de les Moreres (Alicante) was similarly bereft of metal, with flint and stone tools in abundance: J. Aparicio Perez, *Archivo de Prehistoria Levantina* 13 (1972), 23–50; J. L. Ro-man Lajarin, *Archivo de Prehistoria Levantina* 14 (1975), 47–63.

37 Bronze Age occupation in the Cueva del Volcan del Faro, Cullera, yielded evidence of sheep- or goat-herding, with deer and pig as other important animals: I. Davidson, *Trans. Cave Res. Group Gt Britain* 14 (1972), 23–32.
38 Savory 1968, 204–5. Local production of bronze axes, F. M. Jasmet, *Ampurias* 31–2 (1969–70), 105–52; J. Rovira Port, *Pyrenae* 10 (1974), 67–78.
39 The extent of gold work in the peninsula is considerable, and earlier Bronze Age discs (Oviedo), basket earrings (Ermegeira, Lisbon), lunulae (Cabaceiros de Basto, Braga), bracelets (Bonabal, Lisbon), and diadems (Puentes de Garcia Rodriguez, Coruna; Murcielagos, Malaga) are known. The distribution is essentially west coastal: Savory 1968, fig. 68.
40 The Mediterranean and Atlantic elements in local north-west Iberian metalwork have been listed by P. Harbison, *Madrider Mitteilungen* 8 (1967), 100–22, e.g. Valderimbre (León). To suggest that the Early Bronze Age in Galicia consisted of locals in contact with west Europeans, Argaric and Beaker elements seems to us to ask more questions than provide an answer, Savory 1968, 210; yet this area above all others may hold a key to the problems of west European sea-borne contacts, as the rich cist grave at Atios, Pontevedra, may attest: the grave-goods include two tanged daggers with gold foil mounts, and two spiral silver rings. The former have been claimed to be west, i.e. north-west European, the latter to be Argaric, Harrison 1974.
41 Harrison 1974.
42 Schubart 1975; 1976.

43 Schubart 1975, pl. 85, Giraldo; p. 267, Coroa de Frades.

44 Schubart 1975.

45 Atalaia grave systems IV and V have radiocarbon dates of 820 ± 50 and 920 ± 40 bc; Schubart 1975, 170–1. Other sites such as Alcacer do Sal, Evora, have yielded comparable pottery; H. Schubart, TP 28 (1971), 153–82.

46 Schubart 1975, pls 93–94.

47 These are usefully summarized in various papers in Guilaine 1976, sections A and B.

48 G. Jalut in Guilaine 1976, 74–81.

49 T. Poulain in Guilaine 1976, 104–115; P. Ducos in Guilaine 1976, 165–7.

50 Clottes and Costantini 1976: Grotte de la Bergerie, Lot: 40 per cent rodent, 16 per cent pig, 31 per cent domesticates (cattle, sheep, horse, dog), 11 per cent wild (red deer, wolf, fox). Sargel II, Aveyron: 75 per cent domesticates (sheep, then pig, then cattle and horse), 25 per cent wild (incl. rabbit and birds). Marsa I, Lot: cattle, sheep, pig and badger are reported.

51 The deposit may be 1 m thick, but rates of accumulation are unknown; seasonality preferences are likely to have operated in these locations.

52 Clottes and Costantini 1976.

53 Phillips 1975, ch. 5.

54 Guilaine 1976a: the plateau of Ger and the region around Tarbes are areas where polypod vessels are abundant (e.g. Grotte de St Marnet, Haute-Garonne), but they occur across to the Mediterranean coast. It is suggested that the dissemination of such vessels was most easily done through a pastoral-based economy. The evidence as it stands does not seem entirely conclusive.

55 Champ des Granges, Lot: Clottes and Costantini 1976.

56 E.g. Marsa cave with late Neolithic,

57 Clottes and Costantini 1976. The Rhône-type dagger from Corent, Puy-de-Dome, is one of a relatively low number of distinctive products probably brought into the upland regions through some form of distributive mechanism, Daugas 1976, fig. 1, 12.

58 E.g. Grotte à Colombiers and Camp Allaric à Aslonnes: Cordier 1976, 558 refers to other possible locations. Coastal sites of the Loire, including La Roussellerie, Briard 1974.

59 Poulain 1976.

60 Oxen 27 per cent out of domestic total 85 per cent.

61 G. Camps in Guilaine 1976, 192–201.

62 Briard 1973, 133.

63 E.g. Singleyrac and Cissac: Coffyn 1976; and there are many stray flat and flanged axes in the valleys of the Dordogne, Garonne and Loire rivers, e.g. Agen, Loire-et-Garonne: Coffyn, 1976, fig. 1, 7.

64 In coastal Vendée: Cordier 1976.

65 Coffyn 1976: Médoc area; also H. Savory, PPS 14 (1948). The hoards of St Denis-de-Pile in the Dordogne valley and St Vivrien on the coast (Gironde) containing flanged axes and other implements are typical, Coffyn 1976, figs 2, 3, 16–18.

66 Handled cups in earlier Bronze Age contexts include vessels with incised decoration recalling material from the middle Rhine area, e.g. Amboise (Indre-et-Loire), Cordier 1976, fig. 1, 17.

67 Riguet 1976.

68 M.-T. Morzadec-Kerfourn in Guilaine 1976, 88–94.

69 G. Jalut in Guilaine 1976, 74–81.

70 J. Briard, C. Guerin, M.-T. Morzadec-Kerfourn and Y. Plusquellec, Soc. Géol. et Mineral. de Bretagne C.II 2 (1970), 45–60. There is also

Chalcolithic and Early Bronze Age levels.

evidence for grassland conditions at Spézat (to 900 bc), and for elm decline and plantain, bracken increase at Saint Michel de Brasparts (c. 1800 bc): Morzadec-Kerfourn in Guilaine 1976.

71 J. Nicolardot and G. Gaucher, Typologie des objets de l'âge du bronze en France. 5. Outils, 1975; Courtin, Guilaine and Mohen 1976.

72 B. Hallegouet, P.-R. Giot and J. Briard, Annales de Bretagne, 1971, 59–72.

73 Trémargat, Ploubazlanec: Briard 1976a.

74 Giot 1960, 128; Briard 1976a, 569.

75 E.g. Saint-Jude en Bourbriac: J. Briard and P.-R. Giot, Annales de Bretagne 70 (1963), 5–24; Lescongar en Plouhinec: J. Briard, Gallia Préhistoire 11 (1968), 247–59.

76 Giot 1960, fig. 11, 16; Briard 1965, 54–9; 1975a for discussion of continuity.

77 Giot 1960, 116; this stone, 20 m long, and over 350 tonnes in weight, is of course an exceptional piece, never perhaps erected successfully due to engineering problems, but the vast array of other stones in this area of Brittany, as in other regions of north-western Europe, bear witness to the capabilities of third and second millennium stone workers.

78 Giot 1960 for useful and cautious summary, unlike wilder comments elsewhere.

79 P. R. Giot, Compte rendu 15 Session, Congrès préhist. de France 1956, 524–528, discusses some of the human remains evidence, admittedly slender.

80 300 Finistère, 50 Morbihan, 30 Côtes-du-Nord: map Giot 1960, 129.

81 Briard 1976a; J. Cogné and P.-R. Giot, L'Anthropologie 55 (1951), 425–44, basic divisions.

82 Saint-Jude en Bourbriac: Briard 1975a, 21.

83 Briard 1975b; 1975a; 1973.

84 J. Briard, L'Anthropologie 74 (1970), 5–56.

85 Briard 1975b; J. Briard, Archäol. Korrespond. 8 (1978), 13–20.

86 Briard 1973, 145.

87 Giot 1960, 143; Briard 1973, 145; Briard 1976b, 133. These cross-Channel links are further reinforced by the careful work on gold lunulae by J. J. Taylor, PPS 36 (1970), who can point to similarities in technique and style between the major Irish-British series and the North French lunulae, including the St. Cyr (Manche) specimen and the Kerivoa (Côtes-du-Nord) hoard of 3.

88 Giot 1960, 135–6.

89 'Cenotaph' barrows, without recognizable chambers for human burials, may of course have served for surrounding unstructured burials, representing ideologically the provision of a protected resting-place for certain strata of society.

90 Giot 1960, 142.

91 Briard 1965, maps fig. 22, 79–108.

92 Briard 1965, ch. 2.

93 These extend as far south as the Pyrenées, e.g. St-Sever (Landes): Coffyn 1976, fig. 3, 1.

94 Verron 1976a; 1976b.

95 Verron 1975a; 1976a; Gaucher and Mohen 1974; Gaucher 1976.

96 Briard 1973, 147.

97 References in Sandars 1957; Briard 1973, 133.

98 G. Bailloud, Mem. Soc. Préhist. Française 5 (1958), 192. Mohen 1977.

99 G. Gaucher and Y. Robert, Gallia Préhistoire 10 (1967), 169–223.

100 Summaries with references in Burgess 1974, 172–5; Herity and Eogan 1977, ch. 5; see also Ap-Simon 1969, and de Laet 1976; the precise groups and distributions do not concern us here, but Ren-

frew 1973 discusses the social structural evidence. See H. Case in *Beakers in Britain and Europe: four studies* (ed. R. Mercer) 1977, 71–101.

101 The concept of a pastoral highland zone and an arable lowland zone for Britain, with social and political connotations as well, the boundary being a line from the Bristol channel to the Humber river, has some merit in theoretical terms, but recent research has tended to show far greater variety in human actions in both zones, and many tendencies common to both. The original concept: C. Fox, *The Personality of Britain*, 1952; adoption with modifications: J. and C. Hawkes, *Prehistoric Britain*, 1958; recent discussion, Evans 1975, 147.

102 Pennington 1974; Evans 1975, 142; the evidence is far from conclusive.

103 Pennington 1974, 75.

104 Evans 1975, ch. 9.

105 C. Bowen in Fowler 1975, 44–56.

106 Royal Commission Hist. Mons., *Inventory of Historical Monuments in the County of Dorset*, 2, southeast, part 3, 1970, 628.

107 Fowler 1971.

108 Helbaek 1952.

109 Royal Commission Hist. Mons, op. cit. f.n. 106, 511.

110 Evans 1975, 130–4; A. Fleming, *Agric. Hist. Review* 19 (1971), 1–24; Pennington 1974, 78; Smith 1975; Barrett, Hill and Stevenson, in Burgess and Miket 1976, 283–8.

111 E.g. Fowler 1971, 168 with refs; R. W. Feachem, *PPS* 39 (1973), 332–53; much recent work is unpublished. See now H. C. Bowen and P. J. Fowler (eds), *Early Land Allotment in the British Isles*, Brit. Arch. Rep. 48 (1978).

112 Brief description of some important sites in N. Thomas, *A Guide to Prehistoric England*, 1960; E. Mackie, *Scotland: An Archaeological Guide*, 1975; R. Feachem, *A Guide to Prehistoric Scotland*, 1963; J. Dyer, *Southern England: an Archaeological Guide*, 1973. The Royal Commission's volumes on prehistoric field monuments provide much basic data for England, Scotland and Wales.

113 G. T. Denford, *BIA* 12 (1975), 175–96; A. Fox, *South-West England*, 1964.

114 A. Fox, *PPS* 20 (1954), 92.

115 C. Bowen, *Ancient Fields*, 1961; A. Ellison and J. Harriss in D. L. Clarke (ed.) *Models in Archaeology*, 1972, 911–62.

116 R. Mercer, *Cornish Arch.* 9 (1970); Mercer 1975.

117 Fowler 1971, with references.

118 Fleming 1976; A. Fleming and J. Collis, *Proc. Devon Arch. Soc.* 31 (1973), 1–21; e.g. Danby Rigg in N. Yorks; cairns, fields, circles, standing stones and earthworks. Dating of such monuments is notoriously difficult.

119 The dating of these reave systems is uncertain, but is likely to be second millennium bc on the basis of peat formation.

120 Calder 1956; the burnt mounds are described in the late Bronze Age section.

121 Herity and Eogan 1977; ApSimon 1969; J. Coles and J. J. Taylor, *Proc. Soc. Antiq. Scot.* 102 (1970), 87–100.

122 Coney Island on Lough Neagh: P. Addyman, *Ulster J. Arch.* 28 (1965), 78–100.

123 F. Pryor, *Current Arch.* 46 (1975), 332–8; F. Pryor in Burgess and Miket 1976, 29–50.

124 J. Coles and F. A. Hibbert in Fowler 1975, 12–26; *Somerset Levels Papers I* (1975).

125 H. Godwin, *PPS* 26 (1960), 1–36;

J. Roy. Soc. Antiq. Ireland 85 (1955), 77.

126 J. Hillam, *Irish Archaeol. Res. Forum* 3 (1976), 17–20.

127 M. J. O'Kelly, *J. Roy. Soc. Antiq. Ireland* 84 (1954), 105–55.

128 E.g. L. H. van Wijngaarden-Bakker, *Proc. Roy. Irish Acad.* 74 C (1974), 313–83 for late Neolithic; F. Pryor, in Burgess and Miket 1976; Evans 1975, 129; the evidence from most of the British Isles is incomplete and unstudied.

129 See Ashbee 1960 for discussion on British barrows and cairns; Herity and Eogan 1977, chs 6 and 7, and ApSimon 1969 for Irish evidence; Savory 1965 for Wales; Burgess 1975, 176–84 with references for British-Irish general outline.

130 E.g. late Beaker ware: D. L. Clarke, *Beaker Pottery of Great Britain and Ireland*, 1970; J. N. Lanting and J. D. van der Waals, *Helinium* 12 (1972), 20–46; Burgess 1974, 172. Food Vessel Bowls and Vases: Simpson 1968; ApSimon 1969; Waddell 1975; Herity and Eogan 1977, ch. 6; Burgess 1974, 182. Urns including Collared and Cordoned: Waddell 1975; Herity and Eogan 1977, ch. 7; ApSimon 1969; Burgess 1974, 178; I. H. Longworth, *PPS* 27 (1961), 263–306.

131 See R. J. C. Atkinson, in Lynch and Burgess 1972, for overall distribution and number of barrows, and comment on north and south British features of earlier Bronze Age burials. Some e.g. of burials: Bleasdale (Lancs), central pit with cremations and urns under a barrow, surrounded by an oak post circle with entrance, and a ditch lined with birch poles, the whole surrounded by a palisade: W. Varley, *Antiq. J.* 18 (1938), 154–171. Callis Wold (Humber), group of sixteen barrows, including stake circles, and inhumation and cre-

mation burials: J. R. Mortimer, *Forty Years' Researches in British and Saxon Burial Mounds of East Yorkshire*, 1905, 153–6. Knockast (Co. Westmeath) cemetery mound over inhumation and many cremations: Herity and Eogan 1977, fig. 49.

132 Ashbee 1960, 33–5 discusses cemeteries.

133 S. Piggott, *Proc. Soc. Ant. Scot.* 82 (1948), 68–123. Cf. Broomend of Crichie (Aberdeen), a double entry henge and stone circle with cremations in urns and central cist inhumation, possibly linked by a stone avenue to other circles of stones. Many henges are more firmly third millennium.

134 F. Lynch, *Denbigh Historical Trans.* 24 (1975), and 23 (1974) for interim reports; also *Current Arch.* 55 (1976), 230–40.

135 L. N. W. Flanagan, *Irish Arch. Res. Forum* 3 (1976), 7–20, with brief discussion of Irish Bronze Age cemeteries, which on the basis of the maps suggests very dense population concentrations in the north-east of the island.

136 P. Ashbee, *PPS* 23 (1957), 137–166; dugout oak coffins and boat-like coffins are often recorded.

137 Survey in Ashbee 1960, ch. 8; for lists of certain classes of associations see P. Harbison, *Proc. Roy. Irish Acad.* 67 C (1968), 35–91, e.g. Corkey (Co. Antrim) burial in cist with Food Vessel and dagger; Tara (Co. Meath) inhumation with dagger, beads of bronze, amber and jet, and awl.

138 Scotland: A. Henshall in Coles and Simpson 1968, 173–96; A. Henshall, *Proc. Soc. Ant. Scot.* 96 (1963), 145–54; Ireland: Herity and Eogan 1977 do not single out any particular group, but list individual well-furnished graves; England: Ashbee 1960, chs 3–8;

Burgess 1974, 186 and n. 129 states the case clearly.

139 Piggott 1938; Annable and Simpson 1964; Burgess 1974, 187. It is difficult to reconcile the Breton need for Wessex elements, and the Wessex need for Breton elements, to spur each other on, but technical similarities in objects do exist.

140 Henge monuments in particular; the occasional richly-furnished Beaker grave in this area, as elsewhere, provides the beginning of differentiation in burial goods and strengthens local origins.

141 Piggott 1938; Annable and Simpson 1964; S. Gerloff, *The Early Bronze Age Daggers in Great Britain*, 1975; A. Fleming, *PPS* 37 (1971), 138–66; J. M. Coles and J. J. Taylor, *Antiquity* 45 (1971); Burgess 1974, 184–90.

142 Ashbee 1960, 76–7.

143 J. Craw, *Proc. Soc. Ant. Scot.* 63 (1929), 154–89; J. J. Taylor, *P.P.S* 36 (1970), 38–81; e.g. jet spacer necklace: Melfort (Argyll); gold lunula: Athlone (Co. Roscommon).

144 Such small vessels are often found, and they include the series one grape cup, and series two cups decorated with geometric incisions: Annable and Simpson 1964, 24–7.

145 A. M. ApSimon, *Inst. Arch. Lond. Ann. Rep.* 10 (1954), 37–61; Annable and Simpson 1964, 25–7.

146 Other areas also contain richly-furnished graves, e.g. Snowshill (Gloucester), bowl barrow with adult inhumation in a cist, with dagger, spearhead, pin and stone axe. The Folkton (Humber) child's grave contained three chalk drums with decoration, unique to the Early Bronze Age.

147 We do not, however, favour the traditional idea of Wessex middlemen, disseminating gold, tin and copper to all parts of western and northern Europe, nor their receipt of Mediterranean objects or ideas.

148 F. Roe, *PPS* 32 (1966), 199–245.

149 S. Briggs, J. Brennan and G. Freeburn, *Bull. Hist. Metal. Group* 7 (1973), 18–26.

150 Herity and Eogan 1977, fig. 2b; P. Harbison, *N. Munster Antiq. J.* 10 (1966), fig. 1; C. S. Briggs, *Irish Arch. Res. Forum* 3 (1976), 9–15.

151 H. J. Case, *Palaeohistoria* 12 (1967), 141–77; Burgess 1974, 191; J. M. Coles, *Proc. Soc. Ant. Scot.* 101 (1968–9), 69; S. Piggott, in I. L. Foster and L. Alcock (eds), *Culture and Environment*, 1963, 53–91.

152 J. Deady and E. Doran, *J. Cork Hist. Archaeol. Soc.* 77 (1972), 25–27; J. S. Jackson, *Archaeol. Austriaca* 43 (1968), 92–114; a date of 1500 ± 120 bc (VRI − 66) was obtained.

153 H. H. Coghlan and J. Raftery, *Sibrium* 6 (1961), 223–44; D. Britton, *PPS* 29 (1963), 258–325; M. O'Kelly, *J. Cork Hist. Archaeol. Soc.* 75 (1970), 25–8: Lyre (Co. Cork).

154 Burgess 1974, 190–4, 200–2 provides many references. See D. Britton, *PPS* 29 (1963), 258–325: Migdale (Sutherland) hoard; P. Harbison, *Proc. Roy. Irish Acad.* 67 C (1968), 35–91; J. M. Coles, *Proc. Soc. Ant. Scot.* 97 (1964), 82–156, 101 (1969), 1–110; C. Burgess and J. D. Cowen, in Lynch and Burgess 1972, 167–82: Ebnal (Salop) hoard; Rowlands 1976 for assessment of potential explanations.

155 J. J. Taylor, *Antiquity* 45 (1971).

156 J. J. Taylor, *PPS* 36 (1970), 38–81; Taylor 1979.

157 See Butler 1963 for references and opinions.

158 Stone alignments may have sometimes extended over long dis-

tances, linking settlements, ritual sites and burial monuments, e.g. Devil's Arrows (North Yorks.) probably part of a 10–15 km line of sites.

159 P. Ashbee, *Antiquity* 37 (1963), 116–20; A. Ross, in Coles and Simpson 1968, 257; the Wilsford date is 1380 ± 90 bc.

160 Simpson and Thawley 1972, with references to original studies and comments on possible origins in Britain; e.g. the capstone on a cist at Nether Largie (Argyll) is carved with representations of cups and axes. See Herity and Eogan for brief treatment with references. The art on a rock at Clearagh (Co. Cork), consisting of a mass of pecked cups, axes, circles and lines, lies on a hillslope affording extensive views, and this is a typical position for many art sites in Ireland: E. Shee, *J. Cork Hist. Archaeol. Soc.* 73 (1968), 144–51.

161 A. Burl, *The Stone Circles of the British Isles*, Yale, 1977, provides a modern survey of the evidence.

162 W. E. Griffiths, *PPS* 26 (1960), 303–39.

163 G. Eogan, *PPS* 30 (1964), 25–38. The positioning of entire sites such as this is likely to be as important as any precise numbers of stones or internal arrangements. Viewpoints, e.g. Bettany (Co. Donegal) on a hill-top with sixty stones: *Ulster J. Archaeol.* 2 (1939), 293.

164 Atkinson 1956; the problems about the astronomical orientation of the monument will not be considered here: see G. S. Hawkins, *Stonehenge Decoded*, 1965; and R. J. C. Atkinson, *Antiquity* 40 (1966), 212–16 for opposed views; A. Thom, *Megalithic Lunar Observatories*, 1971, *Megalithic Sites in Britain*, 1967. Many others have joined the discussion and views are conflicting.

165 Arribas 1976, 161.

166 *TP* 27 (1970), 22: lab. numbers not given.

6 Northern Europe

The north European area with which we are concerned here stretches from the Rhine delta eastwards across the north European plain, through the floodplains of the great rivers Elbe, Oder and Vistula which flow northwards from the central European uplands into the North Sea and the Baltic. All of this area, over 1,000 km from west to east, lies within about 100 km of the sea, either the North Sea or the Baltic Sea.[1] To the north of the plain is the peninsula of Jutland and the Danish Islands (map 6). Most of these areas of northern Europe lie less than 100 m above sea level, except in the Koszalin-Gdańsk region. Northwards, across the Skagerrak, the Kattegat and the Baltic, are the highlands of northern Europe (Norway, Sweden and Finland to the north-east). Not all of these lands are elevated, and it is significant that the extreme southern part of Sweden (Scania and the coastal zones) are low-lying and have yielded abundant evidence for intensive Bronze Age occupation, whereas the highland areas apparently were excluded from full participation in at least the metallurgical aspects of the Bronze Age. More important than this, however, is the essential fact that all regions of the north were close to maritime waters, which could furnish not only some food supplies but also access from island to island, contact between the Swedish landmass and the north European plain, and communication between communities living along the coasts.

The Early Bronze Age in the north was not initiated by new arrivals; there is nothing in the archaeological record that suggests a dramatic alteration in population, in subsistence technologies, in distributions. What sets the Neolithic apart from the Bronze Age has generally been accepted as metal, at first in small and insignificant quantities, then suddenly in large amounts, and with this last comes some evidence for alteration in social ordering in the population.

Chronology

Studies of the Bronze Age in the north are often associated with the work of Oscar Montelius,[2] but there have been other attempts to provide some chronological ordering of the material, and some of these are noted below. The major difficulty with the basic Montelian periodization of the Bronze Age in the north was and is that it assumes a uniformity both of material culture and of chronological evolution over a large area within which such events are unlikely; at any rate it would seem necessary to demonstrate such uniformities instead of assuming them, and most current work is deliberately aimed at aspects of the Bronze Age outside

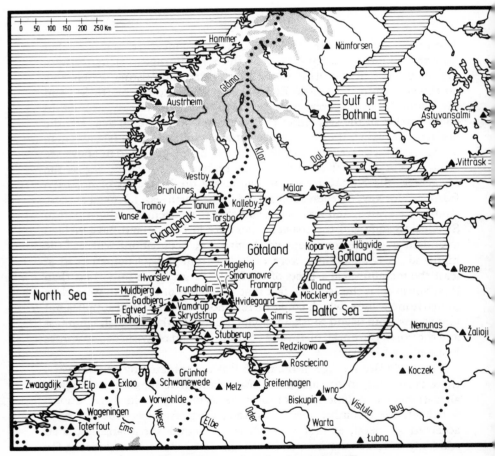

Map 6   Earlier Bronze Age sites in northern Europe

the periodization approach of typology; these developments are proving fruitful, and are noted below. Nonetheless, much of the literature of the Bronze Age continues to record aspects of the Montelian periodization, and a brief description is considered to be necessary here.

In 1885, Montelius produced his sixfold scheme for the Bronze Age. The first period represented almost the initial appearance of metal of any sort in northern Europe; the metal was copper, imported into the north, and its impact is not likely to have been great upon a society in which stone and flint of very high quality was abundant. From Period I to Period II represented a dramatic change, from sparse copper supplies to abundant copper, tin and gold, all of which were not local in their origin.[3] Period II is for us the Early Bronze Age of the north, a significant phase in the evolution of society. Metalwork is abundant, burials by inhumation within barrows and cairns abound, and the preservation of human material in some of these provide the best evidence for Bronze Age clothing that we possess from all of Europe. Period III (when cremation gradually replaced inhumation as the dominant burial rite) falls within our Late Bronze Age, along with Periods IV and V. Period VI is transitional to the Iron Age. Correlations with central European materials, in graves and hoards, suggest that Periods III–V were coeval with Urnfields of the Late Bronze Age. This artificial division between our earlier and later Bronze Age is not that normally employed in the north, where Period III is generally taken into the earlier phase, but we have divided the material in order to correlate it better with the rest of the European picture, where Urnfields mark a convenient start to the later Bronze Age.

Subsequent work on the divisions of the Bronze Age included more detailed groupings[4] and the introduction of geographical zones.[5] The work of Kersten and others suggested that three distinct areas in northern Europe could be distinguished. Zone 1 consisted of northern Jutland, the Danish islands and southern Sweden. Zone 2 lay to the south, southern Jutland, Schleswig-Holstein and Lower Saxony. Beyond this was zone 3, of former Brandenburg, Mecklenburg and Pomerania. The abundant and rich finds from zone 1 were contrasted with the sparser evidence from zones 2 and 3, but this distinction seems today to be less well-founded.

The concept of zonal variation in the north European Bronze Age was important, and Kersten, Sprockhoff[6] and others distinguished several cultural groups, known mostly by graves, existing in zones 2 and 3 in particular. They continued to work, however, within the Montelian chronological scheme, modified subsequently only in minor degree by Broholm.[7]

The logical step was taken by Hachmann, whose work in 1957[8] attempted to provide a much more tightly-controlled chronological basis within the zonal context. Hachmann treated his material, from zones 1 and 2 only, as representing 'horizons' of imports (both finished products and ideas), each of which set off a phase of local duplication and evolution in metalworking. Each horizon contained datable material from central Europe (in the Reinecke scheme) as well as other objects from western Europe, and Hachmann believed that in this way the beginnings of the true Bronze Age in the north could be further refined and organized. His scheme did not touch the copper materials preceding, nor the full Early Bronze Age (Montelius I I) succeeding. The Hachmann scheme has been criticized, principally by Lomborg whose main argument is that the materials in central Europe are not defined well enough to allow such a detailed chronology to be acceptable.[9] This would seem to us an agreeable conclusion, and the result would be a general ordering of the Nordic earlier Bronze Age into an initial phase of the limited introduction of metal into a full neolithic economy, its gradual adoption at a time contemporary with the central European Early Bronze Age, before the distinctive Nordic Bronze Age enters its major phase (Period I I). The marginal alterations to this generalized chronological scheme put forward by all these authors are likely to be of limited significance in any overall survey of the Bronze Age such as is attempted here, although at local level they are undoubtedly important.[10]

The absolute chronology of these events in the north depend upon dates for central European features reliably seen in the north, and radiocarbon dates for north European material. Radiocarbon dates themselves prove to be disappointing, because in many cases the dated material cannot be related to the period scheme for the north, and in any case the reliability of charcoal dates from the later cremations is notoriously suspect. Those dates available indicate that the developed Early Bronze Age in the north (Period I I) was flourishing 1500–1200 bc, and that the final Late Bronze Age (Period V) existed 900–600 bc; the number of dates for Periods I I I – I V is very sparse, but Period I I I may well date to 1200–1100 bc. These dates, and the Montelian scheme, relate only to Scandinavia, and the use of Northern Periods for other areas is unsatisfactory. A more satisfactory periodization of the Bronze Age has been devised for the Netherlands, based upon absolute dating of many sites and relative chronologies of other material.[11] The Early Bronze Age consists of the Hilversum culture, some surviving Late Neolithic groups and various local industries, followed by the Elp group in north and east, and Drakenstein group in south and west. The time range is 1500–900 bc, and a glance at the abundant radiocarbon date list will show the firm base upon which such a local scheme can be set (p. 322). Such internal ordering of material might well be appropriate for other regions of northern Europe.

Settlement and economy

The economic resources of northern Europe were considerable, and as varied as those of any other area. The evidence from settlements of the third and second millennia suggests that relatively stable forms of food production and acquisition existed, involving arable and hoe cultivation, the pasturing of cattle and sheep, and the exploitation of wild plants and animals; for the last, maritime activities played a large part. The areas also yielded abundant timber and adequate supplies of stone, including flint, for the production of implements throughout the Bronze Age. In the northern upland areas, stone tools remained dominant in areas where metal rarely penetrated. Fur trapping was no doubt an important element in the north, and the rock art of the period indicates a significant difference between the low-lying arable and pastoral zone of the south, and the upland zone of the north where hunting and gathering was a dominant economic pursuit.

In all of this, local supplies of metal, copper, tin or gold, were absent; although copper sources do exist in Scandinavia, they lie well to the north, outside the general Bronze Age distribution of metal, and there is no evidence that any local sources of any metal were accessible, known and worked during the Bronze Age. It seems evident, then, that every piece of metal in the north European Bronze Age was imported from other regions; the vast quantities of metal found in the north represent perhaps the finest and earliest example of the organization of a society capable of acquiring and working a material not locally accessible. This was no small matter, and it opens for us the concepts of exchange or distribution networks, the suggestions of deliberate trade, with all that this implies in terms of economic and social organization.

What could be offered in exchange for the metal, some 300 km away from the Baltic coasts, in the Harz and the Bohemian Ore mountains, was doubtless a variety of materials, and of these amber and furs are the most commonly mentioned. Other perishables would include cereals, cattle and sea animals; smoked fish would have made a useful contribution to inland diets. Human slaves have also been suggested as a suitable exchange for the precious metal, and lurid accounts of raiding expeditions into the hunting and gathering groups of the far north have occasionally been advanced. Yet of all of these possible items, only amber can have survived in identifiable form in the recipient areas of central Europe.

Amber, the fossilized resin of pine trees, occurs on the western coast of Jutland, and on the south-eastern shores of the Baltic from the mouth of the Vistula eastwards, as well as in isolated parts of southern Sweden, and in north-eastern Netherlands.[12] Amber is light in weight and therefore large quantities could have been transported in single loads over long distances. Although amber occurs in other parts of Europe as well, including the Mediterranean and the Black Sea, the characteristic spectrum of Baltic and Jutland amber has allowed many of the finds of amber in Bronze Age contexts throughout Europe to be clearly identified as originating in the north. This then demonstrates that a particular material from the north was distributed southwards into central Europe and into the Aegean world of the second millennium BC. There is much amber in Early Bronze Age graves in central Europe, but to agree that northern amber alone brought back central European metal infers a vastly disproportionate exchange, a lightweight material of relatively very small bulk, collected easily from accessible sources and requiring little or no technology, in exchange for tonnes of material of great bulk, mined, separated and smelted at source, cast and beaten into shapes, with other metals (gold and tin) from other sources added to the consignments.

Of course we do not know the relative values of these materials, but amber was certainly abundant in northern Europe prior to the full Bronze Age, and relatively rare thereafter; this suggests the deliberate redirection of gathered supplies. On the other hand, we may be in error in assuming the need for an exchange system of purely economic character; the rarity of metals and amber, in ordinary circumstances, in settlements, and the nature of the deposition of metals in particular, noted below, may indicate a rather more complex and less mundane situation which might well not necessitate any form of material exchange at all.

The north European Bronze Age may be said to begin when metal, whether copper or bronze, appears in sufficient quantities so that a large number of tools, and many ornaments, can be made from non-local supplies. The appearance of local metallurgical workshops also seems to be a significant departure. These features may be seen early in the second millennium BC. For some time before, metal, in the form of cast copper axes and beaten copper ornaments, had been known in the north, in north Jutland, the Ems-Weser region, and the middle Elbe basin,[13] but this does not seem to have played much part in the subsequent establishment of metal industries of the Bronze Age early in the second millennium. It was within the societies of the Single-Grave and Late Neolithic cultures of northern Europe that Bronze Age metallurgy was established. The third and second millennium settlements were essentially agriculture-based, with cattle particularly important, but also with hoe and ard cultivation. Ard-marks sealed beneath the burial mounds suggest a sedentary cultivation process but we know little of field size, and forest clearance, while intensive in places, is likely overall to have been of restricted character. Barley as well as wheat were cultivated, but more open land was devoted to pasture, for sheep, goats and cattle. Wooden carts, drawn by oxen, were available, and the horse is also documented from this time. The working of stone, and more particularly flint, was an important element in industry, and amber was common.

In the Low Countries, the Beaker communities of the late third and early second millennia were the first to obtain metals from central Europe,[14] possibly from the Atlantic coasts as well. In Jutland, and in some other northern areas, the same general time-range for the first introduced metal also seems appropriate, for here within a Late Neolithic context we can see a gradual transition from a stone- and flint-dependent society to one wherein copper, then bronze, appears increasingly important. Although settlements are rare, graves were furnished with flint copies of metal daggers, and metal axes, daggers and ornaments also appear in hoards; most of these are copper but some few are of tin-bronze, and are believed to represent not central but west European imports. Further east, along the Baltic shores, the earliest metal objects are of central European character, and contemporary with the Mierza-nowice group of southern Poland (p. 71).

The impact of this exotic material is likely to have been slight upon a firmly-based locally self-sufficient society, and its importance should not be over-emphasized; there is little evidence that metallurgy at this stage created opportunities for those societies able to obtain the new materials, and this can be seen in the settlements, where data are rapidly accumulating through systematic search and excavation.

Settlements of the earlier Bronze Age in the north European area are unevenly recorded, but this is as much a reflection of preservation as any prehistoric activity or archaeological study. The conditions for the preservation of settlement traces over moorland, over heavy boulder clays, over sands and rocks, are generally poor, yet the major difficulty is probably that stratified settlements seem to have rarely developed; yet increasing numbers of Bronze Age settlements have been discovered, often by accident, and we are therefore able to point to some particular evidence in certain areas.[15]

Recent studies of land-use patterns through time have begun to indicate the extent of the impact of Bronze Age communities on the land. In the Mälar region of Västmanland, late second and first millennia expansions of activity have been recorded.[16] Further south, in Scania, some indication of earlier Bronze Age crops has been provided by a study of grain impressions on pottery,[17] and general assessments of the surviving cultural record in Scania have indicated that most of the best-quality land was worked in the earlier Bronze Age, with clearance of less-fertile soils only in the later Bronze Age.[18] Pollen analyses in Östergötland also indicate continuous open land for both wheat crops and grazing around Lake Striern during the Bronze Age.[19] Further intensive field work and excavation in south-eastern Scania has allowed close identification of the positioning of settlements and cemeteries, generally placed upon light and fertile soils near water, perhaps obvious enough but not often demonstrated.[20] Pollen analyses of many sites in the Netherlands have suggested a continuing series of woodland clearances through the second millennium, often small in extent;[21] the rise in sea levels and the growth of peat during this time are also factors affecting early Bronze Age occupations and a majority of sites lie upon sand ridges and other slightly raised positions.[22]

In the Low Countries, settlements of the developed Bronze Age appear to have consisted of rather small hamlets of a few houses associated with barns and other sheds. North of the Rhine, a farmstead at Elp (Drenthe) was sited on a sandy ridge and was rebuilt several times over a period of four or five centuries (fig. 97).[23] Each time it consisted of one long house, of three-aisled type, 25–36 m in length, which provided a dwelling at one end (west) and stalls for 20–30 cattle at the other, and several other

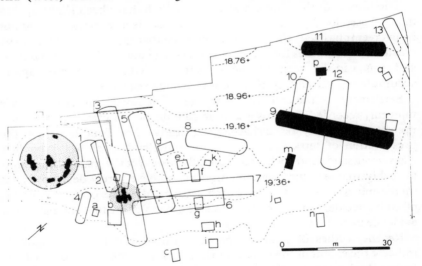

Fig. 97   Plan of the settlements at Elp, Drenthe. Black: stage 1; barrow and graves at left.
(From H. T. Waterbolk, *Helinium* 4 (1964))

smaller buildings including sheds with heavy posts to support timbers for raised storage of grain. Pits had been dug within the side-aisles of some of the long houses, and near the ends of others. The population of such a farmstead, which dates to *c.* 1300–800 bc, may have been an extended family of twelve to twenty persons. Beside the farmstead was a barrow containing about ten individuals, and six flat graves lay within the settled area; these all probably relate to the earlier occupation. The domestic debris consisted of coarse domestic pottery as well as some finer wares, flints, grinding stones, querns, stone hammers, charred wood fragments and traces of wheat and barley, and a spindle whorl. There were a few metal objects in the graves, but none in the settlement debris.[24] Other settlements in this region include Zwaagdijk (North Holland);[25] although the surviving remains were sparse, the small site had arable fields under the ard, and pasture drained by narrow ditches. Domestic debris included plain barrel-like pots, a few flints and hammer-stones, and bones of cattle, sheep or goat, and pig, as well as a few remains of dog, wild boar, roe-deer and fox. The site dates to *c.* 1650 bc, and it suggests that some need was felt to occupy marginal lands at this time; it is not likely that the settlement was a temporary seasonal camp.

Continuing programmes of pollen analytical work in this area have yielded important data about land-use; for example, analyses from barrows at Weelde (Kempen) have indicated that little or no agricultural or pastoral activity was taking place on the upland sands of the southern Netherlands and adjacent Belgium, in contrast to the western Netherlands. Instead, intensive agriculture was only practised in the lower and damper valleys, and settlements and cemeteries themselves were placed away from the valleys on the upland light soils. In the later Bronze Age, the sandy uplands were brought into agricultural use, elm and lime woodlands were cleared, and the valleys were less intensively used.[26]

Other settlements in the southern part of the Low Countries are associated with a late second millennium group, the Hilversum culture. The tradition of houses here is that often associated with the south British Bronze Age, the post-built round house with wattle-and-daub walls. The farmsteads, such as that from Nijnsel (North Brabant), Dodewaard (Gelderland) and Zijderveld (South Holland), contain one or two long houses, circular buildings and smaller rectangular barns or huts (fig. 98).[27] The long houses are of four- or three-aisled type, and average 20 m in length, 5–6 m in width; subsequent Iron Age houses were generally 15 m long. Each long house was divided into two sections, one for livestock, the other for human occupation. The round buildings, so like the contemporary south British houses, are not associated with much domestic debris, in contrast to the British sites; these buildings are 6–8 m

Fig. 98　Plan of the settlement at Nijnsel, Belgium. The scale is approximate. (From de Laet 1974)

in diameter. It is likely that all these structures had wattle walls, perhaps of double thickness in places. The Nijnsel settlement was positioned on a sand ridge and covered an area of 2,000 sq m; storage pits and small barns lay around the central house. At Elp and Angelsloo (Drenthe), the buildings of the settlement were close to the (presumed) local cemetery, but at Laren (North Holland) and Bergeijk (North Brabant) the contemporary cemetery was 500–600 m distant.[28]

Settlements elsewhere in northern Europe have not been so closely characterized. Throughout lowland Denmark and lowland and coastal Sweden, Bronze Age occupation and activity was intensive, but there are few well-documented settlements of the earlier Bronze Age. However, if these were as impermanent as some of the immediately preceding settlements, it is likely that few would be recognized. The houses at Myrhoj (North Jutland), associated with Late Neolithic flint tools and

Beaker pottery, were in part slightly dug into the ground surface; the largest house was c. 20 × 7 m, with a central row of posts. No entrances could be determined in the excavation. The domestic debris consisted of querns, many flints, a few bones and shells, and potsherds. Arable farming is suggested by the querns, corn impressions, and sickles; stock-rearing is attested by the animal bones and teeth. The houses probably consisted of no more than light wooden frameworks with mats or rush or branches providing protection. Normal recent agricultural activities would soon erase most of the structural features.[29] Such houses contrast with the substantial long-houses of the developed Early Bronze Age, such as at Elp. The substantial long house at Trappendal in Denmark, 24 × 8 m with two rows of internal roof-supports and two hearths, may have been a domestic establishment, but was used to hold a burial and then was covered by a barrow; no domestic debris was recovered, and it may be that the whole construction was designed as a mortuary house.[30]

Semi-subterranean houses at sites such as Norrvidinge and Löddesborg (Scania) were smaller, yet strongly built.[31] The Norrvidinge houses, 10 × 5 m in size and built of horizontal logs or wattle-and-daub, were situated on light sandy soil near a large river, the Saxån. Both settlements yielded prolific flint and pottery industries, and cattle and sheep were kept, with fishing also important. Marshland settlements in Belgium, such as Dentergem (Flanders),[32] were doubtless also situated to exploit watery conditions, but in general the sand ridges of morainic country in the north seem to have been the preferred location.

In the area of Baltic coastland stretching from the Gulf of Danzig (Zatoka Gdańska) eastwards into Lithuania and southern Latvia, earlier Bronze Age settlements of the Baltic group defined by Gimbutas[33] reflect their origin in Corded Ware communities whose substantial wooden houses have been recognized at Rzucewo and Suchacz.[34] The Bronze Age village of Biskupin near Znin[35] consisted of a ditched enclosure 90 × 30–60 m in extent, probably with an internal rampart and double entrances; small wattle-and-daub houses yielded domestic debris including much stone and bone, loom-weights, but hardly any metal. The main enclosed area is interpreted as a cattle corral; other animals represented were sheep, pigs and horses, and fish-bones and fresh-water shells were also recovered. The development of earlier Bronze Age communities in this eastern Baltic region is particularly marked by abundant settlements near the rivers and major streams flowing into the Baltic, positioned upon terrace sands and gravels, or on dunes near the coast.[36]

The evidence for food subsistence activities in the north European area is very inadequate for the earlier Bronze Age, and only a few generalizations may be made. The principal one must be that the food

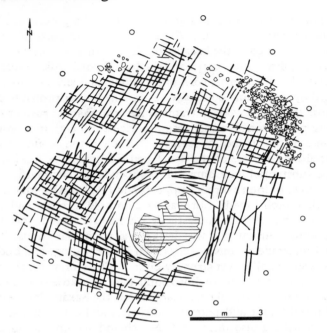

Fig. 99   Plough-marks beneath a barrow at Vesterlund,
Jutland. Charcoal areas at centre and 14 post-holes around
the grave.
(From H. Thrane, *Kuml* (1967))

supplies were varied. From graves, rubbish pits and other sites there is
certain evidence for the cultivation of barley, wheat and millet, and flint
and bronze sickles were no doubt used in the harvest.[37] Ard marks
beneath burial mounds (fig. 99) point to arable cultivation, and the
ashwood crook ard from Hvorslev (Jutland), dated to *c.* 1500 bc,[38] may
be compared with the ard-teams depicted in the rock art of Sweden,
where paired oxen are shown with a ploughman. Shifting cultivation
around an established settlement was one of the procedures adopted
during the Bronze Age in the Mälaren plain (Västmanland, Sweden),
but here as elsewhere the herding of cattle and sheep was increasingly
important.[39] Other animals available within the community were the
dog, pig and horse. The domestic horse is first seen in the Netherlands in
the later second millennium. Cattle were particularly important;
settlements such as Elp (Drenthe) may have had a herd of 20–30 cattle
stabled in one part of the long house, and these animals may have been
used not only for local consumption but also for barter as meat on the

hoof, or as cow hides, in any organized attempts to obtain adequate supplies of raw materials not available locally.

During the Bronze Age, the erection of many thousands of round barrows, generally made of turf, often heather-turf, must have depleted large patches of land in many areas. Study of the turves, and sediments from the burial coffins themselves, have yielded remains of plants generally found on open ground. Old land surfaces preserved beneath the mounds also indicate an open landscape covered with rough grasses, heather, sedges and moss, with sorrel and goose-foot also present; these have been interpreted as showing a Bronze Age hard-grazed land previously cultivated but now allowed to grass over. However, the substantial oak-coffins so commonly used in the Bronze Age of the north also indicate that extensive stands of mature timber were still readily available. Only near or at the end of the Bronze Age did climatic deterioration seriously affect the open land. The forests of the north remained mainly unaltered by both human and climatic change, and sheltered numerous wild animals.

The weapons of the Early Bronze Age in the north included the bow as well as the short javelin, and these may well have been principally employed for hunting. The only surviving Bronze Age bow from Sweden was of yew, but the rock art shows both simple and composite bows in use. There is evidence for hunting of red and roe deer, wild pig, and for birds such as swan and geese.[40] The depiction of many of these animals, and the weapons, in rock art is an important element. Fishing activities are represented by remains of pike, cod, halibut and seal, and of the boating activities of Bronze Age groups there can be no doubt in view of the thousands of depictions of boats on both west and east coasts of Sweden, and elsewhere. Such art, remains of a double fish trap made of willow, as well as pine-bark floats and bone fish-hooks, all dated to the Early Bronze Age on the island of Öland, demonstrate the varied range of attack on the Baltic fish.[41] At Otterböte, on the islands of Åland, bones of grey seal dominated a Bronze Age midden, but eider duck, cattle and pig were also present;[42] no fish bones were found. The site was probably seasonally occupied, with processing of oil from seal fat a major concern, and the likely time of year for this was April–May, when seals could have been clubbed; the Otterböte site yielded few weapons, but many sherds from large coarse pottery vessels probably represent parts of seal oil containers.

Land transport during the Bronze Age in the north was by cart and wagon, by sledge and ski. Metal models of wheeled vehicles exist, rock art shows many two-wheeled carts drawn by paired oxen or horses, and the art also depicts many sledges as well as ships. Finds of wooden skis have been made in northen Sweden and Finland. Winter travel across frozen lakes and rivers would have been in some ways preferable to travel at other seasons. Dugout canoes for inland streams and lakes have been dated to the Bronze Age.[43] Travel across land was sometimes eased by the construction of wooden footpaths and trackways across marshy ground, and there are several finds of wooden wheels which indicate that carts or wagons were employed; the Glum (Oldenburg) wheels were split and adzed from alder, with birch axles.[44]

All of these aspects of settlement and economy suggest that the Early Bronze Age populations in the north were basically self-sufficient, and possessed all of the necessary skills to handle the variety of raw materials available to them. Less easy to interpret are the funerary practices, which demonstrate very considerable variation in both structure and content.

Burial monuments

The most common monument of the Bronze Age in the north European area is the round burial mound.[45] In the relatively small area of Denmark, estimates of the original number of barrows range from 25,000 to 50,000, and the total from the entire north European area must be truly enormous. Almost all of these barrows contained at least one, and often several, bodies, and many barrows were rebuilt for subsequent burials. Above all else, the Early Bronze Age barrows of the north indicate the capacity of the land to support a large population, and the traditions of funerary procedure that developed in the second millennium. They have also yielded the most complete record of Bronze Age equipment, including clothing, from anywhere in Europe.

The variety of burial rites that are represented in these barrows is substantial, and we are not in a position to try to quantify the data; a very large majority of the mounds have been damaged, and many entirely destroyed. The structures within the barrow, the bodies themselves, and the accompanying grave goods, have not often survived undamaged; nevertheless, it is possible, through the excavations of the past 100 years, to reconstruct certain graves, and, as important, to provide a generalized picture of the monuments within different regions of northern Europe.

From the Late Neolithic and throughout the entire Early Bronze Age a single-grave burial tradition was retained, although the more dominant Late Neolithic burial customs in central and southern Scandinavia were collective burials in stone cists; these megalithic-type tombs disappear at the transition to the Bronze Age. The body was generally inhumed, but already in the Early Bronze Age some cremation was carried out and this rite grew in popularity throughout the second millennium. In certain areas a transitional stage took the form of a full-size grave or coffin containing a cremation; this is sometimes called a 'cremated skeleton grave'. But it is also clear that both inhumation and cremation were practised in the Early Bronze Age. The most important aspect is the variety of rites that were practised, each variation representing the individual preference of the particular community.

Of the many thousands of barrows in northern Europe, a large majority occur in groups or cemeteries. These cemeteries may consist of only three or four barrows set out along a ridge, or they may contain many barrows, ten or twenty, arranged in a close group, linear or nuclear, with other groups nearby (fig. 100). Some small areas may contain several hundreds of such inter-connected barrows. In low flat country, such as the Low Countries, the Lüneburg heath and Mecklenburg, the cemeteries were often placed upon ridges of sand or other material, so that the mounds are at their most prominent. On higher ground, in Denmark and Sweden in particular, the mounds were often positioned on hilltops or on plateaux, where again they appear as large as possible when viewed from below. Natural prominences were sometimes used as bases for mounds which would then look the larger. In the north, the cemeteries have been claimed

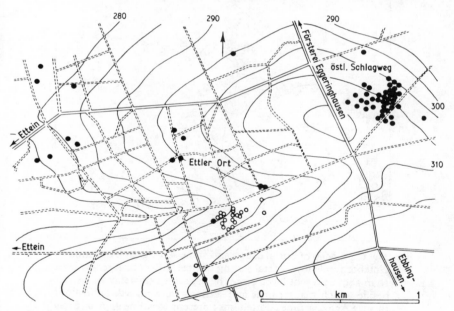

Fig. 100 Cemetery of 39 Early Bronze Age barrows at Etteln, North Rhine-Westphalia
(From Lange and Nowothnig 1971)

to mark the lines of natural routes across country, either lying directly upon the upland route, or as markers for nearby lower routes. Some of the mounds are on the offshore islands of Sweden and Denmark, where they might have served the same purpose for sea passages. Surveys of cairns in Sweden have suggested that they were positioned along the waterways, on coasts looking out to sea, along inlets of the sea, and beside narrow straits dividing islands (fig. 101).[46] The sea level of the second millennium was from 0 to 20 m higher than that of today (depending on latitude), and in some cases this would have created straits into and through present-day valleys.

The character and composition of these burial mounds are regionally

Fig. 101   Map of burial cairns and stone settings at Torslanda nr Göteborg, to show coastal setting of sites at Bronze Age sea-level 10 m above present level. Note the presumed existence of a strait beside which many cairns and settings were placed. Solid line: Bronze Age coastline; dotted line: present coastline approx. Sites off the Bronze Age coasts represent activities after land emergence, but some of the dots on the map obscure small islands.
(After *Fyndrapporter* (1973))

different. Many are built of turf or sods cut from the barrow position or from adjacent pasture. Others, particularly in upland areas of the north, are cairns made entirely of stone and including slabbing as well as the more common rounded cobbles. Barrows may also be built of both stone and earth, with a central stone cairn and earthen covering, or a stone kerb may have served to wall the mound. Some of the workmanship in the mounds is of a high standard in the selection of uniform material and in its careful positioning (fig. 102).

Many of the mounds have been damaged in the course of time, and most were originally of modest size, perhaps 10 m in diameter and 2 m high. Many, however, were rebuilt during the Bronze Age to contain additional burial or burials and were therefore greatly expanded in size. Others seem to have been built very large originally, and some of these exceptional mounds are over 50 m in diameter and 8 m high; the building of these would involve many people.

An important cemetery in the Netherlands is the Toterfout Halve Mijl group (North Brabant), excavated 1948–1951.[47] The cemetery extended over 2 km and consisted of about forty barrows set in several groups. Some of the barrows were surrounded by circular banks, others by ditches, but most by timber circles. Timber circles around barrows are a feature of this region; single, closely-set posts in a narrow trench are of late Neolithic origin, but in the Bronze Age the variation in post-settings is great. The posts may be single closely-set, single widely-spaced, paired widely-spaced, or there may be several concentric circles of posts; in

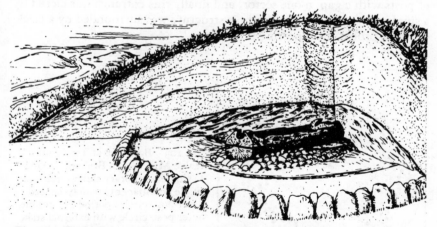

Fig. 102   Early Bronze Age barrow built of sand with stone-encircled central turf-mound covering tree-trunk coffin laid on stone base, Harrislee, Schleswig-Holstein.
(From Ellmers 1971)

addition, slender stakes were sometimes used to mark temporary circles during the building of the barrow.

Although the grave rituals for the region show considerable variation, barrow 8 of this cemetery demonstrates one particular sequence of events quite clearly (fig. 103). The body, that of a child less than 7 years old, was cremated on a pyre near the burial position, and was placed without any grave goods in a shallow oval pit; this was protected by a small mortuary shelter made of four stakes holding up a roof, the whole surrounded by a mortuary enclosure of stakes set in a circle and probably holding hurdle-fencing. Outside the enclosure a fire was made, as part of the funeral ceremony (funeral feast? or actual pyre?), and after a short period the mortuary enclosure and shelter were removed. The barrow was then built over the area, covering the cremation, stake-holes and the fireplaces; the core of the barrow was of turf cut from the site and the upper part of the barrow was of turf cut from the adjacent fenland. The barrow was then covered with sand to form a domed mound, and around the edge a circle of widely-spaced posts was set in position. Extra posts were placed at one position on this circle, as if to block-off a former entrance through the circle; this may mean that the posts were joined to one another by horizontal cross-pieces except at this entrance. This would mark the final act of barrow construction. Thereafter, the barrow was left, the posts decayed, and vegetation covered the mound. After a number of years, a cremation was placed in the top of the mound, and the barrow was enlarged; the barrow edge was marked again by a closely-set double circle of posts with a gap in one sector, and finally this entrance was closed by a single row of posts and the whole structure was surrounded by a circle of stakes probably supporting hurdles.

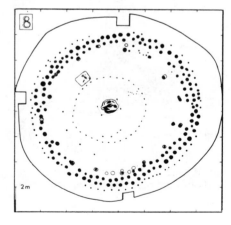

Fig. 103   Barrow 8 at Toterfout-Halve Mijl, North Brabant. Period I: single temporary stake-circle and single (permanent) widely-spaced outer post-circle; period II: double outer post-circle with external stake-circle. The primary grave held a cremation within a four-post structure.
(From Glasbergen 1954)

Although this burial was of a cremation, inhumations in barrows are also known from the region, and in some cases, as at Mol-Postel (Antwerp),[48] log coffins of full body size contain only cremations. Grave-goods are in general not abundant. The pottery sometimes associated with cremations in the southern region are of Hilversum and Drakenstein type, mostly local forms with some suggestion of contact with southern Britain; the urns are barrel-shaped with impressed cordon decoration on the upper part and occasionally with zig-zag decoration.[49]

In Drenthe, inhumations were the traditional earlier Bronze Age rite, and this may reflect a general widespread dominance of inhumation from here across Lower Saxony and beyond. Plain vessels and derivative beaker forms occasionally occur in this northern region. In north Brabant, Campine and Flanders, cremation was a strong tradition even in the earlier Bronze Age. The dates of these burials in the Low Countries range from c. 1500 to 1000 bc.[50]

On the Lüneburg heath of Lower Saxony the single-grave tradition of the later Neolithic was perpetuated in the earlier Bronze Age, and the barrows sometimes contain elaborate mortuary structures. Inhumation was most common, the body often extended in a tree-coffin and furnished with grave-goods. This contrast in grave-goods with the Netherlands is quite marked, but it might be worth noting here that the Low Countries are positioned as far from any metal sources as any other region in Europe, and difficulties of movement into this area from central Europe were probably considerable. However, other regions in the north are also remarkably barren not only in metal but also in any characteristic and recognizable Bronze Age burial monuments, and in these areas, for example in the basin of the Rhine in western Nordrhein-Westphalia, there is little evidence of any Bronze Age impact on the sparse Neolithic communities;[51] the wide and marshy nature of the Rhine itself is not a complete explanation of this absence of recorded Bronze Age activity. More comparable to the Low Countries is southern Lower Saxony, where barrow cemeteries are common, but the metal content of the grave is sparse.[52] Further north, in the lower Weser valley, larger barrow cemeteries occur, and although conditions for preservation of human remains and non-lithic grave-goods are generally poor, the constructional details suggest that most are of the Early Bronze Age. The three cemeteries at Schwanewede, near Bremen,[53] consisting of five, seven and eleven barrows, plus a few isolated mounds, occur within an area only 500 × 300 m; this appears to be a common feature in the region, the barrows forming relatively tight clusters, perhaps representing the traditional burial ground of members of a particular family or hamlet.

However, cremation was also practised in the region in the Early

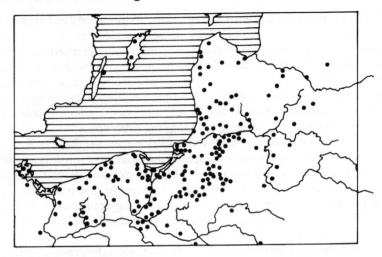

Fig. 104   Distribution of typically Baltic stone and bronze artifacts:
flanged axes, spiral-headed pins, wide-bladed axes, 'Nortycken'
type axes, and snake-headed hoes.
(After Gimbutas 1963)

Bronze Age, and burnt mortuary houses of substantial character have
been recovered.[54] One of these, at Hamburg-Marmstorf, had a stone
paved floor extending about one metre beyond the house itself on each
side; there were twelve posts, five on each side and one at each end, and
the house measured 6.2 × 4.7 m. The posts had been carefully erected in
deep holes with stone packing at the base and around the posts. The
structure with its contained female body had been burnt, and a barrow
12 m in diameter erected over the remains. At Sottorf, a fourteen-post
house was associated with the cremated remains of a very young child.[55]

The best-known burials of Lower Saxony and Schleswig-Holstein,
however, are the inhumations of the Sögel and Wohlde groups. On the
basis of the grave-goods, the burials have been classified in part into an
earlier Sögel group, found mainly in southern Jutland, Schleswig-
Holstein and Lower Saxony (Kersten's zone 2), and a somewhat later
Wohlde group, found in the same area and also farther north, Kersten's
zone 1; the two type-fossils of the groups are short sword or dagger types,
and each figured in Hachmann's scheme for the introduction of metal
into the north.[56] The chronological, or indeed geographical, separation
of these types in the north does not seem to us to be fully established, but
the impact of these impressive productions must have been considerable.
Their inspiration quite clearly lies in central European weaponry, in

upper and middle Danubian types, and this is where the chronological separations should be more clearly defined.

Large barrows, often with massive stone cairns and circles incorporated, cover inhumations.[57] At Vorwohlde (Sulingen), five barrows contained inhumations associated with a variety of grave-goods.[58] Barrow 1, 14 m in diameter, 1 m high, covered an extended male accompanied by two bronze pins, a small spearhead, a flint pick and eight arrowheads of flint. Another barrow held a primary male burial with bronze dagger, nicked flanged axe, arrowhead and bracelet, while four secondary burials had a few metal ornaments. An important barrow at Baven (Celle) contained an impressive mortuary house measuring 5 m × 4 m wide, with a full-width porch. The walls were probably wattle-and-daub. Within the house was an inhumation associated with a short sword, a dagger, a pin, all of bronze, and a point, two picks, and seventeen arrowheads, all of flint.

Other burials in the region are quite clearly related by grave-goods to the full Nordic Bronze Age, with swords, daggers and axes in male graves, ornaments in female graves (fig. 105); the Backsberg (Harburg) barrow,[59] 20 m in diameter, contained metal fittings for a folding wooden stool characteristic of the 'rich' burials of the Danish Early Bronze Age (see below). The separation of these graves from those of the Sögel-Wohlde group may be as much cultural as chronological. In absolute dating terms, these impressive barrow cemeteries and individual graves in Lower Saxony and Schleswig-Holstein fall within a time-range 1500–1300, insofar as correlations with the developed Early Bronze Age of central Europe are possible; radiocarbon dates for the graves in Lower Saxony are in the range 1550–1200 bc.

The same range applies to many of the burial mounds which litter the southern Baltic shores, in Mecklenburg and Pomerania.[60] These barrows are particularly dense upon the island of Rügen, just as upon other Baltic islands, and also in the lower reaches of the Oder, not around the bay of Zalew Szczeciński itself but upstream. The barrows themselves are of general north European form, and the grave goods include varieties of plain pottery vessels occasionally called 'Kümmerkeramik', which generally signifies a plain bucket-shaped pot lacking decoration; the term has been applied throughout the north German area but does not infer any culturally diagnostic feature. Here the Kümmerkeramik occurs primarily on Rügen. Comparable 'featureless' pottery has been noted occasionally from other regions in northern Europe, and may account for the lack of recognizable settlement debris on open sites.

In the Oder valley the associated pottery is of Buchholz type, so-called after a cemetery in Greifenhagen; jugs, beakers and bowls, sometimes with perforated double-lugs, sometimes with a single bar-lug, occur with

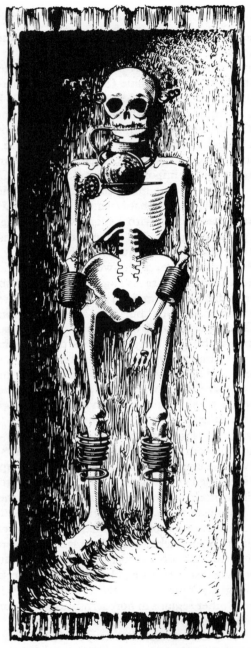

Fig. 105 Inhumation with ornaments from Wardböhmen, Celle.
(From Piesker 1958)

flint daggers, metal (generally bronze) knives, flat waisted axes, or ornaments of metal or amber. Inhumations, and some cremation, were practised. These rather poorly-furnished graves may precede or be contemporary with other graves which have a range of grave-goods absolutely typical of Denmark and southern Sweden in the full Early Bronze Age, swords, palstaves, spearheads and heavy ornaments; these graves lie to the west of the Oder, and those to the east are more aligned towards material from north-central Europe. The mounds containing these burials often have stone cists or internal cairns or kerbs. The region as a whole is of course very closely linked with the major amber sources lying to the east of the Vistula, but the quite clear-cut division in the metal grave-goods along the Oder may indicate a real social boundary between two distinct groups. Amber in graves to the west of the Oder is not as common as in those to the east.[61] Beyond this we can hardly go, but it is probably important to note the same divisions in the material culture of the succeeding Late Bronze Age.

From the lower Vistula valley eastwards, Baltic earlier Bronze Age cemeteries also contain inhumations beneath round barrows. Grave goods include small pottery vessels with slender applied cordons or with incised decoration, often with a boss and radiating lines placed near the rim;[62] this style is replaced in the Trzciniec group vessels with false cordons and horizontal or arc-like incision on the upper part.[63] The Trzciniec settlement is the type-name for a widespread earlier Bronze Age group on the Baltic coasts and beyond (pp. 79, 84, 98, fig. 37).[64] One of the cemeteries, at Łubna in Sieradz, contained about thirty barrows covering inhumations which were wholly or in part (heads) protected by slabs of stone;[65] the barrows were otherwise without major structural features of wood or stone. Other burials in the region, perhaps somewhat later in time, were of cremated remains, placed in stone-settings or in pits. Grave goods of metal are mainly ornaments, and the forms relate quite clearly to central European types; the appearance of amber in southern areas is generally believed to represent the material exchanged for this metal. Comparable graves and related settlements have been recovered from the valleys of the Bug, Narew and Neman-Vilija, which flow towards the south-eastern shores of the Baltic.[66]

The cemeteries of Jutland, the Danish islands and southern Sweden are probably the best-known of all of the Early Bronze Age burial monuments in northern Europe. Many thousands of burial mounds are known from this region, which includes southern Schleswig-Holstein, and doubtless there was considerable variation in the rituals of burial, just as there are in the actual structural features of the barrows and cairns. The cemeteries were often positioned along ridges of sand or gravel (pl. 11), and hill tops were favoured for particularly large monuments. There can be no doubt that the burials were meant to be seen. Many linear cemeteries occur, but there are also groups of barrows and numerous apparently isolated mounds. On the island of Sylt, five or six barrow cemeteries are positioned on what heights there were, to overlook the sea approaches from the north and the east, and western open waters are left unobserved.[67]

The barrows themselves were often made of both stone and turf, but rock areas generally contain true cairns in the absence of thick turf on deep soils. The stripping of turf from a large area to make just one moderate barrow must have seriously depleted the arable or grazing-land in the immediate vicinity;[68] similarly, the collection of suitable stone, including quarrying on occasion, must have involved considerable organization of man-power. The former, however, is on the face of it a much more dramatic and deliberate loss of valuable land; beneath many barrows are the marks of ard or spade suggesting that burials were placed on ordinary cultivated land, perhaps the land of the recently deceased.[69] The collection of stones for a cairn would of course have helped to prepare the land around for cultivation.

The barrows and cairns in these regions are sometimes single-phase monuments of large size, 20–25 m diameter and 3–4 m high; many were re-built for further burials and the result could be a mound 40 m across and 8 m high.[70] These rebuilt barrows may contain thirty or more individual graves.[71] Within these mounds the body was inhumed in a stone cist or in a tree-trunk coffin, or was laid in a shallow trench.[72] Generally the burial was covered by at least a small cairn of stones, with further stones or turf forming the mound itself. The edge of the mound was often marked by a stone wall, sometimes by wooden posts. A typical monument is that from Harrislee (Flensburg) (fig. 102).[73]

On occasion, the technique of stone-working was extremely sophisticated; on Gotland in the Baltic, limestone slabs were extensively used in the building of the several hundred cairns.[74] At Koparve, the cairn had a surrounding wall 0.5 m high, within which there was a drystone 'tower' 3 m high enclosing a space which contained, at its base, a stone cist with two inhumations furnished with a quantity of metal objects; the effect is of course like an internal ring-cairn but here the workmanship was elaborate.[75]

Normal cairns with stone cists have been noted far to the north along the former coasts of the Gulf of Bothnia (Norrland), and although erosion has removed all traces of bodies and grave-goods, they may well belong to the Early Bronze Age of the north;[76] if so, this might represent an extension of the burial tradition first established in the later Neolithic of more southern areas, and it would suggest that the abrupt halt in the recoverable Bronze Age artifacts, in Svealand, was misleading.[77] The Bronze Age population in these northern areas, if permanently settled, could have combined hunting, fishing, sealing and some slight arable farming and stockbreeding.

Further south, conditions for the preservation of material are better, and a number of Early Bronze Age barrows from Jutland have yielded exceptional evidence for clothing; these are noted below. Other barrows, recently excavated, have indicated yet again the great variety, and inexplicable nature, of many grave rituals.

At Stubberup (Lolland), a barrow covered a pit (fig. 106); at its base was a wooden coffin containing a double burial, with the heads of the bodies at opposite ends of the coffin, their legs entwined.[78] Beside one of the bodies were a flint dagger and a bone pin, and on top of the legs of both were an ox-tooth and a human thigh-bone. The pit was partly filled with stone cobbles, and scattered among these were some bones from at least three persons; the pit itself was sealed by a stone carpet laid on the original land surface beneath the barrow. Other double burials of the Early Bronze Age in the north occasionally combine cremation and inhumation, but more are of double inhumations; it has been said that

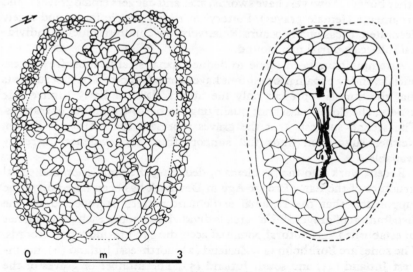

0   m   3

Fig. 106 Early Bronze Age grave at Stubberup, Denmark. Left: lower level of cairn with edge of dug grave shown by dashed line; right: paved area at base of dug grave, with two inhumations (heads shown by circles) with legs entwined.

(From E. Lomborg, *Kuml* (1963))

such double burials are often of a female adult and a child, but the evidence for this interesting statement is not well documented.

Another barrow, at Gadbjerg near Vejle (Jutland), was turf-built, and covered by stones; the body had a belt-plate and probably a bronze dagger.[79] During the building of the mound, a second wooden coffin was placed on a stone paved area, and the body had a bronze dagger in its wooden sheath. The land had been ploughed twice before the barrow was erected, and beneath these marks were some Neolithic graves. Later in the Bronze Age, a pit was dug in the barrow and another wooden coffin was inserted; a stone cairn was put over this burial and the whole mound was enlarged with a very heavy stone wall placed around its edge. The final monument was probably 20 m across and 5 m high. This final inhumed burial was accompanied by bronze weapons and a gold ring. The site demonstrates a continuity of interest and use as a cemetery over several centuries.

It is probably worth noting that of the many thousands of barrows and cairns of the Early Bronze Age in northern Europe, only a small percentage contained burials furnished with very elaborate grave-goods; many burials are without surviving grave-goods or have only one or two small objects such as a stone or metal knife, or razor, or ornament; many other burials, however, have swords, axes and daggers (male graves), and ornaments (female graves). Pottery, of rather simple forms and rarely decorated, occasionally occurs. Relatively few children achieved individual full-scale burial in a mound.

Attempts have been made to deduce social stratification from these burials, and two main propositions have been advanced. The first suggests that the burials represent only the 'upper class' of Early Bronze Age society, the 'lower class' not qualifying for barrow building operations. The second suggests that the graves represent the entire population. Neither suggestion finds full support from the evidence currently available.

Recent work into the problems of deducing the population and social structure of the Early Bronze Age in Denmark has been based upon the supposition that the regional settlement pattern is reflected by the distribution of graves.[80] The area is divided into zones each of which has an established agricultural potential according to pre-industrial records. The zones are Bornholm (1), Zealand (2), north-east Jutland (3), north-west Jutland (4), and south Jutland (5). The number of graves of the respective archaeological periods, I, II and III, in each zone are calculated and are compared with each other in terms of their correlation with deduced agricultural yield-potentials; in this way it is hoped to discover if any particular period or area contains more graves, representing settlements, in relation to food-supplies, than the other periods or areas. For period II, the developed Early Bronze Age of the north, the number of graves in all of the zones correlates with the agricultural potentials, and they do so as well for period III except in zone 4. Here, the density of graves in north-west Jutland is greater, that is, the population is higher for this period than in any other zone. This of course depends upon the presumption that graves equal population in the zone, and there may be doubts introduced here. If these doubts are ignored, and if the level of technology for food-production in the zone did not alter from period II to III, it is possible that the greater density represents a change in economic procurement activities, such as increased farming or greater exploitation of marine resources. Either of these may represent a more complex organization of the society, which is the point of the archaeological study. Alternatively, of course, the densities of population in all of the zones and at all times may have been well below the agricultural capacities of the lands, so that no pressures, no complex re-organizations, no alteration in society, were necessary to maintain a naturally increased population in zone 4.

The study continues by attempts to deduce personal wealth from the individual grave goods found with the burials. In all other zones and periods there are always poorly-furnished graves in abundance, and fewer richly-furnished graves, but in zone 4 period III, where the density of graves was high, the rich graves with males outnumber the poor graves. The wealth of a grave is determined by its weight of metal, with gold assigned a value of 100 times that of bronze. The complexity of metal objects, and their number, might have been equally relevant here. However, there is substantial evidence that graves containing gold often also contain much bronze, and it is also important that such rich graves have also yielded almost all of the particularly fine swords, as well as gold rings, bronze tweezers and razors. In period II graves, objects commonly interpreted as status symbols are always in rich graves although their weight in metal may be slight; these include the bronze fittings for finely-constructed wooden stools, as well as metal discs in male graves. Discs also occur in female graves along with fine bronze daggers. The evidence for rich graves in zone 4 period III is in substantial contrast to that from other zones and periods.

Divisions between male and female graves are also noted. Of the total number of graves for all zones, female burials are only about 50 per cent of male burials, and burials of children are rare. It is inescapable that only a part of the population achieved status sufficient to ensure burial in a mound with grave-goods. From this it is deduced that the society was not egalitarian, and was male-dominated. Further, as population density increased over time, so do the number of rich female graves and the male degree of social stratification and separation also increases. In period II of zone 4, the spread of graves over the region is generally uniform, but in period III there are distinct concentrations of graves which may indicate social groupings based upon male dominions.

These conclusions of this study are based upon several assumptions which have been noted above, but the greatest assumption must be that the evidence available for the study is truly representative of the zones and periods; in view of the widespread destruction of the burial mounds in the past, this may be unwarranted, yet the work opens up other possible lines of approach which may well lead to greater understanding of the societies of the Early Bronze Age.

Other studies of material with the same aim in mind have included the conjectured use of bronzes as status symbols, leading on to discussions of distributions and social ordering;[81] another suggests that the acquisition of metal products may have been the primary duty of the Bronze Age leaders (chieftains) of Gotland, and their importance is reflected in the monumental burial cairns erected for them.[82] The full investigation of two cemeteries in Scania, one containing a rich and elaborate grave, the other only poor and simple graves, also suggests that social and economic divisions existed in the Bronze Age.[83]

The evidence from other areas in northern Europe is not even as specific as this; nevertheless, the building of so many thousands of burial mounds in the second millennium represents considerable undertakings in manpower and time, and must point to strong beliefs in the procedures to be followed when death occurred in the farming and hunting communities of the north. A glimpse of the actual appearance of such people may be afforded by the remarkable state of preservation within some few burial monuments.

The manufacture of textiles and other materials is generally attested in the archaeological record only by spindle-whorls and loom-weights, and many of these are known from Bronze Age contexts. Traces of fabrics are occasionally encountered in graves throughout Europe, often as corrosion-products on bronzes, and it is therefore of considerable importance that well-preserved articles of clothing have been recovered from some Early Bronze Age graves in Jutland. But before describing these it is as well to remember that this is funerary clothing and may not be representative of the apparel of the living.

The preservation of this material is due to several circumstances. The use of a tree-trunk coffin, often of oak, produces a tanning action which helps to conserve certain substances. More important, the coffins were often placed upon a clay soil which created water-logging conditions, aided by the sealing-over of the burial by other layers of soil which hardened into a crust. The excavation of these coffins requires rapid conservation procedures once the drying-out begins.

Inside the coffins have been found both males and females, and it should be noted that their grave goods are not particularly abundant or unusual; in this respect these few well-preserved graves may indicate the extent of our loss of information through the decay of most organic material. The clothing worn by males consists of a kilt-like garment (extending from the breast to the knees), a cloak, a cap, and some form of footwear. Females wore either of two types of dress (a corded skirt and jacket, or a long dress worn either from neck to feet or from breast to feet with a covering jacket), a hair-band or hair-net, a belt with bronze disc, and socks and leather shoes. It is interesting that bronze figurines also depict the short corded skirt on females. Individual graves differ in their composition.[84]

At Skrydstrup (South Jutland), the oak coffin had been placed on a stone base and was covered by stones.[85] The burial was of a young (18- or 19-year-old) female about 1.7 m tall, with a narrow face, large teeth, long eyelashes and long ash-blonde hair, a Nordic type (pl. 10). The body had been placed in the coffin on a cow-hide which itself covered the remains of a bouquet of grass and flowering plants; the funeral had taken place in summer. The girl's body was covered from waist to foot by a plain cloth forming a skirt; she wore a single-piece jacket with decorative embroidery on the sleeves and at the neck (fig. 107), and it seems that this too was a funerary object only, as the stitching was 'false'. A belt with tassel, and foot-bindings of cloth, completed her covering, but she also wore a horse-hair net and a cap tied beneath her chin;[86] two gold earrings and a horn comb emphasize the attention paid to the head. Over the body were two pieces of brown woollen cloth.

The female burial at Egtved (East Jutland) also took place in summer; flowering yarrow was recovered on top of the ox-hide which had lined the coffin and had been folded over the body.[87] A young (18- to 25-year-old) female, 1.6 m tall with light blonde hair, was clad in a short jacket of brown work, and a woollen cord skirt (fig. 108). This skirt is a remarkable garment; it is made of one continuous cord looped up and down and twisted before being gathered at the bottom; its length was only 38 cm and it was wound twice round the body to provide a rather thick and dense covering. A belt round the waist of the body held a bronze disc and a horn comb, and there were also two bronze armlets and a bronze earring. A birch-bark box placed near the head held a hair-net, like the Skrydstrup find, and an awl. A second bark bowl, near the feet, had held a drink of beer or fruit wine. The body had been covered with a cloth

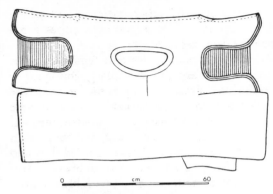

Fig. 107   The Skrydstrup
jacket. Upper: the jacket
pattern; lower: embroidery
plan at the neck.
(From Broholm and Hald
1948)

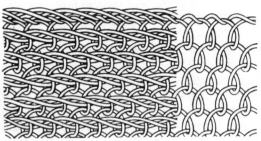

before the hide was folded over; another piece of cloth placed near the left
leg held the cremated remains of a young child.

A female grave from Ølby provides some further support for the corded
skirt as a common form of dress.[88] Here the body wore a skirt made of
individual cords each of which held several bronze tubes. At the waist
there was a large spiked disc, with short sword and other metal ornaments.
Around the neck was a heavy bronze collar.

Male clothing has been recovered from a number of tree coffins in
Jutland. At Trindhoj, the body had decayed but blonde hair was preserved
at the head and pubic region; there was no beard. The man wore a long
gown, made of four pieces of cloth sewn together, and held around the
body by a woven belt with tassels.[89] Cloth wrapping around the feet
served as socks under leather shoes. White wool blanket pieces were
wrapped around the feet and placed beneath the head. A round cap on the
head was made of a round crown and a side-piece of several layers, the
whole covered by short threads sewn-in to form a smooth pile, and with
embroidery stitching on the inside; a second more tubular cap was also
found in a wooden box in the grave. A cloak was spread over the body,
and had been sewn-over with separate threads to form a long hairy pile.
The body had a sword in a wooden sheath by its left side, and a razor,

horn comb and the second cap lay inside a wooden box itself inside a larger wooden box.

Other graves tend to duplicate this male clothing, although in some cases the workmanship is more elaborate. The Muldbjerg cloak, for instance, had a roll-collar, and the cap was covered with a thick pile, with pairs of long threads stitched-in, each thread neatly knotted at its end and also near the stitch. The threads are finely spun two-ply wool (fig. 108).[90]

The grave-goods of these burials in the tree-coffins are not exceptional in the amount of bronze or gold, but they probably indicate a general range of equipment that was placed in many graves; this material is further noted below. What is uncertain is the relationship of individual

Fig. 108   Bronze Age clothing in Denmark, as deduced from grave finds. (Drawing by R. Walker)

burials to one another, within one barrow, within a cemetery, or within a region. Without better preservation, and anthropological examinations, little more can be said. The presumed 'family' graves at Borum Eshoj (Jutland) are a case in point; a central coffin held an elderly male, another coffin nearby held an aged female, and a third coffin held a young male (fig. 109). The males are said to have been related, and the female might represent the wife or associate of the older man; proof is unlikely.[91]

Not all of the mounds have graves with clearly explicable contents. In the truly enormous barrow of Løfthoj (Zealand), a mound 35 m across and 7 m high, a tree-coffin yielded a male furnished with a sword, a gold armlet, and a leather bag containing a bronze knife, razor, tweezers, a piece of wood wrapped in skin, two leather cases tied with string, and a flint knife also wrapped in leather.[92] More remarkable still were the grave-goods found at Hvidegaard near the Løfthoj barrow.[93] Here a stone coffin lined with hide held a cape and cloak, a bronze sword in its scabbard, a bronze brooch and an adult male cremation. A leather purse, closed by an ingenious almost zip-like mechanism using a straight pin, held a piece of amber, shells, a wooden cube, a flint flake, dried roots, bark, a grass-snake tail, a falcon's claw, bronze tweezers, a knife and razor each in a leather case, a flint knife stitched into a bladder or internal organ, a squirrel's jaw in a leather case, and other small organic articles (fig. 110). Belt-bags with comparable objects are now known from about thirty graves in Denmark, and it is tempting to see these as the equipment of 'medicine-men' or their equivalents.

Although these particular graves are exceptional, the general impression provided by a bulk of graves is that of an abundance of material equipment placed with the dead. The tradition of burying personal or community possessions with the dead, or with selected dead, correlates well with other evidence for massive production of equipment in the second millennium.

Metalwork

The evidence for Early Bronze Age metal products in northern Europe is uneven, in quantity and in quality. For the Low Countries, the number of bronze or gold objects of this time is very small, counted in the low hundreds, yet in Denmark there are many hundreds of these objects and often these are heavy and elaborate productions. Neither area possessed metal of its own, and the ability of north Europeans to acquire ample supplies from other regions is an important feature.

A second feature to note is that many of the northern areas did not delay in establishing their own metallurgical processes of casting and

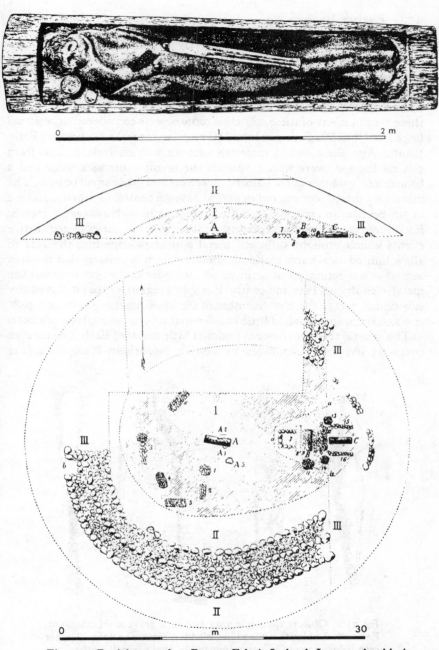

Fig. 109 Burial mound at Borum Eshoj, Jutland. Lower: A. elderly male, B. young male, C. elderly female. Excavated 1850-1875. Upper: young male in coffin B.
(From Glob 1974)

hammering, so that relatively few directly imported objects escaped the melting-pot.[94] Because of the rarity of metals in the Low Countries, it may be an exaggeration to point to the number of actual imports that have survived, and to suggest that local metallurgy was therefore restricted; it is, however, remarkable that almost every large hoard, and there are not many of these, contains some objects considered to be actual imports.[95] The Wageningen hoard (Gelderland) marks a developed Early Bronze Age phase, when materials ostensibly from Ireland, and from central Europe, were widely spread; the hoard contains a stone and a bronze axe, a dagger and a halberd, bracelets and other small objects. The metals are mixed, considered in part to be from central Germany, and are of tin-bronze, in contrast with the preceding Beaker-associated metals. Each however is likely to represent a rather sporadic series of acquisitive events which brought sufficient metal and knowledge into the area to allow limited local participation in metallurgy; it is unlikely that the area served as a meeting-point or impetus for wider exchanges between the metal-rich British Isles and central European region, or that it played any substantial part in the establishment of the more northern Bronze Age.[96] It was too distant, and had little to offer that was not available elsewhere.

The same is true for adjacent regions; little metal of Early Bronze Age character has been recognized in western Nordrhein-Westphalia (the

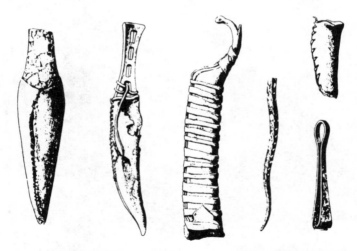

Fig. 110 Objects from a leather bag in a grave at Hvidegaard, Zealand: flint knife stitched in a bladder, bronze knife in a leather case, bronze razor in wrapping, tail of snake, small leather case with jaw of squirrel, and bronze tweezers.
(From Glob 1974)

lower Rhine valley) or in southern Lower Saxony (the mid-Weser valley).[97] This may be the case for the north-west European area in general, but there are exceptions. Throughout the Bronze Age, the communities in the north-east Netherlands could acquire abundant, or at least adequate, supplies of metal, and this gave rise to a series of local industries with restricted distributions. It has been suggested that the ability to acquire metal in this area is a reflection of the locally-available amber supplies.

To the east, however, Lower Saxony and Schleswig-Holstein were positioned on direct routes between central Europe and the north, with the Elbe and Weser rivers providing access, and easily-traversable land-routes also allowing contact and exchange. In many respects, Lower Saxony is a part of the central European Bronze Age unlike the Low Countries, yet it is also distinct. Here the establishment of metallurgy was abrupt and impressive; the materials associated with the barrow inhumations include long daggers or dirks, nicked-flanged axes and a variety of ornaments. The Sögel daggers, perhaps ultimately a southern central European idea, are perhaps the most characteristic earlier Bronze Age weapon, and they seem to have been popular from the Ems river eastwards into southern Jutland.[98] Other graves are less well-furnished, with flint daggers, stone beads and lightweight bronze objects.

Other metal forms of the Early Bronze Age in this region include the Wohlde dirk, a trapeze-hilted weapon, and a very large variety of ornaments, bracelets, armlets and anklets, neck-rings and collars, earrings and pins. Many of these are strictly of local style, and allow quite clear definition of stylistic areas; they may signify the limits of distribution agencies or the gradual 'drift' of objects through use, loss, gift or exchange.[99] It is significant that this region, with its well-defined metal industries, in effect forms a western boundary to the very widespread distribution of central European 'Únětician' products which extend well outside the Únětician culture area and up to the Baltic coasts of Mecklenburg and Pomerania.[100] The inter-relation between these two industrial complexes, and indeed with a third, the Nordic Bronze Age, is a subject that cannot be pursued here. The Sögel-Wohlde industry, the north Únětician industry, all were dynamic and inventive, and to a great extent exclusive, at least at the beginning of the Early Bronze Age.

The area of Baltic coastlands east of the Vistula was similarly without local metal resources, and in the earliest phases of the Bronze Age both settlements and graves contain few metal objects. In time, however, many products of central European character were transmitted into the Baltic lands, and perhaps correlate with the appearance of Baltic amber in the Únětician and related groups of central Europe. The metal products include both bronze and gold, and some of these were melted or beaten into local Baltic forms, both ornaments and heavier equipment, and the range is quite considerable.[101] A number of hoards and other finds of metal within and around the area of amber deposits contain objects that seemingly copy the extensive range of 'Koszider' bronzes (p. 93) from the middle Danube region, as well as a selection of 'Tumulus Bronze' forms, and it is not possible to point to specific areas in central Europe for the direct supply of objects.

The inception of metallurgy in North Jutland, the islands and southern Sweden must be bound up with the introduction of materials and knowledge from central Europe. Although very detailed typological work has distinguished a number of innovating horizons of imports, recent work suggests that a general episode early in the second millennium was sufficient to initiate a local industry or industries that assumed full control over available resources.[102] At first, objects of copper were made in imitation of copper and bronze imported pieces, but soon full tin-bronzes were produced (fig. 111).

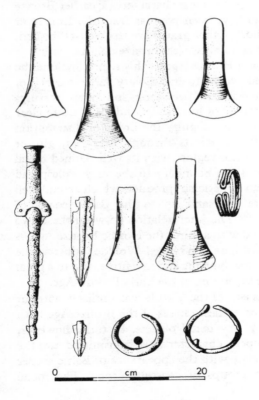

Fig. 111   Metal axes, daggers and ornaments in the Pile, Denmark, hoard.
(From Hachmann 1957)

0   cm   20

The discovery of metalworking sites[103] where conditions could be controlled for melting and casting, as well as hammering, of objects, and the very high quality of products, demonstrates that sufficient confidence existed in the ability to maintain a regular supply of metal from outside the region. The extreme rarity of metal north of Svealand and outside the southern part of Norway is notable.

A recent survey of Bronze Age metal in Finland[104] suggests that much of the earlier Bronze Age objects were brought into the region as finished products from eastern Europe, and metal is generally rare both here and in the many burial mounds of southern Norway.[105]

The Nordic metal industry produced, among other things, daggers, spearheads and heavy axes or palstaves.[106] From the first, these were decorated with geometric designs, dot and concentric circles, arcs and running spirals being most popular. Most of these large objects, which occur in graves and in hoards, are solid metal. Smaller ornaments, particularly bracelets, brooches, necklets and collars, and various discs, were also cast and decorated. The inspiration for much of this material is often believed to have stemmed from the middle Danubian industries, and there are strong typological links in the conception of the shapes and designs, but basically it was a Nordic phenomenon.[107]

The developed Early Bronze Age industries in the north were among the first to create long castings in two-piece moulds, and a whole series of

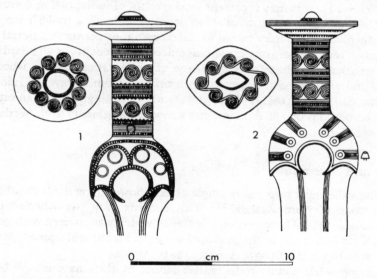

Fig. 112 Metal hilts on swords from Lyngsaa, Denmark.
(From H. Ottenjann, *Die Nordischen Vollgriffschwerter* (1969))

straight-bladed metal-hilted swords were produced; some of the hilts were gapped, to be filled with plates or rings of amber, bone or wood, and sheet-gold was sometimes pressed into prepared areas of cast decoration (fig. 112).[108] The swords were often sheathed in wooden scabbards lined with hide or other soft substances. Very large battle-axes were also produced, occasionally with clay cores, and therefore not for utilitarian use.[109]

Smaller objects, most often found in graves, include animal-headed razors, tweezers, single-edged knives and other cosmetic accessories. Two-piece brooches, double-buttons or studs, and large decorated spiked discs, as well as heavy armlets, sometimes of gold, completed the personal equipment.[110] The wealth in some of these graves was occasionally of such attraction that Bronze Age tomb-robbers acted soon after burial and, by means of hooked sticks inserted into small holes cut through the coffin lids or ends, the valuable relics were removed (fig. 113).[111]

Heavier metals are often found in hoards, buried in moorland for a variety of reasons still under debate. The forty spearheads, found closely-packed together within a heap of stones at Thorsted (Jutland) is a case in point,[112] but hoards of palstaves, swords and mixtures also occur; a hoard from Smorumovre (Zealand) contained sixty spearheads and eighty-eight axes. The weight of metal found in hoards and that from graves is unequal, more coming from graves, but burial in a grave is more explicable. Hoards may represent local wealth, of individual or community, a metal-smith's stock of scrap or saleable items, a trader's storage hiding-place, temporary burial for safekeeping, or permanent burial for religious reasons; any one explanation need not account for all hoards.

Remarkable perhaps only by virtue of preservation are the wooden stool and wooden bowl decorated with tin nails from a grave at Guldhoj (Jutland).[113] The stool is of ash and stands 33 cm high; it had an otter-skin seat, and is one of about twenty known in fragments from northern Europe (fig. 114).

Art and ceremony

Perhaps the most impressive single object, however, is the Trundholm 'sun chariot' from Zealand.[114] This consists of a two-wheeled cart carrying a vertical bronze disc, one side of which was covered with gold-leaf. This find is one of the principal supports for the widespread idea of sun-worship in the Bronze Age (pl. 12a).

Among other metal products that cannot by their nature have been useful in the purely functional terms of work or warfare are the heavy clay-core filled wide-bladed axes of the north, and the extraordinary

Fig. 113   Robbing the grave at Storehoj, Denmark, in the Bronze Age; below, the remains left by the robber including his or her forked stick.
(Based on *Skalk* 1964/4 and Glob 1974)

Ommerschans (Overijssel) type of rapier; the latter is known from finds at Plougrescant (Côtes du Nord, Brittany), Beaune (Côte d'Or), and Jutphaas (Utrecht), as well as Ommerschans.[115] The rapiers are very large and heavy, have thick points, blunt edges and no rivet holes for hilt attachment. They must have been prestige or ceremonial objects, and all seem to have been made by one craftsman. The wide-bladed metal axes of the north (Denmark and Sweden)[116] are also represented on rock engravings in several regions (pl. 13). Associated with these

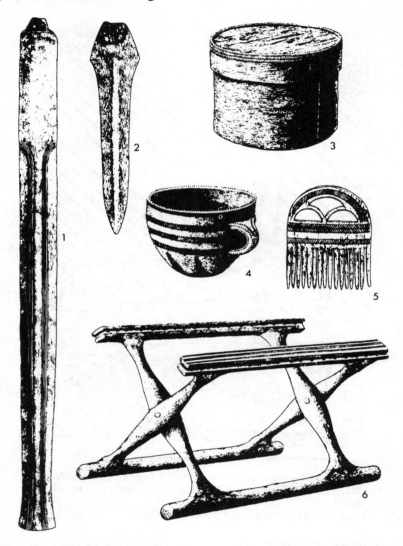

Fig. 114 Objects from Early Bronze Age graves at Borum Eshoj (1, 2, 5) and Guldhoj (3, 4, 6) 1–2. bronze dagger in sword scabbard, 3. birch-bark box, 4. birch wood cup with tin-tack decoration, 5. bone comb, 6. folding ash-wood stool, formerly with otter-skin seat. Scales: 1, 2, 5 about $\frac{1}{2}$; 3, 4 about $\frac{1}{3}$; 6 about $\frac{1}{4}$.
(From Glob 1974)

representations are abundant cup-marks and discs, which are sometimes considered to indicate a Trundholm-type of sun worship, but the content of the rock art is far more varied than this.

Little of this is securely dated, but representations of similar objects on metal weapons allow us to state that at least some of the rock-art is of the Early Bronze Age (fig. 115). One of the earliest metal swords in the north, from Rørby (Zealand),[117] has a slender ship engraved upon its blade, and this is the earliest evidence for such vessels in the north. Many thousands of comparable engravings of ships occur upon the living rock of Norway (Rogaland and Ostfold), and Sweden (Bohuslän, Uppland, and down the eastern coasts to Blekkinge and Scania) and occasionally upon rock in Denmark.[118] These engraved ships may be several metres in length, but most are quite small, perhaps 20–60 cm long, and they depict a great variety of craft; strokes shown above the gunwales are generally interpreted as crew members, and there are often larger figures within the ships or just above them (pl. 24). Some of these ships are probably

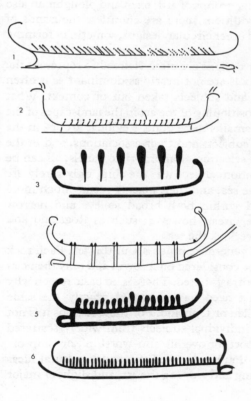

Fig. 115   Ships of the Bronze Age, as seen on rocks and bronzes: 1. Rørby, Zealand (engraving on a sword), 2. Wismar, Mecklenburg (engraving on a horn), 3. Kivik, Scania (rock grave slab), 4. Viemose, Zealand (engraving on a razor), 5. Åmoy, Rogaland, 6. Himmelstalund, Östergötland (rock). Various scales.
(From M. P. Malmer, *Kuml* (1970))

sledges, but others are clearly sea-going vessels, perhaps skin-covered boats, wooden boats or much larger ships. Sails are hardly ever shown, and few distinct oars or paddles.[119] However constructed, these vessels demonstrate the maritime nature of Bronze Age society in the north as does of course its coastal distribution which includes many islands, from Åmoy in Rogaland to Gotland and Bornholm. The eastern coast of Sweden is particularly well-furnished with ship engravings, including the large horizontal rock pictures at Mockleryde in Blekkinge.[120]

Associated with the ships on many rock panels are other representations (fig. 116). Humans holding battle-axes, spears or bows, or unarmed, often appear as singles or in groups, and occasionally they seem related to animal figures of deer, cattle and horses (pl. 13). Human and animal figures are found in abundance in Uppland, in Scania, in Bohuslän and Ostfold, almost always associated with ships.[121] Some humans are depicted very large, as if to dominate a particular scene, but the whole question of association and contemporaneity is difficult. Carts pulled by paired horses are shown, the Frannarp group having only carts and wheels (fig. 190), and ploughing groups of ard, oxen and ploughman also occur regularly (pl. 13). In addition, there are countless thousands of cup-marks and many discs and other circular designs, sometimes forming the bodies of humans.

The discs and other circular designs are often claimed to represent the sun,[122] but in fact these symbols are not nearly as dominant as is often argued from selective panels and subjects taken out of context. What seems more important is the positioning of the art in the landscapes of the north, and here much work remains to be done. Regional groups in the methods of engraving, in the subjects and their associations, and in the style of depictions, and in the selection of appropriate panels, all can be seen. Although the most common subject was the ship, only rarely are such vessels within sight of the sea, and their placing seems much more closely related to arable land within both broad valleys and narrow openings in the hills. In other areas, however, such as Rogaland and Scania, the art may directly overlook the sea.

It is not, in fact, possible to generalize much about this art. Each rock panel or small area must first be considered on its own, and only then can comparisons be drawn, and contrasts noted. There is no basic reason why the decorated rocks of Scania need have signified exactly the same concepts as did those of Bohuslän or Uppland. For these reasons it is not valid or even useful to select individual subjects from widely-scattered sites and present them as support for overall 'sun-worship', or 'ship-of-the-dead' ideas. Each site no doubt expressed particular cultural ideas and images to the society making and viewing the art, and slight or major

Fig. 116 Rock engravings from Himmelstalund, Sweden.
(From Burenhult 1973)

319

differences in style, size, positioning, composition and proximity to other panels were doubtless of some significance, possibly major.

This is not the place to try to present detailed site reports, but we consider that a generalized view, such as has already been indicated, may not be sufficient treatment of this art. One site alone may demonstrate the variations within the art, although it does not by itself represent the full range of artistic motifs and positions. Torsbo is one of the larger sites in an important group near Kville (Bohuslän);[123] the decorated rock face on the ridge extends for *c.* 100 m along the southward-facing slope. The slope itself is relatively shallow, and the exposed rock surfaces with the art lie at angles of 0° (horizontal) to 10°. The art is positioned quite consistently at *c.* 5 m above the level of the smooth fields at the base of the rock ridge, which represents about 15–25 m of rock surface between art and level ground. Other discoveries of decorated surfaces have been *c.* 150 m away from the main area, in otherwise similar positions, and it may be that the entire central ridge carries decoration, over 250 m in extent, but much is still covered by soil and trees; other sites in Bohuslän extend over such great distances.

The art at Torsbo consists of about seventeen panels within the major 100 m length; these panels each contain a number of representations placed closely together, rarely but occasionally overlying one another, and they give the impression of deliberate grouping, if not composition, separated from other panels by blank gaps of undecorated (= unengraved) rocks. The panels are from 6 m to 10 m apart, with one or two further apart than this. The panel sizes are on average *c.* 2 m high and 2–5 m wide, and almost all of the individual representations are placed to be viewed from downslope, from the flat fields to the south of the ridge.

The panels in total contain the following representations, all approximate quantities: 150 ships, 40 animals, 30 humans, 5 footprints, 5 circles or discs, 200 cupmarks and 120 other squiggles. Within the panels, however, considerable variations exist: if we take only simple numbers of ships, animals and humans, different large panels have totals of 8–0–6, 32–5–1, 12–21–4, 11–2–5, 48–4–7. The ships may be fully 2 m long (one is 4.5 m long), or minute (only 20–30 cm), and comparable differences occur in animals and humans. It appears that compositions were deliberate, but it is not possible to assert that actual scenes of events, or hoped-for events, are represented; the panel at Torsbo with 48 ships (a flotilla), and little else, gives the impression of a deliberate grouping and alignment, but this need not exclude the opinion that the individual subjects were actually drawn on the rock from time to time and not all at once.

The problems of the study of this art are very considerable. The overall distribution of the art is well-known, but there are many hundreds of sites along the west coasts of Sweden in particular, where detailed work of high standard has only just begun. The panels of the large known sites in Bohuslän have sometimes been taken to represent central social areas, but much more geographical and archaeological fieldwork is required.[124]

All of these great regions of rock art lie within the distribution of Early Bronze Age settlement, as marked by burials and metal finds. The general northern limit of arable agriculture in Scandinavia, and the southern rock art, is about 66° N, and this is one of the reasons for associating the art with agricultural interests and beliefs. Recent finds of rock art of southern character have extended the range almost to the North Cape, about 71° N, but the general correlation remains true.[125]

In northern Scandinavia, another rock art province has long been known (fig. 117). The art consists of engravings and some paintings of wild animals, reindeer, elk, fish, seabirds, bears and humans.[126] They are associated with the hunting and gathering groups of the far north, but are likely to be contemporary with the Bronze Age rock art of the south,[127] representing as clearly as anything else the divergencies in lifestyles of the two areas. A few sites seem to show a mixture of both art types; at Nämforsen (Angermanland) some 400 km to the north of Uppland, many panels depict both the naturalistic wild animals and the more stylized southern elements of discs, footprints and ships. The rock paintings, not engravings, of southern Finland, now being discovered or re-discovered,[128] which combine geometric designs and human or animal figures, should also be considered here as complementary to the other art provinces (fig. 118). These sites, and the many hunting settlements of the north, probably represent second millennium occupation of vast regions untouched by the defining features of the 'Bronze Age'.

Fig. 117   Rock engravings at Nämforsen, Ångermanland.
(From Fredsjo, Janson and Moberg 1969)

Fig. 118 Painted rock at Ristiina Uitta-monsalmi, Finland.
(After P. Sarvas and J.-P. Taavitsainen, *Suomen Museo,* 1976)

Table 8   Radiocarbon dates, northern Europe, earlier Bronze Age

Site	Lab no.	bc
Low Countries		
Anlo, pit	GrN–852	1670 ± 65
	GrN–1997	1645 ± 85
Nordsleen, barrow	GrN–3036	1310 ± 70
Toterfout-Halve Mijl		
barrows and burials, range of 24 dates		
(Gr–N) 1500 ± 100 to 1105 ± 90		
Vogelenzang, settlement	GrN–2997	1190 ± 70
Oostwond, barrow	GrN–797	1075 ± 80
Mander, barrow	GrN–2388	1960 ± 55
	GrN–2982	1670 ± 70
	GrN–2969	1710 ± 55
Heemstede, bow	GrN–4070	1550 ± 100
Hilversum, barrow	GrN–4885	1290 ± 35
Zwaagdijk, settlement	GrN–4243	1250 ± 60
Renkum, Gelderland, burial	GrN–5034	1510 ± 40
Molenaarsgraaf, burial	GrN–5177	1400 ± 35
Eersel, Nord-Brabant, ?burial	GrN–5350	1510 ± 35
Zijderveld, Zuid-Holland, settlement	GrN–5376	1420 ± 80
Putten, Gelderland, barrow	GrN–4957	1370 ± 85
	GrN–4958	1110 ± 35
Anner Tol, Drenthe		
burials	GrN–6412	1425 ± 35
burials?	GrN–6411	1385 ± 35

Table 8—cont.

Site	Lab no.	bc
Elp, settlement	GrN–2881	805 ± 65
	GrN–4171	1280 ± 80
	GrN–4170	1050 ± 70
	GrN–4172	1030 ± 60
	GrN–4173	910 ± 60
	GrN–5266	1155 ± 65
Deventer	GrN–955	1110 ± 70
	GrN–967	1180 ± 70
Angelsloo, Drenthe, settlement	GrN–5183	1455 ± 35
	GrN–5184	1060 ± 40
	GrN–5186	880 ± 35
	GrN–5185	920 ± 30
	GrN–5015	960 ± 35
	GrN–5265	620 ± 55
Emmerhout, Drenthe, settlement	GrN–5588	1370 ± 60
	GrN–5862	940 ± 35
	GrN–5861	955 ± 35
	GrN–5777	945 ± 35
	GrN–5776	1015 ± 35
	GrN–5775	1140 ± 60
Vasse, settlement	GrN–2978	1220 ± 55
	GrN–2983	1070 ± 70
Emmererfscheidenveen, trackway	GrN–4149	1170 ± 50
	GrN–4342	1195 ± 55

Germany

Site	Lab no.	bc
Ipwegermoor, Oldenburg, trackways	GrN–3527	1700 ± 75
	GrN–3134	1370 ± 70
	GrN–3530	1160 ± 80
	GrN–3514	1410 ± 70
	GrN–3529	1470 ± 75
	GrN–3509	1465 ± 65
Dienste, L. Saxony, burial	Hv–824	1520 ± 80
	Hv–825	1460 ± 100
Ohlenstedt, L. Saxony, burial	Hv–827	1450 ± 105
Luttum, L. Saxony, burial	Hv–773	1710 ± 70
Walkemühle, L. Saxony, barrow	Hv–587	1470 ± 60
Glum, Oldenburg, wheels	GrN–5419	1495 ± 45
	GrN–5420	1530 ± 40
	Hv–4058	1165 ± 140
	Hv–4057	1275 ± 90
Melz, Kr. Röbel, Mecklenburg halberd shafts	Bln–982	1770 ± 100
	Bln–983	1725 ± 100
	Bln–984	1865 ± 100

Table 8—cont.

Site	Lab no.	bc
Scandinavia		
Bornholm, pit	K–585	1920±100
Faarup, wooden wheel	K–989	1510±100
Klosterlund, Jutland, wooden pole	K–1009	1560±110
Nonnebo Mose, Fyn, wooden wheel	K–1112	1400±120
Nymölla, burials	Lu–443	1210±60
	Lu–442	1210±60
	Lu–444	1120±60
Hvorslev, Jutland, ashwood ard	K–1301	1490±100
Lundergaards Mose, N. Jutland, carved tree	K–1339	1520±100
Löderup, Scania, burials	Lu–657	1770±60
	Lu–799	1410±60
	Lu–808	1890±60
Norridinge, Scania, settlement	Lu–836	1670±135
	Lu–837	1010±55
Löddesborg, Scania, settlement	Lu–838	1490±55
Stogaros, Telemark, occupation	T–1445	1860±90
Löderup, Scania, well	Lu–1109	1770±60
Å, Snillfjord, Sör-Trondelag, cist	T–989	1420±170

Notes

1 The modern or recent territories included in this are the Netherlands with Belgium, Lower Saxony, Schleswig-Holstein, Mecklenburg, Pomerania, Koszalin, Gdańsk, Kaliningrad and into coastal Lithuania and Latvia.

2 Montelius 1885 and 1900; for a recent discussion of the development of chronological methods in the north, see Gräslund 1974.

3 Montelius worked before the chronological ordering of the central European Bronze Age was attempted by Reinecke, but eventually he tried to create a relative and then absolute dating system by transferring implement typology into central Europe and beyond, southwards to historically-dated cultures: Montelius 1903. The vast distances involved, the mechanisms of distribution, and the imprecise nature of much of the Mediterranean chronology, all make Montelian schemes difficult to endorse.

4 S. Müller, *Aarbøger* (1909), 1–119, created a different scheme, which survives today only in his phase 2, which fell beyond Montelius I, yet before the full Early Bronze Age of Montelius II.

5 Kersten 1935; J. E. Forssander, *Der Ostskandinavische Norden während der ältesten Metallzeit Europas*, 1936, also tackled this problem, and distinguished a number of finds that characterized his periods: Pile, Tinsdahl, Valsømagle, the last marking the early phase of Period II, the full Early Bronze Age.

6 E. Sprockhoff, *Altbronzezeitliches aus Niedersachsen*, 1940; also *Prähistorische Zeitschrift* 18 (1927), and

21 (1930); Sprockhoff's work concerned northern Germany in particular, and his prolific papers provided much basic data about Bronze Age equipment and their possible relationships with the south and west. His *Nordische Bronzezeit und frühes Griechentum*, 1954, refers mainly to later Bronze Age events.

7 Broholm 1952, 1953; this seems to be the standard framework now employed, although many studies have demonstrated its need to be much less rigid, Randsborg 1972, Thrane 1975.

8 Hachmann 1957; the concept of horizons is a useful one although authors have rarely provided definition of the use of the term. Hachmann's sequence of four horizons: (1) central German and Bohemian objects, plus west European objects (into zone 1 only), dated to Br A1/A2; (2) west Alpine (zone 2) and middle Danubian (zone 1) objects, dated to Br A2; (3) south German (zone 2) objects, dated to Br B1; (4) south German (mainly zone 1) objects, dated to Br B2. The scheme was elaborate and relied upon detailed typology and associations in the north, and in the ability to precisely date various objects in the Reinecke scheme.

9 Lomborg 1959, 1968; the latter is an attempt to define the metals of the Period I–II boundary.

10 Randsborg 1968, the transition from Period II to Period III; Randsborg 1972, from Period III to Period IV; Baudou 1960, an important corpus; Thrane 1975, external relations. See also Gräslund 1974, summary in *Norw. Archaeol. Rev.* 9 (1976), 69–126, for commentary on the development of Bronze Age studies in the north.

11 *BROB* 15–16 (1965–6), 7–11.

12 J. Jensen, Bronze for Rav, *Skalk* 3 (1967), 4–7. The literature on amber and its distribution is large; the initial publication was J. M. de Navarro, *Geographical Journal* 66 (1925), 481–507. Recent assessments show how abundant Baltic amber was in areas far to the south, e.g. J-L. Roudil and M. Soulier, *Gallia Préhistoire* 19 (1976), 173–220, in Languedoc. Brongers and Woltering 1973 comment upon the wide distribution of amber in the north, and point to the Bronze Age settlement at Velsen which yielded a find of amber beads in unfinished states as well as unworked lumps; the amber could have been collected locally. Glob 1974 points to a find of over 2 kg of amber in a Bronze Age pot on the shore between Saeby and Frederikshavn (Jutland) as a possible collection for export. See also I. Loze, *Przegl. Arch.* 23 (1975), 49–82 for amber in early contexts in Latvia. There are conflicting views about the original amber trade definitions: see J. Jensen, *Kuml* (1968), 93–100.

13 B. Ottaway, *PPS* 39 (1973), 294–331.

14 Butler and van der Waals 1966; the Exloo grave-group consists of Bell Beaker, flints, amber, copper tanged knife, awl and spiral bracelet, and two sheet gold fragments. The dagger had been hammered from a cast blank, and its metal was a high As (arsenical), moderate Ni (nickel) type. The awl has high Sb (antimony) and Ni, moderate As and Ag (silver) trace elements, which is a metal characteristic of the Early Bronze Age in central Europe.

15 Good summaries of the Low Countries evidence in Butler 1969 and de Laet 1974, ch. 8; see also Stjernquist 1969 for problem-orientated approach.

16 Welinder 1975.

17 H. Hjelmquist, *Meddelanden från*

Lunds Universitets Historiska Museum, 1971–72, 144–50: barley, emmer, einkorn, spelt and rye.

18 S. Welinder, Det förhistoriska kulturlandskapet i Sydvästskåne. *Skånen Naturskyddsförenings Årsskrift* 61 (1974).

19 H. Göransson, *Meddelanden 1972 fron Ostergotlands och Linköpings stads museum*, 1973, 24–50.

20 M. Stromberg, *Meddelanden från Lunds Universitets Historiska Museum*, 1973–4, 101–65.

21 E.g. J. de Jung, *BROB* 20–21 (1970–1), 75–88; A. V. Munaut, *BROB* 17 (1967), 7–27; Brongers and Woltering 1973; A. D. Verlinde, *BROB* 23 (1973), 109–22.

22 H. T. Waterbolk, *BROB* 15–16 (1965–6), 13–35.

23 H. T. Waterbolk, *Helinium* 4 (1964), 97–131.

24 There are comparable settlements known from Drenthe, including Emmerhout, Deventer and Angelsloo; at the last, the houses are as much as 60 m in length: Butler 1969.

25 P. J. R. Modderman, *Berichten van de rijksdienst voor het oudheidkundig bodemonderzoek* 14 (1964), 27–36.

26 W. Groenman-van Waateringe, *Arch. Belgica* 193 (1977), 42–9.

27 Beex and Hulst 1968; R. S. Hulst, *BROB* 23 (1973), 65–76, 103–7.

28 R. S. Hulst, *BROB* 19 (1969), 275.

29 J. A. Jensen, *Kuml* (1972), 114; A. Steensberg, *Den danske bondegård*, 1974, discusses farm buildings of prehistoric date.

30 H. Neumann, *Sønderjysk månedskrift* 51 (1975), 225–6; The substantial house at Norddorf (Amrum) was 10 m long and 4 m wide, but its post-holes are difficult to interpret in terms of a particular structure; Ellmers 1971, 36. In northern Germany, the practice of providing mortuary houses for selected dead suggests that heavy timber-built houses, with shallow porch, were a common form of construction. In areas with much timber, log-cabins would be entirely suitable, and would leave little trace in the ground. The simulated Bronze Age house at Hjerl Hede, Jutland, based upon an excavated plan, suggests that a foundation trench would not have been necessary for such heavy buildings.

31 J. Callmer, *Meddelanden från Lunds Universitets Historiska Museum*, 1971–2, 120–50; M. Strömberg, *Fornvännen*, 1971, 237–54; M. Strömberg, *Acta Archaeologica Lundensia*, 1975.

32 De Laet 1958, 118.

33 Gimbutas 1965, 402–19, defines this, and extends the distribution farther south than we do here; it is not possible to draw distinct boundaries between this and the Únĕtice and its component groups.

34 Rzucewo, on western shore of bay of Gdańsk: L. Kilian, *Haffküstenkultur und Ursprung der Balten*, 1955; Suchacz, east of the Vistula on the bay of Wiślany (Vistula): B. Ehrlich, *Altschlesien* 5 (1936).

35 K. Rajewski, *Archaeology* 11 (1958).

36 A. Gardawski, *Mat. Staroz.* 5, 1959, 7–189; Gimbutas 1965, 409–19.

37 A hoard of four flint and one bronze sickle is known from the Netherlands, and a flint-working area occurred at the Hilversum culture settlement of Vogelenzang: Brongers and Woltering 1973.

38 G. Lerche, *Tools and Tillage* 1 (1968), 56; other ards have dates in the earlier first millennium bc: alder crook ard, Vebbestrup (Jutland), and alder bow ard from Døstrup; Glob 1951.

39 Welinder 1975; fragments of plain-woven woollen fabric are known from Bronze Age Netherlands: Brongers and Woltering 1973.

40 U. Møhl, *Kuml* (1970), 324, dis-

cusses the evidence for seal and whale hunting off the Danish coasts, activities which were carried on from Stone Age to recent times. S. Welinder, *Fornvännen* 68 (1973), 185–93, describes a settlement at Dalkarlstorp (Västmanland) on the edge of a small marsh with open running water which was apparently a seasonal camp for hunting beaver, with skins exchanged for flint 25 km to the south at the agricultural settlements on Lake Mälaren. Debris at Dalkarlstorp included quartzite, quartz and flint tools, much of it fire-cracked, and four hearths, all within an area 5 × 4 m. The importance of this site is its apparent seasonal nature, and the evidence for a regular exchange system in operation over at least 25 km. Inland water resources have recently been surveyed, and the generally undated pit-falls and other trapping procedures can be seen to have been employed by Bronze Age hunters, probably working part-time, L. G. Selinge, Fångstgropar. *Jämtlands vanligaste fornlämningar* 1974, 1–39. For inland waters, see U. Haberg, 13 *Nordiska arkeologmøte i Tromsø* 1970 (1973).

41 U. E. Hagberg, *Kungl. Vitterhets historie och antikvitetsakademien, Monografier* 46 (1967).

42 Meinander 1954; A. Forsten, *Fynskt Museum* 81, 1974 (1977) 56–60.

43 E. Manker, *Fornvännen* 66 (1971), 77–91 discusses Fennoscandian skis; dugouts, H. Nielsen, *Skalk* 6, (1973), describes a dugout from Varpelev (Zealand) dated to *c.* 1050 bc.

44 Many of these trackways are of the later Bronze Age, but some are earlier; see Hayen 1957 for an extensive range of approaches to path-building in northern Ger-

many; wheels, H. Hayen, *Die Kunde* 23 (1972), 62–86.

45 General summaries in Stenberger n.d.; Glob 1974; Butler 1969; de Laet 1974; but variations in grave and mound are considerable.

46 H. Olsson, *Göteborgs arkeologiska museum Årstryck*, 1970, 33–7; see also K. Cullberg, *Fyndrapporter*, 1973, map p. 250.

47 Glasbergen 1954.

48 De Laet 1974, 333.

49 The complexity of some barrow rebuildings is considerable, and the problem of Late Neolithic tradition vs Bronze Age innovations in the N. Brabant-Antwerp area has been interpreted as marking the arrival of Bronze Age immigrants from the British Isles: Butler 1969; de Laet 1974; I. Smith, *Helinium* 1 (1961), 97–118, discusses the Hilversum-Drakenstein urns from the British viewpoint. Re-use of barrows, J. Butler, J. Lanting and J. van der Waals, *Helinium* 12 (1972), 225–41.

50 De Laet 1974; Butler 1969.

51 Driehaus 1969; Schaaff 1969.

52 Lange and Nowothnig 1971,

53 J. Deichmüller, *Die Kunde* 8 (1957), 200.

54 Wegewitz 1967, 48.

55 Wegewitz 1967.

56 K. Kersten, *Offa* 1 (1936), 56; Hachmann 1957; Lomborg 1959.

57 Piesker 1958; K. Kersten, *Offa* 1 (1936), 56; E. Sprockhoff, *PZ* 18 (1927), 21 (1930); Bergmann, *Germania* 30 (1952). The cemeteries of Schleswig-Holstein, however, are more often associated directly with material in the graves of Danish character. The Luneberg local groupings, based upon grave-contexts, are described by F. Laux, *JIVUF* (1974), 22–8.

58 Piesker 1958.

59 Wegewitz 1967, 44.

60 H. J. Eggers, *Historischer Atlas von Pommern*, karte 4, 1963; K. Kersten,

Die ältere Bronzezeit von Pommern, 1958; H. Schubart, *Die Funde der älteren Bronzezeit in Mecklenburg*, 1972; Neugebauer 1968.

61 The amber finds in western Lithuania indicate that preliminary work was carried out on most of the collected lumps, and indeed that amber beads of various basic shapes were produced at source, before distribution to west, south and east.

62 Iwno group: Gimbutas 1965, 407, fig. 258.

63 E.g. Gimbutas 1965, fig. 266.

64 K. Jażdżewski, *Poland*, 1965, 112–113.

65 A. Gardawski, *Wiadomości Archeologiczne* 18 (1951), 1–85.

66 E.g., the settlement of Żalioji, Vilnius, and the burial at Koczek, Waldersee. See Gimbutas 1965, fig. 244 for distributions and 1963, fig. 10 for general spread of related materials eastwards to the Urals.

67 Ellmers 1971.

68 It has been estimated that a normal barrow required the turf from 1–2 ha of land.

69 Suggestions have been made that all of these plough-marks represent ritual disturbance of the soil prior to the burial. For a recent discussion of burials in south Halland, with plough-marks beneath barrows, see L. Lundborg, *Undersökningar av bronsåldershögar och bronsåldersgraver i södra Halland*, 1974.

70 Some large barrows have deliberate flat tops, and other monuments were made by linking two adjacent round barrows with intervening earth or stones, to form a long mound, as at Muldbjerg, Glob 1974, fig. 27; it has been suggested that these may represent places of assembly, the audience or the protagonists positioned on the platform of such barrows.

71 E.g. the Morsum, Isle of Sylt, barrow held thirty-five burials.

72 Cremations of the earliest Bronze Age are not abundant, but a few have been recorded; their dating must depend upon associated surviving grave-goods, Ellmers 1971.

73 Ellmers 1971, 33.

74 Various forms of internal and external stone-settings are known. The 'tarand graves', in which long stone-settings with internal stone divisions into burial chambers, of a character like that seen in Iron Age graves of eastern Baltic shores, have now been shown to be of the Bronze Age in eastern Sweden, although the tradition continues later; A. Bennett, *Fornvännen*, 1975, 59–67. See also A. Hyenstrand, *Nord Svensk Forntid. Skytteanska Samfundets Handlingar* 6 (1975), 123–132.

75 Stenberger n.d., 80.

76 E. Baudou, *Arkiv för norrländdsk hembygdsforskning* 17 (1968), 5–209.

77 The abundant cairns of the west coast of Sweden have recently been suggested to date to both the earlier and the later Bronze Age, in opposition to the traditional view that all are of the late phase, L. Lundborg, *Rapporter över Göteborgs Arkeologiska Musei undersökningar*, 1970, 71–3. South-west Norwegian cairns and barrows are known in abundance (Hagen 1967) including coastal cemeteries such as Vansa (Wagder), Brunlanes (Vestfold) and Tromöy (Aust Agder), and these too are likely to have been constructed throughout the Bronze Age.

78 E. Lomborg, *Kuml* (1963), 14–32.

79 H. Thrane, *Aarbøger* (1967), 27–90.

80 Randsborg 1974; see also K. Randsborg, *Kuml* (1973–4), 207–8.

81 O. Johansen, *Kontakstensil* 10 (1975), 107–20.

82 E. Nylen, *Die Kunde* 25 (1974), 103–10.

83 M. Strömberg, *Die Kunde* 25 (1974), 89–101.

84 Broholm and Hald 1935; short summary, H. Broholm and M. Hald, *Bronze Age Fashion*, 1948, and descriptions repeated in Glob 1974; E. Munksgaard, *Oldtidsdragter*, 1974. Reconstructions in J. Hinning-Almgren, *Tor* (1949–51), 46–50, and L. Eshildsen and E. Lomborg, *Skalk* (1976), n. 5, 18–26. The short skirt is generally interpreted as summer wear, the long dress as winter wear, but the view has also been advanced that the long dress was worn by unmarried women, the short skirt by married women.

85 H. C. Broholm and M. Hald, *Skrydstrupfundet*, 1939.

86 For hair-net, see E. Lomborg, *Aarbøger* (1963), 31–49, and *Skalk* (1964), no. 2; it may be said that hair-nets have been found so consistently that they formed an essential part of Bronze Age coiffure, certainly in death.

87 T. Thomsen, *Egekistefundet fra Egtved, fra den aeldre Bronzealder*, 1929.

88 Glob 1974, 44.

89 Broholm and Hald 1935.

90 Broholm and Hald 1935.

91 Glob 1974; the role of women in Bronze Age society has recently been assessed on the basis of burials, rock art and votive deposits; Louise Cederschiöld, *O forna tiders Kvinnor*, 1975, 77–87.

92 Glob 1974, 114–15.

93 Glob 1974, 114–17.

94 Settlements in the north, where recognized, often have signs of local metalworking, as if small home-based industries had been in operation.

95 Butler 1967; Butler and van der Waals 1966.

96 The problem of connections across the North Sea between Britain and the north European plain has been examined by J. Butler, *Palaeohistoria* 9 (1963), and P. Harbison, *Palaeohistoria* 14 (1970), 175–86. The existence of small 'home-industries' in the Early Bronze Age of the Netherlands is undoubted; J. Butler, *Nieuwe Drentse Volksalmanak* 81 (1963), 181–212. The Voorhout hoard however has eighteen palstaves of British type and must represent some deliberate traffic.

97 Driehaus 1969; Schaaff 1969; Lange and Nowothnig 1971. S. Gollub, *FvfD* 33 (1977), 13–37 and 34 (1977), 13–21.

98 E. Sprockhoff, *Altbronzezeitliches aus Niedersachsen. Studien zur Vor- und Fruhgeschichte*, 1940; Hachmann 1957; J. Bergmann, *Die ältere Bronzezeit Nordwestdeutschlands. Kasseler Beiträge zur Vor- und Frühgeschichte* 2 (1970), provides a corpus of finds and materials. See also G. Sudholz, *Die ältere Bronzezeit zum Niederrhein und Mittelweser. Münstersche Beiträge zur Vorgeschichtsforschung* 1 (1964), for related materials and discussion. G. Jacob-Friesen and H. Aust, *FvfD* 29 (1976), 105–55 for Elbe-Weser area.

99 The Overloon hoard (Limburg) contains characteristic bronzes of the Wohlde group in a western region, Butler 1969, and the Drouwen find contains Sögel dagger and axe, with gold spirals and other bronzes and flints.

100 The halberds from Melz (Röbel) in Mecklenburg represent quite clearly this central European flavour: their shafts of ash and lime have provided dates c. 1800 bc. U. Schoknecht, *Bodendenkmalpflege in Mecklenburg*, 1971, 233–53.

101 E.g. Brzeźno, Starogard; Rościęcino, Kołobrzeg; Redzikowo, Slupsk; see Gimbutas 1965, figs. 261–3, pp. 410, 418.

102 Hachmann 1957; Lomborg 1959; the literature is enormous.

103 E.g. S. Vestergaard Nielsen, *Kuml* (1956), 41–9.

104 C. Carpelan, *Kuml* 1973–74, 286–287; see also Meinander 1954.

105 Hagen 1967; the Vestby (Akershus) sword in a burial cist is a notable exception.

106 Illustrations of the range in Broholm 1952; A. Oldeberg, *Die ältere Metallzeit in Schweden* 1 (1974).

107 A. Oldeberg, *Die ältere Metallzeit in Schweden* 1 (1974) provides an essential catalogue for future work.

108 H. Ottenjann, *Die Nordischen Vollgriffschwerter der älteren und mittleren Bronzezeit*, 1969. For Mecklenburg, U. Schoknecht, *Bodendenkmalpflege in Mecklenburg*, 1972, 45–83. Scabbards: B. Sylvest, *Kuml* (1957) 44–8.

109 E.g. Skogstorf; the shaft-tube battle-axe from Halland is 32.5 cm long and richly decorated; Stenberger n.d. fig. 35.

110 Bracelet with tally marks or identity signatures: H. Thrane, *Skalk* (1964) no. 2, 18–19. Recent survey of Danish prehistoric gold, M. Schou Jørgensen, *Guld fra Nordvestsjaelland*, 1975, 29–110, 220–2.

111 I. and E. Lomborg, *Skalk* (1964) no. 4; Glob 1974, 94–7.

112 C. J. Becker, *Skalk* (1964) no. 1, 10–11; the spearheads are described by G. Jacob-Friesen, *Bronzezeitliche Lanzenspitzen Norddeutschlands und Skandinaviens*, 1967.

113 Glob 1974, 89–92. It was associated with an adult male dressed in cloak and cap, and with leather shoes laid beneath his head; grave goods included a dagger, battle-axe, fibula, six split hazel sticks, and two wooden bowls, decorated with nails of tin in a star-pattern. The folding stool from Guldhoj has been compared with similar seats from the east Mediterranean, but such connections do not seem to us essential for the presence of wooden seats in the north.

114 Widely illustrated, e.g. Broholm 1952; Glob 1974, 102; *Kuml* (1955) for night and day sides of the disc.

115 J. J. Butler and J. A. Bakker, *Helinium* 1 (1961), 193–210; J. J. Butler and H. Sarfatij, *BROB* 20–21 (1970–1), 301–9; Briard 1965, 91.

116 Broholm 1952, 252–3; Stenberger n.d., figs. 35–6.

117 T. Mathiassen, *Aarbøger* 1952; but the style of ship engraving is unlike that elsewhere on the sword.

118 Vast literature: useful summaries in Stenberger n.d.; A. Fredsjo, S. Janson and C.-A. Moberg, *Hällristningar i Sverige*, 1969. More detailed studies, Glob 1969, Burenhult 1973, Marstrander 1963, with important conceptual reviews of the last in *Norw. Archaeol. Review* 3 (1970), 89–112; also A. Wihlborg, *Meddelanden från Jönköpings läns henbygstörbund* 45 (1972), 7–19. Dating: M. P. Malmer, *Kuml* (1970), 206–7; Sprockhoff 1962 provides many illustrations of curvilinear decoration on metal objects, and relates these to rock art engravings. General belief that the rock engravings began as pecked outlines, later ground down evenly, is technically necessary: see E. Johansen, *Wiwar* 2 (1974), 15–17, but the overall dating is complex and problematical. The current view is that the art was practised throughout the Bronze Age and into later periods as well. The few associations with burials include the stone slabs from Jönköping, Småland, decorated with horses and ships.

119 G. Burenhult, *Meddelanden från Lunds Universitets Historiska Museum*, 1971–72, 151–62, investigates the possibility of sailed vessels in the art, and interprets the strokes as timbers holding hay-cargo. The Kalnes (Østfold) ships were the basis for reconstructing Bronze Age boats as skin-covered, a view not universally accepted. If the Nordic later Bronze Age axe found near Brantford, Ontario, Canada, got there in the Bronze Age then our views about boats will need re-thinking: G. Rausing, *Skalk* (1977) no. 1, 9–10.

120 Particularly on the islands of Gotland (Hägvide site), Öland and on coastal mainland sites, both eastern Sweden and western Norway from Rogaland (Åmoy site) northwards to Sogn og Fjordane (Austrheim site) and beyond.

121 Uppland sites, see now E. Kjellén, *Upplands Hällristningar*, 1976: sites include Rickeby and Himmelstalund. Scanian sites include Simris and Jarrestad. Bohuslän sites include a group around Tanum, such as Vitlycke, Litsleby and Aspeberget. Østfold sites include Kalnes. All of these are associated with ships in some way or another.

122 E.g., P. Gelling and H. E. Davidson, *The Chariot of the Sun*, 1969; Glob 1974 *passim*.

123 Not fully published. A small area in the region, near Kville, has been surveyed and a full documentary publication produced: A. Fredsjö, *Hällristningar Svenneby socken*, 1971; *Hällristningar Bottna socken*, 1975. These books demonstrate the potential number of sites that await recognition in other areas. Torsbo lies just outside Svenneby parish.

124 S. Welinder, *Meddelanden från Lunds Universitets Historiska Museum* 1973–4, 244–75, suggests that for Scania, three separate rock art groups can be identified on the basis of geography, content and chronology: 1. ships of the Early Bronze Age, associated with burials. 2. wheels and wagons, also of the Early Bronze Age, associated with burials. 3. footprints, late Bronze Age.

125 P. Simonsen, *Kuml* (1970), 241.

126 G. Hallström, *Monumental Art of Northern Europe from the Stone Age*. 1, *The Norwegian localities*, 1938. 2. *Namforsen and other localities*, 1960. G. Hallström, *Hällristningarna vid Nämforsen*, Svenska Fornminnesplatser 50, 1967.

127 C.-A. Moberg, *Kuml* 1970, 230; A. Hagen, *Studier i Vestnorsk Bergkunst* 1969; E. Bakka, *Arkeologiske Skrifter Historisk Museum Universitet i Bergen* 2 (1975) describes rock carvings geologically dated to a time earlier than a 26 m sea level, here in Nord-Trøndelag of the fourth millennium bc. This would take the dating of some of this art well before anything generally conceived.

128 V. Luho, *Fundamenta monographien zur Urgeschichte* 1.A, 2 (1970), 402–8; recent discoveries, e.g. P. Sarvas and J.-P. Taaritsainen, *Suomen Muinaismuistoyhdistys* 1976, 30–52. Important sites include Vitträsk, Astuvansalmi and Uittamonsalmi.

PART II
Later Bronze Age

7 Central Europe

We have seen in an earlier chapter how the progress of the central European Bronze Age may be traced in separate ways in settlements, burials and artifacts. We saw that settlement evidence is really too scanty for detailed conclusions to be drawn from it concerning the state of the population, and that the artifacts are in a continual state of development. Burial rites, on the other hand, do show a degree of stability in each area, and it is in the burial rites that the change from earlier to later Bronze Age is customarily discerned. By the end of the Únětice period, burial under a barrow was quite common; by the end of the Tumulus period it was, in some areas, pretty nigh universal. At the same time, however, some groups – particularly those in the east – were cremating their dead, putting the ashes in an urn and the urn in a pit. It is with the widespread adoption of this latter rite that we are particularly concerned in this chapter. Over the whole of central Europe, except in certain local areas, the dominant practice was that of cremation, with the subsequent deposition of the cinerary urn in a delimited area or cemetery, traditionally called an 'urnfield'.

When we refer to the Late Bronze Age as the 'Urnfield period', however, we are talking of more than a universal cremation rite. We can include under the same heading a range of bronzes, pottery, settlement-types, and even house-types; more to the point, though harder to distinguish, we can suggest specific ethnic identities for the people responsible for the strictly archaeological evidence listed. It is this last point which, more than anything else, lends the concept of the 'Urnfield culture' some sort of meaning as an entity higher than merely a collection of artifacts.

The later Bronze Age, in the sense in which we employ the term, began around 1300 BC and continued until about 700 BC. Those six centuries – as long as the time-span from the Black Death and Wat Tyler to the present day – were undoubtedly times of change and chance. On the one hand the martial arts must have flourished, to judge by the quantity of offensive weapons, defended hill-top sites, and settlement discontinuity that can be traced. On the other, the arts of peace and progress were in an intensely productive and formative stage. Technological advances include the development of hollow-casting in bronze (using plugs), sheet metal-working with bosses and buckles, new alloys, the invention of new types such as the safety-pin, true glass production, advances in musical instruments, in architecture, in transport, in pottery production. Our main problem is to pinpoint the time and place where each of these major advances took place, for we can normally only proceed by pointing to the first known occurrence of each. Accompanying these purely technical achievements were those of a religious or even scientific nature. Religious symbolism acquired a mature and unified expression: nor were its connections with scientific, possibly astronomical, matters forgotten, for this, we must remember, is the period when Stonehenge had just reached its final form, and even if the date of the final constructional phases precedes our later Bronze Age, one can hardly suppose that the arts which erected it had been so quickly forgotten, or that they were restricted to Britain alone. Yet it is an incontestable, if disappointing, fact that the later Bronze Age in continental Europe has produced no great monuments of grandeur or beauty to lighten the misty dawn in which it lies. Imposing sites there certainly were, with elaborate and intricate defences; holy places there were, though perhaps of a more natural than artificial sanctity; but nothing on the scale of Stonehenge, or Mycenae, or the Mycenaean *tholos* tombs.

In some measure this may be attributed to the uncertainties of the age. The only thing of which we can be sure is that events were on the move, and, no doubt, people with them. Mycenaean civilization came to an end, the Hittite Empire fell, and most Levantine cities suffered at least one major destruction. The role of European tribes in these happenings is unknown, but they could hardly have been unaware of or unaffected by them, and it is certainly possible that they were instrumental in bringing them about. The rise in the numbers of central European sites at precisely the time of the decline of Mycenaean ones has been noted before now, and it is tempting to believe that the two phenomena are directly connected.[1] The idea of a great 'migration of peoples' has often been broached, though never resolved.[2] The hypothesis of a Lausitz migration, or even a Lausitz folk, reaching down to Macedonia has long been considered implausible,[3] but the fact that central European culture was homogeneous continues to suggest a unified racial situation. The problem is complicated, of course, by the fact that when the western part of our area finally emerges into history it is occupied by the Celts and other tribes described by classical historians. It is assumed that these peoples arrived in the area from elsewhere and were not indigenous; the question then arises, when and whence did they come? Detailed treatment of this question is beyond the scope of this book, but it may be remarked that most recent writers have envisaged a proto-Celtic, if not a full Celtic society in later Urnfield times, for it is hardly possible to introduce the Celts suddenly either with the start of iron-working or with that series of graves described as Hallstatt C.[4] Further east, it used to be thought that an 'Illyrian' homeland could be descried; this theory is not now widely accepted, but it is certainly true that a different (non-Celtic?) archaeological grouping was present.[5]

Environment

Pollen analysis contributes to the general picture of Late Bronze Age life, though few diagrams refer specifically to archaeological events within the period. The indications from Poland are that pasture plants, together with weeds accompanying cultivation, reached a peak during the later Bronze Age; during the late Sub-boreal an intense phase of deforestation occurred, causing dramatic drops in the values of hornbeam, lime and hazel, and made manifest by charcoal layers and increasing values for cereals and grasses.[6] This activity is seen in the upland zone no less than the lowland.[7] Of considerable interest is the evidence of increased precipitation in the Carpathians at the start of the sub-Atlantic, as shown by the remains of trees uprooted by floodwater and preserved in alluvial fans,[8] for this compares with evidence from other sources. In general it is believed that the climate was becoming gradually colder, with a particular cold spell occurring from around 850 bc and lasting for more than a century.[9] This picture was obtained, for instance, from the wells at Berlin-Lichterfelde (below, p. 354). There birch increased in frequency throughout the life of well 2 until it accounted for over 70 per cent of all pollen near the top. The appearance of grasses and weeds is irregular, but the contents of the vases thrown into the well are interesting: much pine and birch, but also linden, willow, cereals, grasses, ferns and wild flowers – mugwort, *Umbelliferae*, *Compositae* and several others – perhaps the remains of offerings of plants of various kinds.[10]

Of greater potential value, because datable in archaeological terms, is the evidence from soil profiles, especially in central Europe. Nearly forty years ago Lais showed how soil profiles in the upper Rhine area contained a 'red-weathering phase', attributed to increased dryness and dated in different cases to Eneolithic and Late Bronze Age,[11] and a classic paper by Zeuner, building on this foundation, attributed this and the formation of brown earths and podsols in other areas to a period of increased rainfall following a dry spell – tentatively attributed to the Sub-boreal/Sub-atlantic sequence.[12] Recently this line of evidence has been followed afresh with work on sediments mainly in limestone and karst areas, and on mollusc sequences.[13] A series of profiles, such as in the Pennickental near Jena, provided evidence of interruption in the subaquatic sedimentation, with a temporary replacement by dry-land conditions; part of this profile is archaeologically dated prior to Ha A2 (eleventh century), while a slightly later date is suggested elsewhere. The development of steppe soils in later prehistory has long been a matter for discussion, and the increase in xerothermic land-snails in soil profiles archaeologically dated to the Urnfield period again suggests that increasing dryness may have prevailed in continental Europe as the first millennium progressed, later being replaced by a much wetter spell.

Terminology and relative chronology

We saw in chapter 2 that the chronology of the central European Bronze Age is based on the divisions of Reinecke, and this remains true for the later no less than the earlier Bronze Age, though Reinecke's chronology has been greatly elaborated. For Reinecke, phase D of the *Bronzezeit* referred to the material coming from south Bavarian tumuli containing cremation burials (like Riegsee) – the period when the cremation rite greatly increased in distribution.[14] Immediately following this, but normally sharply distinguished from it, was the first of four phases of the *Hallstattzeit* (A), so named after the material from the great cemetery of Hallstatt. Cremation tumuli occurred now also, but most characteristic was the appearance of urnfields – restricted, according to Reinecke, to the early Hallstatt period.[15] Hallstatt B was then taken as the period of the first appearance of iron swords, starting around 1000 BC, and comprised grave material from tumuli, flat cemeteries and urn cemeteries, as well as pottery from hill-settlements and lake-dwellings.[16] It was subsequently realized that much of this material, in particular the iron objects and the painted pottery, in fact comes rather later than Reinecke at first suggested – some of it actually belongs to his phase C (said to be eighth century in date), some dates to the latest part of B. The most detailed analysis of Urnfield chronology, and the currently accepted modification of Reinecke's scheme, is that of Müller-Karpe, who divides Hallstatt (Ha) A into two parts, and Ha B into three – in effect, therefore, splitting the Urnfield period up into six more or less equal parts (Br D, Ha A1 and 2, Ha B1, 2 and 3). In some areas this scheme works better than in others. Müller-Karpe's own work on the cemetery of Kelheim (lower Bavaria) provides the rationale as far as Bavaria is concerned; elsewhere the individual phases may be hard to distinguish. Ha B2, as defined by Müller-Karpe, is hard to identify in Hesse and western Germany, for instance; the Br D-Ha A1 transition is very blurred in the eastern Alps; while 'Ha A2' in western Bohemia has produced no typical bronzes.[17] In each of these areas a separate system of phasing has been worked out; we present the whole as a table rather than discuss each country individually (table 9).

More recent analyses have distinguished detailed differences between the various phases of the Urnfield period: three phases in Franconia, for instance,[18] four for Hesse, where Ha B2 is very poorly represented, with several local groups (mainly pottery)[19]; and four for north Württemberg, where, similarly, Ha B is divided into only two phases.[20]

Settlement (fig. 119)

While the Urnfield world of central Europe was essentially a homogeneous one, employing everywhere biconical funerary urns for the ashes of the deceased, post-framed houses, and particular types of bronze objects, it is nevertheless possible to distinguish in the broad area covered different local groups homogeneous within themselves but related to the overall pattern in general terms.[27] Much the largest single grouping is the *Lausitz culture*, found in varying forms in Poland, eastern Germany, Czechoslovakia and the western Ukraine, though the name refers to the small upland area of Germany between Dresden and the Neisse where the group was first identified. Numerous local groups and sub-groups have been recognized in this material.[28] To the west, in Germany, come a collection of specific cultural groupings: the *Unstrut* group ('stone-packing graves'); the local representative of the *Nordic* groups – the *Saale mouth* group (stone cists); and the *east Thuringian, Vogtland, Franconia-Palatinate, Rhine-Swiss* and *Lower Main-Swabian* Urnfield groups. In Bohemia are the *Knovíz* and *Milavče* groups; in Moravia and adjacent Austria the *Velatice-Baierdorf* group; in west Slovakia the *Čaka* group; in southern Austria the *Hötting-Morzg* group; in south Slovakia the *Chotín* group; in western Hungary the *Vál* group and in eastern Hungary the *Gáva* group. Similarly, further west still in the middle and upper Rhine basin and neighbouring eastern France the later Bronze Age is marked by the appearance of both urnfields and many settlements along the major river valleys of the Rhine, Main and Moselle. In addition to distinguishing such small local groupings, it is also possible to see wider groups: Bohemia, for instance, was closely related to east Bavaria, eastern France to Württemberg, and a whole collection of small groups on the Middle Danube hang together. To describe each one of these groups in detail would be tedious; we rather try to discern order in the mass of evidence, picking out those elements that seem common to the whole area rather than regional peculiarities.

Attention has normally focused on the burial aspects of the Urnfield groups, but in some areas, settlement studies are well-developed. A very large number of sites is known, and house-plans have been recovered from many. Less work has been done on the examination of settlement patterns, but a notable exception is the case of north-west Bohemia where a pioneer study has made available a detailed picture of settlement in the Knovíz group.[29] Several situations were distinguished in the 158 settlement locations analysed: on river or stream banks (much the commonest), near springs, on lake shores or on hills with natural or artificial defences (cf. below, p. 341). All sites were near water, a pattern that is repeated throughout the Urnfield world and, after all, not really very surprising.[30] Most of the sites were at a medium height above sea-level, between 150 m and 350 m, and the density of occupation is fairly even at around one site per 6 sq km, though the authors express doubt that this represents the true prehistoric picture. In the Rhine-Main basin abundant sites contrast with much sparser evidence for the preceding centuries.[31] Pollen analysis suggests that woodland clearances continued, and that some occupation was extended onto upland areas, but there is no dramatic evidence for sudden widespread clearances near the end of the Sub-boreal,[32] and the settlements themselves indicate more of an infilling, an increase in density, than a major expansion outwards into new topographical areas. In the valley of the Main, occupation occurs along the river itself, beside smaller streams flowing into the river, and on the hills up to 300 m, which reflects the Early Bronze Age preferences insofar as the latter have been recorded. As in Bohemia and most other areas, many of the later Bronze Age sites were fortified with walls and ramparts, and positioned on promontories, on hill-tops, or on islands. Others were placed along river banks, on low terrace-gravels, where defensive outlooks were not considered necessary.[33] In some of these low situations, the cemeteries were placed immediately beside the settlements.[34]

In western Hungary settlements of the earlier Urnfield period have been shown to lie either on ridges surrounded by water (the commonest situation), on hill-tops, or on the banks of the great rivers. The first type is frequent but does not, apparently, include deeply stratified sites which would indicate a lengthy occupation; this role is left to the hill-top sites. Some of these continued in use right through the Urnfield period, whereas the low-lying sites were soon deserted. It is claimed that later

Urnfield settlement lies almost exclusively along the great natural lines of transport, indicating the importance of trade and exchange.[35] Finally, in upper Silesia settlements are most often found on the edge of raised terraces above flood plains or on isolated hills; settlements in the valleys themselves are not common.[36] In the east of the area are found 'zones of colonization', where small amounts of pottery are found scattered over a very wide area, sometimes several kilometres. In some areas very dense groupings of sites occur, as on the Głubczyce plateau; it has been suggested that a group of settlements and one major cemetery would occupy 25–30 sq km.

The picture of Urnfield settlement is, thus, a full one, and as a result it is possible to draw certain conclusions concerning social and economic structure. Some areas with Urnfield occupation had not been settled before, nor were they again to be settled until the Middle Ages: this must imply pressure on land and a high population. On the other hand, the settlement spread is not continuous: there are gaps in some places, on the edges of established groups, which appear to form a kind of 'no-man's land', and can be interpreted as the border zones between different tribes. If this is correct, life in Urnfield times was relatively prosperous; we should envisage a tribal political structure and an agricultural basis for the economy.

Perhaps the most remarkable settlement type to be found in the later Bronze Age of central Europe is the fort or stockade. It is common in English to refer to these as 'hill-forts', but we intentionally avoid this term so as not to give the impression that all forts were on hills. Many were; but on the flat or rolling country of the north European plain many sites were naturally defended or made defensible by other means. We have already seen how in parts of central Europe complicated ramparts could be erected in the earlier part of the Bronze Age; but it was not until the latter part of the Late Bronze Age and the beginning of the Iron Age that fort-building became a major preoccupation and defensive engineering an important industry. It was above all the Lausitz group which made use of forts, but many other groups used them too; the distribution of forts is, then, especially dense in eastern Germany and Poland, with extensions to northern Czechoslovakia, but they occur too in south-central Europe, in Hungary, in Jugoslavia, in Romania (cf. below, pp. 406, 443). Certainly it was in the Lausitz area that the longest sequence and most elaborate developments occurred – in fact a majority of Lausitz forts date to the Early Iron Age; the excellent excavation and analysis of (amongst recent authors) W. Coblenz and J. Herrmann have enabled a detailed comparison to be made between different forts and different areas.[37]

Table 9 Comparative chronological sequences for central Europe, later Bronze Age

Century	Müller-Karpe[21]	S. Bavaria[21]	Hesse[22]	E. Alps[23]	Moravia/Slovakia[24]	Bohemia[25]	Saxony/Lausitz[26]	Montelius
13th	Br D	Riegsee	Wölfersheim	Baierdorf	Pre-Čaka Blučina	Modřany Vrhaveč	'Early' (I)	III
					Čaka Mostkovice	Knoviz-Milavče II	'early Middle' (IIa)	
12th	Ha A1	Hart	Hanau I	Grossmugl Unterradl	Velatice, Očkov	K-M III 'early phase'	'transitional groups (IIab)'	IV
							'late Middle' (IIb)	
11th	Ha A2	Langengeisling	Hanau II	Jurkendorf	Oblekovice 'transitional horizon'	K-M IV 'middle phase'	'early Late' (IIIa)	V
						K-M V 'classic phase'		
10th	Ha B1	Kelheim	Pfeddersheim	Ruše I	Klentnice I	K-M VI 'post-classic phase'	'late Late' (IIIb)	
		Kelheim			Klentnice II			
9th	Ha B2	Kelheim	?	Ruše II	Brno-Obřany I	Štitary-Nynice I	Silesian I	
						II	Silesian II	
8th	Ha B3	Mauern	Wallstadt	Ruše III	Brno-Obřany II Podolí	III	III	
7th	Ha C							VI

342

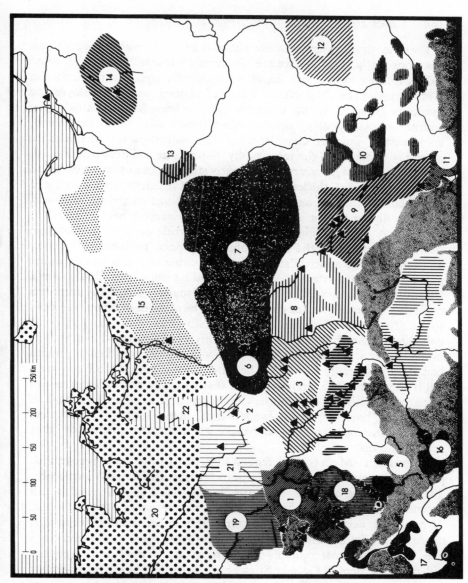

Fig. 119   The distribution of north European Urnfield groups and fortified sites:
1. Saale mouth, 2. Spindlersfeld, 3. Lower Lausitz, 4. Saxo-Lausitz, 5. Vogtland,
6. Aurith, 7. Great Polish, 8. Lower Silesian, 9. Middle Silesian, 10. Upper
Silesian-Little Polish, 11. Głubczyce, 12. Kielce, 13. Kujavian-Chełmo,
14. Warmian-Masurian, 15. Pomeranian, 16. Bohemian, 17. South German,
18. Unstrut, 19. North Harz-Middle Elbe, 20. Nordic, 21. Elbe-Havel, 22. Area
of Urnfield influence.
(After Herrmann 1969)

343

Forts in the Lausitz area are situated in three main topographical positions[38] (fig. 120). There are hill-forts on low hills or knolls, or on ledges formed by moraine deposits – especially common in north-east Germany and the Oder-Neisse valleys; hill-forts on steeper slopes and knolls, or on spurs in hilly country; and low-lying forts in flattish open country or wide valley bottoms, often beside lakes or in marshland, composed of sand or clay 'islands'. The nature of the fortifications naturally depends on the topography. Sometimes a simple palisade was thought sufficient, at any rate in the early stages; more usually a bank and ditch was provided, the length and strength of which depended on the lie of the land. Hill-forts on gentle hills typically had encircling ramparts, those on higher hills or spurs made use of the steep slopes to reduce the amount of construction required and provide sections of rampart (*'Abschnittswälle'*) at the most vulnerable spots. In some cases these sections could be multivallate; they would either cut off a spur or would join up a plateau settlement with its defending slopes (e.g. Pfaffendorf). By contrast, of course, low-lying forts had massive encircling ramparts enclosing a roughly oval or circular area. The amount of labour required to fortify one of these sites was naturally very great, and it is no coincidence that hill-forts which are only partly fortified can enclose much bigger areas than low-lying stockades where every foot of ground had to be artificially fortified. The latter do not exceed 1.8 ha in area, while the former are rarely less than that and may run to some tens of hectares, as with the 35 ha of the Goldkuppe near Seusslitz (Riesa). It is remarkable, however, that in every case the plan is regarded as complete and self-contained, and does not make use of annexes, baileys or other accessory plots.

In the Rhine-Main basin defended sites, being more easily recognized, provided a majority of the observations for later Bronze Age settlement. The positioning of these on naturally protected sites allowed a full defensive system to be obtained with a minimum of artificial slope. Although the necessity for fortification may have been evident for several centuries before the ninth and eighth centuries, most of the excavated sites have yielded material only of the final phases of the Bronze Age; the hill-top settlement of Grosser Stiefel near St Ingbert in the Saarland has tenth-century material,[39] and many others may well be as early or earlier, but excavated examples are mostly later, and contain material of the Iron Age as well. The Knetzberg and the Schwanberg, in the middle Main valley, have occupation dated by radiocarbon to the tenth or ninth centuries.[40]

The natural positions chosen for these settlements include hilltops, promontories and ridges; the hilltops occasionally needed no human

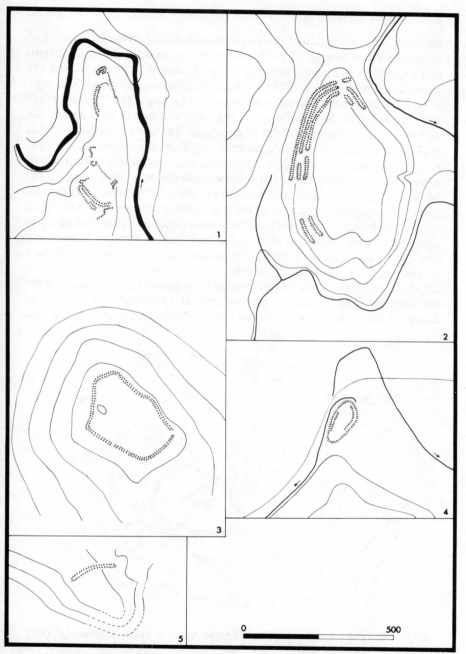

Fig. 120   Plans of Late Lausitz hill-forts (Late Bronze to Early Iron Ages): 1.
Eisenberg near Pöhl, 2. Gühlen-Glienicke, 3. Schafberg near Löbau, 4. Görne,
5. Sörnewitz. Scale in metres.
(After Herrmann 1969)

345

defences to be erected, if the slopes were sufficiently steep, but many had artificial strengthening. The Schwedenschanze, in the valley of the Main, had a 2 m high rampart to complete an enclosure of 260 × 120 m, and the Bleibeskopf fort, near the Rhine-Main confluence, had a wall 3 m wide at its base to help enclose an oval area of 1.4 ha (fig. 121).[41] Promontory sites such as the Schwanberg needed only a rampart to separate the settlement from the remainder of the ridge, but there is nothing in this region to match the Wittnau promontory fort in massiveness (below, p. 429). Occasionally a ridge was selected, and two ramparts built across to provide a central defended area between them; the Vogelsburg, in the Main valley, had an area 400 × 100 m enclosed in this way.[42] Although there are many defended sites in the region, established on high terraces, ridges and hilltops, very few have been excavated, and their dating relies upon surface collections of sherds; the distinctions between Bronze and Iron Age wares may well not be precise enough to allow separation, and in any case the association between defences and internal occupation debris is uncertain. Only in cases where undisputed Bronze Age material has been found in abundance and without later additions, such as on the dozen or so settlements in the upland valleys of Baden-Württemberg, can

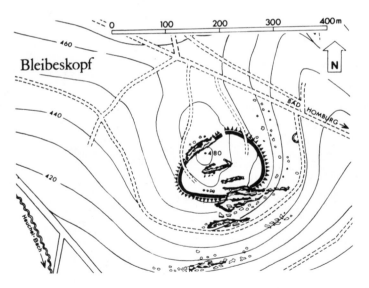

Fig. 121   Plan of the defended Late Bronze Age fort at the Bleibeskopf (Bad Homburg) on the flank of the Taunus hills. There is a single entrance to the north facing the promontory.
(After D. Baatz, *Führer* ... 21 (1972), 150)

we assume establishment of the defences in the ninth and eighth centuries.[43]

The actual techniques of rampart construction vary with topography and with time.[44] The normal type in the Lausitz group is the *plank and palisade shell type* (fig. 122, 1–2), in which two plank walls were erected some 2–3 m apart, with anchoring beams joining front and rear, and space in between being filled with earth and rubble. This type could take various forms: at Senftenberg, for instance, an outer wall of vertical planks was joined to two inner palisade walls providing walkways at two levels; at Podrosche the planks were fitted horizontally between pairs of upright posts. Closely comparable, but restricted to upland areas with abundant stone, is the *dry stone shell type* (fig. 122, 5), where two stone walls were similarly tied in with anchoring beams, as at the Schafberg near Löbau. Perhaps earlier than these is the *grid type* (*Rostbauweise*) (fig. 122, 4), in which parallel rows of timbers were laid in consecutive layers, one layer being laid along the axis of the rampart, the next at right-angles to it, the interstices being filled with wood chips, earth and stone, and the whole being finished off with a capping plank wall at Podrosche. The most famous example of this type of construction is at Nieder-Neundorf

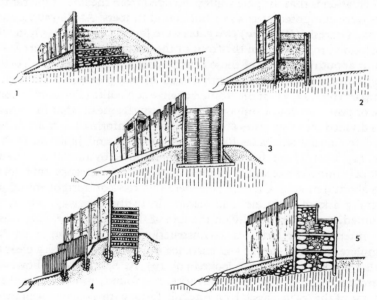

Fig. 122 Diagrammatic reconstructions of Lausitz fortifications: 1–2. plank and palisade types, 3. box type, 4. grid type, 5, dry stone wall type.
(After Coblenz 1974)

(Niesky), where a substantial quantity of the lowest layer, apparently set in a clay bedding socle, was found in excavation. The latest type, probably exclusively of Ha C and later dates, is the *box-type* (*Kastenbauweise*) (fig. 122, 3), in which a series of wooden 'boxes' was constructed (i.e. continuous wooden frames) and filled with rubble. This is the type which became popular at, for instance, Biskupin and other Polish sites. The boxes were built up from rows of timbers laid at right angles to each other and mortised in, the exterior being coated with clay to prevent firing and the interior being supported by massive revetting timbers. Though the upper levels were not preserved at the Polish stockade of Biskupin they were no doubt finished off with a crenellation and protected walkway, the whole being 5–6 m high. Outside the stockade was a series of wooden posts inserted into the ground at an angle of about 45° pointing towards the fort, eight or nine to the square metre (thus 35,000 around the whole site); this is thought to have served as a breakwater, but would have done duty equally well for repelling attackers.

Gateways in Lausitz forts are not generally well-known.[45] At Nieder-Neundorf (fig. 123, 6) Coblenz found evidence of a funnel-like construction, though all that can really be said from the published information is that the gate walls protruded from the line of the rampart, and were composed of rows of horizontal timbers. At Zawada Lanckorońska (Brzesko, Tarnów) two gates were found (fig. 123, 4–5), in which a palisade projected from the front of the rampart, though there is some doubt about the dating of these constructions. At Kamieniec (Toruń) a long entrance-way framed with a wall of oak planks led through the rampart (fig. 123, 3); at the Römerschanze at Nedlitz (Potsdam) a central line of posts, no doubt supporting a gate-tower, meant that the entrance was divided into two aisles (fig. 123, 7). Most information is available on the late Lausitz stockades like Biskupin (Żnin) and Jankowo (Pakość) (fig. 123, 1–2). There the rampart was interrupted by a street of horizontal parallel timbers, averaging about 3 m wide; the entrance thus formed was about 9 m long. On each side were two rows of upright round posts forming a kind of funnel and leading in to the doorway, which, it is assumed, would be actually on the line of the rampart, i.e. very close to the interior. The brilliant reconstruction of the Biskupin gateway, complete with gate-tower and entrance causeway, makes very clear how such a stockade must have looked (pl. 19). At Senftenberg, however, a completely different style of entrance was found, much more like the scheme of things in classic Iron Age hill-forts, with a curtain wall thrown out to protect a narrow passage running longitudinally along the middle of the rampart (fig. 124). It is interesting that in the later phase of this site this arrangement was dispensed with.

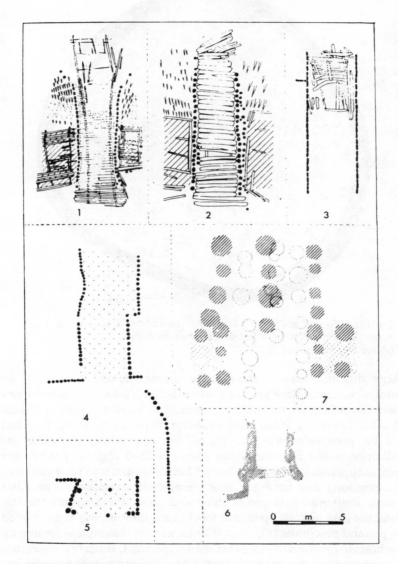

Fig. 123 Gateways in Lausitz forts: 1. Jankowo, 2. Biskupin,
3. Kamieniec, 4–5. Zawada Lanckorońska (west and east), 6. Nieder-
Neundorf, 7. Nedlitz.
(After Ostoja-Zagórski, *Slavia Antiqua* 20 (1973))

349

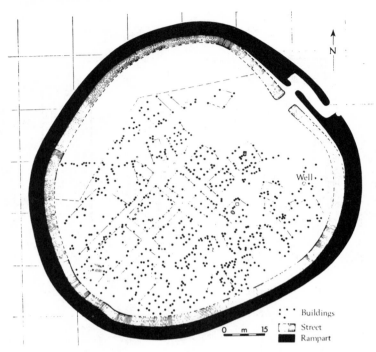

Fig. 124   Plan of the fortified Lausitz stockade of Senftenberg, first phase. Billendorf phase of Lausitz, seventh century. (After Herrmann 1969)

After this discussion of the external appearance of Lausitz forts we must devote a little time to asking what their purpose was. Here no one answer can suffice. On the one hand some sites, notably the late stockades and other low-lying forts, have evidence of intensive occupation and must be permanent dwelling-places. On the other, sites like the Goldkuppe or the Eisenberg near Pöhl (Plauen) (fig. 125) have only scanty occupation traces. None has yet been shown not to have *any* trace of occupation; few have yet been completely examined. The Altes Schloss, Senftenberg, is one of those that have: the area immediately behind the gate was left open, but most of the interior was densely filled with pits and post-holes (fig. 124). The excavators' attempts at joining up these holes to form structural plans are not, perhaps, entirely convincing, but one must agree that the evidence for total occupation is overwhelming. Further evidence for the ordinary domestic use of these sites comes from agricultural and industrial activity in the form of smelting hearths, quernstones and so on.

Fig. 125   Reconstruction of the Lausitz hill-fort of Eisenberg near Pöhl (Plauen, Saxony).
(After Coblenz 1972)

On the other hand some sites are clearly placed where they are for strategic purposes. The selection of naturally defensible sites and the erection of ramparts speaks, of course, not only for skilful engineering but also for troubled times, that such defences should be necessary at all. Some areas had an intense concentration of sites; in other cases a fort or series of forts was clearly placed with the intention of guarding a pass or river valley – as in the upper Elbe valley or several other major river valleys. It is not possible to ascribe a single reason for the existence of many diverse sites; the rise of forts is rather to be seen as the fashion of the age, and the standard practice in many areas of Europe. Quite different reasons in different areas are likely for their foundation; some, where the fortifications are scanty and evidence for settlement negligible, have even been regarded as cultic in purpose (p. 368).

It has been argued for Biskupin that the likely population figure would be around 700–1,000 (based on a figure of between 13 and 18 sq m per person).[46] Taking 15 sq m per person as an average, most of the smaller forts would hold between 500 and 1,000 people, the larger ones – if intensively occupied – many thousands. That such a straight correlation between size and population numbers is unrealistic, however, is shown by the Goldkuppe near Seusslitz, which would theoretically hold more than 23,000 people! It goes without saying that such a figure is at variance with other evidence and most unlikely to be right. That large numbers were needed to construct the forts at all is shown by the Biskupin calculations, where it was suggested that 50,000 to 80,000 man-days were required for its erection – that is, half the potential population for five months.[47]

We have seen that some of these hill-sites and forts were actively settled, and this raises the question of house-types. In fact most of the well-studied settlements were open sites in low-lying situations, after the lines of the analyses presented above; and it is to these that we turn first. Over such a vast stretch of land it would not be surprising to find a great variety of house-types, but they are in fact remarkably homogeneous as a group. The lack of research in the past has meant that little attention has been paid to this aspect, but recent excavations have revealed a large number of house-plans. One of the most extensive sites is that of Lovčičky (Vyškov) in south Moravia, extending over 3 to 4 ha; by 1972 more than 1 ha had been excavated and forty-four houses found, the majority belonging to the Velatice group (fig. 126).[48] These the excavator has divided into four groups, those with the posts well-separated, those with the posts close together, those with both systems, and a single example with foundation trench on three sides and the fourth left open. The first group was made by mortising horizontal tie-beams into the vertical posts and filling in the spaces between with daub (remains of which showing post and beam impressions were found). The second group is thought to have had a light wall of wattle-and-daub pressed against the framing posts. The actual house forms are all square or rectangular, but show considerable variation in detail – different positioning of doors, hearths, internal posts etc. In some cases a central row of posts indicates a ridge-roof, in others these are lacking but a ridge construction is likely all the same, the horizontals of the roof-triangle resting on the walls as in modern houses. Most of the houses were simple one-roomed affairs a few metres either way, but three houses have an additional room in megaron style, and one (E) is described as a 'hall'. It is unusually long and contains not only internal posts on the long axes but also transverse divisions, with a central door on one of the long sides. Parts of comparable buildings, which can be interpreted as chieftains' houses (chemical analysis did not support the idea that these were byres at Lovčičky), have been found in several other parts of the Urnfield world, though the details vary considerably. Houses G, H and J were arranged beside one another so as to enclose a courtyard, a feature which clearly recalls the later houses at Buchau (below, p. 354).

Another recent find is that of an Urnfield settlement under the Roman fort at Künzing (Deggendorf) on the Danube in lower Bavaria.[49] Parts of ten separate houses were recovered, the complete ones varying between about 5 and 8 m in length and 5 and 3 in width – mostly rectangular, but

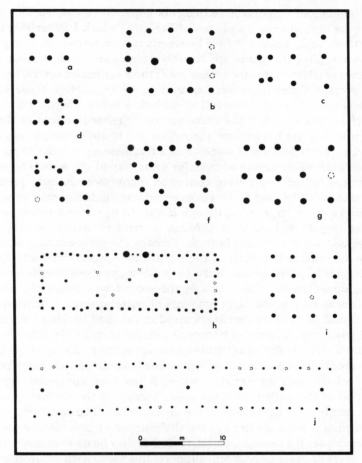

Fig. 126   Houseplans from Urnfield sites: a, b, d, e, g, h, i, j,
Lovčičky (Vyškov); c, f, Pécsvárad-Aranyhegy (Pécs).
(After Říhovský 1972, Dombay 1958)

approaching square in one instance. Only one of these houses has a central
row of post-holes, and this same house appears to have double posts –
perhaps for functional purposes, perhaps only the result of rebuilding.
The reconstruction of walls and roof by Zippelius at this site is similar to
that adopted by Říhovský at Lovčičky. At Künzing there was clearly a
sizeable settlement, but, as with many of the recently discovered Urnfield
houses in Germany, it was found by chance in the excavation of a later
site, so that the full extent of the Urnfield settlement has not been
investigated.

A number of important settlements come from eastern Germany. There are several sites in and around Berlin, of which Lichterfelde is the most thoroughly known.[50] Five house-plans were recovered, along with numerous pits; the plans are roughly rectangular and without clear evidence of central posts for a ridge-roof; three contained central hearths. The average dimensions were around 10 × 8 m, though these varied considerably. The pits were full of rubbish – bones, sherds, and burnt material – and some had the characteristic bell shape noticed in Knovíz pits (below, p. 358). A granite quernstone was found in the corner of one house, supported by small stones, and a fragmentary grinder to go with it; a cylindrical stone-walled oven lay some way to the west. The whole settlement, which must have contained many more houses, probably extended over 3 ha, and there was an encircling ditch that may once have enclosed a much larger area, though it was cut by rubbish pits in several places; the ditch itself cuts through a mass of stones, which, it is suggested, was a working platform. Perhaps the most exciting finds are two wells outside the ditch to the north-east – wood-lined and full of stones, sherds, plant remains and other rubbish; medieval sherds occurred in the upper layers. The depth of the second well below the ground surface was 1.55 m and large amounts of pottery, some of it complete, were found in it; other sherds occurred in the sand backing behind the wood (fig. 127). A complex history of use and re-use followed, with the deposition of cult offerings (small vessels) apparently playing a significant role; since their deposition may be presumed to post-date the main period of use of the well for drawing water, it has been suggested that the desertion of the settlement came about because of the drying-up of the wells, that is, a fall in the level of the groundwater. The vessels thrown in would then represent offerings for the purpose of propitiating the god responsible for the drought, and the fact that they lie more or less in rows, with layers of grass in between, supports this view. Rich environmental evidence was also recovered (above, p. 337). Another fully excavated site is at Perleberg, where sixteen rectangular houses, including two with entrance porch, were found.[51]

Perhaps the best-known Urnfield settlement in the southern area is the fortified island site (*Wasserburg*) in the Federsee near Buchau (Biberach) in Württemberg.[52] The island, 90 × 80 m, was protected by several outer palisades of pine poles, with several entrances defended by wooden towers. Bridges connected the palisades with the wooden and stone-paved edge of the island settlement. Two phases of occupation were recognized by the excavators, although these probably mask many episodes of rebuilding. The earlier settlement consisted of thirty-seven one-roomed houses, about 4 × 4 m; a single example was of a larger megaron type and

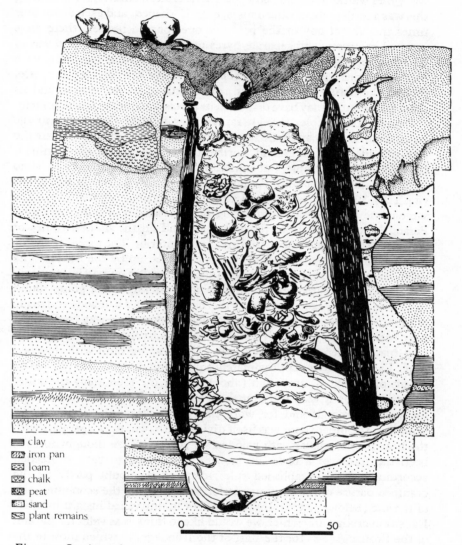

	clay
	iron pan
	loam
	chalk
	peat
	sand
	plant remains

0   50

Fig. 127 Section of a well from the Late Bronze Age settlement at Berlin-Lichterfelde.
(After von Müller 1964)

is assumed to have been a chieftain's house. The method of construction was either wattle-and-daub on a post frame or horizontal logs. Succeeding this was a settlement of nine houses, each U-shaped, and each about four times the size of any of the previous one-roomed houses; there were internal partitions and separate byres nearby. Again, one house was of double size, with six rooms. These later houses were log-built, with plastered inner walls. The site is believed to have been destroyed by fire, though the nature of its position, the length of its occupation and its subsequent burial may have disguised its precise manner of abandonment.

Closely comparable, though rather later in date (belonging to the Lausitz culture, but attributed to its Iron Age phase, Ha C and D) are the lake-side sites of Great Poland, north-east of Poznań. Biskupin (Żnin) is the best-known example, but similar or larger sites are found – Izdebno (Żnin), Jankowo (Pakość), Komorowo (Szamotuły), Sobiejuchy (Żnin) (fig. 128). Biskupin itself lies on a peninsula jutting into the lake of the same name in the gently undulating sandy lowlands of northern Great Poland,[53] in a strongly fortified position and on the natural routes of commerce from the Baltic coastal area to the interior. The fortress extends over 1.3 ha, rather over half of that being taken up by the houses. The defences we have already described (above, p. 348); on passing through the gateway one came immediately to an encircling street going round the whole interior except at the northern end. It was 2.9 m wide and made of squared oak beams resting on a wooden support; one-way traffic must have been the rule (pl. 18). Twelve straight transverse streets ran off this ring-road, bordered by thirteen rows of houses, log-built with thatched roofs. Each house was approximately square and divided into two parts; details of threshold, anteroom (about 0.25 of the total area) and inner room are virtually identical over the whole site. The anteroom was used for stalling animals and for work like wood-chopping, grinding and skinning; the inner room was itself divided into two, the larger part with the hearth, the smaller with wooden supports that are thought to have been the frame of a bed. Life at Biskupin seems to have proceeded according to well-established rules, dictated no doubt partly by the cramped nature of the accommodation and partly by the economic basis of the site (below, p. 377). Biskupin offers an unrivalled insight into late Lausitz everyday life, which we would like to think is as valid for the end of the Bronze Age as for the start of the Iron Age, to which most of the material recovered belongs.

In Hungary house-plans are not commonly found in the Urnfield settlements and forts. The most extensive series comes from Pécsvárad-Aranyhegy, where Dombay found a considerable number of post-framed houses belonging to both earlier and later Hallstatt periods, and to the

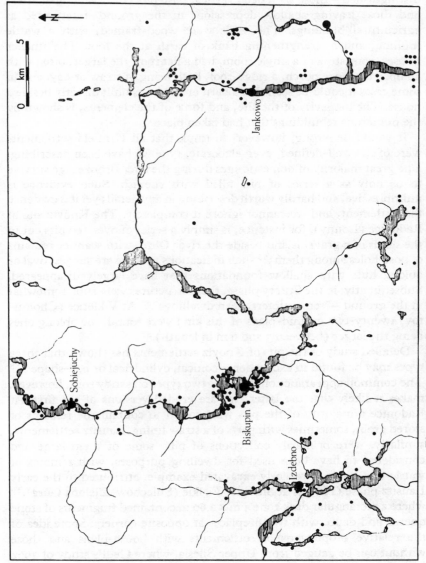

Fig. 128 Map of the Biskupin-Jankowo area showing Lausitz sites.
(After Ostoja-Zagórski 1974)

early Iron Age (fig. 126).[54] Numerous pits were found, in and around square or irregularly quadrangular post-structures. Two main types were distinguished – those with deep vertical post-pits (the dwelling-houses) and those leaving shallow depressions in the ground, interpreted as agricultural buildings. The walls were wood-framed, with a wattle infilling, and a strengthening bank of earth at the foot. The smaller houses, consisting of a single room, had a flat roof, the larger, often with an open entrance porch, a ridge-roof, both being of straw or hay, and in some cases it could be seen that a barn or shed was built directly beside a house. The longevity of the site, and force of the elements, is shown by the numerous rebuildings that had taken place.

It would be wrong, however, to think that all Urnfield settlements were of the well-defined, even elaborate, type we have been describing. The great majority of domestic sites during the later Bronze Age survive to us only as a series of pits filled with rubbish. Such evidence is unimpressive, and hardly worth describing in any detail; yet it *is* evidence for settlement, and we cannot ignore it completely. The Knovíz site at Radonice (Louny), for instance, is simply a series of over 100 pits cut in the sands of a gravel island beside the river Ohře, with scantier remains of post-holes among them;[55] such indications as there are suggest oval or oblong huts with shallow foundations that have largely disappeared. Subsequently, in the Štítary phase, these structures were sunk somewhat in the ground – 'semi-subterranean dwellings'.[56] At Vikletice (Chomutov) twenty-two ground-plans of this kind were found, the oblong ones being the larger (between 3 and 6 m in length).[57]

Detailed study of the pits of Knovíz settlements has shown that three types may be found in excavation – conical, cylindrical or bell-shaped.[58] The common appearance of the latter two types on sandy soils, however, makes it likely that the latter two are eroded versions of the first. At Radonice a majority of the pits were found to contain the remains of stored grain, sometimes with parts of a straw lining. Lausitz settlements, similarly, were primarily collections of pits, some of them large and considered to have been used for dwelling purposes, with remains of wattle-and-daub. A recently excavated example, attributed to the early Lausitz phase (III), is at Smolno Wielkie (Sulechów, Zielona Góra),[59] where a rectangular dark zone 4 m × 2.60 m contained fragments of stone querns and daub, with two fireplaces at opposite corners. Some idea of the relative proportions of settlements with house-plans and those without can be gauged from Upper Silesia, where Gedl's study of 1962 includes 116 habitation sites, of which thirty had been systematically excavated, and only nine had remains of post-framed huts, all dating to the latter part of the Lausitz period.[60]

Urnfield settlements no doubt *did* all contain houses, and probably they were mostly of the post-framed type we have described. It seems most likely that two separate settlement areas can be distinguished: one for habitation, and one for grain-storage and rubbish-disposal. The latter is much more readily recognized in rescue-excavation than the former, which is why there seem to be so many settlements without houses.[61]

Burials

We have already mentioned that during the later Bronze Age the standard method of disposing of the dead was that of cremation, the ashes being deposited in an urn and the urn in a pit in the ground. So ubiquitous was this practice that our discussion of burials will be brief. Cremation was very common throughout central Europe in this period, but it was by no means universal, and in some areas inhumation was the commoner. As a general rule of thumb, however, it remains true to see this period as one dominated by the spread of the cremation rite, earliest in the central area, and reaching out towards the oceans rather later; few places were immune from the new rite by the end of the period. The change of rite must have been a sufficiently radical step for a major shift in attitudes to have been necessary. We may compare the reaction which took place in Britain to the reintroduction of cremation in the late nineteenth century; beliefs, especially religious or ritual beliefs, die hard.[62] The very fact of the widespread adoption of the cremation rite in the central European Bronze Age has been taken as one of the most significant pointers to a change in population in some areas.

Cremation was the dominant rite, but the actual method of disposing of the ashes varied considerably (fig. 129). The commonest method, putting them in more or less randomly disposed pits in an 'urnfield', by no means accounts for all the variations. For a start, urns were sometimes used and sometimes not. A setting of stones was sometimes built around the urn. Quite often urns were inserted into a barrow, or put in a pit and a barrow heaped up over them. To these elaborations we shall return: first let us look a little more closely at the most common practices.

Much the most information is available from the northern Urnfield branch – the Lausitz area. Huge numbers of cemeteries, many containing hundreds of graves, occur on the north European plain, and the literature of the countries concerned – especially Poland – is densely packed with excavation reports and analyses of Lausitz cemeteries. Synthesizing accounts of Lausitz funerary practices have been provided by Coblenz and Malinowski.[63] In Poland, 2,832 cemeteries were analysed, and the main types of grave distinguished: tumuli, 'stone border graves', and

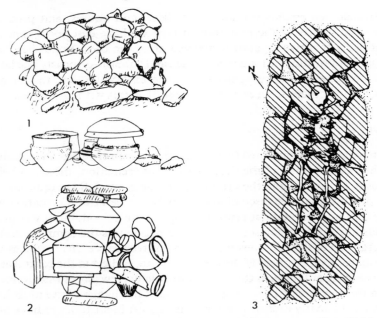

Fig. 129 Types of Urnfield burial: 1–2. Saxony, 3. Grundfeld, Franconia, 1–2. cremation, 3. inhumation; all with stone settings. (After Grünberg 1943, Radunz 1966)

deposition of ashes in a pit, with or without an urn. Inhumations occur sometimes, though they are restricted to certain areas at certain times; 'biritual' cemeteries are also found. Of considerable interest are the tumulus burials, to which we return, for these provide a link with the preceding period – indeed in some areas Lausitz burials continue in unbroken sequence from period II, when they were quite frequently under barrows (cf. above, p. 57).

The choice of sites is truly vast, but selecting some representative examples we may mention as typical cremation cemeteries Kosin (Kraśnik, Lublin),[64] where there were some 400 graves, all cremations, and the overwhelming majority of those in urns; Malá Bělá (Mladá Boleslav) with 181 cremations;[65] Třebušice (Most) of the Knovíz group with fifty cremations to four inhumations in the excavated part, with stone settings appearing quite often;[66] thirty-four cremations, twenty-six of them with urns, and most having stone settings, at Grosseutersdorf (Jena);[67] the list would be endless. More specific cremation types include such forms as the stone cists of the Saale mouth group, where the burial urns were themselves placed inside cists; the 'bell-graves' of the middle

Elbe, where a second large urn was inverted over the first;[68] 'house-urns' or their substitutes as in the cemeteries of Vollmarshausen (Kassel) or Diebzig (Köthen), and their associated ritual;[69] pyre-graves; and so on. Even in Hungary and Jugoslavia (below, p. 444) the cremation rite was dominant, as large cemeteries like Csabrendek and Gáva show, the cremations being put, as elsewhere, in stone settings or cairns.[70]

But there are plenty of exceptions to such general rules. One of the largest and most thoroughly published Lausitz cemeteries is at Przeczyce (Zawiercie) in Lower Silesia.[71] 874 burials were discovered in rescue excavations, of which 727 were inhumations, 132 cremations, one mixed, and fourteen uncertain. The grave-goods indicated a date late in the Bronze Age (period V). The inhumations were invariably oriented north-south and placed in irregular rectangular or oval pits, sometimes covered over with stones or a wooden construction. The body lay on its back, head to the south, usually alone and often without grave-goods. The cremations were usually placed in simple pits rather than urns, and were, according to the grave-goods found with them, contemporary with the inhumations. Flat inhumation cemeteries were common in other areas, though they do not necessarily outnumber cremations. Chief among these is the Knovíz group.[72] An especial feature of the burials was their apparently casual nature: most are simply deposited in rubbish pits, and only some 10 per cent were laid in specially prepared graves. Regular inhumation cemeteries are thus not found. In parts of eastern Germany, on the other hand, cemeteries of inhumations are the rule: in the Unstrut group around Halle in particular the standard burial form was the 'stone packing grave', a rectangular pavement of stones, on which the skeleton is laid, commonly measuring 3×1–1.5 m.[73] Over the skeletons was erected a stone cover, often enclosing a cist-like construction that actually protected the body. An example at Hedersleben (Eisleben) was even divided into three internal compartments, presumably for multiple burial.[74] In various other parts one may find biritual cemeteries, as for instance in upper Franconia at Grundfeld (Staffelstein), where stone settings enclosed both cremations and inhumations (fig. 129, 5–7).[75]

A special case is the extraordinary group of burials from the Velatice levels of the ditch at Cezavy near Blučina (Brno-venkov). Here the scattered and battered skeletal remains of some 205 individuals were recognized, in various positions and with a variety of grave-goods.[76] Some were deposited intentionally and carefully, others casually; the bones were not damaged by injury in life, but their deposition and occurrence along with animal bones suggest unusual practices such as cannibalism. Only one grave, no. 132, had a true grave-pit, and this was also the richest grave on the site. It is hard to avoid the conclusion that this was no ordinary cemetery but the result of special circumstances –

not, according to the excavator, a war-cemetery but some ritual deposition. Cannibalism has also been suggested at sites in Bohemia and elsewhere.[77]

Much fewer in number than burial in urns and stone settings are tumulus burials, but they do nevertheless constitute an important type and are found quite widely. In Slovakia, for instance, Lausitz burials under tumuli are not uncommon in the earlier phases – at Trenčianské Teplice (Trenčín) the grave-goods indicated a date of Br D (fig. 130).[78] Most of the Slovak tumuli have a ring of stones retaining an earth mound, though a few have earth only or a double stone covering. The diameter varies between 2 and 10 m, most falling between 4 and 8 m – that is, rather small. Most contained a single urn, more rarely two; these were commonly standing on or covered with flat stones, or encircled by a small ring of stones. The cremation process had in at least some cases taken place on the spot. Of some interest is the adjacent presence of ordinary flat graves, much poorer in grave-goods, suggesting a marked degree of social differentiation. In Bohemia one can find comparable things, as for instance at the cemetery of Mladá Boleslav-Čejetičky, Choboty I.[79] This cemetery consists of more than sixty-three tumuli, belonging to the

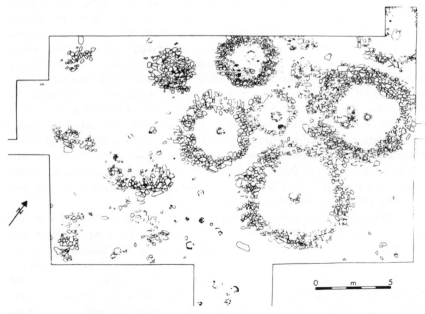

Fig. 130   Plan of early Lausitz barrows at Trenčianské Teplice (Trenčín). (After Pivovarová 1965)

Únětice, Tumulus, Lausitz and Hallstatt periods, with the graves of a flat cemetery scattered in between. Many of the Lausitz mounds had stone encircling walls with a central stone setting or else a complete stone covering; Plesl has been able to make chronological distinctions between the various types of construction. Other Lausitz tumuli may be mentioned from Saxony, such as Sachsendorf (Grimma) or examples from some thirty other sites, though it must be mentioned that these finds are strictly localized.[80] It is worth recording here that although tumulus burials were by no means infrequent in the Urnfield groups, we believe Gimbutas to be mistaken in attributing a much wider currency to the form in antiquity. Her contention that many 'Urnfield' tumuli have simply been ploughed out since the Bronze Age takes no account of the differential distribution of the mounds through central Europe, or of the really colossal numbers of graves that may appear on one site. On most ordinary 'urnfields' it is quite impossible that anything more than small stone covers were used.

In some areas tumuli were used to cover burials of more-than-ordinary elaborateness and splendour. Chief among these is the series of very large mounds in south-west Slovakia and adjacent areas attributed to the Čaka and Velatice groups. At the eponymous site of Čaka (Levice) a large tumulus covered a series of graves, some stratigraphically later than others.[81] The central grave chamber with timber construction was apparently of Tumulus Bronze Age date, while the most famous grave (which produced many fragments of a sheet bronze corslet) was in a large rectangular pit 4 × 2.5 m at the south-eastern side, with a niche in one side to contain the armour (fig. 131). Other rich graves were found on the perimeter of the same mound, with heaps of burnt material that suggested the remains of a pyre to the excavators, kindled *in situ* on a prepared area just outside the main tumulus. At Kolta (Nové Zámky) a central grave-pit, robbed in antiquity, was initially covered with a small mound which had been flattened off and used for further burning processes at one point in its construction.[82] Clearly visible in the section of the mound were the remains of inclined layers of material representing the successive phases of construction and indicating a total height of 5.5 m for the first mound. Under each of the capping layers was found a cremation (interpreted as a sacrificial burial); under the latest, which brought the height up to 14 m and the diameter to nearly 50 m, were two richly furnished graves of the Čaka group. A ditch surrounded the whole. The rich cremations appeared simply as discolorations of the soil, with piles of sherds and ashes – in other words, the remains were laid on the surface and covered over. Other recently excavated mounds are at Lužany (Topolčany)[83] and Dedinka (Nové Zámky),[84] also with central and secondary pits, large

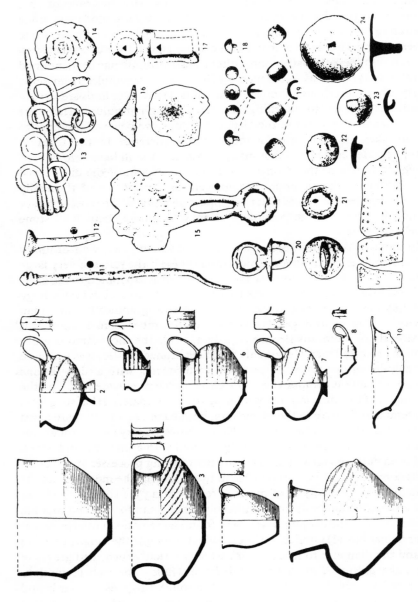

Fig. 131   Finds from the rich tumulus burial of Čaka (Levice). Left, pottery; right, bronzes. Thirteenth century BC. (After Točík and Vladár 1971)

mounds, remains of funeral pyres, and rich bronzes and pottery. On the other hand a barrow apparently of this type at Palaríkovo (Nové Zámky) contained no burial.[85]

Another well-known site of this Slovakian group, though closer in its finds to the Moravian-Austrian group, is Očkov (Trenčín), rather to the north of those described so far. The essential features may be described briefly, but for full details Paulík's invaluable account is recommended.[86] Right round the outside ran a circular stone retaining wall, 25 m in diameter, mostly of limestone blocks whose nearest occurrence is some 2 km away. Upon removal of the upper layers of the mound material an inner ring of stones was found 17 m in diameter and about 2.5 m wide: the stones had been put in place in at least two and probably three layers separated by earth. In the centre was a large deep pit, which had been dug down through a thin layer of burnt material that originally extended over an area 10 m in diameter. This layer contained charcoal and pottery and bronze fragments showing signs of damage by intense heat, and so it is interpreted as the remains of the funeral pyre. The central pit or grave chamber was about 3 m deep and measured about 5 × 4 m, with a wooden lining round its lowest part; this pit was full of debris from the burnt layer and stones which had collapsed in from the capping. In the floor of this 'grave chamber' was a smaller rectangular pit 2 m deep, 2.5 m long and 1.5 m wide, containing only a small amount of debris from upper levels and no intentionally placed goods; its purpose is not known, but Paulík has remarked that it is not too small to contain an inhumation burial. Whether or not this was so, the fact of elaborate pit-burial in a large mound certainly suggests a continuation of practices from an earlier period.

Rich cremation burials of early Urnfield date under or in barrows occur elsewhere in the same area and to the west in Moravia and Austria.[87] Comparable tumuli are also found in Hungary (e.g. Hövej, Zirc-Alsömajor, Bakonyszucs-szászhalom etc.) where a considerable variety of local types of construction is represented. One may further compare the rich tumuli of Bohemia in the Milavče group – in this case perhaps the richest in the series of tumuli from the region.[88] In the case of the Slovakian tumuli Paulík has stressed that they stand out from the run of burials by their size, the richness of their central graves, their placement away from the burials of the rest of the population and on the fringes of a given culture area, and their apparent similarity to the funeral monument described by Homer as having been erected for Patroclus. We can hardly doubt that we are here dealing with the special burials of a special class of people, and the warlike apparatus that is found (armour, weapons etc.) indicates that these were warriors and chiefs.

Rich burials occur not only under tumuli but also in the ordinary urn and pit burials of the great mass of urnfield cemeteries. Most Lausitz burials were accompanied by up to three pots and the odd bronze, but occasionally these numbers can be greatly augmented. A grave at Liegau-Augustusbad (Dresden-Land), for instance, contained the remains of twenty-three vessels including a single urn, glass beads and rings, bronze rings, a bronze sickle, spirals, and two pins.[89] The cist of an old man at Acholshausen (Schweinfurt) in the middle Main valley contained not only thirty-eight pottery vessels, but a wealth of other objects in bronze, including a miniature waggon 18 cm long and 12 cm high, carrying a metal vessel.[90] Such a find compares closely with a life-size find of a waggon from Hart an der Alz, dating to Ha A1, along with beaten bronze cups and other finds.[91] Graves like these suggest that society was fragmented, the few being favoured in death as in life, though information about social structure is sparse and entirely conjectural. It is of some interest that rich burials occur in a 'horizon' in early Urnfield times (Br D–Ha A1) and then again in the late period (Ha B2–3); in between they are almost totally absent. This, too, should have social implications.

In conclusion we may say that Urnfield burial rites show both innovative and conservative elements, the interpretation of which is extremely hard. On the one hand the spread of the cremation rite certainly suggests major changes in beliefs about death and the afterlife; on the other the continuity shown in tumulus-building in some areas raises the whole question of the ethnic allegiance of the Urnfield tribes. At present the most reasonable line to take should probably combine both features: continuity at least as far as the Lausitz group is concerned, but the gradual building up within that and most other groups of a body of belief which saw pit cremation as the natural burial mode.

Such ideas seem, on present evidence, to appear earliest in the Hungarian plain whence they may have spread to other parts of central Europe (cf. above, p. 86). On the other hand urn-burial is known even from the Middle Danubian Tumulus group, so that there is little cause for envisaging shifting populations.[92]

How are we to account for the urnfields in historical terms? Are we to take the spread of cremation burial over much of central (and, later, western and southern) Europe as indicative of a change in population? Or should we rather imagine that this spread merely reflects a temporary fashion which was widely adopted? Herodotus and the other ancient historians leave us in no doubt that by the fifth century BC west-central Europe was occupied by the Celts.[93] Are we to assume that they had arrived at some time between the end of the Bronze Age and Herodotus' own day? Or were they already present in Europe before that – in other words, during the Bronze Age?

1   Early Bronze Age ornaments. (Photo Prähistorische Abteilung Naturhistorisches Museum,
Wien)

a

2 (a) Jászdózsa-Kápolnahalom tell, Szolnok. (b) Wietenberg hill settlement, near Sighişoara. (Photos A. F.
Harding)

b

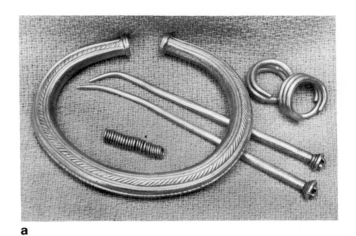

a

3   (a) Gold ornaments from the Leubingen
grave. (b) Reconstruction of the Leubingen
burial. (Photos Landesmuseum für Vorgeschichte, Halle/Saale)

b

a

4 (a) Handled cup from Marnbach, Bavaria. (Photo Prähistorische Staatssamm-
lung, Munich) (b) Únětice handled jug
from Halberstadt. (Photo Landesmuseum
für Vorgeschichte, Halle/Saale)

b

a

5 (a) Querns from Dívčí Kámen; length of central quern 20 cm. (Photo J. Poláček) (b) Hoard from Bresinchen, Kr Guben. (Photo Museum für Ur- und Frühgeschichte, Potsdam)

b

a

6 (a) Settlement at Spišský Štrvrtok, central Slovakia; the site lies within the trees. (b) Stone walling at Spišský Štrvrtok. (Photos A. F. Harding)

b

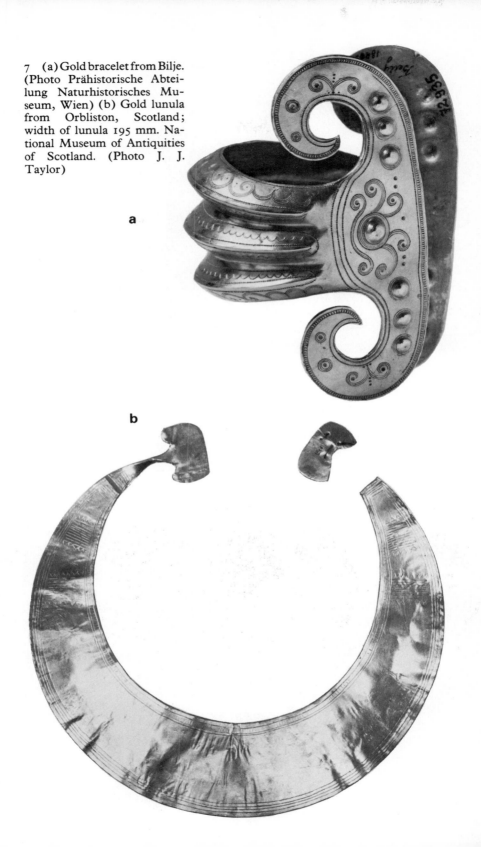

7 (a) Gold bracelet from Bilje. (Photo Prähistorische Abteilung Naturhistorisches Museum, Wien) (b) Gold lunula from Orbliston, Scotland; width of lunula 195 mm. National Museum of Antiquities of Scotland. (Photo J. J. Taylor)

a

b

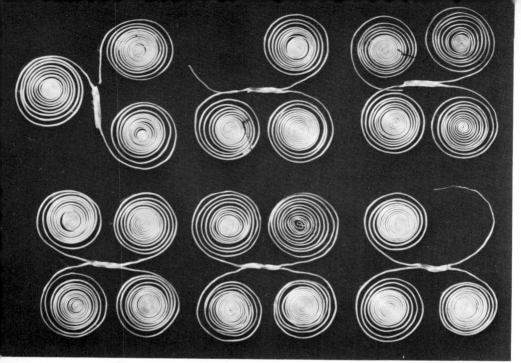

a

8 (a) Gold spiral ornaments from Zvornik, Jugoslavia.
(Photo Prähistorische Abteilung Naturhistorisches Museum, Wien) (b) Gold twisted torc from Grunty Fen,
England. (Photo University Museum of Archaeology
and Ethnology, Cambridge)

b

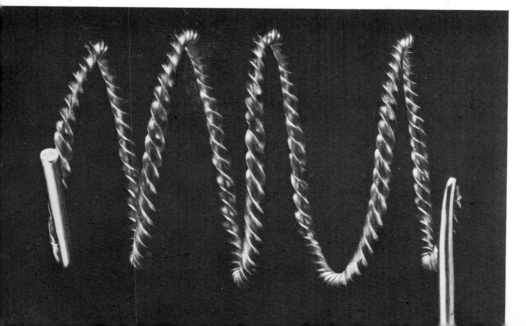

a

9 (a) Hurdle trackway, Somerset, England, Early
Bronze Age; scale 1 m. (Photo J. M. Coles) (b) Part of
the tell at Tószeg, Hungary. (Photo A. F. Harding)

b

10   Head of the woman buried at Skrydstrup, Jutland. (Photo from P. V. Glob 1974, fig. 24)

11   Burial mounds in Thy, Denmark. (Photo from P. V. Glob 1971, fig. 53)

a

12 (a) The Trundholm horse and disc, Zealand.
(Photo from P. V. Glob 1974, fig. 38) (b) Stonehenge.
(Photo West Air Photography)

b

a

13 Rock engraving from Aspeberget, Bohuslän. (b)
Rock engraving from Fossum, Bohuslän. Scales with 5
cm divisions. (Photos J. M. Coles)

b

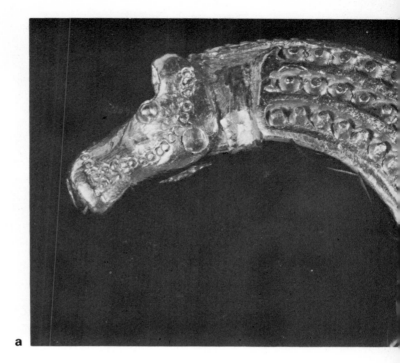

14 (on facing page) Bronze Age barrows on Oakley Down, Dorset. (Photo J. White, West Air Photography)

15 (a) Detail of terminal on gold bracelet from Vad. (b) Detail of engraving and punched decoration on dagger from Maiersdorf. (Photos Prähistorisches Abteilung Naturhistorisches Museum, Wien)

a

b

a

16 (a) Lausitz clay horn from Malitzschken-
dorf, Cottbus; length 8 cm. (b) Bronze cult
wagon from Eiche, Potsdam; length *c.* 20 cm.
(Photos Museum für Ur- und Frühgeschichte,
Potsdam)

b

a

17 (a) Lausitz urn from Drebkau, Cottbus; height 22 cm. (b) Lausitz armlets from Golssen, Cottbus; diameter of left armlet 11 cm. (Photos Museum für Ur- und Frühgeschichte, Potsdam)

b

18   Biskupin; internal view of the reconstructed Lausitz
stockade. (Photo A. F. Harding)

19 (a) Clay chariot from Dupljaja, Banat. (Photo National Museum, Belgrade) (b) Gold bowls from Skrea, Halland and Nättraby, Blekinge. (Photo Historiska Museet, Stockholm)

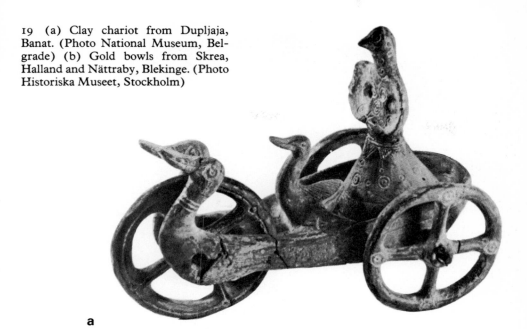

a

b

a

20 (a) Lausitz pottery vessel with bird figures, from
Klein Döbbern, Cottbus; diameter at mouth 148 mm.
(b) Lausitz urn from Wilmersdorf, Frankfurt/Oder;
height 255 mm. (Photos Museum für Ur- und Frühgeschichte, Potsdam)

b

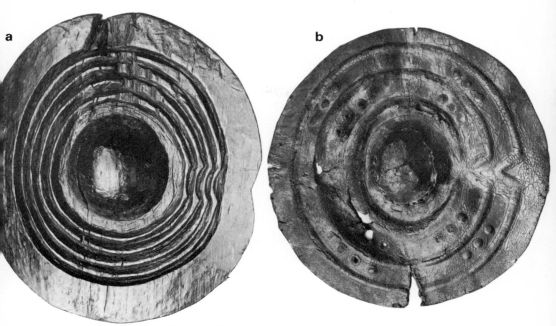

21 (a) Wooden shield from Cloonlara, Co. Mayo, Ireland; diameter 48 cm. (b) Leather shield from Clonbrin, Co. Longford, Ireland; diameter 50 cm. (Photos National Museum of Ireland) (c) Planks of ash and oak, 800 bc, Somerset, England; scale 1 m. (Photo J. M. Coles)

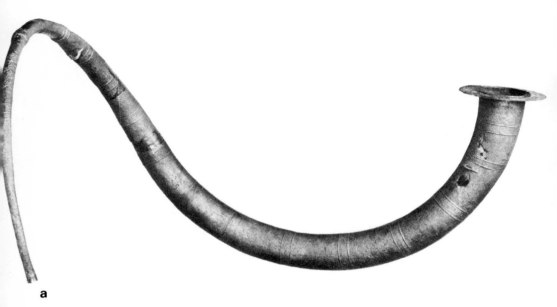

a

22 (a) Bronze *lur* from Rørlykke, Langeland, Denmark. (Photo National Museum of Denmark) (b) Bronze shields and Urnfield swords. (Photo Landesmuseum für Vorgeschichte, Halle/Saale)

b

23 (a) Bronze figure from Grevensvaenge, Zealand; total height 9 cm. (b) Bronze figure from Kaiserberg, Holstein; height 6 cm. (Photos from P. V. Glob 1974, figs. 57 and 65) (c) Bronze figure of warrior, Sardinia; height 17 cm. National Museum, Denmark. (Photo from Torbrügge 1972) (d) Bronze figure of mother and child, Domu s'Orku. Museo Archaologico Nazionale, Cagliari. (Photo from Lilliu 1962)

a

b

c

d

a

24 (a) Rock engraving from Fossum, Bohuslän. (b) Rock engraving from Kalleby, Bohuslän; scales with 5 cm divisions. (Photos J. M. Coles)

b

The latter question is currently, and seems likely to remain, unanswerable, until some infallible method is devised for identifying racial affinities in prehistoric populations. There is little that is specifically 'Celtic' in Urnfield Europe; equally there is no particular reason for introducing Celtic warriors at the end of the Bronze Age, unless the rich graves of Ha C are theirs. Childe suggested, and he was not alone, that Beakers could be the tangible expression of Celtic race – which would mean that the whole Bronze Age was 'Celtic', though the question of origins would remain insoluble. Our own feeling is that the process of Celticization was much more gradual, and that no one culture or time should be sought as the immediate source of Celtic origins. We know nothing of Celtic language until well into the historical period, and precious little even then; let us wait patiently for a little longer, to see if the chances of discovery may not surprise us with unexpected information from sources like this.

Racial questions apart, Gimbutas' view that Urnfield culture continued without a break from Tumulus seems to us reasonable. Apart from anything else, large numbers of urnfields speak for a greatly increased population in the later Bronze Age, which may alone be sufficient to account for the widespread adoption of the new rite. Such an explanation would allow for the differential rates of development and change in the different parts of Europe, and would obviate the awkward necessity of having to introduce an important cultural element from outside.

It would be idle to pretend that sacred sites are at all well-known from the Urnfield world. For the most part our information is derived from 'enigmatic features' in the ground, and artifacts of cultic significance. Occasionally there is some clearer indication, as at the Knovíz sites of Čakovice (Prague north) and Mutějovice (Rakovník). At the first[94] were found three houses, numerous pits, five pottery ovens and – outside the habitation area – three 'ritual' cremations with rich ceramic grave-goods; separated from these by an empty space was a ring-ditch and palisade 17 m in diameter with a sandstone stele placed off-centre in the central part. A single narrow causeway broke the line of the ditch, at the opposite side to the settlement. The excavator spoke blithely of a 'sanctuary of the solar cult', but such an explanation leaves many questions unanswered. It is tempting to see parallels far afield: the circular form recalls the henges of Britain, and the addition of a central post suggests an analogy with the Goloring near Koblenz in western Germany.[95] Furthermore the discovery of 'hengiform' monuments in western Bohemia, one having a central stone setting, means that Čakovice need be no isolated occurrence.[96] One can recall also that the Early Iron Age sanctuary of Libenice (Kolín) contained an upright stele at its business end, though there need be no specific connections between the sites.[97] Comparable to Čakovice is Mutějovice, where a horseshoe-shaped enclosure with entrance was found in the midst of a Knovíz settlement.[98]

Of a very different kind are the hill-top sanctuaries of Silesia and elsewhere, mostly attributable to the Early Iron Age but at least in some cases starting in the Bronze Age. The most famous is the group of three sites near Sobótka (Wrocław) in lower Silesia: Góry Kościuszki, Ślęża and Radunia.[99] Each of these hills, some 700 m above sea level, has a rough stone circuit wall enclosing an oval area; Ślęza has outlying works as well. Animal statues must be of later date, but stone *menhirs* may well date to the Bronze Age. These hills must presumably mark the centre of some open-air cult, and the use of hill-tops recalls certain scenes on Creto-Mycenaean religious art.

A further type of site used for cult practices is the well or river. We have already mentioned the ritual use of the well at Berlin-Lichterfelde (above, p. 354); this was by no means the only such site. A well at Lüdersdorf (Luckenwalde) contained a bronze sword, and pottery was in the well of the fort at Senftenberg.[100] Other examples are known from Denmark. It has often been remarked that water offerings, or rituals in wet places, were an especial feature of the later Bronze Age in Britain; much the same was true of central Europe, where the abundant hoard and other finds from bogs and rivers have been chronicled by Torbrügge.[101]

It has been shown very clearly in the Main-middle Rhine region that the deposition of objects of all sorts, but especially weapons, increased greatly during the Urnfield period, and thereafter fell away to negligible proportions.[102] Several theories have been advanced to account for this; the two principal ideas are the 'catastrophe theory' and the 'votive offering theory', or a combination of both.[103] Modern authors tend to the second view, which is indeed more plausible. The dramatic decline in numbers after Ha B3 (eighth century) could then be attributed to a change in cult form – even a change in population. As we have already mentioned, increased precipitation is recorded during some parts of the Bronze Age, but most of the evidence we have for the earlier Urnfield period indicates a dry spell. Could it actually have been for the purpose of entreating the river-gods for water that offerings were made during this time?

Commoner than obviously sacred sites are cult objects and religious paraphernalia. The Lausitz group was especially prolific in zoomorphic vases (pl. 20), miniatures, rattles, horns and so on, at least some of which we may interpret in this way (fig. 132).[104] By far the most popular motifs in Urnfield symbolism are birds and sun symbols. The birds come in many forms: typically only their heads and necks ('protomes') are represented, and frequently they are conjoined with boat motifs to

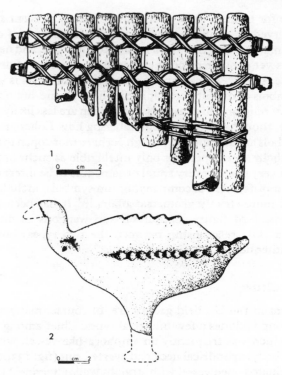

Fig. 132 Finds from the Lausitz cemetery of Przeczyce (Zawiercie): 1. pan-pipes (reconstructed), 2. bird-shaped rattle.
(After Szydłowska 1972)

suggest that they are water-birds. In addition to zoomorphic pots one finds bronze pendants and figurines, and attachments on larger objects – cauldrons, waggons, 'double-picks' etc. – which appear all over Europe, from Denmark (Skallerup in Zealand) to Greece (the Tiryns treasure). On the one hand actual examples of birds in the round drawing waggons are found (Burg an der Spree); on the other they are depicted in two dimensions on beaten bronze-work, frequently placed antithetically (Lúčky, Hajdúböszörmény). Waggons themselves are of great interest (pl. 16). We consider Trundholm and Dupljaja elsewhere (pp. 316, 408), but in central Europe one can mention Milavče or Szászvarosszek among other examples, some being masterpieces of the bronzesmith's art.[105] Two main candidates for interpretation present themselves; one, the traditional view, is that these are funerary vessels which it is perhaps appropriate for birds to draw over water or land; a recent suggestion is that they served as symbolic containers for the purpose of calling forth (and, presumably, collecting) rain in times of drought, and have therefore been seen as yet another piece of evidence for a period of dryness in the Late Bronze Age.[106] The symbolic significance of birds is well-known; birds as symbols of divinity or epiphanies have a time-honoured place in the history of religion. Birds as beasts of burden are less likely (unless they are swans?), though it is worth remembering how Lohengrin travelled.

Sun-symbols are ubiquitous, though perhaps more open to speculation. The Trundholm disc is perhaps only intelligible as such, but it does not follow that every disc or every spiral ornament is to be interpreted in this way. Other motifs, often accompanying sun symbols, include hour-glass designs and more strictly geometric affairs.[107] It has been pointed out that the same bird figures appear on sun-waggons as on cauldrons, suggesting a close relationship between the two types: both allegedly refer to weather deities.[108]

Material culture

Pottery forms in the Urnfield groups are, of course, many and various, but each group includes a few universal types. Chief among these is the urn itself, which was frequently an amphora-like vessel, with spherical or biconical body, cylindrical neck and everted rim (fig. 133, 1); a related form is a carinated open vessel with straight walls ('terrine') (pls. 17, 20). A Knovíz speciality, for instance, was the 'storied vase' (*Etagengefäss*) – essentially a globular urn with high neck on which the belly has been pinched in (fig. 133, 3). The urns were accompanied by a standard range of accessory vessels. Perhaps the commonest is the low conical one-handled cup with omphalos base, as the usual accompaniment of Lausitz burials. Another standard form is the ovoid pot with lug-handles. In the Czech groups bellied one-handled cups are common; in Slovakia and Austria high loop handles are found, as well as pedestal bowls.

Surface treatment and decoration similarly vary by regions. In general Urnfield funerary ware is well-made (by hand), slipped (generally dark and often black) and polished. Especially important is fluted decoration, which may be vertical or diagonal in Austria, Hungary and Czechoslovakia, or horizontal in late contexts (fig. 134). Bosses or semi-bosses are very common, as is channelling in patterns (sometimes around bosses or together with fluting). Incision, by contrast, is relatively less common, and painting is exceptional until the very latest stages. On domestic pots a range of rustication techniques is found.

In pottery sequences that have been worked out in great detail (e.g.

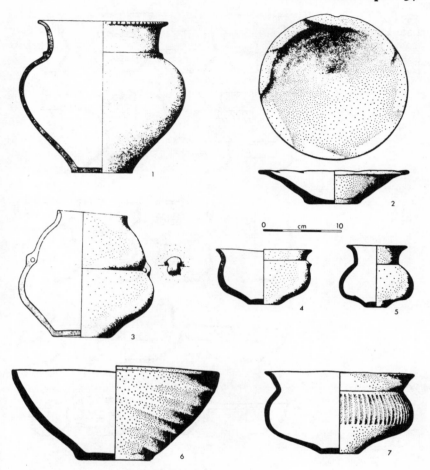

Fig. 133 Pottery from the early Urnfield cemetery of Grundfeld (Staffelstein). (After Radunz 1966)

Knovíz and Lausitz) many phases have been distinguished. In the Lausitz sequence, for instance, it is especially obvious how simple rounded and undecorated forms, or vessels with bossed decoration, develop into more elaborate types and later into angular, highly decorated forms some of which give the impression of having been made on the wheel. In this connection the categories distinguished for Saxony by Grünberg in an important book published in 1943 and by Coblenz in 1952 should be mentioned briefly.[109] Characteristic of the 'Middle Bronze Age', that is, period III (early Lausitz) are a series of vessels especially

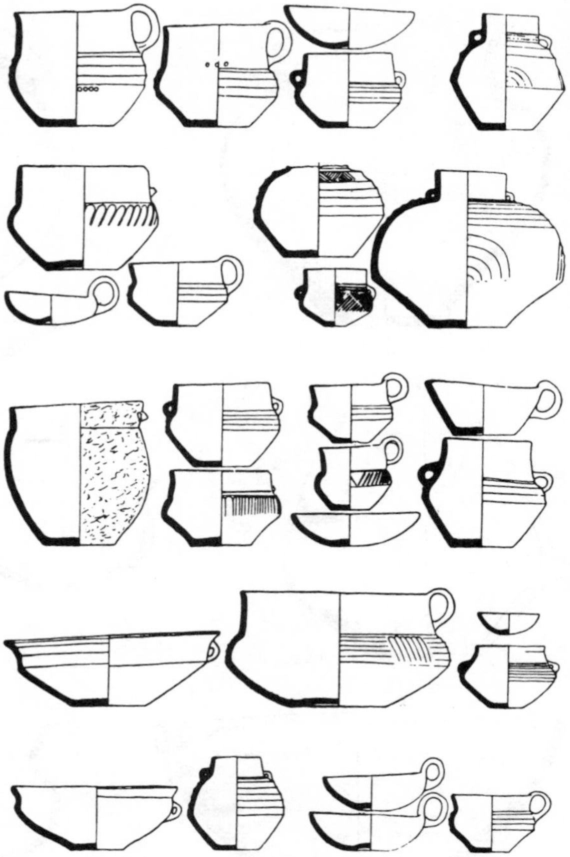

Fig. 134
Late Lausitz pottery
from Saxony.
(After Grünberg
1943)

decorated by bossing and fluting, and coming in quite simple shapes –
ovoid jars, terrines, low bowls with flaring mouth, one-handled jugs and
so on. Following this is a group of pottery characteristic of the northern
graves that immediately follow, but mark a distinct break with, these
bossed wares; Grünberg called this the 'foreign group of straight-walled
incised wares' (*Fremdgruppe*). These types are found in association with
the bossed wares, though this is not the case any more with the next
group, the 'foreign group with plastic fluting'. On the other hand a local
style, derived from the bossed wares, continues alongside the 'foreign
groups', eventually fusing with them. Somewhat later comes a rather
different style, the 'angular rilled and facetted ware', and finally the
'horizontally fluted ware' (fig. 134), which takes us on into the Early Iron

Age, and for which Grünberg was able to distinguish the products of different workshops.

These divisions compare quite closely with at least part of the sequence in southern Germany.[110] Again a group of 'foreign cultures' was distinguished, and subdivided into local types – the Mels-Rixheim and Riegsee groups (in which pottery was not well-known), the 'lightly fluted wares' (*leichtgerillte Ware*, after Kraft),[111] and Dixenhausen pottery (so named by Vogt after the type-find near Hilpoltstein Kr. Weissenburg). These styles, which are mostly characterized by fluting, bossing and incised ornament on polished fabrics, especially on low bowls with flaring mouth, have recently been the subject of further very detailed examination.[112] A speciality of the Rhine basin was the occasional application of haematite as a colour coat to shallow vessels. In some areas of southern Germany detailed pottery sequences covering the whole Urnfield period have now been worked out.[113]

A ceramic curiosity is the finding of an Únětice polypod bowl from a nearby grave reused as a cinerary urn in a final Bronze Age grave at Altlommatzsch (Meissen), indicating that the latest pot forms were not invariably considered essential, especially when the ground was already hallowed.[114] Further products in clay could include occasional figurines, as in the Billendorf cemetery at Niederkaina (Bautzen),[115] and the zoomorphic vessels and rattles already mentioned.

In metalwork, which constitutes the principal typological indicator of the period, the number of types is very great.[116] Of the main innovations in each succeeding century we may mention the following:

13th (Br D): the earliest beaten bronze vessels and cult waggons; Peschiera daggers; heavily ribbed bracelets; ring-ended knives; tanged daggers; Rixheim swords; Nenzingen swords; violin-bow fibulae; Riegsee solid-hilted swords; spike-grip swords; 'turban-headed' pins; flange-hilted and flat-hilted knives; belt plates; etc.

12th (Ha A1): vessels of *Friedrichsruhe* type and early buckets; violin-bow fibulae with straight bow or extended foot; early *Dreiwulstschwerter* (solid-hilted swords with three raised ridges on the hilt); early crescentic razors; vase-headed pins; flange-hilted knives; spike-grip knives; Erbenheim and Letten swords; 'plate-headed' pins and pins with faceted head; etc.

11th (Ha A2): vessels of *Fuchsstadt* type; late crescentic or pennanular razors; late tanged knives; late *Dreiwulstschwerter*: fibulae with serpentine or leaf bow.

10th (Ha B1): vessels of Jenišovice-Kirkendrup type ('point-boss system') (fig. 136, 2–3); bowl-pommel swords; spearheads with wave ornament; eyelet pins; special types of spike-grip knives, bracelets etc.; end-winged axes; cauldron with cross-attachment (fig. 136, 1); one-edged crescentic razor-knives (these latter characteristic of the entire 'Late Urnfield period'); etc.

9th (Ha B2): early antenna swords; Auheim grip-tongue swords; one-edged crescentic razors with peaked back; richly decorated curved-back knives with spike-grip; large vase-headed pins, harp fibulae; spectacle fibulae; vessels of Haslau-Regelsbrunn type; etc.

8th (Ha B3): vessels of Stillfried-Hostomice type; late antenna swords; late flange-hilted and solid-pommel swords; socketed knives; horse-harness; fibulae with extended foot; harp fibulae; simpler arc fibulae; socketed chisels; v-shaped pendants; spike-tang knives with ribbed tang; late crescentic razors; looped end-winged axes; small vase-headed pins; 'ring-hooks'; etc.

Universal types: socketed axes (earliest in the east); winged axes; bracelets; flange-hilted swords; sickles; etc.

Each of these types occurs in isolated finds; more useful, however, is their occurrence with other objects. The Late Bronze Age was the great period of hoard finds, and these may take on a variety of forms. Much metal, often of high quality, was placed deliberately in the ground or in lakes or streams (cf. above, p. 368), whether for recovery or as some form of ceremonial gift to the elements is not at all certain. The two hoards from Bad Homburg (Rockenberg, Friedberg), for instance, found only 2 m apart, contained 22 kg of metal, mostly domestic equipment and ornaments,[117] but other deposits of material, particularly those in water, are often of finer quality, including beaten metal vessels and elaborate weapons.[118] Some of these hoards exhibit concentrations on particular types – for instance the sickle hoards or ornament hoards of central Germany[119] – while others contain a very general range of material, especially waste pieces from casting, broken objects for re-use and so on. Clearly one can distinguish at the very least founders' hoards as one type, and ritually deposited hoards of various kinds as another. Large numbers of stone and clay moulds are also known, for this was clearly a period of metallurgical experimentation.

Skill in the fine arts was not restricted to pottery and bronze, however. True translucent glass, mainly in the form of small beads, is regularly found, especially in the later part of the period, indicating that the mastery over the material that was lacking in the Early Bronze Age had now been found with the development of efficient firing technology.

Fig. 135   The Urnfield warrior, *c.* 800 BC.

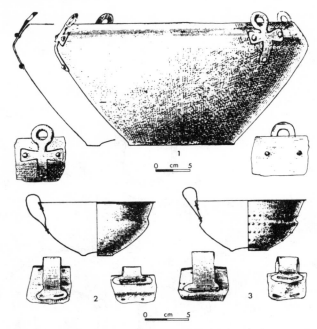

Fig. 136   Beaten bronze vessels of Jenišovice type (2,3) and cauldron with cross-attachments (1) from Liptovská On-drašova (Liptovský Mikuláš, central Slovakia). Ninth century BC.
(After Furmánek 1970)

Amber and other raw materials continued to be worked for ornaments. An interesting recent find is of a set of bone pan-pipes from a grave at Przeczyce (fig. 132); this is so far unique in Bronze Age Europe and has been connected with depictions of pan-pipes on Early Iron Age *situlae*.[120] We feel sure that the form must have been a widespread one.

Economy

The economic life of the later Bronze age in central Europe must have been full and varied. Though the evidence for regular long-distance trade is not so full as in previous centuries, more local exchange and intermingling of ideas is very well-documented. Numerous well-studied areas have produced evidence of the products of one area turning up in another. In any case the community of material culture through continental Europe meant that innovations in one area were speedily adopted in another. Where evidence for traded commodities, like amber, is present, there are signs that during the Urnfield period interest was revived in promoting such exchanges. Another commodity that was becoming increasingly important was salt; the Halle production area continued in operation, while in Poland vessels connected with salt production by evaporation are found, though not tanks or larger constructions; in one vessel was a cylindrical lump of salt weighing half a kilo.[121] By this time the great site of Hallstatt was well-settled; indeed, if the flowering of Ha C is to be attributed to Hallstatt's dominance of the salt market, production must already have been well under way in Ha B or earlier. The elaborate system of mining, and the finds of organic materials like cloth, rope, basketry and leather from the Hallstatt salt-mines, belong to another book, but it is not unreasonable to claim some of this activity for the Bronze Age.

Metal ore must have been the subject of much trade and exchange, but the mixed nature of the metal pool by this time means that analysis cannot tie objects down to ore-sources. One can assume, however, that the mines of Austria continued to flourish, and that the sources in the Ore Mountains and elsewhere continued to be intensively exploited.

Greece and Italy were importing amber again during the eleventh and succeeding centuries, and this trade must, it seems, have passed through central Europe. What, if anything, passed in the opposite direction, we do not know; most of the supposed Mycenaean connections date to an earlier period. It is interesting to note, however, how similar the armour and equipment of late Mycenaean Greece was to that of central Europe (fig. 135).[122]

The basis of economic life in Urnfield sites was broad in all cases where good indications are available. Numerous finds of agricultural implements (especially sickles) and grain storage pits indicate the importance of arable agriculture. At Buchau, for instance, granaries held wheat, barley, and millet, and supplies of broad beans, peas, flax and poppy seeds, apples, various berries and nuts were also kept.[123] Sickles and querns, antler hoes and hammers, were among the equipment used for the cultivation and processing of plants. Cattle, sheep, goats, horses, pigs and dogs were kept, and hunted animals included deer, boar and elk. Fishing was represented by net-sinkers. The island position of the site did not prevent arable cultivation of nearby land, nor pasturing and feeding of animals, and wooden waggons for large-scale transportation were used. An especially good array of information is available from the Polish lake-sites.[124] The basic corn plants at the end of the Bronze Age comprised various types of wheat (principally emmer), barley (six-row), millet, and, less commonly, rye and oats; the relative proportions of these vary considerably and no doubt depend on varying site conditions. Pulses are also present in varying quantities, as the following figures show:

Table 10 Quantities of various crops recovered from Lausitz stockades (after Ostoja-Zagórski 1974)

	Wheat	Barley	Millet	Oats	Rye	Pea	Bean	Lentil
Biskupin	6865	733	514	–	–	234	83	209
Wrocław-Osobowice	1	8	3	40	1	–	–	–
Smuszewo	101616	28025	76460	71	–	8885	13762	9684

(individual species identifications)

These main cultigens also occur regularly on Urnfield sites elsewhere in central Europe, though emmer wheat does not always predominate.[125] In addition at Biskupin oleaginous plants such as poppy and rape were cultivated, and there are a few seeds of flax. This combined evidence speaks for a high degree of agricultural organization – based, it has been suggested, on a burning or fallow rotation system. On the other hand large numbers of edible weeds have been taken to indicate the poverty of other available resources, at least towards the end of the period.

Stock animals vary similarly, though the preponderance of cattle is practically universal:

Table 11 Percentage proportions of animal bones recovered from Lausitz stockades (after Ostoja-Zagórski 1974)

	Cattle	Pig	Sheep/ goat	Horse	Dog	% Domestic animals
Biskupin	54.8	23.4	21.4	+	+	76.6
Wrocław-Osobowice	57.0	17.0	15.0	10.0	+	98.0
Smuszewo	41.7	34.8	8.3	8.3	+	95.6

(percentages of total domesticated animals; figures = average of all levels)

Only at one site, Szczecin-Zamek, did pig predominate, but the high proportions of pig elsewhere are significant. Sheep/goat is consistently in third place. The role of non-domestic animals was generally small, but larger at Biskupin: wild species include red and roe deer, boar, bison and elk as well as small mammals. To judge from the situation prevailing at Biskupin today frogs' legs may well have been a speciality of the house! Fishing was naturally important too, as is shown by the finding of fish scales and of net sinkers, bark floats, and bone, horn and bronze fish-hooks.

What information there is from other sites bears out this general picture, but it must be recorded that these are still too few for any real conclusions to be reached.

Absolute chronology

The two main points of contact that give us a historical chronology are, first, the correlation between Br D in central Europe and late LH IIIB in Greece and, second, the supposed dates for the founding of Greek colonies in Italy. A considerable range of new bronze types (flange-hilted swords, leaf-shaped spearheads of particular forms, 'Peschiera daggers', violin-bow fibulae, and armour of sheet bronze) seem to have been first adopted in Greece towards the end of the LH IIIB period (thirteenth century), and these are precisely the forms that typify the Br D phase in central Europe. Bronzes of this general nature at Scoglio del Tonno in southern Italy (below, p. 418) are similarly accompanied by Mycenaean pottery which includes, albeit without stratigraphical definition, LH IIIB. The date for LH IIIB is far from being well-established, but it cannot go beyond certain limits: the surest evidence at present available shows that the later part of the period (LH IIIB2 in certain contexts at Mycenae) must be contemporary, at least in part, with the reign of the Egyptian king Merneptah (accession date 1224 BC), while there are indications that it may not have ended until some time after 1200 BC. Br D, which includes types identical to those of late LH IIIB, must partly fall in the thirteenth century. The next indications of absolute date come from the first Greek towns in Italy, notably Kyme and Pithekoussai, traditionally attributed to the later eighth century. A date of c. 700 BC for the start of Ha C has been obtained by comparison of bronze types from the Italian peninsula and central Europe, but the situation in Italy is changing – as the finding of Middle Geometric skyphoi with pendent semi-circles at Veii and elsewhere has shown[126] – so that this date may soon have to be revised upwards. The chronology adopted by Müller-Karpe places each succeeding phase of the later Bronze Age squarely in a given century from 1300 BC down to 700 BC ; this neat division has been questioned on more than one occasion, and it has recently been demonstrated that Müller-Karpe's dating is too high at the start of the period.[127]

Radiocarbon dates seem to suggest a date somewhere around 1300 bc for the start of the later Bronze Age, and a date around 700 bc for its end (table 12). The apparent agreement of these figures with the historical chronology is obvious, and the implications of calibrating the dates are unfortunate, for they will then be 200 to 300 years 'too early'. The number of dates is still too small for detailed discussion of the chronology of each phase to be worthwhile. Of some interest are the dates from Biskupin, almost the only sequence we have; it is clear that the material they refer to cannot be much, if any, later than the true Bronze Age in central Poland.

Table 12   Radiocarbon dates, central Europe, later Bronze Age

Site	Lab no.	bc
Lausitz and related		
Chodouny (Litoměřice), grave 7, Br D	P–1902	1130 ± 60
Dneboh-Hrada (Turnov)	P–1904	1050 ± 50
	P–1905	1080 ± 60
	LJ–2042	860 ± 150
Berlin-Lichterfelde, late M. I V	K–	1080 ± 55
Iwanowice (Miechów, Kraków)	M–2167	1240 ± 160
Kratzeburg (Neustrelitz), M. I V-V	Bln–78	815 ± 100
Ichtershausen (Arnstadt), Unstrut group	Bln–398	910 ± 120
Perleberg (Golm), hearth	Bln–97	635 ± 100
Biskupin (Żnin), first settlement	Gif–494	720 ± 150
later settlement	Gif–495	560 ± 150
fortifications	Gif–492	620 ± 150
A2 4C, V I I	Gif–493	620 ± 150
Knovíz		
Radonice (Louny)	P–1906	1100 ± 50
Vikletice (Chomutov), Štítary phase	P–1907	780 ± 60
Čaka		
Lužany (Topolčany), upper	Ba–38	1090 ± 160
lower	Ba–90	1310 ± 110
Other Late Bronze Age		
Volders (Tirol), Ha B2	GrN–1691	910 ± 50
Pitten (Nö), pyre from pyre-grave	VRI–93	1100 ± 90
Loretto (BG), pyre grave	VRI–41	1040 ± 120
Brno-Líšeň, Staré Zámky, pit	Bln–434	1085 ± 150
Hallstatt, (Oö), tools from mine shafts	VRI–345	860 ± 90
	VRI–258	860 ± 90
	VRI–267	970 ± 100
Dürrnberg bei Hallein, salt mines	VRI–290	720 ± 80
Buchberg (Bischofshofen), mine	U–134	1220 ± 90
Brno-Obřany, Hradisko, hillfort	GrN–2087	870 ± 70
Grosser Knetzberg, Knetzgau (Hassfurt), hillfort	GrN–4705	980 ± 40
Schwanberg (Kitzingen), hillfort	GrN–4466	910 ± 50
	GrN–4467	910 ± 50
Cronenburg (Bas-Rhin), pottery kiln	Gsy–85	1265 ± 150

Notes

1 Suggested by J. Bouzek, *Beiträge zur Lausitzer Kultur*, 1969, 25ff., and elsewhere.
2 Most notably by W. Kimmig 1964.
3 Discussion and review by Kimmig 1964, 259. It is distressing to find this old 'red herring' repeated anew: e.g. N. G. L. Hammond, *A History of Macedonia*, vol. 1, 1972, 305ff.; *Migrations and Invasions in Greece and Adjacent Areas*, 1976, 148.
4 E.g. Piggott 1965, 171; J. Filip, *Celtic Civilisation and its Heritage*, 1960, ch. 1 esp. 24.
5 See e.g. Malinowski 1974. The evidence from physical anthropology seems nugatory, that from philology disputed.
6 M. Ralska-Jasiewiczowa, *Folia Quat.* 29 (1968), 163–82; *Acta Soc. Botan. Pol.* 33/2 (1964), 461–8; W. Koperowa, *Acta Palaeobot.* 11/2 (1970), 42pp.
7 M. Ralska-Jasiewiczowa, *Ber. Deutsch. Bot. Ges.* 85 (1972), 101–12.
8 M. Ralska-Jasiewiczowa, *Studia Geomorph. Carp.-Balc.* 6 (1972), 5–19.
9 E.g. K. Rybníček and E. Rybníčková, *Folia geobot. et phytotax.* 3 (1968), 117–42; F. Kral, *Pollenanalytische Untersuchungen zur Waldgeschichte des Dachsteinmassivs*, 1971, 92f.; Frenzel 1974, 108ff.
10 Müller 1964, 71ff.
11 R. Lais, *Germania* 24 (1940), 157–166.
12 F. E. Zeuner, *7th Ann. Rep. Inst. of Arch.* (1961), 46–53.
13 J. Bouzek, *Actes du IXe Congrès Intern. SPP*, Nice, 1976, forthcoming. K.–D. Jäger and V. Lozek, *Tagung Deutsch. Hist. Ges. Dresden*, 1975 (quoted *AR* 29 (1977), 201). We thank Dr Bouzek for permission to quote his paper.
14 Reinecke 1911/1965, 1ff., esp. 8ff.
15 Reinecke 1911/1965, 25ff. A more logical scheme was that suggested by Childe in 1948, that Ha A and B should rather be called Br E and F. This was never adopted on the continent, though some scholars seem to be aware of its possible merits: W. A. von Brunn, *JIVUF* (1974), 20f.
16 Reinecke 1911/1965, 37ff.
17 A. Jockenhövel, *JIVUF* (1974), 57, 65.
18 Hennig 1970, 33ff. (early phase = Br D, middle phase = Ha A1, Ha A2 and Ha B1; late phase = Ha B2/3).
19 Hermann 1966, 30ff: *ältere Urnenfelderkultur*, divided into early (Ha A1) and developed (Ha A2); middle period (Ha B1); and 'end phase' (Ha B3).
20 Dehn 1972, 55ff. Phase 1 – Ha A1b, 2 – Ha A2, 3 – Ha B1, 4 – 'Ha B2' (Ha B3 of Müller-Karpe).
21 Reinecke 1911/1965, 1–33; Müller-Karpe 1959, 141ff., and *JIVUF* (1974), 14ff.
22 F. Holste, *Die Bronzezeit in nordmainischen Hessen*, 1939; Herrmann 1966; W. Kubach, *JIVUF* (1974), 29ff., table p. 50.
23 Müller-Karpe 1959, 100ff.; Vinski-Gasparini 1973.
24 Podborský 1970; A. Jockenhövel, *JIVUF* (1974), 57ff.; table p. 69.
25 J. Böhm, *Základy halštattské periody v Čechách*, 1937; Kytlicová, Vokolek and Bouzek 1964.
26 Quoted by Kytlicová *et al.* 1964.
27 The most useful synthesizing studies for central Europe (and Italy) are Müller-Karpe 1959 and von Brunn 1968. The following areas are dealt with in specific studies: Württemberg: Dehn 1972; Hesse: Herrmann 1966; Baden: W. Kimmig, *Die Urnenfelderkultur in Baden*, 1940; Franconia: Hennig 1970; Austria: K.-H. Wagner, *Nordtiroler*

Urnenfelder, 1943; Pittioni 1954, 403ff.; Bohemia: J. Filip, *Popelnicová pole a počátky doby železné v Čechách*, 1937; J. Böhm, *Základy halštattské periody v Čechách*, 1937; Bouzek *et al.* 1966; Hrala 1973; Moravia: Podborský 1970; Slovakia: see under Lausitz, and in text under Čaka group; Hungary: Patek 1968; F. Köszegi, *AAH* 12 (1960), 137–86 (Vál and other Urnfields); cf. now contributions by F. Köszegi, T. Kovács and T. Kemenczei in *AAH* 27 (1975), 297–336; East France-Rhineland: W. Kimmig, *Rev. Arch. Est* (1951), 65–81; Zumstein 1966; Sandars 1957 (especially for local groups, as acknowledged by others, e.g. Briard 1974); enclosures, Chertier 1976.

28 Groups of the Lausitz culture:
  A *Saxo-Lausitz* groups, comprising: *Aurith* (middle Oder area): J. Schneider in *Studien*, 1958, 5–70; R. Breddin in *Beiträge*, 1969, 45ff. with refs. *Göritz* (middle to lower Oder): S. Griesa, *Beiträge*, 1969, 115ff. with refs. *Billendorf* (late (M.VI) group in Lausitz area and adjacent Poland): W. Kropf, *Die Billendorfer Kultur auf Grund der Grabfunde*, 1938; D.-W. Buck in *Beiträge*, 1969, 49–52. *Lower Lausitz, Neisse mouth, Elster*: R. Breddin, *Beiträge*, 1969, 41ff. with refs.
  B *Bohemian*: Plesl 1961.
  C *Moravian*: V. Dohnal, *Die Lausitzer Urnenfelderkultur in Ostmähren*, Studie Arch. Ústavu ČSAV v Brně, 2, 3 (1974); J. Nekvasil, *AR* 16 (1964), 225–264.
  D *Slovakian*: Z. Pivovarová, *AAC* 9 (1967), 11–23; A. Točík and J. Vladár, *Beiträge*, 1969, 295ff. with refs; Z. Pivovarová, *Sl.A.* 20 (1972), 253–312; Pivovarová 1965.

  E *Pomeranian*: J. Kostrzewski, *Kultura łużycka na Pomorzu*, 1958.
  F *Central Polish* groups, including the Konstantynów group (Łódź phase): H. Wiklak, *Początki kultury łużyckiej w Polsce srodkowej*, 1963.
  G *East Polish* groups: in general, Dąbrowski 1972, 120ff. *Mazury-Warmia*: Dąbrowski 1972, 129ff. *Tarnobrzeg* (material in Rzeszów Museum): after Gedl, pers. comm.; K. Moskwa, *Grupa tarnobrzeska kultury łużyckiej*, 1976. *Chełm*: Chudziakowa 1974. *Ulvivok* (Ulwówek) (south-east Poland and west Ukraine, middle Bug area): Dąbrowski 1972. *Northern Masovian, Masovian-Podlasian*: Dąbrowski 1972.
  H *Middle Silesian* groups: Ślęża, Trzebnica: Gollub 1960, Gediga 1967.
  I *Upper Silesian – Little Polish* groups (Kraków, Częstochowa-Gliwice, Kępno): Durczewski 1939–46; Gedl 1962. Also Głubczyce group: Gedl 1962.
29 Bouzek, Koutecký and Neustupný 1966.
30 Cf. Hrala 1973, 117.
31 E.g. Zumstein 1966, fig. 2, 5, 11.
32 B. Guillet *et al.* in Guilaine 1976, 82–7; G. Jalut, in Guilaine 1976, 180–5; Zumstein 1976, 630ff.; the clearance noted for parts of the Upper Rhine valley on the edges of the Haguenau forest are likely to represent Sub-atlantic activities of the Final Bronze Age and Early Iron Age communities.
33 E.g. settlements along the terraces of the rivers Lauch and Malsbach, Haut-Rhin: Zumstein 1966, fig. 11.
34 E.g. Ballern-Rech, Saarland; A. Kolling, *Führer*.... 5 (1966).
35 Patek 1968, 15ff.
36 Gedl 1962, 125, 421.

37 General articles: Coblenz 1963, 1964, 1974; Herrmann 1969.

38 Herrmann 1969, 59ff. A. Niesio-łowska-Wędzka, *Początki i rozwój grodów kultury łużyckiej*, 1974.

39 A. Kolling, *Führer* ... 5 (1966).

40 C. Pescheck. *Führer* ... 27 (1975).

41 Ibid.; D. Baatz, *Führer* ... 21 (1972), 149–52.

42 C. Pescheck, *Führer* ... 27 (1975); the dating of this site, and of others too, is uncertain as sherds of both later Bronze Age and early Iron Age character have been recovered.

43 O. Hockmann, *Führer* ... 23 (1973).

44 Herrmann 1969 has the most convenient summary.

45 J. Ostoja-Zagórski, *Slavia Antiqua* 20 (1973), 73–85.

46 Herrmann 1969, 78; Ostoja-Zagórski 1974, 137 with refs.

47 Archaeological experiments often show that particular tasks took much less time than one would expect. In this case the work-rate (based on medieval sources) of 1 cu m of wood requiring 6–10 man-days, and 1 cu m of earth $\frac{1}{2}$–1 man-day, may be excessively slow.

48 J. Říhovský, in *Beiträge*, 1969, 229–252; *AR* 24 (1972), 173–81.

49 F.-R. Herrmann, in *Ausgrabungen in Deutschland*, 1975 (ed. K. Böhner), Teil 1, 155–70.

50 Müller 1964. The finds from Buch are described by Gimbutas (1965, 304ff.); the original 1923 publication of this site by A. Kiekebusch is not easily found in Britain. Other sites in the Berlin area are described by Müller (p. 1).

51 H. Schubart, *AuF* 3 (1958), 215, 221.

52 H. Reinerth, *Die Wasserburg Buchau*, 1928; *Das Federseemoor als Siedlungsgebiet*, 1936.

53 Not Pomerania, as stated by some authors: e.g. Piggott 1965, 202. On Biskupin generally: *III Sprawozdanie z prac wykopaliskowych w grod-zie kultury łużyckiej w Biskupinie w powiecie żninskim ze lata 1938–9 i 1946–8*, Poznań 1950.

54 J. Dombay, *AJPME* (1958) 75–97.

55 Bouzek et al. 1966, 78.

56 Cf. Hrala 1973, 120.

57 Bouzek et al. 1966, 79.

58 J. Bouzek and D. Koutecký, *AR* 16 (1964), 28–43.

59 J. Ostoja-Zagórski, *FAP* 24 (1973), 33–47.

60 Gedl 1962, 122, 420.

61 We thank Dr J. Bouzek for this suggestion.

62 G. E. Daniel, *Antiquity* 44 (1970), 86f.

63 Coblenz 1952, 21ff.; Gollub 1960, 5; T. Malinowski, *Przeg. Arch.* 14 (1961), 5–135 (French résumé, 124ff.). A very detailed account, essential for those interested in the details of Lausitz burial.

64 J. Miskiewicz and T. Wegrzynowicz, *WA* 39/2 (1974), 131–204.

65 J. Hralová, *Das Lausitzer Gräberfeld in Malá Bělá*, 1962.

66 J. Bouzek and D. Koutecký, *PA* 63 (1972), 432–97.

67 K. Peschel, *Alt-Thüringen* 12 (1972), 131–249.

68 Brunn 1954a; B. Schmidt and W. Nitzschke, *AuF* 19 (1974), 6–17.

69 J. Bergmann, *Germania* 51 (1973), 54–72.

70 Gimbutas 1965, 325ff.; Patek 1968, 81ff.

71 E. Szydłowska, *Cmentarzysko kultury łużyckiej w Przeczycach, pow. Zawiercie* (Rocznik Muzeum Górnośląskiego w Bytomiu, 5, 8, 9, 1968–72, 4 vols); German summary in 9 (1972), 239–47.

72 V. Spurný, *PA* 43 (1948), 13–20, 136 (French résumé).

73 Brunn 1954a, esp. pp. 18ff., map p. 21; more recent finds: B. Schmidt, *AuF* 9 (1964), 29–32; G. Billig, *JMV* 52 (1968), 81–130 (Rumpin, Saalkreis).

74 O. Marschall, *AuF* 16 (1971), 18–21.
75 Radunz 1966.
76 K. Tihelka, *Velatice Culture Burials at Blučina*, 1969.
77 E.g. Velim-Skalka in Bohemia and several other sites: information from Dr J. Bouzek.
78 Z. Pivovarová, *Sl.A.* 13 (1965), 107–62.
79 E. Plesl in *Beiträge*, 1969, 211–20.
80 W. Coblenz, *AFSB* 1945–50 (1951), 46–56.
81 A. Točík and J. Paulík, *Sl.A.* 8 (1960), 59–124; J. Paulík *Sl.A.* 11 (1963), 269–338.
82 J. Paulík, *Sl.A.* 14 (1966), 357–96.
83 J. Paulík, *Zborník Slov. Nar. Muz.* 63 (1969), *Historia* 9, 3–51.
84 J. Paulík *JIVUF* (1975), 57–60; *AR* 28 (1976), 369–73.
85 J. Paulík, *AR* 28 (1976), 369f.
86 J. Paulík, *Sl.A.* 10 (1962), 5–96.
87 In some cases, e.g. Velatice (Brno), the existence of a barrow is doubtful: J. Říhovský, *PA* 49 (1958), 67–118; cf. J. Bayer, *MAGW* 61 (1931), 209ff.; Patek 1968.
88 E.g. E. Jílková, *PA* 49 (1958), 312–346; E. Jílková, A. Rybová and V. Šaldová, *PA* 50 (1959), 54–119; J. Bouzek, *SNMP* 17/2–3 (1963); V. Šaldová *PA* 56 (1965), 1–91.
89 W. Coblenz, *AuF* 16 (1971), 70–7.
90 C. Pescheck, *Führer* ... 27 (1975): the cremation grave also contained a sword, two spearheads, two knives, two pins and other ornaments.
91 Müller-Karpe 1959, 156f.; *BVgbl.* 21 (1956), 46–75.
92 Benkovský-Pivovarová 1975.
93 Herodotus II. 34, IV. 49. In both cases he refers to the fact that the Danube rises among the Celts 'near Pyrene' and that the Celts were the most westerly people of Europe apart from the Cynetes.
94 B. Soudský in *Investigations*, 1966, 159.
95 J. Röder, *Bonner Jahrb.* 148 (1948), 81–132.
96 E. Čujanová-Jílková, *AR* 27 (1975), 481–7.
97 A. Rybová and B. Soudský, *Libenice*, 1962.
98 J. Hrala and J. Fridrich, *AR* 24 (1972), 601–14.
99 Mus. Wrocław, and J. Gassowski and A. Kempisty, *Przewodnik Archeologiczny po Polsce*, 1973, 66, 79 and map, pl. 15. Gediga 1970, 28f. with refs.
100 K. Hohmann, *BBVF* 2 (1953), 62ff.; Müller 1964, 29.
101 Torbrügge 1970–1.
102 G. Wegner, *Die vorgeschichtlichen Flussfunde aus dem Main und aus dem Rhein bei Mainz*, 1976, 30ff.
103 H.-E. Mandera, *Fundb. aus Hessen* 12 (1972), 97ff.
104 Kossack 1954; J. Hralová-Adamczyková, *Acta Universitatis Carolinae* 3 (1959); Gediga 1970.
105 Reinecke 1911/1965, 3; Stocký 1928, pl. LII; Gimbutas 1965, pl. 62.
106 J. Bouzek, *AR* 29 (1977), 197–202.
107 Gimbutas 1965, 319, 328.
108 J. Bouzek, *AR* 29 (1977) 200.
109 Grünberg 1943; Coblenz 1952. For Coblenz *Mittelbronzezeit* is the same as period III, Grünberg's *Buckelware*; Grünberg's scheme is as follows: (1) Bossed ware, equivalent to Montelius III; (2) *Fremdgruppe*, equivalent to Montelius IV; (3) Horizontally fluted ware, equivalent to Montelius V; (4) Billendorf wares, equivalent to Montelius VI (EIA).
110 Holste 1953a, 86ff.
111 G. Kraft, *Die Kultur der Bronzezeit in Süddeutschland*, 1926.
112 C. Unz, *PZ* 48 (1973), 1–124.
113 E.g. by Herrmann 1966, Hennig 1970, Dehn 1972.
114 W. Coblenz, *AuF* 19 (1974), 89–94.

115 W. Coblenz, *AuF* 15 (1970), 75–85.

116 On each bronze type, a series of volumes of *Prähistorische Bronzefunde*, by areas. Some other works: *Knives*: H. Müller–Karpe, *BVgbl* 20 (1954), 113–19; *Germania* 41 (1963), 9–13; J. Říhovský, *Studie Arch. Ústavu ČSAV* 5 (1972). *Flange-hilted swords*: Sprockhoff 1941; Cowen 1956. *Solid-hilted swords*: Sprockhoff 1934; Holste 1953b; Müller-Karpe 1961. *Spearheads*: G. Jacob-Friesen, *Bronzezeitliche Lanzenspitzen Norddeutschlands und Scandinaviens*, 1967. *Sheet bronzework*: Sprockhoff 1930; several important papers by G. von Merhart, collected and reprinted under the title *Hallstatt und Italien*, Mainz 1970; O. Kytlicová, *PA* 50 (1959), 120–57; Furmánek 1970 (convenient summary of research).

117 F.-R. Herrmann, *Führer* ... 21 (1972), 121–4.

118 Torbrügge 1970–1.

119 Brunn 1968, 202ff.

120 Malinowski 1974, 219.

121 A. Jodłowski in *Salt, the Study of an Ancient Industry* (eds K. de Brisay and K. A. Evans), 1975, 86.

122 H. Müller-Karpe, *Germania* 40 (1962), 255–87; A. Snodgrass, in *The European Community in Later Prehistory*, 1971, 33–50; J. Paulík, *BRGK* 49 (1968), 41–61.

123 H. Reinerth, *Das Federseemoor als Siedlungsgebiet*, 1936.

124 Summarized by Ostoja-Zagórski 1974.

125 Cf. for instance J. Schultze-Motel and W. Gall, *Alt-Thüringen* 9 (1967), 7–15; K.-H. Knörzer, *Bonner Jahrb.* 172 (1972), 395–403.

126 D. Ridgway and O. T. P. K. Dickinson, *BSA* 68 (1973), 191–2.

127 N. Sandars in *The European Community in Later Prehistory*. (eds J. Boardman, M. A. Brown and T. G. E. Powell), 1971, 1–29. Sandars' proposed lowering of the dating seems to us too extreme.

8 Eastern Europe

A historical reconstruction of the events of the later Bronze Age in the Balkan area is a difficult task, but the proximity of historical cultures and the archaeological evidence of change and upheaval compel us to attach here a brief consideration of developments in the area during the centuries succeeding the rise of the Mycenaean civilization, that is, the second half of the second millennium BC.

In mainland Greece the development of Mycenaean culture and settlement reached its apogee in the thirteenth century BC, while in Anatolia the Hittite Empire was still dominant. Northern Greece was 'Mycenaeanized' only gradually; features of Mycenaean type appear in central and southern Thessaly from Late Helladic II (fifteenth century BC), with several tholos tombs and even a 'palace' at Iolkos, but not in northern Thessaly until LH IIIA (fourteenth century). In Macedonia, similarly, there is little Mycenaean material until LH IIIB, and then not a great deal; pottery is said to have been both locally made and imported at sites like Agios Mamas, Saratse and Gona. Limnotopos (Vardina) and Axiochorion (Vardaroftsa) on the river Axios have attracted a disproportionate amount of attention because of the presence in them of 'fluted wares' and twisted handles, connected by Childe with Urnfield groups far to the north, and especially with Lausitz. The balance is being redressed today by excavation at Assiros (near Thessaloniki) and Kastanas, so that a complete and detailed stratigraphical picture should enable us to tie down the appearance of these 'intrusive' wares more precisely in relation to the end of the Mycenaean period. In any case, it is clear that the fluted wares of Vardaroftsa have nothing to do with Lausitz, but are related to a group of cultures distributed in the Thracian area from Troy to the Danube.[1] The alleged occurrence of similar wares, as well as possible Trojan forms, in south Greece at this time[2] can also be seen in connection with possible population movements and cultural innovations in the whole south-east European area.

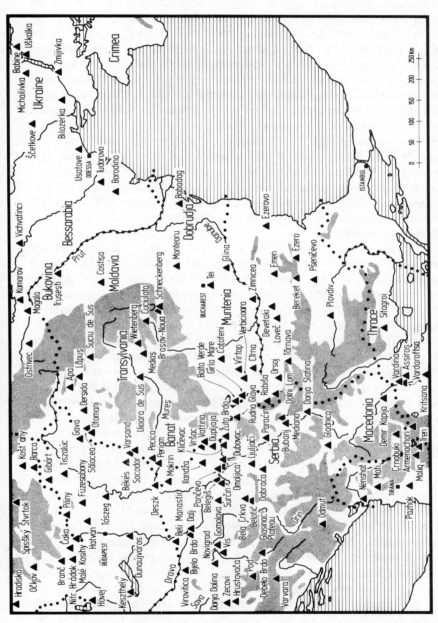

Map 7 Bronze Age sites in eastern Europe

We may briefly consider here the problem of the causes of the end of Mycenaean civilization, and any possible connection between it and the area to the north of Greece. Historically, the established facts are few. The only event which is recorded by the later historians,[3] apart from the fall of Troy, is the 'Dorian invasion', an immigration of Greek-speaking peoples into the Peloponnese and elsewhere, displacing existing communities. The inference is that they came through, if not from, central and northern Greece, so that attention naturally focuses on these areas and the lands immediately to their north. Archaeologically, Mycenaean sites fall in number dramatically from a peak in LH IIIB to a much smaller number in LH IIIC (twelfth century). At more or less the same time, many sites are sacked and deserted; and new types of swords, spearheads, body armour and safety-pins appear, distinctively 'European' and non-Mycenaean. At the end of LH IIIC the situation is hard to reconstruct; some sites were abandoned, others continued in use, while new bronze types, some of them identical to those known in other parts of Europe, are found.

Theories that account for the fall of Mycenaean Greece, and the problems in identifying the Dorians in the archaeological record, are numerous.[4] It has not proved possible to show with any degree of certainty that any of the innovations in Greece from 1200 BC onwards are attributable either to the 'Dorians' or to peoples coming from north of Greece. Pottery analogies are vague; and the influx of bronze types, though striking, is not necessarily any more than one would expect from the spread of technologically and functionally superior objects from one area to another. Most parts of Europe received such types at this time; and it is only the fact that Greece was by now open to such influence that lends their appearance here any special significance. The Dorians were, in any case, Greeks, so that one would not expect them to have come from a non-Mycenaean area outside Greece; indeed, it has been argued that a Dorian invasion would leave no trace at all in the archaeological record.[5]

Whatever the truth about the Dorians, it is clear that northern Greece in general, and Macedonia in particular, are crucial to any question of invasion from further north, so that a brief survey of the material found there will help to set the scene in perspective.[6] On most Macedonian Late Bronze Age sites three general categories of pottery are found: coarse domestic ware, painted wares in dark-on-light, and incised wares. The painted ware has as its most common shapes shallow bowls with angular or sagging body and thumb-grip or wish-bone handles, jugs with cutaway neck, and jars with globular body, conical neck and everted rim.[7] The decoration is geometric, with hatched pendent triangles of various forms, multiple triangles, 'pot-hook spirals' and so on, executed rather roughly in purple paint on yellow-buff or orange-slip ground. The incised wares are dark-faced and include most commonly deep globular bowls with narrow mouth and high loop-handles, jars with 'broken' profile and lug-handles, open bowls with wish-bone handles, small jugs etc.[8] The decoration is in large bold patterns, very often ribbon spirals or parallel lines, and often framed, with accessorial dots and dashes. The time-span of this latter class of pottery is very large, unlike that of the painted ware, which occurs only at the very end of the Bronze Age.

Onto this basis of local pottery Mycenaean ceramics were introduced, and have been found in surface collections at some forty sites in central Macedonia, though at very few in the west and south-west, away from the natural landing-area of the Thermaic Gulf.[9] Most of the motifs indicate a date in LH IIIB and C, though a few are earlier. One of the sites where it was most prolific was Axiochorion (Vardaroftsa), and the occurrence of the 'fluted ware' there makes a consideration of this site necessary. Some 150 Mycenaean sherds were found, from the twentieth half-metre to the eighth (in the composite section); the eleventh to eighth levels were 'burnt', and it was here that the 'fluted wares' occurred.[10] These are said to be in a gritty fabric with a dark polished surface; shapes include a low, wide two-handled urn with ring-base, low bowls with fluted rims, plain cups with cylindrical necks and high loop handles etc.; handles are often twisted.[11] These last occur at Mediana near Niš in Serbia[12] but also more generally through the central Balkan area; comparable forms are found in Troy VIIb2 and at Babadag on the Danube (below, pp. 391, 406). The same can be said for the decorative techniques (fluting, incised joined circles and 'quirks' etc.) which occur at these sites and in Bulgaria[13] (fig. 137). The detailed analysis of these stylistic similarities must await further excavation in Macedonia; but it seems possible that we should regard the Thracian area as a unified culture-province at this time, so that Vardaroftsa (and, now, Kastanas and Assiros)[14] can most properly be seen as belonging to the northern, not the Aegean, province.

In Bulgaria relatively little material can be attributed to the later Bronze Age. The only exception to this statement is in the north-west of the country, where a number of finds of Cîrna-Gîrla Mare type have been made (p. 406). Elsewhere, pottery attributable to this period is scarce.[15] Pottery of the Zimnicea-Plovdiv (Čerkovna) style continued to be produced; probably dating to a late phase of it is a cemetery of inhumation graves from Krušovica (Vraca).[16] The most characteristic style in Bulgaria is knobbed, incised and stamped ware, which is paralleled in Troy phase VIIb2.[17] Notable finds come from Pšeničevo (Stara Zagora), Kozloduj (Vraca), Rabiša cave (Vidin), Gabarevo (Kazanlâk), Bukjovci

(Vraca), Dolni Lom (Belogradčik), Čatalka (Stara Zagora) and Čepina (Pazardžik). The fabric of these pots is usually polished black, the decoration incised, stamped and occasionally channelled (fig. 137). Shapes include one-handled cups and jugs, biconical jars and low bowls, quite alien to the standard Bulgarian forms known hitherto. The incised ornament has running dot-and-line decoration, wavy lines, lozenge-bands etc. as well as hatched triangles which appear to start rather earlier in the Bronze Age. Tall, bossed cremation urns, described as 'Thracian',

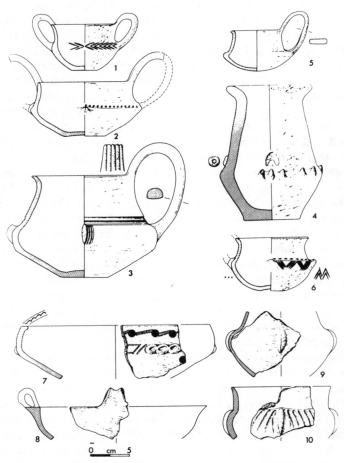

Fig. 137   Late Bronze Age pottery from Romania and Bulgaria.
1–6. Insula Banului, 7–10. Pšeničevo.
(After Hänsel 1976)

but not necessarily so advanced in date, have been found at sites in the east of the country.[18]

The study of the later Bronze Age in Bulgaria is practically impossible without proper excavation of stratified settlement sites – and of cemeteries, which are almost totally lacking – and one can only look forward to a change in this situation. At Pšeničevo itself there are post-framed rectangular houses, but it is not yet clear to what precise period they belong.[19] Only in metalwork is there any quantity of material, and even that is small by comparison with what occurs in Romania.[20] Socketed axes and sickles are the commonest finds, but sword and spearhead fragments do occur. Ornaments are rare. A notable feature of Bulgaria is the relatively high proportion of moulds known, especially for axes; the hoard of Pobit Kamâk (Razgrad) contained numerous limestone moulds, and it is interesting that moulds also occurred at Assiros.[21] Finally, one must mention the finds of 'Mycenaean' metalwork: an imported sword from Galatin (Vraca) and possible imitations elsewhere; several imported spearheads; and a 'Mycenaean' double-axe from Semerdžievo (Ruse). Most of these pieces should date to the earlier centuries of the period under consideration. The rapier fragment of Romanian 'Mycenaean' type from Sokol (Silistra), however, is dated by its association to Br D, and is convincing evidence that the Romanian rapier series is quite independent of the Mycenaean (fig. 138).[22]

Little is known of grave-rites, but it has been suggested that the earliest megalithic tombs in Bulgaria – in the south-east of the country – may date to the Late Bronze Age. A 'dolmen' near Mladinovo (Haskovo) is said to have had sherds of knobbed ware around it (though not in it), which would put it in the same chronological horizon as the Troy VIIb2 – Pšeničevo horizon we have been considering.[23] This monument is a simple one-chamber affair, a rectangular slab construction with narrow doorway and short *dromos,* with a small cairn of stones piled up around it and a ring of stones enclosing the earth barrow. Most Bulgarian 'dolmens' date to the Iron Age, so that this could be important evidence for Late Bronze Age – Early Iron Age continuity if substantiated by similar finds from excavation.

North of the Danube, the period succeeding the Verbicioara – Tei grouping in lowland Romania is hard to define. Some authors[24] call the period 'Horizon V' in the local terminology, referring to elements of later culture appearing in the lowland groups of the preceding phase; in effect this means that the major groups, especially Tei, Zimnicea, Coslogeni and Monteoru, continue on into the later Bronze Age, contemporary with the early Urnfield period elsewhere.

If lowland Romania is something of a blank at this stage, we are

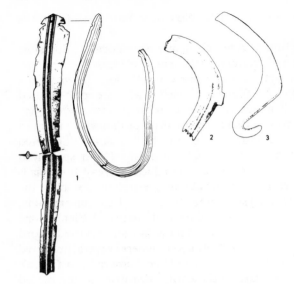

Fig. 138
Part of bronze hoard
including 'Mycenaean'
rapier from Sokol
(Silistra) Thirteenth-
twelfth centuries.
(After B. Hänsel, *PZ* 48
(1973))

fortunate in having a good deal of evidence from Moldavia and Transylvania as well as the western Ukraine. In both areas – and the eastern wing of the Carpathians seems here not to have acted as the barrier one would expect – the previous cultural groups were succeeded by, or, as we shall argue, developed into, what is known in Romania as the *Noua* culture, in the north-west Pontic area as the *Sabatinivka* culture, and in Podolia as the *Bilogrudivka* culture. Noua itself is the site of an inhumation cemetery in Braşov, investigated early in the present century;[25] but the concept of a culture for which that would be the type-site was not formulated until 1953, even though the non-funerary aspect of the group had been recognized by Nestor.[26] In general, the culture is characterized over most of its extent by unfortified encampment sites, frequently by rivers, with large amounts of ash in the archaeological deposits – hence the name *zolniki* ('ash-pits') (fig. 139). It is not established quite why such large quantities of ash should be present, nor have houses as such been identified in the Romanian sites; presumably this situation is one in which temporary camps were regularly, if seasonally, used for habitation, during the occupation of which numerous fires for cooking and heating were lit. It is suggestive that in these masses of ash recent excavations have found traces of hearths, clay benches, calcined daub etc. Typical *zolniki* have been excavated at sites like Truşeşti – Movila (Botoşani),[27] Lichitişeni and Lozinca-Bărboasa (Bacău),[28] Piatra Neamţ-Ciritei[29] and many other localities.

In the Soviet part of the Noua distribution, however, a certain number

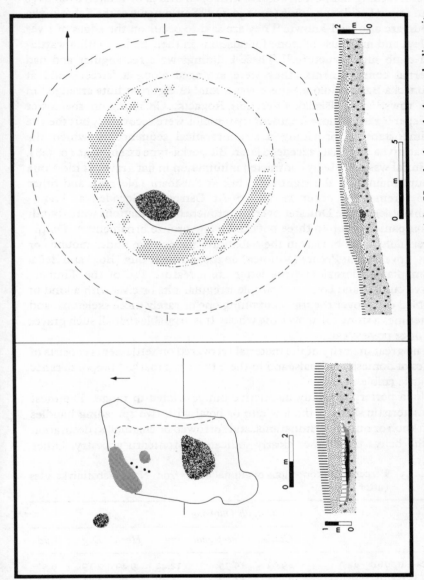

Fig. 139   *Zolniki* from Moldavia and the Ukraine: 1. Magala, 2. Adamivka. Hearths shown by heavy shading, pits by dense hatching and beaten clay by light stipple. (After G. I. Smirnova. *Arch. Sbor.* 14 (1972))

of house-plans *have* been recovered. At Magala (Sadgar, Černivcy) several rectangular post structures with open hearth or vaulted oven have been found beside the *zolnik* (fig. 139,1).[30] Settlements of the Sabatinivka group are also well-known. They are said to occur on the edges of river valleys and made use of stone foundations in their houses with a wattle-and-daub superstructure.[31] These buildings were rectangular and had internal compartments; they were arranged along a 'street', and at Zvonecka Balka (Solone) there was a total of eighteen huts arranged in two rows.[32] At Uškalka (Verchnij Rogačik, Cherson) on the lower Dnieper[33] rather more fragmentary remains were recovered, but the site is important in providing a stratigraphical sequence in which the Sabatinivka material precedes a later, Bilozerka-type assemblage (p. 398).

Burial was usually by contracted inhumation in flat graves in the Noua group, mainly on the right side; but at Săbăoani (Neamţ), and other sites, cremations occur as well.[34] At Ostrivec (Gorodenka, Ivano-Frankovsk) on the Dniester over 150 crouched inhumations were found, accompanied by up to three pots and a few bronze ornaments.[35] On the other hand some burials in the Sabatinivka group are under mounds or stone covers, as at Pečora (Vinnica) on the southern Bug (Bog) and Balka Basmatka (Zaporožje);[36] the latter are a feature also of the Timber-Grave culture and consist of simple irregular pits or cists with a kind of cobbled cover over the top, containing one or rarely more skeletons, and sometimes a stone cairn over the whole. It is arguable that all such graves did once possess cairns.

The great majority of the material recovered on settlements consists of bones of domestic animals, and in these there is a marked preponderance of cattle (table 13).

Noua pottery is highly distinctive but restricted in range. The most characteristic shape is the low cup or bowl with two spreading handles with knob or button terminations, and furrowed or channelled decoration on the belly: these vases clearly indicate a Monteoru ancestry. Other

Table 13   Percentage proportions of animal bones from Noua-Sabatinivka sites (after Florescu)[37]

| Site | Individuals (min. nos.) % | | | | | |
	Cattle	Sheep/goat	Pig	Horse	Dog	Wild
Valea Lupului – Iaşi	49.63	19.75	12.41	9.49	2.19	6.57
Piatra Neamţ – Ciritei	47.72	12.50	11.36	7.96	3.41	17.04
Bîrlad	40.98	22.95	11.48	13.11	1.64	9.84
Zmijivka (Berislav)[38]	45	18	18	26		

popular shapes are one-handled cups, ovoid storage jars (from the *zolniki*) and low conical bowls (fig. 140). Decoration on the settlement pottery is crude – usually raised bands with or without finger-impressions. On settlements other material is rich and varied: stone hammer-axes and flint *Krummesser* (curved sickle-knives), bone awls, discs, horse cheek-pieces, weaving combs and other objects: at Gîrbovat (Tecuei, Galaţi) the bone-work was especially numerous, including notched scapulae, sickles, hafts and many other strange-looking objects of unknown use.[39] An eastern (Timber Grave) origin is suggested for much of this. A ritual element may be visible in the 'sceptres' in stone from various sites.[40] In metalwork, knot-headed and roll-top pins are commonest; bronze knives and awls occur in the Sabatinivka group, and the earliest iron objects are found in the latest sites of this type. A few hoards, which include both 'European' types like hook sickles, and 'eastern' types like spatulate daggers, are found.[41]

Chronologically, the Noua-Sabatinivka group can be seen to span a wide range, and the available radiocarbon dates bear this suggestion out (below, p. 410). Two Noua phases have been distinguished on the basis of pottery typology,[42] and Sabatinivka can be similarly divided;[43] various elements can be seen as going to make up the whole – drawn on Timber Grave, Monteoru and Wietenberg stock. It seems likely that Noua represents a local pottery tradition, but the steppe elements in bonework appear undeniable.

The *Bilogrudivka* group (Uman', Čerkasy) is in many respects similar to the Noua-Sabatinivka culture, though it has been considered to fall a little later in time.[44] *Zolniki* are found here too;[45] the pottery includes the same general shapes, with the exception of the two-handled cup;[46] miniature vases, spindle-whorls, figurines, bone and stonework are common, and bronzes commoner than in the Noua area; faunal remains indicate a comparable economic basis.

An interesting recent settlement find was that of Velika Andrusivka (Novo-Georgijvs'ke, Kirovograd),[47] where the remains of ten sunken wood-built huts were found, varying between 5 × 6 m and 10 × 12 m. Fig. 141 shows one which measured 5 × 10 m and included a clay oven and many sherds, some of them Iron Age in date. Most of the pottery here is domestic in nature, and includes many ovoid and globular storage jars, one-handled cups, and inverted-piriform cheese-strainers. The only decorative motifs are zig-zags of the 'eyebrow' type, no doubt reflecting the same decorative elements as are found on later Lausitz pottery. Related material, perhaps a little later and connected with what some authors call the *Čornij-Lis* group,[48] comes from Kompanijci (Kobeljaki, Poltava) on the Dnieper.[49]

Fig. 140   Pottery and other objects of Noua types from Romania.
Varying scales.
(After Florescu 1964)

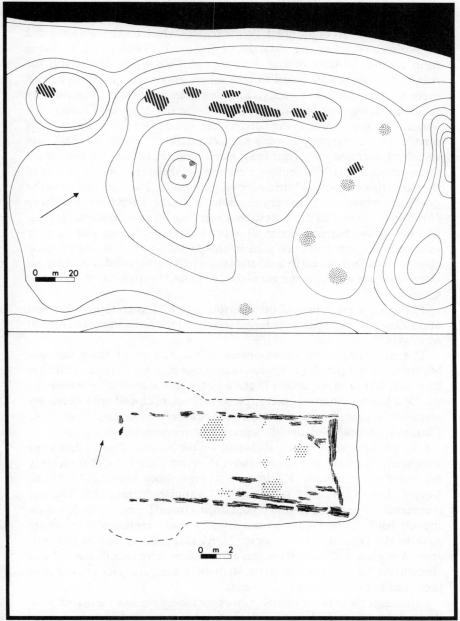

Fig. 141   Upper: The Velika Andrusivka settlement, Ukraine, placed on a low terrace adjacent to a river. The houses are shown hatched and ash mounds dotted. Lower: House plan; daub is shown stippled.
(After E. F. Pokrovs'ka and E. O. Petrovs'ka, *AK* 13 (1961))

397

The eastern part of the north Pontic region, which had been dominated by Kurgan burial of the Catacomb type, gradually changed its burial form during the later Bronze Age, though barrow-burial was still the rule. Settlements now begin to take on an importance hitherto denied them because of their scarcity. The new burial type can be shown by relative typology to originate further east – on the steppeland beyond the Volga. The graves under the barrows are square or rectangular and, to start with at any rate, lined with oak planks;[50] ochre or chalk was sprinkled over the floor (fig. 142). Burial was, as before, by contracted inhumation, and animal skulls – or even whole skeletons – may accompany the dead, though giftless burials are very common. The name given to the group as a whole – and it is very generalized – is the *Timber-Grave* culture (*Srubnaja kultura*). By contrast to the preceding Pit and Catacomb graves, Timber-Grave barrows occur all over the steppe and not just in river valleys. Some scholars have seen in this fact a reaction to the climatic change from Sub-boreal to Sub-atlantic, when wetter conditions enabled large-scale use of the steppe grassland to be used for pasture or even crop agriculture.[51]

Though the main part of the distribution of Timber-Graves lies east of the Dnieper, extensions are found west of it; the same rite even reached Moldavia.[52]

The most important development in the culture of these barrow-builders, for our present purposes, is the large number of settlement sites they have left to us, especially in the western end of their distribution. In the Don basin numerous open sites, sometimes equipped with defensive earthworks, provide us with vivid evidence of settlement conditions.[53] At Chutor Ljapičev (Volgograd) square and rectangular hut-plans were recovered, apparently wattle-and-daub on timber post-frame; they were irregularly disposed on a terrace above the river Carica.[54] Other recently excavated sites include Kapitanovo (Luganskoe, Doneck),[55] Nižnij Vorgol (Elec, Lipeck),[56] and Mosolov (Anninsk, Voronež).[57] The last is especially interesting in that it contained a metal foundry: the site is on the left bank of the Don, and the foundry was a rectangular structure sunk in the ground, 8.5 × 19.5 m. Many clay moulds and mould-lids, stone hammers and other tools, jets and runners were found; the site was specializing in the production of shaft-hole axes and sickles, but also produced hoes, knives and spearheads.

Other aspects of the material culture include wide low carinated pots, decorated with incised and comb-stamped geometric designs[58] (a local variant found in the lower Dnieper basin is characterized by conical and biconical jars with multiple raised cordons round the body),[59] and bone-work, which included horse cheek-pieces (e.g. at Kapitanovo) (fig. 143);

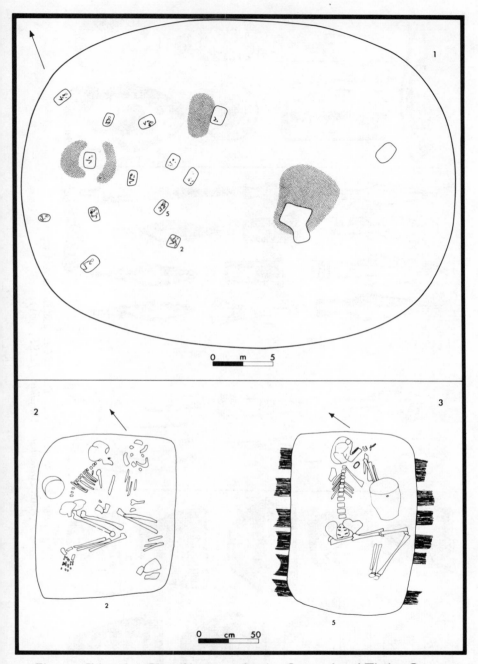

Fig. 142   Il 'men': 1. Plan of barrow 6 showing Catacomb and Timber Graves,
2. Grave 2,   3. Grave 5.
(After Kačalova 1970)

399

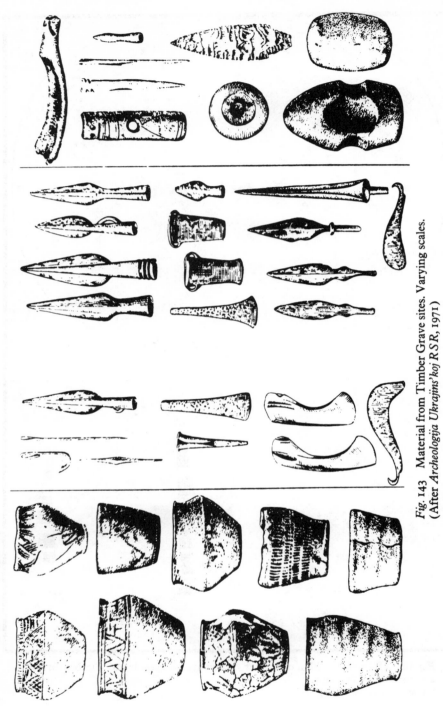

Fig. 143   Material from Timber Grave sites. Varying scales.
(After *Archeologija Ukrajins'koj RSR*, 1971)

but it is the rich and well-developed metal industry which deserves the widest attention. Some metal hoards rival those of central Europe in size, and the range of forms represented is very large. Bronze foundry sites[60] and collections of stone moulds[61] provide a vivid illustration of the scope of Pontic metallurgy.

One aspect of the Timber-Grave culture deserves special mention: the abundant evidence of horses. Numerous horse-bones as well as bridle and harness apparatus indicate a reliance on the horse for traction and food, and it can be no coincidence that the spread of the 'Thraco-Cimmerians' (below, p. 403) is largely chronicled by the spread of horse-harness.

A late aspect of the same cultural traditions may be seen in sites on the lower Don of *Kobjakovo* type. The type-site is a defensive earthwork not far from the mouth of the Don (Rostov/Don); several habitation sites have been dug in the same area;[62] they contained sunken rectangular stone-built houses and production areas. The material recovered included rich finds of settlement debris, especially weights, pounders, grinders and large faunal samples.

Other cultural groups of the later Bronze Age in the Soviet Union require less attention.[63] In Volynia, the west of the Ukraine and in White Russia the *Visocko* group is to be seen as a late aspect of the Lausitz culture group (above, p. 339); in the north Carpathian foothills the Komarov barrow-culture developed into the *Goligrady* (Holihrady) culture. On the middle Dnieper and upper Donec are sites named after *Bondaricha*; further west are hill-top sites named after *Milograd* and *Juchnov* which are concentrated in White Russia. Finally, in central Russia we have elements of the *Balachna-Volosovo* group. In general we may note the predominance of settlement sites, and in the Bondaricha group these are large and have provided ample evidence for houses, economic activities and bronze-working: the type-site near Izjum (Char'kiv) on the river Donec,[64] Mali Budki (Nedrigajlove, Sumy) on the Sula, and Studenok, site 5 (Krasnij Liman, Char'kiv) on the northern Donec may be singled out for special mention.[65] Burials are much less well-known; the main points of note are the grave-goods, among which the horse harness and the bronze arrowheads are of special importance and no doubt indicate a Scythian element.[66] Material from settlement sites is informative but unremarkable (fig. 144); moulds and crucibles were found at Studenok, where the two-loop socketed axe, a new and characteristically Pontic form, was being produced.

The development of the bronze industry in the Soviet area is extremely complicated and hard to synchronize. We are too far from central Europe for the Müller-Karpe system to be of much use, so that we have to proceed by reference to events in Europe, the Caucasus, Anatolia, Greece

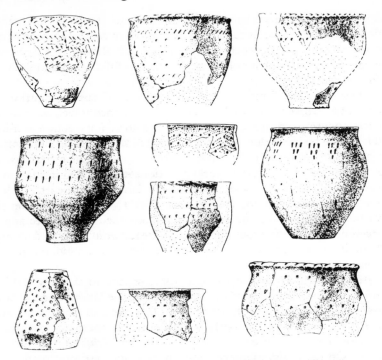

Fig. 144　Late Bronze Age pottery from the Ukraine (sites of
Mar'janivka, Mali Budki and Bondaricha type). Varying scales.
(After *Archeologija Ukrajins'koj RSR*, 1971)

and the Near East. Little is known of metallurgical events following the
time of the Borodino hoard. Shaft-hole axes, long flat chisels, and hook
sickles were standard. Double-axes of Aegean type in finds of this period,
as at Kozorezovo and Ščetkovo, may attest direct contact with the south,
while the trunnion axe may have arrived now via the Caucasus.[67] Rather
late on the scene is the socketed axe, which increases in popularity, and
acquires two loops, probably indicating that it was mounted on its haft
adze-wise. A marked change is discernible between the metalwork before
1100 BC and that after. Numerous hoards and foundry sites attest
increased working of the metal; Caucasian and Volga types, like tanged
leaf-shaped daggers and distinctive socketed spearheads, predominate,
and the forms are highly distinctive and quite un-European. Only in the
sub-Carpathian area was a standard range of 'European' types
represented.[68]

The development of metalworking, and the sequence of settlement
sites, take us to the threshold of history. The early historians preserve

mention of tribal names and movements which must originate in the Bronze Age. Most notable of these are the Scythians and the Cimmerians. Herodotus records the expulsion 'from Europe' of the Cimmerians by the Scythians, and the subsequent presence of both tribes in parts of Asia Minor.[69] Their homeland, however, he clearly places north of the Black Sea: the Scythians had themselves been forced out of Asia by the Massagetae across the Araxes (?Volga) into 'Cimmeria'. At the time Herodotus wrote, the Scythians occupied the entire north Pontic region as far west as the southern Bug, and as far north as 'eleven days' sail' up the Borysthenes (Dnieper). North of these were the 'Neuri' to the west, the 'Androphagi' (Man-eaters) in the centre, and the 'Melanchlaeni' (Black-cloaks) to the east, the latter two having no racial connection with the Scythian tribes.[70] If we ignore the fascinating details of Scythian life that Herodotus provides and concentrate on archaeological identification of these peoples, it is at least possible that the ancestors of the historical Scythians are to be seen in the Timber-Grave culture which Soviet scholars agree is earliest in its eastern, north Caspian, branch, and only secondary in its Pontic distribution. This would allow us to put the Cimmerian homeland along the north coast of the Black Sea at an earlier stage – the Catacomb Grave culture? Be that as it may, the spread of new techniques and artifacts in the earlier first millennium BC has often been attributed to the displaced Cimmerians – above all the use of iron and the abundant exploitation of the horse, as shown by bridle-bits and horse-harness. Such a movement into Europe is not, however, mentioned by the historians, unless one may read into a story of Herodotus the germ of such an idea. He records the division of opinion among the Cimmerians at the time of the Scythian invasions, some wishing to flee, others to stand and fight.[71] Is it possible that a division of opinion really did occur, not as to the course of action to be taken but as to the course of the flight before the invaders? By this means we might be able to reconcile the historical and archaeological sources, for on the one hand the Cimmerians crossed the Caucasus into Phrygia and Urartu, on the other elements of supposed Cimmerian derivation are found in east-central Europe from this time. To our mind the crucial weakness of this argument is the lack of any artifacts that can be uniquely attributed to either the Scythians or the Cimmerians. Since we do not know for sure what Scythian or Cimmerian culture was like in its place of origin, it is optimistic to try to identify it on its path east- or westwards. The spread of iron technology, and of horse-riding, must have been but part of the innovations of the day, and though the 'Thraco-Cimmerians' may have had some part in their diffusion, the techniques can hardly be attributed solely to them.

Gimbutas' explanation may perhaps come close to the truth.[72] She sees the Čornij-Lis group as the immediate ancestor of the Scythian tribes, and the Timber-Grave group as 'proto-Scythian'; the Neuri are to be seen in, first, the Bondaricha and later in the Milograd and Juchnov groups – both, ultimately, of Baltic stock. For the Man-eaters and Black-cloaks we must presumably look to the safe obscurity of the Abaševo group of central Russia.

In contrast to the inhumation cemeteries which were almost universal in the Noua groups of Transylvania, Moldavia and the eastern sub-Carpathian Ukraine, adjacent areas of north-eastern Hungary and Ruthenia (the upper Tisza basin) were occupied by a cremating group of urnfield type, with very distinctive local pottery. This is best known in north Romania, where it is named after the site of *Suciu de Sus* (Maramureş);[73] in Hungary it is known as the *Felsöszöcs* group (= Hungarian for Suciu de Sus) with various sub-groups;[74] in the Ukraine it is called *Stanovo*[75] (Beregiv, sub-Carpathian region). Settlements are quite well-known from Ruthenia, where they are either open sites in raised positions on marshy areas or river-banks, or else hill-sites with large accumulations of rubbish and debris in the many habitation levels. Houses are said to be 'semi-subterranean' or wooden-framed daub affairs. At Culciul Mare (Satu Mare) on the Someş, a village of twelve houses was recovered, with model wheels and a 'cult waggon' being found in one of them.[76]

The urnfield burial rite may take on a number of variations: urns were placed in a shallow pit, or incineration may have taken place on the spot and then been covered over, with the ashes of the dead in a cup in the centre. Usually – as at Suciu de Sus itself – the cemeteries were true 'urnfields', but at Lăpuş mounds were raised over the cremated remains; this site is considered by its excavator to represent a developed stage of the culture. Another exception is the richly furnished tumulus burial at Nyírkarász-Gyulaháza in north-eastern Hungary.[77]

The richly-decorated pottery of the Suciu de Sus group is its most characteristic feature. The commonest decorative technique is excision and encrustation with white paste, and the motifs are markedly curvilinear, including spiraliform and foliate designs, as well as rectilinear geometric decoration (fig. 145). Though some features link it with the Komarov group, it is with Füzesabony-Otomani that it has most in common, and it is tempting even to see it as a direct continuation of that culture. At Garneşti (Mureş)[78] these designs were amply represented on low globular bowls and one-handled jugs, and elaborate knob-handles are an additional feature. At Lăpuş, a number of individual forms are present, including urns with tall cylinder neck and protruding shoulder-knobs, vase-supports, lids, fluted cups, zoomorphic handles and so on.

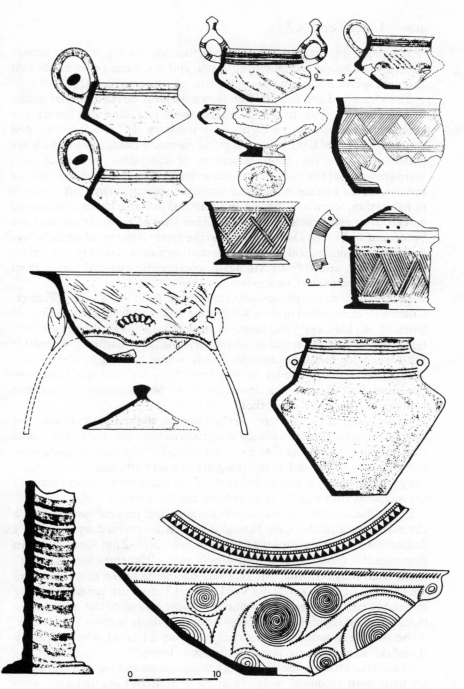

Fig. 145   Pottery of Suciu de Sus type from Lăpuş (Satu Mare). Scales in cm.
(After C. Kacsó, *Dacia* 19 (1975))

It is to the time of this cultural group that one can attribute the bronze hoards to be found on the Upper Tisza, and there can be no doubt that this area was one of numerous metallurgical centres (fig. 146).[79]

Elsewhere in Late Bronze Age Romania most of the material comes from settlement sites. In the Dobrogea, the site of Babadag (Istria) is of great importance.[80] It is a fortified promontory on Lake Babadag, and contains a cultural layer up to 2 m thick. As usual, storage pits (which are bell-shaped) are the main indication of habitation; traces of huts recovered are said to be either 'semi-subterranean' or, in the middle of the site, on the surface. A long and intensive occupation had left six levels of habitation, all rich in incised and stamped pottery, bones, carbonized cereals, iron and bronze fragments. Other sites of a similar nature have been identified in the Dobrogea, and so the group is named after Babadag; two main chronological horizons are distinguished, roughly equivalent to Hallstatt A and B.[81] In Moldavia, comparable material comes from sites attributed to the Cozia group (Iaşi).[82]

In Oltenia, multi-phase *zolnik*-like sites such as Vîrtop (Pleniţa, Craiova)[83] correspond in time to hill-forts in Transylvania like Mediaş,[84] Şeica Mică (Mediaş)[85] and Someşul Rece (Cluj).[86] The former are low-lying terrace sites often full of ashy layers; the latter naturally defensible hill-tops, with fortifications added only where necessary. Their main occupation actually occurs in the Iron Age, but enough sites have produced true Bronze Age levels for it to be reasonable to envisage continuity from one to the other.[87]

In the south of the country, on the Danube, the transition to the Iron Age is marked by the appearance of a group named after the site of Insula Banului, an island in the Danube (Mehedinţi).[88] Here house-plans were recovered from the sand, roughly square to start with, and later circular; the group's pottery is said to indicate a Gîrla Mare ancestry, but traits of the incipient Iron Age Basarabi culture are also present.

In the Banat, Oltenia, north-west Bulgaria and parts of eastern Serbia the earlier part of the Late Bronze Age is still occupied by the highly distinctive urn-using group of Gîrla Mare-Cîrna-Žuto Brdo type. In Romania this grouping is known simply as the 'Funerary Urn Culture'. Cîrna itself may continue into this period; among the largest cemeteries are Cruceni (Timiş) and Balta Verde (Dolj).[89] Inurned cremation is the invariable rule and went on in much the same way until flat inhumation burial characteristic of the Iron Age Basarabi culture became fashionable. A comparable situation occurs at the site of Pecica (Arad), where typically 'Urnfield' biconical urns occur in the upper levels.[90]

In material culture, the pottery is homogeneous and varies little: there are urns with biconical body, cylindrical neck and everted rim, with

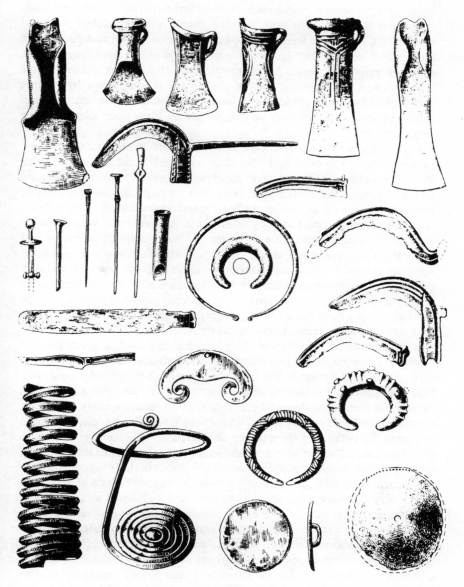

Fig. 146   Late Bronze Age metalwork from the Subcarpathian region. Varying scales.
(After *Archeologija Ukrajins'koj RSR*, 1971)

cord-impressed decoration in parallel bands; accessory vessels (bowls and cups); simple bronzes that hark back to an earlier period (heart-pendants, triangular daggers, pins with swollen shank, plain bracelets of round section, etc.). As time went on, the urns acquired bosses and knobs with channelled semicircles around them and pendent arcading motifs. Bronzes remained rare. An interesting 'cult complex' comes from Timişoara: two huge but typical urns were accompanied by a large pedestalled bowl, an ovoid vessel, and a two-handled jug with vertical fluting; the bowl is extraordinary in having six large pointed projections on the rim.[91]

It is perhaps to this period (late Dubovac-Žuto Brdo) that the famous figurine from Kličevac and the 'cult waggon' from Dupljaja (south Banat) should be assigned. The figurines are usually stylized standing female figures, with bell-shaped skirt, though there are several variants of this form: the upper part of the body may be solid and the skirt hollow; the hands may rest on the belly or on the breast. Alternatively the body may be flat and massive. In either case the techniques of execution and decoration are the same as on pottery, with elaborate impression or incision infilled with white paint; the fabric is grey, black or red and polished. The commonest ornaments indicating dress are concentric circles and spiraliform designs. Typologically these figurines can be arranged into a developmental sequence, though such subjective criteria may not reflect the true chronological situation.[92]

The famous 'chariot' from Dupljaja has received a great deal of attention, though we are no nearer a final solution of the many problems it presents.[93] The basis of the group is a typical bell-skirted figure with beak-like head, arms akimbo and concentric-circle decoration. It stands on the platform of a three-wheeled cart which is apparently drawn by three aquatic birds – two in front and one behind. The wheels, tie-beams and even the bottom of the cart are decorated with concentric circles, as is a small conical object with suspension loop that was associated with the chariot group. Some reconstructions of the group include this object over the figurine's head as a 'parasol'; others see it simply as a sun symbol which may not have been attached to the central group at all (pl. 19a).

While interpretation of this extraordinary object is very hard, certain parallels may be drawn. Cult waggons and birds were a regular feature of Urnfield symbolism (above, p. 368), and the Dupljaja chariot must belong in the Urnfield sphere, though its precise chronological position is harder to define. The hand-made pottery and figurines of the Submycenaean period in Athens (Kerameikos cemetery) have been said to be related to this middle Danubian plastic art style:[94] this must imply a date as late as 1050 BC or later. A similarity has also been seen between the Kličevac idol's dress and the dress of the Philistines as known from Egyptian reliefs at Medinet Habu, but this can only be a parallel of the most general nature.[95]

The material culture of all these groups has in common the great development of bronze-working, especially in Transylvania (320 of 360 hoards). Huge hoards, like that from Uioara de Sus (Aiud, Cluj) with its 1,300 kg of metal (nearly 6,000 pieces) occur in most areas, though the repertoire of shapes is strictly limited and quite in line with general developments everywhere. One hoard, that of Băleni (Bujor, Galaţi)[96] in south Moldavia, consists of 269 pieces, of which thirty-seven are parts of horse-harness; culturally speaking it belongs in the Noua area, but the presence of rhomboid-headed pins (like that in the Borodino hoard) and Caucasian-type spearheads suggests manufacture outside the Carpathians.

Table 14　The sequence of Romanian hoards, later Bronze Age

Century	Müller-Karpe 1959	Hoard phase[97]	Other notable finds (Romania)
13th	Br D	Uriu-Domăneşti	Sfîrnas, Drajna de Jos
12th	Ha A1	Cincu-Suseni	Uioara de Sus, Şpălnaca 1, Guşteriţa
11th	Ha A2	Turia-Jupalnic	Slimnic (not well-represented)
10th	Ha B1	Moigrad-Tăuteu	Sălard, Şpălnaca 2
9th	Ha B2	Fizeşul Gherlei-Sîngeorgiu de Pădure	Bîrlad
8th	Ha B3	Şomartin-Ugra	

Some bronze types continue through all these phases, and only detailed typological distinction can separate them. Such forms are solid- and flange-hilted swords, socketed axes, winged axes, flange-grip sickles, and elaborately incised solid bracelets. In other cases, particular types are characteristic of, or invented in, particular phases. Thus the Peschiera dagger, the flame-shaped spearhead, the double-pick, and the shaft-tube axe are especially noteworthy in von Brunn's phase 1; the pommel-cup sword in phase 4. By phase 5 (Ha B2) the first iron objects are starting to appear.[98] It is natural enough that iron-working should have reached the east of Europe before the centre; Ha B3 in Romania belongs to the full Iron Age.

Other skills, such as the production of glass and faience beads and the working of gold foil, are found less universally: in the case of Cioclovina (Hunedoara) a ritual intention is suggested since all the 2,000 bronzes, 1,000 amber beads and 2,000 faience and glass-paste beads are new and unused.[99] Pottery production was of a high order, and the urns of the Urnfield-type cremating groups are in a fine shiny black ware decorated with bosses and channelling. The coarser wares, as found at Babadag or the Oltenian hill-forts, are technically much inferior, though covering a wide range of forms. Other domestic objects, like spindle-whorls and loom-weights, are also well represented.[100]

Chronology

We have seen how various schemes for pottery and bronzes have built up detailed relative chronologies in restricted areas; for absolute chronology our information is scanty indeed. In the south, the end of Mycenaean

Table 15   Radiocarbon dates, eastern Europe, later Bronze Age

Site	Lab	bc
Timber Grave		
Kudinov (Rostov), kurgan 1 grave 7	UCLA	
	–1274	1575±80
	LE–511	1230±80
Archadinskaja (Volgograd), kurgan 9 grave 4	UCLA	
	–1272	1440±80
Vibla (Kiev), Krest kurgan	LE–731	970±80
		890±110
Il'men', (Borisoglebsk, Voronež), kurgan 8	LE–708	1460±50
Bondaricha		
Cikalovka (Poltava)	LE–413	660±100
Kob'jakovo		
Kob'jakovo (Rostov), occupation layer of earth-work	RUL–105	900±110
	LE–406	670±130
Noua-Sabatinivka		
Ivanice (Dubno) pyre, late Komarov	GrN–5250	1285±35
Magala (Sadgar, Cernivci)	GrN–5135	1150±35
	LE–489	1430±80
Goligrady		
Magala (Sadgar, Cernivci)	LE–573	540±90

pottery production gives us a date in the early eleventh century BC for the ceramics of Troy VIIb2 type, as the latest Mycenaean pottery at Troy, assigned by Blegen to the Granary Class, is in level VIIb. Most other cross-dating is by bronze types. The LH IIIB/Br D synchronism is of relatively little value in the east; more useful are fibulae and other specific types, which provide a yardstick of progress. A Vrokastro-type arc fibula, for instance, from Bradu in central Moldavia shows us that the Basarabi culture dates later than the ninth century BC.[101] But only the arrival of datable Greek ceramics in the colonizing era puts the sequence firmly back on its feet, by which time the Iron Age was well under way.

Radiocarbon dating is, so far, of little help because of the small number of available dates, and the ambiguity of those. Dates for the Timber Graves span nearly 600 years, with the earliest dates coming from the western part of the distribution. A start by 1500 bc is suggested, continuing to at least 900 bc. This is more or less in agreement with the dates for the succeeding Bondaricha and Kob'jakovo groups, between 900 and 600 bc. In the western area, Noua-Sabatinivka seems to fall between 1450 and 1150 bc, Goligrady to be late, even Iron Age, in date.

Notes

1 The wider connections of these wares have been documented most fully by Kimmig (1964, 257ff.), but only recently have the Romanian and Bulgarian finds been brought into the picture: Morintz 1964; Čičikova 1968; M. Stefanovich, *Actes du VIIIe Congrès UISPP III*, 1973, 148–59; Sandars 1971; Hänsel 1976, esp. 86, 243.

2 J. Rutter, *AJA* 79 (1975), 17–32 (cf. too *AJA* 80 (1976), 186ff.).

3 Herodotus, i. 56; Thucydides, i. 12.

4 Convenient summary and bibliography: P. Betancourt, *Antiquity* 50 (1976), 40–7.

5 A. M. Snodgrass, *The Dark Age of Greece*, 1971, 312.

6 Heurtley 1939, 93ff., 214ff. The results from the excavations of K. Wardle and B. Hänsel are providing more reliable data.

7 Heurtley 1939, 94, 218f., nos 421–425.

8 Heurtley 1939, 95, 214f.

9 Heurtley 1939, xxiif., 96f.; D. French, *Index of Prehistoric Sites in Central Macedonia*, 1967.

10 Heurtley 1939, 36ff., 98f.

11 Wardle (pers. comm.) has suggested that the stratigraphy at Vardaroftsa is much more complicated than Heurtley believed; the strata are terraced and the precise relative positions of Mycenaean and fluted wares are not, therefore, certain. Heurtley 1939, 216 fig. 87.

12 C. Blegen *et al.*, *Troy IV*, 1958, I, 169 no. B47; II, fig. 263; M. V. Garašanin, *Arch. Iug.* 10 (1969), 87, pl. I.3, IV, 19; Morintz 1964, 109, fig. 6,3.

13 C. Blegen *et al.*, *Troy IV*, 1958, 177ff.; Garašanin, op. cit. pls II, 9–10, III, 13–14 etc.; Morintz 1964, 107, fig. 4,3, figs 7–8; Čičikova 1968, figs 8, 9, 11, 12; Dimitrov 1968, 10, figs 3–7; Hänsel 1976.

14 Unpublished information from Prof. B. Hänsel and Dr K. A. Wardle. Their results (from Kastanas and Assiros respectively) will be of the greatest importance in elucidating these connections. We thank both scholars for their kind help.

15 Hänsel 1976, 76ff., 113ff., 169ff. etc. This important book appeared too late for us to take it into full account.

16 B. Nikolov, *Arch.* 6/2 (1964), 75f., figs 11–13; Hänsel 1976, 77f., pl. 35, 5–11.

17 Dimitrov 1968; Čičikova 1968; N. Djambazov and R. Katinčarov, *Arch.* 3 (1961), 56–64 figs 5, 6, 8 (Magura); B. Nikolov, *Arch* 6/2 (1964), 72 fig. 6 (Kozloduj). For a full description of regional styles and find catalogue, see Hänsel 1976, 169ff.

18 G. Tončeva, *INMV* 8 (1972), 260–263. These vessels are comparable to material from Stoicani in Romania (Hänsel 1976, 140ff.).

19 M. Čičikova, *Arch.* 16/4 (1974), 21ff., fig. 2.

20 Distribution map in V. Mikov, *Arch.* 12/3 (1970), 60, fig. 11; Hänsel 1976, 25ff., esp. 37ff.

21 Information from Dr K. A. Wardle. Bulgarian moulds: important finds from the Vraca region, B. Nikolov, *Arch.* 16/1 (1974), 41–50 (including forms like those from Assiros); N. Kojčev, *IAI* 17 (1950), 218ff. (from Sokol, Nova Zagora); Hänsel 1976, pls 1–3.

22 B. Hänsel, *PZ* 48 (1973), 200–6.

23 V. Mikov, *IAI* 19 (1955), 31ff., figs 8b, 10; Hänsel 1976, 191ff.; D. Peev, *Arch.* 16/1 (1974), 24–31.

24 Berciu 1967, 102f.

25 J. Teutsch, *Mitt. der präh. Komm. Wien* 1 (1903), 395, figs 169–72.

26 The original definition was by M. Petrescu-Dîmbovița, *SCIV* 4 (1953), 443–86 and *Dacia* n.s. 4 (1960), 139–59; detailed discussion by Florescu 1964. Pottery from some of the *zolniki* was discussed by Nestor (1932, 117 n. 481).

27 *SCIV* 4 (1953), 29ff., 450ff.; *SCIV* 5 (1954), 19ff.; *SCIV* 6 (1955), 172.

28 M. Florescu and V. Căpitanu, *Carpica* 1 (1968), 35–47.

29 A. C. Florescu, *Memoria Antiquitatis* 1 (1969), 83–92.

30 G. I. Smirnova, *KSIIMK* 70 (1957), 99–107; *MIA* 150 (1969), 7–34; *Arch. Sbor.* 14 (1970), 12–31.

31 The main concentration of sites occurs along the main rivers between the Dniester and the Dnieper: I. N. Šarafutdinova, *SA* 1968/3, 16–34, fig. 1.

32 Sulimirski 1970, 343.

33 D. Ja. Telegin, *AK* 12 (1961), 3–15.

34 U. Minodora, *Carpica* 2 (1969), 35–48.

35 E. A. Balaguri, *AK* 13 (1961), 145–154.

36 Sulimirski 1970, 345.

37 Florescu 1964, 147.

38 Sulimirski 1970, 346.

39 A. C. Florescu, Şt. Rugină and D. Vicoveanu, *Danubius* 1 (1967), 75–87.

40 I. Mitrea, *Memoria Antiquitatis* 1 (1969), 311–17.

41 O. I. Terenožkin, *AK* 16 (1964), 202–7: hoard from Solonec, (Cjurupinsk, Cherson).

42 Florescu 1964, 196ff., 214.

43 Sulimirski 1970, 343f. after Šarafutdinova.

44 Florescu 1964, 191ff., 214ff.

45 Cf. S. S. Berezans'ka, *AK* 24 (1970), 20–31: *zolniki* from Adamivka and elsewhere.

46 S. S. Berezans'ka, *AK* 16 (1964), 49–75: material from Sobkivka (Uman', Čerkasy).

47 E. F. Pokrovs'ka and E. O. Petrovs'ka, *AK* 13 (1961), 129–44.

48 Sulimirski 1970, 378ff.; Gimbutas (1965, 440) prefers 'Černolesska'.

49 E. V. Machno and I. M. Šarafutdinova, *AK* n.s. 6 (1972), 70–81.

50 Later Timber-Grave burials in the west were often inserted into existing barrows without a wooden frame: Sulimirski 1970, 342.

51 Sulimirski 1970, 337.

52 A. I. Meljukova, *KSIAM* 89 (1962), 30–7; V. L. Deržavin, *SA* 1976/2, 118–24.

53 It is customary to refer to the settlement aspect of the Timber-Grave culture by the name Bilozerka type, after the site on the Dnieper near Nikopol.

54 Sulimirski 1970, 337f., fig. 78.

55 N. N. Čeredničenko, *SA* 1970/1, 233–8. The material found includes horse cheek-pieces.

56 A. D. Prjachin, *SA* 1968/3, 182–8.

57 A. D. Prjachin and V. I. Sagajdak, *SA* 1975/2, 176–87.

58 E.g. O. A. Krivcova-Grakova, *MIA* 46 (1966), 88, fig. 17. Other pottery is exceptionally crude and simple: V. P. Šilov, *MIA* 60 (1959), 419, fig. 36, from Kalinov (Volgograd).

59 S. S. Berezans'ka, *Materialy po archeologii severnogo pricernomor'ja* 4 (1962), 5–15. B. A. Latynin (*Arch. Sbor.* 6 (1964), 53–71) seems to be correct (*pace* Sulimirski, *BIA* 8–9 (1970), 128) in seeing this group as a local Timber-Grave variant.

60 A. M. Leskov, *KSIAM* 103 (1965), 63–6; A. V. Bodjanskij and I. N. Šarafutdinova, *Archeologičeskie Issledovanija na Ukraine 1965–6*, 1967, 90ff.

61 I. N. Šarafutdinova, *KSIAK* 10 (1960), 59–64; A. I. Terenožkin, *SA* 1965/1, 63–85, fig. 2 (Krasnomajackij).

62 E. S. Šarafutdinova, *SA* 1973/2, 3–26, with other refs.

63 Details in Sulimirski 1970. Gimbutas (1965, 468–9) follows a different system, distinguishing typological phases on the basis of metalwork.

64 D. Ja. Telegin, *AP* 6 (1956), 75–84.

65 D. Ja. Telegin, *KSIAK* 8 (1959),

74ff; V. A. Illins'ka, *AK* 10 (1957), 50–64; *KSIAK* 8 (1959), 80–4; *SA* 1961/1, 26–45. The multiplicity of site types in Moldavia and the difficulties in dating them have been discussed by A. I. Meljukova, *SA* 1972/1, 57–72.

66 Sulimirski 1970, 387.

67 A. M. Tallgren, *La Pontide Préscythique*, *ESA* 2 (1926), 173, fig. 97.

68 Gimbutas 1965, 569ff. For the north Carpathian area, see p. 404 and note 79.

69 Herodotus i. 103, iv. 1, 11, 12.

70 Herodotus iv. 16–20.

71 Herodotus iv. 11.

72 Gimbutas 1965, 443.

73 T. Bader, *SCIV* 23 (1972), 509–35 for general summary and discussion; C. Kacsó *Dacia* n.s. 19 (1975), 45–68 on new material from Lăpuş; N. Chidioşan, *SCIV* 21 (1970), 287–93 for sites in Crişana, where Suciu de Sus material is associated with phase III of Otomani and Wietenberg.

74 N. Kalicz, *AE* 87 (1960), 3–15 (study of Felsöszöcs and original definition of Berkesz-Demecser group); Mozsolics 1960 (tumulus of Nyírkarász-Gyulaháza); T. Kemenczei, *AE* 90 (1963), 169–88, esp. 182–6 (distinction of Berkesz-Demecser as a phase later than Felsöszöcs); T. Kovács, *FA* 18 (1966–7), 27–58 (dating of Berkesz-Demecser to Br D).

75 E. A. Balaguri, *SA* 1969/2, 147–59 and Kalicz, op. cit.

76 T. Bader, *SCIV* 23 (1972), 512, pls 1–12.

77 Mozsolics 1960.

78 Mus. Cluj.

79 K. Bernjakovič, *Sl.A.* 8 (1960), 325–392; S. I. Penjak and A. D. Šabalin, *SA* 1964/2, 193–201; S. I. Penjak, *KSIAM* 115 (1969), 39–44 (Negrov hoard).

80 Morintz 1964.

81 Morintz 1964, 101–18 (*pace* Berciu

1967, 109, fig. 51, where the whole culture is placed within Ha A; this would hardly allow time for the substantial local working of iron to have developed). For other pottery sites, see Hänsel 1976, 120ff.

82 Hänsel 1976, 134ff.

83 D. Berciu, *Arheologia preistorica a Olteniei*, 1939, 142ff.

84 E. Zaharia, *Dacia* n.s. 9 (1965), 83–104.

85 K. Horedt, *SCIV* 15 (1964), 187–204.

86 Şt. Ferenczi, *AMN* 1 (1964), 67–77.

87 Cf. D. Berciu in *Istoria Rominiei*, I, 1960, 151. Cf. now Hänsel 1976, 88ff.

88 S. Morintz and P. Roman, *SCIV* 20 (1969), 393–423; Hänsel 1976, 151ff. ('Ostrov group').

89 D. Berciu and E. Comşa, *MCA* 2 (1956), 251–489 (Balta Verde).

90 Mus. Arad. Nestor 1932, 115; Hencken 1968, 440ff.

91 Muzeul Banatului, Timişoara.

92 Z. Letica, *Starinar* n.s. 19 (1968), 47–57.

93 Dj. Bosković, *Arch. Iug.* 3 (1959), 41–5, with full bibliography; V. Trbuhović, *Starinar* n.s. 13–14 (1962–3), 177–9; Gimbutas 1965, 342 pl. 67; in greatest detail concerning the symbolism, Kossack 1954.

94 E.g. by J. Bouzek, *Homerisches Griechenland*, 1969, 115 fig. 45, with refs.

95 Gimbutas 1965, 335.

96 I. T. Dragomir, *Danubius* 1 (1967), 89–105.

97 Most recently, M. Petrescu-Dîmboviţa, *Actes du VIIIᵉ Congrès ISPP*, 1971, 175–92; cf. also M. Rusu, *Dacia* n.s. 7 (1963), 177–210, with other refs.

98 Cf. K. Horedt, *Dacia*, n.s. 8 (1964), 119–32, who lists four Ha B2 and B3 hoards with iron objects; Z. Székely, *Dacia* n.s. 10 (1966), 209–19.

99 E. Comşa *AAC* 8 (1966), 169–74.

100 From the Babadag-type site of Cozia (Iaşi) come wheels for tooth-stamping pottery: A. László, *Memoria Antiquitatis* 1 (1969), 319–26; *Alutia* 2 (1970).

101 A. Vulpe, *JIES* 2/1 (1974), 1–21.

9 Southern Europe

The events that caused turmoil in the eastern Mediterranean and change in central Europe found a reflection too in the south. Most notably, settlement sites occupied more or less continuously through the earlier Bronze Age fell out of use or were abandoned, and almost simultaneously the practice of cremating the dead and placing the ashes in an urn was adopted. This 'Urnfield' rite is found, eventually, throughout Italy and over much of Jugoslavia; in Albania, on the other hand, tumulus burial continued the dominant rite. Naturally enough, the appearance of cremation burial in Italy, and with artifacts that are clearly ancestral to the Early Iron Age 'Villanovan' culture (itself arguably one ancestor of Etruscan civilization), has led to speculation that invaders arrived in Italy at the time of the great upheavals in the east, bringing with them the distinctive hallmarks of the Urnfield world in the north. Italy certainly adopted Urnfield practices, not only in burial rites but also in artifact types, symbols and techniques; so much so that from this moment on the yardstick of progress in the north, and the method by which Müller-Karpe established the chronology of the Urnfields north of the Alps, is the cross-comparison of artifact-types, principally bronzes, in Italy and in central Europe. For by 800 BC – though some traditions placed the date as early as 1000 BC – the first Greek colonists were to appear in southern Italy, bringing with them ceramics that are, by European standards, as closely datable as anything one could expect. Such finds are not, of course, present in Jugoslavia, where we must follow the course of events in terms of the central European sequence.

Italy

In north Italy the Late Bronze Age saw the end of the lake-sites and the *terremare*, and their replacement by open sites and hill-forts with

415

Protovillanovan material. In the north-west the *Canegrate* group of cemeteries is found. In central and southern Italy the Apennine sites continue, albeit sporadically, side by side with urnfield cremation cemeteries, while Mycenaean imports become much scarcer. Finally, in Sicily and the Aeolian Islands the acropolis sites were abandoned, and a new culture, called *Ausonian* by Bernabò Brea, arrived; rock-cut tombs continued on Sicily the dominant form, including now material of the *Pantalica* group.

For a while the settlement patterns of the earlier Bronze Age continued unchanged in northern Italy. The best-known settlement-type was, as before, the lake-dwelling, and the most famous series is again concentrated on Lake Garda. At the 'mouth', or rather outflow, of the river Mincio lies the site of Peschiera – Imboccatura del Mincio, and other similar stations lie not far away.[1] The lack of systematic work on this site means that we know nothing of its construction or layout, only that it was a pile site on the lake-edge. Of the great quantity of material recovered, the most informative element is the bronze-work, which we discuss below. Most of this dates to one period only, contemporary with Br D north of the Alps, and in southern Europe usually named after the site of Peschiera itself. Subsequent to this there is nothing. One is forced to the conclusion that the sites were abandoned, unexpectedly and simultaneously, during or at the end of Br D, perhaps around 1200 BC. For this the most likely explanation is undoubtedly that of flooding. Lake-side settlements would have had a constant battle against the water-level, and continual renewal of the floor-levels must have been necessary. A sudden cloud-burst at night in a wet season could easily have been the last straw; the inhabitants would have had no chance of saving even their personal possessions or tools in their rush to escape. That such things can happen even today is clearly seen in the disastrous floods in Florence in 1966 or by many another example nearer home.

On the Po plain, too, things were happening to cause an abrupt change in the cultural sequence.[2] Several of the *terremare* have cultural levels attributed to Br D, though again little is known of their nature. Cavazzoli, Gorzano, Monte Venera and Montecchio (Reggio Emilia), for instance, have Late Bronze Age levels, but perhaps the most notable thing is the appearance in them of late Apennine pottery, as at Toscanella (Imola), where formerly influences had gone in the opposite direction. We should not read too much into this; but that the *terremare* shortly came to a complete end *is* a matter of importance. A majority of the bronzes on the *terremare* date to the early Late Bronze Age (Br D); their contemporaneity is not surprising, since the metal would have been constantly re-used, and at any one moment most of the tools present would have been typologically representative of that moment. The latest forms found include, for instance, the simple violin-bow fibula, just as at Peschiera, and it seems as clear as such things can be that the *terremare* were deserted, *en masse,* at about the same time as the northern lake-sites. What was the cause of this desertion? Säflund and others thought that a climatic change – or some similar *causa naturale catastrofica* – was responsible, just as flooding was suggested for the Peschiera sites. But the known climatic deterioration did not take place until the eighth century BC, and in any case an increase in rainfall would hardly be sufficient to account for widespread desertion over the entire Po plain.[3] At S. Caterina-Tredossi the desertion apparently took place actually during road- and dyke-building operations. Furthermore the abandonment of the *terremare* practically coincides with the start of new centres of settlement, as in the Polesine area. For these reasons it has been suggested that the end of the *terremare* is connected with historical, not natural, events, the contemporary turmoil in the Aegean lending support to this idea. 'Natural causes' are not, of course, a panacea, nor appropriate in all instances; yet the evidence of the lake sites may lend some support to the 'climate' hypothesis. The alternative is to see an invasion of people who sweep through Italy destroying existing sites before setting themselves up in wholly different centres. To this problem we return, connected as it must be with the question of the cremation burial rite.

Nothing is known of the Protovillanovan settlements that succeeded the *terremare* except that they existed. Sites like Mariconda di Melara and Frattesina (Rovigo) have produced abundant surface indications but, at the time of writing, little from excavations. Frattesina is believed to have covered 9 ha, and has produced much settlement debris, with at least one roughly rectangular wattle-and-daub building.[4] Perhaps the most interesting aspect of this site was the prolific workshop material found there – cut but unworked ivory, glass fragments and waste, crucibles and so on – and the imported material – a late Mycenaean sherd, and ostrich-egg fragments. Is it possible that this site was the Spina of its period? We have long hoped to find a trading entrepôt at the head of the Adriatic in the Bronze Age. Frattesina is some 50 km from the sea today (40 km from the Lagoon of Comacchio), but the silting-up of the mouth of the Po has extended the distance appreciably since prehistoric times.

Probably dating to this period too are a few defensible hill sites like the Rocca di Rivoli (Verona) near Lake Garda; not closely datable, but certainly in existence by this time are the numerous hill-forts of the Trieste region, Istria and the Julian Alps, known as *castellieri.* As with hill-forts in other areas of Europe, these could either have ramparts completely encircling a knoll, or else segments of rampart cutting off promontories or spurs.[5] There is some evidence of hill-fort construction in central Italy, too.[6]

Further south, the difficulty of dating Apennine material means that we cannot be sure whether, or to what extent, sites occupied during the earlier Bronze Age continued far into the later period. It certainly seems clear that Apennine traditions continued on some sites, such as Santa Paolina near Filottrano (Ancona),[7] where oval hut-foundations were found; at a series of caves in the Apennine foothills such as the Grotta Farneto (Bologna),[8] the Grotta Frasassi above the river Sentino (Ancona) or, higher up, the Grotta a Male (Assergi); at Monte Cetona and adjacent sites like Belverde, where rich bronze-work of Br D – Peschiera type was found;[9] at Narce (Calcata, Viterbo), where phases III and IV date to this period;[10] and at several important sites in the south. At Narce parts of oval or semi-circular cobbled hut floors were found in phase IIIA and substantial post-framed buildings in IIIB with hearths; at the end of phase III water-laid silts, thought to emanate from rainwater rather than the river Treia on which Narce lies, covered the occupation area, probably indicating the temporary abandonment of the site. It was then reoccupied on a larger scale (phase IV), and with still more substantial buildings, though no perimeter wall was found. The top of the acropolis was also intensely occupied at this period. At the end of phase IV burning occurred, for all the floors were sealed by a charcoal layer, prior to the construction of the phase V buildings – rectangular timber-framed affairs, as far as one could tell, and attributable culturally to a post-Apennine, 'Protovillanovan' or early Villanovan phase. At Narce many features of Apennine pottery continue into the Protovillanovan phase, though true Protovillanovan seems to be present already in phase III and gradually to increase in quantity – one of the strongest arguments for a peaceful continuity from one to the other.

At Luni sul Mignone the excavators have seen a gradual transition from the Apennine Bronze Age into the 'Iron Age'; house-types and material culture are not dissimilar in each, but the recovered pottery is attributed to a late stage of Protovillanovan. If continuity this really was, a Bronze Age origin for the 'monumental building' of Iron Age Luni will have to be sought.[11]

In the south of the peninsula, the trade with Greece was undoubtedly a factor of the greatest importance, with Mycenaean pottery reaching its maximum distribution and quantity in LH IIIB and early C. This period saw the greatest flourishing of the best-known trading-port in Bronze Age Italy, Scoglio del Tonno (Tunny Reef), the promontory facing Taranto. We know of this site's importance from the finds recovered (fig. 147), but of the find circumstances virtually nothing is

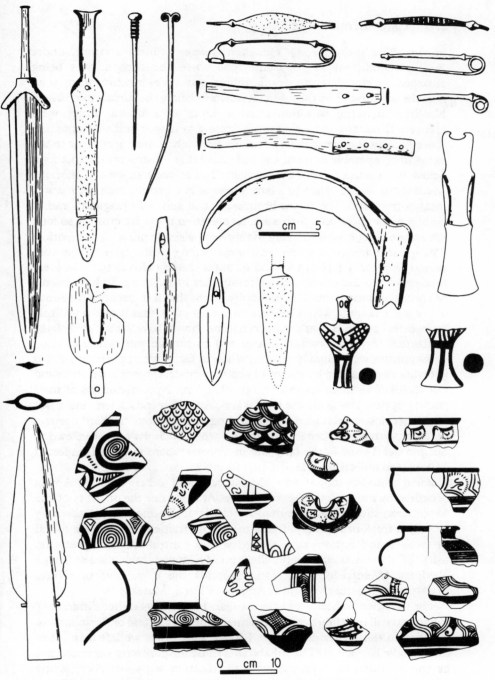

Fig. 147 Scoglio del Tonno, Taranto: bronzes (above) and imported Mycenaean pottery (below), including figurines.
(After Müller-Karpe 1959)

419

known. The excavator, Q. Quagliati, made a valiant attempt, under 'rescue' conditions in 1899 and 1900 when the harbour was being enlarged, to elucidate the stratigraphical sequence, but his information is of the scantiest.[12] In the lowest levels, 2 m below the surface and below, Neolithic material was found. At a depth of 1 m, hut floors were recovered, rectangular, with in one case a vestibule and side-apse. On these floors was a dense mass of occupation debris, not, according to the excavator, separable into phases, and above that, sealing the deposit 0.5 m below the surface, a stone pavement. It has been suggested that the Mycenaean sherds relate to a later phase of occupation than the mass of local pottery and *Terramara* bronzes, but in spite of Quagliati's rather ambiguous indications, such a reinterpretation is hardly possible so long after the event; it is most likely to represent a single phase of occupation. The great majority of imported sherds belong to the later Mycenaean period, especially L H I I I A2 and B, but including also I I I C. The great interest of the site lies in the possibility that it may actually have been a Mycenaean settlement. We can hardly doubt that if it were not, its *raison d'être* was the trade with Greece. Our own view is that it seems unlikely on political grounds that the Mycenaeans should have set up an isolated settlement (or even several settlements) on foreign soil, where existing communities were already settled, when as far as we can tell they could get what they wanted by means of ordinary trade. Cyprus apart, they did not establish settlements in the Levant, where large quantities of their pottery appear alongside the local wares. A further indication, and a fact of the greatest importance, is the finding of numerous 'Italian' bronzes together with the Mycenaean material – which includes also bronzework. Scoglio del Tonno is the only site in Europe where local and imported Mycenaean objects mingle on equal terms.

Porto Perone, too, Torre Castelluccia and other sites in Apulia benefited by the commercial connection. At P. Perone the quantity of late Mycenaean sherds is greater than at Scoglio del Tonno, though this may be only a freak of recovery. Remains of post-framed houses were found in levels b and c, horseshoe-shaped with a central entrance-post (fig. 148).[13] Substantial settlement, albeit poorly-known, took place at Coppa Nevigata (Manfredonia) in (and around) the huge cave of Grotta Manaccora (Peschici),[14] and at Anglona (Tursi, Matera).[15]

The situation in Sicily and the Aeolian Islands was rather different.[16] We may recall how flourishing settlements like Milazzese or Portella were founded in the earlier part of the Bronze Age. Since we left them, dire things have happened. The inhabitants must have bitterly regretted not having provided their villages with fortification walls, for every single one was destroyed, and when Lipari was reoccupied it was with a very

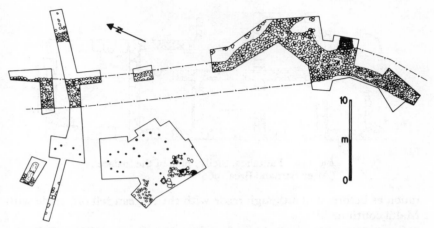

Fig. 148   Porto Perone, Leporano (Taranto): plan of the later Bronze Age settlement showing defensive wall and horseshoe shaped huts. (After Lo Porto 1963)

different cultural assemblage. The excavations of Bernabò Brea and Cavalier on the acropolis at Lipari have provided extensive information.[17] The earlier Bronze Age houses were burnt down, and in the succeeding layer the pottery is very similar to that of the late Apennine culture of the mainland. A few sites on Sicily, like Milazzo, have also produced some of these wares. This is not a long-lived period, however, for in the succeeding strata the material is different again, and, what is more, corresponds to that known from a series of cremation cemeteries on the Italian mainland. Bernabò Brea calls it 'Ausonian' (this is phase II) after the tradition recorded by Diodorus Siculus that Liparos with a band of Ausonians from southern Italy first occupied the islands. At Lipari there are extensive remains of houses, subrectangular in shape, timber-framed, with a clay-lined gravel floor and hearth; one of these was nearly 14 m long and 7 wide. We can assume that something similar once stood at Milazzo in north-eastern Sicily, but now only the pottery it contained survives. Elsewhere in Sicily the indications of settlement are slight, in spite of the great numbers of tombs known. The best-known site is Pantalica (Siracusa), where a truly Cyclopean palace (*Anaktoron*) has been excavated, long and narrow, containing half a dozen squarish rooms (fig. 149). Other houses no doubt existed at this site, which is massively defended both by walls and by a naturally fortified position.[18] It is unfortunate that the cultural position of the palace is not more secure. The 'palace' at Thapsos continued to be occupied during this period; some reconstruction took place, but the main lines seem to have been

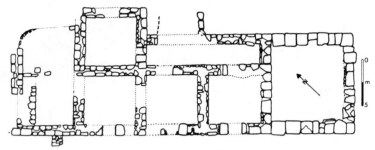

Fig. 149   Pantalica, Sicily: plan of the 'palace'.
(After Bernabò Brea 1966)

much as before, and although trade with the Aegean fell off, trade with Malta continued.[19]

Scantier remains have been found at Morgantina (Serra Orlando, Aidone) and La Motta, Rometta (Messina), at both of which an Ausonian II level was represented.[20]

The burial rite of later Bronze Age Italy was almost invariably that of inurned cremation. Most authorities have, however, divided those burials which can be seen as part of the wider 'Urnfield movement' from those which cannot, the validity of which distinction we shall discuss shortly. Many correspondences, not only in the fact of cremation and the artifact types, but also in the specific manner of deposition of the ashes in a large biconical urn, link Italy in its 'Urnfield' phase with other parts of the Urnfield world, especially the middle and lower Danube.[21] In contrast to this, early cremation burials in northern Italy were in simple bowl-like urns, often in cemeteries of limited extent. From the Peschiera phase, for instance, we have the cemeteries at Croson di Bovolone and Franzine (Verona), where both inhumations and cremations are found, the cremations in low globular or ovoid urns, the inhumations extended and in one case provided with long dress pins at either shoulder.[22]

In the north-west, too, cremation cemeteries appear: cemeteries at Scamozzina (Lombardy) and Monza are true urnfields in all but name. The urns were sunk into pits and sometimes covered by a stone slab, while remains of the funeral pyre are found round about.[23]

More famous is the urnfield from Canegrate (Milan) and others in the same region.[24] The site is on a low terrace above the river Olona, the tombs being rather shallow pits in the sub-soil. Many urns were placed upside-down, no doubt filled up with earth to prevent the ashes falling out. The urns placed the right way up were sometimes covered with a stone slab, and sometimes too a stone setting lay around the urn, or in one case a cist.

To a similar period must belong a certain number of finds in the *Terramara* area, in particular Montata (Reggio), Copezzato (Parma) and Casinalbo (Modena).[25] Cremation seems to have started here by Br C and certainly continued into Br D, though Montata does not look like a real urnfield, since it is composed of two superimposed lines of urns. Säflund was of the opinion that the urnfield of Bismantova was of *Terramara* date, but it is in fact later.[26] Whether or not 'urnfields' were present during the *Terramara* phase, inhumation was, in the *Terramara* area, at least as popular as cremation; in some cases, both rites appear on the same site.[27]

By Ha A1 (twelfth century), however, it is possible to descry a much more extensive series of cremation cemeteries, which appear not merely in the north but down the whole peninsula and in Sicily and the Aeolian Islands. Urn burial was universal, and a markedly uniform collection of bronzes accompanies the dead. Urn forms vary locally, but the biconical shape is much the commonest and decorative motifs recur in different areas. Angarano (Veneto) in the north-east, Ascona (Locarno) on Lake Maggiore, Fontanella (Mantova) on the Po plain, Bissone (Pavia) in southern Lombardy, Bismantova (Reggio Emilia) in the Apennine foothills south of Reggio, Pianello (Ancona) in the Marche (fig. 150), Allumiere (Civitavecchia) in Latium, Timmari (Matera) in northern Apulia, Torre Castelluccia (Tarento) in southern Apulia, Milazzo (Messina) in north-eastern Sicily, and Lipari in the Aeolian Islands – all are characterized by large Urnfield cemeteries (with the characteristic biconical urns and accompanying grave-goods, and a bronze industry of remarkable uniformity, which compares also with what is found north of the Alps). What is the origin of this universal spread of culture? Does it bespeak purely local fashions or can it be seen as part of some wider movement?

The existence of some cremation burials already in the latter part of the earlier Bronze Age certainly suggests that it is unnecessary to introduce invaders from outside the peninsula to account for the spread of the Urnfield rite, but on the other hand some stimulus must have been necessary to bring about its universal dispersal within a relatively short space of time. In this respect, the problem is part of the wider European one of Urnfield origins. In Italy, however, the situation is much more complicated since these later Bronze Age cemeteries, often called 'Protovillanovan', are in some ways ancestral to the 'Villanovan' sites of the Early Iron Age, and these in turn form at least one part of Etruscan culture. The cremating groups of the later Bronze Age can thus be considered directly ancestral to Etruscan civilization. If this were so, then 'Protovillanovan' might seem an appropriate term; but what of earlier cremating groups, what of the other cultures in Italy, what in particular of the Apennine culture?

These questions are much discussed, and we cannot treat them in detail.[28] The ancient writers were agreed that the Etruscans had been in the Italian peninsula for a very long time, and certainly before the time

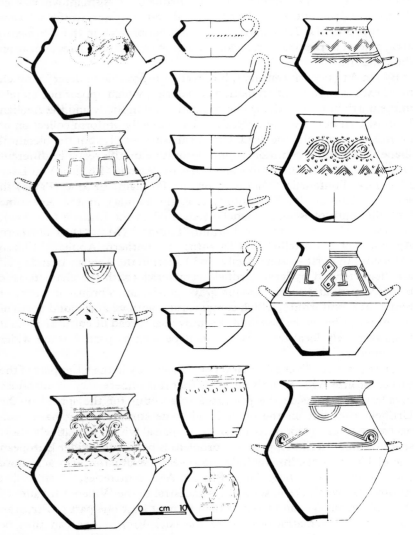

Fig. 150   Pianello (Ancona): cremation urns from the Protovillanovan cemetery. (After Müller-Karpe 1959)

of the first Greek colonies. This alone implies their existence in Italy early in the Iron Age. Other traditions record movements of people – Arcadians and other 'Pelasgian' tribes, Greek and Trojan heroes – from the east to Italy at a still earlier date, though these are almost certainly to be seen in terms of late attempts to derive Roman genealogies from the pre-classical Greek world. Does any of this find a reflection in the archaeological record?

It is surely right to refer to the cremation cemeteries of Italy earlier than Villanovan not as 'Protovillanovan' but 'Previllanovan', in order to avoid the implication, whether correct or not, that the 'Protovillanovan' cemeteries were ancestral to the Villanovan. The term was coined by A. Colini in 1914 to describe a group of material in central Italy that he recognized as earlier than the classic Villanovan of Bologna or Tarquinia.[29] Since then the term has been applied to groups over the whole peninsula, with varying degrees of accuracy. Today the term is used to refer to the whole period between, for instance, the *terremare* and the Villanovans, perhaps 300 years; but in the early, true Bronze Age, part of this span the amount of material is very small. The urnfields of Pianello-type are the main sites (apart from the settlements already discussed), but more information comes from bronze finds (see below). In fact, very few sites *or* finds can be firmly attributed to the crucial period, the twelfth century, though those that can show the start of a typological sequence that is thereafter unbroken. Pianello, for instance, still has violin-bow fibulae, while the 'double bird-protome' motifs on its pottery can be cross-dated by an identical motif on a bronze bowl from a LH III C chamber tomb at Pylos in Greece;[30] the actual motif suggests a connection with the Urnfield world of central Europe (fig. 150). Violin-bow fibulae are less common in the south, though other forms show that sites like Torre Castelluccia have at least some material from the twelfth century.

The scientific world is divided into those who favour an indigenous development for Protovillanovan and those who see it as intrusive. As far as the non-ceramic finds are concerned, we would say simply this: most of the forms found are variants of universal European types which occur throughout Europe at this time (Ha AI in the north). Their appearance in Italy can certainly be explained in terms of the spread of social and technological ideas, just as it can in Greece. Beaten bronze-work, certain types of winged axe, arc fibulae and so on are all found very widely and are by no means specifically 'Italian'. The question of change and continuity must proceed by other arguments, and the desertion of the *terremare* may be a relevant consideration. Unfortunately, we know far too little about that elusive century, 1200-1100 BC, to be able to reach any firm conclusion about the nature of the next two.

The bronzework is one aspect of Late Bronze Age Italy that is reasonably well-known and may help to shed light on the period as a whole. Peschiera, in fact, is most notable for its bronze industry (fig. 151). The most characteristic forms are violin-bow fibulae (usually with twisted bow), two-part razors, 'wheel-discs', median-winged axes, tanged and flange-hilted knives, simple tanged daggers, 'Peschiera daggers', and pins with spiral, serpentiform, poppy, vase, spherical, seal or ribbed head. Most of these forms are directly linked to Br D types north of the Alps, but it is of great interest that many of them are found at Scoglio del Tonno and a few (more important still) in Greece. Identical fibulae and daggers at Mycenae and elsewhere seem to indicate that a special relationship between the two areas had been established; one that was to continue through the ensuing centuries.[31] Bronzes of Peschiera type are, however, not widely found in Italy.

In the succeeding phase there are several famous hoards, though hardly a standard range of forms.[32] Notable finds are that from Surbo (Lecce), which includes a Mycenaean sword fragment, shaft-hole hammers and single-bladed axes, a gouge or chisel and a median-winged axe;[33] or from Coste del Marano (Rome), where a hoard of 147 objects was buried in a pottery vessel.[34] Most notable there are the three beaten bronze cups with boss ornament, two of them decorated with horned handles. Rather later come the huge hoards like that from Piediluco.[35] Elaboration of existing forms rather than the development of new ones is characteristic of succeeding phases of Italian metalwork: for instance violin-bow fibulae with flattened bow are decorated with double bird-protomes, just as pots and larger-scale bronzes are; the bow becomes stilted or serpentiform; and, with the arrival of the arc fibula, semicircular.

It has long been realized that some aspects of the Italian Late Bronze Age, particularly in the north, are similar to those of the Hungarian plain across the mountains to the north-east. It used to be thought, in the heyday of *Terramara* research, that Tószeg and other tell-sites were *terremare*. Such notions are today regarded as red herrings, but it has recently been demonstrated with some force that the bronzes of each area are remarkably similar.[36] This similarity, which amounts in some cases to identity, starts with the Keszthely and Boiu swords of the Middle Bronze Age, becomes strong in the Peschiera phase (equivalent to Mozsolics' Ópályi group), and reaches a peak in Protovillanovan with median-winged axes, swords with pommel-tang, greaves, certain types of fibula, and buckets being represented in the same forms in each area. At the very least this must indicate that smiths in both areas were in close contact; it could even mean that smiths travelled between the two lands, selling their wares to both.

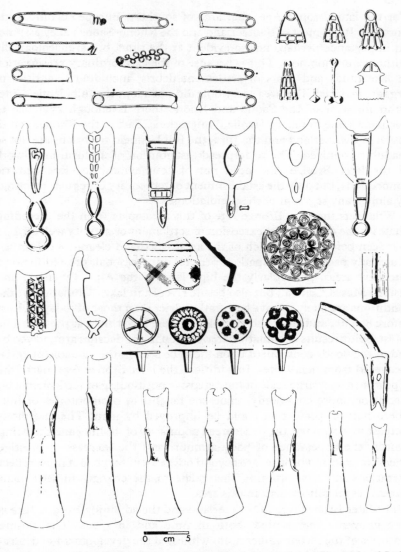

Fig. 151   Peschiera-Imboccatura del Mincio: bronzes from the muds of Lake Garda.
(After Müller-Karpe 1959)

427

Switzerland and the Rhône Valley

For the later Bronze Age, that area of southern Europe encompassing northern Italy, most of Switzerland and the Rhône-Saône valley assumes an importance perhaps not so evident at the time, but archaeologically without question now. This is because of the extraordinary preservation in lake muds and peats of settlement debris, including quantities of organic material. The area as a whole did not adopt the full Urnfield rite, although west of the Saône and Rhône there is enough evidence to persuade some to talk of Urnfield migrations. East of the Rhône, and in much of Switzerland and the Jura, the full Urnfield traditions are not so readily recognized. The widespread distribution of uniform metalwork of the later Bronze Age need not of course indicate close cultural connections, but only the establishment of temporary or regular meetings by almost any segment of the populations.

What sets the later Bronze Age of this area apart from the preceding phases is the evidence for extension of settlement or activity well beyond that seen before. Over much of the area, woodland clearance continued at a steady pace, and occupation, perhaps only seasonal, pressed forward into new areas, particularly the high land of the Alps, Pyrenees, and eastern Massif Central, but also beside rivers and lakes. Climatically, the conditions are likely to have been rather drier than those of today, at least before 800 bc, and lake- and river-levels were lower than at present. The catastrophic results of climatic deterioration in the decades around 700 bc and of the floods consequent upon it can be seen in the valuable material recovered from many sites. In addition, the later Bronze Age marks the appearance on a large scale of the defensive positioning of settlements, on islands or, more commonly, upon the heights of promontories or hills where natural protection could be improved by man. The enormous increase in weaponry, the widespread popularity of slashing and thrusting swords, the appearance of body-armour, and the increase in prestige objects of gold and bronze, are beyond our present scope, but must reflect alterations in social ordering that relate to the changes in settlement patterns especially evident in this area.

The later Bronze Age in Switzerland and the adjoining French Jura is very unevenly represented, both in time and in space. The closing centuries of the second millennium witnessed the development of central European Urnfield groups, but their influence upon the Alpine zone was negligible (other than in eastern Switzerland, where cremation burials from 1200 BC onwards have been recorded).[37] With the adoption in the early first millennium of Urnfield customs in the Rhine valley, parts of northern Switzerland appear to relate more closely to traditional central

European practices, but one should not force the evidence. More local and Alpine is the *Melaun* group,[38] characterized by pottery with applied incised ribs and high bossed handles, and representing part of a central Alpine province in western Austria, eastern Switzerland and north Italy in the closing centuries of the Late Bronze Age.[39]

The southern slopes of the Alps, in Ticino or Tessin, have yielded only sparse evidence of intensive occupation; what there is relates logically to the north Italian developments of the later Bronze Age.[40]

The Alpine passes[41] – St Bernard in the west at 2,473 m, five others further east at 1,800–2,330 m – must have allowed contact across the mountain barriers; indeed, evidence from metalwork suggests quite close contacts between north and south, but it is unlikely that more than a few hardy souls would have ventured regularly over these heights.

The major evidence for later Bronze Age activity on the plateau and the Jura belongs to the early centuries of the first millennium. Before this, only burials and bronzes are recorded in any quantity, and the former exhibit a complexity of cremations and inhumations, with or without pottery vessels, in trench, pit or cist, and with a rich variety of metal grave goods. In the first millennium, this range of burial practices persists, and there are no large cemeteries of urned cremations such as we might expect.[42] Instead, there are many substantial settlements, both on heights and beside lakes and streams. We shall look more closely at some of these; let us note in passing that many of these early first millennium settlements housed substantial populations. At the Kestenberg near Möriken, lines of log-built cabins up to 5 × 6 m in size were set along the slope of the hill, with poles holding up the roofs on the downward side only. The promontory fort at Wittnau enclosed an area suitable for seventy houses (fig. 152), and some of the lakeside settlements are believed to have been laid out in a similarly orderly manner;[43] some contained their own workshops for the production of special pieces in metal or pottery. These facts and figures suggest that the communities involved may have been well over 200 strong, which in itself carries connotations for leadership and control.

The number of such communities on the plateau and Jura regions is uncertain, but about 100 lakeside settlements have been recognized, most of them contemporary to judge from the character of associated debris (fig. 153). Nearly forty are on Lake Neuchâtel, and twenty-five on Lake Léman. The conditions under which the wooden piles and platforms, the house foundations, collapsed walls and fences survived, have meant that plans of settlements cannot be reconstructed today; clearly much organization and planning were necessary. At Mörigen, over 11,000 heavy oak timbers were apparently required for foundation work, and at

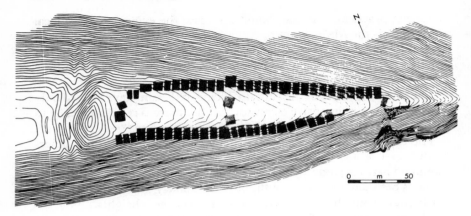

Fig. 152   Plan of the defended settlement at the Wittnau with rampart on west, and positions of houses along the ridge sides.
(After Drack 1971)

Zug-Sumpf the houses were supported on the lakeshore by poles fixed into heavy plano-convex base-plates; mortice and tenon fittings were common.[44]

Within the settlements, many industries and economic activities were carried on, including bronze-casting, pottery-making, wood-carving, and weaving of textiles. It is significant that while the vast array of bronzes recovered from these sites includes swords, spearheads and many ornaments, it also contains large numbers of tools such as axes, chisels, gouges, hammers, anvils, saws, sickles and knives.[45] Very few of the last group would normally be placed in a grave, where the typical offering would be a weapon or ornaments; clear proof, this, that without settlements and their debris, we can obtain only a biased view of economic interests in the Bronze Age.

Among the specialized activities carried out, graphite-coated pottery in black and red, white-inlaid wares and tin-band decorated vessels were produced. Some limited work with a new metal – iron – was attempted, and harnesses for horse-riding and fittings for carts were produced in bronze.

The nature of recovery methods used in the past on many of these sites does not allow us an unbiased view of the evidence for subsistence practices, but more modern excavations have begun to supply quantitative data to control the qualitative already available. Pollen analyses at Zug-Sumpf show forest clearance and concomitant increases in grasses, clover

Fig. 153 Reconstruction of a lakeside settlement according to Keller 1878. Many of these settlements are now believed to have been built on the shorelines rather than over open water as shown here. (After Keller 1878)

and plantain,[46] which compare with the animal bone evidence from Zürich-Alpenquai for sheep pasturing on a large scale.[47]

The presence there of pigs signifies that woodland was still within reach of the settlement, but it seems likely that sheep and cattle were particularly important animals.[48] The high proportion of adult sheep suggests an interest in wool, while the killing age of pigs was 2 years, a practice yielding the maximum return of meat for labour and fodder. The high proportion of adult cattle at Zürich-Alpenquai, more than at any other site studied, indicates successful over-wintering practices, and a majority of these were males; as not all would be breeding bulls, most were probably oxen for ploughing and for meat. A tentative reconstruction of the herd would be two breeding bulls, eighty cows, and 100 oxen, the cows yielding forty male and forty female calves each year of which eight and twenty-five respectively were slaughtered, leaving thirty-two oxen and fifteen breeding cows for the future. The maintenance of oxen until they were 3 years old would yield 500 kg of meat per animal. If these estimates are near the truth, it suggests that a wide area of land had been taken into the community care, serving the needs of the large population which maintained it.

The evidence for plant remains cannot by its nature be so precise; from Mörigen was recovered a wide range of cultivated plants: millet, peas, lentils, horsebeans, flax and opium poppy, as well as wild gathered plants, hazelnuts, acorns, apples, various berries and cherries.[49] Other wild life was also exploited, including deer, birds and fish, the last doubtless being an important commodity.

The lakeside settlements of the later Bronze Age existed, with rebuilding episodes, until the eighth century when they were abandoned. Why this should be has not yet been determined, but the evidence that hundreds of precious objects of clay and bronze and wood were left behind indicates a sudden catastrophe. Climatic indications suggest an increase in rainfall and humidity at this time, and there is geological evidence for 'backing-up' of the major river system around lake Neuchâtel, and for a rise in the level of Lake Léman of 9 m. Any or all of these would eventually force widespread evacuation and economic chaos; particularly so a sudden flood, maybe of a temporary nature, but sufficient to disrupt and destroy forever the established patterns of existence along the shores of the lakes.[50]

A major gap in our knowledge of these societies is the absence of associated cemeteries which would yield data about population structure; in other parts of the plateau and the Jura, cemeteries and isolated burials have been recorded, and show the mixed nature of burial practices, reflecting both earlier Bronze Age and Urnfield traditions. The twelve graves in the Boiron cemetery at Tolochenaz included supine inhumations as well as cremations in pits or pottery vessels, some of each kind having stone slab covers (fig. 154).[51]

This variety of practices is also a feature of later Bronze Age burials in the French Jura and southern Alps, where cremation cemeteries on level ground, beneath barrows and in caves have been recorded;[52] at Gondenans-Montby, the funeral pyre was outside the cave and the ashes and bones were then placed in crevices in the cave, with pots broken beside them. At Dampierre, the bodies were cremated in pits dug in open ground, and grave-goods were subsequently added to the deposit. The funerary pottery in the region consisted of globular or biconical jars and bowls, with flared rims and decorated with horizontal or vertical channelling and occasional bosses; metal objects included various pins and bracelets with incised geometric decoration. Heavy metal objects such as axes and swords were not abundant (fig. 155).

The contemporary settlements include defended promontories and hilltops, and the approach to defensive walls at Mont-Ceint at Rahon, Mont-Guérin and Mont-Bart was probably comparable to the Wittnau example although less massive.[53] Other settlements on heights were undefended, at Schafrain and Kestenberg, just as were the villages placed on lower ground in the valleys and plains; a settlement at Mont-Ceint lay below the fort, and at one of the two sites at Dampierre on the edge of a small lake near the river Doubs a fence separated settlement from cemetery. This site extended over some 30 × 30 m; the second, which

Fig. 154   Late Bronze Age burial positions in the cemetery at Le Boiron (Vaud). (After Sauter 1976)

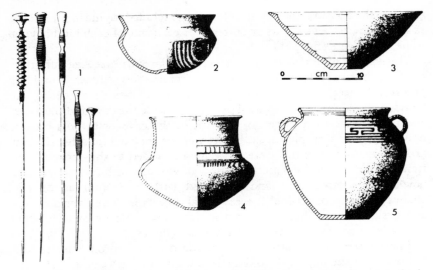

Fig. 155 Late Bronze Age material from the Jura: 1. hoard of pins, Arinthod-Vogna, 2–5. urns: 2. Bavans, 3–4. Gonvillars, 5. Sancey-le-Long. (From Guilaine 1976)

intruded onto a previous cemetery, was larger, 80 × 60 m (fig. 156). The houses at Dampierre were of wattle and daub, about 6 × 5 m in size, and were apparently rectangular, oval or circular, probably performing different functions. The huts at Kestenberg were log-built, about 4 × 6 m in size, and smaller storage huts were also erected.[54] Other settlements were positioned beside lakes and major rivers, but little information has been yielded by sporadic and uneven exploration. Caves and rock shelters were extensively employed for habitation, and some had been subdivided into separate chambers at the entrance, and paved.[55]

At Gonvillars, the food animals were primarily pig (60 per cent), with cattle (28 per cent) and a few sheep and deer. The Kestenberg settlement yielded more cattle than pig, but no sites have suggested much interest in wild animals. Carbonized cereals have been noted from both caves and open settlements, and bronze sickles and some pollen evidence indicates that woodland clearance was progressing, at least in part for arable cultivation. Extensive textile weaving may be assumed from the finds of loom-weights at many sites, and one large bronze foundry at Larnaud indicates some production for the local market (fig. 157, 2).[56]

South of the Rhône, in the upland regions of the French Alps, cave settlement was abundant, and the pollen evidence suggests a greater interest in highland clearances over 1,500 m. The lakeside settlements,

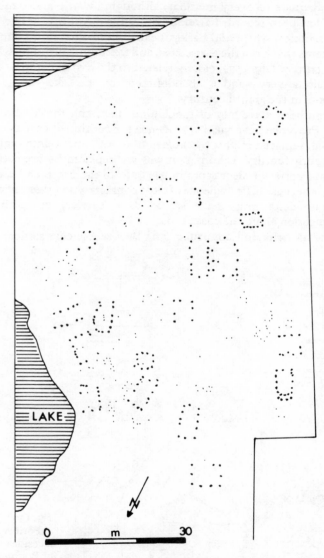

Fig. 156   Plan of later settlement at Dampierre sur-le-Doubs (Doubs) with post-hole alignments forming house-plans shown as larger dots.
(After Petreguin, Urlacher and Vuaillat, *Gallia Préhistoire* 12 (1969))

such as the sites around Lake Bourget,[57] have – to put it mildly – suffered from inadequate recovery methods, although a wattle-and-daub house, 5 × 3 m, has been recorded from Sévrier, Lake Annecy.[58] The yield of organic remains, wheat and barley, beans, acorns, hazelnuts and apples, supplements that from the Swiss sites, and the abundance of metal objects and fine pottery (fig. 157), closely related to the Swiss material, suggests once again a very sudden abandonment of the lake- and riverside settlements in the eighth century.

The southern extremity of the Alpine chain and the Mediterranean shore of Provence have yielded evidence for continued cave occupation and burial, replaced in part by extensions of settlement onto higher land in the eighth century. Inhumation was not replaced by cremation, but metals and pottery reflect types in use both to the north and the east.[59] There is otherwise little evidence of close contacts with other regions, and the Rhône delta must have served as a barrier, preventing land communication along the coastlands.

West of the delta, in Languedoc, later Bronze Age cave settlements and

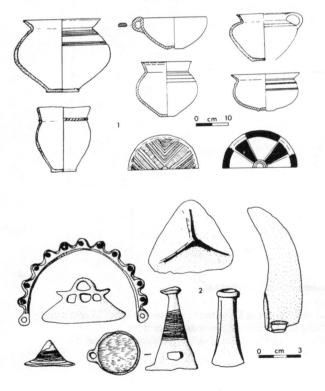

Fig. 157
1. Pottery from the lakeside settlement of Bourget (Alpes).
2. Launacian bronzes.
(After Bocquet 1976, Roudil and Guilaine 1976)

open sites are well-represented. Local metal industries were developed, and pottery from graves is as varied as in the preceding phases. Only in the first millennium do cylinder-neck urns of true Urnfield shape occur, in flat cremation cemeteries. The settlements at Roc de Conilhac, and Portal-Vielh yielded traces of houses, circular, oval and rectangular with a majority quite small (3 m long), although a wattle-and-daub house from Baous de la Salle was 75 sq m in extent.[60] The settlement at Cayla had numerous houses, and a possible defensive rampart, but records are uncertain. What is clearer is that woodland was being removed, upland areas were put into pastoral use, and occupation sites were increasing in the early first millennium.

The many sites yielding animal remains indicate some reliance upon wild game, red deer and boar in particular, but also roe deer, badger, hare, rabbit and fox, with occasional aurochs, bear and wolf. Fish are likely to have been important in areas of major streams, in the eastern Pyrenees for example. Domestic animals form 70 to over 80 per cent of totals, with pig perhaps the most abundantly represented. At the cave of Gaougnas at Cabrespine, pig and sheep formed two-thirds of the total population represented, with some cattle. The evidence for decline in sheep, and increase in pig, from the earlier Bronze Age, requires further documentation and may represent a local event rather than a regional one.[61]

Carbonized wheat and barley have been recovered from several caves, and a few bronze sickles also indicate some arable cultivation. Most of this evidence has been obtained from the Languedoc region; comparable data from the Pyrenees and the Massif Central are lacking. In the latter, however, settlement traces in upland areas probably represent abandonment of the lower wetter valleys in the first millennium.[62] To the north, in Burgundy, upland pastures were established; heights were occupied and sometimes fortified with ramparts – at Vitteaux for example – but valley settlements were also established. The riverside farmsteads at Vauvretin consisted of a house of 18 sq m facing the river, with internal storage jars for produce and possibly with a palisade around the house.[63] More significant is the settlement at Ouroux-Marnay, placed immediately beside the river Saône; activities included agriculture, hunting, fishing, weaving and basketry, and probably pot-making and metal-working as well. Wooden implements and planks have been recovered from the debris which now lies well beneath the river levels; this suggests that the abandonment of the site may have been contemporary with the desertion of many other sites beside lakes and rivers in the Alpine region.[64]

The burial traditions of this region, from the Mediterranean and Pyrenees northwards to Burgundy, reflects the variety of social groups already present and their reactions to new ideas and materials. The problem of actual immigrants in the south must also be considered. In the north, the practice of inhumation in cist or coffin, which was sometimes placed under a barrow, became less common; increasingly popular were cremations, surrounded by circular or rectangular ditches. Barrows continued to be built throughout however. The accompanying grave goods included local pottery styles of bowls, jars and dishes decorated by incision; cylinder-necked urns remained very rare. The evidence from the Massif Central is much more sparse, and it is not until the close of the Late Bronze Age that cremation graves, sometimes under barrows, sometimes within megalithic tombs, become a significant element. Metalwork here and in Burgundy was in general a regional industry, and a variety of tools and weapons were produced, for local use as well as, perhaps, for exchange with neighbouring groups, especially to the east. The Villethierry hoard of 876 ornaments is an outstanding example of these industries.[65]

Along the Mediterranean coast west of the Rhône, and into the eastern Pyrenees, later Bronze Age groups have been identified with clarity only in the final phases,[66] and rather small regional assemblages based upon pottery and metalwork have been presented;[67] these may well represent individual communities or settlements, the products of which were gradually distributed over a defined or partly random territory. Channelled decoration, later supplanted by geometric incision, on cylinder-necked urns is characteristic of earlier phases, and the appearance of cremation cemeteries at Le Moulin, adjacent to the Cayla settlement, and at other sites, has suggested a movement of displaced peoples from further north and east.

The cemetery at Le Moulin contained many cremations set with urns in pits, accompanied by other vessels, metal ornaments, razors and weapons.[68] The pottery includes a variety of urns decorated with geometric designs as well as with schematic human and animal forms. Metal products were the work of an industry called the Launacian, which created various tools and ornaments for regional use. These objects occur in the eastern Pyrenees at heights up to 2,200 m. Within the assemblages of hoards and cemeteries there are occasional iron pieces, and a majority of the larger cremation cemeteries are likely to be contemporary with the emergence of the Celtic Iron Age in this region. This leaves unanswered the problem of Urnfields in southern France, the relationship between these and comparable materials in the Rhône and Rhine provinces; it is, however, tempting to equate in some way the chronological position of widespread abandonment of settlement in lake- and riverside areas of the Rhône-Alpine region, and the appearance among the Mediterranean coast and Pyrenées of groups whose material culture does not conflict in character with that further north and east. The Urnfield burial rite is not consistently enough represented in the south to allow such an equation, however, nor are the words 'cylinder-necked urn' sufficient to evoke human populations. Nonetheless, the 'Urnfield migrations' postulated by some authorities should not be lightly discarded, even if we cannot see any evidence for widespread traffic rumbling its way southwards to avoid climatic or human interference.

Sardinia and Corsica

In Sardinia, the full Bronze Age begins with the Nuraghic phase which appeared *c.* 1500 BC.[69] This is characterized above all by the *nuraghi* themselves, great stone towers numbering between six and seven thousand. Ten metres in diameter and often ascending to 15 m in height, they contain a central roofed chamber and a staircase in the walls which leads up to a second and sometimes a third floor. The walls are of large stones without mortar, and the chambers have corbelled roofs. The earliest *nuraghi* were probably set as isolated towers, perhaps with one or two huts around, but a characteristic village soon developed where the tower itself was surrounded by many circular stone-built houses. *Nuraghi* occur all over Sardinia, but most are on upland plateaux, especially in the

Fig. 158   Decorated slab from Substantion (Hér-ault) showing notched shield, wheels and other designs.
(After Briard 1974)

north-west, at heights between 200 and 700 m above sea level. The size of some of the defensive circuits, with main tower, outer walls and supplementary towers, suggests garrisons of up to 200 men. These represent a late evolution of the concept, which at first was concerned only with a single structure, as at Sa Corona and early Barumini.

The completed forts, dating to the first millennium, are among the most impressive monuments from Bronze Age Europe (fig. 159). Towers with jutting parapets supported by corbels, and outer defensive walls with corner towers, were built to withstand the siege artillery and battering rams of Carthaginian forces; that they failed need not surprise, for their constricted nature internally must have presented insuperable problems of mobility and escape.

The sequence of building phases has been established at Barumini. A central tower 17 m high contained three chambers, one on each floor. The entrance was guarded by a side-room. Niches for sleeping were provided, possibly with cork lining. Subsequently a four-towered wall was added, and external huts were built with extra single towers. Later these single towers were joined by walls to provide a double defensive system for the original central tower.

Contemporary sacred wells and springs, stone-built temples and tombs are also known in Sardinia; collective successive burials in enormous megalithic monuments occur, probably the *nuraghi* builders or at any rate their occupants.[70] Stone and metal-working was practised, and copper mines were exploited; quarries, galleries and shafts, smelting and casting

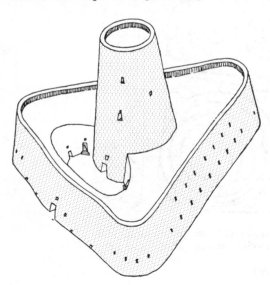

Fig. 159   Reconstruction of Sant'Antine (Torralba), with central tower and triple defensive towers linked by wall.
(After Guido 1963)

places, ingots and moulds all attest the interest in metalwork, and the products included axes, spearheads, daggers and sickles. Imported copper ingots from the eastern Mediterranean have been found, as well as west European axes and swords. Maritime traffic was well-established in the first millennium BC, and had much earlier beginnings. The Monte Sa Idda hoard, probably from a Nuraghic foundry, contains a vast array of bronzes, unfinished castings and scrap metal representing Spanish objects as well as local copies and inventions.[71]

The most instructive metalwork, however, consists of the large series of bronze figures, cast in a lost-wax or lost-lead process and recovered from hoards, foundries, settlements, tombs and sacred sites. Over 400 figures exist, ranging in height from 2 to 40 cm. They depict peasants carrying animals, fruit, loaves, jars of water, skins or musical pipes. Wrestlers, cripples on crutches, warriors with spears, slings or bows, and a few women, rarely with a child or youth, are also represented (pl. 23). Peasants wear loin-cloths, the warriors have tunics and vests, with greaves and various helmets or caps; some warriors have pointed beards, and hair is generally short. The women have long skirts or cloaks, and the upper body is generally left bare; their hair is long and plaited, and may be covered by a hood. Particularly large bronze figures depict males with cloaks and caps, bearing a knobbed club in one hand while the other hand is raised. The animals include oxen, deer, sheep, goats, pigs, dogs and wolves, and there are other less intelligible figures. The date for many of these figures is the earlier first millennium, perhaps 800–600 BC. Because of the unbroken succession of levels at the *nuraghi*, we may see in these human figures some of the very rare representations of European Bronze Age people, not perhaps as authentic as the *in corpore* survivors from Denmark but welcome nonetheless.

The pottery from the Nuraghic settlements contains Monte Claro, Ozieri and Bonnanaro forms, carinated bowls, tripods and large jars with incised or punched decoration. The later Nuraghic pottery, however, included finer wares copying Etruscan forms, with elaborate shapes and decorations.[72]

In spite of this full and interesting information about defence, industry and religion, we still lack reliable data about subsistence and population in Bronze Age Sardinia. Nonetheless, the evidence from the figurines, biased though it may be, provides a useful comparison with the representations of warriors on the statue-menhirs of neighbouring Corsica, just as the immense effort put into the construction of *nuraghi* invites comparison with the Corsican *torri*.

The development of prehistoric settlement in Corsica has been divided into a pre-Torrean and Torrean phase.[73] The colonization of the island

and the construction of dolmens, alignments and statue-*menhirs* were undertaken in the third and early second millennia by neolithic pastoralists, according to current views, and it was not until the later second millennium that a new group arrived or emerged. This group, called Torrean, was responsible for the building of many circular towers on the island, for the occupation of established settlements such as Filitosa, for the introduction of metallurgy and for the re-use and modification of statue menhirs bearing representations of the Torreans themselves. The southern part of the island was the principal area of Torrean occupation, and the *torri* were placed on hills or promontories, sometimes dominating groups of stone houses. Similar though they are to the *nuraghi* of Sardinia, their central corbelled chambers are small and it is suggested that they are not dwellings but cult centres. The towers are 10–15 m in diameter and range from 3 to 7 m in height. The internal deposits often contain hearths and cattle bones, and there is some suggestion that fires were a permanent feature of these centres. Pottery within the deposits is sometimes of Sardinian Monte Claro and Bonnanaro types, but a majority is of Torrean character, rather heavy handled ware lacking much ornamentation. Metalwork is rarely found because of the acidity of the soils.

The statue-*menhirs* carved and erected by pre-Torrean communities continued in use, but now the *menhirs* were shaped to depict the Torreans, warriors with metal swords, wearing loin-cloths and helmets, with provision in the stone for detaching the horns. Other human features are sometimes shown, ribs and hearts, backbone and shoulder-blades.[74]

In the earlier first millennium, the establishment of Torrean settlements in Corsica was consolidated by fortifications around villages and by the erection of additional towers. At Filitosa, major modifications were made to the settlement, and here and elsewhere the *torri* were brought into use as defensive fortifications for human occupation. Abandonment of many such sites in the first millennium may have been brought about by external invaders, but whether these were from Sardinia, Italy or Africa remains to be determined.

These two societies, Sardinian and Corsican, together with comparable evidence from the Balearics reflect the evidence for war and upheaval in western seas. Warlike representations on stelae in the South French and Iberian later Bronze Age (fig. 158), and the gradual emergence of hillforts in the middle of the first millennium BC, show that the transformation of the Bronze Age into the Celtic Iron Age was no peaceful process.

Jugoslavia and Albania

During the later Bronze Age, as in most other periods, Jugoslavia contained a mixture of cultures. Most of the northern and central area was an integral part of the Urnfield group; the east was a part of the west Romanian culture province (above p. 406), that is, the late Žuto Brdo and Balta Verde grouping; the south and south-west, with Albania, were following their own lines of development and for the most part still using tumulus burial.

In the Urnfield area settlements are extremely sparse. In the Srem, Gomolava (Hrtkovci, Sremska Mitrovica) on the Sava is again the best example; the later Bronze Age material is typical of the settlement aspect of the eastern Urnfields. [75] A similar situation prevails further up the Sava at Novigrad (Slavonski Brod), where separate layers of three Urnfield phases are represented.[76] In the Vojvodina sites are undistinguished affairs on loess terraces near rivers, marked only by pits;[77] similar settlement debris, including post-holes, comes from the important site of Brzi Brod (Mediana) near Niš and other sites in the vicinity.[78]

An extremely important, though relatively little-known, site is Donja Dolina on the Sava.[79] It has long been known as an Iron Age pile-dwelling site, but only comparatively recently has extensive Bronze Age settlement been recognized as a result of further excavation. It is said to be the only site in central Europe having continuity from Ha A through to the Roman period. The picture of Bronze Age settlement on the site is scanty, though clear stratigraphical divisions were observed and the phases there can be regarded as the type-sequence for the area.

Different in situation, though comparable in stratigraphical detail, are a series of Bosnian and Dalmatian hill-sites, in defensible, though not necessarily defended, positions.[80] Vis near Derventa (Doboj) is one such, where Ha A-B settlement is well attested, and attributed by the excavator to the Urnfield peoples;[81] others include Velika Gradina at Varvara (Prozor, Sarajevo) in Bosnia, where fortifications were added during the Late Bronze Age,[82] Zecovi level I I I (Prijedor),[83] and Radovin (Zadar).[84] These 'hill-forts' are found in quantity in Bosnia, where the terrain is admittedly most favourable. They are also typical of the succeeding 'Illyrian period', going on well into the Iron Age, and several authorities have seen in this a reflection of the arrival of Illyrians, or the founding of an Illyrian culture, already in the Bronze Age.[85] As far as one can tell, these sites appear only at the end of the Bronze Age; their main period of use is in the Early Iron Age.

Much better known are cemeteries. In the north of the country these follow the standard Urnfield pattern, from the well-known site of Ruše[86] (formerly Maria Rast, Maribor) in Slovenia, through Croatia where Virovitica is typical of the earliest phase,[87] to Serbia where the *Dalj* and *Belegiš-Surčin* groups are representative, or, according to N. Tasić, the 'Urnfield Plain Culture' found around Belgrade.[88] Only occasionally does the form of the grave diverge from the norm, as at Zagreb-Vrapče where stone cists were found.[89] At the southern limit, in Kosovo-Metohija, a late cremation cemetery from Donja Brnjica (Priština) had groups of ten to twenty tombs in pits or cists, or in a storeyed arrangement.[90]

By contrast, in most of Bosnia and parts of south Croatia tumulus burial was still the favoured rite. On the Glasinac plateau in Bosnia many hundreds of mounds of this period are known.[91] In other parts of Bosnia the tumulus was still standard, and though inhumation was the rule, cremations do occur as well, urns being put in stone settings in the body of the mound.[92] In a few instances, at the very end of the Bronze Age or start of the Iron Age, cist graves are found,[93] and we should not forget local peculiarities as at the Bezdanjača cave near Vrhovine, where burials continued through this period (cf. above, p. 198). More unusual things were happening in the cave of Skočjan, where votive bronzes attest a sacred purpose, and at other caves in Slovenia.[94]

What little we know of Albania and Macedonia tells its own story. The Maliq site continues, as finds of Macedonian matt-painted ware show; these are, however, the latest finds on the site. More information comes from the important cave-site at Tren (Korçe) beside the Little Prespa Lake, 856 m above sea-level.[95] Levels III–V here contain material attributable to the Late Bronze Age/Early Iron Age transition, and, most important, imported Mycenaean sherds.[96] Nearby, high up on the rocky mountain-side, are rock-paintings depicting horse-mounted warriors; these are attributed to the Early Iron Age.[97] The dating of sites in this hazy period is very difficult, and until the entire collection from Tren is published, certainty cannot be achieved. The matt-painted ware found through the Macedonian region is considered to be of Bronze Age date by Albanian scholars, though it is found in Greece and Jugoslavia in Iron Age contexts. If the Albanians are right, an ancestry in Albania should be considered.

Tumulus-burial continued the standard rite in Albania, while in Jugoslav Macedonia a few cist-burials are known from the Bronze Age/Iron Age transition.[98] Of the various Albanian tumuli, the group at Pazhok in the Devoll valley contains the greatest variety and the richest grave-goods.[99] Twenty-five tumuli are known from this locality, which is on the right bank of the Devoll in central Albania where the river emerges from the mountains. They are preserved up to 5 m high and can be of impressive diameter. The body was usually placed in a central pit, which could be round or rectangular, and is stone- or wood-lined and surrounded by a stone pavement. The body was laid on the right side, knees bent, cheek resting on the right hand, and head looking west (i.e. oriented north-south). The earth mound which was then heaped up would be surrounded by a circle of stones and in some cases was subsequently re-used, heaped up again, and provided with a second retaining wall. In the 'Great Tumulus' the central pit contained the head and other bones of a bovine; in 'tumulus I', grave 7 contained a sword said to be a Mycenaean imitation and, most interesting, an imported Aegean Vapheio cup of Late Helladic I-II: such an importation does not necessarily have any great chronological value.[100] In the body of this and other mounds were set later burials, on which details are lacking. The burial rite in other areas of Albania was similar: a central cairn and cists are known from Vodhinë in the Drin valley,[101] while in the Mati valley both inhumation and cremation are recorded (fig. 160). Since, however, most of the Mati burials date to the Iron Age, we cannot be sure that the introduction of cremation is not an Iron Age rather than a Bronze Age feature.

The material found in these Balkan graves varies greatly according to its locality. In the Urnfield area of Jugoslavia the regular paraphernalia of Urnfield burial turns up – pins, rings, fibulae, razors, swords, knives, tutuli and so on in bronze, urns, with (less frequently) cups or other accessory vessels in pottery (fig. 161). At the end of the period, on the threshold of the Iron Age, finds of horse-harness (as at Dalj) indicate the arrival of 'Thraco-Cimmerian' elements (above, p. 403), and these are accompanied by bangles, spectacle and arc fibulae and other 'Macedonian bronzes'.[102] In the Bosnian tumuli the finds are less rich but rather similar; the violin-bow fibula serving as a central chronological point, and pins, rings and bracelets being the commonest finds. Albania has its own characteristic collection of material, insofar as one can pin the finds down to one phase rather than another. The dominant pottery is 'Macedonian matt-painted ware', whose shapes include two-handled bowls or kantharoi and beak-spouted jugs, the bowl forms apparently going back into the Bronze Age if the available reports on Pazhok are interpreted aright (fig. 163). The bronzes include both Mycenaean and European swords, spearheads, knives and other tools.[103] We may specifically mention imported Mycenaean swords at Vajzë (Vlorë), the Mati valley, Nënshat (Shkodër) and at Tetovo in Jugoslav Macedonia.

Hoard finds in the Late Bronze Age are very numerous (fig. 162).[104] The forms represented belong, for the most part, to the standard European repertoire, and we will not discuss them in detail. Hoards like Otok-Privlaka (Otok, Vinkovci), which consists of 276 pieces, contain

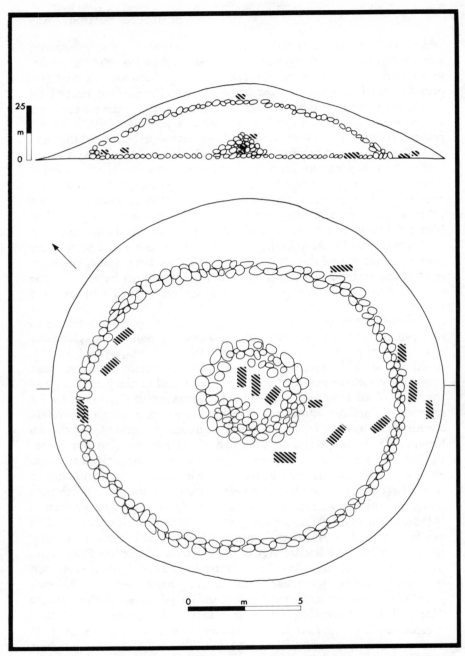

Fig. 160   Vodhinë (Gjirokastër), south Albania: plan and section of barrow with burials shown hatched.
(After N. G. L. Hammond, *BSA* 66 (1971))

fragments of weapons, tools and ornaments, and ingot pieces; there are also hoards of new and unused objects, presumably deposited with some votive purpose in mind. Sheet-bronze-working, as shown in the greaves from Ilijak in Bosnia or the T-handled cauldron from Požarevac, was also becoming a standard technique.[105]

The interpretation of the Urnfield period in Jugoslavia is not easy. One thing is quite clear: the southern Urnfield border lies *in* Jugoslavia, and roughly corresponds with the southern edge of the Sava valley, following the Morava south into Serbia to include the Banat 'Urnfields'. Upland Jugoslavia and Albania were not affected, and the tumulus traditions

Fig. 161   Belegiš (Osijek): urns and other pottery from the cremation cemetery. Varying scales.
(After *Epoque préhistorique*, 1971)

continued as before, with the addition of 'hill-forts' or *gradina*-type sites. The arrival of the Urnfield rite in Jugoslavia must be seen as part of the wider movement; if the origins of the culture are to be sought in an area with a local ancestry of cremation, then a movement southwards from Hungary is obviously a possibility. The presence of fluted wares and various decorative forms has even suggested to one author an element of Lausitz influence in northern Jugoslavia.[106] The situation in southern Jugoslavia and Albania is different. In Serbia, sites like Mediana contain pottery that links them with areas to the south and east – Greece, Bulgaria, Romania, and even Troy. If tribal names can be assigned on

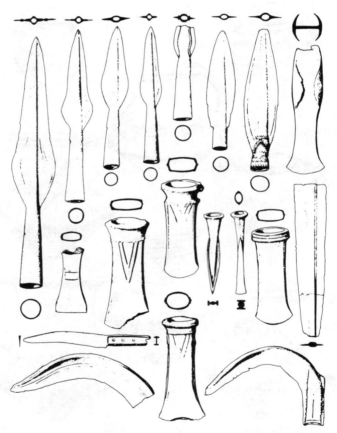

Fig. 162   Donja Bebrina (Slavonski Brod, Croatia): bronze hoard, eleventh century BC. Varying scales.
(After Vinski-Gasparini 1973)

such scanty evidence, we should presumably think of the makers of these pots as Thracian or Moesian.[107] In Albania and Dalmatia, the historical inhabitants were the Illyrians, first mentioned by Herodotus in the fifth century BC as one-time neighbours of the Dorians and Pelasgians,[108] and later known to extend over the whole Dalmatian area from Greece to the Sava-Danube line in the north, and to the Morava-Vardar line in the east. We have plainly seen that this area is not archaeologically homogeneous in the Late Bronze Age, so there can be no simple equation of sites and races. Kossinna used to believe, on the basis of the Urnfield developments in Jugoslavia, that the Illyrians must have come ultimately from Lausitz stock; few would follow such a theory today. Albanian scholars, who naturally do not like the idea of a descent from north Europe, point to the alleged continuity of culture at Maliq, from Neolithic to Late Bronze Age (and thence on into the Iron Age) as proof that the Illyrians were indigenous and aboriginal. Jugoslav scholars have also remarked on the impossibility of linking Illyrians directly with the Urnfields, or with the movement of peoples in the Aegean area.[109] In the present state of knowledge there is no strong reason to suppose that the Albanian view is not correct; one must simply remember that none of the Late Bronze Age artifacts can of itself be called 'Illyrian'.[110] Only with the start of hill-towns in the Albanian Early Iron Age, and Bosnian *gradina* sites in Ha B, do the distinctive features of later Illyrian settlement appear.

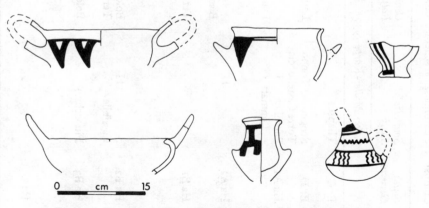

Fig. 163   Tren cave (Korcë), eastern Albania: painted pottery from the latest Bronze Age layers.
(After M. Korkuti and S. Anamali, *Bulletin d'arch. sud-est européen* I (1969))

Table 16 Comparative chronological schemes for southern Europe, later Bronze Age

Absolute Date BC	South Germany	South Italy/ Sicily	Central Italy	North Italy	East Alps	Croatia (after Vinski-Gasparini)	Hungary (after Mozsolics)
		(after Müller-Karpe 1959)					
1300	Br C	Thapsos				Urnfield Phase I	IVa Forró
1200	Br D	Scoglio del Tonno Torre Castelluccia	Late Apennine	Peschiera	Baierdorf	II	IVb Ópályi
	Ha A1	Pantalica I Timmari	Pianello I	Protovillanovan	Grossmugl Unterradl		Va Aranyos
1100	Ha A2	II	II Bismantova	Fontanella	Jurkendorf	III	Val I Vb Kurd
1000	Ha B1		Terni I		Ruše I	IV	VIa Hajdúböszörmeny
900	Ha B2	Cassibile III	Bologna I Terni II	Este I	II		Val II VIb
800	Ha B3	Finocchito	Bologna II	II	III	V	
700	Ha C		III	III			'Thraco-Cimmerians'

Chronology

We have tabulated the relative chronology of the later Bronze Age in southern Europe, following Müller-Karpe and others, in Table 16. Almost all of these synchronisms are based on typological cross-comparison, and such forms as the violin-bow fibula are among the most-used. This type was probably invented somewhere in the area under discussion about 1200 BC – perhaps at or near Peschiera itself? – and adopted universally thereafter, in Italy, Jugoslavia and Greece. Its first appearance thus acts as an accurate chronological indicator. In the south of the area, imported Aegean pottery provides absolute dates (radiocarbon determinations are still too few to be of much value) for the successive stages of the Italian sequence, and these are expressed in absolute centuries BC at the left of the table.

Other dates can be derived from detailed typological study. As the later Bronze Age proceeded, links across the Adriatic became very common, and identical production of some objects (certain types of amber beads, bronzes, etc.) has been suggested. It is, indeed, hardly possible to deny the closeness of such contacts.[111]

Table 17   Radiocarbon dates, southern Europe, later Bronze Age

Site	Lab no.	bc
Central Italy		
Luni sul Mignone, Tre Erici, level 6, Apennine IVb	St–1341	825±100
Luni sul Mignone, Tre Erici, level 3, Iron Age	St–1340	915±80
Iron Age building on west of hill	St–1346	835±70
Grotta del Farneto (Bologna), 'sub-Apennine'	Pi–53	1290±110
Fucino (Avezzano), 'sub-Apennine'	Pi–80	1416±130
Narce, phase III (Apennine-Protovillanovan)	St–2395	1040±100
phase IV (Protovillanovan)	St–2396	960±105
Grotta Misa, late Apennine	R–9	920±60
	R–24	750±60
	Pi–54	1080±75
S. Michele di Valestra, phase II, LBA–PVN	R–734a	710±50
phase III, PVN	R–735a	880±50
Ripara di Romagnano III-Loc, Luco culture, equiv. to Ha A	R–768	1050±50
South Italy		
Porto Perone, Leporano, LBA house	R–117	1150±60

Table 17—cont.

Site	Lab no.	bc
Lipari, acropolis, Milazzese	R–365a	950 ± 50
Ausonian I I, destruction	R–181	605 ± 50
	R–367a	820 ± 50
	R–367	870 ± 50
Filicudi, Capo Graziano, hut 8	R–369	1050 ± 60
Morgantina (Enna), Ausonian I I	St–1339	745 ± 70
Sardinia		
Nuraghe Albucciu, (Sassari)	Gif–242	1220 ± 250
Nuraghe Brunku Madili, Gesturi, (Cagliari)	Gif–243	1820 ± 250
Barumini (Cagliari), tower	K–151	1970 ± 200
Malchittu, tower	R–344A	920 ± 70
Oridda, megalithic tomb	R–1060	1220 ± 50
Nuraghe Genna Maria, Villanovaforru	P–2403	970 ± 50
Ortu Comidu, Sardara. 4 dates, range 960 ± 250 – 1130 ± 60		
Corsica		
Castello de Cecica, Porto-Vecchio	Gsy–120	1345 ± 150
	Gsy–94A	680 ± 200
	Gsy–94B	1915 ± 125
Sartène, Cucuruzzu	Gif–239	660 ± 150
	Gif–240	825 ± 150
	Gif–241	880 ± 150
Bonifacio, Abri de Araguina	Gif–776	1090 ± 110
	Gif–777	1350 ± 120
	Gif–778	1600 ± 120
Sartène, Castello d'Araggio	Gif–898	550 ± 110
	Gif–899	940 ± 110
	Gif–1001	980 ± 120
Sollacaro, Filitosa	Gsy–58	1200 ± 150
	Gif–150	600 ± 170
	Gif–2398	1130 ± 110
	Gif–2399	1430 ± 110
Sartène, Curacchiaghiu	Gif–1958	660 ± 110
	Gif–1959	1280 ± 130
Sartène, Stantare	Gif–1396	1000 ± 110
Bilia Castello d'Alo	Gif–478	1150 ± 110
	Gif–479	1550 ± 120
	Gif–480	1870 ± 200
Serra di Ferro Basi	Gif–1846	1400 ± 110
	Gif–1847	1620 ± 110
Jugoslavia		
Mediana, Brzi Brod (Niš), "in front of LBA construction"	BC–6	1280 ± 90
Pit 1, Lj xvii	BC–8	1000 ± 200

Table 17—cont.

Site	Lab no.	bc
Bezdanjača cave (Vrhovine), sticks	Z–186/I	1036±75
torches	Z–186/II	1349±61
grave 19, sticks	Z–219	1110±58
wooden construction	Z–220	917±75
Switzerland		
Mottata, Ramosch, cave occupation	B–147	1370±100
Montbec, Neuchâtel (Vaud), lake-side settlement	LV–87N	980±120
	LV–87	890±220
wooden spear	LV–208	1310±160
Champreveyres, lake-side settlement	LV–88	730±150
Aare river, sword	B–484	1230±130
Bevaix, Neuchâtel, dugout	LV–270	940±110
Zug-Sumpf, lake-side settlement	GI–12	1220±110
Petit-Cortaillod, Neuchâtel, lake-side settlement	LV–452	560±90
	LV–453	520±65
	LV–454	570±85
	LV–455	590±85
South France		
Niaux, (Ariège), cave	Gif–2396	1160±100
Esclauzels, G. du Noyer, (Lot), cave	Gif–1160	1090±110
	Gif–1631	1200±110
	Gif–1159	1300±110
Sauliac, L'Igue Blanche, (Lot), cave	Gif–1882	850±70
Cahors, (Lot), pit	Gif–1881	740±70
Cabrespini, G. du Gaougnas, (Aude), cave	Gif–483	1210±200
Tharaux, G. du Hasard, (Gard), cave	Gif–1359	1000±130
Montclus, G. de Prével, (Gard), occupation	Gif–1910	700±110
Ardagne, Chaos de Targasonne (Pyr. Or.), occupation	Gif–1883	500±70
Llo (Pyr. Or.), occupation	Gif–3072	1070±110
Saillagouse (Pyr. Or.), occupation	Gif–2803	790±110
	Gif–2804	1090±110
G. de Camprafaud, Ferrière-Poussaron (Hérault), cave	Gif–1091	1130±110
Bedoin (Vaucluse), rock shelter	Gif–2868	1070±100
Salies de Béarn, (Pyr. Or.), salt site	LV–246	1260±170
	LV–247	1120±120
Craz de Michaille, (Ain)	Ly–233	1310±100
St André de Cruzière, (Ardèche)	Gif–274	780±150
Brisson St Innocent, (Savoie), pilotis	Ly–508	890±300
Chindrieux, Chatillon, (Savoie), occupation	Ly–18	780±160
	Ly–17	750±100
	Ly–9	1110±100
	Ly–274	720±110

Table 17—cont.

Site	Lab no.	bc
Annecy, Duingt, (H. Savoie) lake-side settlement	Mc–81	550 ± 100
	Ly–63	1450 ± 600
	Ly–191	810 ± 150
	Ly–192	1080 ± 150
Port de Thonon les Bains (H. Savoie), lake-side occupation	Sa–228	490 ± 180
St Alban, Aiguebelette (Savoie), lake-side occupation	Ly–19	1090 ± 140
	Ly–689	760 ± 90
Seyssinet-Pariset, G. des Sarrasins, (Isère), cave	Ly–238	990 ± 170
	Ly–239	1290 ± 120
	Gif–1202	1030 ± 105
	Gif–1203	1370 ± 110
Solignac, Champs Vieux (H. Loire), occupation	Ly–872	920 ± 100
Epervans, Vauvretin (S.-et-Loire), hearth	Ly–664	840 ± 190
Dampierre sur le Doubs (Doubs) settlement	Gif–2656	790 ± 110

Notes

1 This material is in Verona Museum; cf. Müller-Karpe 1959, 89ff., Taf. 103–7. For comparable material further north, see R. Lunz, *Studien zur End-Bronzezeit und älteren Eisenzeit im Südalpenraum*, 1974, esp. table p. 541.

2 De Marinis 1975, 43ff.

3 De Marinis 1975, 47f., 52, note 33. He also disposes of the 'hydraulic clay' theory.

4 A. M. Bietti Sestieri, *Padusa* 11 (1975), 1–14; note 1 for full bibliography (all in numbers of *Padusa*).

5 Barfield 1971, 99, 126f.; the classic work is C. Marchesetti, *I Castellieri Preistorici di Trieste e della Regione Giulia*, 1903.

6 M. Cipelloni, *Origini* 5 (1971), 149–191.

7 U. Rellini, *Mon. Ant.* 34 (1931), 177ff.; Müller-Karpe 1959, 65; Trump 1966, 131f.

8 G. Montanari and A. M. Radmilli, *BPI* n.s. 9 vol. 64 (1954–1955), 137–69.

9 Müller-Karpe 1959, 65f. with refs.; M. Cipelloni, *Origini* 5 (1971), 149–91.

10 Potter 1976, 48ff., 317ff.

11 T. Wieselgren, *Luni sul Mignone*, vol. II fasc. 1, 1969; P. Hellström, vol. I I fasc. 2, 1975, esp. 93ff.; the late dating is hardly discussed (p. 97).

12 Q. Quagliati, *BPI* 25 (1899), 202f.; 26 (1900), 12ff.; Müller-Karpe 1959, 30ff. A subsequent attempt at deciphering the stratigraphy: G. Säflund in *Dragma M. P. Nilsson*, Skrifter Inst. Rom 1 (1939), 458ff.

13 Lo Porto 1963, 285ff., fig 5.

14 Coppa Nevigata: A. Mosso, *Mon. Ant.* 19 (1908), 305ff. Grotta Manaccora: E. Baumgartel, *PBSR* 19 (1951), 23–38; 21 (1953), 1.

15 D. and R. Whitehouse, *PBSR* 24 (1969), 34–75.

16 On Sicily generally: Bernabò Brea 1966, 130ff.

17 L. Bernabò Brea and M. Cavalier, *BPI* n.s. 10 vol. 65 (1956), 8ff.; 67ff.

18 Gentili, *Not. Scavi* 1956, 165ff.; Bernabò Brea 1966, 157f.; Tinè and Vagnetti 1967, 21, pl. 29, 132.

20 E. Sjöqvist, *AJA* 62 (1958), 157; R. Stillwell, *AJA* 67 (1963), 171; H. Allen, *AJA* 74 (1970), 369ff. Mycenaean finds: Tinè and Vagnetti 1967.

21 Hencken 1968, 440ff.

22 Peroni 1963, 78ff.

23 Scamozzina: Castelfranci, *BPI* 3 (1877), 1; 28 (1902), 130; 35 (1909), 1; Monza: id., *BPI* 14 (1888), 208; 17 (1891), 34; *Not. Scavi* 1888, 615 (quoted Rittatore 1953–4).

24 Rittatore 1953–4.

25 Säflund 1939, 197ff.; Peroni 1963, 94ff.; M. Degani, *Preistoria dell'Emilia e Romagna* 1 (1962), 63–110.

26 Säflund 1939, 204; Hencken 1968, 452f.

27 De Marinis 1975, 46.

28 Hencken 1968, esp. chs 21, 22, 30, 32; cf. too Schuhmacher 1967, where the material from each area is listed and briefly described.

29 A. Colini, *BPI* 39 (1914), 19ff.; 40 (1914), 121ff. (quoted Schuhmacher 1967).

30 W. D. Taylour, in *The Palace of Nestor at Pylos,* vol. III, 197, fig. 291, a-e.

31 Fibulae: C. Blinkenberg, *Fibules grecques et orientales,* 1926; J. Sundwall, *Die älteren italischen Fibeln,* 1943. Peschiera daggers: R. Peroni, *Badische Fundberichte* 20 (1956), 69–92; V. Milojčić, *RGZM* 2 (1955), 157ff.; unpublished lists by J. Bouzek and A. F. Harding; cf. Müller-Karpe 1962.

32 Bietti Sestieri 1973.

33 E. Macnamara, *PPS* 36 (1970), 241ff.; Bietti Sestieri 1973, 387f.

34 R. Peroni, *Inv. Arch. Italia* 1 (1961), I.1, 1–147. Bietti Sestieri attributes this hoard to the eleventh century, earlier than previous dates assigned by Peroni and Müller-Karpe; a dating with which we concur.

35 Müller-Karpe 1959, pls 48–52.

36 A. Mozsolics, in *The European Community in Later Prehistory,* eds Boardman, Brown and Powell, 1971; *RSP* 27 (1972), 373–98; *AAA Szeged* 21 (1973), 8ff.

37 Including the Mels poppy-pin graves of Br D and the Binningen graves of Ha A1 in the Müller-Karpe terminology.

38 B. Frei, *ZSAK* 15 (1954), 129–73, including description of stratification at the Montlinger Berg hill settlement; B. Frei in Drack 1971, 87–102.

39 Sauter 1976, 90, 97; M. Primas, *JIVUF* (1974), 51–6, on later Bronze Age groupings in the Alpine area; M. Primas and U. Ruoff in Drack 1971, 55–86.

40 See also M. Primas, *ZSAK* 29 (1972), 5–18 for description of final Bronze Age cemeteries and other finds in Tessin.

41 The beginnings of high Alpine activity, and the exploration of the passes, have been discussed by R. Wyss in *ZSAK* 28 (1971), 130–145, esp. the maps, figs 1–2.

42 V. Rychner, *Archaeologia* (Dijon) 101 (1976), 39–45; Y. Mottier in Drack 1971, 145–56.

43 U. Ruoff in Drack 1971, 71–86; R. Wyss in Drack 1971, 103–22; G. Bersu, *Das Wittnauer Horn im Kanton Aargau.* Monog. zur Ur- und Fruhgeschichte der Schweiz I, 1945.

44 Keller 1878 with many illustrations; J. Speck in Guyan 1954,

275–333; R. Wyss (Drack 1971, 103–22) provides a summary of the settlement evidence; see also U. Ruoff, in Drack 1971, 71–86.

45 J. Speck, in Guyan 1954, 275–333.

46 W. Lüdi, in Guyan 1954, 92–109.

47 E. Wettstein, *Vierteljahresschrift der Naturforschenden Gesellschaft in Zürich* 69 (1924), 78–127.

48 Higham 1968.

49 J. Renfrew 1973, 206.

50 Historical reasons for the abandonment, involving invaders, have sometimes been advanced, but we find these unpersuasive.

51 Sauter 1976, fig. 44.

52 Millotte 1963 and 1976.

53 Millotte 1963.

54 Millotte 1976, 502.

55 Such as the Gonvillars cave.

56 Millotte 1963.

57 Bocquet 1976, 483; Sandars 1957.

58 Bosquet 1976, 493.

59 Legrand 1976.

60 Roudil and Guilaine 1976; Roudil 1972; Guilaine 1972.

61 Guilaine 1972: Chalcolithic: domestic 89% (sheep 61, pig 11, and others); Middle Bronze: domestic 98% (sheep 44, pig 26); Late Bronze: domestic 83% (sheep 28, pig 38). The evidence for 'decline' in sheep, and 'increase' in pig, from the earlier Bronze Age, requires further and more extensive documentation.

62 Daugas 1976.

63 Bonnamour, Mordant and Nicolardot 1976.

64 This is one of the principal supports for the idea of 'Urnfield migrations' from the central European (including Alpine) areas into Southern France and southeastern Spain (pp. 439, 464).

65 C. and D. Mordant and J.-Y. Prampart, *Le Dépot de bronze de Villethierry* (Yonne). *Gallia Préhistoire* 1976. This is a very detailed study of an impressive hoard

weighing 12,000 g and containing 488 pins, 22 brooches, 43 pendants, 80 bracelets, 249 rings and 1 pair of tweezers, as well as fragments of tools. The Cannes-Écluse hoard, found nearby, contained a comparable range of objects. We have not touched here upon the detailed typological studies made on the region's pottery and bronzes, studies which may allow more precise local groups to be identified, and external relations assessed, e.g. Sandars 1957.

66 Sandars 1957; Briard 1974; Guilaine 1972; Roudil 1972.

67 E.g. Guilaine 1972, fig. 130; Roudil 1972, figs. 93–97. Guilaine 1976a, fig. 3, 12: Le Bazacle, H.-Garonne, sword; fig. 4, 5: G. du Hasard and fig. 5, 2–5: Roc de Conilhac, Aude, Urnfield wares of regional character.

68 Mailhac: Guilaine 1976, fig. 6.

69 Guido 1963; Lilliu 1962.

70 The radiocarbon date at Oridda has confirmed a Nuraghic use of a 'Giant's Grave': R–1060, 1220 ± 50 bc.

71 Guido 1963, 158–9.

72 Guido 1963, fig. 57–8.

73 Grosjean 1976; Briard 1974, 148; Daniel and Evans 1967, 32.

74 R. Grosjean, *Antiquity* 40 (1966), 194.

75 B. Jovanović, *RVM* 14 (1965), 121; N. Tasić, *RVM* 14 (1965), 198ff.; B. Brukner in *Epoque préhistorique*, 1971, 175f.

76 Vinski-Gasparini 1973, 36, 196.

77 N. Tasić *Starinar* n.s. 17 (1966), 15–26.

78 M. V. Garašanin, *Arch. Iug.* 10 (1969), 85–90; *Praistorijske kulture pomoravl'a i istočne Srbije*, Niš, 1971, 75ff. The two main levels are attributed to Br C-D and Br D. Other material is later.

79 Z. Marić, *GZMS* n.s. 19 (1964), 5–128, esp. 23ff., 58ff. Phase I of

Marić's classification is of the Urnfield culture; Ia equivalent to Ha A1–2 in the west and Glasinac IIIb; Ib to Ha B1–2 and Glasinac IIIc; Ic to Ha B3 and part of Glasinac IVa. The amount of material from each of these phases is, however, very unequal.

80 B. Čović, *GZMS* n.s. 20 (1965), 27–145.

81 Z. Marić, *GZMS* n.s. 15–16 (1960–1), 151–71; *Epoque préhistorique*, 1971, 76ff.

82 B. Čović, *Epoque préhistorique*, 1971, 74–6.

83 B. Čović, *GZMS* n.s. 11 (1956), 147–66; Trbuhović 1968, 92ff.

84 S. Batović, *Diadora* 4 (1968), 53–74. A well-published excavation with a good series of house-plans of the Early Iron Age, as well as a consideration of other similar sites.

85 E.g. Kusače (Rogatica): C. Truhelka, *GZMS* 2 (1890), 387ff.; 3 (1891), 310ff.; *WMBH* 1 (1893), 67f. cf. Benac and Čović 1956, 42.

86 S. Pahič, *Razprave* 4,3 (1957); cf. too Pobrezje (Maribor): S. Pahič, *Pobrezje*, 1972.

87 On Croatia generally, Vinski-Gasparini 1973.

88 N. Tasić, *Starinar* n.s. 17 (1966), 15–26.

89 Vinski-Gasparini 1973, 187, 199.

90 D. Srejović, *Glasnik Kos. i Met.* 4–5 (1959–60), 83–135. Such cemeteries are rare, even in central Serbia; a few urns have turned up elsewhere (Fafos, Ljušta etc.).

91 Benac and Čović 1956, e.g. 42.

92 M. D. Kosorić, *Članci i grada* 11 (1975), 5–9, 15–20. In the north of Bosnia urnfields are found near the Sava: e.g. Barice near Gračanica (Tuzla), B. Čović, *GZMS* 13 (1958), 77–96; Krcevina and Mala Gradina, B. Belić, *Zbornik Krajiskih Muzeja* 2 (1963–4), 19–35.

93 J. Mladin, *Jadranski Zbornik* 4 (1959–60), 211–25: Oser on Cres Island, Ha B.

94 J. Szombathy, *Mitt. der prah. Komm.* 2/2 (1912), 127–190; cf. J. Alexander, *Jugoslavia*, 1972, 91.

95 M. Korkuti *Stud. Alb.* 4/1 (1967), 139–156; *Shqiperia arkeologjike*, 1971, pl. 26; *Iliria* 1 (1971), 31–45. For the latest finds and divisions at Maliq, *Iliria* 3 (1975), 401–6.

96 Unpublished. In Tirana Museum the exhibition includes a kylix fragment (monochrome) and some other possibly Myc sherds, but it must be stressed that the find circumstances of these are unknown to us.

97 *Shqiperia Arkeologjike*, 1971, pls 27–9.

98 The burials at Vergina (Verroia) in western Greek Macedonia are also in tumuli, though of clear Iron Age date. A cist-grave at Prilep: C. Truhelka, *Glasnik Skopje* 5 (1929), 59–62.

99 Islami and Ceka 1964, 94ff. Hammond 1967, 77ff. M. Korkuti, *Stud. Alb.* 7/2 (1970), 46; for latest finds, mostly Iron Age in date, and including vases with diagonal fluting on the shoulder, see *Iliria* 3 (1975), 407–14.

100 Information provided in Tirana in 1972 has suggested that grave 7 lay directly above the bovine grave in the 'Great Tumulus' (i.e. Tumulus 1 *is* the Great Tumulus). Other groups of finds in the same barrow, mainly swords, spearheads and daggers, seem late in the Bronze Age or even Iron Age in date.

101 F. Prendi, *BUSS* 1956/1, 180f. N. G. L. Hammond, *Epirus*, 1967, 201–4.

102 Vinski-Gasparini 1973, pls 119–120; for Macedonian bronzes, J. Bouzek, *Graeco-Macedonian Bronzes*, 1974, and *PA* 65 (1974), 278–341.

103 M. Korkuti, *Stud. Alb*, 7/2 (1970),

43–50; cf. A. F. Harding, *Stud. Alb.* 9/2 (1972), 218ff.; Harding 1975.

104   F. Holste, *Hortfunde Sudosteuropas,* 1951; Z. Vinski and K. Vinski-Gasparini, *Opusc. Arch.* 1 (1956), 57–109.; F. Holste, *Zur Chronologie der südosteuropäischen Hortfunde der Urnenfelderzeit,* 1962; von Brunn 1968; Vinski-Gasparini 1973. M. Kosorić, *Arch. Iug.* 13 (1972), 1–25, distinguishes three horizons of Late Bronze Age hoards; Ha A, Ha A-B, and Ha B-C.

105   G. von Merhart, *BRGK* 37–38 (1956–7), 91ff., 107ff. figs. 3; 5–6;

M. D. Kosorić, *Starinar* n.s. 15–16 (1964–5), 191–2.

106   V. Trbuhović, *Starinar,* n.s 13–14 (1962–3), 181–4.

107   Cf. Dimitrov 1968.

108   Herodotus i. 56.

109   M. V. Garašanin, *Diadora* 2 (1960–1961), 117–34; A. Benac, *ARR* 4–5 (1967), 319–36.

110   Cf. A. F. Harding, *Stud. Alb.* 9/2 (1972), 221, in contrast to the standard and oft-repeated remarks in the Albanian literature, as seen most recently in F. Prendi, *Iliria* 3 (1975), 109–38.

111   A. F. Harding, op. cit.; cf. above, notes 25 and 26.

10 Western Europe

The later Bronze Age in Atlantic Europe developed imperceptibly from the preceding earlier Bronze Age. In Iberia, in western and northern France, and in the British Isles, the evidence for cultural change and innovation is relatively slight, although the onset of deteriorating climatic conditions near the end of the second millennium had substantive effects upon the established farming practices in some upland regions. In many areas of western Europe, progressive expansion of settlements and forest clearance, with more and more land-take, may have resulted in permanent deforestation, if the processes of soil podsolization through human interference were substantial.[1] The growth of peat which swamped many areas of previous, second millennium, agricultural activity, was probably both a cause and an effect of human exploitation in many regions of the west.[2] We should not, however, attempt to translate particular climatic and anthropogenic factors, applicable to well-studied areas, into other situations of western Europe, where different elements may well have been the principal reasons for changes in social patterns. In more southerly areas, it is possible, if not proved, that increased rainfall and lowered temperatures would have helped to redress any soil exhaustion, by bringing into potential circulation new areas of land not previously suitable for cultivation.[3]

The chronological basis for the later Bronze Age in Atlantic Europe must be radiocarbon dating, in the absence of any major cultural change. Elsewhere, the appearance of the true Urnfields makes a convenient point, but in western Europe this phenomenon is absent, and Urnfield 'influences' are shadowy, elusive, and archaeologically indefinable. The evidence for continuity within the entire Bronze Age of the west is strong, and an arbitrary division is therefore made near the end of the second millennium BC, separating earlier from later. The subsistence economies, settlement patterns and industrial activities throughout Atlantic Europe remained as before, with some small alterations in areas and emphases. Burial practices also did not alter substantially except that in certain regions the methods of disposal of the dead became less archaeologically visible.

Schemes for the later Bronze Age generally have been based upon elaborate typological divisions of metalwork; often a threefold system has been proposed as a general principle, but all seem unnecessary in the present context.[4]

Iberia

The later Bronze Age developments in Spain and Portugal have only

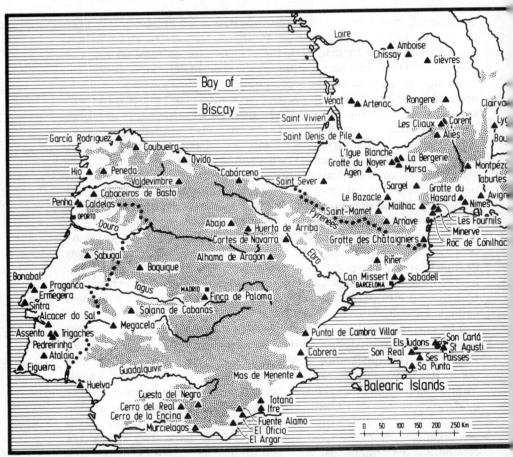

Map 8   Bronze Age sites in south-western Europe

recently been the subject of intensive exploration, except for studies of metalwork and pottery. The earlier Bronze Age Argaric material of south-eastern Spain still remains the predominant and best-known Bronze Age cultural group, but recognition of post-Argaric sites has allowed a greater measure of cultural continuity to be demonstrated. The separation of Argar A and Argar B (see p. 222) into discrete episodes appears less formal than hitherto, and work at Cerro del Real in Granada has revealed dated occupations which follow-on from the late Argar of Cerro de la Virgen.[5] The early settlement at Cerro del Real consisted of a group of oval or circular houses, built of mud brick, averaging 12 m in diameter; the area of settlement was 500 × 200 m, which is substantially larger than most Bronze Age occupation sites in western Europe. The houses had vertical walls, not domed, and their roofs were probably of wood and grass. The layered plastered walls and repaired floors indicate prolonged occupation, as does the 5–6 m of associated deposit, and some pottery from this settlement at Cerro del Real suggests an early first millennium date.

This site is likely to be the contemporary of Cerro de la Encina in the same region of southern Spain. A narrow plateau above the river Monachil was occupied by a late Argaric group who built in stone and clay;[6] the settlement was subsequently strengthened near the end of the second millennium, and was then abandoned. In the early first millennium, and contemporary with Cerro del Real, the plateau was again occupied, and a small settlement of mud-brick and wattle-and-daub houses was built; the inside walls were plastered with yellow and white mud, decorated with geometric grooves. The occupants had sheep and goat, with some cattle and pig, but their arable interests are unknown; wild animals formed 25 per cent of the total.

Rather more substantial structures have been recorded from another contemporary settlement at Cuesta del Negro, on a high plateau at 1,000 m and within a region of uplands which ensure a continental climate of cold winters and short but hot summers. The settlement lies between a river valley system and the fringes of the Sierra Nevada but was positioned near arable land, pasture for animals and freshwater springs. Succeeding the late Argaric phase, which was of long duration, was an early first millennium occupation covering 200 × 100 m and representing at least four rearrangements of houses. The houses were rectangular, 7 × 4–5 m in size, with deeply-cut foundations of stone dug into the Argar or virgin soil levels. One house had a semi-circular clay wall containing storage jars and querns, and remains of wheat. Apparently contemporary with this domestic arrangement was a stone and mud-brick enclosure, built during the Argaric phase and repaired during the later Bronze Age, perhaps providing a defensive element to the settlement.[7]

These three settlements are but the forerunners of a number and variety of later Bronze Age occupation sites currently under investigation, and when their economic practices have been fully explored through environmental and subsistence studies, our information for the post-Argaric Bronze Age will be as complete as that for the Argaric itself. There will still remain, however, an unfortunate lack of well-documented settlements from much of the remainder of the Iberian peninsula. Contemporary occupations at El Oficio and Fuente Alamo, following on from the Argaric, have been suggested on the basis of later Bronze Age pottery from these and other sites.

At Cerro del Real, carinated bowls and everted dishes with burnished surfaces were abundant, but there were also sherds of Urnfield-related ware. Coarser pottery included flat-based vessels and lugged jars. At Cerro de la Encina, pottery and loom weights believed to have been traded or brought in from central Spain, the Ebro Valley and south-central Spain, have been recorded.[8] The domestic ware from Cuesta del Negro included flat dishes and carinated vases, mostly plain although some excised ware and channelled ware is noted. Some of this pottery is of Boquique type; known from the Boquique cave, this consists of shallow bowls with stab and drag furrows arranged in pendent semi-circular designs, with zigzag and other barbed designs.[9] The contemporary excised wares, where clay has been cut-out to form geometric designs, are often compared with east French pottery of the second millennium although no cultural connections can be suggested.

Elsewhere in Spain and Portugal, except for the north-east, large settlements of the later Bronze Age are mostly unknown or unexplored. The well-organized town-plan of Cortes de Navarra, in the Ebro valley, covering at least 300 sq m provides a continuity between the latest Bronze Age and the Iberian culture which emerged by the mid-first millennium BC. The tell consisted of successive mud-brick houses built in groups and separated by wide streets (fig. 164). Most houses had an entry through a narrow end, with the main room placed behind a vestibule.[10] Stone moulds from Cortes de Navarra and from other sites in the Ebro valley, including Cabazo de Monléon,[11] indicate extensive metalworking in copper and bronze. Further south, at Villena (Alicante), the enormous hoard of over 20 kg of gold and silver vessels shows that more precious metals were also available to some sectors of the population in the later Bronze Age.[12]

The economic basis behind these extensive settlements of the first millennium must have been well-established and reliable. The size of

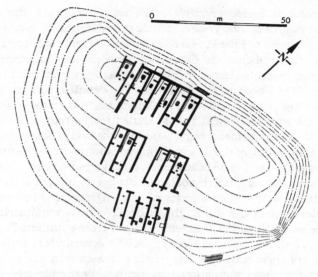

Fig. 164   Plan of the settlement at Cortes de Navarra in the Ebro valley.

Fig. 165   Reconstruction of part of the settlement.
(From Savory 1968)

population housed necessitated wide areas of controlled land, and the
length of occupation, attested in part by the depths of deposit, suggest a
series of successful exploitations of resources. The evidence for increased
aridity, soil erosion, the need for irrigation, is not well-documented, nor
is the evidence for animal husbandry and cereal agriculture.[13] A further
gap lies in the scarcity of known large cemeteries associated with some of
the major settlements.

In north-eastern Spain, however, the evidence for burial practices in
the later Bronze Age is abundant. In place of the more regular
inhumations of the earlier Bronze Age there now appears widespread
cremation, usually in urns accompanied by small vessels and occasional
metal ornaments. The cemeteries may be large, with over 100 graves,

each marked by a slab or circle of stones. Caves were also used for sepulchral purposes. The vessels include cylinder-necked urns and other forms which seem to relate to Urnfield material from southern France of the earlier first millennium. Coastal settlements and cemeteries of this time suggest careful selection of the best-quality agricultural land, and the valley of the Ebro was also exploited. The detailed work on metal and pottery forms from north-eastern Spain has suggested that several different groups of Urnfield people settled in the region in successive episodes of folk movement[14] and certainly the wider occupation of the area at the beginning of the first millennium is an important feature of the archaeological record. The occurrence, however, of objects from widely spread regions to east, north and south, suggests human activities of a more complex nature than a series of folk migrations. The evidence of large settlements in the south, the evidence of major industries in the north (see below) and the Urnfield evidence from southern France and elsewhere, all should be considered as possible contributory factors to the appearance of apparently new features in north-eastern Spain. The local earlier Bronze Age population was neither negligible nor inactive, however, and there is great variety in its products (fig. 166).

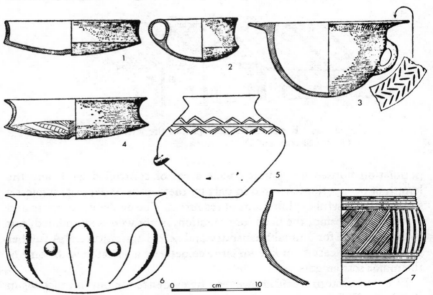

Fig. 166   Late Bronze Age pottery from Spain and Portugal: 1. Castro Marim, Algarve, 2. Pragança, Lisbon, 3. Caldelas, Guimarães, Braga, 4. Ervidel, Beja, 5. Azaila, Teruel, 6. Pedra d'Oiro Alemquer, Lisbon, 7. Penha, Guimarães, Braga. (From Savory 1968)

Elsewhere, the evidence for innovation is not lacking, and from the varied materials of the later Bronze Age two provinces have been singled out. One of these is north-western Iberia, where major settlement evidence is lacking, but where substantial activity is nonetheless attested. This takes the form of a bronze industry, part of a tradition of metal-working that was established in the second millennium along Atlantic shores of Britain and France (p. 234), but which now apparently was in part transferred to north-western Iberia where metal supplies were available. The objects manufactured included palstaves, both double-looped and single-looped, socketed axes, and sickles. The major distribution of these products extends from north-western Iberia down the Atlantic coastal zone to the valley of the Tagus, but stray specimens occur more widely along Atlantic shores of France and Britain, and into Mediterranean Sardinia.[15] A few of these bronzes have been recovered from upland settlements in north-western Iberia, but mostly in unstratified positions. Associated materials are rare, although character-istic pottery of 'hat-bowl' type, with cremations, are believed to be contemporary.

The second province, in south-western Iberia, is equally uneven in its surviving remains. Few settlements and burials, supplemented by carved stone slabs and metalwork, form the basis for identification of an area which must have seen few innovating elements, other than those by trade or exchange, to seriously alter the well-established earlier Bronze Age traditions of behaviour. The great hoard from Huelva, found in the estuary of the river Odiel, and probably from a shipwreck, represents the major features of the metal industry of the region. The hoard contains metal-hilted swords, as well as carp's-tongue swords with characteristic elongated tips, daggers, spearheads, helmet fragments, belt hooks and brooches. The distribution of some of this material is essentially Atlantic, and Huelva represents some of the major evidence for some form of trade or distributive mechanism in the early first millennium. This is but one aspect of the Tartessian culture of south-western Iberia.[16] Another is the carved stone cist-covers and stelæ which depict various pieces of weapons, sword, spear, shield, helmet, and sometimes the warrior himself;[17] there are also wheeled vehicles, brooches and other equipment shown on the stones, and associated material includes earlier Bronze Age pottery forms such as fine carinated bowls. The date of this rather unevenly represented culture-group is likely to be mid-first millennium, and it merges evenly into the earlier Iron Age of the peninsula. It is tempting to refer part of this complex to Phoenician activities in and around the western Mediterranean.[18]

The contemporary developments in the Balearic Islands of the western

Mediterranean reflect these, and earlier, maritime activities. The two main islands, Majorca and Minorca, contain abundant and unusual stone monuments, and although chronologies remain imprecise, it seems probable that the emergence of the *talayot* culture commenced in the later second millennium.[19] Metallurgy had been established at an earlier time, although it always remained a relatively minor aspect of economic life in the islands.[20] The basis of subsistence was agriculture on the fertile lowlands, particularly of Majorca, but stock-breeding was also important; water resources from the limestone base would have been valuable. The distribution of settlement tends to concentrate on the lowland fertile regions, but coastal sites were naturally also favoured, as maritime activities are likely to have been important.

The characteristic stone-built *talayots* or towers of the islands are today some of the most impressive free-standing monuments of the European Bronze Age (fig. 167). Although many varieties of towers exist, the earliest seemed to have formed nuclei for small enclosed settlements. On a hill at Ses Paisses, Majorca, an area 106 × 96 m was enclosed by a massive slab-faced wall with four entrances, and contained a central tower *c.* 10 m in diameter, with stone-built huts around.[21] This is the basic plan for these settlements, with *talayots* serving either as watch-towers, as refuges or as dwellings; some had upper floors accessible by external ramps or internal steps. The Minorca settlement of San Carla was larger than Ses Paisses, and had a *talayot* at each end of the elongated enclosure, with a central *taula* consisting of an upright pillar supporting a horizontal slab, each of considerable size.[22] The *taula* at Trepúco had an upright pillar 4 m high, and a slab 3.7 × 1.8 × 0.6 m; these megaliths are interpreted as cult centres.

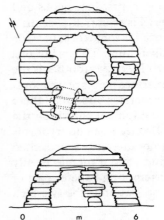

Fig. 167   Plan and section of San Agusti Vell *talayot*, Minorca.
(After Pericot Garcia 1972)

0   m   6

Dwelling-places within and outside the enclosures consist of either circular stone-built houses, or, on Majorca, boat-shaped houses called *navetas*;[23] these can be 20 m long, with slightly convex longer sides, and they occur singly or in groups. At Boquer, a small village of *navetas* was enclosed by a wall. One such house at Sa Punta contained occupation debris of pottery, querns, bone tools, bronze spearheads and carbonized wheat and barley. The boat-shaped stone structures of Minorca in contrast were built or used for burials; that at Els Tudons contained over 100 inhumations with bone buttons, bone discs and bronze bracelets.[24] Burials at the Son Real cemetery on Majorca were placed in smaller stone-built enclosures of various shapes (fig. 168), with the earliest likely to be the boat-shaped tombs, 3 × 2 m with slab roof, each holding one or two contracted inhumations, sometimes more. Grave-goods were sparse, mainly bone buttons, ovoid handled pots, some bronze spearheads, discs and chisels. Some bodies had been trepanned after death.[25]

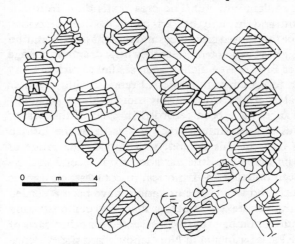

Fig. 168
Plan of part of the Son Real, Majorca, cemetery, showing stone-built tombs, circular, rectangular and boat-shaped. (After Pericot Garcia 1972)

0 m 4

The dating of the *talayot* phase of the Balearic Islands remains imprecise, due principally to the ruinous state of most occupation deposits, and the dismantling of the stone structures, but careful investigations suggest a period of active building from *c.* 1200 bc, which eventually evolved into a period of participation in Mediterranean contacts in the closing centuries of the first millennium when the Bronze Age origins of the *talayot* group had been long submerged. Perhaps the most interesting aspect of the Balearic Islands *talayot* phase is its probable relationship with the Nuraghic and Torrean phases of Sardinia and Corsica, and the invention and necessity for tower fortifications in the western Mediterranean.[26]

Apart from the Balearic Islands, where earlier Bronze Age episodes are very imperfectly known, the evidence for the development of the later Bronze Age in the western Mediterranean regions of Spain and Portugal, taken as a whole, does not suggest essentially significant alterations from the patterns of subsistence and social organization established earlier in the second millennium. The differences between the earlier and the later Bronze Ages are matters of degree; the evidence for particularly wealthy graves is less abundant in the later Bronze Age, perhaps due in part to lack of excavation; the evidence for metal industries along the western coasts is greatly increased in the later Bronze Age.

Western France

These same two observations can be made for Atlantic France in the late second and early first millennium BC. The area, extending from the Pyrenées northwards into and through the Paris basin, has been described (p. 229) and the evidence for limited clearances and regions of exploitation in the earlier Bronze Age has been noted. Relatively little dramatic change is attested from the later Bronze Age. Pollen analyses fail to pick out any significant alteration in forest cover in western France during the later Bronze Age, but at local levels there is naturally more evidence of small-scale activities.[27] Clearances have been recorded in parts of the Massif Central when *Abies* was at a maximum level, but most of the human impact was in eastern parts of this upland, well outside the range of western France;[28] in the Pyrenées, little variation from second millennium conditions has been noted.[29] In Armorica, in contrast, clearances of woodland, with cereals and weeds of cultivation, have been recorded from early first millennium contexts.[30] Further diagrams demonstrating clearances and cereal cultivation have been constructed for other parts of northern France, in the Paris basin and in Normandy[31] and the evidence from carbonized cereals (wheat and barley) and bronze sickles, helps to supplement the impression that agricultural practices throughout western France were well-developed and successful, if of no great impact on the landscape as a whole.

The relationship between cultivation of crops, involving woodland clearances, and herding of animals, also necessitating some forest management, can hardly be ascertained for later Bronze Age western France.[32] The restricted evidence from settlement sites suggests, perhaps inconclusively, that domestic animals were increasingly occupying the attention of Bronze Age communities, and that fewer wild animals were being taken. In upland areas, sheep and goats were naturally dominant, and in the river valleys and lowlands cattle were herded; however, the evidence is far from abundant.[33]

The later distribution of known settlements of the later Bronze Age is sporadic through western France. The settlements at Videlles and Misy-sur-Yonne, in the valley of the Seine, where continuity of occupation throughout much of the Bronze Age can be demonstrated, exhibit some of the character of settlement debris and some of the problems. Metalwork, so abundant in stray finds and in hoards, is rare, pottery of domestic character, unlike funerary wares, is abundant, as is stone-working in flint. A mixed economy was practised, with pigs, some cattle and sheep, a certain amount of hunting, and clearances for cultivation.[34] Other settlements at Fort Harrouard, Aulnay-aux-Planches, and at many other sites in the Paris basin suggest substantial concentrations of population, organization of labour and sharing of produce. Evidence for wider regional connections is not abundant.[35] Elsewhere in western France, caves and shelters were occupied both for the living and for burial of the dead; open settlements at river-mouths and in upland areas are also indicated by the wealth of data at present being assembled by prehistorians, data which are fragmentary and inadequate yet nonetheless welcome.[36] Although constructional details of house shapes and disposi-tions are sparse, the positions of some of the settlements suggest not only proximity to high-quality agricultural land or resources of marine character, but also careful alignment to control or direct major riverine traffic with its possible regional or long-distance distributive potentials. The large settlement at Cannes-Écluse, near the confluence of the Seine and Yonne rivers, extended over 150 m. along the river bank. Fifteen houses were noted during its destruction, some with heavy post-walls supporting wattle and daub panels; there were many large hearths, both inside and outside the houses, and both clay and metal were fired.[37]

Caves were used extensively for burials in southern and western France, but flat cemeteries, megalithic tombs, and earthen or stone barrows are more commonly encountered in the later Bronze Age. From the late second millennium, a variety of burial traditions was practised; the cemetery at La Colombine, in the upper Seine, in essence a part of the west-central European development, yielded over 100 flat graves among which at least one was of a female richly furnished with metal ornaments,[38] and other smaller cemeteries exhibit those mixed features of inhumation and cremation, flat graves and barrow graves, that characterize the burial practices of central Europe near the close of the second millennium.

The early first millennium burial traditions of western France fall within two rather broad groups. The first is necessarily the native,

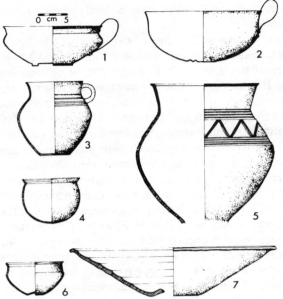

0 cm 5

Fig. 169
Late Bronze Age vessels from France: 1–2. hoard of metal cups, Carnac, Lozère, 3–4, 6. Grotte de Clapade, Aveyron, 5. Grotte du Luc, Gard, 7. Grotte des Blanquets, Lozère.
(From Clottes and Constantini 1976)

previously-evolved, practice of inhumation, in a flat grave or under a mound, which was never wholly supplanted by the rapid adoption of urned cremation which became the dominant treatment of the dead throughout most of France in the later Bronze Age. The details of the transition, the bewildering variation in recognizable practices, are not discussed here.[39] The essential character of later Bronze Age burials in much of eastern and central France, and in parts of the west, was the adoption of individual cremation on a single or communal funeral pyre, the ashes and bone sometimes placed in an urn and buried in a cemetery. The grave marking may have been a stone, a mound, or an organic or withdrawn marker; few graves overlap one another.

The development of the Urnfield tradition in western France was sporadic. The characteristic cemeteries along the Loire and its tributary streams[40] mark a natural route westwards; at Chissay-en-Touraine, nineteen cremations were found in a flat cemetery, with two burials in channelled urns. Northwards, at Aulnay-aux-Planches, a large cemetery spanning perhaps 500–600 years contained among its earliest burials a group of cremations in urns or in pits lined with small stones; the grave-goods included bronze knives, biconical urns with incised or fluted decoration, and other pottery dishes.[41] Subsequent burials in the cemetery were sometimes enclosed within ring-ditches 5–8 m in diameter with a single causeway entry at or near the south; the urns and other wares are more elaborately decorated, with polychrome, fluting, and geometric designs. Adjacent to the cemetery were house structures of a contemporary settlement.[42] Further excavations of enclosed Urnfield burials at Saint-Gond (Marne) have amplified our knowledge of the variation in burial practices in the early first millennium; four main tomb types have been recognized, urned cremations, cremations placed in shallow pits, cremations within ring-ditches, and funerary enclosures (fig. 170).[43] Among the pottery vessels in these cemeteries are not only cylinder-necked urns of typical Urnfield shape but also a wide range of shallow bowls and dishes (fig. 171). Detailed studies of this material, using typological analysis as well as horizontal stratigraphies, has allowed a number of groups to be recognized.

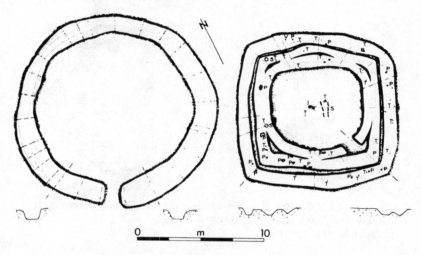

Fig. 170 Cemetery enclosures at Broussy le Grand, Saint-Gond, Marne: I. cremation, T. potsherd, P. stone, OS. human bones, V. non-human bones, S. inhumation.
(After Chertier 1976)

Cemeteries in the Paris basin at the beginning of the later Bronze Age have been described as marking the appearance of a new society, the Saint-Gervais group.[44] The material culture of this group is restricted to the eastern and southern regions of the basin. Early burials of males contained rapiers and daggers, as well as razors; female burials had beads and bracelets and pins. These assemblages differ from the preceding Chéry group which has Atlantic character palstaves and rapiers, and is believed to be contemporary with settlements at Videlles and Fort-

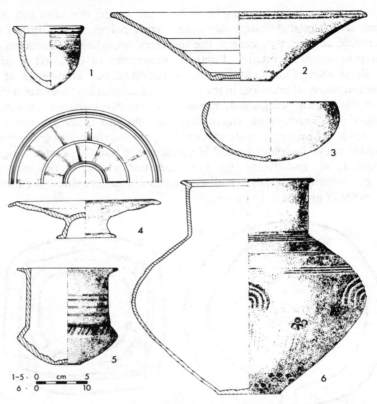

Fig. 171   Late Bronze Age vessels from Saint-Gond, Marne:1–3.
Aulnay-aux-Planches, 4–6. Broussy-le Grand.
(From Chertier 1976)

Harrouard. Cremation appears with the developing Saint-Gervais group;
at Marolles, one such burial within a circular enclosure consisted of a
cremation in a large urn with small bowl lid, and various other pots in the
urn and in the pit grave. The full Urnfield tradition emerges in the
succeeding Longueville group, with central European metal forms and
cylinder-neck urns, and the final Plainseau episode of metalwork is
basically an Atlantic tradition. This region of northern France was better
positioned than most to receive and transmit ideas and objects from both
east and west (fig. 172).

The distribution of true Urnfield cemeteries in western and northern
France is severely restricted. Those described above are essentially part
of the west-central European province, and the impact of Urnfield

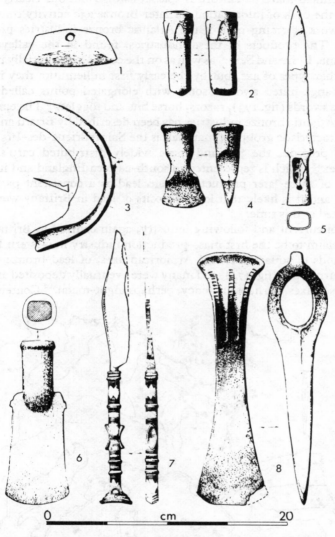

Fig. 172   Late Bronze Age implements: 1. knife, 2. hammer,
3. sickle, 4. chisel, 5. knife, 6. hatchet, 7. knife, 8. axe. Various sites
in Centre-Ouest.
(After Cordier 1976)

473

culture on the west was negligible. On the Atlantic coasts, the evidence for Urnfield material culture is sparse, as distributions clearly show.[45] Here, the bulk of information for later Bronze age activity comes from metalwork, forming part of the Atlantic bronze industries previously noted. The products of these industries, found in the valleys of the Garonne, Loire and Seine, as well as on the coasts, were initially palstaves and other types of axe, but by the early first millennium they included long flange-hilted swords, some with elongated points called carp's-tongue swords (fig. 173), razors, horse bits and toggles.[46] The emergence of the Atlantic bronze industries has been described by Briard and one of its characteristic groups of materials is the Saint-Brieuc-des-Iffs hoard[47] which precedes the full and more widely distributed carp's-tongue complex[48] which is represented in south-eastern England and in Iberia. Many of these later products contain lead as a consistent part of the metal, and it is likely that local deposits of lead in Brittany were being exploited at this time.

A concurrent and following industry, again centred in Brittany, has some claim to be the first mass-production industry in western Europe; thousands of square-socketed Armorican axes, of lead-bronze or lead, were turned out (fig. 174), and many were eventually deposited as hoards of unused axes, perhaps currency, perhaps ingot-metal.[49] Contemporary

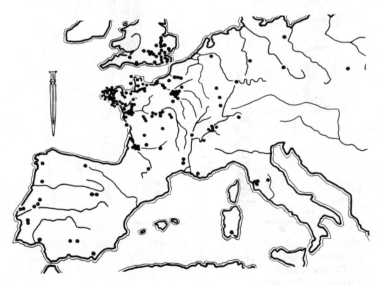

Fig. 173　Distribution of carp's-tongue swords in Europe. (From Briard 1965)

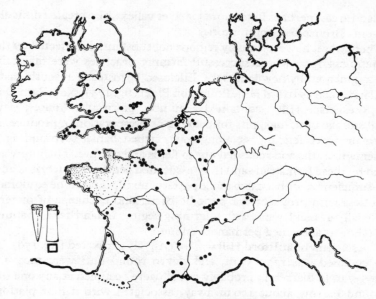

Fig. 174   Distribution of Armorican socketed axes.
(From Briard 1965)

settlements and other economic practices are scarcely known[50] but domestic pottery, flints and very rare metal objects have been noted from coastal sites in north-western France. One of these, at Ploubazlanec, on the mouth of the Trieux river, may represent a fortified later Bronze Age village.[51] The final episodes of the Bronze Age in Atlantic France are difficult to decipher, represented as they are by masses of metal products, scatters of domestic pottery and fragmentary earthworks or pits, and no clearly stratified settlements or cemeteries.

The British Isles

For the British Isles, the later Bronze Age is marked by quite dramatic alterations to the subsistence practices, and therefore settlement patterns, in western areas. Climatic deterioration, through increased rainfall and inadequate summer temperatures, created grave problems for the maintenance of upland farms in western Britain and Ireland, and cereal cultivation must have become increasingly difficult from late in the second millennium. The growth of peat over moorland, caused by a combination of both climatic and human factors, led to the abandonment of many earlier Bronze Age farms and settlements; flooding in restricted lowland areas, perhaps in some major river valleys, also created difficulties for some Bronze Age communities.

There were, however, many regions not substantially affected by these climatic changes, where successful farming practices were maintained and augmented by new land-take. Enclosed farmsteads in south-eastern England, such as Itford Hill, Plumpton Plain (fig. 175), New Barn Down and Shearplace Hill[52] contained a number of circular houses,[53] with small storage buildings, pits for cooking or preservation of produce, and thorn or other fencing set along low earthen banks surrounding the settlement. Paths and roads led out to fields and pasture. The impression given by these farmsteads and their associated occupation debris is one of self-sufficiency, with locally-made pottery, textiles and stone equipment, doubtless with provision for periodic barter and exchange of materials not locally available, and with a farming regime of land-take, manuring and fallow that seemed permanent enough.

The settlement at Itford Hill was extensively excavated (fig. 176). The area enclosed was 125 × 50 m, and eleven round huts were recovered, each 5–7 m in diameter; probably not all were occupied at any one time. A round barrow about 100 m away, associated with a flint platform, contained about fifteen cremations and potsherds from the cemetery related directly to pottery from the settlement.[54]

Other contemporary sites in southern England include banked and ditched enclosures, up to 1 ha in area, and these have been suggested as part of a pastoral system in operation on the chalklands, where long linear

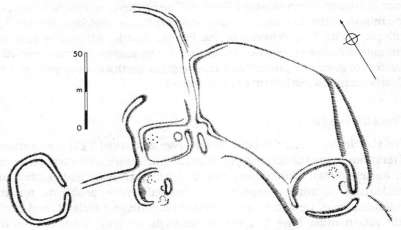

Fig. 175 Plan of the settlement enclosures, roadways and fields at Plumpton Plain, Sussex.
(After E. C. Curwen, *Archaeology of Sussex.* 1954)

Fig. 176   Reconstruction of the settlement at Itford Hill, Sussex.
(From G. P. Burstow and G. A. Holleyman, *PPS* 23 (1957))

ditches marked off ranch boundaries; certainly in places these linear
ditches run across Celtic fields, but their dating is otherwise difficult.[55]
They may in fact mark settlement boundaries, or arable–pastoral
divisions; considerable variation in position occurs.

The evidence of animal bones from the farmsteads and enclosures
suggests a mixed economy, with cattle and sheep on most sites, as well as
horse and deer. Emmer and barley have been recorded, and saddle quern
fragments occur. Loom-weights and traces of loom-posts demonstrate
textile manufacture, and flint-working was a major source for small
equipment.

Although the distribution of these settlements is far from completely-
known, it seems likely that each had its component of arable land, grazing
pasture and woodland, the last providing essential food for pigs, shelter
for deer and other wild animals, and supplies for wooden equipment
which has rarely survived.

Copper or bronze, is very rarely encountered, and gold is practically absent; it is not certain, of course, how precious bronze and gold were to these farmers and herdsmen, but it is likely that broken metal objects would be put back into circulation through the melting-pot rather than abandoned as flint and pottery were.

The settlements themselves suggest one major living house, with subsidiary hut or huts and various storage structures, and there are no indications of larger or more impressive buildings such as might indicate increased status for a person or a family.

Similar isolated farmsteads or hamlets are known from the centuries either side of 1000 bc in many parts of Britain and Ireland. In the south-west, the upland settlements of the earlier Bronze Age were undergoing gradual abandonment at this time, and population pressures due to displacement must have been present locally. Low-lying settlements in this region, such as those at Trevisker[56] and at Gwithian,[57] show established farming practices involving ard cultivation of regular fields (fig. 177), probably with manuring, and the repair and rebuilding of round houses.

Another coastal settlement of this period lies 1,100 km away from Gwithian, at Jarlshof in Shetland.[58] The small village consisted of several oval houses, each with a central hearth and internal cubicles; one house was a metal workshop for casting bronze weapons and tools. Copper was locally available, but the nearest tin was probably in Cornwall. Hardly any bronze implements have been recovered from the Shetland Islands, and metal must have been a precious commodity. Domestic equipment at Jarlshof included slate clubs, stone querns, bone tools and coarse barrel-like pottery. Cattle were herded, cereals were probably cultivated, shellfish were gathered and deep-water fishing was practised. Again the impression of this settlement is one of self-sufficiency in all things except metal.

The contemporary occupations on other islands in the north and west of the British Isles are less well-known, but recent work has suggested that the quantity of boiling mounds, heaps of burnt stones associated with cooking troughs, in Orkney and elsewhere, represent early first millennium settlements utilizing peat as fuel in the absence of wood.[59]

Elsewhere in Britain and Ireland, river valley settlements perhaps positioned for upriver and cross-river traffic as well as for agricultural potential, were occupied in the earlier first millennium. The sites at Old Brentford and Runnymede, on the Thames, are notable for their yield of metalwork, in contrast to the scarcity of such material from almost all other settlements.[60] Bridle pieces, clay loom weights and spindle whorls, amber and lignite ornaments, domestic coarse pottery bowls and jars as

Fig. 177 Plan of later Bronze Age fields at Gwithian, Cornwall.
(From J. V. S. Megaw in Burgess and Miket 1976)

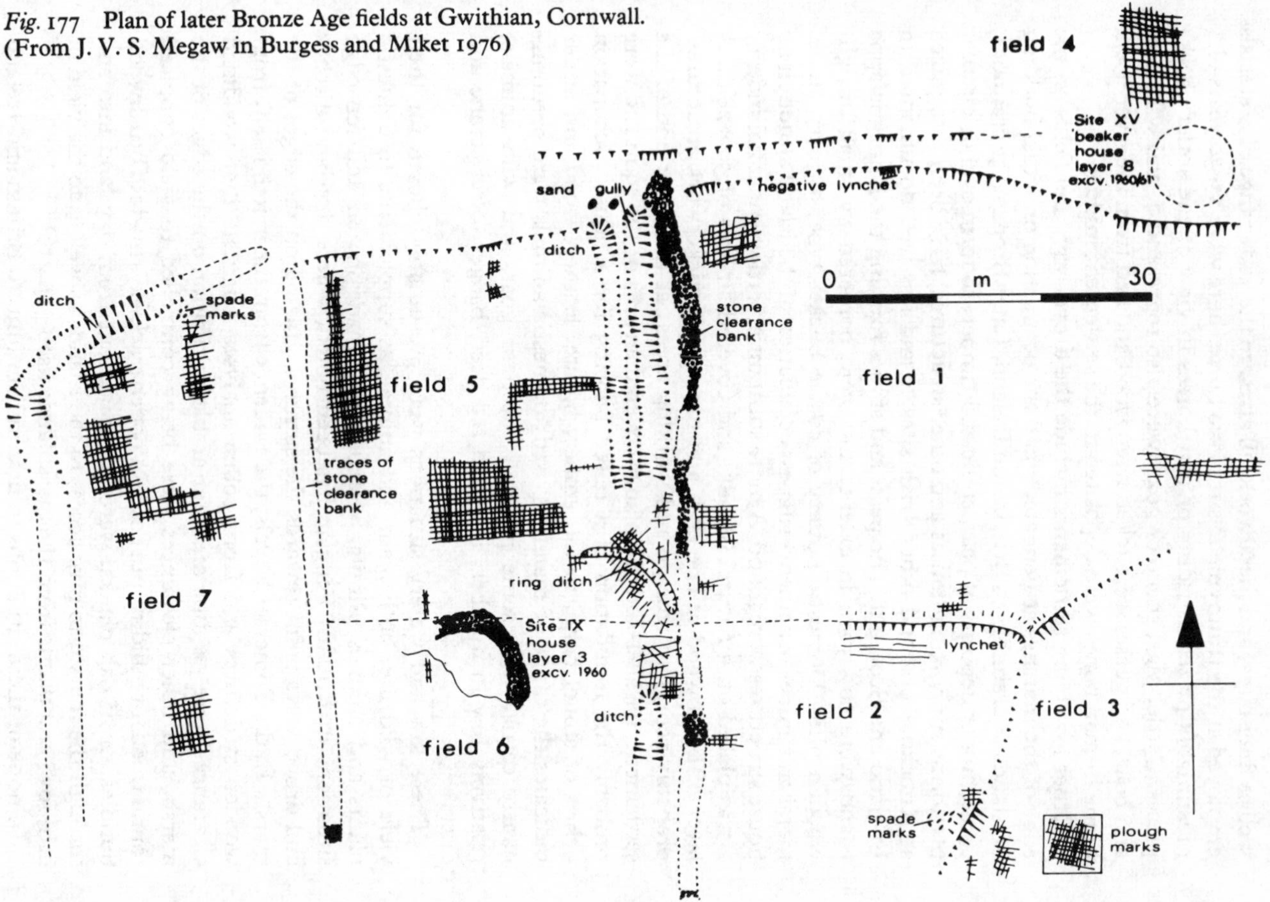

field 4

Site XV
beaker
house
layer 8
excv. 1960⁄61

30

m

0

negative lynchet

stone
clearance
bank

sand

gully

ditch

field 5

traces of
stone
clearance
bank

spade
marks

field 7

ditch

ring ditch

Site IX
house
layer 3
excv. 1960

ditch

field 6

field 1

lynchet

field 2

field 3

spade
marks

plough
marks

479

well as finer cups, and metalwork, all attest to the wide range of materials employed at the Runnymede site. Two horses here were 25–30 years old, presumably prized as riding or cart horses in view of the antler cheek-pieces. Cattle, pigs, sheep or goats were also represented, and wild deer and boar, and geese, were taken from woodland and from the river itself. Some human bones were deposited in the settlement midden.

Other low-lying settlements include the drove-ways and fields on the edge of the marshes at Fengate,[61] and the occupation or actual building of islands or crannogs in Britain and Ireland. Later Bronze Age crannogs, consisting of deposits of peat, stone and timber, to form oval or circular platforms supporting houses and other structures, have been recognized at Knocknalappa and other Irish sites,[62] and less well documented in England and Scotland. The peats and stones forming the Knocknalappa island were 60 × 30 m in extent, and were bordered by small upright wooden piles. Domestic pottery of coarse bucket type, a quern stone, metal and amber ornaments suggest occupation of the island although no house structures were found. A more substantial settlement at Ballinderry 2 was placed on a natural island[63] and covered an area of 50 × 28 m. A layer of brushwood at one end, and nine small wickerwork structures, probably represent storage and working areas; at the other end of the settlement, parallel-laid oak planks covered an area of 120 sq m and were probably the foundation of a raised flooring for a house. Occupation debris of stone, bone, metal, amber, lignite, leather, wood and antler indicates the range of materials used; domestic animals were predominantly cattle, with some pig and sheep or goat, and wild animals, relatively few in number, included red deer, badger, otter, crane and duck.[64]

These low and watery situations were presumably chosen for their yield of wild life, both plant and animal, as supplements to domestic plants and animals. Similar selection was made in fen and fen-edge situations in Britain; Fengate has been noted, where dry-land ditches and drove-ways point towards the summer grazing on the edges of the marsh. In the Somerset Levels, the evidence from the marsh itself, from wooden structures and from pollen analyses, suggests that woodland clearances were yielding areas for arable cultivation on the edges of the marsh, and other clearances were being controlled to yield coppiced round wood for building purposes. Wooden trackways made of brushwood bundles, or of oak planks, were being laid out from dry land into and through the marsh, to give access to the islands as well as to the yield of fish, fowl and plants from the marshlands itself (pl. 21c).[65]

In none of these situations in first millennium BC Britain and Ireland is there much or any evidence for defensive fortification. The upland farmsteads, where an individual house and outbuildings may have been surrounded by a fence or shallow ditch, are similarly undefended except against wild or domestic animals. Palisaded enclosures in southern Scotland and northern England protected farm buildings at first millennium sites such as West Plean and Glenachan Rig,[66] and unenclosed platform settlements with buildings set on terraces scooped from hillslopes, were probably subsistence-orientated in the same way towards a predominantly but not exclusively pastoral economy.[67] The ubiquitous hut-circle settlements of upland areas of Britain and Ireland are likely to represent in part contemporary occupations, perhaps seasonal rather than year-round.[68] The Dalnaglar group of three circular enclosures, 15 m diameter, is only one of about twenty such groups at 300 m altitude in the valleys of the Garry and Isla streams, and pollen analyses indicate phases of forest clearance likely to be contemporary with the occupation.

Rather more substantial palisaded or banked enclosures, categorized as hill-forts, have recently been recognized as originating in Bronze Age societies rather than in the full Iron Age of the middle first millennium, but the evidence for abundant later Bronze Age defensive fortification is still sparse.[69] Hilltop settlement in positions subsequently heavily defended is known from many regions; the substantial occupations on Traprain Law in central Scotland, Portfield Camp in northern England, and Ham Hill in south-west England, recall a late Bronze Age interest in such withdrawn positions, but without the need or desire for humanly-devised defences.[70]

The Dinorben (Denbigh), the Breiddin (Powys) and Grimthorpe (Yorkshire) hill-forts are dated to the Bronze Age by radiocarbon analyses, and their evidence for Bronze Age occupation now seems firmly established.[71] The occupation of hill-top sites in Ireland is equally as suggestive; the Rathgall Bronze Age settlement included a workshop for casting bronze implements, and the defences here may be contemporary with the extensive Bronze Age occupation debris.[72] The hill-top settlement at Downpatrick included a considerable later Bronze Age element, but the defensive organization is not certainly tied to this earliest occupation.[73] The recognition of coarse domestic pottery of the later Bronze Age at Rathgall and Downpatrick supports suggestions that the vast array of bronze tools now available were for wood-working, and that quality wooden vessels were used for all purposes except those involving heat. The character of domestic pottery, bucket and barrel shapes, often thick and with heavy grits, is strangely at variance with the high-quality metal and wooden products.

The industries of the later Bronze Age settlements included the working of stone, wood, bone, antler, bronze, gold, lead, amber and flint into tools, weapons and ornaments. Local pottery and textiles were produced, and animal skins were tanned. Relatively few organic products have survived, although there are some traces of clothing, a number of wooden artifacts, and rare leather objects. (pl. 21a–b).[74]

Metal industries were prolific in their output, and all available resources of copper, tin, lead and gold must have been exploited in the British Isles as in neighbouring northern France, and in northern Iberia as well. The very numerous bronze rapiers and swords, spear-heads and wood-working tools such as chisels, punches, gouges, palstaves and socketed axes, as well as ornamented bracelets, necklets and rings, demonstrate not only the general abundance of metal products, but also the variety of local tastes and consumption.[75] In these workshops were craftsmen who specialized in sheet-metal and in gold. Their products included buckets and cauldrons, shields and other large and impressive objects.[76] Gold ornaments involving massive weights of metal included bar-torcs and solid bracelets, but much fine light sheet-gold work was also produced; most, though not all,[77] of this was Irish (pl. 8b).

Many of the impressive metal objects, of gold or of bronze, occur in hoards and in situations involving water, in former marsh, peatbog or river. Some hoards are large, involving dozens of items, and some, such as the Dowris (central Ireland) hoard, have been interpreted as the cumulative offerings made into a ritually-important marsh or lake; the Dowris finds also contained many bronze musical horns of types found only in Ireland, as well as metal rattles (fig. 179).[78]

Pottery of the later Bronze Age in Britain and Ireland is again regionally distinct. Domestic ware from northern and western settlements tends to

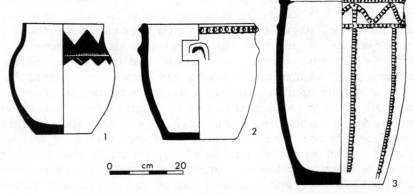

Fig. 178 Burial urns from cemeteries in Southern England. 1. globular urn, 2. bucket urn, 3. barrel urn. Various sites.
(From Annable and Simpson 1964)

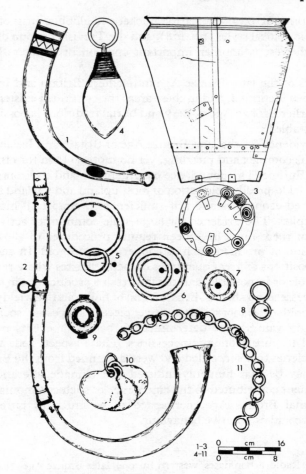

Fig. 179   Late Bronze Age horns, rattle, bucket and
harness-fittings from Ireland. 1–2. horns, side-blow and
end-blow, 3. bucket, 4. crotal or rattle, 5–11. rings and
jangles. Various sites.
(From Eogan 1964)

be plain, bucket- or barrel-shaped, and rather coarse, the so-called Flat-
Rimmed ware, and comparable pottery has often been recovered from
the settlements in southern Britain as well. Only in southern Britain is
there much evidence for funerary pottery, in the Deverel-Rimbury
groups; cremation in urns, or unaccompanied, was practised, and
cemeteries were flat or placed beneath or in the sides of newly-built or

pre-existing barrows. The barrel, bucket and globular urns of the region have various local styles (fig. 178), and the Trevisker group of pottery in the south-west is another important component of later Bronze Age wares.[79]

Burials of the later Bronze Age in northern Britain and Ireland have rarely been identified, and in these areas the continued existence and use of the earlier Bronze Age pottery and burial traditions is possible but not demonstrable.[80]

The evidence for the later Bronze Age of Britain and Ireland, taken in totality, is complex and puzzling, yet no more so than for other areas of western Europe. The abundance of settlements and environmental data suggests widespread exploitation of most upland and lowland landscapes, with mixed economies and self-sufficiency in almost all materials and food supplies. The evidence for large-scale community activities is not great, but there must have been regular procedures to allow the even distribution of products such as copper, tin and gold. In addition, the watery positions of great quantities of metal, in sites where recovery was undesirable or impossible, and the impressive productions in sheet metal of large vessels and shields, in cast metal of horns and unwieldy weapons, and in gold of elaborate decorative pieces, suggest a society where community values were determined by beliefs or events not entirely restricted to pure economic necessities. These aspects reflect upon the Celtic societies that succeeded and were descended from the Bronze Age, and it may be that humanly-induced and climatic alterations in the environment contributed to the emergence of such ceremonial activities in the final Bronze Age, perhaps even as much as purely human acquisitive and ostentatious behaviour.

Table 18   Radiocarbon dates, western Europe, later Bronze Age

Site	Lab no.	bc
France		
Videlles les Roches, Essonne, settlement	Gsy–110	980±150
Porte Joie, Eure, burials	Ly–702	1090±280
	Ly–705	1310±190
Flamanville, Manche, hearth	Ly–83	710±220
Merri, Le Camp de Bièrre, Orne, occupation	Ly–465	860±120
	Ly–466	790±110
Erquy, Cap Fossé de Catuelan, C.-du-Nord, hillfort	Gif–715	550±110
Créac'h Kiliet, C.-du-Nord, megalith	Gif–197A	900±170
	Gif–197B	840±150
Penguilly, Finistère, barrow	Gif–2380	550±100

Table 18—cont.

Site	Lab no.	bc
Le Curnic, Guisseny, Finistère, hearth, saltpan	Gif-159	1225 ± 160
	Gif-160	800 ± 150
	Gsy-47C	1270 ± 110
Ile de Geignog, Finistère, megalith	Gif-161	800 ± 150
	Gif-162	890 ± 150
Kerlande, Finistère, occupation	Gif-2378	870 ± 100
Monteneuf, Finistère, burial	Gif-719	900 ± 110
Crée de Carate, Finistère, barrow	GrN-1973	700 ± 60
	Gsy-33	510 ± 150
	Gsy-46	590 ± 150
Préfailles, le Boucaud, Loire-Atl., briquetage	Gif-410	750 ± 200
Saint Brévin l'Ocean, Loire-Atl., settlement	Gif-193A	1225 ± 200
	Gif-193B	825 ± 200
	Gif-193C	515 ± 200
	Gif-194	770 ± 200
Champtocé, Maine-et-Loire, megalith	Gif-234A	805 ± 150
Chazelles, G. du Quéroy, Charente, occupation	Gif-2739	1090 ± 110
	Gif-2740	870 ± 110
	Gif-3284	810 ± 110
Rancogne, Charente, cave occupation	Gif-724	1200 ± 110
La Rochette, Charente, cave occupation	Gif-2263	1210 ± 100
	Gif-2266	910 ± 100
	Gif-2344	1020 ± 100
Courcoury, Charente Maritime, barrow	Gif-2347	850 ± 70
Aslonnes, Camp Allaric, Viènne, settlement	Gif-3008	610 ± 110
La Viaube, Vienne, settlement	Gsy-62	1125 ± 175
Villegouge, Roanne, Dordogne, occupation	Gif-782	900 ± 135
Biarritz, Pyr-Atl., cave	Gif-3043	940 ± 110
	Gif-3044	1050 ± 110
Les Rives de Thorey, Saône-et-Loire, settlement	Ly-1026	830 ± 230
	Ly-1027	820 ± 260
Puy Saint-André, Puy de Dôme, occupation	Ly-1230	830 ± 130
Moulin de Géline, Hautes-Pyrénées, burial	Ly-1024	550 ± 160
	Ly-660	510 ± 180
Fontaines Salées, Yonne, well	Sa-56	1020 ± 170
Saint-Bugan, C-d-Nord, socketed axe hoard	Gsy-42	570 ± 110
Rancogne, Charente, well	Gif-724	1200 ± 110
Griny, Rhône, wooden axe handle	Ly-952	1120 ± 110

Iberia and Balearics

Cerro de La Encina, Granada, settlement[81]	GrN-?	c. 1150
Cerro de Juan Climaco	S-177	990 ± 140
	HAR-177	790 ± 110
Atalaia, Bajo Alemtejo cemetery	KN-201	790 ± 120
	KN-I-204	920 ± 40
	KN-I-201	820 ± 50

Table 18—*cont.*

Site	Lab no.	bc
Monte da Penha, Guimaraes, spearhead shaft	GrN–5568	930±65
Son Matge, Majorca	Y–2667	1250±100
Son Real Escombrera, talayot	Y–1856	1010±80
S'Illot, Majorca, talayot	Hv–1716	1130±75
	Hv–1717	1010±90
	Hv–1718	640±60
Poblado de ses Paises, Majorca, talayot	Gif–1247	950±110
Son Oms, Majorca	Y–2666	580±80
British Isles		
Shearplace Hill, Dorset, settlement	NPL–19	1180±180
St. Eval, Cornwall, settlement	NPL–134	1110±95
Barmston, ER Yorkshire, occupation	BM–122	1010±150
	BM–123	940±150
Weston Wood, Surrey, settlement	Q–760	510±110
Itford Hill, Sussex, settlement	GrN–6167	1000±35
Grandtully, Perth, cremation	GaK–1397	930±90
Ryton-on-Dunsmore, Warwick, burial	Birm–26	751±41
	Birm–228	920±106
	Birm–227	835±120
Ampleforth, Yorkshire, barrows	BM–369	582±90
	BM–368	537±90
Sharpstones Hill, Shropshire, cremation	Birm–206	1255±130
	Birm–207	1020±118
Carkenny, Co. Tyrone, cremation	UB–599	865±50
Meare Heath, Somerset, track	HAR–943	1030±70
Kate's Pad, Lancashire, track	Q–68	810±120
Fordy, Cambridge, track	Q–310	610±110
Brigg, Lincoln, track	Q–77	602±120
Thorne Moore, Yorkshire, track	Birm–336	1140±90
Carn Bog, Co. Mayo, wooden handle	D–50	1050±140
Short Ferry, Lincoln, dugout	Q–79	846±100
Brigg, Lincoln, boat	{ Q–1199	680±100
	{ Q–1200	593±100
Tormarton, Gloucester, skeleton with spearheads	BM–542	977±90
Gwithian, Cornwall, cremation	NPL–21	1120±103
Croft Ambrey, Hereford, grain in hillfort ditch	Birm–144	1050±200
Rams hill, Oxford, enclosure	HAR–461	1030±70
	HAR–232	1060±70
Liddle farm, Orkney, cooking site	SRR–701	876±75
Dinorben, Denbigh, settlement, fortified	V–123	945±95
	V–122	895±95
	V–125	765±85
Kaimes, Midlothian, occupation	GaK–1970	1191±90
Mam Tor, Derby, settlement	Birm–202	1180±132
	Birm–192	1130±115

Table 18—cont.

Site	Lab no.	bc
Grimthorpe, Yorkshire, settlement, fortified	NPL-137	970 ± 130
Simons Ground, Dorset, barrow and cemetery range of 8 dates 71 ± 50 to 917 ± 55		
Breiddin, Powys, settlement, fortified	BM-798	754 ± 50
	BM-878	800 ± 41
	BM-879	828 ± 71
	BM-880	868 ± 64
Knighton Heath, Dorset, barrow cemetery range of 7 dates 1102 ± 40 to 1205 ± 49		
Cadbury, Somerset, occupation	I-5971	925 ± 90
	I-5973	985 ± 90

Notes

1 Dimbleby 1962.

2 Evans 1975, 149.

3 The evidence for such conditions and exploitation is not yet established.

4 E.g. Burgess 1974, 170; Guilaine 1976a, 19–20; Briard 1965; this should not be taken as criticism of the essential internal ordering of industrial materials, as these provide the detailed systems necessary for regional studies.

5 Arribas 1976, 155.

6 Arribas 1976, 156, fig. 1–2; Arribas et al. 1974.

7 Arribas 1976, 160–1; Molina Gonzalez and Pareja López 1975.

8 Arribas 1976, 158.

9 Wide distribution: Savory 1968, 216–17.

10 Savory 1968, fig. 81; J. M. Maluquer, *El Castro de los Castellejos en Sanchoreja*, 1958.

11 A. Beltran, *V Congresso Nac. de Arqueología*, 1959, 149–50.

12 W. Schüle, *Madrider Mitteilungen* 17 (1976), 142–79; probable date 1200 BC; other gold work, Almagro Gorbea 1974, Cardoso 1968. The quantity of such objects in the Early

and Late Bronze Age is remarkable. See also chapter 5.

13 The excavation of cave occupations has indicated that a fauna including *Ovis, Oryctolagus, Sus scrofa* and *Bos taurus* may have been typical of some upland areas, J. Vilaseca, *Ampurias* 25 (1963), 105–36.

14 Pins, bracelets, combs, razors and tweezers in the graves: Savory 1968, fig. 75. See F. M. Jusmet, *Ampurias* 31–2 (1969–70), 105–52 for local Catalonian industries producing axes, and J. Malaquer de Motes and M. Fuste, *Zephyrus* 13 (1962), 5–16, for metal finds in Andorra; Savory 1968, 228–32 for urnfields of Sabadell and Can Missert, Barcelona.

15 Savory 1949, figs 2, 3, 6; 1968, 221–227, figs 77–8; wide distribution includes antenna-hilt swords of Castro de Coubueira (Lugo); palstaves of Penha (Braga), Padilla de Abajo (Burgos), Pragança (Lisbon); leaf-bladed swords of Vila Maior Sabugal (Guarda), Alhama de Aragón; cauldron of Peneda (Pontevedra), Cabárceno (Santander). There are gold products as

well; the Sintra gold collar, probably of late second millennium date, is perhaps the most outstanding piece of gold-work in the peninsula: C. F. C. Hawkes, *Brit. Mus. Quarterly* 35 (1971), 38–50. M. Almagro, *Ampurias* 26–7 (1964–5), 226–33 discusses the sparse but wide distribution of shaft-tube axes, found from southern England to Sicily, but in total numbering well under fifty. Such objects as these add little to the evidence for organized exchange systems in Atlantic Europe. The evidence for distributions of objects such as cauldrons, n. 76, is more substantive by virtue of the products themselves. Hat-bowl pottery: Savory 1949, 134–5; e.g. Caldelas (Braga). R. J. Harrison, *Madrider Mitteil.* 18 (1977), 18–29 for Mérida gold grave group and comparable finds.

16 Savory 1968, 232–6, fig. 83; the carp's tongue material of southwestern Iberia is restricted to ornaments and weapons, and there is little of the domestic equipment found in Britain and Atlantic France. The Hio hoard (Pontevedra) has a carp's tongue sword and parts of a flesh fork known from Britain and Ireland as well. Horse-riding gear also appears in Iberia at about this time, with wider connections. R. J. Harrison, *Ampurias* 36–37 (1974–5), 225–33, for distribution of carp's tongue swords.

17 M. Almagro, *Les Estelas Decoradas del Suroeste Peninsular. Biblioteca Praehistorica Hispana* 1966; Solana de Cabañas (Cáceres): warrior, sword, mirror, brooch, vehicle; Megacela (Badajoz): warrior, horned helmet, sword, shield; Figueira (Algarve): shield. M. V. Gomez and J. P. Monteiro, *TP* 34 (1977), 155–204.

18 Savory 1968, 236.

19 Perricot Garcia 1972; radiocarbon

dates, W. Waldron and J. Kopper, *Pyrenae* 3 (1967), 45–66.

20 Copper sources in the islands were accessible, but the extent of their exploitation is unknown; copper ore from the rock-cut tomb of Sa Font de Sa Teula suggests an early interest: Pericot Garcia 1972. C. Veny, *TP* 34 (1977), 111–54; *TP* 33 (1976), 227–54.

21 G. Lilliu *I. Naz. d'Arch e Storia* 9 (1960); *Arch. Studi. Sardi* 28 (1962); *Ann. Fac. Lettere Cagliari* 27 (1959).

22 J. Macaró Pasarius, *Las Taulas*, 1968.

23 G. Rossells Bordoy, *Studi Sardi* 19 (1966). C. Veny, *TP* 31 (1974), 101–36.

24 M. L. Serra Belabre, *X Congreso Nacional de Arquelogia*, 1964.

25 M. Tarradell, *Mateu Excavaciones Arquelógicas en España* 24 (1964); the cemetery also contains many burials of later date, with iron objects.

26 This problem cannot be explored here, but see Guido 1963; Grosjean 1976; Piggott 1965, 158–60.

27 Planchais 1976.

28 Beaulieu 1976.

29 G. Jalut in Guilaine 1976, 74–81, 182.

30 M.-T. Morzadec-Kerfourn in Guilane 1976, 88–94.

31 G. Jalut in Guilaine 1976, 180–5.

32 This is not a problem restricted to France alone.

33 Poulain 1976.

34 Videlles: G. Bailloud, *Mémoires Soc. Préhist. Française* 5 (1958) 192ff. At Misy-sur-Yonne, the proportions of domestic animals to wild animals remained at a constant 90:10 ratio throughout the later Bronze Age, except in the final phase when birds and fish made up 27 per cent of the total. The domestic animals were pig, cattle, sheep and horse, with pig a dominant form: C. and D.

Mordant, *Bull. Soc. Prehist. Française* 74 (1977), 420–71. Mohen 1977.

35 J. Philippe, *L'Anthropologie*, 1937, 253. A. Brisson and J. J. Watt, *Rev. Arch. Est.* 4 (1953), 193; 18 (1967), 7.

36 E.g. Clottes and Constantini 1976; Cordier 1976; Gaucher 1976; Verron 1976; Chertier 1976; Sandars 1957, 248, 253, 255, 261, 265, 268; Giot 1960, 166–7. The estuaries of Loire, Charente and Garonne in particular, which must surely dispose of the belief in vegetation-choked, muddy and inaccessible river deltas for traffic.

37 Mohen 1977, 204.

38 B. Lacroix, *La nécropole préhistorique de la Colombine*, 1957.

39 See for example the detailed descriptions in Sandars 1957, 78–154; a more general statement, Briard 1974, 144–54; regional studies, Guilaine 1976, 445–653 *passim*.

40 G. Cordier, *L'Anthropologie*, 1961, 184; 1976; the channelled decoration on many vessels from small cemeteries or stray finds is a characteristic feature, e.g., Les Cliaux (Puy-de-Dome): Daugas 1976, fig. 4,15; Chissy (Loire-et-Cher) and Gièvres (Cher): Cordier 1976, fig. 6,1–3.

41 A. Brisson and J. J. Hatt, *Rev. Arch. Est.* 4 (1953), 193.

42 A. Brisson and J. J. Hatt, *Rev. Arch. Est.* 18 (1967), 7.

43 Chertier 1976; B. Chertier, Les Nécropoles de la Civilisation des Champs d'Urnes dans le région des marais de Saint-Gond, Marne. *Gallia Préhistoire* IV (supp. 1976).

44 Gaucher 1976.

45 E.g. H. Savory, *PPS* 14 (1948), fig. 2, 3; cf. fig. 1, 4, 5.

46 In the upland areas of these river basins of central France, metal is rather rare, but the sheet gold cup from Rongère (Allier), Daugas 1976, fig. 3,8, is an outstanding piece. Bronzes include slashing swords, e.g. Aliès (Cantal), Daugas 1976, fig. 4,1–3, and the Vénat hoard (Charente), Coffyn 1976, fig. 4.

47 Briard 1965, ch. 11; the recent discovery of a hoard of bronzes from *c.* 10 m of water off the coast of Dover (Kent) may represent part of a boatload of material in transport from France; the objects are primarily of continental forms, of the early first millennium, D. Coombs, *Archaeol. Atlantica* 1 (1975), 193–5; hardly any trace of such objects have been found on British land.

48 Briard 1965, ch. 12; 1974, 153 map.

49 Briard 1965, ch. 13; Giot 1960, ch. 9; Briard 1976a, 571.

50 Giot 1960, 166–8.

51 Giot 1960, 167.

52 G. P. Burstow and G. A. Holleyman, *PPS* 23 (1957), 167–212; E. C. Curwen and G. A. Holleyman, *PPS* 1 (1935), 16–38; E. C. Curwen, *Sussex Arch. Coll.* 75 (1934), 137–170; P. Rahtz and A. M. ApSimon, *PPS* 28 (1962), 289–328.

53 Possible interpretations of houses: original reports, cf. M. Avery and J. Close-Brooks, *PPS* 35 (1969), 345–51, cf. C. R. Musson, *Curr. Arch.* 21 (1970), 267–75.

54 *Curr. Arch.* 32 (1972), 232–5.

55 Fowler 1971; C. C. Taylor, *Fields in the English Landscape*, 1975.

56 A. M. ApSimon and E. Greenfield, *PPS* 38 (1972), 302–81.

57 J. V. S. Megaw, in Burgess and Miket 1976, 51–65; J. V. S. Megaw, A. C. Thomas and B. Wailes, *Proc. West Cornwall Field Club* 2 (1961).

58 J. R. C. Hamilton, *Jarlshof*.

59 J. Huxtable, M. J. Aitken, J. W. Hedges and A. C. Renfrew, *Archaeometry* 18 (1976), 5–17.

60 D. Longley, *London Arch.* 3 (1976), 10–17.

61 F. Pryor, in Burgess and Miket 1976, 29–50.
62 Knocknalappa: J. Raftery, *North Munster Archaeol. Jour.* 3 (1942), 53–72; Lough Eskragh: A. E. P. Collins and W. A. Seaby, *Ulster. Jour. Arch.* 23 (1960), 25–37; Lough Gara: crannog with possible association with hoard of gold ornaments, G. Eogan, *PPS* 30 (1964), 268–351.
63 H. Hencken, *Proc. Roy. Irish Acad.* 47 C (1942), 1–76.
64 Wooden traps, e.g. J. G. D. Clark 1952, 53.
65 J. M. Coles and F. A. Hibbert, in Fowler 1975, 12–26; the flooding horizons in the peats may indicate one reason for track building, to preserve traditional passages, but the creation of new opportunities here and elsewhere should not be discounted.
66 K. A. Steer, *Proc. Soc. Antiq. Scot.* 89 (1956), 227–51; R. W. Feachem, *Proc. Soc. Antiq. Scot.* 92 (1959), 15–24.
67 R. W. Feachem, *Proc. Soc. Antiq. Soc.* 94 (1961), 79–85.
68 M. E. C. Stewart, *Proc. Soc. Antiq. Scot.* 95 (1962), 134–58.
69 Summarized in Burgess 1974, 197, 207, 219.
70 E. Burley, *Proc. Soc. Antiq. Scot.* 89 (1956), 118–226; E. Mackie, *Scotland: an archeological guide*, 1975, 96–7; J. D. Blundell and I. H. Longworth, *Brit. Mus. Quarterly*, 32 (1968), 8–14; Burgess 1974, 220; and see A. Ritchie, *Scot. Arch. Forum* 2 (1970), 54–5.
71 H. Savory, *Antiquity* 45 (1971), 251–6; but see also *Antiquity* 46 (1972), 330–1; I. H. Stead, *PPS* 34 (1968), 148–90; survey of evidence to date in D. W. Harding (ed.) *Hillforts. Later Prehistoric Earthworks in Britain and Ireland*, 1976,
especially articles by H. N. Savory, 237–92 and C. R. Musson, 293–302, for Wales, and B. Raftery, 339–358 for Ireland.
72 B. Raftery in de Laet 1976, 193; *Antiquity* 44 (1970), 51–5.
73 V. B. Proudfoot, *Ulster Journal Arch.* 17 (1954), 97–102; 19 (1956), 57–72.
74 Textiles: A. Henshall, *PPS* 16 (1950), 130–62; wooden objects: Herity and Eogan 1977, 202, 217, 212 (dugouts); leather: J. Coles, *PPS* 28 (1962), 156–90.
75 Many studies: surveys and references in Burgess 1974, 203–14; and in Herity and Eogan 1977, 169–73, 183, 193–7; distributive mechanisms: M. J. Rowlands 1976. The Wilburton, Cambridge hoard is one of the characteristic hoards of the period, containing swords, spearheads and axes: C. Fox, *Archaeology of the Cambridge Region,* 1923, pl. X.
76 C. F. C. Hawkes and M. A. Smith, *Antiq. Jour.* 37 (1957), 131–98; J. M. Coles, *PPS* 28 (1962), 156–90; e.g. Lisdromturk (Monaghan) cauldron, Herity and Eogan 1977, fig. 84.
77 Herity and Eogan 1977, 173–209; Taylor 1979.
78 Dowris and Bog of Cullen gold hoard: G. Eogan, *PPS* 30 (1964), 268–351; horns: J. M. Coles, *PPS* 29 (1963), 326–56; the horns and rattles have suggested the possibility of a 'bull cult' in western Europe, *Antiquity* 39 (1965), 217–19.
79 Deverel-Rimbury, its history and recent expansion: Burgess 1974, 214-17. Trevisker, A. M. ApSimon and E. Greenfield, *PPS* 38 (1972), 326–41.
80 E.g. B. Raftery, in de Laet 1976, 195–6; Burgess 1974, 220–1.
81 Arribas 1976, 161.

11 Northern Europe

The Late Bronze Age in northern Europe is not dramatically distinct from the Early Bronze Age, but it is marked by the opening-up of new lands for agriculture, by the development of larger settlements and cemeteries, by a wider distribution of metalwork, and by the deliberate disposal of valuable objects. The transition from the Early to the Late Bronze Age is, however, indistinct, and there seems little evidence for any outside stimulus or internal upheaval that might have caused an abrupt change in the evolution of society in the closing centuries of the second millennium.

The defining features of central European Urnfields, the urnfield burial rite, Urnfield pottery and metal objects, are not encountered in northern Europe. Cremation in the north was an important Early Bronze Age characteristic, as it was in other regions too, and it gradually became the dominant way of disposing of the dead in most regions in the Late Bronze Age, but northern European ceramic and metallurgical industries, settlement dispositions, and other cultural developments remained firmly independent of other regions.

The divisions of the Late Bronze Age in the north are periods III–V, with period VI marking a transitional phase to the full Iron Age.[1] Regional concepts within these divisions have recently been examined, and these allow a better impression of the development of material culture in Scandinavia.[2] On the north European plain, local groups and traditions have been recognized; in the Low Countries, an extension of true western Urnfield culture in its closing phases has been suggested, and along the south Baltic shores the Early Bronze Age combination of Scandinavian traditions and purely local developments was continued.

In radiocarbon years, the later Bronze Age of northern Europe represents a period from c. 1200 bc to c. 600 bc. There are many dates that apply to the various periods within this, and these suggest that period III is 1200–1100 bc, and period V 900–600. The correlations with the central

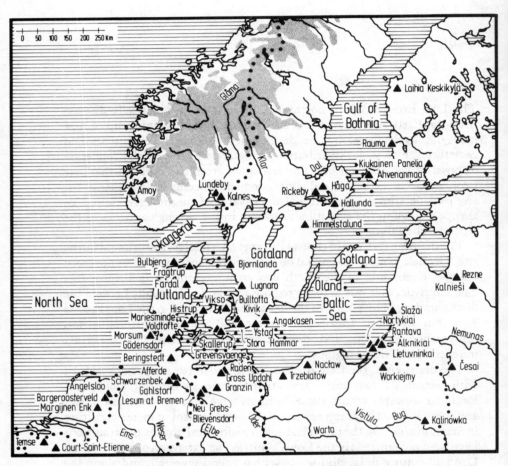

Map 9   Later Bronze Age sites in northern Europe

European sequence of Urnfields, on the basis of imported metal goods in the north, are quite satisfactory so far as these dates are concerned.[3]

The later Bronze Age in northern Europe is represented by settlements, cemeteries, hoards of metal objects, megalithic monuments, trackways, rock engravings and a number of other finds that can be explained best by the vague term 'votive deposits'. All of this evidence suggests that the concentration of population is likely to have been greater than previously, in that settlements where known are larger, cemeteries are much larger, there is increasing specialization in crafts, and wider exchange or distribution systems were developed. The overall spread of material is greater than previously, with more metal (bronze and gold), in circulation over almost all the north European area.[4]

The major distinctions between the earlier and the later Bronze Age, other than those of degree noted above, are the widespread and almost total adoption of cremation of the dead, the appearance of ship-settings in the cemeteries, evidence for horse-riding, and the greatly increased activity in the production of prestige objects for ritual deposition in marshy ground. Most of these features can be traced back to the Early Bronze Age, but their abundant appearance in the Late Bronze Age gives the impression of a dramatic and relatively rapid development.

Finally, near the end of the Bronze Age, there are two doubtless far-reaching events; the first of these is the appearance of iron in increasing quantities, and this has given rise to the uncertain 'period VI', within a Bronze Age system but including iron as a significant element. The second event is the evidence for climatic deterioration which would have had profound effects upon many areas of the north; the development of peat bogs gradually restricted areas of pasture through the growth of moss and other unsuitable grazing plants, and localized flooding and waterlogging in the lower reaches of some rivers would have seriously hindered travel and disrupted other activities; on the other hand, increased climatic moisture may well have allowed new areas, of sand for example, to be more actively cultivated.[5] The overall effect of climatic deterioration must have been adverse to the communities of the north European plain and Scandinavia.

Settlements and economy

The distribution of the later Bronze Age settlement in the north European plain, from the Low Countries and Lower Saxony in the west, across the south Baltic shores to coastal Lithuania and Latvia, is considerably more extensive than that of the earlier Bronze Age. Cemeteries and other finds in the west point to more archaeologically-recognizable activity, perhaps indicating denser occupation, and the same can be seen on the Baltic coastal zone. The popularity of certain selected regions, such as Rügen, the lower Oder valley, and around the Gulf of Danzig, already noted for the Early Bronze Age, continued in the Late.

For southern Scandinavia, the distributions of Early and Late Bronze Age material are generally uniform, although the isostatic recovery of the land accounts for the more immediately coastal distribution of Late Bronze Age sites. Other than this, there are few dramatic alterations in distributions in Denmark and southern Sweden between c. 1400 and c. 1000 bc; for central Sweden, however, the appearance of abundant evidence for occupation in Västmanland and Uppland in the later Bronze Age is dramatically new.[6] A similar but less novel appearance of late material has been recorded from the eastern and northern shores of the Skagerak, but western Norway, even in its southernmost regions, is remarkably free of substantial finds of metal.[7] Stone working here remained a dominant industry, but elsewhere in the north the working of stone also remained important, and is found in quantities in settlements where the usual rarity of metal is still a feature.[8]

The overall picture of actual settlements of the later Bronze Age is still uncertain, and it is not possible to make many generalizations about the structural details of houses, the size and disposition of settlements, and their subsistence bases.

Recent regional studies in southern Sweden and Denmark have begun to point to the relationships that existed between landscape, settlement and cemetery, and these may well lead to a far greater understanding of population size and organization in the later Bronze Age than we possess at the moment.[9] Yet there must remain many difficulties; for instance, investigations near Malmo in Scania have revealed traces of later Bronze Age settlements, but hardly any of the earlier Bronze Age, yet many graves of the earlier period are known.[10] The use of pollen analysis and other approaches can provide some evidence for land use that may otherwise not be recognizable, and in the Mälar region of Sweden studies of land use patterns have suggested an impact on the landscape of the later Bronze Age not seen before;[11] this evidence points to communities with permanent settlements which served as central bases for shifting cultivation practices in peripheral areas (fig. 180). In Scania, less fertile lands were taken into cultivation in the later Bronze Age,[12] and similar traces of land-take during the early first millennium have been indicated by pollen analyses in Finland.[13]

Although many Late Bronze Age settlements have recently been recognized in the north, their precise sizes and original appearances are still indistinct. Both small oval houses and large rectangular houses have

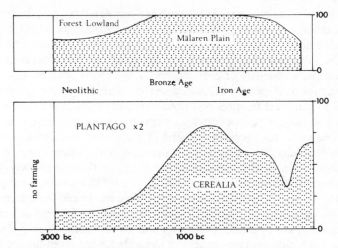

Fig. 180 Upper: Distribution of farming population in the region of Lake Mälaren, showing a movement onto the Plain in the later Bronze Age. Lower: Ratio of Cerealia: Plantago lanceolata in the region of Lake Mälaren, showing the increase of Cerealia in the later Bronze Age.
(After Welinder 1975)

been recorded from the Late Bronze Age of the north. The houses were most commonly post-built with wattle-and-daub walls, but log-walls between such uprights are also suggested. Stonework for lower walls, and turf as well, was also used on occasion. Slighter dwellings, perhaps of a more temporary nature, were semi-subterranean or had their floors slightly beneath the land surface.

Post-built long houses, of Elp type, with the animals tethered at one end, the human occupation at the other, have now been recognized. At Fragtrup near Alborg (North Jutland), three long-houses with roofs supported on double rows of internal posts have been recorded, and the significant point about this site is its resemblance in basic constructional details to both the earlier Elp type, and the later houses of the Iron Age in northern Europe. It is therefore likely that continuity in house type existed from the later second millennium well into the first millennium bc, and we might expect more such houses to be recognized; it may still be premature to argue that this was the dominant house type of the later Bronze Age.[14]

Many sites, presumed to be settlements, have yielded only a series of pits and scoops, often filled with domestic rubbish. Although these do not provide the evidence for structures, they do yield preserved material that reflects economic activities. At Kvarnby (Scania) a large number of refuse pits, hearths and possibly a pit-like house contained much domestic material including pieces of moulds for casting metal.[15] The site at Voldtofte (Funen) also consisted of a series of rubbish pits, from which was obtained a quantity of pottery, metal and stone objects. The site lay on the southern slope of a hill and covered an area of about 1,600 sq m.[16] The only structural features recorded in the excavations of 1909–16 were the pits, although the occupation deposits were apparently over 1 m thick. The associated pottery consists of barrel-like pots, biconical urns, handled jugs, slender-necked vases, open bowls, shallow dishes and lids. Decoration consists of horizontal channelling on the upper body of some vessels, but others are plain. The storage jars of bucket-shape are plain or decorated with a cordon; several of these were recovered from outside the occupation area and contained deposits of wheat, barley and millet. Near the settlement are a number of burial mounds which are likely to be of the same date as Voldtofte: a cemetery of mounds 1.5 km from the settlement yielded several very richly-furnished graves, and there are other contemporary graves, nearer.[17] Also within the settlement's immediate area of activity was a group of metal objects deposited in a small marsh or pool. All of these finds are of the early first millennium and probably represent permanent occupation of a favourable situation in Funen, but it is not possible to carry out further reconstruction in the absence of better recorded investigations of all these sites. However, we can say that the economy here was mixed, with arable land yielding barley, wheat, millet and oats. Domestic cattle were kept, and sheep, pig and horse as well. Most of the bones of these animals were mature. Wild animals were sparse, and may be explained by the situation of Voldtofte, on an island (although large) and in an area where Bronze Age activity was quite intensive judged by overall finds. That some at least partly-specialized activities were carried on at the site is shown by the remains of a crucible and a sword mould, and it is worth noting that other evidence for localized industries has been recovered from other settlements of this period.

At the settlement of Bulbjerg on the northern coast of Jutland, the domestic debris included sufficient amber lumps to warrant describing this site as a centre for the collection of amber for ultimate distribution into northern Europe and probably beyond. The occupation debris was 25–60 cm deep, which might indicate something more than a temporary seasonal encampment. The settlement remains consisted of pits and post holes, and suggested a rather small house without side aisles, probably with wattle-and-daub walls.[18]

Similar houses were probably built at the three settlements of Hötofta (Scania). Lying on gravel ridges, the precise character of the houses could not be determined, but the domestic remains were abundant even although the occupations seem to have been of rather short duration. The economy was based on arable farming and stock-breeding of cattle. The main cereal was barley, but emmer wheat, possibly einkorn wheat, and oats, were also cultivated. Cattle were the most important beasts, but sheep, goats, horses, pigs and dogs were also kept; there were few wild animals captured, and the young age of the slaughtered cattle and horses suggests that these were primary food animals.[19] Pottery in the settlements consisted of coarse barrel-like storage jars, as well as finer biconical vessels and bowls; the total number of such pots in all three settlements was under 100. Flint work techniques were rather poor, and the products restricted to awls, sickles, knives, scrapers and strike-a-lights. There were a few fragments of crucibles and moulds for casting metal, and a stone axe and horn axe. This site demonstrates two important features; the first is that a mixed economy, combining arable cultivation and stock-breeding, was in operation, and the second is that relatively small settlements conducted their own metal-working.

At Björnlanda, on an island in Gothenburg (Halland), a small settlement established on the east side of a valley occupied a former Mesolithic camp.[20] The Bronze Age occupation dates to c. 650 bc and shelter was provided by a large house 30 × 10 m in size, with turf walls 2–3 m thick at base; interior posts probably supported the roof. The domestic debris consisted of potsherds from barrel-like and biconical jars, flints including arrowheads, and crucible fragments. Other large rectangular houses have been recorded from the major settlement at Hallunda near Stockholm.[21] The settlement extended over 1.5 ha, and was positioned on the crown of a hill which had been slightly terraced for the houses. Three large houses, and possibly as many again, may have sheltered a population of 100; the largest house, 20 m long, had large boulders and stones forming at least the lower parts of the walls. It held twelve ovens, each 0.5–1.25 m in diameter, and some of these were provided with vents for forced air draught; the temperature achieved in these was as much as 1,200°C. Crucibles, fragments of moulds and ten narrow bronze rods were associated, and the site must have served as a major metallurgical centre for at least the immediate region if not farther afield.

The other houses were not so substantial but the occupation debris is extensive and thick, which suggests a relatively long period of habitation. Fire-cracked stones occur in abundance, and many thousands of potsherds include fragments of plain jugs, bowls, handled cups, pedestal bowls, and a range of ornamented vessels with twisted cord, stab, slash, groove, cordon and channel decoration, as well as concentric circle stamps. The evidence for subsistence economy suggests both arable-land agriculture and stock-breeding of cattle, sheep or goats, and pigs. Within the settlement area itself was a cemetery of at least thirty cremations placed beneath small stone-settings; grave-goods consisted mainly of potsherds with a few bronze ornaments. Radiocarbon dates for the settlement are c. 775 bc. About 1.5 km away from the settlement a rock carving has recently been recorded; it lies characteristically at the edge of a rock overlooking the valley where Bronze Age sites are situated. The art consists of thirteen ships, one human (standing in a ship), three animals, one footprint, one ring and 150 cups.[22]

The Hallunda settlement was probably a small village rather than a single farmstead, and its importance at the present time is its impressive evidence for a substantial metal industry, much larger than would seem to be appropriate to a small village, and its support for other evidence that a mixed economy combining arable cultivation and stock breeding was standard practice in the later Bronze Age.

Several of the sites described above support the idea that permanent settlements with concentrated populations were a feature of the later Bronze Age of the north, and the same may be said for long houses of the later Bronze Age in the Low Countries, at Margijnen Elk (Overijssel).[23] But much other evidence suggests that many small impermanent farmsteads or encampments were also a characteristic element. Small round or oval houses have been discovered at numerous sites such as Igelsta (Södermanland), and in the Mälaren valley.[24]

The Igelsta hut measured 4 × 3 m, and had a clay and pebble floor with wattle-and-daub walls. Probably associated with this small dwelling were some cairns and stone settings with cremation graves, the complex dated to the later Bronze Age (c. 1100–600 bc). Also occurring here were mounds of split stones which are generally interpreted as debris from settlement activities; many of these mounds lie in a region of central Sweden from south-east Västmanland to south-west Uppland, in an area rich in rock carvings, and associated with cairn cemeteries. Contained within these mounds are potsherds, daub, hammers and grinders of stone.[25] Other settlement heaps have been noted on the island of Hisingen (near Göteborg) near the Björlanda site. One mound, dated to 630 bc, was 4 m in diameter and 0.4 m high, and contained parts of over twenty pots, including barrel-like jars and polished bowls.[26] Other mounds, dated to c. 800 bc, also yielded pottery and one site contained crucibles for melting metal. The high phosphate content of the adjacent ground supports the interpretation of these heaps of scattered stones as part of occupation or activity areas.[27]

Along the southern shores of the Baltic, major settlements are still indistinctly known, yet the abundance of other evidence, large cemeteries and hoards of material, must indicate that we are dealing with communities whose construction of houses was of a nature to leave little trace; log-built houses, earthen foundations for wooden superstructures, and other procedures, would leave little trace. Some few exceptions are known; the Ulvivok group of settlements and cemeteries in north-western Ukraine is a case in point.[28] Occupation sites, such as that at Bondaricha on the upper Donecs river (p. 401), and those in the valleys of the Desna, Sejm and other rivers, were positioned on terrace gravels and sands. They have yielded quantities of domestic debris, querns and sickles, crucibles and stone moulds, a few metal objects, and animal bones of cattle, sheep, goats, pigs and horses. These sites are all of the ninth and eighth centuries.[29]

Although we have been able to point to a large number of settlements and houses in the north, it is not possible to describe these as typical settlements of the later Bronze Age. The number of such permanent or temporary occupation sites must have been enormous, yet a large majority have been destroyed, and others unrecognized. To the evidence from settlements we must add that from cemeteries, hoards, stray finds, and locational studies, in order to gain some impression of later Bronze Age society. A small part of this approach is concerned with actual routes, traditional roads and paths overland, and established waterways, which can often be identified by pure distributions of materials, and sometimes by surviving parts of such roadways.

A number of such trackways have been dated to the Late Bronze Age of the north, in the Low Countries and Lower Saxony in particular, and their yield of information about wood technology is impressive.[30] The Angelsloo (Drenthe) trackway was built of carefully-adzed planks with square holes cut to allow the planks to be held in place with long wooden pegs.[31] Such wood working should provide a guide to the character of the wooden parts of houses, and may allow a closer identification of fragmentary remains.

Of far greater importance for travel in northern Europe were the marine and inland waterways. Although the use of these cannot easily be attested through finds of surviving boats,[32] the known distributions of objects of stone and metal, the presence of many settlements and burials on islands, and the representations of ships on the rock engravings, all suggest that the movement of people and materials was often by sea, and probably easier by sea than by land. The overall distribution of Late Bronze Age objects and sites tends to be coastal rather than inland, although there are few parts of the north European area that are totally isolated from access to the marine waters of the North Sea and Baltic Sea.

Burials

The number of burials in the later Bronze Age of the north exceeds that of the earlier Bronze Age by a very large amount. It is perhaps too easy to infer from this that there was a population increase in the Late Bronze Age; the demonstration, for the Early Bronze Age, of gross inequality in the numbers of male and female graves suggests that a proportion of the population did not receive archaeologically recognizable burial, and the same may be true for the Late Bronze Age.

The major alteration in the treatment of the dead was the transition from, basically, the inhuming rite of the Early Bronze Age to the cremating rite of the Late. In Denmark, the developed Early Bronze Age (period II) has over 1,150 inhumations known, and under forty cremations; in the subsequent period III, which we take as the beginning of the Late Bronze Age, the known burials are c. 1,300 inhumations and 330 cremations. Subsequently, in the developed Late Bronze Age, there are hardly any inhumations known, and thousands of cremations.[33] In southern Sweden it appears that cremation was becoming an important rite sooner than this, and many graves of the earlier Late Bronze Age are cremations. The same is true in parts of the south Baltic coasts, west of the Oder river, but to the east, inhumation continued to be a dominant rite well into the later Bronze Age. The bodies of the dead were burnt on pyres generally outside the area of proposed burial, and were then collected and placed in the grave (fig. 181). In terms of the bodies themselves, the change from inhumation to cremation appears drastic, but the form of burials demonstrate that the change was gradual, and at first there were hardly any alterations in the monument built to hold the dead.

In the Early Bronze Age, the body was placed in a tree-coffin or stone-setting, along with suitable grave goods, and the barrow or cairn was erected to cover all. At the beginning of the Late Bronze Age, a major change was in the actual body treatment, and the burnt bones, cleaned of the pyre's charcoal, were placed in a full-sized coffin or setting of stones,[34] with unburnt grave goods, and a mound put over the remains as before. The cairn at Valhall (Scania) covered a stone cist containing a cremation with an unburnt bronze sword in its wooden sheath; a similar type of transitional burial in the Bulltofta (Scania) mound had a coffin 1.5 m long containing a cremation; an unburnt bronze fibula and two rings was positioned below a second tree coffin 2.8 m long holding another cremation.[35] These examples show that the traditions of burial were scarcely altered from the earlier local rites and, as expected, a number of particularly rich burials of this period are known; the significance of some of these, in Jutland, has already been commented upon (p. 302).

Fig. 181 Cremations and burials in urns in the south Baltic area: a reconstruction of some possible events.
(Drawing by R. Walker)

The very large mound at Håga (Uppland), however, is an exception even in a general 'rich grave' context.[36] The mound was 9 m high and was positioned on a low ridge overlooking the sea in the late second millennium; today isostatic recovery of the land has land-locked the mound. The mound consisted of an inner cairn of stones covered by turves. The central burial was a cremation, in a tree coffin, and the grave goods included a fine sword of bronze with gold-decorated hilt, as well as ornaments, razors and tweezers, some of which also had gold decorative components. Although this is an impressive burial, it is basically in the same tradition, an inhumation-sized grave-chamber with unburnt grave-goods, and is different only in degree from the much more common and smaller barrows or cairns holding similar burials furnished with objects of lower value.[37]

The cairns and barrows built to conceal yet distinguish the dead tended at first to be of comparable size to the mounds of the Early Bronze Age, but in time there was a marked diminution in size which coincided with a gradual reduction in the coffin size built to hold the cremated remains. Grave goods were at first of normal size, but then special miniature versions were created to accompany the dead in their smaller containers. The burial mounds of the later Bronze Age are often quite inconspicuous, of small diameter and low height; an average size might be 5–10 m in diameter, 1–2 m height. Cemeteries of mounds still occur, but often each mound may contain not one but several, or many, cremations. Many hundreds of such low mounds have been destroyed by relatively recent agricultural activities. Others have survived for recording or preservation, and often the internal stone structures have been the first indication of a ploughed-out burial's presence (fig. 182).

Throughout the later Bronze Age, the low barrows and cairns

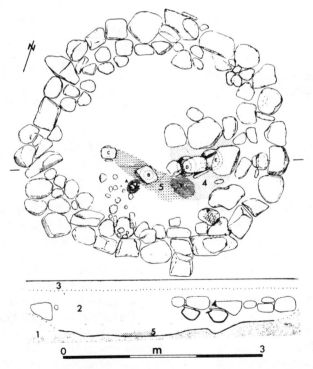

Fig. 182 Cremation graves in enclosure at Simris, Scania: 1. sandy subsoil, 2. sandy humus, 3. humus, 4. charcoal, 5. charcoal and burnt bone.
(After B. Stjernquist, *Acta Archaeologica Lundensis* 1961)

containing the cremated dead were placed in clusters over the landscape of Denmark, southern Sweden and adjacent regions.[38] In Norrland, several thousand small cairns have been recorded, positioned along the coast yet often in inaccessible places such as crags and cliffs. They must represent a continuity of settlement in this remote area, from the Stone Age through the Bronze Age and into the Iron Age, but mostly lacking metal of any sort.[39]

Many earlier barrows contained the traditional stone kerb or internal stone-setting or cist, and often these stones were arranged in complex patterns. At Hårbolle Hestehave (Møn), a small mound had a well-chosen selection of stones forming an outer kerb, and a small heap of stones at the centre protecting the cremation. At Hostrup (Røsnaes), four concentric stone circles surrounded a central stone-setting beneath an earthen mound.[40] Similar stone circles have often been noted beneath cairns in Sweden, and these can have been of little structural advantage; they are likely to represent buried versions of stone circles which are noted below.

In Uppland and Gotland, some circular settings of stone beneath cairns also have crisscross lines of stones, to form wheel-like figures beneath the covering cairn, and it has been suggested that the plain circles and the wheel-like circles, reproducing rock art symbols of disc and wheel, may represent similar religious ideas as does the rock art.[41]

There are many stone-circles in northern Europe, and a large number can be dated to the Iron Age or later periods. Some, however, are by association of the Bronze Age. They may represent a version of the kerb or internal stone-circles of barrows and cairns of the earlier Bronze Age, at a time when the tradition of large burial mounds had ceased to dominate. The small stone-heaps or settings over cremations may also represent versions of the previous tradition. The circles often, but not always, contain cremations at their centre, and some of these have been dated by radiocarbon to the early first millennium bc.

At Askim (Halland), a small circle of 4 m diameter had been formed of upright slabs up to 2 m long; at the centre of the circle, a cremation in a shallow pit had been covered by stones.[42] Other stone circles in the same area may also have contained cremations of the Late Bronze Age, but the dating of unassociated stone circles is virtually impossible. The three large circles at Lundeby (Østfold), each about 12 m in diameter and consisting of about the same number of large stones, are a case in point; they may be of Late Bronze or Early Iron Age date, but there is often little evidence to distinguish these periods in similar traditional monuments.[43]

What may seem clearer, however, is the group of stone-settings which take the form of double-pointed ovals, generally described as ship-settings.

There are many hundreds of such settings in northern Europe, many of them dated to the Iron Age, Viking or later periods. Some, however, are certainly of the Late Bronze Age. They consist of rather small elongated stones set up to form a ship-plan; sometimes the stones are graduated so that they rise upwards to a prow which may be 2 m high. The ships are generally pointed north-south and occasionally the stern is shown by a transverse stone, like a transom. The lengths of the ships range from 6 to 20 m in general, but some are larger.

The distribution of these Bronze Age ship-settings is restricted to the island of Gotland, a large number on the north-east coast of Småland, with smaller numbers elsewhere in Sweden, a few on Åland to the north, and a group in northern Latvia. There are strays elsewhere in Denmark and coastal Norway, but Gotland seems to be the centre of a Baltic tradition.[44]

The earliest-known ship-setting of the Bronze Age is perhaps a small, 2.5 m long, cist in the shape of a boat beneath a mound at Dömmestorp (Halland); within the cist was a cremation associated with a dagger and a pin of the earliest Late Bronze Age (period III, 1200–1100). Better known is a large barrow at Lugnaro (Halland), beneath which a careful outline of a ship was marked by lines of flat stones on edge.[45] The ship was 8 m long, and outside it was a stone-setting with urned cremation and miniature sword, tweezers, and awl; the date of this grave is early first millennium. A few other barrows or cairns of the Late Bronze Age in Scania and Småland also cover ship-settings, but most of the settings are unprotected and exposed like stone-circles.

At Ängakåsen in Scania, a large ship-setting lies on a low ridge parallel to the Baltic shore, and separated from it by a dip and second ridge; this other ridge carries a substantial stone circle. Within and around the ship-setting are 130 small stone settings marking Late Bronze Age cremation graves which extend over about 150 m of the ridge. A similar association, insofar as such a physical relationship can signify contemporaneity, exists at Wenningstedt (Sylt).[46]

The ship-settings of the Baltic region emphasize again the interest of north European Bronze Age people in the sea, and it has been suggested that some close relationship in belief existed between the ship-settings and the many representations of ships in the rock-art of the north.

In the early first millennium, cremations began to be placed in pottery vessels which no doubt acted as substitutes for stone or wooden coffins, and these urns were buried in low mounds, most often in pre-existing mounds or in flat cemeteries; these cemeteries may well have been distinguished by wooden marker-posts to avoid disturbance of previous graves, but today they are totally unmarked. They are of Periods IV–V.

The urn-burials of Denmark and southern Sweden are bereft of consistent grave-goods. The usual accompanying objects, where present at all, are small toilet articles such as tweezers and razors, and knives, pins and other ornaments also occur. These were not burnt with the dead. The pottery vessels used to hold cremations are of varied shapes and sizes. Among the earlier forms are cylinder-necked urns often with small paired handles at the base of the neck; biconical urns with or without handles also occur, as well as handled jugs and vases with long necks (fig. 183). Regional preferences may be distinguished, such as the spherical flagons of Zealand.[47] Decoration on the vessels is generally rather sparse, often consisting of incised zigzag lines in groups, or arcs. The quality of the pottery is in general not high although of course some particularly fine wares do occur. Pottery lids for the urns are common, and there are a few pottery boxes from Zealand, Schleswig-Holstein and Brandenburg.

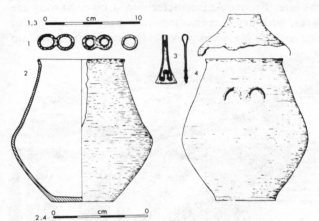

Fig. 183
Bronze Age urns
from Jutland,
with grave goods:
1–2. Snede, 3–4.
Fårdal.
(From Baudou
1960)

More remarkable are series of urns, from Denmark, southern Sweden and northern Germany, which are known as house urns and face urns. Both of these types are generally dated to the end of the Bronze Age, period VI in the terminology.[48] The house urns are cylindrical or slightly rounded upright jars, often with small openings at the top and a rectangular pottery door cut out of the body; the door was replaced after the cremated remains had been placed inside. These urns occur in Denmark and Holstein, with a few others elsewhere. One of these, from Stora Hammar (Scania) is remarkable in that the urn had been painted and the paint survived the burial in the earth.[49] The urn has a domed top and a door in the body; the presumed wall-posts beside the door, and other wall pillars, as well as the incised radiating lines on the roof, are painted in black or yellow. Many other urns may well have been painted originally.

Over 100 face-urns are known from Denmark,[50] particularly Jutland, and there are some north German examples as well. The representation of a human face may take the form of eyes, nose and mouth, or eyes and nose, or eyes alone, and the use of ribbon handle or boss for the nose is economical if amusing.

In Schleswig-Holstein, a region where finds of the later Bronze Age are not as abundant nor generally as impressive as those farther north, urn cemeteries or urnfields are known from areas near pre-existing barrows, in the sides of barrows and beneath low barrows. A barrow at Morsum (Sylt) contained both a primary urned cremation and secondaries (fig. 184).[51] Grave-goods are generally rare, and this is perhaps the most dramatic and important change between the earlier and the later Bronze Age (see p. 526, n. 1).

Further south, the later Bronze Age cemeteries of Lower Saxony are true urnfields in places, with urned cremations in flat cemeteries, but in others the cremations may be placed in previously-existing barrows; up

Fig. 184   Late Bronze Age barrow with primary cremations in urns in stone cairn, secondary cremations in cist and pit. Morsum, Sylt.
(From Ellmers 1971)

to 100 burials are reported from some of these cemeteries. The urns are said to be closely related to south German types, but the plain double conical form is very widespread in northern Europe generally; the division between Late Bronze Age and Early Iron Age is not apparent in these cemeteries, and continuity of population is stressed.[52] The northern part of Lower Saxony, including major areas of the Lüneburg heathlands, is more closely related to the north European later Bronze Age, but here the cremation rite had been a dominant form since the Early Bronze Age.[53] The later burials, however, are urned and occur in large cemeteries often placed near the largest of pre-existing barrows, or in the sides of barrows. The urns are cylinder-necked, and some carry decoration said to be of Lausitz character from across the Elbe. Grave goods are sparse, consisting of northern types such as pins, razors or tweezers; the Gödenstorf burial was associated with tweezers and a razor decorated with ship motif. The large urnfield at Schwarzenbek yielded 61 urns covered by stone-paved areas up to 4 × 2 m in size which in some cases seem to have been the sites of pyres, presumably for subsequent cremations. A large cemetery at Tiefensohl consisted of low barrows, 4–12 m in diameter, scattered around larger Early Bronze Age mounds; stone-packed graves at the centres or around the stone rings at the edges of the barrows contained urned cremations, and within the region the cylinder-neck urns continued in use well into the Early Iron Age, judging by the iron grave goods.[54]

The same situation may be seen in the Late Bronze Age cemeteries of the Low Countries, where the division into Bronze Age and Early Iron Age is arbitrary at times.[55]

The Lower Rhine valley in the later Bronze Age represents a complex situation not at all related to the remainder of the north European area, particularly the classic Nordic region, and the distinction between Early and Late Bronze Age is not clear-cut. The appearance of cremations in bucket urns, in the banked and ditched barrows of the lower Rhine basin, is an Early Bronze Age feature, and the Hilversum and Drakenstein groups are known from both settlements and cemeteries (p. 293). The beginning of the Late Bronze Age in the lower Rhine area does not represent any major alteration in social ordering, and the viewpoint that major immigrations were involved is no longer universally accepted. Urnfields appear in the southern part of the Low Countries in the eleventh century (Hallstatt A2 in the south German sequence),[56] with features slightly different from those of the preceding centuries. The burials consist of cremations, some in urns and others unurned, placed in small groups on the old land surface and each covered by a small mound; a circular ditch often surrounded the mound. Grave goods were rare or absent.[57] The tradition is clearly comparable to that of the earlier Bronze Age in the area, and the later burials were often placed near or around traditional earlier cemeteries.

The urns used to hold the cremated remains include Urnfield forms comparable to those of the south German and Swiss Urnfield groups, although locally made,[58] and also urns with excised decoration (*Kerbschnitt*), also of upper Rhine character; in addition, rather coarse pots with finger-tip decoration around the neck recall closely the local earlier Bronze Age Drakenstein and Laren urns. There is some debate about the nature of these urnfield cemeteries, and continuity with the preceding traditions of the Lower Rhine is generally believed to be the most important aspect, rather than immigration from upstream.[59] Considerable variation in burial monuments occurs: flat graves in Belgian Brabant and Flanders,[60] low wide mounds in Campine,[61] and ditched barrows in North Brabant and Limburg.[62]

North of the Rhine, in Overijssel, Drenthe, Groningen and Frisia, the cremation rite was not universal, and some inhumations still continued; the grave was placed under low rather oblong mounds with ditch around, and rectangular post-settings still occur within the grave area. Urns were not consistently used for cremations. Rather later, burials in the region were cremations surrounded by a keyhole-shaped ditch. Grave goods were scarce, and urns were not consistently used; urns are biconical or globular, some with two handles.[63] The plain *Kümmerkeramik* wares of the earlier Bronze Age probably continued to be manufactured and used in both cemeteries and settlements; the Elp settlement continued in use well into the Late Bronze Age (p. 285).

All of these Late Bronze Age groups in the Low Countries have distinctive characteristics and have been considered to represent different societies; their local ancestries in Early Bronze Age communities seems very strong, and they provide clear evidence of their gradual transition from final Bronze Age to the Iron Age in a smooth and uninterrupted fashion,[64] doubtless imperceptible to those experiencing it.

Along the southern shores of the Baltic, burial practices of the Late Bronze Age were varied, but one generalization can be made. To the west of the Oder valley, in Mecklenburg, cremation burials in urnfields became a dominant rite; to the east, inhumation of the dead remained traditional until the first millennium bc.

The grave-goods of the Baltic coastlands west of the Oder river are more consistently of Nordic character, as this region (Mecklenburg) is generally recognized as a part of the northern Bronze Age territory. Yet there are certain differences in the burial practices which are of considerable interest. The principal feature of all the Mecklenburg later

Bronze Age cemeteries is that cremation was absolutely dominant, whereas, to the north and east, the inhumation rite was still an important element in the earlier phases of the late Bronze Age. In addition, flat cemeteries, low stone cemeteries, and large mounds, were all used to contain the dead. It is probably better to look for continuity in these monuments rather than to emphasize their differences, because in almost all cases the cremated remains were enclosed in an urn and/or placed within a shallow stone-setting which served to separate the individuals within a large cemetery, and to provide a covering for the grave; the effect is a small rather shapeless cairn placed around and over the burial, and in the absence of evidence that the burials were set in scoops or shallow pits, the stone settings provided a marker for the grave readily visible so that future burials rarely encroach and disturb.

Cemeteries of the late second millennium were either flat, with low stone settings around or over the urned cremations,[65] or were beneath or within mounds.[66] Many bodies were apparently burned wearing clothing decorated with bronze studs.[67]

The practice of barrow-building continued into the first millennium in Mecklenburg, and barrow-cemeteries often occur. That at Gross Upahl consisted of c. 30 barrows ranging from 5–12 m in diameter, 0.5–2.5 m in height, but on the edge of the group was a very large mound 15 m across and 4 m high. Most had a stone kerb around or just inside the earthen mound, and the cremations in urns or on the ground were often protected by stone settings. The funeral pyre was positioned at times within the kerb. Cylinder-neck urns and Nordic metal types such as razors, pins and miniature swords were associated, as well as decorated bone cylinders. The largest barrow contained a central urned cremation in a stone cairn, and other graves within the barrow also yielded urns including a fine decorated vase and a house-urn with square door.[68]

One of the largest cemeteries of the later Bronze Age in the region is near Blievenstorf, in the Elbe basin. Over an area of c. 1,800 sq m occurred 169 graves, 123 potsherd deposits, eight scoops or pits, and various burnt areas, probably the sites of pyres for cremating bodies. Many of the burials were within or near stone settings, and many cremations were enclosed in plain urns generally with a pottery lid; the urns are biconical or have rounded bases and conical necks. Metal grave-goods were rare; only thirty-six out of 169 had a single metal piece, and one grave had two pieces. Spiral rings or wire were the most common item, but the weight of bronze from the entire cemetery was very slight. Of 164 identified bodies, the ages were as follows: 0–7 years (39), 7–14 (16), 14–21 (12), 21–40 (56), 40–50 (33), over 50 (8). Males and female adults were almost equally represented.[69]

The cemeteries in Mecklenburg appear to represent a greater density of population in the later Bronze Age when compared with the earlier Bronze Age, but the absence of diagnostic grave-goods from many graves suggests that numbers alone cannot be relied upon for accurate estimates. In any case, the evidence from cemeteries often indicates a continuity of use over long periods; the very large cemetery at Lanz began only in the latest Bronze Age and continued in use, spreading eastwards, well into the late La Tène period.[70]

Along the south-eastern shores of the Baltic, burial practices continued to be varied, and inhumation remained a dominant form until well into the Late Bronze Age.[71] The sequence can be seen in a single barrow of the Rantava cemetery, Samland; the barrow consisted of a central cairn 10 m in diameter, surrounded by two stone circles or kerbs, and all covered by an earthen mound 20 m across and about 2.5 m high. Within the cairn itself and later within the earthen mound, a series of burials was made which span the later Bronze Age of the area.[72]

The primary burial was an inhumation with a bronze sword, battle-axe, bracelet, necklet and pin, as well as glass beads and a plain small pot; comparable grave-goods are known from other cemeteries in the region, and they are probably of the tenth and eleventh centuries. Other inhumed bodies from the Rantava barrow, placed in the upper part of the cairn, were provided with heavy ribbed pins, bracelets, studs, amber beads and plates, and undecorated bowls and small lugged vessels. Again, grave-goods of these types occur over a wide coastal area from the Oder eastwards to Lithuania, and are associated on occasion with early central European Urnfield forms and Nordic Period III types.[73]

The final graves in the Rantava barrow are cremations in urns placed in the earthen mound over the cairn; the pots are plain with cylindrical or tapered necks, but even simpler barrel-like urns also occur. The adoption of cremation as the burial rite in this region came rather late, but its absolute dominance from about 1000 BC is striking. The cemeteries may be flat but more often are in barrows,[74] the primary cremations placed within a small stone vault-like cairn surrounded by circles of stones and all buried under an earthen mound. Other cremations in urns were placed within the barrow, and at Workiejmy (Warminski), a barrow only 13 m in diameter and 1.8 m high contained about 600 graves, all cremations. The earlier were mere piles of burnt bones, the later were urned cremations, and this cemetery spanned perhaps 600 years.[75] The urns are mostly plain, with cylinder-necks, but some grooved decoration occurs. Other cemeteries of this latest Bronze Age consist of a number of barrows with individual cremations, occasionally up to 100 mounds. Grave goods of stone or metal are generally rare, but they have included a few objects from outside the region, such as Nordic razors and tweezers.

Metalwork

The metalwork of the later Bronze Age of Scandinavia is rather more widely distributed than was that of the earlier Bronze Age, but it is a question of degree rather than of fundamental change. Much of central and most of northern Scandinavia remained outside the compass of metallurgical practice, unless it is argued that conditions for preservation of metal in these regions are so poor as to cause the disappearance of almost all surviving traces; this seems unlikely in view of the quite abrupt line, from Rogaland in western Norway across to Uppland in eastern Sweden, beyond which metal rarely appears. The limit is, in effect, the northern edges of the central lowland belt which extends across from the Oslofjord through the inland waters of Vänern and Mälaren to the Baltic waters at Åland; in adjacent Finland, some few metal objects are known, and are clearly in the fashion of northern metallurgy, but this region too seems generally to have been outside the major distribution networks of the important industries of the south.[76] The southern boundary of these metal industries receives comment below,[77] but it may be noted here that the markets for Nordic products were restricted (fig. 185).[78]

The transition from earlier to later Bronze Age metalwork in the north is marked by an alteration in the types of weapons and ornaments produced, and in their decoration. Although we do not believe that separation of industries along these lines can be relied upon in any way except as a general trend, a gradual alteration in tastes and preferences, nevertheless the disappearance of the heavy palstaves and spearheads marks a firm horizon, and so does the decline in interest shown in the running spiral decoration. The emergent decorative motifs in metalwork are zigzag lines, triangles, arcs and concentric circles, and these continued to be preferred thoughout the entire later Bronze Age.[79]

Weapons of the earlier phase of the later Bronze Age included long swords with straight or mildly leaf-shaped blades; their hilts were cast metal but often contained grooves for inserts of bone, wood or leather. Flange-hilted swords, with provision for entire grip plates of organic substances, are new forms, and are often linked with central European swords, particularly the Nenzingen or Type II swords.[80] Later types of sword include long straight-bladed weapons with cast-on metal hilts; a number of these recall central European forms, such as the antenna-hilted type. Some swords are miniatures, 15 cm long, fitting more readily into the small container, of pottery, wood or stone, holding the cremated dead. Knives and bracelets, studs and fibulae, necklets and razors are often associated with cremation graves, and there are heavier pieces as well including small circular boxes with cast ornament of circle and arcs, generally called belt boxes.

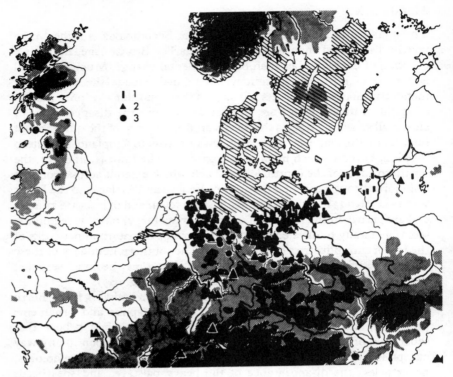

Fig. 185 Distribution of Nordic bronze products in north and central Europe. Nordic area hatched. 1. swords, 2. fibulae, hanging vessels, belt buckles, 3. other bronzes.
(From Thrane 1975)

Succeeding phases of bronzework demonstrate the variety of individual industries that were established in the north during the earlier first millennium. The general range of weapons, tools and ornaments has been carefully described in a number of important studies,[81] and many individual workshops can be distinguished from their specialized products;[82] this is not the place to list these, but it will be apparent that the presence of metalworking areas within many settlements of the later Bronze Age would have yielded a large variety of local forms. Spearheads, socketed axes, and single-edged knives are particularly well defined in terms of individual industries, and certain of the axes can be shown to represent perhaps ten or fifteen different production workshops.[83]

The characteristic ornamentation of metalwork in the later Bronze Age is the circle, arc and ribbon; the ribbon style takes a variety of forms, sometimes a wavy line ending in a short spiral, or an elaborate interlaced pattern of joined arcs. The styles are best seen as entirely local in origin, and continuity through the later Bronze Age, and emanating from the earlier, can be demonstrated.

The cheek-pieces of bronze and antler recovered from graves, hoards and as stray finds in the north have been interpreted as indicating a wide adoption of chariots and carts in the late second millennium. The questions concerning the introduction of horse-harness and horse-riding in the north are fairly complex, but the evidence, from cheek-pieces, models of wagons and carts, and rock art, is extensive and we cannot doubt that the improvement in transportation involving the horse, whether ridden or a draught animal, was progressive throughout the Bronze Age.[84]

Perhaps of outside origin is the decoration seen on beaten metal vessels, involving dot-and-circle and duck-like designs.[85] These metal vessels, handled cups and bowls, and larger buckets and cauldrons (fig. 186), have generally been interpreted as imported pieces, made in central Europe in Late Bronze Age workshops.[86] The typological similarities within major groups of these, and their distributions, appear to support this general idea, but from it there has come an opinion that north European metalsmiths were not capable of sheet metalwork. This seems extreme in the presence of a number of sheet objects which are likely to

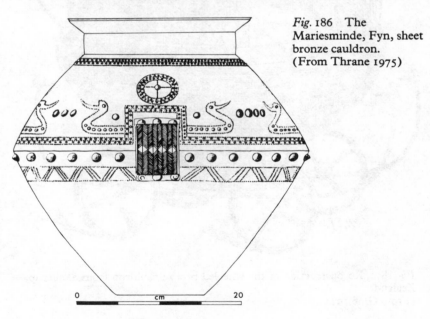

Fig. 186 The Mariesminde, Fyn, sheet bronze cauldron.
(From Thrane 1975)

be of northern inspiration and manufacture. They include metal shields and some of the rather simpler metal vessels which are not matched elsewhere in style, as well as the exquisite gold cups from Mariesminde (Fyn),[87] and elsewhere (pl. 19).

Other metal vessels are more unusual. At Skallerup (Zealand), a large grave of the earlier part of the Late Bronze Age was found with a sword, razor, tweezers, gold armlet and a wheeled bronze cauldron containing a cremation.[88] The undercarriage consists of four wheels joined by two rods ending in ducks; the cauldron itself, only 30 cm in maximum diameter, has ribs of embossed dots, a splayed base and flattened wide rim supporting wire rods attached to the body, and spear-shaped pendants (fig. 187).

The chassis of a somewhat similar vehicle was found at Ystad (Scania), and at Peckatel (Mecklenburg) a complete wheeled cauldron was recovered from a burial mound; a fourth example comes from Milavče (Bohemia), and the idea, whatever it was, behind these cauldrons seems to be north European rather than external.[89]

Fig. 187   Reconstruction of the wheeled bronze cauldron from Skallerup, Zealand.
(From Glob 1974)

Much has been written about the 'trade links' that may have existed between northern Europe and other regions in the later Bronze Age. It can be demonstrated that particular objects were subjected to transportation over long distances, and a series of maps produced by Thrane shows the joint distribution of some few articles; these are winged axes, horse fittings, vase-head pins and ribbed armlets and various swords, but of these, only the pins, armlets and winged axes can claim to show that certain types (and these not over-specialized) were in common use over wide areas from the lower Rhine to Jutland.[90] The distinction between actual imports and local copies or developments is difficult to judge, and although we may regard the mechanism of long distance trade as theoretically demonstrated[91] there does not seem to be very substantial evidence of this occurring at this time; the matter is discussed elsewhere (p. 15, 281). The winged axes are, however, of some interest; hoards of these in Denmark often contain no local northern types yet sometimes other 'exotic' forms and particular routes into the north have been suggested.[92] Local production in northern Germany is not excluded,[93] and this emphasizes the problems of distinguishing long distance trade from all the other possibilities for transmission of material or inspiration.[94]

The appearance in northern Europe, however, of craftsman-produced sheet metal vessels of very distinctive types can hardly be interpreted in any other way than as a form of exchange system which resulted, eventually, in long-distance movement of specialized materials. The peculiar character of these objects suggests that the impetus and arrangements for their acquisition in northern lands may not have been typical for other materials.[95]

In contrast to these southern products in the north, there are very few Nordic objects that found their way southwards into central Europe. The distribution of Nordic bronzes stops quite abruptly, the practical limit being an arc from just across the Ems river in Drenthe through the lower reaches of the Elbe, the Oder and the Vistula rivers.[96] This is hardly outside the immediate Baltic coastlands, and what there is beyond can be nothing more than sporadic drift of objects through random time and hands (fig. 185).

In concluding the discussion here of the Nordic metal industries, and its presumed receipt of objects and ideas from further south, it may be worth endorsing Thrane's remark about the character of the north in this respect: 'The essence of the Nordic Bronze Age and that which makes it unique is the talent for transforming every foreign impulse into something special marked by the hallmark of local tradition.[97]

The metal types which have precise or close relationships with central European forms have prompted several authors to attempt cross-correlations with the central sequence. The results of this work is the suggestion that the beginning of the later Bronze Age in the north (period III) relates to Br D – Ha A1 – Ha A2 except in Zealand where local developments characteristic of period IV are associated with Ha A2 forms. Ha B1 and part of Ha B2 correlate with general period IV in the north, which leaves the final Urnfield phase, Ha B3, coinciding with period V. Considerable overlaps within this general sequence doubtless exist, but the picture appears clearly defined by the recent work of Baudou, Randsborg and Thrane.[98]

The metalwork of the Low Countries never achieved the wide internal circulation of the northern industrial production, but greater quantities of materials were available to the smiths during the later Bronze Age than had been present in earlier times. Products of the Nordic areas are found only as far west as the Ems river and eastern Drenthe, and west of this the metalwork is to a great extent local.[99] Individual styles of axes, palstaves, bracelets have been recognized, and moulds for some of these have also been found.[100] That local production was necessary is also shown by the apparently deliberate avoidance of the region by the mechanisms bringing central European metalwork northwards into Lower Saxony and beyond.[101] The products of the British Isles occasionally found in the Low Countries and other northern areas have probably received far more attention than they deserve, and there are few now who would see these as anything more than occasional exchanges.[102]

The areas immediately to the east of the Low Countries assume contrasting characters in later Bronze Age metalwork; Lower Saxony, the Weser and western Elbe region, continued to acquire metal supplies successfully, but the Rhine valley in Nordrhein-Westphalia remained a peripheral and fringe area in terms of metalwork, although urnfields are common.[103] Farther east, in the mid-Weser valley, metals of the later Bronze Age are more abundant, and a few substantial hoards are known; the Afferde group contained bracelets, axe and spearhead.[104] The vast bulk of metalwork, however, occurs farther north, in Lower Saxony itself as well as Schleswig-Holstein; the latter is quite clearly within the Nordic industrial province in which the overall types of preferred implements were standard, but considerable local variation in details was developed by individual smiths. The sheet gold vessel from Albersdorf is an outstanding piece; the bronze knife from Beringstedt with a handle in the form of a female wearing a corded skirt, necklet and huge earrings is also unusual.[105]

Although the Lüneburg heathlands were to a great extent the centre of an earlier Bronze Age community with its own particular burial traditions and metal industries, it is possible to see these merge with customs and preferences of the north, and east, in the later Bronze Age. The Ilmenau metal industry of the late second millennium, with its own types of bronze ornaments and other objects, appears to fade into a general merger with the Nordic industries which dominate the area of Lower Saxony in the later Bronze Age.[106] Within the area there are a number of moorland and riverine finds which fall within the framework of presumed Nordic votive deposits; the sheet bronze helmet out of the Lesum at Bremen, the bronze bracelet of Bassum-Hassel, the gold bracelet of Gahlstorf, all are of the final Bronze Age or early Iron Age of the region and demonstrate the quite widespread distribution of prestige products over the north European plain.[107]

Farther to the east, the Mecklenburg province remained a part of the Nordic metallurgical tradition in the later Bronze Age but a clear boundary to this south Baltic area is the lower Oder valley. The region to the east of the Oder is not one noted for its abundance of metalwork, yet in the later Bronze Age locally-strong metal industries were established and maintained. It is significant that the products include heavy solid weapons and tools, which suggest that supplies of metal were not scarce. The Nortycken (Nortykiai) or Baltic bronze battle axe may be 20 cm long, and hoards of up to 24 occur along the coastal belt from Latvia as far west as southern Jutland, and individual styles can be determined.[108] Other products included ornaments (necklets, pins and bracelets), a few gold spiral rings, and tools such as flanged axes with wide blades, sickles, spearheads. The Lietuvninkai hoard contained sixty-four sickles, eleven spearheads, seven socketed axes, and thirty-six bracelets, all of them unusable through breakage or other defects in production.[109]

Ceremonial activities

The significance of much of this metalwork remains imprecise, principally because of its rarity in settlements, and its appearance in hoards of metal alone. One of the features of later Bronze Age metalwork in the north is its regular association with moorland and marshland, and this has led recently to an extreme (to us) view, which sees almost all the metalwork hoards as votive offerings to Bronze Age deities.[110] Not all subscribe to this, partly no doubt because it is difficult to comprehend the reasons behind such an economically wasteful activity, more particularly in the light of the necessity to import all metals into the region. Yet this could be the exact reason for the deposition of metal, because it was exotic and the most valuable possession of communities. Others would interpret the hoards of metal as partly votive, and partly economic; the latter could include hoards of finished products, and scrap metal. Here we are concerned with the evidence for votive offerings.[111]

Among the objects called to witness the existence of ritual actions in the later Bronze Age, ceremonial axes, helmets, shields, cauldron-carts, human figurines, and *lurer* (horns) are most often advanced, other than art itself.

Large wide-bladed axes, occasionally with clay core beneath a thin bronze shell, are a good example of the equipment which in appearance is physically functional but which in effect is nothing of the sort. These axes, such as those from Skogstorp (Södermanland), Galstad (Västergötland), and Egebak (Jutland, 48 cm, 7.1 kg) can be classed only as display equipment in our opinion,[112] and in the same category are the few but large sheet-bronze shields, demonstrably impressive in appearance but without value against slashing swords or projectiles.[113]

The two bronze helmets from Viksø (Zealand) would also appear to represent the display element within later Bronze Age society and their resemblance to bronze figurines, and representations in rock art and on a metal razor from Vestrup (Jutland), bring together many of the elements claimed to be of ritual significance[114] particularly if the horned aspect of the helmets is linked with the origins of the metal horns or *lurer*.

The *lurer* represent one of the more spectacular technological feats of the northern Bronze Age.[115] Made in segments by the lost wax or equivalent process, the *lurer* are 1.5–2.1 m long. They occur most often as pairs, each pair consisting of a right-hand and left-hand *lur,* with opposing bends and curves; the similarity to a pair of animal horns is obvious. The *lurer* dated by decoration to the earlier part of the Late Bronze Age (*c.* 1200) are closer in form to the organic prototype than are the later more elongated *lurer* of the final Bronze Age (*c.* 700) (pl. 22a). The mouthpieces of all of the instruments are primitive, and although the exteriors of the *lurer* are carefully smoothed, the interiors have been left with the original casting-marks and occasional repair-patches. For these reasons it is considered that the actual musical notes produced by the *lurer* were not as important as the appearance and occasion upon which they were exhibited. Most of the fifty *lurer* that have been found come from moors or marshlands of Jutland and the Danish islands, although a few have been recovered from southern Sweden, Norway, Schleswig-Holstein and Mecklenburg; the distribution is strictly within the northern Bronze Age region and not beyond. Some of the *lurer* were buried after their mouthpieces had been broken off, as if to prevent 'unofficial' use. Those that survive intact can yield up to 12 or 15 notes, and much has been written about their musical capabilities.[116] The *lurer* are best interpreted as elements in ceremonial displays of particularly impressive metal products, but what these displays signified to society is unknown; hints may be provided by rock art where humans are depicted playing instruments like the *lurer* (Kalleby, Bohuslän), and are associated with scenes which may represent sacrifices or merely processions (Kivik, Scania). The humans at Kalleby are shown wearing horned helmets, and these are often compared with the Viksø metal helmets, and certain small figurines (pl. 24b).

The metal figurines of the later Bronze Age are of considerable interest, not only for their possible ritual significance but also for their representation of actual humans wearing clothing; there are otherwise very few traces of Late Bronze Age costume to compare with the extensive earlier Bronze Age finds. The two major finds are from Fårdal (Jutland) and Grevensvaenge (Zealand), but there are others as well (pl. 23a–b).

The Fårdal group consists of figurines set upon perforated pegs as if for mounting upon a rod or structure such as a model wagon, ship or similar shape. The figurines are two gracefully-curved horned animal heads, one similar but double-headed mount with a small bird between, a snake-like creature with broad snout, and a human female wearing a cord-like skirt, and whose eyes are gold-leaf covered.[118]

At Grevensvaenge there were six figurines, now mostly lost, but drawings exist of the find. Three of these were females wearing cord-like skirts and bent backwards; two other humans were kneeling and wore Viksø-like helmets and held large axes of the display type. The sixth figurine was female with a long skirt and outstretched hand.[119]

It is not possible to state more than the obvious here, that these figurines almost certainly relate to some ceremonial actions; what these were we cannot at this time say, but the resemblances to rock-art depictions are probably significant. The females bent backwards, as if doing a backward somersault, the figurines holding enormous battle-axes, the style of the Stockhult legs,[120] the snake-like figure, all can be seen in rock art sites and it seems logical to connect the two forms of evidence.

A site directly combining burial mound and rock art is Bredarör at Kivik (Scania).[121] The cairn here, originally 70–80 m in diameter, is the largest in all Scandinavia, and was systematically robbed for building purposes up to and beyond 1748 when a central stone chamber was discovered and rifled (fig. 188). The character and contents of the burial are not known, although the cist itself, 3.8 m long and 1 m wide, has been considered to represent a fitting place for the most wealthy and powerful of all Bronze Age leaders. The cist was formed of ten dressed slabs, four along each side, and was covered by three large capstones; each slab was over 1 m high, about 1 m wide and relatively thin (20–25 cm). Seven of

Fig. 188   The Kivik grave, Scania: top left, the chamber as allegedly found; top right, excavations and emptying of the chamber in 1748; below, the eight decorated slabs, several now damaged or lost.
(From *Skalk* 1965/3)

the side-slabs were decorated on their inner faces, and the designs have for long intrigued prehistorians. Representations of ships, animals, hafted axes, wheels and other curved shapes occur on five of the slabs; two others carry scenes interpreted as processions of robed humans, with other humans, animals, a chariot and other symbols possibly involved in some sort of ceremonial action. The interpretations of the scenes are of course subjective, but most often the words 'ritual' and 'sacrifice' occur, and these may well be correct. Beyond this we cannot proceed, except to indicate that the dating of the cist to the Late Bronze Age is not certain, and there may be a case for suggesting an earlier period.

It is not merely the chronological position that is often in doubt; far more fundamental is the question of function and significance. For some monuments, the question is unanswerable; at Rønninge Søgård (Funen), *c.* 500 pits, aligned east-west in fifteen parallel rows, are not unique to northern Europe but their significance to the societies of *c.* 1000 BC is almost beyond conjecture.[122]

A particularly inexplicable burial, one among many, is a cremation in a small stone cist beneath a mound at Maglehøj (Zealand); the grave goods consisted of a belt box, a stud, a knife and a fibula of bronze. The box held two horse's teeth, weasel bones, a wild cat's claw, a lamb or deer bone, part of a bird's windpipe, snake vertebrae, burnt bone pieces, fragments of wood, pebbles of quartz, pieces of clay and pyrites, and a small bronze sheet and wire hook.[123] General comparisons with the Hvidegaard grave are obvious (p. 308). Finds such as these are perhaps indications of the presence of 'medicine-men', but analogies with schoolboys' pockets are also possible.

One of the few structures of the later Bronze Age that can certainly be shown to fall within the ceremonial or ritual category is the wooden building at Bargeroosterveld in Drenthe.[124] Here a position in a marsh, 250 m from the dry land, was selected and a ring of stones, 4 m in diameter, was placed upon the waterlogged surface. Within the circle, two wide oak planks with other smaller pieces of wood had been pegged into the peat beneath (fig. 189). The site had been extensively disturbed upon discovery, and, of the possible upper parts of the structure, little remained. Several curved oak pieces, and other fragments, suggested an open-air structure with horizontal horn-like projections on the uppermost timbers. What function this performed in later Bronze Age society is totally unknown, as no finds of stone, metal or pottery were made. However, it appears that the structure was deliberately destroyed in the Bronze Age, when much of it may have been removed along with any other elements present on the site. In the same area, three hoards of metal have been found, and it has been suggested that these may represent votive deposits associated in idea with the Bargeroosterveld structure; the hoards contain objects of British, Nordic and south German types, and their time range is c. 1100–800. The structure has been dated to c. 1050 bc.

The rock art of the north has already been discussed briefly (p. 317), but it is important to realize that a large proportion of it must belong to the later Bronze Age rather than to the earlier phase. The work of dating this art is difficult, if not impossible, and there is a general absence of motifs in the art which can be directly related to dated designs on metal or pottery. Stylistic and evolutionary sequences of ship representations have been established by Marstrander and sometimes comparable designs occur on metal razors and, rarely, on other objects;[125] all that seems reasonably certain is a general dating to the later Bronze Age for many rock art panels or isolated pictures, and the precise relationship between the art of different regions remains uncertain. In terms of the discussion on ceremonial and possible ritual actions of the later Bronze Age, the art depicts humans bent backwards over ship designs, large display-axes

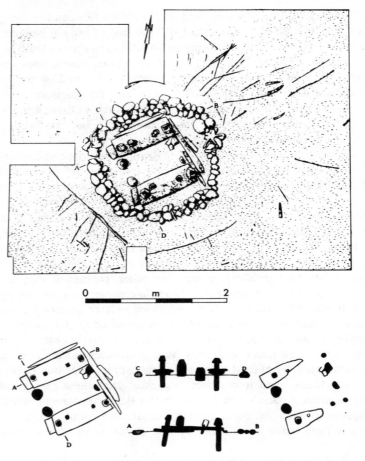

0   m   2

Fig. 189   Plan and sections of the wooden 'temple' at
Bargeroosterveld, Drenthe.
(From H. T. Waterbolk and W. van Zeist, *Helinium* I (1961))

placed amidships or held by humans, *lur*-blowers, snake designs, vehicles
(fig. 190) and a large variety of other motifs that remain without exact
identification and without interpretation.[126] Probably the only way by
which the art can successfully be studied is through detailed regional
surveys of discovery and location, in their relationships to settlements,
cemeteries, hoards and land-use of the Bronze Age. Some first steps have
been taken in this programme.

The end of the Bronze Age in the north cannot be determined with
precision. What evidence there is suggests a transition, not only from a

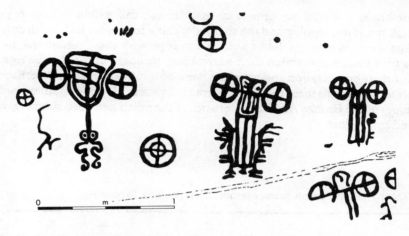

Fig. 190   Rock engraving of wheeled vehicles at Frannarp, Scania.
(From Fredsjo, Janson and Moberg 1969)

bronze-based to iron-based metallurgical tradition, but also an alteration
in social and economic activities. 'Period VI' of Denmark, as originally
proposed, marked this change, with a basic Late Bronze Age range of
equipment in hoards and graves but with the addition of material which
was either of iron or bronze with central European Hallstatt Iron Age
character.[127] Continuity between the Bronze Age and the Iron Age in
northern Europe is attested in many ways; and although this is not the
place for a detailed discussion, we can point to comparable subsistence
strategies, continuities in industries of bronze, gold, and pottery, and
continuity in burial sites and practices. However, that changes occurred
cannot be doubted; among these were some alteration in traditions which
allowed, or demanded, the breakage or burial of ceremonial objects such
as the *lurer* and elaborate gold or bronze vessels,[128] and the apparent
cessation in rock engravings. How much these changes were created by
human social developments, how much by environmental changes, we
cannot say.

The most significant alteration in the first millennium was probably
climatic. There is ample evidence for a deterioration in conditions,
beginning early in the millennium and culminating perhaps in the final
centuries. Summer temperatures had been higher than those of today,
but gradually a change to cooler and wetter summers must have altered
some of the established subsistence patterns. Marshland peats began to
increase in extent, and drowned forests demonstrate their impact. Some
agricultural lands were affected but possibly the greatest adaptation
required was for pasturing of cattle, because it may not have been possible

for outdoor winter pastures to be maintained; this would involve hay-making, leaf-cropping and the stalling of cattle indoors. The later Bronze Age societies were no doubt well able to cope with these conditions just as they had demonstrated their adaptability throughout the Bronze Age, but their organization and activities were no doubt affected, and perhaps imperceptibly to them the changes gradually succeeded one another until many of the Bronze Age characteristics of the north had been submerged and totally lost.

Table 19   Radiocarbon dates, northern Europe, later Bronze Age

Site	Lab no.	bc
North European plain		
Wingst, Lower Saxony, occupation	Hv–170	850 ± 200
Moers, Nordrhein-Westphalia, settlement	Hv–324	1020 ± 80
Ipwegermoor, Oldenburg, trackways	GrN–4394	1100 ± 55
	GrN–5422	1160 ± 65
Tarmstedt, Lower Saxony, burial vault range of 6 dates (Hv—)850 ± 85 to 1030 ± 155		
Gräpel, Lower Saxony, burial	Hv–821	700 ± 75
Mollenknob, Sylt, ditched site	KI–244	1110 ± 65
Asva, Estonia, fortified site	TA–81	570 ± 60
Bargeroostervelt, Holland, building	GrN–1552	1290 ± 65
Wervershoof, Holland, barrow	GrN–2359	1065 ± 55
	GrN–2168	1015 ± 45
Holsloot, Holland, barrow	GrN–1563	1110 ± 70
	GrN–1561	930 ± 70
	GrN–1562	940 ± 50
Hilvarenbaek, Holland, cemetery	GrN–1674	900 ± 60
Hoogkarspel, North Holland	GrN–5050	1070 ± 40
burial	GrN–5051	730 ± 50
settlement	GrN–5048	700 ± 45
Weelde, Flanders, Belgium	IRPA–49	930 ± 130
?occupation	IRPA–51	965 ± 160
	IRPA–52	1205 ± 160
Bovenkarspel, North Holland	GrN–7508	790 ± 40
Goirle, Holland, cemetery	GrN–4919	870 ± 50
	GrN–4920	830 ± 50
	GrN–4921	920 ± 50
Neerpelt, Belgium, cemetery	IRPA–2	517 ± 100
	IRPA–7	760 ± 150
	IRPA–18	311 ± 340
Hamont, Belgium, barrow	Lv–191	570 ± 120
	Lv–192	930 ± 150

Table 19—*cont.*

Site	Lab. no.	bc
Haps, Holland, cemetery	GrN–5687	1250±70
	GrN–5689	1060±45

Scandinavia
Simris, Scania, burials
   range of 6 dates (U–) 560±80 to 780±70

Slettebö, Rogaland, settlement	T–457	900±100
Lunden, Hedmark, elk antler mattock	T–2132	1020±70
Alstad, Oppland, elk antler mattock	T–2133	1050±80
Broby, Uppland, foundry pit	St–490	780±90
	St–491	520±90
Ö. Vemmerlöv, Sweden, burial	U–168	1135±120
Byneset, Norway, wooden bowl	T–23	560±140
	T–26	420±140
Andesta, Västmanland, burnt mound[129]	St–1869	745±106
Kirkebakkegaard, Zealand, occupation	K–1218	830±100
Dragby, Sweden, burials	U–80	550±90
	U–82	540±90
	U–81	1170±90
		and 675±90
	U–148	670±90
Broby, Uppland, burial	St–489	745±100

Hagestad, Scania[130]
   series of dates in first millennium bc

Garahaugen, Hordaland, Norway, burials	T–858	1380±80
	T–859	1080±70
	T–860	1130±80
Stenmark, North Jutland, occupation.	K–1373	1220±100
	K–1374	1120±100
	K–1375	1130±100
Vebbestrup, Jutland, alder ard	K–1495	910±100

Jyderup Skov, Zealand, burials
   range of 5 dates (K–)790±100 to 1040±100

Bjergagerojård, Denmark, pit	K–575	630±100
Löderup, Scania, burial	Lu–800	570±55
Valleberga, Scania, barrow	Lu–965	1140±55
	Lu–966	1190±55
Nordmannslågen, Hordaland, occupation	T–1230	1300±150
	T–1231	840±240
	T–1229	470±140
Stogaros, Telemark, occupation	T–1450	1030±170
Lonelega, Rogaland, rock shelter	T–1427	830±110
Bringsjord, Vest-Agder, ?burial	T–1041	520±80

Saerheim, Klepp, Rogaland pits and cairn
   range of 5 dates (T–) 390±70 to 660±80

Table 19—cont.

Site	Lab. no.	bc
Ingelstrop, Scania, burial	Lu–1177	1070±55
	Lu–1196	1140±60
	Lu–1210	780±55
Sörheim, Hordaland, barrow	T–1278	990±130
	T–1280	1800±90
Hunn, Borge, Ostfold, stone circle burial	T–1166	750±160
Håga, Uppland, buria, range of 5 dates *c.* 900		
Gårdlösa, Scania, cult site	Lu–996	810±55
Valleberga, Scania, settlement and cemetery	Lu–1092	940±55
	Lu–1093	1010±55

Notes

1 The divisions are conveniently set out by Broholm 1953. We include period III here in the later Bronze Age, unlike the traditional view referred to in chapter 6. A major distinction between periods III and IV–V is that grave goods are not consistently present in IV–V, whereas III is similar to EBA II in the presence of abundant grave goods.

2 Randsborg 1968, 1972 examines the transitions between periods II and III, and III and IV; Baudou 1960 has catalogued regional types. The Scandinavian terminology is often employed for other areas of northern Europe.

3 These are presented here as a general guide; the precise dating of the phases is not yet established.

4 Except in more northerly areas where metal products have rarely been recovered from sites.

5 The rise of the land relative to the sea during the second millennium resulted in the creation of valleys and the exposure of new areas of coastline, both suitable for Late Bronze Age occupation.

6 Compare the maps in Stenberger, n.d. fig. 32 (EBA), fig. 38 (LBA).

7 Baudou 1960.

8 E.g. a round house at Nordmannslagen (Hordaland), and rock shelter occupations also in southern Norway, all dated to the first millennium bc, demonstrates the metal-less nature of settlements in the north.

9 M. Strömberg, *Meddelanden från Lunds Universitets Historiska Museum,* 1973–4, 101–68; H. Thrane, *National Museums Arbejds* 1 (1975), 172–82; G. Kossack *et al., Bericht Römisch-Germanisch Kommission* 55 (1974), 261–427.

10 B. Salomonsson, *Forntid för framtid,*

1972, 144, 153; *Ale* 1973/3, 53–4; D. Widholm *Ale* 1974/3, 1–10.

11 Welinder 1975: cereal pollen increases in relation to plantain pollen, suggesting an augmented arable system at the expense of pastureland. It is believed that the Mälaren plain was exploited mainly for arable farming, with permanent settlements employing a shifting cultivation process.

12 S. Welinder, *Skånen Naturskyddsförenings Årsskrift* 61 (1974).

13 E.g. S. Hicks, *Terra* 87:3, 167–176, for Lake Kuusamo, Finland.

14 S. Andersson, *Göteborgs Arkeologiska Museums Årstryck*, 1970, records a long house, 30 m in length, from western Sweden, and the seven long houses from Lens-Saint-Servais (Liege), De Laet 1958, 134, may also be compared. The excavations at Bovenkarspel (N. Holland) have yielded house-plans, ditches and pits, as well as abundant domestic refuse; one carbonized seed of flax has been noted, J. Buurman and J. P. Pals, *BROB* 24 (1974), 107–11.

15 D. Widholm, *Kring Malmöhus* 4 (1973–4), 43–89; the animals represented were cattle, sheep or goat, and pig. A similar sunken dwelling from Högatorp (Scania) yielded pottery, a stone shaft-hole axe and a bronze pin, B. Salomonsson, *Ale* 1969/3, 54–5.

16 Jensen 1967.

17 The recent re-excavation of one of these has shown that the old land surface beneath the barrow had a wooden mortuary hut with straw mats on its floor, H. Thrane, *Fynske Minder*, 1973, 5–18.

18 The house compares well with north-German post-built houses at Norddorf and Berlin-Lichterfelde.

19 Stjernquist 1969.

20 S. Andersson, *Fyndrapporter*, 1970, 345–432.

21 H. Jananusson, *Fornvännen* 66 (1971), 171–85; H. Jananusson and G. Vahlne, *Riksantikvarieämbetet Rapport* 1975, B23, B64. Stockholm; the excavations are not yet complete.

22 A. Hyenstrand, *Fornvännen* 67 (1972), 35–44.

23 De Laet 1956, 126; a comparable structure at Bucholtwelmen (Dinslaken) in the western Ruhr was 11.5 × 3.3 m in size, with rather lightweight posts set about 1 m apart, R. Stampfuss, *Siedlungsfunde der jüngeren Bronze- und älteren Eisenzeit im westlichen Ruhrgebiet*, 1959, 73.

24 A. Hyenstrand, *Fornvännen* 61 (1966), 90–8.

25 A. Hyenstrand, *Tor* 12 (1967–8), 61–80.

26 S. Andersson, *Fyndrapporter*, 1973, 129–93.

27 J. Wigforss, *Fyndrapporter*, 1972, 193–224.

28 Gimbutas 1965, 434.

29 A. Il'inskaja, *SA* 1961, 26–45.

30 The establishment of trackway types, constructions and many sites are in Hayen 1957.

31 Butler 1969, pls 19–20; survey of Dutch finds, W. van Zeist and W. A. Casparie, *Spiegel Historiael* 2 (1967), 195–210.

32 See H. Christensen, *Sjöfartens historia baserad på undervattensarkeologi*, for descriptions of Bronze Age ship building; E. Nylén, *Antikvariskt Arkiv* 49 (1973), 3–51, and *Archaeologia Baltica Symposium*, 1974, for discussion on the role of ships in Gotland's Bronze Age.

33 Glob 1971, 139.

34 Called a 'cremated skeleton grave', perhaps more clearly a 'skeleton grave cremation'.

35 Stenberger n.d., 92; another grave, at Smerup (Thyholm), consisted of a cist containing cremated remains and a long bronze sword which just

fitted into the cist, Glob 1971, figs 55–6.

36 Stenberger n.d., 93; radiocarbon dates from the central grave are in the range 940–815 ± 100 bc. Other impressive graves of the later Bronze Age are not uncommon: the Lusehoj barrow near the Voldtofte settlement is a case in point, H. Thrane, *Fynske Minder*, 1973, 5–18.

37 A cairn at Syrhala (Halland), for example, only 10 m diameter, with small stone cist holding a cremation with one jet bead, J. Wigforss, *Fyndrapporter*, 1970, 101–37.

38 The tendency for the cairns to be situated near the sea is a reflection of the continued interest in maritime resources and transport throughout the Bronze Age, as well as the advantage that coastal area had for agriculture. During the late second and early first millennia, the levels of the sea in relation to the land was higher than it is today, and many cairns now inland were positioned along former bays and straits. One of these straits divided parts of the peninsula and the west of Gothenburg, and within the strait itself, a number of small islands were selected for cairn-building, while other cairns were placed along the contemporary shoreline. Stone-settings were positioned rather further inland: B. Sandberg, *Fyndrapporter*, 1973, 237–58. The contents of these cairns are varied, but some contain only cremations, while others have burials with grave-goods. One of the cairns contained a cist 3.2 m long placed near one edge of the cairn; it was divided into three compartments by two slabs. Cremated human bones in one segment were probably associated with some small gold rings, a bronze razor and miniature sword; there were later Iron Age deposits:

H. Olsson, *Fyndrapporter* 1970, 199–238.

39 E. Baudou, *Arkiv för norrländsk hembygdsforskning* 17 (1968), 5–209; review in *Fornvännen* 64 (1969) 122–5.

40 Glob 1971, fig. 59–60.

41 A. Hyenstrand, *Fornvännen* 63 (1968), 185–9.

42 K. Rex, *Fyndrapporter*, 1972, 511–530.

43 Many stone circles are firmly dated to Iron Age and later periods by association in the north, e.g. Viking graves at Lindholm Hoje at Norresundby.

44 Müller-Wille 1968–9.

45 L. Lundborg, *Svenska Fornminnesplatser* 5 (1974).

46 Ellmers 1971.

47 Baudou 1960, maps 53–5 demonstrates several North Jutland ovoid vessel forms, as well as more widespread biconicals.

48 Period VI represents a transition to the Iron Age; grave goods include characteristic Bronze Age bronzes as well as a few small iron objects.

49 Stenberger n.d. 106.

50 Broholm 1953 provides a range of illustrations.

51 Ellmers 1971.

52 Lange and Nowothnig 1971.

53 Wegewitz 1967.

54 The variation in burial practices in this region is remarkable. W. Urban, *Führer zu vor- und frühgeschichtliche Denkmälern* 7 (1967), 87–89, describes the major barrow of Grünhof-Tesperheide (Herzogtum-Lauenburg) which covered only a pair of burials. The barrow was placed on a high terrace of the Elbe, and was over 30 m in diameter and 2 m high. Incompletely excavated, it contained two primary burials in stone settings, and, off centre, a substantial burnt mortuary house, 4.4 by 3.8 m, set upon a larger pavement of stones; the

house had contained two burnt wooden coffins with a cremated adult female and a 2-year-old child. The adult had worn a bronze fibula and neckring, and a corded skirt decorated with spiral rolls of sheet bronze. The burning of the house and its contents had reddened a clay packed floor inside the house, and subsequently the remains of all had been buried by stones, both inside and outside the house. The barrow had then been piled over the cairn. The grave-goods date this particular burial to c. 1200 bc. K. Kersten, *Offa* 1 (1936), 56.

55 E.g., M. Desittere, *Helinium* 14 (1974), 105–34.

56 S. de Laet, J. Nenquin and P. Spitaels, *Contributions a l'Etude de la Civilisation des Champs d'Urnes en Flandres*, 1958; W. Kimmig, *Helinium* 10 (1970), 39–51; useful survey in De Laet 1974, ch. 9; Desittere 1968; Verwers 1969.

57 Driehaus 1969; Schaaff 1969.

58 De Laet 1974, ch. 9.

59 Called 'Niederrheinische Grabhügelkultur'.

60 Important cemeteries: Court-Saint-Etienne (Belg. Brabant) with Urnfield and Iron Age graves, including richly-furnished 'warrior' graves; Temse (Flanders).

61 E.g. Lommel-Kattenbos (Campine).

62 Riethoven and Goirle (Limburg and N. Brabant); one grave at Goirle contains five inverted urns, one of which held four small pots, one held other pots, and three held cremated remains, G. J. Verwers, *Analecta Praeh. Leidensia* 2 (1966), 33–48.

63 E.g. Oldenzaal, Gasteren: De Laet 1958; Butler 1969, 75, fig. 32, 34, 35.

64 M.-E. Marien, *Trouvailles du champ d'urnes et des tombelles hallstattiennes de Court-Saint-Etienne* 1958; de Laet 1974, ch. 10.

65 In the cemetery at Raden (Güstrow) stone settings were spaced over an area 250 × 150 m, and most of the cremated remains were contained in rather plain cylinder neck urns. The grave-goods, burnt along with the bodies, consisted of bronze rings, armlets or a brooch. The cemetery contained 10 identifiable individuals: 2 infants, 2 juveniles, 4 adults, 1 mature adult, 1 'senile' adult: H. Keiling, *Bodendenkmalpflege in Mecklenburg*, 1970, 193–224.

66 The cemetery at Neu Grebs in the Elbe valley consisted of a series of cremations placed beneath a number of small cairns or settings and sealed by a turf barrow 20 m in diameter and at least 1.6 m high. The central cremation grave was furnished with a gold ring and flint arrowhead, with a stone cairn (4 × 5 × 0.6 m) over the remains. A contemporary second grave, with smaller cairn, yielded an amber bead, a heavy bronze pin and a bronze box; the box has a cylindrical body, and flat lid held by a bar passing through loops. The sides and base of the box are heavily-decorated with ribs and grooves in bands and arcs. Other, later, graves contained metal and flint arrowheads, bracelets, studs, pins and rings; the contrast in grave-goods with other cemeteries is striking, although barrow-building is more common than flat cemeteries at this time: F. Just, *Bodendenkmalpflege in Mecklenburg* 1968, 191–210.

67 U. Schoknecht, *Bodendenkmalpflege in Mecklenburg*, 1965.

68 F. Just, *Bodendenkmalpflege in Mecklenburg*, 1960, 7–90.

69 H. Keiling, *Bodendenkmalpflege in Mecklenburg*, 1968, 211–64.

70 H. Keiling, *Bodendenkmalpflege in Mecklenburg*, 1962, 1–440.

71 The Rezne (Estonia) cemetery of barrows contained several hundred burials, both inhumations and cremations, of the later Bronze Age, with subsequent inhumations believed to be of the Iron Age; it appears that the cemetery was used for many decades, Gimbutas 1963, 68; 1965, 432.

72 Gimbutas 1965, 420 with refs.

73 The Nacław barrow in eastern Pomerania yielded a conical necked urn, local forms of ornament and a short sword claimed to represent an import from the south, Gimbutas 1965, 427; the inhumation from Trzebiatów in the same region was associated with ornaments and plain pottery vessels, mostly representing the products of active ceramic and metal industries in the immediate area, Gimbutas 1965, 428.

74 Other important barrow cemeteries are those at Šlažai (Lithuania), Alknikiai (Samland), and Kalnieši (Latvia): E. Šturms, *Die ältere Bronzezeit im Ostbalticum* (1936); Gimbutas 1965, 425.

75 C. Engel, *Untersuchungen über Siedlungstätigkeit und Kulturgruppen im vorgeschichtlichen Ostpreussen* I (1935).

76 Baudou 1960 provides a useful set of maps to illustrate these points. For Finland, see Meinander 1954; C. Carpelan, *Kuml* 1973–4, 286–7 identifies local industries in the later Bronze Age but many products were probably made in the centres in Denmark and Sweden. The finds from e.g. Laihia, Rauma, Kiukainen, are but a few of the objects found in mainly coastal situations. The island of Åland, between Sweden and Finland, has also yielded supplies of Nordic metal objects. The Lake Inari region of Finland, at 69° North, represents one of the most northerly find-spots for bronzes.

77 Thrane 1975, esp. fig. 128.

78 U. Schoknecht, *Bodendenkmalpflege in Mecklenburg*, 1969, 1974.

79 Randsborg 1968 discusses the transition from period II to III in detail; illustrations most conveniently in Broholm 1952.

80 Swords have a vast literature. For the ubiquitous Nenzingen type, E. Sprockhoff 1931 presented one of the first surveys.

81 Broholm gives a view of the major forms, 1953, but Thrane 1975 provides more meaningful detail with full references; Randsborg 1972 discusses the change from period II to IV.

82 Baudou 1960 has provided subtypes and maps, including some treatment of northern Germany.

83 E.g. Baudou 1960, maps 8–15.

84 H. Thrane, *Aarbøger* 1963, 50–99; J. Nenquin, *Helinium* 15 (1975), 38–42. For the metal wheels from Stade: *FvfD* 29 (1976), 132.

85 The range of decorative elements is best seen through the general descriptive works noted above, but, e.g., Sprockhoff 1962 presents a useful corpus of selected designs, particularly of ship-like and bird-like figures.

86 The pair of decorated buckets from Granzin (Lübz), and amphora from Mariesminde (Fyn) carry dot and circle designs incorporating bird or duck designs; the workmanship on vessels such as these is likely to have emanated from specialists, but whether full-time or not cannot be said. Granzin: P. Patay, *Bodendenkmalpflege in Mecklenburg* 1971, 265–72; Mariesminde: Thrane 1975, fig. 87.

87 For metal vessels, Sprockhoff 1930: H. Thrane, *Acta Archaeologica* 33 (1962), 109–63; Thrane 1975. For shields, Coles 1962; B. Gräslund,

Acta Archaeologica 38 (1967). Gold vessels: Broholm 1953, nos 114–16.

88 Broholm 1952, no. 335.

89 Sprockhoff 1930, 124; cf. Acholshausen in the mid-Main valley, Pescheck 1975.

90 Winged axes: Thrane 1975 fig. 55; horse-fittings fig. 74; pins and armlets fig. 103; swords figs 208–9.

91 E.g. Stjernquist 1967.

92 E.g. H. Thrane, *Skalk* 1971 no. 4, 8–12; H. Thrane, *Aarbøger* 1972, 71–134, suggests that these axes were brought in for their weight in metal, presumably destined for the melting-pot.

93 K. Tackenberg, *Die jüngere Bronzezeit in Nordwestdeutschland.* Hildesheim 1971; this is a useful source book for material culture.

94 Rowlands 1976.

95 Thrane 1975 shows the range and variation of types and their scattered find places, maps 81, 89, 95; full description, H. Thrane, *Acta Archaeologica* 36 (1965), 157–207.

96 Thrane 1975, 231.

97 Thrane 1975, 263.

98 Baudou 1960; Randsborg 1972; Thrane 1975.

99 De Laet 1974, 349–63; de Laet 1958, 128–31; Thrane 1975, 231.

100 J. Butler, *Palaeohistoria* 8 (1960), 108–22; *Nieuwe Drentse Volksalmanak* 83 (1965),163–98; Butler 1969.

101 Thrane 1975, 163.

102 Butler 1963 has presented the evidence.

103 Driehaus 1969; Schaaff 1969.

104 Lange and Nowothnig 1971.

105 Ellmers 1971; the earlier Bronze Age Gönnebek gold cup is also a product of this region.

106 E. Sprockhoff, *Studien zur Vor- und Frühgeschichte* 1940; *Bericht der Römisch-Germanischen Kommission* 31 (1941); *Offa* 11 (1952); J. Butler 1963, 219 (map); Urban 1967; Thrane 1975, fig. 128.

107 Brandt 1965; C. F. C. Hawkes and R. R. Clarke in I. L. Foster and L. Alcock (eds), *Culture and Environment*, 1965, 193–250.

108 Gimbutas 1965, 422, map p. 431; H. Arbman, *PZ* 24 (1933), 3–22; hoards of many local axes, Kalinówka Kóscielna, and Česai, Merkine: Gimbutas 1965, fig. 295.

109 Gimbutas 1965, fig. 284.

110 E.g. Glob 1969, 315; H. Hundt, *J. Römisch-Germanisch Zentralmuseum Mainz* 2 (1955), suggests the same for Mecklenburg.

111 E.g. *Inventaria Archaeol.* DK5, 6, 9 1967: Basland (Jutland), socketed axes, spearheads, sickle, possibly for distribution; Lovskal (Jutland), broken axes etc, for the melting-pot; Kostraede (Zealand), strainer, belt-box, belt-plates, fibula, 2 gold spirals, probably personal possessions.

112 Stenberger n.d.; see also Broholm 1952 no. 253; *Skalk* 1978/2, 3–7.

113 Coles 1962; B. Gräslund, *Acta Archaeologica* 38 (1967), 59–71; Z. Bukowski, *Archeologia* 22 (1971), 42–76.

114 H. Norling-Christensen, *Acta Archaeologica* 17 (1946).

115 Broholm, Larsen and Skjerne, 1949.

116 Most recently, C. Lund, *Musik i forntiden. Klang i flints och brons.* Stockholm 1974; *Fran istid till vikingen i norden. Kland i flints och brons,* Stockholm, 1974; full assessment in Broholm, Larsen and Skjerne 1949; various gramophone records exist, Nationalmuseet, *Klange fra Danmark's Bronzealder-Lurer,* 1966.

117 The Pinedalen (Scania) hoard, found in a stone-covered pit, contained two *lur*-discs, four rattles, two large and two small bridle pieces, two curved tubes and two armlets. The tubes are decorated with horned heads, and the hoard

itself is probably the most remarkable 'votive' deposit recently found in Sweden, L. Larsson, *Meddelanden från Lunds Universitets Historiska Museum*, 1975.

118 Complete set of illustrations, Broholm 1953, nos 313–17; 320–3 for other figures.

119 The original drawing is exhibited in Glob 1974, 164; see also *Aarbøger*, 1952, *Kuml*, 1961.

120 Another find, from Stockhult (Scania), contained axes, spear, collars and belt-plates, armlets and rings, as well as two human male figurines wearing loin cloths and conical hats with narrow brims; the arms were separate and are lost, L. Cederschiöld, *Objets* 3 (1970), 37–47. Other figurine finds, perhaps also wheeled carts and sun-bearing chariots, have been reported from the north, but only dismal records exist of their discovery and destruction.

121 A. Norden, *Bildgatan i Bronsaldersgraven vid Kivik*, 1917; C.-A. Moberg, *Kiviksgraven. Svenska Fornminnesplatser* 1 (1963). The nature of the burial in the great cairn is not known; the suggested date is *c*. 1000 bc.

122 H. Thrane, *Fynske Minder*, 1974, 96–114.

123 Glob 1974, 162.

124 H. T. Waterbolk and W. van Zeist, *Helinium* 1 (1961), 5–19; the hoards: J. J. Butler, *Palaeohistoria* 8 (1960) 103–26.

125 Marstrander 1963; C.-A. Moberg, *Norwegian Archaeol. Review* 3 (1970), 98–102. E.g. Horsefeld, Kr. Stade, grave with razor and knife each decorated with ship engraving; *FvfD* 29 (1976), 122.

126 For further references to the art, see n. 116–26, page 332; Burenhult 1973 provides objective illustrations of much of southern Swedish art; Fredsjö, Janson and Moberg 1969 give a survey of the areas of engravings in Sweden, including the northern art provinces.

127 Broholm 1953; Baudou 1960, map 58. A find at Hassle (Närke) represents both the transition and the continuity: the hoard consists of an enormous cauldron containing the squashed remains of two grooved buckets and two swords, as well as twelve bronze and iron bosses. The buckets and swords are of central European Hallstatt type, and the cauldron is believed to have been made in Etruria in the seventh or sixth century, Stenberger, n.d., 112. The traditional date for the transition is the seventh century, possibly the sixth, but E. Nylen, *Antikvariskt Arkiv* 44 (1972) has examined the evidence for the transition from a full Late Bronze Age to the Iron Age, and suggests that 300 bc is a more likely date; this conclusion has not been examined by us in detail, but its implications are considerable.

128 E.g. the Rezne barrow in Estonia was apparently used by communities over several centuries, with alternating inhumations and cremations, and with long-standing traditions of deposition of horse teeth, pottery, animal bones and axes: Gimbutas 1963, 68; see also L. V. Vankina, *KSIIMK* 42 (1952).

129 See *Radiocarbon* 9, 417 ff. for other mounds.

130 *Hist. Tidskrift för Skåneland*, 1961–1965.

12 Conclusion

We have left many parts of Europe hovering on the threshold of history. By the end of the Late Bronze Age we are able to speculate with some pretension at accuracy on the identity of many of the peoples of eastern, southern and even central Europe. Within two centuries they were starting to emerge into the relative light of historical day. By that time they were mostly using iron as a primary material for tools, and as such do not concern us here. In no case do we have any definite historical records of European peoples – outside the Aegean area – in the period before iron-using became standard. From written sources in the eastern Mediterranean we may catch glimpses of possible non-Greek Europeans, but they are no more than glimpses: the Shardana, the Shekeresh and others (?Sardinians, Sikels), who formed part of the confederation of 'Peoples of the Sea' responsible for so much destruction in the Near East around 1200 BC.[1]

Apart from this we have to depend on later classical sources which speak of barbarian tribes or groups of tribes, mostly on the fringes of the classical world but in some cases extending far beyond it. Chief among these are the Illyrians and the Celts, both of whom we know were present in central and southern Europe early in the Iron Age. We have touched on the possible reasons for attributing them to an earlier period, but certainty is unfortunately not within our reach. It seems possible that all of them reached their later positions at much the same time, in a 'migration of peoples'; but the archaeological record is powerless to speak more precisely of the date of such a migration. The most commonly accepted hypothesis is that the period of turmoil in the historical areas – the Aegean, Anatolia, the Levant and Egypt – might also be a troubled time for the barbarian world, that is, from the mid-thirteenth century BC on; it is tempting to see a causal connection between the supposed events in each area. If movements of peoples did take place around this time – which is possible, but hardly susceptible of proof – then most of the

Urnfield period in continental Europe must have been occupied by Celts, Illyrians and the numerous other tribal groupings who appear subsequently. This is the likeliest theory; would that the archaeological record could supply clear proof that it really was so.

By the end of the Bronze Age the use of iron was becoming widespread and, of course, in the succeeding period it was standard in some areas. Iron-smelting first appears in the Near East towards the end of the third millennium BC, and through the second millennium it seems to have been restricted to that area. Objects of hammered iron do occasionally appear in Europe, but smelting is not found until the first millennium. In Greece the first iron objects begin to appear in the eleventh century;[2] in Romania and Jugoslavia the odd piece is datable to the ninth but more comes from the eighth;[3] in central Europe objects of iron become frequent in the eighth century but are known already in the tenth, and the distinctive signs of their use indicate their presence even in the eleventh.[4] In western and northern Europe the signs are less clear until the seventh century, but the finding of an iron awl dated 1170 bc on a trackway at Bargeroosterveld (Drenthe) shows us that the metal was known, maybe even well-known, to the inhabitants of Late Bronze Age Holland.[5] There can therefore be no clear-cut division between Bronze and Iron Ages; rather, we have to assume that the knowledge of ironworking and the quest for iron sources were already of paramount importance in most of Europe by the seventh century; in some areas the use of iron for weapons was widespread, in others its start was delayed, but its desirability no smaller. The Bronze Age ends when people's minds had turned to the important matter of securing iron and making iron objects demonstrably more efficient than bronze ones; but at the same time they continued to produce bronze objects, much as stone continued in use into the Bronze Age.

We have seen that the basis of life throughout the Bronze Age was a mixed economy wherever conditions permitted, with relatively minor shifts of emphasis between types of production. Settlement was generally on low-lying sites near water except in those special cases where defence was necessary – and sometimes even then. In spite of the underlying continuity of economy, each part of the Bronze Age does seem to have its special character. The early stages appear somewhat tentative, mostly without large-scale habitations but already with rich burials. Large monuments, especially in the west, were being built, perhaps in continuation of Neolithic practices. Subsequently the course of events changed; new horizons of metalwork appear as if out of the blue, hill-top fortifications begin; settlements are abandoned and re-settled. This time, c. 1500–1200 BC, was perhaps especially one of change. Later, a markedly homogeneous material culture became spread over most of Europe: this was the time of climax and maturity, the period of the great flowering of the Bronze Age.

During the course of the Bronze Age a number of important changes took place – changes that lend the period its characteristic appearance and distinguish it from anything that had gone before. Many of these changes were in settlement and material culture which we have attempted to describe in this book. Others were of a more general nature. Perhaps the most obvious of these is the rise of the privileged. In most parts of Bronze Age Europe one finds – in distinction to Neolithic practice – 'rich' graves and 'poor' graves side by side. The rich graves vary in richness, but the richest are remarkable not only for their splendour but also for the amount of potential wealth encapsulated in them and thus lost to the society that produced them. It is hard to think of this process in terms other than those of aggrandisement of the few, the rise of the élite, and the start of social stratification. Once acquired, this habit was never lost: it persists to the present day.

Another feature of the Bronze Age is the development of long-distance trade. In the Neolithic, stone, flint, obsidian, shells and amber were exchanged, sometimes on a large scale and in an organized fashion. During the Bronze Age the extent of this commerce was greatly increased as was its range. Movement of metal – in ingot form or as finished objects – took place on a large scale; workshops may have been set up specifically to deal with the satisfaction of these commercial demands; travelling smiths, entrepreneurs and organizers must have been at work. Perhaps most remarkable is the establishment of long-distance trading channels, regularly connecting widely separated areas. The amber trade from the Baltic to Greece is a prime example of this.

Especially characteristic of the later part of the Bronze Age is the rise of fortified hill-top settlements and stockades. In many parts a fashion for fortifying settlements set in, perhaps around 1000 BC, or even earlier. Ramparts were elaborately constructed of timber, earth and stone; the practice of 'timber-lacing' also seems to have been common to more than one area. The existence of these forts speaks for a prolonged period of inter-tribal warfare; it may be that their start should be seen in connection with the spread of Celtic and other people across Europe. Alternatively it may be that the box rampart was an invention like any other, designed to improve the means of defence, and therefore widely adopted throughout Europe.

By the end of the Bronze Age many of the skills and features of daily life that were to prevail over the next millennium and a half were already present. From the start of the Bronze Age one can descry an acceleration in the development and variety of these skills, some of which were in an embryonic state already in the Eneolithic. The use of most of the metals, the cutting of precious stone, the making of glass and of very fine (though not glazed) pottery, the development of trade and the means of transport (both vehicles and trackways) to promote it, the mining and panning of salt, and – perhaps most important – the rise of proto-urban communities in which craft specialization must have played an increasingly important role: these skills and customs are ones which survived unchanged or developed into and through the Iron and on into the Middle Ages.

One can perhaps best assess prospects for the future of European Bronze Age studies by mentioning what seems to us the most important work of the last few years. Broadly speaking, such work can be divided into field-work and its publication on the one hand, and analysis, with results from related disciplines, on the other. As far as excavation is concerned there has been a welcome shift from cemetery to settlement excavation, though this process could well go further. Until radically new techniques present themselves, the excavation of graves does not seem likely to add greatly to our knowledge, except in areas where they are very few (like Bulgaria) or very poorly studied in the early days of barrow excavation (Britain or the Soviet Union). Settlement excavation, on the other hand, has much to offer, particularly total and area-excavation in skilful hands. The recent work at Tószeg illustrates this, and we look forward to comparable work elsewhere.

Specific goals in excavation should, then, be detailed and careful examination of settlements of all sorts. Here the use of ancillary techniques is essential. It goes without saying that macrofaunal and floral remains should be preserved and analysed; work on microscopic material, though less well-advanced, is potentially even more fruitful. Here the excavation of waterlogged deposits will be most helpful; witness the wells at Berlin-Lichterfelde or recent work on Swiss lake-sites.

Systematic excavation of hill-forts is also needed, especially in south-central and southern Europe. The north is quite well-served, but very few southern forts have had more than the odd rampart section cut. Area-excavation inside the forts, and more extensive examination of the ramparts, should pay rich rewards.

Side by side with excavation should go field surveying. In many areas few sites are yet known; in many the pattern is haphazard. The practice of positively *looking for* sites has yet to be developed in some areas. Until it is, our knowledge of settlement location will remain scanty.

On the whole, however, we feel that it is in the second bracket, comprising analysis, that the most fruitful advances will be made. Analysis, in the past, has usually proceeded by means of typology, and in spite of our professed intention to avoid typological description it will not have escaped the reader's notice that some has crept in: indeed it would be impossible for it to be otherwise in a period at present dominated by objects rather than events. Typological study, however, cannot ultimately help to *understand* the Bronze Age; much good time has to be spent simply trying to understand the typologies rather than the human element behind them.

The typological approach has dominated Bronze Age studies throughout this century and the objective observer may justly wonder whether it is any longer significantly increasing our knowledge. In this connection the magnificent series *Prähistorische Bronzefunde* must be mentioned. Unlike so many series in the past, this has set out to provide *complete* coverage of bronze finds in each area, principally in Europe. It is obvious that this is a vast undertaking and will eventually run to many scores of volumes; but precisely because it aims to be comprehensive it should facilitate the detailed unravelling of complicated production networks. We would even go so far as to suggest that typological analysis in publications should halt until the series is complete: let us first be sure what the finds are, then let us analyse them.

Analysis of Bronze Age social organization has until recently been conducted on an unacceptably subjective level. A number of studies have now shown how a more objective standard can be achieved, principally by detailed examination of grave contents. This work is potentially of great importance; we would like to see it increased in scope and taking in large numbers of cemeteries in different parts of Europe. The use of ethnographic parallels for the understanding of social organization is more risky, however; we would prefer to see their application restricted to the study of technical matters, in which they can be of great value.

Physical anthropology undoubtedly also has a part to play, though the value of its contribution so far is arguable. The application on a larger scale of techniques from other fields – like blood-group testing on skeletal remains – may provide the specific information that metrical analysis has so far failed to give. For this, however, very large numbers of tests will be necessary, and any programme aiming at providing answers along these lines will take many years to complete.

The most hopeful lines of approach – environmental and economic studies – are already being applied, but their scope needs to be extended greatly. Pollen analysis, sedimentology and pedology can all be used to tie down more firmly the major climatic and other natural events that occurred during the period. There is a danger of circular argument in that archaeological finds are sometimes used to date pedological or palynological events, when what we really need is the reverse; but applied with caution these disciplines have a great deal to offer (cf. pp. 5, 32, 337). The role of economic studies is a little harder to assess, as it has barely got beyond the descriptive to the interpretative stage. There are several prerequisites for success in this field. The problem must first be tackled in excavation with improved sampling techniques for the recovery of floral and faunal remains (froth flotation, water-sieving) and their painstaking subsequent identification; then such a programme must be applied across a wide range in time and space. Only then will patterns of economic exploitation begin to emerge. Recent work in Italy and, to a lesser extent, Poland is starting to fill out some of the details of economic life in the Bronze Age by these means.

We leave till last two purely technical matters, but ones which can have a profound effect on our knowledge of the Bronze Age: physical analysis, particularly of metal; and scientific dating methods. We have already discussed the uses (and abuses) of metal analysis (pp. 13, 18); in the future, programmes of work using such analyses will have to be thought out very carefully. Many objects have now been drilled more than once; this cannot go on indefinitely, as there is some onus even on scientists to preserve the past, not destroy it. But more important, it is essential that any future programme is able to define very clearly at the outset what it hopes to achieve and how it hopes to do it. Only if the answers are likely to be absolutely specific will it be worth proceeding.

The other scientific method, radiocarbon dating, is of course subject to correction and change, but one may still hope that it will eventually provide an accurate absolute chronology. Certainly it can provide a relative chronology by indicating synchronisms, and for that alone it can prove of very great value to Bronze Age studies. The chronology of the Eneolithic and Bronze Age in the USSR, for instance, would be quite unknown if it were not for the long series of dates available. But there are still many areas with few or no dates at all; central Europe is among the most poorly served, although it is one of the most important areas of Europe during the course of the Bronze Age. Only absolute dating methods, whether this or any other, can ultimately solve the main controversies over contact between cultures. The acquisition of samples from good contexts in central Europe must be a high priority, especially in the early Bronze Age. Such a dating programme may also help to resolve some of the difficulties over calibration that we have mentioned. At present the calibrated radiocarbon chronology is still in direct conflict with traditional notions of chronology, and it looks as if one or the other must be in error. At present we can do no more than state the problem, and look forward to its solution.

We have attempted in this book to trace the main developments in

European prehistory between *c.* 2000 BC and 700 BC. It will have become evident that those 1300 years were a time of great change for the communities who lived in them. The Bronze Age, in fact, is *the* great formative period for later European history, the period when most of the subsequent social, economic and technical developments occurred that continued unchanged, except for shifts of emphasis, until the Renaissance. Only a few of the major arts and skills, most notably writing, were not present somewhere in 'barbarian' Europe during the Bronze Age, and most of the rest were present in Greece. It is this above all that makes the Bronze Age a period of crucial importance in the development of European culture and society.

Notes

1 R. D. Barnett, *CAH*, II, 2, 3rd edn, 1975, ch. 28; Kimmig 1964; N. Sandars, *The Sea Peoples*, 1978.

2 A. Snodgrass, *The Dark Age of Greece*, 1971, ch. 5, esp. 217ff.

3 M. Rusu, *Dacia* n.s. 7 (1963), 177–210; K. Horedt, *Dacia* n.s. 8 (1964), 119–32; Z. Székely, *Dacia* n.s. 10 (1966), 209–19; R. Vasić, *Kulturne grupe starijet grozdenog doba u Jugoslaviji*, 1973, 19ff. with refs.; A. László, *SCIV* 26 (1975), 17–39, with some earlier finds (Ha A).

4 Kimmig 1964, 274ff. (list of early iron finds in Europe). R. Pleiner, *Základy slovanského železářského hutnictví v Českých zemích*, 1958, 72–80, and *Staré evropské kovářství*, 1962; J. Bouzek, *ZfA* forthcoming (article kindly lent prior to publication).

5 J. J. Butler, *IXᵉ Congrès UISPP, Nice*, 1976, Résumés, 431.

Bibliography

ADLER, H. (1967) *Frühe Bronzezeit in Linz-St. Peter* (Linzer Archäologische Forschungen, 3); *Das Urgeschichtliche Gräberfield Linz-St. Peter, Teil 2, Die frühe Bronzezeit.* Linz : Archaeological Museum.

ALMAGRO GORBEA, M. (1972) La espada de Guadalajara y sus parallelos peninsulares. *Trabajos de Prehistoria* 29, 55–82.

ALMAGRO GORBEA, M. (1974) Orfebreria del Bronce Final en la Península Ibérica. *Trabajos de Prehistoria* 31, 39–100.

ANATI, E.(1961) *Camonica Valley.* New York: Knopf.

ANNABLE, F. K. and SIMPSON, D. D. A. (1964) *Guide Catalogue of the Neolithic and Bronze Age Collections in Devizes Museum.* Devizes: Wilts. Arch. Nat. Hist. Soc.

APARICIO PEREZ, J. (1976) *Estudio económico y social de la Edad del Bronce Valenciano.* Valencia.

APSIMON, A. (1969) The earlier Bronze Age in the north of Ireland. *Ulster J. Arch.* 32, 28–72.

ARRIBAS, A. (1976) A new basis for the study of the Eneolithic and Bronze Age in south-east Spain. In J.V.S. Megaw (ed.) *To Illustrate the Monuments: Essays on Archaeology presented to Stuart Piggott.* London: Thames and Hudson.

ARRIBAS PALAU, A., PAREJA LOPEZ, E., MOLINA GONZALEZ, F., ARTEAGA MATUTE, O. and MOLINA FAJARDO, F. (1974) *Excavaciones en el Poblado de la Edad del Bronce 'Cerro de la Encina' Monachil (Granada).* Excavaciones Arqueologicas en España 81.

ASHBEE, P. (1960) *The Bronze Age Round Barrow in Britain.* London: Phoenix.

ATKINSON, R. J. C. (1956) *Stonehenge.* London: Hamish Hamilton.

BANNER, J. and BÓNA, I. (1974) *Mittelbronzezeitliche Tell-Siedlung bei Békés.* Budapest: Akad. Kiadó.

BARFIELD, L. (1971) *Northern Italy Before Rome.* London: Thames and Hudson.

BARKER, G. W. W. (1975) Prehistoric territories and economies in central Italy. In E. S. Higgs (ed.) *Palaeoeconomy*, 111–75, Cambridge: Cambridge University Press.

BATTAGLIA, R. (1943) La palafitta del Lago di Ledro nel Trentino. *Memorie del Museo di Storia Naturale della Venezia Tridentina* 7, 3–63.

BAUDOU, E. (1960) *Die regionale und chronologische Einteilung der jüngeren Bronzezeit im Nordischen Kreis.* Stockholm: Almquist and Wiksell.

BEAULIEU, J.-L. La végétation pendant le Post-Glaciare dans le Massif Central et les Alpes Méridionales. In Guilaine 1976, 59–66.

BEEX G., and HULST, R. S. (1968) A Hilversum-Culture settlement near Nijnsel, Municipality of St Oedenrode, North Brabant. *BROB* 18, 117–30.

BEITRÄGE (1969) *Beiträge zur Lausitzer Kultur.* (Arbeits-und Forschungsberichte zur sächsischen Bodendenkmalpflege, Beiheft 7) Berlin.

BENAC, A., and ČOVIĆ, B. (1956) *Glasinac. Katalog der Vorgeschichtlichen Sammlung des Landesmuseums in Sarajevo.* Teil I *Bronzezeit.* Sarajevo: Archaeological Museum.

BENKOVSKY-PIVOVAROVÁ, Z. (1975) Zur Genese der Urnenbestattung in der Lausitzer Kultur Mährens, der Slowakei und Südpolens. *JIVUF* (1975), 61–72.

BERCIU, D. (1961) Die Verbicioara-Kultur. Vorbericht über eine neue, in Rümanien entdeckte bronzezeitliche Kultur. *Dacia*, n.s. 5, 123–63.

BERCIU, D. (1967) *Romania before Burebista.* London: Thames and Hudson.

BERNABÒ BREA, L. (1966) *Sicily Before the Greeks* (2nd edn). London: Thames and Hudson.

BIETTI SESTIERI, A-M. (1973) The metal industry of continental Italy, 13th to the 11th century BC, and its connection with the Aegean. *PPS* 39, 383–424.

BILL, J. (1973) *Die Glockenbecherkultur und die frühe Bronzezeit im französischen Rhonebecken und ihre Beziehungen zur Südwestschweiz.* Schweizerische Gesellschaft für Ur- and Frühgeschichte.

BILLIG, G. (1958) *Die Aunjetitzer Kultur in Sachsen.* Leipzig: Veröff. des Landesmus. für Vorgeschichte, Band 7.

BLANCE, B. (1964) The Argaric Bronze Age in Iberia. *Revista de Guimarães* 74, 129–42.

BLANCE, B. (1971) *Die Anfänge der Metallurgie auf der Iberischen Halbinsel.* Berlin: Römisch-Germanisches Zentralmuseum.

BOCQUET, A. (1976) Les civilisations de l'Age du Bronze dans les Alpes. In Guilaine 1976, 483–94.

BÓNA, I. (1958) 'Chronologie der Hortfunde vom Koszider-Typus. *AAH* 9, 213–43.

BÓNA, I. (1975) *Die mittlere Bronzezeit Ungarns und ihre südöstlichen Beziehungen*. Budapest: Akad. Kiadó.

BONNAMOUR, L., MORDANT, C. and NICOLARDOT, J.-P. (1976) Les civilisations de l'Age du Bronze en Bourgogne. In Guilaine 1976, 601–617.

BOUZEK, J., KOUTECKÝ, D. and NEUSTUPNÝ, E. (1966) *The Knovíz Settlement of North-West Bohemia*. Prague: National Museum.

BRANDT, K.-H. (1965) *Bremen, Verden, Hoya*. FvfD 2, Mainz: Philipp von Zabern.

BRIARD, J. (1965) *Les Dépôts Bretons et l'Age du Bronze Atlantique*. Rennes: Laboratoire d'Anthropologie Préhistorique de la Faculté des Sciences de Rennes.

BRIARD, J. (1974) Bronze Age Cultures: 1800–600 BC. In S. Piggott, G. Daniel and C. McBurney (eds), *France before the Romans*, 131–56, London: Thames and Hudson.

BRIARD, J. (1975a) Acculturations Néolithiques et Campaniformes dans les tumulus Armoricains. In de Laet 1976, 34–44.

BRIARD, J. (1975b) Nouvelles découvertes sur les tumulus Armoricains. *Archaeologia Atlantica* 1, 17–32.

BRIARD, J. (1976a) Les civilisations de l'Age du Bronze en Armorique. In Guilaine 1976, 561–73.

BRIARD, J. (1976b) *L'Age du Bronze en Europe Barbare*. Toulouse: Editions des Hespérides.

BROHOLM, H. C. (1952-3) *Danske Oldsager*. III *Aeldre Bronzealder* (1952), IV *Yngre Bronzealder* (1953). Copenhagen: Gyldendal.

BROHOLM, H. C. and HALD, M. (1935) *Danske Bronzealders Dragter*. Nordiske Fortidsminder 2, Hefte 5–6.

BROHOLM, H. C., LARSEN, W. P. and SKJERNE, G. (1949) *The Lures of the Bronze Age*. Copenhagen: Gyldendal.

BRONGERS, J. A. and WOLTERING, P. J. (1973) Prehistory in the Netherlands; an economic-technological approach. *BROB* 23, 7–47.

BRUKNER, B., JOVANOVIĆ, B. and TASIĆ, N. (1974) *Praistorija Vojvodine*. Novi Sad: Monogr. Institute za izucavanje istorije Vojvodine.

BRUNN, W. A. VON (1954a) *Steinpackungsgräber von Köthen. Ein Beitrag zur Kultur der Bronzezeit Mitteldeutschlands*. Berlin: Akad. Verlag.

BRUNN, W. A. VON (1954b) Eine unbekannte Bronzeschale aus Ostdeutschland. *Germania* 32, 284–93.

BRUNN, W. A. VON (1959) *Bronzezeitliche Hortfunde*, Teil 1 *Die Hortfunde der frühen Bronzezeit aus Sachsen-Anhalt, Sachsen, Thüringen*. Berlin: Akad. Verlag.

BRUNN, W. A. VON (1968) *Mitteldeutsche Hortfunde der jüngeren Bronzezeit*. Berlin: de Gruyter.

BURENHULT, G. (1973) *The Rock Carvings of Götaland*. Acta Archaeologica Lundensia 8.

BURGESS, C. (1974) The Bronze Age. In C. Renfrew (ed.) *British Prehistory. A new outline*, 165–233. London: Duckworth.

BURGESS, C. and MIKET, R. (eds.) (1976) *Settlement and economy in the third and second millennia BC.* Brit. Arch. Rep. 33.

BUTLER, J. J. (1963) Bronze Age Connections Across the North Sea. *Palaeohistoria* 9.

BUTLER, J. J. (1969) *Nederland in de Bronstijd.* Bussum: Fibula-van Dishoek.

BUTLER, J. J. and VAN DER WAALS, J. D. (1966) Bell Beakers and early metal working in the Netherlands. *Palaeohistoria* 12, 41–140.

CALDER, C. S. T. (1956) Stone Age house sites in Shetland. *Proc. Soc. Ant. Scot.* 89, 340–97.

CARDOSO, M. (1968) Bibliografía das jóias arcaicas da Península Ibérica. *Revista de Guimarães,* 68, 85–8.

CHERTIER, B. (1976) Les civilisations de l'Age du Bronze en Champagne. In Guilaine 1976, 618–29.

CHILDE, V. G. (1929) *The Danube in Prehistory.* Oxford: Oxford University Press.

CHILDE, V. G. (1948) The Final Bronze Age in the Near East and in Temperate Europe. *PPS* 14, 177–95.

CHRISTLEIN, R. (1964) Beiträge zur Stufengliederung der frühbronze-zeitlichen Flachgräberfelder in Süddeutschland. *BVgbl.* 29, 25–63.

CHUDZIAKOWA, J. (1974) *Kultura łużycka na terenie międzyrzecza Wisły, Drwęcy i Osy.* Warsaw, Poznań: Tow. Nauk. w Toruniu.

ČIČIKOVA, M. (1968) Keramika ot starata željazna epocha v Trakija. *Arch.* 10/4, 15–27. (French résumé.)

CLARK, J. G. D. (1952) *Prehistoric Europe: the Economic Basis.* London: Methuen.

CLOTTES, J. and COSTANTINI, G. (1976) Les civilisations de l'Age du Bronze dans les Causses. In Guilaine 1976, 470–82.

COBLENZ, W. (1952) *Grabfunde der Mittelbronzezeit Sachsens.* Dresden: Landesmuseum.

COBLENZ, W. (1963) Bemerkungen zur Funktion der Lausitzer Burgen Sachsens. In *Munera Archaeologica Iosepho Kostrzewski...oblata,* 193–200. Poznań: Poznańskie towarzystwo pryzyjaciół nauk.

COBLENZ, W. (1964) Burgen der Lausitzer Kultur in Sachsen. In *Studien aus Alteuropa,* 189–204. Beihefte der Bonner Jahrbücher, Bd 10/1.

COBLENZ, W. (1974) Die Burgwälle und das Ausklingen der westlichen Lausitzer Kultur. In *Symposium zu Problemen der jüngeren Hallstattzeit in Mitteleuropa, 1970, Smolenice,* 85–99. Bratislava.

COFFYN, A. (1976) Les civilisations de l'Age du Bronze en Aquitaine. In Guilaine 1976, 532–42.

COLES, J. M. (1962) European Bronze Age Shields. *PPS* 28, 156–90.

COLES, J. M. and SIMPSON, D. D. A. (eds.) (1968) *Studies in Ancient Europe*. Leicester: Leicester University Press.

CORDIER, G. (1976) Les civilisations de l'Age du Bronze dans le Centre-ouest et les pays de la Loire moyenne. In Guilaine 1976, 543–60.

COURTIN, J. (1976) Les civilisations de l'Age du Bronze en Provence. Le Bronze ancien et le Bronze moyen en Provence. In Guilaine 1976, 445–51.

COURTIN, J., GUILAINE, J. and MOHEN, J.-P. (1976) Les débuts de l'agriculture en France. In Guilaine 1976, 172–9.

COWEN, J. D. 1955 (1956) Eine Einführung in die Geschichte der bronzenen Griffzungenschwerter in Süddeutschland und den angrenzenden Gebieten. *BRGK* 36, 52–155.

CROSSLAND, R. A. and BIRCHALL, A. (eds) (1973) *Bronze Age Migrations in the Aegean*. London: Duckworth.

ČUJANOVÁ-JÍLKOVÁ, E. (1970) *Mittelbronzezeitliche Hügelgräberfelder in Westböhmen*. Prague: Archeologické Studijní Materiály.

DĄBROWSKI, J. (1972) *Powiązania ziem polskich z terenami wschodnimi w epoce brązu*. Warsaw: Ossolineum.

DANIEL, G. and EVANS, J. D. (1967) The Western Mediterranean. *CAH*, 3rd edn, II/2, ch. 37. Cambridge University Press.

DAUGAS, J.-P. (1976) Les civilisations de l'Age du Bronze dans le Massif Central. In Guilaine 1976, 506–21.

DEHN, R. (1972) *Die Urnenfelderkultur in Nordwürttemberg*. Stuttgart: Müller and Gräff.

DE LAET, S. J. (1958) *The Low Countries*. London: Thames and Hudson.

DE LAET, S. J. (1974) *Prehistorische Kulturen in het Zuiden der Lage Landen*. Wetteren: Universa.

DE LAET, S. J. (ed.) (1976) *Acculturation and Continuity in Atlantic Europe mainly during the Neolithic Period and the Bronze Age*. Diss. Arch. Gandenses 16, Bruges: De Tempel.

DE LUMLEY, H., FONVIELLE, M.-E. and ABELANET, J. (1976) Les gravures rupestres de l'âge du Bronze dans la région du Mont Bégo (Tende, Alpes-Maritimes). In Guilaine 1976, 222–36.

DESITTERE, M. (1968) *De Urnenvelden Kultuur in het Gebied tussen Neder-Rijn en Nordzee (Periodes Ha A en B)*. Diss. Arch. Gandenses, 11. Bruges: De Tempel.

DIMBLEBY, G. W. (1962) *The Development of British Heathlands and their Soils*. Oxford Forestry Memoir 23, Oxford.

DIMITROV, D. P. (1968) Troja VII b2 i balkanskite trakijski i mizijski plemena. *Arch*. 10/4, 1–15.

DRACK, W. (ed.) (1971) *Ur- und Frühgeschichtliche Archäologie der Schweiz. III Die Bronzezeit*. Schweizerische Gesellschaft für Ur- und Frühgeschichte, Basel.

DREISCH, A. VON DEN (1973) Fauna, Klima und Landschaft im Süden der Iberischen Halbinsel während der Metallzeit. In J. Matolcsi (ed.), *Domestikationforschung und Geschichte der Haustiere*, 245–54. Budapest: Akad. Kiadó.

DRIEHAUS, J. (1969) *Linker Niederrhein, Krefeld, Xanten, Kleve. FvfD* 14, Mainz, Philipp von Zabern.

DUMITRESCU, V. (1961) *Necropola de incineraţie din epoca bronzului de la Cîrna*. Bucharest: Edit. Acad. R.S.R.

DURCZEWSKI, Z. (1948) *Grupa górnośląsko-małopolska kultury łużyckiej w Polsce*. Polska Akademie Umiejetności. Prace Prehist., 6. Katowice: Wydawnictwa Śląskie.

DUŠEK, M. (1960) Patince – pohrebisko severopanónskej kultúry. In B. Chropovský, M. Dušek and B. Polla, *Gräberfelder aus der älteren Bronzezeit in der Slowakei* 1, 139–296. Bratislava: Slovenská akadémia vied.

DUŠEK, M. (1969) *Bronzezeitliche Gräberfelder in der Südwestslowakei*. Bratislava: Slovenská akadémia vied.

ELLMERS, D. (1971) *Schleswig, Haithabu, Sylt. FvfD* 9, Mainz: Philipp von Zabern.

EPOQUE PRÉHISTORIQUE (1971) *Epoque préhistorique et protohistorique en Yougoslavie - Recherches et résultats*. G. Novak *et al.* (eds). Beograd: Comité National d'Organisation du VIIIe Congrès International des Sciences Préhistoriques et Protohistoriques.

EVANS, J. D. (1959) *Malta*. London: Thames and Hudson.

EVANS, J. D. (1971) *The Prehistoric Antiquities of the Maltese Islands, a Survey*. London: Athlone Press.

EVANS, J. G. (1975) *The Environment of Early Man in the British Isles*. London: Elek.

FEUSTEL, R. (1958) *Bronzezeitliche Hügelgräberkultur im Gebiet von Schwarza (Süd-Thüringen)* (Veroff. des Museums f. Ur-und Frühg. Thüringens, I). Weimar: Böhlaus.

FISCHER, U. (1956) *Die Gräber der Steinzeit in Saalegebiet. Studien über neolithische und frühbronzezeitliche Grab- und Bestattungsformen in Sachsen-Thüringen*. Vorgeschichtliche Forschungen, Heft 15.

FLEMING, A. (1976) The Dartmoor reaves. *Curr. Arch.* 55, 250–2.

FLORESCU, A. C. (1964) Contribuţii la cunoaşterea culturii Noua. *Arh. Mold.* 2–3, 143–216.

FOWLER, P. J. (1971) Early prehistoric agriculture in western Europe: some archaeological evidence. In D. D. A. Simpson (ed.) *Economy and Settlement in Neolithic and Early Bronze Age Britain and Europe*, 153–82. Leicester: Leicester University Press.

FOWLER, P. J. (ed.) (1975) *Recent work in Rural Archaeology*. Bradford-on-Avon: Moonraker.

FREDSJÖ, Å., JANSON, S. and MOBERG, C.-A. (1969) *Hällristningar i Sverige*. Oskarshamn: Forum.

546   Bibliography

FRENZEL, B. (1966) Climatic change in the Atlantic/Sub-boreal transition on the Northern hemisphere: botanical evidence. In *Proceedings of the International Symposium on World Climate 8000 to 0 B.C.*, 99–123. London: Royal Geographical Society.

FURMÁNEK, V. (1970) Hromadný nález bronzových předmětů v Liptovské Ondrašové. *Sl. A.* 18/2, 451–68.

GARAŠANIN, M. V. 1958 (1959). Neolithikum und Bronzezeit in Serbien und Makedonien. *BRGK* 39, 1–130.

GAUCHER, G. (1976) Les civilisations de l'Age du Bronze dans le bassin parisien et le Nord de la France. In Guilaine 1976, 574–84.

GAUCHER, G. and MOHEN, J.-P. (1974) *L'âge du bronze dans le nord de la France*. Amiens: Société de Préhistoire du Nord.

GEDIGA, B. (1969) *Plemiona kultury łużyckiej w epoce brązie na Śląsku środkowym*. Warsaw: Ossolineum.

GEDIGA, B. (1970) *Motywy figuralne w sztuce ludności kultury łużyckiej*. Wrocław-Warszawa-Kraków.

GEDL, M. (1962) *Kultura Łużycka na Gornym Śląsku*. Warsaw: Ossolineum.

GERLOFF, S. (1975) *The Early Bronze Age Daggers in Great Britain and a Reconsideration of the Wessex Culture*. (Prähistorische Bronzefunde, Abt.VI, Bd. 2). Munich: Beck.

GILMAN, A. (1976) Bronze Age Dynamics in south-east Spain. *Dialectical Anthropology*, 1, 307–19. Amsterdam: Elsevier.

GIMBUTAS, M. (1956) *The Prehistory of Eastern Europe. Part 1. Mesolithic, Neolithic and Copper Age cultures in Russia and the Baltic area*. Cambridge, Mass.: Amer. School of Prehist. Research.

GIMBUTAS, M. (1963) *The Balts*. London: Thames and Hudson.

GIMBUTAS, M. (1965) *Bronze Age Cultures in Central and Eastern Europe*. The Hague: Mouton.

GIOT, P. R. (1960) *Brittany*. London: Thames and Hudson.

GLASBERGEN, W. (1954) *Barrow Excavations in the Eight Beatitudes*. Groningen: Wolters.

GLOB, P. V. (1951) *Ard og Plov i Nordens Oldtid*. Jysk Arkaeologisk Selskabs Skrifter Bind 1. Aarhus.

GLOB, P. V. (1969) *Helleristninger i Danmark*. Jysk Arkaeologisk Selskabs Skrifter Bind 7. Odense.

GLOB, P. V. (1971) *Danish Prehistoric Monuments*. London: Faber.

GLOB, P. V. (1974) *The Mound People*. London: Faber.

GOLLUB, S. (1960) *Endbronzezeitliche Gräber in Mittel- und Oberschlesien*. Bonn: Habelt.

GRÄSLUND, B. (1974) *Relativ Datering. Om kronologisk metod i nordisk arkeologi. Tor*, 16.

GROSJEAN, R. (1976) Les civilisations de l'Age du Bronze en Corse. In Guilaine 1976, 644–53.

GRÜNBERG, W. (1943) *Die Grabfunde der jüngeren und jüngsten Bronzezeit im Gau Sachsen.* Vorgeschichtliche Forschungen, 13. Berlin: de Gruyter.

GUIDO, M. (1963) *Sardinia.* London: Thames and Hudson.

GUILAINE, J. (1972) *L'Age du Bronze en Languedoc Occidental, Roussillon, Ariège.* Paris: Société Préhistorique Française.

GUILAINE, J. (ed.) (1976) *La Préhistoire Française. II. Les Civilisations Néolithiques et Protohistoriques de la France.* Paris: Centre national de la Recherche Scientifique.

GUILAINE, J. (1976a) Les civilisations de l'Age du Bronze dans les Pyrénées. In Guilaine 1976, 522–31.

GUYAN, W. (ed.) (1954) *Das Pfahlbauproblem.* Monog. zur Ur- und Frühgeschichte der Schweiz 11.

HACHMANN, R. (1957) *Die frühe Bronzezeit im westlichen Ostseegebiet und ihre mittel- und südosteuropäischen Beziehungen.* (Atlas der Urgeschichte vol. 6). Hamburg: Kartographisches Institut.

HAGEN, A. (1967) *Norway.* London: Thames and Hudson.

HAMMOND, N. G. L. (1967) Tumulus-burial in Albania, the Grave Circles of Mycenae, and the Indo-Europeans. *BSA* 62, 77–105.

HÄNSEL, B. (1968) *Beiträge zur Chronologie der mittleren Bronzezeit im Karpatenbecken.* Bonn: Habelt.

HÄNSEL, B. (1976) *Beiträge zur regionalen und chronologischen Gliederung der älteren Hallstattzeit an der unteren Donau.* Bonn: Habelt.

HARDING, A. (1971) The earliest glass in Europe. *AR* 23, 188–200.

HARDING, A. (1972) Illyrians, Italians and Mycenaeans: trans-Adriatic contacts during the Late Bronze Age. *Stud. Alb.* 9/2, 215–21.

HARDING, A. and WARREN, S. E. (1973) Early Bronze Age faience beads from central Europe. *Antiquity* 47, 64–6.

HARRISON, R. J. (1974) Ireland and Spain in the Early Bronze Age. *J. Roy. Soc. Ant. Irel.* 104, 52–73.

HARTMANN, A. (1970) *Prähistorische Goldfunde aus Europa. Studien zu den Anfängen der Metallurgie,* 3. Berlin: Mann.

HÄUSLER, A. (1974) *Die Gräber der älteren Ockergrabkultur zwischen Ural und Dnepr.* Berlin: Akad. Verlag.

HAYEN, H. (1957) Zur Bautechnik und Typologie der vorgeschichtlichen, frühgeschichtlichen und mittelalterlichen hölzernen Moorwege und Moorstrassen. *Oldenburger Jahrbuch* 56, 83–170.

HELBAEK, H. (1952) Early crops in southern England. *PPS* 18, 194–233.

HENCKEN, H. (1968) *Tarquinia, Villanovans and early Etruscans.* (Amer. School of Prehist. Research, Bull. no. 23) Cambridge, Mass: Peabody Museum.

HENNIG, H. (1970) *Die Grab- und Hortfunde der Urnenfelderkultur in Ober- und Mittelfranken.* Kallmünz/Opf.: Lassleben.

548 Bibliography

HERITY, M. and EOGAN, G. (1977) *Ireland in Prehistory*. London: Routledge and Kegan Paul.

HERRMANN, F.-R. (1966) *Die Funde der Urnenfelderkultur in Mittel- und Südhessen*. Berlin: de Gruyter.

HERRMANN, J. (1969) Burgen und befestigte Siedlungen der jüngeren Bronze- und frühen Eisenzeit in Mitteleuropa. In K-H. Otto and J. Herrmann (eds) *Siedlung, Burg und Stadt: Studien zu ihren Anfängen*. Berlin: Akad. Verlag.

HEURTLEY, W. (1939) *Prehistoric Macedonia*. Cambridge: Cambridge University Press.

HIGHAM, C. F. W. (1968) Patterns of prehistoric economic exploitation on the Alpine foreland. *Vierteljahrsschrift der Naturforschenden Gesellschaft in Zürich* 113, 41–92.

HOLSTE, F. (1953a) *Die Bronzezeit in Süd- und Westdeutschland*. Handbuch der Urgeschichte Deutschlands, 1. Berlin: de Gruyter.

HOLSTE, F. (1953b) *Die bronzezeitlichen Vollgriffschwerter Bayerns*. Munich: Beck.

HOREDT, K. (1960) Die Wietenbergkultur. *Dacia* n.s. 4, 107–37.

HOREDT, K. and SERAPHIN, C. (1971) *Die Prähistorische Ansiedlung auf dem Wietenberg bei Sighişoara-Schässburg*. Bonn: Habelt.

HRALA, J. (1973) *Knovízská kultura ve středních Čechách*. Prague: Inst. of Arch.

HUNDT, H.-J. (1958) *Katalog Straubing. I. Die Funde der Glockenbecherkultur und der Straubinger Kultur*. Kallmünz/Opf: Lassleben.

INVESTIGATIONS (1966) *Investigations archéologiques en Tchéchoslovaquie*. J. Filip (ed.), Prague: Academia.

ISLAMI, S. and CEKA, H. (1964) Nouvelles données sur l'antiquité illyrienne en Albanie. *Stud. Alb.* 1, 91–137.

JENSEN, J. (1967) Voldtofte-Fundet. *Aarbøger for nordisk Oldkyndighed og Historie*, 149–54.

JUNGHANS, S., SANGMEISTER, E. and SCHRÖDER, M. (1960) *Metall analysen kupferzeitlicher und frühbronzezeitlicher Bodenfunde aus Europa*. Studien zu den Anfängen der Metallurgie 1. Berlin: Mann.

JUNGHANS, S., SANGMEISTER, E. and SCHRÖDER, M. (1968) *Kupfer und Bronze in der frühen Metallzeit Europas*. Studien zu den Anfängen der Metallurgie 2. Berlin: Mann.

KAČALOVA, N. K. (1970) Il'menskie kurgany. *Arch. Sbor.* 12, 7–34, 117.

KALICZ, N. (1968) *Die Frühbronzezeit in Nordostungarn*. Budapest: Akad. Kiadó.

KATINČAROV, R. (1975) Traits caracteristiques de la civilisation de l'âge du bronze ancien et moyen en Bulgarie *AAC* 15, 85–111.

KELLER, F. (1878) *The Lake Dwellings of Switzerland and other parts of Europe*. London: Longmans, Green.

KERSTEN, K. (1935) *Zur älteren nordischen Bronzezeit.* Neumünster: Wachholtz.

KERSTEN, K. (1958) *Die Funde der älteren Bronzezeit in Pommern.* 7 Beiheft zum Atlas der Urgeschichte. Hamburg: Hamburgisches Museum.

KIMMIG, W. (1964) Seevölkerbewegung und Urnenfelderkultur. Ein archäologisch-historischer Versuch. In *Studien aus Alteuropa*, Teil I Beihefte der Bonner Jahrbücher 10/1, 220–83.

KOSORIĆ, M. (1976) *Kulturni, etnički i hronološki problemi ilirskih nekropola podrinja.* Tuzla: Musej istočne Bosne.

KOSSACK, G. (1954) *Studien zur Symbolgut der Urnenfelder- und Hallstattzeit Mitteleuropas.* Berlin: de Gruyter.

KOSTRZEWSKI, J. (ed.) (1950) *III Sprawozdanie z prac wykopaliskowych w grodzie kultury Łużyckiej w Biskupinie w powiecie żnińskim za lata 1938–1939 i 1946–1948.* Poznań: Nakladem polikiego towarzystwa prehistorycznego.

KYTLICOVÁ, O. (1959) Ein Beitrag zum Problem der getriebenen Bronzegefässe aus der jüngeren und späten Bronzezeit. *PA* 50, 126–57.

KYTLICOVÁ, O., VOKOLEK, V. and BOUZEK, J. (1964) Zur urnenfelderzeitlichen Chronologie Böhmens. *Acta Musei Reginaehradensis S.B.: Scientiae Sociales* 7, 143–80.

LAGRAND, C. (1976) Les civilisations de l'Age du Bronze en Provence. Le Bronze final. In Guilaine 1976, 452–8.

LANGE, W. R. and NOWOTHNIG, W. (1971) *Hameln, Deister, Rinteln, Minden. FvfD* 4. Mainz: Philipp von Zabern.

LAUTENSACH, H. (1964) *Iberische Halbinsel.* München: Geographische Handbücher.

LEAHU, V. (1966) *Cultura tei.* Bucharest.

LILLIU, G. (1962) Las Nuragas. *Ampurias* 24, 67–145.

LOMBORG, E. (1959) Donauländische Kulturbeziehungen und die relative Chronologie der frühen nordischen Bronzezeit. *Acta Archaeologica* 30, 51–146.

LOMBORG, E. (1968) Den tidlige bronzealders kronologi. *Aarbøger* (1968), 91–152.

LO PORTO, F. G. (1963) Leporano (Taranto) – La stazione protostorica di Porto Perone. *Not. Scavi* 8th ser. 17, 280–380.

LYNCH, F. and BURGESS, C. (eds) (1972) *Prehistoric Man in Wales and the West.* Bath: Adams and Dart.

MALINOWSKI, T. (1974) The Question of a Northern Proto-Illyrian Borderland. *JIES* 2/3, 213–22.

MARINIS, R. DE (1975) L'età del bronzo. In M. Cremaschi (ed.), *Preistoria e Protostoria nel Reggiano, Ricerche e scavi 1940–1975*, 31–55.

550   Bibliography

Reggio Emilia: Municipio di Reggio Emilia, Civici Musei e Gallerie d'Arte.

MARSTRANDER, S. (1963) *Östfolds Jordbruksristninger*. Oslo: Institute of Comparative Research in Human Culture.

MATTHIAS, W. (1976) Die Salzproduktion – ein bedeutender Faktor in der Wirtschaft der frühbronzezeitlichen Bevölkerung an der mittleren Saale. *JMV* 60, 373–94.

MEINANDER, C. F. (1954) *Die Bronzezeit in Finnland*. Finska Form-minnesföreningens Tidskrift 54.

MELLOR, R. E. H. (1975) *Eastern Europe: a Geography of the Comecon Countries*. London: Macmillan.

MERCER, R. (1975) Settlement, farming and environment in south west England to *c*. 1000 BC. In Fowler 1975, 27–43.

MILLOTTE, J. P. (1963) *Le Jura et les Plaines de Saône aux âges des métaux*. Paris: Annales Littéraires de l'Université de Besançon 59.

MILLOTTE, J. P. (1976) Les civilisations de l'Age du Bronze dans le Jura. In Guilaine 1976, 495–505.

MOHEN, J-P. (1977) *L'Age du Bronze dans la région de Paris*. Paris: Musées Nationaux.

MOLINA GONZALEZ, F. and PAREJA LÓPEZ, E. (1975) *Excavaciones en la Cuesta del Negro (Purullena, Granada)*. Madrid: Excavaciones Arqueologicas en España, 86.

MONTELIUS, O. (1885) Om tidsbestämning inom bronsåldern med särskild hänsyn till Skandinavien. *Kongl. Vitterhets Historie och Antiquitets Akademiens Handlingar* 30. Stockholm.

MONTELIUS, O. (1900) *Die Chronologie der ältesten Bronzezeit in Nord-Deutschland und Scandinavien*. Braunschweig.

MONTELIUS, O. (1903) *Die typologische Methode. Die ältere Kulturperioden im Orient und in Europa. 1*. Stockholm.

MORINTZ, S. (1964) Quelques problèmes concernant la période ancienne du Hallstatt au Bas-Danube à la lumière des fouilles de Babadag. *Dacia*, n.s., 8, 101–18.

MOUCHA, V. (1961) *Funde der Únĕticer Kultur in der Gegend von Lovosice*. (Fontes Arch. Pragenses 4) Prague: National Museum.

MOUCHA, V. (1963) Die Periodisierung der Únĕticer Kultur in Böhmen. *SbČSSA* 3, 9–60.

MOZSOLICS, A. (1952) Die Ausgrabungen in Tószeg im Jahre 1948. *AAH* 2, 35–69.

MOZSOLICS, A. (1957) Archäologische Beiträge zur Geschichte der grossen Wanderung. *AAH* 8, 119–56.

MOZSOLICS, A. (1960) Der Tumulus von Nyírkarász-Gyulaháza. *AAH* 12, 113–23.

MOZSOLICS, A. (1967) *Bronzefunde des Karpatenbeckens. Depotfundhorizont von Apa und Hajdúsámson*. Budapest: Akad. Kiadó.

MOZSOLICS, A. 1965–6 (1968) Goldfunde des Depotfundhorizontes von Hajdúsámson. *BRGK* 46–7, 1–76.

MOZSOLICS, A. (1973) *Bronze- und Goldfunde des Karpatenbeckens. Depotfundhorizont von Forró und Ópályi.* Budapest: Akad. Kiadó.

MÜLLER, A. VON (1964) *Die jungbronzezeitliche Siedlung von Berlin-Lichterfelde.* Berlin: Hessling.

MÜLLER-KARPE, H. (1959) *Beiträge zur Chronologie der Urnenfelderzeit nördlich und südlich der Alpen.* Berlin: de Gruyter.

MÜLLER-KARPE, H. (1961) *Die Vollgriffschwerter der Urnenfelderzeit aus Bayern.* Munich: Beck.

MÜLLER-KARPE, H. (1962) Zur spätbronzezeitlichen Bewaffnung in Mitteleuropa und Griechenland. *Germania* 40, 255–87.

MÜLLER-KARPE, H. (1974) *Handbuch der Vorgeschichte. Band III: Kupferzeit.* Munich: Beck.

MÜLLER-WILLE, M. (1968–9) Bestattung im Boot. *Offa* 25–26.

NENQUIN, J. (1961) *Salt. A Study in Economic Prehistory.* Bruges: Tempel.

NESTOR, J. (1932) Der Stand der Vorgeschichtsforschung in Rumänien. *BRGK* 22, 11–181.

NEUGEBAUER, W. (1968) *Hansestadt Lübeck, Ostholstein, Kiel. FvfD* 10. Mainz: Philipp von Zabern.

NEUMANN, G. (1929) Zur Entwicklung der Aunjetitzer Keramik in Mitteldeutschland. *PZ* 20, 70–144.

NITRA KOMMISSION, 1958 (1961). *Kommission für das Äneolithikum und die älteren Bronzezeit, Nitra, 1958.* Bratislava: Slovenská akadémia vied.

NOVOTNÁ, M. (1970) *Die Bronzehortfunde in der Slowakei, Spätbronzezeit.* Bratislava: Slovenská akadémia vied.

ONDRÁČEK, J. (1962) Únětické pohřebiště u Rebešovic na Moravě. *SbČSSA* 2, 5–100.

ORDENTLICH, I. (1969) Probleme der Befestigungsanlagen in der Siedlungen der Otomanikultur in deren rumänischem Verbreitungsgebiet. *Dacia* n.s. 13, 457–74.

ORDENTLICH, I. (1972) Contribuţia săpăturilor arheologice de pe 'Dealul Vida' (com. Sălacea, judeţul Bihor) la cunoaşterea culturii Otomani. *Satu Mare-Studii şi Comunicări,* 1972, 63–84.

ÖSTENBERG, C. E. (1967) *Luni sul Mignone e problemi della preistoria italiana.* Lund: Gleerup.

OSTOJA-ZAGÓRSKI, J. (1974) From studies on the economic structure at the decline of the Bronze Age and the Hallstatt period in the north and west zone of the Odra and Vistula Basins. *Przeg. Arch.* 22, 123–49.

PATAY, P. VON (1938) *Frühbronzezeitliche Kulturen in Ungarn.* (Dissertationes Pannonicae, ser II, no. 13) Budapest.

PATEK, E. (1968) *Die Urnenfelderkultur in Transdanubien.* Budapest: Akad. Kiadó.

PENNINGTON, W. (1969) *The History of British Vegetation.* London: Unibooks.

PERICOT GARCIA, L. (1972) *The Balearic Islands.* London: Thames and Hudson.

PERONI, R. (1959) Per una definizione dell'aspetto culturale subappenninico come fase cronologica a sè stante. *Atti. Accad. naz dei Lincei* 8th ser. 9, 3–253.

PERONI, R. (1963) L'età del bronzo media e recente tra l'Adige e il Mincio. *Memoria del Museo Civico di Storia Naturale di Verona* 11, 49–104.

PERONI, R. (1971) *L'età del bronzo nella penisola italiana.* 1. *L'antica età del bronzo.* Firenze: Olschki.

PESCHECK, C. (1975) *Würzburg, Karlstadt, Iphofen, Schweinfurt. FvfD* 27. Mainz: Philipp von Zabern.

PHILLIPS, P. (1975) *Early Farmers of West Mediterranean Europe.* London: Hutchinson.

PIESKER, H. (1958) *Untersuchungen zur älteren Lüneburgischen Bronzezeit.* Lüneburg: Landesmuseum.

PIGGOTT, S. (1938) The Early Bronze Age in Wessex. *PPS* 4, 52–106.

PIGGOTT, S. (1965) *Ancient Europe.* Edinburgh: Edinburgh University Press.

PITTIONI, R. (1954) *Urgeschichte des österreichischen Raumes.* Wien: Denticke.

PIVOVAROVÁ, Z. (1965) K problematike mohýl v lužickej kultúre na Slovensku. *Sl. A.* 13, 107–62.

PLANCHAIS, N. (1976) La végétation pendant le Post-Glaciaire: aspects de la végétation holocène dans les plaines françaises. In Guilaine 1976, 35–43.

PLESL, E. (1961) *Lužická kultura ve severozápadních Čechách.* Prague: ČSAV.

PODBORSKÝ, V. (1970) *Mähren in der Spätbronzezeit und an der Schwelle der Eisenzeit.* Brno: Univ. J. E. Purkyně.

POPESCU, D. (1944) *Die frühe und mittlere Bronzezeit in Siebenbürgen.* Bucharest: Biblioteca Muzeului Naţional de Antichităţi din Bucureşti.

POTTER, T. W. (1976) *A Faliscan Town in south Etruria: excavations at Narce 1966–71.* London: British School at Rome.

POULAIN, T. (1976) La faune sauvage et domestique en France du Néolithique à la fin de l'Age du Fer. In Guilaine 1976, 104–18.

PRENDI, F. (1966) La civilisation préhistorique de Maliq. *Stud. Alb.* 3/1, 255–80.

PROX, A. (1941) *Die Schneckenbergkultur.* Kronstadt: Braşov.

PUGLISI, S. (1959) *La civiltà appenninica. Origine della comunità pastorali in Italia.* Firenze: Sansoni.

RADUNZ, K. (1966) Urnenfelderzeitliche Bestattungssitten im Gräberfeld von Grundfeld (Reundorf), Ldkr. Staffelstein/Ofr. *BVgbl.* 31, 49–67.

RAGETH, J. (1974) Der Lago di Ledro im Trentino und seine Beziehungen zu den alpinen und mitteleuropäischen Kulturen. *BRGK* 55, 73–259.

RANDSBORG, K. (1968) Von Periode II zu III. *Acta Archaeologica* 39, 1–142.

RANDSBORG, K. (1972) *From Period III to Period IV.* Copenhagen: National Museum.

RANDSBORG, K. (1974) Social stratification in Early Bronze Age Denmark: a study in the regulation of culture systems. *PZ* 49, 38–61.

REINECKE, P. (1911/1965) *Mainzer Aufsätze zur Chronologie der Bronze- und Eisenzeit.* Bonn: Habelt.

REINERTH, H. (1928) *Die Wasserburg Buchau. Eine befestigte Inselsiedlung aus der Zeit 1100–800 v. Chr.* Augsburg: Filser.

RENFREW, C. (1973) *Before Civilisation. The Radiocarbon Revolution and Prehistoric Europe.* London: Cape.

RENFREW, J. (1973) *Palaeoethnobotany.* London: Methuen.

RIQUET, R. (1976) L'Anthropologie protohistorique française. In Guilaine 1976, 135–52.

ROUDIL, J.-L. (1972) *L'Age du Bronze en Languedoc Oriental.* Paris: Société Préhistorique Française.

ROUDIL, J.-L. and GUILAINE, J. (1976) Les civilisations de l'Age du Bronze en Languedoc. In Guilaine 1976, 459–69.

ROWLANDS, M. J. (1976) *The Organisation of Middle Bronze Age Metalworking.* Oxford: Brit. Arch. Rep. 31.

RUCKDESCHEL, W. (1968) Geschlechtsdifferenzierte Bestattungssitten in frühbronzezeitlichen Gräbern Südbayerns. *BVgbl.* 33, 18–44.

SÄFLUND, G. (1939) *Le Terremare delle provincie di Modena, Reggio Emilia, Parma, Piacenza.* Lund: Skrifter utgivne av Svenska Institutet i Rom, VII.

SANDARS, N. K. (1957) *Bronze Age Cultures in France.* Cambridge: Cambridge University Press.

SANDARS, N. K. (1971) From Bronze Age to Iron Age: a sequel to a sequel. In J. Boardman, M. A. Brown and T. G. E. Powell (eds) *The European Community in Later Prehistory,* 3–29. London: Routledge and Kegan Paul.

SARNOWSKA, W. (1969) *Kultura unietycka w Polsce,* vol. I. Wrocław: Mus. Arch.

SAUTER, M.-R. (1976) *Switzerland. From earliest times to the Roman Conquest.* London: Thames and Hudson.

SAVORY, H. N. (1949) The Atlantic Bronze Age in south-west Europe. *PPS* 15, 128–55.

554 Bibliography

SAVORY, H. N. (1968) *Spain and Portugal. The prehistory of the Iberian peninsula*. London: Thames and Hudson.

SAVORY, H. N. (1965) The Bronze Age. In I. L. Foster and G. E. Daniel (eds) *Prehistoric and Early Wales*, 71–107. London: Routledge and Kegan Paul.

SCHAAFF, U. (1969) *Essen, Düsseldorf, Duisburg. FvfD* 15. Mainz: Philipp von Zabern.

SCHUBART, H. (1975) *Die Kultur der Bronzezeit im südwesten der Iberischen Halbinsel*. Madrider Forschungen 9. Madrid: Deutsches Archäologisches Institut.

SCHUBART, H. (1975a) Cronologia relativa de la ceramica sepulcral en la cultura de el Argar. *TP* 32, 79–92.

SCHUBART, H. (1976) Eine Bronzezeitliche Kultur im südwesten der Iberischen Halbinsel. In de Laet 1976, 221–34.

SCHUBERT, E. (1973) Studien zur frühen Bronzezeit an der mittleren Donau. *BRGK* 54, 1–105.

SCHUHMACHER, E. (1967) *Die Protovillanova-Fundgruppe; eine Untersuchung zur frühen Eisenzeit Italiens*. Bonn: Habelt.

SIMPSON, D. D. A. (1968) Food vessels: associations and chronology. In Coles and Simpson 1968, 197–211.

SIMPSON, D. D. A. and THAWLEY, J. E. (1972) Single grave art in Britain. *Scottish Archaeological Forum* 4, 81–104.

SIRET, H. and L. (1887) *Les premiers âges du métal dans le Sud–Est de l'Espagne*. Anvers. *Las primeras edades del metal en el Sudeste de España*. (1890) Barcelona.

SIRET, L. (1913) *Questions de Chronologie et d'Ethnographie Ibériques. 1. De la fin du Quaternaire à la fin du Bronze*. Paris: Geuthner.

SKLENÁŘ, K. (1974) *Památky pravěku na území ČSSR*. Prague: Orbis.

SMITH, A. G. (1975) Neolithic and Bronze Age landscape changes in northern Ireland. In J. G. Evans, S. Limbrey and H. Cleere (eds) *The Effect of Man on the Landscape: the Highland Zone*, 64–73. London: Council for British Archaeology.

SPROCKHOFF, E. (1930) *Zur Handelsgeschichte der germanischen Bronzezeit*. Berlin: de Gruyter.

SPROCKHOFF, E. (1931) *Die germanischen Griffzungenschwerter*. Berlin: de Gruyter.

SPROCKHOFF, E. (1934) *Die germanischen Vollgriffschwerter der jüngeren Bronzezeit*. Berlin: de Gruyter.

SPROCKHOFF, E. (1962) Nordische Bronzezeit und frühes Griechentum. *Bremer Archäologische Blätter* 3, 28–110.

STEIN, F. (1968) Beobachtungen zu Tracht- und Bestattungssitten der frühbronzezeitlichen Bevölkerung von Gemeinlebarn. *BRGK* 49 1–40.

STENBERGER, M. (n.d.) *Sweden*. London: Thames and Hudson.

STJERNQUIST, B. (1967) *Models of commercial diffusion in prehistoric times.* Lund: Scripta Minora.

STJERNQUIST, B. (1969) *Beiträge zum Studium von bronzezeitlichen Siedlungen.* Acta Archaeologica Lundensia.

STOCKÝ, A. (1928) *La Bohème à l'âge du bronze.* Prague: Štenc.

STUDIEN (1958) *Studien zur Lausitzer Kultur.* Leipzig: Barth.

SULIMIRSKI, T. (1968a) The Bronze Age in the U.S.S.R. *BIA* 7, 43–83.

SULIMIRSKI, T. (1968b) *Corded Ware and Globular Amphorae north-east of the Carpathians.* London: Athlone Press.

SULIMIRSKI, T. (1970) *Prehistoric Russia: an outline.* London: Baker.

TARRADELL, M. (1965) El problema de las diversas áreas culturales de la península Iberica en el edad del bronce. In E. Ripoll Perelló (ed.) *Miscelánea en Homenaje al Abate Henri Breuil (1877–1961)* 2, 423–30. Barcelona.

TAYLOR, J. J. (1979) *Bronze Age Goldwork of the British Isles.* Cambridge: University Press.

THÉVENIN, A. (1976) Les civilisations de l'Age du Bronze dans l'Est de la France. In Guilaine 1976, 640–3.

THRANE, H. (1975) *Europaeiske forbindelser.* Copenhagen: National Museum.

TIHELKA, K. (1965) *Hort- und Einzelfunde der Úněticer Kultur und des Věteřover Typus in Mähren.* Brno. Fontes Arch. Moravicae, vol. IV.

TIHELKA, K. 1958 (1961). Der Věteřov (Witterschauer)-Typus in Mähren. *Kommission für das Äneolithikum und die ältere Bronzezeit, Nitra*, 77–109. Bratislava: Slovenská akadémia vied.

TINÉ, S. and VAGNETTI, L. (1967) *I micenei in Italia.* Taranto: Museo Arch.

TOČÍK, A. (1963) Die Nitra-Gruppe. *AR* 15, 716–74.

TOČÍK, A. (1964) *Opevnena osada z doby bronzovej vo Veselom.* Bratislava: Slovenská akadémia vied.

TOČÍK, A. and VLADÁR, J. (1971) Prehl'ad bádania v problematike vývoja Slovenska v dobe bronzovej. *Sl.A.* 19, 365–422 (German résumé).

TOMPA, F. 1934–5 (1937). 25 Jahre Urgeschichtsforschung in Ungarn 1912–1936. *BRGK* 24/25, 27–115.

TORBRÜGGE, W. (1959a) *Die Bronzezeit in der Oberpfalz.* Kallmünz: Lassleben.

TORBRÜGGE, W. (1959b) Die Bronzezeit in Bayern. Stand der Forschungen zur relativen Chronologie. *BRGK* 40, 1–78.

TORBRÜGGE, W. 1970–71 (1972) Vor- und frühgeschichtliche Flussfunde. Zur Ordnung und Bestimmung einer Denkmälergruppe. *BRGK* 51–52, 1–146.

TRBUHOVIĆ, V. B. (1968) *Problemi porekla i datovanja bronzanog doba u Srbiji.* Beograd: Arh. Inst.

TRUMP, D. H. (1958) The Apennine Culture of Italy. *PPS* 24, 165–200.

TRUMP, D. H. (1966) *Central and Southern Italy before Rome.* London: Thames and Hudson.

ULLRICH, H. (1972) *Das Aunjetitzer Gräberfeld von Grossbrembach. Teil 1. Anthropologische Untersuchungen zur Frage nach Entstehung und Verwandtschaft der thüringischen, böhmischen und mährischen Aunjetitzer.* Weimar: Böhlaus.

VERRON, G. (1975) Préhistoire de l'Eure. *Nouvelles de l'Eure* 56, 3–24.

VERRON, G. (1976a) Les civilisations de l'Age du Bronze en Normandie. In Guilaine 1976, 585–600.

VERRON, G. (1976b) Acculturation et continuité en Normandie durant le Néolithique et les Ages des Métaux. In de Laet 1976, 261–83.

VERWERS, G. J. (1969) The beginning of the Late Bronze Age in the Lower Rhine area. *BROB* 19, 17–25.

VINSKI-GASPARINI, Z. (1973) *Kultura polja sa žarama u sjevernoj Hrvatskoj.* Zadar: Filozofski Fakultet.

VLADÁR, J. (1973a) Osteuropäische und mediterrane Einflüsse im Gebiet der Slowakei während der Bronzezeit. *Sl. A.* 21, 253–357.

VLADÁR, J. (1973b) *Pohrebiska zo staršej doby bronzovej v Branči.* Bratislava: Slovenská akadémia vied.

VOZA, G. (1972) Thapsos, primi resultati delle più recenti ricerche. *Atti della XIV Riunione Scientifica dell' Istituto Italiano di Preistoria e Protostoria (Puglia 1970)*, 175–205.

VOZA, G. (1973) Thapsos: resoconto sulle campagne di scavo del 1970–71. *Atti della XV Riunione Scientifica dell' Istituto Italiano di Preistoria e Protostoria (Verona-Trento 1972)*, 133–57.

WADDELL, J. (1976) Cultural interaction in the Insular Early Bronze Age: some ceramic evidence. In de Laet 1976, 284–95.

WEGEWITZ, W. (1967) *Hamburg-Harburg, Sachsenwald und die nördliche Lüneburger Heide. FvfD* 7. Mainz: Philipp von Zabern.

WELINDER, S. (1975) *Prehistoric Agriculture in eastern middle Sweden.* Lund: Acta Archaeologica Lundensia.

WILLVONSEDER, K. (1937) *Die mittlere Bronzezeit in Österreich.* Vienna: Schroll.

ZIEGERT, H. (1963) *Zur Chronologie und Gruppengliederung der westlichen Hügelgräberkultur.* Berlin: de Gruyter.

ZSCHOCKE, K. and PREUSCHEN, E. (1932) *Das urzeitliche Bergbaugebiet von Mühlbach-Bischofshofen.* Materialien zur Urgeschichte Österreichs, VI.

ZUMSTEIN, H. (1966) *L'Age du Bronze dans le Département du Haut-Rhin.* Bonn: Habelt.

ZUMSTEIN, H. (1976) Les civilisations de l'Age du Bronze dans l'Est de la France. A: Les Civilisations de l'Age du Bronze en Alsace. In Guilaine 1976, 630–9.

Index

References to figures are given in italics